Reconsidering a Balanced Approach to Reading

Reconsidering a Balanced Approach to Reading

Edited by
Constance Weaver
Western Michigan University

National Council of Teachers of English
1111 W. Kenyon Road, Urbana, Illinois 61801-1096

Staff Editors: Michael Greer and Tom Tiller

Interior Design: Tom Kovacs for TGK Design

Cover Design: Carlton Bruett

NCTE Stock Number: 02344-1450

Library of Congress Cataloging-in-Publication Data

Reconsidering a balanced approach to reading / edited by Constance Weaver.
    p. cm.
    Collection of articles, some previously published.
    Includes bibliographical references and index.
    ISBN 0-8141-0234-4
    1. Reading (Primary) 2. Language acquisition. I. Weaver, Constance.
LB1525.R39   1997
372.41—dc21
                                        97-29868
                                              CIP

Contents

VI From Instructional Myths to Meaningful Instruction

Foreword
Research as Inquiry

Diane Stephens
University of Hawaii

On the inside of one of my kitchen cupboard doors, I have taped up part of a newspaper article. It begins, "It's important to keep your shower clean and fresh, whether it's a separate shower, shower stall or shower in a tub. Here are some hints." One of the hints explains that "dull and filmy glass shower doors" should be wiped with a "soft cloth saturated with a distilled white vinegar." Now, I currently don't have glass shower doors, but I keep that article because I used to have glass shower doors that were hard to keep clean, and if I ever have them again, I want to try vinegar. I will most definitely wipe them down as directed and see if vinegar "works" to clean them.

Charles Sanders Peirce was a U.S. philosopher who would have referred to my experiment as the fourth way people "fixate belief": by trying things out on their own to see what happens, and by believing their own "test results." The other three ways were believing what one wants to believe; believing what one has always believed; and believing what an authority says is true. Of these, only the fourth way, Peirce argued, would lead to knowledge or truth (Peirce, 1955). Peirce went on to explain that once a person "fixated belief" they would be willing to take action. In my case, if vinegar worked, I would believe in its usefulness. I would consider it "true" that vinegar cleans shower doors and take the action to keep on using it. If it did not work, I would not consider it "true" and so not take further action.

"Truth" and "proof" are more complicated for professional researchers. During the last thirty years people who conduct research for a living have had enormous debates about what constitutes "proof" that something is or is not "true." If a researcher wanted to know if vinegar cleans glass shower doors (or not), for example, she or he would most likely carefully design an experiment and draw a conclusion based on the findings. Other researchers, however, might argue that the design of the experiment was flawed. It might be argued, for example, that not enough shower doors were tested or that the brand of vinegar was not consistent across wipings or that different people wiped in different ways, causing different results.

Studies like this, studies that test hypotheses, are called "quantitative" studies. For a long time, in education and in some other fields, this was the only kind of research that professional researchers accepted. To determine the truthfulness of these quantitative studies, researchers developed elaborate rules for determining whether or not the hypotheses were "proved": rules that, in this case, would assess the adequacy of the number of shower doors washed, the kinds of vinegar used, and how the wiping was done. The "findings" from these kinds of studies are published as "research reports," and there are "rules" for writing up such reports. They are supposed to begin with a rationale, include a review of the literature, clearly delineate the methodology, state and discuss the findings, and conclude with remarks that include a discussion of the limitations of the research—e.g., "In this study, however, only left-handed male subjects wiped the shower doors. Further research is needed to determine if using females and/or right-handed males would lead to the same results."

For the last thirty or so years in education, a second sort of research has been published. This kind of research is called "qualitative" research. When qualitative researchers first tried to get their work published, they had a hard time; sometimes they still do. That was, and is, because qualitative research does not follow the rules of quantitative research and so, at first, qualitative research was dismissed as *not* research or as not *good* research.

Over time, however, the research community has come to understand and accept that qualitative research does not follow the rules of quantitative research because both the means and the ends of quantitative and qualitative research are different. Quantitative researchers seek to "prove" the truth of an hypothesis; qualitative researchers seek to better understand a particular situation. Quantitative researchers make up rules for determining truth—that is, they carefully define means and methods; qualitative researchers focus on systematically examining particular situations to see what they can learn from their inquiry. It is similar to my planned experiment with vinegar—except that most of the time it is considerably more interesting. Very few people would be interested in a detailed examination of how I cleaned my shower doors with vinegar and what happened when I did—but a lot of people might be interested in understanding what happened when I personally helped a particular child succeed as a reader or when I helped a particular teacher or group of teachers learn how to help children succeed as readers.

Quantitative studies are generally published as research reports. Qualitative studies, in contrast, are most often published as narratives, as stories of experiences. As a reader of my narrative, you would not be expected to consider my particular experiences "proof" of anything—neither my method for cleaning shower doors nor for teaching children—but you might get ideas from reading my narratives and you might try those ideas out for yourself. In this way, you would "fixate belief" based on your own experience. In this way, qualitative research is considered useful not because it proves answers but because it can be generative and lead to new inquiries (including quantitative research).

Of course, it is also possible to read and use quantitative research in the same way one reads and uses qualitative research. That is, both "research reports" and "narratives" can be considered as "stories" of particular experiences, rather than as proof or truth. Both can be generative. Rather than lead us to conclusions or proof, both can serve as starting points for personal inquiries.

When Connie Weaver was considering what to include in this book, she had to think about these kinds of things. Would she limit herself to one kind of research or would she include both? She decided to include both but to approach them similarly. Rather than offer these studies—quantitative and qualitative—as "proof" of some truth, she has simply gathered together work that she considers especially important for informing our understanding of what we call "reading" and "learning to read." She expects her readers to fixate their own beliefs—to read both quantitative and qualitative studies and summaries as stories of other people's experiences and to determine for themselves, through their own experimentation, what they believe to be true.

In the past, when the research that counted most was quantitative research, researchers made up rules for gathering together and making sense of multiple quantitative studies. One of the rules was called meta-analysis. In the mid-1980s, I was involved in a rather large meta-analysis (Harste & Stephens, 1985). We read all the reading comprehension research that had been conducted from 1974 to 1984 and if the study included an experimental group and a control group and if statistical data resulted, we used a formula to draw conclusions across studies. We took the mean of the treatment group, subtracted the mean of the control group, and divided by the standard deviation of the control group to get a "gain effect size." We could then compare studies by comparing gain effect sizes.

Now that both quantitative and qualitative studies are being published, the rules are different: old rules apply for old patterns (e.g., meta-analysis for particular kinds of quantitative studies), while new rules are emerging. One time, for example, I became interested in making sense of multiple studies, some of which were quantitative and some of which were qualitative (Stephens, 1991). In contrast to the 1985 meta-analysis, I used a different set of rules for what I would and would not include. Rather than look for studies with true control groups and standardized test data, I looked for studies that fell into a particular category. That category was "whole language." I defined what I meant by the term, so that readers would understand my rules for inclusion or exclusion, and I used my selection criteria consistently. I annotated the studies that met my criteria and wrote a narrative that was published along with them. Some professional researchers did not like or agree with my criteria. I considered that their choice. Others argued that my collection of studies did not "prove" anything, and I agreed. I did not intend to "prove" anything. I simply wanted to gather together what was known in a particular category, using a particular definition of that category, so that it would be easier for people to find and know about the studies in the category. I hoped that such an effort would prove generative for readers.

Connie Weaver has done a similar thing in this collection. She has defined her category as research studies and summaries that she believes particularly inform our understanding of the reading process, learning to read, and teaching children to read. It would have been impossible to include everything, and she makes no claims for having done so. Concerned that policy is too often grounded on a few particular studies, she believes that policy and practice should instead be grounded in a broader, deeper knowledge base. Therefore, she has chosen articles that she believes may help the reader expand her or his own knowledge base. Weaver's intent is not to prove, but to inform.

I once heard "objectivity" defined as the responsibility of the writer to say to the reader, "If you stood where I stood and looked as I looked, you would see what I saw." Throughout this book, Weaver provides us with just such an opportunity. She tells us in her introduction and in the first chapter where she's stood and how she's looked, and then she shows us what she's seen. She enables her readers to learn directly from multiple authors and thereby to take ideas from original sources, test them out on their own, and fixate belief based on personal experience.

It is Connie's hope, and mine, that you find this perspective generative as well.

Works Cited

Harste, J. C., & Stephens, D. (Eds.). (1985). *Towards practical theory: A state of practice assessment of reading comprehension instruction.* (Final report #USDE-C-300-83-0130). Bloomington, IN: Language Education Department.

Peirce, C. S. (1955). The fixation of belief. In J. Buchler (Ed.), *Philosophical writings of Peirce.* New York: Dover Publications, Inc.

Stephens, D. (1991). *Research on whole language: Support for a new curriculum.* Katonah, NY: Richard C. Owen.

Introduction: A Perspective

The argument underlying this book is that we need either to reconsider and revise the "balanced approach" to reading as it has been conceptualized in the marketplace, or that we need to reconsider whether a so-called balanced approach is really what will benefit children most. In either case, such reconsideration is in effect mandated by various bodies of research from the last three decades. *Reconsidering a Balanced Approach to Reading* is intended primarily for curriculum specialists dealing with the primary grades, administrators, policymakers, and teachers interested in various kinds of research relevant to reading, learning to read, and the teaching of reading.

What prompted the development of this book was, first, the release of the California Reading Task Force Report, *Every Child a Reader* (California Department of Education, 1995). Then came a follow-up reading advisory that raised even more concerns: *A Balanced, Comprehensive Approach to Teaching Reading in Prekindergarten Through Grade Three* (California Department of Education, 1996). The vision of a "balanced" approach to reading instruction that emerges from these reports is that of a structured program for teaching, assessing, and remediating reading—an approach wherein teachers will explicitly teach phonemic awareness (awareness of what we think of as the "separate" sounds in words), phonics, and other word-attack skills.

To many people, such a "balanced" approach to reading seems to be an eclectic approach, a little of this and a little of that, like a tossed salad, with no particular relationship among the various ingredients. This is what seems to be promoted by *Every Child a Reader* (1995). When I read that document, I saw what it promotes as resting on two sides of a balance scale, with phonemic awareness, phonics, and other word-identification skills on one side of the balance, and the reading and writing of literature and other whole texts on the other side. That is, the document seems to promote a program wherein skills are separate from their use, and are taught prior to their use (the document asserts that children must be taught to read before they can read to learn).

Unfortunately, this vision of a balanced approach to reading rests upon a very narrow research base and ignores much of the research of the past three decades that bears upon the teaching of reading: for example, research on the nature of the reading process itself, on how literacy develops, and on how human beings learn complex processes and concepts. It also ignores a growing body of experimental research that compares children's development as readers and writers in different kinds of classrooms. And it ignores various other lines of research that are represented in this collection.

In the wider public arena, too, competing theories of reading and reading instruction have become central to a number of debates surrounding education, curriculum, and funding. President Clinton's January 1997 State of the Union address, in which he announced the America Reads initiative, was a notable and powerful example of the rising stakes in the ongoing project of reading education. On both the state and national levels, legislation continues to be written, sponsored, and sometimes passed in an attempt to promote one or another form of "balance" in school reading programs. In a politicized climate, it is not surprising that many parents and other members of the public perceive the issue of "balance" in a simplified, either-or perspective—phonics or whole language, skills or whole texts, and so forth. "Reconsidering" thus means, in this context, stepping back and looking more closely at how terms like "balance," "phonics," and "whole language" are defined, and how they are interrelated.

This book, then, grows from a desire to redress the imbalance in the research base from which an alleged balanced approach to the teaching of reading is being derived. Certain articles were chosen to "talk" to one another—that is, to provide different approaches that could be weighed against one another.

What about Teaching Phonemic Awareness and Phonics?

I must say at the outset that I am not opposed to teaching phonemic awareness and phonics explicitly, if they are taught briefly, in the context of reading and writing whole texts. In fact, I agree that some children need more help than they have received in learning to attend to letter/sound patterns, and in trying to sound out problem words in related letter chunks, such as ch-ip for *chip*, tri-ang-le for *triangle*, su-per-sti-tious for *superstitious*—provided that all the while they are trying to come up with a meaningful word that fits the context. Just this morning, in fact, I was talking with a friend, my dentist's assistant, with whom I always exchange book recommendations whenever I'm in the office. Sally reminded me that most of the time, she has three—or even five—novels in progress: one at work, one in the living room, one in the bedroom, one in the bathroom, and one on tape, which she listens to in the car. When I asked how she had become such an avid reader, Sally admitted that after two years of schooling she still could not read. Her teacher discovered that though she could read the Dick and Jane books reasonably well, she was mostly memorizing the texts; she had not yet learned to attend to the letter patterns within words, or to deal with unfamiliar words in chunks. After supplementary tutoring for some time, she became a competent reader. However, it was not until the tenth grade that she became a truly avid reader. At that time, her English teacher helped and encouraged her to design her own "program" for reading: to read numerous books of her choice. Since then, Sally has been an avid reader—indeed, probably the most avid reader I know.

We hear and read of others not as fortunate as Sally, children and adults who have not learned to attend to letter patterns in reading (and therefore not learned to try to sound out words in chunks, in order to get at least many of the words that they have heard spoken). Within the nearly two thousand miscue analyses done by my preservice teachers over the last two decades, I have noticed from some children's miscues (a neutral term in place of "error") that they seem not to process "unfamiliar" words in any coherent fashion, such as by breaking the word into pronounceable chunks of letters. In fact, some readers seem to pick up some letters of a word and then say a word that has those letters—without any regard for whether or not the word makes sense in context, or even for whether it's an actual word. However—and this is a crucial point—I have witnessed such unproductive processing of words from children who have had extensive and intensive phonics training, as well as from children whose reading instruction may have focused more on meaning. For instance, I observed an Orton-Gillingham trained teacher teach three children a lesson on open and closed syllables, then later in the day listened to the boy read aloud. He used what we might call the "random letter pick-up strategy" I described, making no attempt to sound out in chunks some of the words that he might have gotten if he had used this strategy in conjunction with meaning.

So I do agree with the argument that some children need more help with phonics than they have been getting, though this is not necessarily the kind of phonics that has traditionally been taught or that is being currently recommended. They need more help not only or necessarily in recognizing letters and relating them to sounds, but in sounding out words as best they can, while using context and everything they know to get words and meaning. They need help with other strategies, too, such as strategies for continuing to read instead of continuing to struggle unsuccessfully with problem words.

I worry that the two California documents, especially the reading advisory, will be taken as promoting phonics *first,* which in turn will produce many readers who try to sound out words without regard to whether they fit in context (or even to whether what they've said is a real word); many readers who think reading means saying the words, *not* constructing meaning from texts; many readers who avoid reading whenever possible because they think they will not know all the words; and many children who do not do well with isolated phonics teaching and therefore are given more and more skills work and less authentic reading and writing, with the result that they never become independent, much less avid, readers. What makes me fear this? It is partly my experience in analyzing and evaluating my students' miscue projects, wherein they interview children about their reading and their strategies for reading, in addition to having the children read a selection aloud and discuss it afterwards. All too many children seem to fall into one or another of the categories above. But the concern for what happens to such children is also well documented by more formal research (see, for example, Allington's article in this volume).

In addressing an alleged imbalance, then, these California documents threaten to generate an old/new imbalance by focusing on phonics too early and too heavily, with assessment that seems likely to hold some children back as readers, as instruction focuses more and more on isolated skills and leaves less and less time for the reading and writing of whole texts. Research does *not* show phonics first to be the best way to approach reading instruction (as many of the chapters in this volume illustrate). Nevertheless, the cry for phonics first is being widely disseminated. Witness, for example, the following claim from Phyllis Schlafly's *Education Reporter*:

> With true phonics, the child is first taught to recognize the letters of the alphabet and then is drilled in the letter sounds—first vowels, then consonants, then consonant-vowel combinations—so that the child develops an automatic association between letters and sounds. When that is accomplished, the child is then given words, sentences, and stories to read ("Civil Rights," *Education Reporter,* July 1989, p. 3).

This phonics-first concept is what appears to underlie more than twenty bills introduced in state legislatures: bills designed, in one way or another, to promote or require the teaching of phonics intensively and systematically, if not *first.* Originally, this push for phonics came mostly from ultra-conservative groups such as Phyllis Schlafly's Eagle Forum and Pat Robertson's Christian Coalition, but their pro-phonics (and anti-whole language) cry has been widely disseminated and is now being taken up by many others including the media (Weaver & Brinkley, forthcoming).

If phonics first were justified by the available research, that would be another matter, but it isn't.

What about the Research Cited in Support of Phonics First?

The idea that phonics should be taught first, and the idea that this will make a reading approach balanced, have both grown from misinterpretations of the work of particular scholars, such as Marilyn Adams, whose book *Beginning to Read: Learning and Thinking About Print* (1990) has been commonly cited in the political arena and the marketplace. A careful reading of her book shows, however, that Adams argued for extensive exposure to books and print before children would be taught phonics.

Nevertheless, the research of Adams and other scholars has often been misinterpreted and misunderstood. For example, Marilyn Adams and Maggie Bruck (1995) point out that various studies have shown poor word-identification skills to be strongly coupled with poor reading comprehension (on standardized tests, which are usually timed); they cite (p. 13) various sources, such as Perfetti, 1985; Stanovich, 1982, 1991; Vellutino, 1991. In a related vein, Adams and Bruck (p. 15) also point out that the speed and accuracy with which children can read single words predicts their ability to comprehend written text (again, typically when measured via timed, standardized tests); they cite, for example, Curtis, 1980; Stanovich, Cunningham, & Freeman, 1984. Adams and Bruck (p. 14) also cite the earlier research showing that preschoolers' familiarity with letters of the alphabet "is a powerful prognostic of the success with which they will learn to read" (Bond & Dykstra, 1967; Chall, 1967), and they mention the research which suggests that "skillful readers visually process virtually each individual letter of every word" (see reviews in Just & Carpenter, 1987; Patterson & Coltheart, 1987). But the observation that has received the most emphasis in the public and political arenas is this: "Faced with an alphabetic script, the child's level of phonemic awareness [awareness of what we think of as the "separate" sounds in words] on entering school is widely held to be the strongest single predictor of the success she or he will experience in learning to read and of the likelihood that she or he will fail" (p. 15). Adams and Bruck cite a variety of references, including Blachman, 1984; Juel, 1991; Stanovich, 1986; and some references for learning to read in Swedish, Spanish, French, Italian, and Russian.

As research conclusions such as these have reached public awareness, they have been taken to justify the argument for teaching phonics *first*.

This, however, is not what scholars like Adams and Bruck are actually recommending in their own writings. For example, Adams makes clear in *Beginning to Read* (1990) that children need many, many hours of experience with written texts before being taught phonics in any formal way. For children who have had few or no experiences with books in the home, it is especially crucial for preschools and elementary schools to provide extensive and intensive experiences with print: environmental print, certainly (signs, notices, labels, and all the various kinds of print we encounter in our daily or classroom environments), but also extensive and intensive experiences with books. Adams and Bruck (1995) give considerable attention to the many benefits of reading children's books to and with children before they are taught to decode words: children learn concepts of print, such as directionality, and concepts like "word" and "sound"; they learn new words, language, and concepts; they come to understand various creatures and characters and share their experiences; and much more. As Adams and Bruck explain: "These sorts of understandings serve vitally to set up the knowledge, expectations, and interest on which learning to read depend. If children also learn that reading is something they want to be able to do, they are well on their way" (p. 14).

Thus the kind of balanced reading program promoted in the writings of scholars like Adams and Bruck (1995) and Beck and Juel (1995) is actually different in significant ways from what they are often said to be advocating. Their concept of balance is reflected in the three stages they delineate—overlapping stages, they might say, through which word recognition develops. The first of these is "fostering the emergence of early literacy knowledge," as briefly explained above. The second is "helping young readers to break the code," which they believe must include explicit attention to letters, individual letter/sound relationships, and patterns of letters and sounds (but not in any linear order). In other words, these key researchers suggest that developing phonemic awareness and phonics knowledge is second to learning many concepts about language, written language in particular, texts, and the real world, all through various opportunities to listen to, discuss, and analyze texts.

Adams and Bruck's "later stages" include extensive reading. They point out that learning to recognize words is a relatively small component of learning to read, though a critical one. They argue: "Children who quickly master the early stages of reading find reading less aversive, less time consuming, and more rewarding than those who do not. Because of this, better readers are likely to read more than children with poorer skills (Juel, 1988) and, as a consequence, their early facility cascades into a sea of advantages. Most obviously, more reading is clearly the best path to better reading" (p. 17).

For developing preschoolers' knowledge of letters, Adams and Bruck (1995) mention the efficacy of "little books for parent-child sharing" (p. 14, citing McCormick & Mason, 1986). For developing phonemic awareness, they note that "many of the activities (e.g. songs, chants, and word-sound games) that have long been enjoyed with preschoolers are ideally suited toward developing their sensitivity to the sound structure of language," though these can be used far more effectively if used with that goal in mind. Even so, they point to the research indicating that "teaching letters with sounds is more effective than teaching either alone (Ohnmacht, 1969) and related research showing that developing phonemic awareness with letters is more effective than developing phonemic awareness by itself (e.g., Bradley & Bryant, 1983; Byrne & Fielding-Barnesley, 1991; Cunningham, 1990). Adams and Bruck also cite the research showing that "even very beginning readers make associations between larger orthographic units, such as the rhymes of words, and their sounds (e.g., Goswami & Bryant, 1990)."

Beck and Juel (1995) suggest nursery rhymes and tongue twisters, but also recommend reading activities that can have many of the same benefits in developing phonemic awareness and phonics knowledge. For example, they suggest using some children's books like Dr. Seuss's *The Cat in the Hat, Hop on Pop, Fox in Socks,* and *There's a Wocket in My Pocket.* They also recommend using Big Books in a shared reading situation (p. 41).

Thus the researchers whose conclusions are often cited as supporting phonics first do *not*, in fact, advocate teaching phonics before immersing children in numerous reading experiences. In fact, they increasingly promote the development of phonemic awareness and phonics knowledge partly through reading and writing experiences—even in preschool and kindergarten. In other words, such researchers do not themselves seem to have a balance-scale view of what a balanced approach to reading means—nor even a tossed salad view. They have a coherent theory, according to which we must first give children plenty of diverse experiences with reading, writing, and books; a theory according to which phonemic awareness and phonics knowledge arise partly from such experiences, but also from teaching phonics explicitly. (See also Adams, 1991, "Why Not Phonics *and* Whole Language?")

Somehow this notion of a balanced approach to reading seems to have gotten lost as others try to translate the research into recommendations for practice. For instance, the California reading advisory *A Balanced, Comprehensive Approach to Teaching Reading in Prekindergarten*

Through Grade Three (1996) gives the impression, through many pages, of advocating phonemic awareness, phonics, and skills first. Even though the document eventually recommends a variety of learning activities that sound more balanced, the grade-level expectations emphasize the development of skills, in preschool and even more so in kindergarten. Furthermore, in the section on diagnostic tools, the document asserts "[s]tudent skills can be assessed with a list that begins with single letters and progresses to words ordered in complexity." So in this critical area of assessment, the document seems to promote the teaching and assessment of phonics-related skills first, despite the brave attempt elsewhere in the document to promote a balanced approach to reading.

Since the preceding pages of this introduction were written (early in 1996), proponents of phonics first have virtually ignored the research of Adams and these other scholars mentioned—perhaps because they, too, now recognize that such scholars do not, in fact, advocate phonics first. Instead, phonics-first proponents now promote the research funded by the National Institute for Child Health and Human Development. However, that body of research does not provide justification for phonics first, either (see chapters 1 and 4; see also Allington & Woodside-Jiron, 1997).

Reconsidering a Balanced Approach

Regarding the concept of a "balanced" approach, we have noted that one view of a balanced approach is that articulated by Marilyn Adams and others: a view that places a high premium on teaching and learning phonemic awareness, phonics, and identifying words through their letter/sound patterns, but not before children have had extensive experiences with books. We should remember, too, that this emphasis in Adams's book (1993) resulted from her having been asked to summarize the research on teaching and learning phonics, not the fuller body of research on learning to read.

The balance is both similar and different for researchers who have engaged in different kinds of research, such as research on the nature of the reading process itself (e.g., Pearson & Stephens, 1992, reprinted in this volume; Y. Goodman & K. Goodman, 1994, reprinted in this volume, and K. Goodman, 1973; Brown, Goodman, & Marek, 1996); research on emergent literacy (Hall, 1987); and research on the development of phonics *along with* the development of other reading and writing strategies, skills, behaviors, and attitudes (see sources cited in Moustafa, chapter 5; and Weaver's summary of research in chapter 4). These researchers see as paramount not the reading of words (though obviously that is important) but the development of strategies for predicting, monitoring comprehension, and confirming the appropriateness of what has been read or trying to correct what doesn't fit the context. Thus researchers emphasize not only teaching phonemic awareness and phonics in the context of reading and writing whole texts, but in the context of helping children develop appropriate reading strategies. Mindful too of the extensive research showing that phonically regular text like "Nan can fan Dan" is actually harder to read than more natural text (e.g., Rhodes, 1979; Simons & Ammon, 1989; Kucer, 1985; Baddeley & Lewis, 1981), they emphasize using simple patterned and predictable books with children along with various natural texts and trade books that expose children to more sophisticated language.

We ignore decades of these and other kinds of research not only at our own peril, but most critically at the peril of the children we teach. We need a *truly* balanced approach to reading, one that neither ignores the development of skills nor places too much emphasis on learning too many skills, especially prior to and in isolation from reading and writing whole texts. Or we need to abandon the idea of a "balanced" approach to reading in favor of an *integrated* approach that reflects a coherent integration of *all* the relevant bodies of research. It is to this end that this book is dedicated.

For help with this book, I want to thank particularly my longtime friend Diane Stephens, for whom I have the utmost respect as a researcher, thinker, and editor. She read most of the abstracts in this book and made excellent suggestions, most of which I acted upon. In addition, she graciously wrote the foreword at my request (I *knew* she'd think of something better than what I would have drafted). Equally helpful in making decisions has been Michael Greer, Senior Editor for NCTE. He, too, drafted some paragraphs for me when I was suffering from a dry brain in a dry season, and his ideas seemed better than mine. More than that, we seem to be kindred spirits as editors—which probably accounts for both the strengths and the weaknesses of this book. Others, too, contributed directly and indirectly to this book, but I especially want to thank certain staff members at NCTE: Tom Tiller, Marlo Welshons, Jeannette Kent, Kim Peterson, and Jean Forst, whose assistance went far beyond the usual. Finally, I thank my family and the many friends who supported me in this work, including the authors who contributed so generously of their time and expertise. Thank you all.

References

Adams, M. J. (1990). _Beginning to read: Thinking and learning about print._ Cambridge: MIT Press.

Adams, M. J., & Bruck, M. (1995). Resolving the "great debate." _American Educator, 19_ (2), 7, 10–20.

Allington, R., & Woodside-Jiron, H. (1997). _Adequacy of a program of research and of a "research synthesis" in shaping educational policy._ National Research Center on English Learning and Achievement, Report series 1.15. University at Albany; Albany, NY.

Altwerger, B. (1991). Whole language teachers: Empowered professionals. In J. Hydrick (Ed.), _Whole language: Empowerment at the chalkface_ (pp. 15–29). New York. Scholastic.

Baddeley, A. D., & Lewis, V. (1981). Inner active processes in reading: The inner voice, the inner ear, and the inner eye. In C. A. Perfetti & A. M. Lesgold (Eds.), _Interactive processes in reading_ (pp. 107–29). Hillsdale, NJ: Erlbaum.

Beck, I. L., & Juel, C. (1995). The role of decoding in learning to read. _American Educator, 19_ (2), 8, 21–25, 39–42.

Blachman, B. A. (1984). Language analysis skills and early reading acquisition. In G. Wallach & K. Butler (Eds.), _Language learning disabilities in school-age children_ (pp. 271–87). Baltimore: Williams and Wilkins.

Bond, D. L., & Dykstra, R. (1967). The cooperative research program in first-grade reading instruction. _Reading Research Quarterly, 2,_ 5–142.

Bradley, L., & Bryant, P. E. (1983). Categorizing sounds and learning to read—a causal connection. _Nature, 301,_ 419–521.

Bradley, L., & Bryant, P. E. (1985). _Rhyme and reason in reading and spelling._ I.A.R.L.D. Monographs No. 1. Ann Arbor: University of Michigan Press.

Brown, J., Goodman, K. S., & Marek, A. M. (1996). _Studies in miscue analysis: An annotated bibliography._ Newark, DE: International Reading Association.

Byrne, B., & Fielding-Barnesley, R. (1991). Phonemic awareness and letter knowledge in the child's acquisition of the alphabetic principle. _Journal of Educational Psychology, 81,_ 313–21.

California Department of Education. (1996). _A balanced, comprehensive approach to teaching reading in prekindergarten through grade three._ Sacramento: California Department of Education.

California Reading Task Force. (1995). _Every child a reader._ Sacramento: California Department of Education.

Chall, J. (1967/1983). _Learning to read: The great debate._ New York: McGraw-Hill.

Church, S. (1994). Is whole language really warm and fuzzy? _The Reading Teacher, 47,_ 362–70.

Cunningham, A. E. (1990). Explicit versus implicit instruction in phonemic awareness. _Journal of Experimental Child Psychology, 50,_ 429–44.

Cunningham, P. M. (1995). _Phonics they use: Words for reading and writing_ (2nd ed.). New York: HarperCollins College Publishing.

Curtis, M. E. (1980). Development of components of reading skill. _Journal of Educational Psychology, 72,_ 656–69.

Goodman, K. S. (1973). *Theoretically based studies of patterns of miscues in oral reading performance*. Detroit: Wayne State University. (ED 079 708)

Goodman, K. S. (1989). Whole-language research: Foundations and development. *The Elementary School Journal, 90*, 208–21.

Goodman, K. S. (1993). *Phonics phacts*. Portsmouth, NH: Heinemann.

Goodman, Y. M. (1989). Roots of the whole-language movement. *The Elementary School Journal, 90*, 113–27.

Goodman, Y. M., & Goodman, K. S. (1994). To err is human: Learning about language processes by analyzing miscues. In R. B. Ruddell, M. R. Ruddell, & H. Singer (Eds.), *Theoretical models and processes of reading* (4th ed., pp. 104–23.) Newark, DE: International Reading Association.

Gorsky, D. (1991). After the reign of Dick and Jane. *Teacher Magazine,* (August), pp. 22–29.

Hall, N. (1987). *The emergence of literacy*. Portsmouth, NH: Heinemann.

Juel, C. (1988). Learning to read and write: A longitudinal study of 54 children from first through fourth grades. *Journal of Educational Psychology, 80*, 437–47.

Juel, C. (1991). Beginning reading. In R. Barr, M. L. Kamil, P. B. Mosenthal, & P. D. Pearson (Eds.), *Handbook of reading research*, Vol. 2 (pp. 759–88).

Just, M. A., & Carpenter, P. A. (1987). *The psychology of reading and language comprehension*. Boston: Allyn & Bacon.

Kucer, S. B. (1985). Predictability and readability: The same rose with different names? In M. Douglass (Ed.), *Claremont Reading Conference 49th yearbook* (pp. 229–46). Claremont, CA: Claremont Graduate School.

McCormick, C. E., & Mason, J. M. (1986). Intervention procedures for increasing preschool children's interest in and knowledge about reading. In W. H. Teale & E. Sulzby (Eds.), *Emergent literacy: Writing and reading* (pp. 90–115). Norwood, NJ: Ablex.

Mills, H., O'Keefe, T., & Stephens, D. (1992). *Looking closely: Exploring the role of phonics in one whole language classroom*. Urbana, IL: National Council of Teachers of English.

Monson, R. J., & Pahl, M. M. (1991). Charting a new course with whole language. *Educational Leadership, 48*, 51–53.

Newman, J. M., & Church, S. M. (1990). Myths of whole language. *The Reading Teacher, 44*, 20–26.

Patterson, K. E., & Coltheart, V. (1987). Phonological processes in reading: A tutorial review. In M. Coltheart (Ed.), *Attention and performance, XII: The psychology of reading* (pp. 421–47). Hillsdale, NJ: Erlbaum.

Pearson, P. D., & Stephens, D. (1992). Learning about literacy: A 30-year journey. In C. Gordon, G. D. Labercane, & W. R. McEachern (Eds.), *Elementary reading instruction: Process and practice*. Ginn Press.

Perfetti, C. A. (1985). *Reading ability*. New York: Oxford University Press.

Powell, D., & Hornsby, D. (1993). *Learning phonics and spelling in a whole language classroom*. New York: Scholastic.

Rhodes, L. (1979). Comprehension and predictability: An analysis of beginning reading materials. In J. Harste & R. Carey (Eds.), *New perspectives on comprehension* (pp. 100–30). Bloomington, IN: School of Education, Indiana University.

Simonds, H. D., & Ammon, P. (1989). Child knowledge and primerese text: Mismatches and miscues. *Research in the Teaching of English, 23,* 380–98.

Stanovich, K. E. (1982). Individual differences in the cognitive processes of reading, Part 1: Word decoding. *Journal of Learning Disabilities, 15,* 485–93.

Stanovich, K. E. (1986). Matthew effects in reading: Some consequences of individual differences in the acquisition of literacy. *Reading Research Quarterly, 21,* 360–407.

Stanovich, K. E. (1991). Word recognition: Changing perspectives. In R. Barr, M. L. Kamil, P. B. Mosenthal, & P. D. Pearson (Eds.), *Handbook of reading research* (Vol. 2, pp. 418–52). New York: Longman.

Stanovich, K. E., Cunningham, A. E., & Freeman, D. J. (1984). Relation between early reading acquisition and word decoding with and without context: A longitudinal study of first-grade children. *Journal of Educational Psychology, 76,* 668–77.

Stephens, D. (1991). *Research on whole language: Support for a new curriculum.* Katonah, NY: Richard C. Owen.

Vellutino. F. R. (1991). Introduction to three studies on reading acquisition: Convergent findings on theoretical foundations of code-oriented versus whole-language approaches to reading instruction. *Journal of Educational Psychology, 83,* 437–43.

Wagstaff, J. (1994). *Phonics that work! New strategies for the reading/writing classroom.* New York: Scholastic.

Watson, D. J. (1989). Defining and describing whole language. *The Elementary School Journal, 90,* 130–41.

Watson, D. (1996). *Making a difference: Selected writings of Dorothy Watson* (Ed. by Sandra Wilde). Portsmouth, NH: Heinemann.

Weaver, C. (1990). *Understanding whole language: From principles to practice.* Portsmouth, NH: Heinemann.

Weaver, C. (1994). *Reading process and practice: From socio-psycholinguistics to whole language* (2nd ed.). Portsmouth, NH: Heinemann.

Weaver, C., & Brinkley, E. (forthcoming). Phonics, literacy education, and the religious and political right. *Peabody Journal of Education.*

I Reading and Literacy

Reading and Literacy: A Broader Vision

We hear a lot of talk these days about a "balanced" approach to reading. What's typically meant is that teachers should teach the skills needed for reading *and* should also give children many opportunities to read whole texts that interest them. A balance scale seems to represent what many people think of as a balanced approach to reading. Note, however, that reading skills are on one side, while the reading of actual books—and, of course, other texts—is on the other side. The implication is that these are separate or, worse, sequential: that reading skills are taught first, before children are given opportunities to read and reread easy and enjoyable texts together.

This book explicitly rejects that view.

As we shall see later, much of the classroom research since 1985 suggests, instead, that children seem to master and *use* reading skills *as well or better* when such skills are taught in conjunction with actual reading—and with writing. Thus a balanced approach to reading might better be conceptualized as a circle, with reading and writing skills—and strategies—taught in the context of reading and writing and discussing whole, meaningful texts: books, magazines, newspapers, and various kinds of texts we encounter in our daily environments. In this image of a balanced approach, the skills and strategies taught are not confined to reading. That's because writing reinforces reading skills and strategies, and vice versa (as do the oral language arts and skills, too). So a concern for teaching reading must become a concern for teaching writing, as well—and still more broadly, a concern for developing *literacy*.

Even if children do not master reading skills faster when skills are taught in the context of reading and writing whole texts, the children usually make faster progress toward becoming genuinely literate. Literacy is much more than merely being *able* to read and write. Many children learn to read and write at least minimally, but they never become fully literate: they rarely choose to read or write, and thus miss out on the many opportunities to explore ideas and experience other circumstances and worlds, as well as to express and create, to explain and persuade through the written word. As educators, we typically find that learning to read and write proceeds best when we help children simultaneously experience the pleasures of reading and writing.

Furthermore, both experience and research suggest that children most readily become literate if reading and writing skills and strategies are taught and learned while the children are engaging in the kinds of real life experiences that engage all of us outside school—that is, reading and writing to enjoy, learn, inquire, persuade, and so forth. These are the kinds of experiences that children and their teachers may be involved in during theme study, for example—the study of a particular topic, concept, or issue that may even take them beyond the classroom walls to participation in the community. Under such circumstances, literacy is not just a future goal, a dream deferred perhaps forever, but a present and positive experience.

In general, this book reflects the stance that an appropriately balanced approach to reading, writing, and literacy will

- focus not merely on reading, but on literacy, broadly defined;
- integrate language and literacy across modes of language and across disciplines;
- attend to reading, writing, and other kinds of skills and strategies in context—that is, in the context of reading, writing, and learning from whole and meaningful texts (texts that children themselves find meaningful);
- reflect a coherent integration of the best research available.

The last of these principles is addressed below in the first chapter, "Toward a Balanced Approach to Reading." Unfortunately, space limitations prevent the inclusion of an even broader research base in this collection; the articles here have been chosen to address the imbalance that currently exists in the marketplace. Equally unfortunate is the necessary omission of many articles that would have described in greater detail how reading and writing reinforce each other and how theme study can help promote genuine literacy. But this volume is at least a start.

Note

This introduction draws upon material originally presented in a videotape developed by the author (see Weaver, C. [1997]. *A balanced approach to reading and literacy*. Videotape. Plano, TX: Skyhooks.)

A Note on Terms: Conceptualizing Phonics and Whole Language

Both phonics and whole language are sometimes characterized as approaches to reading, especially by the media. In truth, neither one is. Phonics is less than a complete approach to reading, while whole language is fundamentally much more—a research-based theory of learning and teaching, which gives rise to certain kinds of practices in helping children develop literacy, but is not confined to reading and writing. Two other terms used frequently in this volume also require some definition: phonological awareness and phonemic awareness.

Let us start with the least familiar terms, phonological and phonemic awareness. *Phonological awareness* refers to awareness of the sound system of the language and, more specifically, to units of sound within the language. In order of descending size, these include syllables; the major parts of syllables (onsets and rimes, which are defined elsewhere in the book); and phonemes, the sounds that we adults have learned to hear as separate within words. Sometimes the more inclusive term phonological awareness is used as synonomyous with phonemic awareness, awareness of the "separate" sounds in words. Hearing individual phonemes is not an easy task—nor, even, is hearing the "separate" words in a sentence. Take, for instance, "I'm going to go," which is often pronounced /ahm gunna go/ or even as one giant word, /ahmunnago/ (slant lines are used to enclose attempts at indicating pronunciation). Or take "What do you want?", which is often pronounced in two word-like segments, /wadduhyu want?/. Hearing the "separate" sounds within words can be even more difficult, especially with the shorter vowel sounds. For example, the "a" sounds in *bat* and *bank* are not really identical, even though we adults have typically learned to think of them as a single sound. When researchers and educators talk about developing children's phonemic awareness, they are talking about developing children's ability to hear such sounds, and particularly to analyze words into their "separate" sounds.

Sometimes phonemic awareness is considered to be part of phonics. Basically, phonics is the relationship between the spelling system of the language (the orthographic system) and the sound system (the phonological system) (see K. Goodman, 1993). Thus when we speak of phonics relationships, we are talking about correspondences between sounds and letters, or more often between sound patterns and letter patterns. Since one needs to be able to hear the "separate" sounds of the language in order to make connections between single letters and sounds, phonemic awareness is required; thus, phonemic awareness is sometimes included in the term "phonics." Other educators keep the terms separate because phonemic awareness can be taught through oral activities only, as well as through reading itself and through activities with written language. They keep it separate also because phonemic awareness correlates highly with standardized test scores.

The term "phonics" is used in other ways, too, depending upon the writer's purposes. For example, I talk about "phonics knowledge," by which I usually mean a functional knowledge of letter/sound patterns that is not necessarily conscious, but that readers can and do use in processing both familiar and unfamiliar print words. Derived from actual reading and writing as much or more than from any direct instruction in phonics (see Moustafa, chapter 5), a functional knowledge of phonics is much more complex than what can reasonably be taught. A functional knowledge of phonics is typically derived from our knowledge of words that all too often represent alternative pronunciations of the same letters. For example, what about the various pronunciations of "a," as in *cake, above, bat, bar, father, awe* (which is not different from the "a" in *father*, in some dialects)? What about the various pronunciations of "ea," as in *treat, sweat* (the two most common pronunciations), but also *great, heart*, and the ambiguous *lead*? Or *cove, love, move*, and the ambiguous *dove*? Or *slow, grow*, and *know*, versus *cow, plow*, and *now*? Consonants are much more stable in pronunciation, though "c" and "g" at the beginnings of words are usually pronounced one way if certain vowels follow, and another way if other vowels follow. The "th" in *think* is not the same as the "th" in *this*. And what about the "ph" in *telephone* versus *telegraph*? The "s" in *sun* and *suggestion*, versus *sugar* and *sure*? Or the "c" in *medicine* and *medical*? Part of our functional knowledge about phonics is the knowledge, commonly unconscious more than conscious, that there is often more than one relationship between letters and sounds.

It should be clear even from this brief description of phonics that we must use grammar (syntax) and meaning (semantics) as we read, plus everything we know, in trying to make sense of texts. Thus phonics is by no means a complete approach to reading, however phonics may be defined. Phonics refers to only one of the language cueing systems, and readers need to learn to attend to and orchestrate all of them: phonics (the relationships between the orthographic and the phonological systems), syntax, semantics, plus prior knowledge and experience as well. Teaching phonemic awareness and letter/sound relationships is not the same as teaching children how to read.

Whole language, too, is often misunderstood. It is often assumed to be merely a method of teaching children to read, or to read and write. However, whole language has become a full-fledged, though still evolving, theory of learning and teaching that guides instructional decision making. It exemplifies a constructionist view of learning, according to which concepts and complex processes are constructs of the human brain; therefore, research suggests, the greater the intellectual and emotional involvement in learning, the more effectively the brain learns, uses, and retains what is learned. From this basic theory of learning derive other whole language principles: not only that people learn best when actively involved in learning, but the corollary that making many of one's own decisions about what to read, write, and learn will often generate greater involvement and thus deeper learning. Three other principles especially important to whole language are (1) that collaboration and support often enable individual children to do their personal best; (2) that children will not all learn the same things, much less learn them at the same time, no matter how we teach; (3) and that educational assessment of learning should both focus on and promote continued learning. Given these principles, it follows that children will learn to read and write by being supported in actually reading and writing whole texts—not by being required to do limited activities with bits and pieces of language. Given these whole language principles, it also follows that less proficient readers, writers, and learners can still engage in the same kinds of challenging educational experiences as their more proficient classmates; they will simply need more support—for example, in reading and writing whole texts that interest them. In whole language classrooms, children with less developed reading and writing skills are not consigned to do isolated skills work. They still engage in "authentic" reading and writing, though with/of less sophisticated texts and with more support, as needed. They are given help developing needed skills and strategies in the context of reading and writing meaningful, interesting texts. For a deeper understanding of whole language, see such references as Church, 1994; Altwerger, 1991; Gursky, 1991; Monson & Pahl, 1991; K. Goodman, 1989; Y. Goodman, 1989; Watson, 1989; Newman & Church, 1990; and Weaver, 1990.

One popular misconception about whole language is that whole language teachers do not teach phonics. However, phonics—the relationships between letter and sound patterns—has always been at the heart of whole language, acknowledged and taught as one of the three major language cueing systems that must be orchestrated as one reads. (See, for example, Mills, O'Keefe, & Stephens, 1992, and Powell & Hornsby, 1993; Wagstaff, 1994, also relates different ways of teaching phonics to some common whole language experiences.)

In summary, then, neither phonics nor whole language is, properly speaking, an approach to reading. "Phonics," however, is often used, by the media and others, as a synonym for a method of teaching reading in which children are provided with direct, systematic, and extensive instruction in sound/symbol relationships (and now phonemic awareness) before any other reading instruction or reading experiences. I refer to this as "phonics first," or as "phonics first and in isolation." Often it becomes "phonics first and only." Similarly, "whole language" is often considered as synonymous with teaching all cue systems together, including phonics, and teaching the cue systems and reading strategies in conjunction with what children are reading and writing. This can be referred to as teaching "phonics and other cue systems and strategies in context."

These two approaches, phonics first and in isolation versus phonics and other cue systems and strategies in context, are grounded in two very different ideas about how children learn and, in particular, how children learn to read. The first reflects a behavioral model, according to which knowledge is transmitted from (in this case) a teacher to children. From this perspective, children learn only what they are directly shown or told. They do not learn by developing inferences, concepts, and other generalizations through experience. In contrast, the latter approach reflects a constructivist model, according to which knowledge is constructed by the learner, and therefore the more meaningful and natural the context in which something is taught, the more likely it is that what's taught will be learned and used. So the idea of teaching phonics first and in isolation differs sharply from a whole language approach to literacy, according to which phonics is taught gradually and in context. But on the other hand, phonics is not enough to be an approach to teaching reading, while whole language is considerably more than that.

Works Cited

Altwerger, B. (1991). Whole language teachers: Empowered professionals. In J. Hydrick (Ed.), *Whole language: Empowerment at the chalkface,* (pp. 15–29). New York: Scholastic.

Church, S. (1994). Is whole language really warm and fuzzy? *The Reading Teacher, 47,* 362–70.

Goodman, K.S. (1989). Whole-language research: Foundations and development. *The Elementary School Journal, 90,* 207–21.

Goodman, K.S. (1993). *Phonics phacts.* Portsmouth, NH: Heinemann.

Goodman, Y.M. (1989). Roots of the whole-language movement. *The Elementary School Journal, 90,* 113–27.

Gursky, D. (1991). After the reign of Dick and Jane. *Teacher Magazine,* August, 22–29.

Monson, R.J. & Pahl, M.M. (1991). Charting a new course with whole language. *Educational Leadership, 48,* 51–53.

Newman, J.M. & Church, S.M. (1990). Myths of whole language. *The Reading Teacher, 44,* 20–26.

Mills, H., O'Keefe, T., & Stephens, D. (1992). *Looking closely: Exploring the role of phonics in one whole language classroom.* Urbana, IL: National Council of Teachers of English.

Powell, D., & Hornsby, D. (1993). *Learning phonics and spelling in a whole language classroom.* New York: Scholastic.

Wagstaff, J. (1994). *Phonics that work! New strategies for the reading/writing classroom.* New York: Scholastic.

Watson, D.J. (1989). Defining and describing whole language. *The Elementary School Journal, 90,* 129–41.

Weaver, C. (1990). *Understanding whole language: From principles to practice.* Portsmouth, NH: Heinemann.

1 Toward a Balanced Approach to Reading

Constance Weaver
Western Michigan University

Weaver begins by noting that the government's mandating of phonics in some states and locales threatens teacher professionalism and children's learning to read, partly because various documents call for a "balanced" reading approach that is being interpreted as calling for phonics-first-and-only instruction. A balanced reading program, she argues, should be based upon coherent integration of the best from various research studies and different kinds of research bases. Therefore, after discussing the nature of proficient reading, she offers a definition and model of reading designed to incorporate conclusions from different kinds of research related to reading.

In articulating her concern that the oft-cited research not be construed as supporting phonics first, Weaver discusses different phases of the research relating to the teaching of phonics, including the research on phonemic awareness. She concludes this part of the discussion by noting that almost all of the phonemic awareness studies can be interpreted as supporting, or at least not contradicting, the hypothesis that phonemic awareness and learning to read facilitate one another. Noting that some of the classroom-based experimental research since 1985 compares a whole language approach with a skills-intensive and sometimes phonics-intensive approach, she briefly explains several ways in which the children in whole language classrooms typically get off to as good a start or better in reading and writing than their peers in skills-intensive classrooms according to research that includes but is not limited to standardized measures of phonics knowledge. Weaver concludes this discussion of phonics and phonemic awareness by emphasizing points of agreement among researchers of different persuasions, most of whom have taken a stand against phonics first, but also a stand for providing extra tutorial help for children who seem unable to develop phonological awareness sufficiently and/or to use such awareness in decoding, given just regular whole-class instruction (of whatever kind).

Next, Weaver explains her concern about the proposed assessment and diagnosis of children's weaknesses in skills: namely that it will result in intensive skills work for such readers, with little time for the reading and writing of whole texts. She warns that in attempting to implement a balanced approach to reading, we must not fall into this kind of trap, as the educational system has historically done. Next she discusses ten particular concerns about *A Balanced, Comprehensive Approach to Teaching Reading in Kindergarten Through Grade Three*, which is a reading advisory (not binding on any of the schools) from the California Department of Education. Finally, she articulates her own vision of a balanced approach to reading, with three particular recommendations for state policymakers and politicians.

The basis for this article was a presentation made to the long-range planning committee of the Texas State Board of Education in 1996. The present version was last revised in May, 1997.

What is a balanced approach to teaching reading, anyway?

Though that question has no single answer, since the first six months of 1996 (during which most of this article was originally written), it has become increasingly easy to see what a balanced approach to reading is not.[1] It is *not* what is increasingly being mandated by politicians and administrators in various states and locales across the country.

What I wrote in 1996 began like this: We've heard a lot recently about a "balanced" reading approach, courtesy of the California Reading Task Force Report, *Every Child a Reader* (1995). That report called for redressing an allegedly current imbalance and giving more attention to skills instruction. But while skills instruction may be insufficient in some classrooms, and while we do indeed need to adopt a balanced approach to reading, educators and the public also have good reason to fear just the opposite: that there will be too little emphasis on drawing inferences and on analyzing, synthesizing, and evaluating what is read. Furthermore, various documents, plans, and legislation designed to redress the alleged imbalance threaten to push us even further in the direction of skills and away from meaningful and critical reading. They threaten to maintain or restore an old imbalance in the opposite direction: too much skills work, and too little thoughtful reading and discussion of texts read.

From Teacher Professionalism to Mandating Methodology

Those words from 1996 could not have been much more prophetic. Over 40 percent of our state legislatures have seen the introduction of bills to mandate the teaching of phonics, the training of teachers in phonics, and/or the requirement of extensive teacher education in phonics for teacher certification (Paterson, 1996). Such bills have actually been passed in more than a handful of states.

It's true that many preservice and inservice teachers could benefit from more education and mentoring in learning to teach reading effectively, including more effective ways of helping children develop and use phonics knowledge as a crucial part of reading. It's not true, however, that low scores on standardized tests necessarily reflect poor teaching or insufficient teaching of skills (see chapters in this volume by McQuillan, Krashen, Goodman, and Fink). Nor is it true that the demagogues who promote the teaching of phonics first and only have any idea of the complexity of the reading process or the complexities of teaching and learning. And it most certainly is not true that politicians know what they're doing when they mandate reading methodology through one means or another—as, for example, when California politicians included in a 1997 bill (AB 1086) a provision to the effect that Goals 2000 money must be used to promote teaching phonics intensively and systematically, not just as it becomes relevant in the course of reading and writing; or when the reading initiative of the governor of Texas is allegedly to be based only on "scientific" (experimental) research but actually ignores more than 99 percent of that research, in addition to the kinds of research that typify the human sciences. (The proposed Texas limitation seems clear from a talk given by a member of the governor's business council at a reading conference in Houston on May 16, 1997; see Winick, 1997).

Though teachers may not always know everything they ought to in order to teach reading, or to teach reading most effectively to individual as well as entire classes of children, certainly the demagogues, politicians, and administrators with inadequate classroom experience typically know and understand even less.

Part of what they do not understand is that there is a balance, and a very delicate one, between not doing enough to help children learn to draw upon phonics knowledge to recognize familiar and unfamiliar print words, and emphasizing phonics too much. They do not understand the delicate balance between letter/sound knowledge and the other kinds of knowledge and cues that good readers use. They do not understand that a delicate instructional balance will vary from child to child, nor do they understand that teachers need to be flexible and to receive support in meeting children's diverse learning needs. They do not understand that good teaching requires knowledgeable teachers able to teach flexibly, not locked into mandated methodology or a prepackaged curriculum. In short, they do not understand the disaster they seem bent on creating.

If this trend continues, I fully expect to see within the next decade headlines like this: "Too many children not reading for meaning"; "Pleasure reading drops to new lows"; "Teachers not allowed to meet students' needs"; "State sued for mandating intensive phonics rather than balanced reading instruction"; and "The great phonics hoax exposed." Children *do* need to develop and use phonics knowledge: on that, everyone is agreed. But better to promote teacher knowledge and professionalism than to mandate imbalanced reading instruction and/or particular programs.

So, What Might Characterize a Balanced Approach to Reading?

To look ahead briefly, then, what is a balanced approach to reading? Certainly not the phonics-first-and-only that is mentioned above. But I will argue that it should also not be conceptualized as a balance-scale approach to teaching reading, with skills and real reading taught apart from each other, nor an eclectic, theory-less, tossed-salad approach, with everything thrown together randomly—the visions of reading instruction that seem to be promoted by documents like the California Reading Reading Task Force report *Every Child a Reader* (1995), Bill Honig's testimony before the Texas State Board of Education in December of 1995 (see Honig, 1995), Texas Governor George W. Bush's reading initiative document (1996); or the California Department of Education's *A Balanced, Comprehensive Approach to Teaching Reading in Prekindergarten through Grade Three* (1996).

Rather, I argue for instruction based on a coherent integration of the best of differing bodies and types of research and a theory of reading that puts meaning at the heart of reading from the very beginning, rather than as some distant goal.

Understanding Proficient Reading

In general, I am concerned about how we define and characterize reading; how we teach phonemic awareness and phonics; how we assess reading and readers; and how we conceptualize and implement a balanced reading program. Let us consider the nature of proficient reading first.

The research base that underlies the aforementioned documents and related texts is not nearly as limited as that adduced in support of phonics first and only, but it is still quite narrow. By itself, that research focuses too narrowly on word identification, without regard for how readers actually process coherent text.

Judging by the bibliography of *Every Child a Reader* and of Bill Honig's book, *Teaching Our Children to Read* (1995), what seems to have been taken for granted, and what we've been hearing about, is the research that has led scholars like Marilyn Adams (1990) and Keith Stanovich (1991) to conclude that the major hallmark of good readers is that they recognize most words automatically—an observation that should not surprise us, since reading is typically measured by timed, standardized tests that disadvantage those readers who struggle with words. On the other hand, what's missing from that perspective is, first of all, the considerable body of psycholinguistic and socio-psycholinguistic research into how proficient readers read actual texts in relatively natural situations (Pearson & Stephens, 1994; K. Goodman, 1973, 1982; references in Brown, Marek, & K. Goodman, 1994). In other words, what's missing is research on the strategies that good readers use. A balanced reading program must reflect both kinds of research, I think, and a definition and model of reading that integrates them appropriately.

I'd like, then, to begin to round out the picture of proficient reading, in order to develop a better conceptualization of the "product" we want, proficient and eager readers. One line of psycholinguistic research is often associated with P. David Pearson, who has written an excellent article with Diane Stephens (1994) on what we have learned about the reading process from thirty years of research. Another line of psycholinguistic research is that spearheaded by Kenneth Goodman, who coined the term "miscue" to characterize a reader's departures from the actual words of the text. By discovering patterns in the miscues made by good readers, Goodman and his intellectual descendants have contributed significantly to our understanding of the reading process (K. Goodman, 1973, 1982; references in Brown, Marek, & K. Goodman, 1994).

To better understand some important observations about proficient reading, it would help if you have someone read the following passage aloud to you, as you listen. That is, instead of reading the passage yourself, just listen and try to determine what miscues were made as the person reading aloud tries to recapitulate the miscues of a sixth grader named Jay, who was reading an O. Henry story that included some southwestern dialect features ("Jimmy Hayes and Muriel"; Porter, 1936). Jay read the passage as follows:

> After a hearty supper Hayes joined the smokers around the fire. His appearance did not at all settle all the questions in the minds of his brother rangers. They simply saw a loose, lank young with tow-colored sunburned hair and a berry-brown, ingenious face that wore a quizzical, good-natured smile.
> "Fellows," said the new ranger, "I'm goin' to interduce you to a lady friend of mine. Ain't heard much about her beauty, but you'll all admit she's got a fine points about her. Come along, Muriel!"
> He held open the front of his blue flannel shirt. Out crawled a horned toad. A bright red ribbon was tied jauntily around its spiky neck. It crawled to its owner's knee and it sat there motionless.

"This here's Muriel," said Hayes, with an oratorical wave of his hand. "She's got qualities. She never talks back, she always stays home, and she's satisfied with one red dress for everyday and Sunday, too."

"Look at that blamed insect!" said one of the rangers with a grin. "I've seen plenty of them horny toads, but I never knew anybody to have one for a partner. Does the blame thing know you from anybody else?"

"Take her over there and see," said Hayes.

As you listened, you probably noticed the miscue "young" for "youth," as Jay read "a loose, lank young. . . ." The word "young" was a reasonable prediction, based on prior context and sampling of the letter/sound cues, but "young" did not fit with the following grammar. Not surprisingly, therefore, Jay corrected the miscue, reading what the text actually said: "a loose, lank youth." You might also have noticed the miscue "a" in one place. That word was also a logical prediction, in the context "You'll all admit she's got a. . . ." However, the following phrase was actually "fine points," so the word "a" didn't quite fit. This miscue Jay did not correct. Nor did he correct the other miscue that some listeners will have noticed, namely "ingenious" for "ingenuous." Probably Jay didn't know the word "ingenuous." It is very difficult, even for us as proficient adult readers, to sound out words correctly when they aren't already part of our listening vocabulary, the words we know from hearing them. An example from my own reading is the word *demesne*. Derived from Old French, the word's first dictionary pronunciation is given as "demane." However, I mentally pronounced it as "demense" throughout one novel and most of its sequel. I made a classic reversal, because I didn't know the word—and was less interested in its pronunciation than in its meaning, which seemed clear from the context.

But back to Jay. These three miscues—"young," "a," and "ingenious"—are only three of the twenty-three miscues Jay made in this short stretch of text (Weaver, 1994b, pp. 259–261). The other twenty miscues do not reflect a significant difference in meaning, nor do they disrupt the flow of the text. (Figure 1 includes a key for interpreting the miscue markings, while Figure 2 shows Jay's miscues on this segment of text).

Of course as Adams (1990) and Stanovich (1991) have noted, many good readers, those who score well on standardized tests, also read lists of words with a high degree of accuracy. Such readers may indeed make very few miscues, and sometimes none. But when good readers *do* make miscues, we can gain valuable insight into the nature of the reading process itself.

SUBSTITUTION   After a hearty supper Hayes joined the other smokers
around
~~about~~ the fire.

(A word written over another word indicates a substitution. The original
text word(s) may be crossed through, for clarity.)

OMISSION   . . . she always stays(at)home . . . .

(A circle around a word or group of words indicates an omission.)

at all

INSERTION   His appearance did not settle all the questions . . .
                                                ∧

(A caret points to whatever is inserted.)

REVERSAL   They saw╱simply a loose, lank youth . . .

(The typical editors' symbol is used to indicate a reversal.)

                                          ©
                                           young
CORRECTION   They saw simply a loose, lank ~~youth~~ with tow-colored

sunburned hair . . .

(The C indicates that the miscue was corrected, and the underlining indicates
what portion of the text was repeated as the reader made the correction.)

                    ©   4 who'd
                        3 who
                        2 you
MULTIPLE   ~~Who'd've~~ thought jus' a year ago . . . ."
ATTEMPT

(Multiple attempts at a word are numbered consecutively.)

                                               2 wa –
                                               1 w–
PARTIAL WORD They were day laborers who picked cotton for ~~wages~~, . . .

(One or more letters followed by a hyphen indicate that the reader uttered
what he or she apparently considered only part of a word, judging by the
reader's intonation.)

                              ®
REPETITION   I did not feel like messing with Lillian Jean.

(The R indicates that the word or words were repeated, while the underline
indicates *which* word or words were repeated.)

                                          ℘
PAUSE   "I'm going up to Mr. Jamison's . . . ."

(A long-tailed P is used to indicate where the reader paused for a considerable time.)

Figure 1 Miscue markings

After a hearty supper Hayes joined the smokers ~~about~~ the fire. His
① *around*

appearance did not settle all the questions in the minds of his
② *at all*

brother rangers. They saw simply a loose, lank youth with tow-
③   ④ © *young*

colored sunburned hair and a berry-brown, ~~ingenuous~~ face that
⑤ *ingenious*

wore a quizzical, good-natured smile.

"Fellows," said the new ranger, "I'm goin' to interduce you to

a lady friend of mine. Ain't ever heard ~~anybody~~ call her
⑥   ⑦ *much about*   ⑧   ⑨

a beauty, but you'll all admit she's got ~~some~~ fine points about
⑨   ⑩ *a*

her. Come along, Muriel!"
©   ⑪

He held open the front of his blue flannel shirt. Out of
⑫   ⑬

it crawled a horned ~~frog~~. A bright red ribbon was tied jauntily
⑫   *toad* ⑬

around its spiky neck. It crawled to ~~its~~ owner's knee and sat
the ⑭   *it* ⑮

there motionless.

"This here Muriel," said Hayes, with an oratorical wave of his hand,
⑯ *'s*   ⑰ ₀

"~~has~~ got qualities. She never talks back, she always stays at home,
She's ⑱   ⑲

and she's satisfied with one red dress for everyday and Sunday, too."

"Look at that blame insect!" said one of the rangers with a grin.
d ⑳

"I've seen plenty of them horny ~~frogs~~, but I never knew anybody
toads ㉑

to have one for a side partner. Does the blame thing know you
©   ㉒

from anybody else?"

"Take ~~it~~ over there and see," said Hayes.
her ㉓

Figure 2 Miscues of Jay, a good sixth grade reader

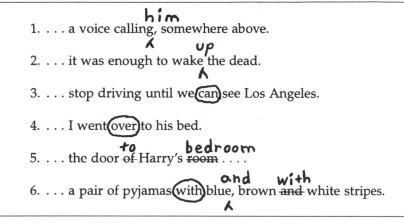

Figure 3 Good readers' miscues

From Kenneth Goodman, *Theoretically based studies of patterns of miscues in oral reading performance.* Detroit: Wayne State University, 1973. (ERIC: ED 079 708)

What kinds of miscues are typical of good readers—by which I mean readers who are good at comprehending texts for which they have sufficient background? In general, good readers make miscues that fit with what came before, whether the miscues consist of an insertion, an omission, a reversal of words, or one word in place of another. Figure 3 shows some examples from children, all of whom had been identified as good readers on measures independent of miscue analysis (K. Goodman, 1973). Most of these miscues involve function words and/or pronouns, and indeed, good readers make such miscues more often than poorer readers (K. Goodman, 1973). As further examples, here are two rather different miscues of my own, both of which involve reading one visually similar word in place of another:

The CES process involves reorganizing not only the curriculum

and the school day and year but reorganizing decision making by
delaying
"delayering" decisions about what to teach and how to teach.

In this first example, the miscue made sense with what came before. In fact, I read all the way to the end of the sentence before concluding that the sentence didn't make sense with the word "delaying." So then I reread and corrected my miscue. The same process occurred when I read "assumes" for *assures*, in the following sentence:

assumes
That sort of visibility ~~assures~~ that everyone knows who is sup-

porting the effort.

"Assumes" fit with what came before, and even with what followed in the same sentence, but the whole sentence did not make sense in the surrounding context. So again, I reread and corrected the miscue.

In reading aloud as performance, I make a wider range of miscues than when reading silently: like Jay and like the children whose miscues are noted in Figure 3, I insert, omit, rearrange, or change words as I try to maintain eye contact while reading the text. But these particular miscues of mine ("delaying" for *delayering* and "assumes" for *assures*) and my experience with the word *demesne* illustrate two kinds of miscue situations that occur even with those of us who read almost all the words of a text "correctly," most of the time (at least when reading silently). How we handle such miscues reveals some important things about proficient reading.

From analyzing the miscues of many other good readers, including those who fairly often insert, omit, rearrange, or change words, researchers (e.g., K. Goodman, 1973; sources cited in Brown, Marek, & Goodman, 1994) have found that good readers exhibit such characteristics as the following:

1. They concentrate more upon constructing meaning from texts than upon identifying all the words correctly (as Jay obviously did). Indeed, good readers may read words better in a list than in context (Nicholson, 1991).

2. They use prior knowledge and context to predict (perhaps unconsciously) what's coming next. Much of the time, prediction prevents miscues or enables readers to identify words by just sampling the visual information. Sometimes, though, this automatic strategy of prediction actually *causes* miscues, because the brain is ahead of the eye. This is often true with Jay, who was reading rapidly and fluently. Because he was using the effective and efficient strategy of predicting, Jay made several

miscues that changed the words or the structure of the sentences. Nevertheless, he produced a fluent rendition of the text that was both *grammatical* and *meaning-preserving*.

3. Good readers are constantly monitoring comprehension (which Jay did), noticing when meaning has gone awry, and when necessary, doing whatever they can to restore meaningfulness (which Jay didn't need to do).

In short, good readers use effective *strategies* for processing text. Strategies are mental plans and operations, which may or not be executed consciously. Strategies enable us to make purposeful, orchestrated use of our various skills, such as phonics knowledge. Three major strategies good readers use are (1) predicting; (2) monitoring comprehension; and (3) confirming or correcting what has been read. (See K. Goodman, 1996a, for an expanded list; see Y. Goodman, Watson, & Burke, 1996 on strategies.)

For instance, almost all of Jay's miscues fit with the preceding context, suggesting that he uses grammar, meaning, and prior knowledge to predict as he reads. For example:

After a hearty supper Hayes joined the smokers ~~about~~ *around* the fire. His
appearance did not settle all the questions *at all* . . .

—

He held open the front of his blue flannel shirt. Out (of)(it) crawled
a horned ~~frog.~~ *toad*

—

"This here *'s* Muriel," said Hayes, with an oratorical wave of his
hand, "~~has~~ *she's* got qualities."

These miscues—indeed, all of Jay's miscues—go with the preceding context and therefore suggest that Jay is predicting. Jay corrected "Out crawled" to "Out of it crawled" in the second example, but usually Jay doesn't bother correcting his miscues when they go with the following context as well as with the preceding, or when he can reconstruct the following context to fit the miscue(s) he has just made—as he did in both the second and third of the preceding examples. On the other hand, Jay corrects the miscue "young" for *youth*, suggesting that he monitors comprehension and grammar and corrects those miscues that don't fit with what follows. (Probably he didn't notice the miscue "ingenious" for *ingenuous*, and he may have decided that the prediction "a," when the text actually says *some*, wasn't worth correcting out loud.) In short, Jay's miscues demonstrate that he's good at predicting and suggest that he monitors comprehension and grammar too, correcting his miscues when necessary to preserve meaning and/or grammatical appropriateness.

If you've been accustomed to thinking of proficient readers as those who identify all or almost all the words correctly and automatically, you may be surprised to learn that Jay was considered the best reader in his sixth grade class. Furthermore, the *kinds* of miscues he made, and the *kinds* of strategies he used, are typical of good readers—even though most of the time, most of us don't make as many miscues as Jay made as he read this selection aloud rapidly.

Furthermore, even first graders make similar kinds of miscues if they're good readers. Take Anne, for instance. Here is a passage she read, with her miscues marked. I suggest you read the passage as Anne read it, complete with miscues:

Now the band began to play. Then the lions roared. Peter the pony

ran ~~around~~ [about] the ring. Bill the circus boy ~~led~~ [© let] Penny the elephant into

the circus ring. ~~Everybody~~ [Everyone] forgot to eat popcorn. They forgot to

drink soda pop. They forgot to wave balloons. ~~The~~ [A] circus man

made a bow.

Trixie ran into the middle of the ring. She sat and waited. Carlo

the clown ~~ran~~ [went] up to Trixie. Trixie jumped up and sat ~~in~~ [on] his hand.

Carlo put Trixie on ~~a~~ [the] box. Trixie stood on her hind legs. Then she

jumped onto Carlo's head. Trixie looked very funny sitting on

Carlo's head. ~~Everybody~~ [Everyone] laughed.

If this passage had been read aloud to you without your seeing it, you might have noticed no miscues whatsoever, yet in this passage Anne made eight miscues, correcting only one. Her miscues reflected *the same* effective reading strategies as Jay's miscues, even though Anne was only a first grader. Note that by *conventional* wisdom, Anne might be thought to have difficulty reading "a" and "the" because she substitutes one for the other in two of her miscues. First we might note, though, that there is another miscue that fits the context even though it doesn't look or sound like the test word: "went" for *ran*, for instance, in the sentence *Carlo the clown ran up to Trixie*. Second, we should note that there are other instances of "a" and "the" that are read as is. That should help us realize that Anne does not have a problem with these so-called basic sight words. More importantly, however, miscue analysis leads us to think of such miscues as *predictions* rather than substitutions: a matter of *processing text* effectively, rather than *reading words* ineffectively. Anne's miscues reveal her mind at work.[2]

These major observations about good readers' miscues demonstrate, in effect, the nature of the reading process itself. True, many effective and efficient readers can and do identify most of the words in a text fluently and automatically. But that is *not* what they are mainly trying to do when they read. On the contrary, their miscues demonstrate that reading is *not* a precise process of identifying every word, but an ongoing construction of meaning from the text (K. Goodman, 1967).

A Comprehensive Research-based Definition and Model of Reading

To guide reading instruction, then, we should have a comprehensive research-based definition and model of proficient reading itself: a description of the target behavior. Taken together, various kinds of research give rise to the following definition of proficient reading:

Reading is processing written symbols and texts to derive meaning. In attending to meaning, proficient readers *automatically*

- predict by using prior knowledge, context, word knowledge, and letter/sound knowledge simultaneously;
- monitor comprehension and use fix-it strategies when meaning has gone awry;
- identify words readily, which makes it easier to attend to meaning.

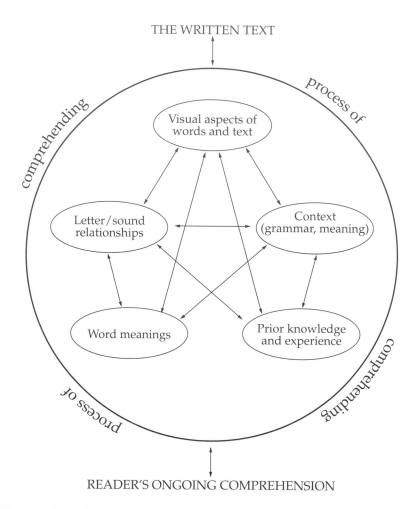

Figure 4 Redundancy model of reading

The model of reading conceptualized in Figure 4 reflects my attempt to put into perspective four major kinds of research (see Weaver 1994b, pp. 209-13): the research from timed, standardized tests which suggests that good readers read words easily and automatically; research from laboratory experiments on word perception; similar research on reading and comprehending sentences and short passages; and the research from observations of the actual reading of whole texts, showing that good readers do not necessarily read all the words as they are on the page, in their overriding quest for meaning. Furthermore, although readers may indeed "see" all the letters of many of the words they read as printed (e.g., Just & Carpenter, 1980), whole words seem to be identified and processed for meaning before the individual letters are seen (Smith, 1994; McConkie & Zola, 1981; Rayner & Pollatsek, 1989).

As I see it, research clearly demonstrates that when a reader reads to *construct meaning from text* (rather than merely to identify words), various interactive processes are going on more or less *simultaneously.*[3] These processes involve the use of prior knowledge and experience, grammar and meaning within the text, visual aspects of the words and text, and the reader's knowledge of concepts of print, word meanings, and letter/sound relationships. The proficient reader orchestrates all of these various kinds and sources of information into strategies such as predicting, monitoring comprehension, and correcting or trying to correct miscues that don't fit the context. A vital, related point is that *even in the primary grades, proficient readers read this way.*

To be balanced, then, a reading program must reflect a definition and model of reading that coherently integrates the best from various bodies of research. A balanced reading program focuses on using skills like phonemic awareness (awareness of separate sounds) and phonics knowledge in the service of strategies for constructing meaning from text.

What about Teaching Phonics First in a Balanced Reading Program?

My response may be obvious: that teaching phonics first makes learning to read more difficult than it needs to be—much more difficult, for many children.

Focusing on phonics first seems logical to many people—perhaps especially to those who have used a phonics program in home schooling their own children. They may not consider the fact that they are probably *not* teaching phonics first: that, in fact, they have been reading to their children for several years and discussing environmental print with them long before starting a phonics program. Therefore, they do not realize that literally teaching phonics first makes learning to read much more difficult for many children, especially those who have not had rich exposure to children's books and other texts (such as the Bible and hymns, perhaps) in the home. Such parents also may not realize that a child can often learn through one-on-one instruction some things that he or she cannot learn well through whole class instruction.

For emergent and less proficient readers, context and prior knowledge are important aids to word identification. Children can often recognize words in context that they could not yet recognize in isolation, or recognize words in familiar contexts that they cannot yet recognize in an unfamiliar context. For example, at the age of fifteen months, Lester Laminack's son Zachary could recognize the McDonald's logo in conjunction with the golden arches outside the restaurant, but he read the logo on his cup of orange drink as "orange" and the logo on his french fries as "fries." By the age of twenty-one months, Zachary read the logo correctly on his father's coffee cup; the logo had become a reliable representation for the name. Zachary then went through much the same process in learning to read "Hardee's," the name of a restaurant that the family went to less often (Laminack, 1991). This process is typical of how a word identified at first only in a familiar or predictable context becomes reliably identified in all contexts.

Without the support of meaningful and predictable (even patterned) texts —with, instead, a relatively unnatural text that emphasizes phonic regularity but makes the use of context and prior knowledge difficult—the less proficient reader lacks the support needed to identify the

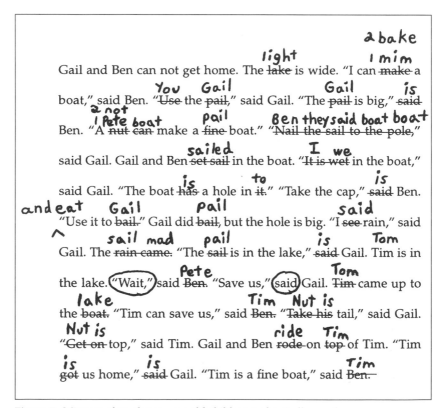

Figure 5 Miscues of an eleven-year-old child on a phonically regular passage

words. See, for instance, Figure 5, which includes the miscues of an eleven-year-old in a resource room who was being taught to read through phonics and through texts that emphasized letter/sound patterns over sense (Weaver, 1994b). Such texts actually make reading harder rather than easier (Rhodes, 1979; Simons & Ammon, 1989; Kucer, 1985; also Baddeley & Lewis, 1981, and Perfetti & McCutcheon, 1982, as cited in Adams, 1990, p. 322). It is not surprising that this struggling reader had considerable difficulty with the text. In fact, a child able to read "Gail," "pail," "sail," "bail," and "tail" in isolation might still miscue on these words in an unnatural, unpredictable text like this one.

Of course we don't want children to remain limited to reading common words only in natural and familiar contexts, but that doesn't often happen. And when reading unfamiliar words *is* a problem, more phonics in isolation is not the best answer, partly because it further encourages readers to deal with each word as if it stood in isolation—a task more difficult than also using context and prior knowledge when trying to read the word. In fact, when children read to identify words *rather than* to construct meaning, both word identification and meaning suffer (K. Goodman, 1973).

In characterizing readers like this with whom she worked tutorially, Carol Chomsky describes her group of eight-year-olds thus:

> These children were not nonreaders. They had received a great deal of phonics training and had acquired many phonetic skills. They met regularly with the remedial reading teacher with whom they had worked intensively since first grade. After much effort, they could "decode," albeit slowly and painfully. What was so frustrating was their inability to put any of this training to use, their failure to progress to even the beginnings of fluent reading. . . . In spite of their hard-won "decoding skills," they couldn't so much as read a page of simple material to me. (Chomsky, 1976)

What made these children into fluent readers and comprehenders was, incidentally, Chomsky's then-experimental technique of having children listen to a book on tape daily and read along with it until they could read it fluently—even if it took a month!

As Chomsky's success with these children helps to illustrate, most children won't remain forever dependent upon context and prior knowledge to identify words they encounter frequently in their reading, if they are given ample opportunities to read and reread familiar texts, along with support from a person or tape recording as necessary.

Do the children simply learn more and more words "on sight" as they read and reread familiar texts? Apparently not. Researchers from varying perspectives agree that what are stored in the brain are not just the visual images of whole words, but letter patterns (and letter/sound knowledge, too, for readers of alphabetic languages). These patterns are not just single letters, but letters (and sounds) that frequently occur together. Furthermore, there is a substantial body of evidence suggesting that we read in "chunks" of letters, and that it is these chunks that facilitate the recognition of even unfamiliar words. We typically read unfamiliar words more by analogy with known words than by identifying letters separately and then sounding words out. And when we do stop to sound out, we frequently do so in chunks—that is, syllables and/or smaller units. This is true not only for adults but for most children as well (Glushko, 1979; Lenel & Cantor, 1981; Bradley & Bryant, 1983, 1985; Perfetti, 1985; Stanovich, 1984; Treiman & Chafetz, 1987; Goswami, 1986, 1988; Kirtley, Bryant, MacLean, & Bradley, 1989; Wise, Olson, & Treiman, 1990; Haskell et al., 1992).

A set of studies by Moustafa (1990; reported also in Moustafa 1993, 1995, and Chapter 5 in this volume), provides evidence of this. In designing the studies, Moustafa drew upon research showing that young children find it relatively easy to hear syllabic chunks known as onsets and rimes (e.g., Goswami & Bryant, 1990; Treiman, 1985). (An onset consists of any consonant[s] occurring before the vowel, as in tip, chip, trap, strap. The rime part of a syllable is the vowel plus anything that comes after it, as in I, tip, past, chain.) Children who aren't yet readers find it substantially easier to divide words into onsets and rimes than to divide them into separate phonemes (the "separate" sounds within words, which aren't really so separate as the alphabetic representation of them would lead us to believe). What Moustafa found in her research was that onset/rime analogy accounted for children's ability to recode printed words into spoken words better than did the theory that we blend phonemes to make words. Or in other words, her research supports the idea that we process words in chunks of letters like onsets and rimes, rather than letter by letter.

We may hypothesize, then, that what happened with the children in Chomsky's study was not—or not merely—that they learned a lot of new words by reading and rereading the books they chose. Rather— or in addition—they internalized more letter/sound patterns that facilitated the reading of unfamiliar words. In other words, the children learned phonics by or while learning words. This explanation fits with Moustafa's results and her hypothesis: that children commonly develop phonics knowledge through repeated exposure to texts and words (including exposure that provides the spoken words that correspond to the written words). This hypothesis also explains the success of readers diagnosed as dyslexic in childhood who have nevertheless become extraordinarily successful as adults, and who read and write complex texts almost daily, even though they still have difficulty with decoding words (see Fink, chapter 13).

To combine two points and generalize, then: after repeatedly identifying a word in context, a reader gradually learns to identify the word without the help of context: the reader has learned to recognize the word, no matter where it occurs (Laminack, 1991). Even more important, the reader has learned to recognize parts of the words, which facilitates reading unfamiliar words in chunks, by analogy. However, insisting on phonics first, or sight words first, makes learning to read much more difficult. Teaching reading by phonics alone is somewhat like making a child learn to walk with one leg tied up and hands tied behind the back, before allowing the child the use of both legs and the arms for balance. Or it's like giving the child training wheels only *after* he or she has learned to ride a bicycle without support. As ridiculous as this sounds, it's not much more ridiculous than insisting that children be taught phonics *first*. Phonics alone is not enough, and phonics first makes learning to read more difficult, especially for children who have not already had rich exposure to books and other texts. Learning to read is easier when children are encouraged to use prior knowledge and context to facilitate their use and development of word knowledge and phonics: when, for instance, they read predictable texts, such as texts they themselves have composed, or familiar songs, rhymes, and patterned stories.

Surely we want to make learning to read as easy as possible, not as difficult as possible.

Teaching Phonemic Awareness, Phonics, and Decoding Skills

No doubt you can already see why my second major concern is that the recent research on phonemic awareness not be misconstrued as evidence for the teaching of intensive, systematic phonics *first*. Research on the teaching and learning of phonics has been fraught with controversy, with claims and counter-claims, with first one kind of evidence and then another. However, conclusions from the first major body of research can be summarized rather briefly. This section is taken nearly verbatim from Weaver, Giymeister-Krause, and Vento-Zogby, 1996, second printing.

The oft-cited research base (research before 1967)

Research summarized in two major reports (Chall, 1967; Bond & Dykstra, 1967) allegedly showed that intensive phonics produces better reading and spelling achievement (scores on standardized tests) than the traditional basal reading programs, which then generally emphasized learning words on sight.

In the wake of a detailed criticism of many of these studies and their summaries (Carbo, 1988), assessment expert Richard Turner (1989) undertook to analyze only the best of the studies that actually compared classroom approaches. He concluded:

> Systematic phonics appears to have a slight and early advantage over a basal-reader/whole word approach as a method of beginning reading instruction. . . . However, this difference does not last long and has no clear meaning for the acquisition of literacy.

The latter point is a crucial one that seems to have been forgotten in today's frenzy to teach phonics and more phonics.

Research on phonemic awareness and decoding

The last decade has seen considerable research on phonological awareness and phonemic awareness. *Phonological awareness* may be defined as the ability to hear and manipulate sound units in the language, such as syllables; the major parts of syllables (onsets and rimes); and *phonemes* (what we have learned to hear as the individual "sounds" in words). One body of research has usually focused on phonological awareness and phonological coding skills in general, but typically included measures of phonemic awareness specifically. Such research has demonstrated that there is a strong correlation between phonemic awareness and reading achievement, as measured by scores on standardized tests (e.g., summaries in Adams & Bruck, 1995; Beck & Juel, 1995; Foorman, 1995). There is also research showing the opposite correlation: low phonemic awareness, low scores on standardized tests (e.g., Lyon, 1995a, 1995b; Vellutino & Denckla, 1991; Goswami & Bryant, 1990; Elbro, 1990; Boder, 1973). These correlations are hardly surprising, since readers with weak phonemic segmentation skills may be slower than those with strong segmentation skills in decoding unfamiliar print words, and standardized tests are commonly timed. Such correlational research has led to the argument that children should be explicitly taught phonemic awareness—not merely to help them sound out words, but to recognize words on sight, automatically (e.g., Stanovich, 1991, 1992). However, a correlation simply means that the two go together, like bread and butter; it says nothing about whether one causes the other—for example, whether phonemic awareness leads to independent reading, whether learning to read results in phonemic awareness, or both. What, then, does the research show?

1. *Various studies demonstrate that children can be trained to hear phonemes and to segment words into phonemes and/or suggest that teaching phonemic awareness causes, or at least facilitates, higher scores on standardized tests.* These studies include, among others, Stanovich, Cunningham, and Feeman, 1985; Fox and Routh, 1976; Bradley and Bryant, 1985; Ball and Blachman, 1991; Vellutino and Scanlon, 1987; Nation and Hulme, 1997. Several research studies focus on children considered to have severe reading difficulties (e.g., Torgeson and Hecht, 1996; Vellutino et al., 1996; Fox and Routh, 1976) and/or on children considered to be at risk of reading failure (Foorman, Francis, Beeler, Winikates, and Fletcher, 1997). Ayers (1993) is exceptional in that the training groups were entire classes of kindergartners, rather than small groups. Some research has been interpreted as demonstrating that phonemic awareness is a necessary prerequisite to learning to read, or at least a necessary but not sufficient cause or facilitator in learning to read. One oft-cited example is Juel, Griffith, and Gough (1986), while another, more recent study is Foorman, Francis, Beeler, Winikates, and Fletcher, 1997. Several studies indicate that phonemic awareness develops best when taught in conjunction with letter/sound correspondences (Ball & Blachman, 1991; Bradley & Bryant, 1983; Byrne & Fielding-Barnsley, 1989, 1991; Goldstein, 1976; Treiman & Baron, 1983; Vellutino & Scanlon, 1987; Wallach & Wallach, 1979; Williams, 1980).

   Particularly noteworthy is Ayers's award-winning study (1993), in which she found that kindergartners who encountered a meaning-emphasis in reading before receiving direct instruction in phonological elements did better on measures of those elements than children who had the direct instruction first (see Ayres, chapter 8 here).

2. *Some research has been interpreted as demonstrating that phonemic awareness is a consequence of learning to read.* These studies include Morais, Carey, Alegria, and Bertelson (1979); Mann (1986); and Wimmer, Landerl, Linortner, and Hummer (1991). Another study that did not focus specifically on phonemic awareness but that supports this conclusion is Moustafa (1990, 1995, and in chapter 5 in this volume).

3. *Some of the phonemic awareness studies explicitly support, and the others do not contradict, a reciprocal hypothesis: that phonemic awareness facilitates learning to read and that learning to read also facilitates phonemic awareness.* Studies explicitly drawing this conclusion include

Perfetti, Beck, Bell and Hughes; 1987; Ayers, 1993, and Chapter 8
here; Wagner and Torgeson, 1987; Wagner, Torgeson, and Rashotte,
1994. Tunmer and Nesdale (1985) found that the correlation
between method of instruction and phonemic segmentation ability did not reach significance, which implies a reciprocal relationship between phonemic awareness and learning to read. In some
instances the researcher did not set out explicitly to test the hypothesis that learning to read promotes phonemic awareness, but found
that by the end of first grade, the control group did as well as the
experimental groups on measures of phonemic awareness and/or
comprehension (e.g., Ayres, 1993). In fact, Ayres found that kindergartners whose reading experiences focused first (for ten weeks)
on getting meaning and enjoyment from texts were better able to
take advantage of direct instruction phonics than those children
who were given direct instruction in phonics first.

4. *Different methods of teaching the recognition of phonological units
   (especially rimes, onsets, and "individual" sounds) and other phonics-
   related concepts and skills do not necessarily produce results that differ very much from one another* (e.g., Torgeson & Hecht, 1996;
   Tunmer & Nesdale, 1985; McIntyre & Freppon, 1994 [chapter 7
   in this volume]). For instance, Tunmer and Nesdale write that
   "the correlation between method of instruction and phonemic
   segmentation ability did not reach significance" in their study
   (1985, p. 424). This is particularly noteworthy in view of the fact
   that children in half of the classrooms received instruction that
   included no incidental or formal instruction in phonological
   decoding skills (p. 421).

5. *With regard to decoding itself, the research is somewhat contradictory.*
   Some research suggests that, like adults, children decode unfamiliar print words by analogy with parts of known words (e.g.,
   Moustafa, 1990, 1995, and chapter 5 in this volume; Goswami,
   1986, 1988). That is, they read unknown print words in chunks
   (Gunning, 1988; Gibson, 1985; Santa, 1976–77; and other sources
   cited in Gunning, 1995). Some studies suggest that phonemic
   awareness precedes the ability to decode unfamiliar print words
   (e.g., Tunmer & Nesdale, 1985; also see Ehri & Robbins, 1992, and
   Moustafa's reinterpretation of that study, chapter 5 in this volume). Other research suggests that the ability to read unfamiliar
   print words in pronounceable chunks precedes the ability to segment words into phonemes (Ehri, 1991, 1994, 1995; Goswami,
   1986, 1988, 1993), and/or that knowing a lot of sight words is

more helpful in decoding unknown words than is letter/sound knowledge (Moustafa, 1990, 1995, and chapter 5 here). More research is needed on these factors, since decoding is an actual reading skill that children need to develop.

6. *No matter how they are taught—whether with intensive phonics, incidental phonics, or no phonics—some children will still need more intensive individual help.* For example, Tunmer and Nesdale write, "although phonemic segmentation ability can be readily improved through training, there remain substantial individual differences after such training (e.g., Wallach & Wallach, 1976; Williams, 1980), suggesting that the cognitive abilities of some children may be such that they require additional, more intensive training" (1985, p. 420).

7. *With such intensive help, however, almost all children can develop adequate phonological skills* (e.g., Clay, 1987, Inversen & Tunmer, 1993; Vellutino et al., 1996). Vellutino and his co-researchers clearly demonstrate that most of these children can benefit from, and become at least average-level readers in one or two semesters of daily tutoring, leaving only a very small percentage—perhaps about 3%—that cannot achieve adequate phonological skills with a year's individual tutoring.

8. *The research on so-called "linguistic" or "decodable" texts (texts with phonically regular words exemplifying patterns already taught) shows clearly that they are harder to read than texts written in more natural language* (e.g., Simons & Ammon, 1989; Kucer, 1985; Rhodes, 1979). One study is currently being cited as evidence for using decodable texts rather than texts with high interest words (Juel & Roper/Schneider, 1985). However, this study compared the effects of reading texts having mostly phonically regular words with the then-typical basal reading texts and concluded merely that the decodable texts were more likely to lead to a letter/sound strategy in reading. However, that strategy *alone* leads to a focusing on identifying words, at the expense of meaning (e.g., K. Goodman, 1973). Furthermore, to date there has apparently been no research that has explicitly compared the effects of decodable texts with "predictable" texts that use more natural language, organized in repeating and predictable patterns.

Typically, the research alleging a high correlation between phonemic awareness and reading scores, and the research showing that many seemingly poorer readers are not strong in phonological or phonemic awareness, has led to the argument that many children need explicit help in developing the ability to segment words into sounds—not merely in order to sound out words, but to recognize words on sight, *automatically*, and thereby to read *fluently* and rapidly. Only a small body of research has addressed or been interpreted as having bearing on alternative hypotheses, such as the hypothesis that there is a reciprocal relationship between phonemic awareness and learning to read, with each facilitating the other. However, that body of research is growing.

Research comparing skills-oriented with literature-based and/or whole language classrooms

In the past decade, quite a few studies have compared the effects of literature-based and/or whole language teaching with the effects of traditional skills-oriented teaching (several are summarized in Weaver, 1994b). Though whole language teaching involves much more than a different approach to reading and writing, one key element of whole language classrooms is that children receive the support they need to read and write whole texts and to develop reading and writing skills within meaningful reading and writing situations. *This includes explicit help in developing phonemic awareness, phonics knowledge, and decoding skills.* Part of what many whole language teachers do in the primary grades is spend significant time each day reading to children from a large text that all can see, then rereading the text with the children chiming in. Repeated rereadings and calling attention to words and letter/sound patterns help the children learn words and phonics, as well as basic concepts of print. For example, extensions of such reading activities may include discussing and making charts of words that alliterate or rhyme. Examining and comparing the spellings of children's names is another way phonics may be taught. Whole language teachers also promote phonics knowledge by helping children write the sounds they hear in words. By teaching phonics through reading, mini-lessons, and writing, whole language teachers help children develop phonics knowledge in the context of the texts they enjoy reading and writing.

In two of these studies, the skills-based classrooms were characterized particularly by programs teaching phonics in isolation from literature and authentic writing; these were Ribowsky (1985) and Kasten & Clarke (1989). Some of the studies focused on at-risk children (Stice & Bertrand, 1990; Dahl & Freppon, 1992, 1994; Knapp and associates, 1995; and some of the studies discussed in Tunnell & Jacobs, 1989, which included some studies involving children identified as having reading difficulties, too). All of these studies used a variety of measures in addition to standardized tests. The following patterns seem to emerge from these studies and others referenced below:

1. *Children in whole language classrooms typically do as well or better on standardized reading tests and subtests, including tests that measure phonemic awareness and phonics knowledge, though the differences are seldom statistically significant.* For example, the whole language kindergartners in Ribowsky's study (1985) scored better on all measures of growth and achievement, including the tests of letter recognition and letter/sound knowledge. In the Kasten and Clarke study (1989), the whole language kindergartners performed significantly better than their counterparts on all subtests of the Metropolitan Readiness Test, including tests of beginning consonant sounds, letter/sound correspondences, and sounds and clusters of sounds in initial and final positions of words. In the Manning, Manning, and Long study (1989), children in the whole language classroom did better on the Stanford Achievement Test's subtest on word parts, even though only the children in the skills classroom had explicitly studied word parts.

2. *Children in whole language classrooms seem to develop greater ability to use phonics knowledge effectively than children in more traditional classrooms where skills are practiced in isolation.* For example, in Freppon's study (1988, 1991), the skills group attempted to sound out words more than twice as often as the others, but the literature-based group was more successful in doing so: a 53 percent success rate compared with a 32 percent success rate for the skills group. Apparently the literature-based children were more successful because they made better use of phonics in conjunction with other information and cues. (For another relevant study, see also A. E. Cunningham, 1990).

3. *Children in whole language classrooms seem to develop the alphabetic principle, vocabulary, spelling, grammar, and punctuation skills as well as or better than children in more traditional classrooms.* For example, see Elley's 1991 summary of studies on learning English as a second language; Knapp and associates, 1995, on a variety of skills; also McIntyre and Freppon, 1994, on development of the alphabetic principle; Clarke, 1988, on spelling; and Stice and Bertrand, 1990, which included spelling. A comparison of standardized test scores before and after implementation of whole language instruction in two school districts reveals essentially no difference in test

scores (Traw, 1996). In addition, see Calkins, 1980; Gunderson and Shapiro, 1988; Smith and Elley, 1995. DiStefano and Killion (1984) is also relevant.

4. *Children in whole language classrooms seem more inclined and able to read for meaning rather than just to identify words.* For example, when asked "What makes a good reader?", the children in Stice and Bertrand's study (1990) reported that good readers read a great deal and that they can read any book in the room. The children in the traditional classrooms tended to focus on words and surface correctness; they reported that good readers read big words, they know all the words, and they don't miss any words. In a study by Manning, Manning, and Long (1989), children in the whole language classroom were more likely to read for meaning, read with greater comprehension, and read with greater accuracy (not counting the errors that resulted in no meaning loss).

5. *Children in whole language classrooms seem to develop more strategies for dealing with problems in reading.* For example, the children in the whole language classrooms in Stice and Bertrand's study (1990) typically described six strategies for dealing with problem words, while the children in traditional classrooms described only three.

6. *Children in whole language classrooms seem to develop greater facility in writing.* For example, in the Dahl and Freppon study (1991, 1994), a considerably larger proportion of the children in the whole language classrooms were writing sentences and stories by the end of first grade. The children in the whole language classrooms in the Kasten and Clarke study (1989) were similarly much more advanced as writers by the end of their kindergarten year.

7. *Children in whole language classrooms seem to develop a stronger sense of themselves as readers and writers.* Take, for example, the Stice and Bertrand study (1990). When asked "Who do you know who is a good reader?", 82 percent of the kindergartners in the whole language classrooms mentioned themselves, but only 5 percent of the kindergartners in the traditional classrooms said "me." During the first-grade year, when the children were asked directly "Are you a good reader?", 70 percent of the whole language children said yes, but only 33 percent of the traditional children said yes.

8. *Children in whole language classrooms also seem to develop greater independence as readers and writers.* In the Dahl and Freppon study (1992, 1994), for instance, passivity seemed to be the most frequent

coping strategy for learners having difficulty in the skills-based classrooms. But in whole language classrooms, those having difficulty tended to draw upon other learners for support: by saying the phrases and sentences that others could read, by copying what they wrote, and so forth. That is, these less proficient literacy learners still attempted to remain engaged in literacy activities with their peers. They didn't just give up.

In whole language classrooms like the ones in these studies, where phonics is taught briefly but explicitly in the context of reading and writing, the concepts of phonemic awareness, phonics, and decoding skills seem to be learned at least as well as in skills emphasis classrooms (Stahl & Kuhn, 1995). Taken together, various studies suggest that about 80-85 percent of our children develop such skills without additional help in phonological skills.

These research results corroborate conclusions from more naturalistic research; they do not stand alone in support of whole language. Furthermore, other comparative studies have generated similar results (see the summaries in Stephens, 1991; Shapiro, 1990; Tunnel & Jacobs, 1989; for the importance of reading and more reading, see Krashen, 1993). Share and his colleagues account for such learning in their self-teaching model of word reading acquisition (Share & Jorm, 1987; Share & Stanovich, 1995). And recent research suggests mechanisms by which such learning may take place (Moustafa, 1995, and chapter 5; Peterson & Haines, 1992, also chapter 6).

In lone contrast is the aborted study by Foorman, Francis, Beeler, Winikates, & Fletcher (1997), which compared a program with direct and intensive phonics instruction to programs wherein phonics was "embedded" in other literacy activities and with a "whole language" approach wherein phonics was supposed to be taught in the context of reading and writing. Preliminary results from this study at least seem to suggest that teaching phonics in isolation may get children off to a better start in developing phonemic awareness and phonics skills and in using these skills in word identification than a program that embeds phonics into a whole literacy context. However, this preliminary report does not indicate whether the time spent focusing on letter/sound relationships in the "embedded phonics" and "whole language" treatments was equal to that in the direct instruction phonics program. If not, this difference might account for why this study showed more positive results for the direct instruction program.

Furthermore, the study included only one independent (multiple-choice) measure of comprehension, on which there were no significant differences among treatment groups. No additional kinds of factors were measured. So the study speaks only to the early acquisition of phonemic awareness and phonics skills, not to the overall issue of becoming a competent and independent reader who uses such skills in the service of constructing meaning. For example, we have no way of gleaning answers to questions like these:

- How and how effectively do the children make use of reading strategies to orchestrate their use of skills and to read for meaning?

- How and how effectively can they retell and discuss what they have read? Draw inferences and make connections across text elements? Analyze, synthesize, and evaluate?

- How willing are they to read texts wherein they cannot identify almost all the words?

- How much reading do they do voluntarily, and what kinds of texts do they read?

The ability to read and comprehend meaningful texts affects one's willingness to read, which in turn affects how much one reads, and that in turn ultimately affects how well one reads. As Marilyn Adams and Maggie Bruck have put it, "Most obviously, more reading is clearly the best path to better reading" (1995, p. 17). This conclusion is amply documented by other research (e.g., Anderson, Hiebert, Scott, & Wilkinson, 1985; Tunnel & Jacobs, 1989; Krashen, 1993; Fink, Chapter 13 in this volume; McQuillan, in progress).

What we need to know over time, then, is, how will children with different beginning reading emphases fare in reading by, let's say, grade 5? Will children from the direct instruction phonics tend to overattend to words at the expense of meaning? Will children from the whole language, skills-in-context classrooms read for meaning and read voluntarily, but have greater difficulty with word identification? Will one group be able to comprehend more sophisticated texts than the other? Or will the differences even out, after several years of instruction?

So, What Are We to Make of These Bodies of Research?

When it comes to implementation, all of this research must be interpreted cautiously. One reason is that both kinds of experimental research—one dealing with phonological and phonemic awareness, and another dealing with the development of a wide range of literate behaviors—have often focused on small numbers of children. Much of the research on teaching phonological and phonemic awareness, in fact, has involved teaching children either in small groups or tutoring them one-on-one (an important exception is Ayres, 1993, and chapter 8 in this volume). Furthermore, while research may sometimes show the greatest effects for direct instruction tutoring, the differences do not necessarily last, nor are they necessarily great enough to be statistically significant. In the Torgesen and Hecht study (1996), for example, the differences among the different tutorial treatments were very slight, while there was a substantial difference between all the tutorial groups and the children receiving no additional tutoring.

Another limitation of both bodies of research is that the studies typically do not assess comprehension on measures other than standardized tests (though, in the latter group of studies, children were sometimes asked to retell what they had read). This is a major limitation that needs to be addressed in future research, and addressed over a period of years, in longitudinal studies—as do various aspects of literacy development.

Given these limitations and caveats, what can we tentatively conclude? The evidence seems fairly strong that whole language teaching usually produces about the same results on standardized tests (including measures of phonics, which *ipso facto* require phonemic analysis) as does traditional skills-oriented teaching, including teaching that has emphasized phonics. There is also some evidence that direct-instruction phonics may produce higher initial scores on phonemic awareness and word attack skills and sometimes on comprehension tests, particularly with children labeled at risk or reading disabled, when they are tutored one-on-one or in very small groups. On the other hand, this advantage appears not to last very long, particularly for comprehension tests. Meanwhile, students in classrooms where skills are taught in the context of reading and writing whole texts have typically made substantially greater advances in a variety of literacy-related skills, strategies, behaviors, and attitudes. Thus, such teaching may be superior overall to skills-intensive and phonics-intensive teaching, at least for a majority of our children.

Toward a Consensus on the Teaching of Phonics

There are still critical differences in how reading researchers conceptualize and characterize reading. Those who have examined the reading process through an analysis of the miscues made by proficient readers have concluded that what most obviously characterizes proficient reading is the reader's drive to construct meaning (Goodman, 1973; Brown, Goodman, & Marek, 1996). Those who have examined word identification and/or correlations among test scores more than the process of reading whole texts have concluded that what most obviously characterizes proficient reading is the ability to read most words in a text automatically and fluently (e.g., Adams & Bruck, 1995; Beck & Juel, 1995; Stanovich, 1991).

The former group of researchers point out that too much attention to phonics can detract from the construction of meaning and the development of effective reading strategies, while the latter cite correlations between tests of phonemic awareness and scores on standardized tests as evidence that phonemic awareness and phonics must be taught early to promote reading achievement—that is, high standardized test scores. Note, however, that the two ideas are compatible: children may have developed phonemic awareness *in the process* of becoming independent readers and writers.

How has this partial convergence begun to come about? On the one hand, whole language researchers and educators have done research and written books, articles, and other documents demonstrating how phonics is learned and/or taught in the context of reading and writing whole texts (McIntyre & Freppon, 1994; Mills, O'Keefe, & Stephens, 1992; Powell and Hornsby, 1993; Weaver, 1994a; Routman & Butler, 1995). On the other hand, some researchers who most adamantly insist on teaching phonemic awareness and phonics are suggesting teaching methods and materials that resemble those of the whole language educators (Adams & Bruck, 1995; Beck & Juel, 1995; also P. Cunningham, 1995; Griffith & Olson, 1992). For example, some educators within both groups recommend using nursery rhymes, tongue twisters, and books like the rhymed Dr. Seuss books. Both groups recognize the importance of reading to and with children. One remaining difference, however, is that phonemic awareness researchers and educators often advocate oral language play and games in the preschool years (Yopp, 1992), while whole language educators typically are convinced this is unnecessary and that children will learn more in less time when the teacher focuses on phonemic awareness in the context of written texts (e.g., see Kasten & Clarke, 1989; Richgels, Poremba, & McGee, 1996; and the aforementioned studies showing that phonemic awareness is best learned when letter/sound correspondences are also taught).

As someone who once advocated systematic phonics (Stahl, 1992) now puts it, "there is little evidence that one form of phonics instruction is strongly superior to another" (Stahl, McKenna, & Pagnucco, 1994). And considering the major theoretical differences among reading researchers and the resulting emphases, it is particularly noteworthy that researchers and educators from various backgrounds are beginning to converge on the following major points about the teaching of phonics:

1. Phonemic awareness facilitates learning to read, and learning to read—and write—also facilitates the development of phonemic awareness (the reciprocal hypothesis).

2. Worksheets and mindless drill are not the best means of developing phonemic awareness and phonics knowledge (e.g., A. E. Cunningham, 1990), nor is focusing on rules as helpful as focusing on patterns.

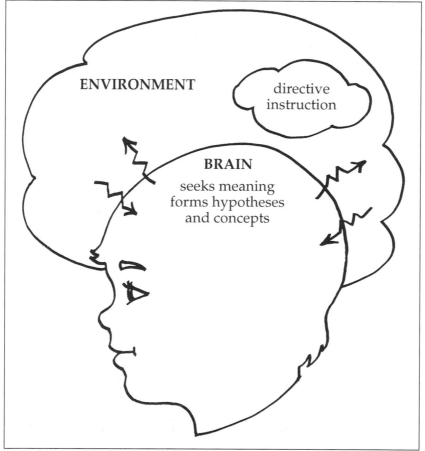

Figure 6 A Constructivist Model of Learning

From *Creating Support for Effective Literacy Education* by C. Weaver, L. Gillmeister-Krause, & G. Vento-Zogby, © 1996. Portsmouth, NH: Heinemann. Reprinted with permission.

3. Learning in general, and the learning of phonics in particular, are primarily intellectual acts of pattern detection and hypothesis and concept formation, even though some children will need more directive instruction to make comprehensible the patterns in the words they encounter (see Figure 6 for a constructivist model of learning that includes directive instruction provided as needed, to meet individual readers' needs).[4]

4. Effective teaching of phonics:

   • is derived from and embedded within a rich literacy context that also integrates reading, writing, and literature with the use of oral language across the curriculum;

   • requires children to think, not passively complete worksheets or engage in drill;

   • focuses on patterns, not rules;

   • focuses on rimes and onsets before single phonemes (other than onsets);

   • combines attention to phonemic awareness with attention to letter/sound correspondences;

   • is interactive and collaborative, involving discussion.

5. Children should be given some explicit, direct help in developing phonemic awareness and a functional command of phonics.

6. Such direct teaching does not, however, have to be intensive and systematic to be effective for a majority of our children. Indeed, at least three-fourths of our children typically develop phonemic knowledge and phonics knowledge without much direct teaching.

7. Nevertheless, some children will need and benefit from additional help in developing phonemic awareness, phonics knowledge, and/or decoding skills (as predicted by the constructivist model). Various sources suggest that somewhere between 15 and 20 percent of our children show a need for such additional instruction, whether it be provided in the classroom or without (Lyon, 1996).

Such additional teaching is still not a panacea, though, as a small percentage of children continue to have difficulty in developing phonemic awareness and phonics knowledge no matter how they are taught and tutored (e.g., Dahl & Freppon, 1992; Vellutino et al., 1996; Torgeson & Hecht, 1996). However, teaching phonics in context and through discussion and collaborative activities seems to be effective with a majority of our children, and additional, more intensive and systematic teaching of phonemic awareness and phonics skills can be provided in daily tutorial sessions for children who appear to need it—either within the classroom (see articles in the companion volume, *Practicing What We Know: Informed Reading Instruction* [Weaver, 1998]), or in pull-out programs (e.g., Clay, 1987; Iversen & Tunmer, 1993). Meanwhile, most of the children in classrooms where skills are taught in the context of reading and writing whole texts get a better start on becoming proficient and independent readers, not mere word-callers (e.g., Dahl & Freppon, 1992, 1994; Stice & Bertrand, 1990; Kasten & Clarke, 1989).

Helping Children Develop Phonics Knowledge

Without using programs for teaching phonics intensively and systematically, parents and teachers can do various things to help children gain phonics knowledge and develop phonemic awareness in the context of meaningful reading and writing and language play. Educators differ as to which particular practices they adopt or recommend, but many educators and researchers advocate at least some of the following (Fountas & Pinnell, 1996; Mills et al., 1992; Powell & Hornsby, 1993; Freppon & Dahl, 1991; Griffith & Olson, 1992; Weaver, 1994a and b; Routman & Butler, 1995; P. Cunningham, 1995; Wagstaff, no date; Adams & Bruck, 1995; Beck & Juel, 1995):

1. Read and reread favorite nursery rhymes, and enjoy tongue twisters and other forms of language play together.

2. Reread favorite poems, songs, and stories; discuss alliteration and rhyme within them; and play with sound elements (e.g., starting with *cake,* remove the *c* and consider what different sounds could be added to make other words, like *take, make, lake*).

3. Read alphabet books to and with children, and make alphabet books together.

4. Discuss words and make lists, word banks, or books of such words that share interesting spelling/sound patterns.

5. Discuss similar sounds and letter/sound patterns in children's names.

6. Emphasize selected letter/sound relationships while writing with, for, or in front of children.

7. Encourage children to play with magnetic letters and to explore letter/sound relations.

8. Help children write the sounds they hear in words.

9. When reading together, help children use prior knowledge and context plus initial consonants to predict what a word will be, then look at the rest of the word to confirm or correct. This is especially important for helping children orchestrate prior knowledge with context and letter/sound cues in order not merely to identify words but to construct meaning from texts—which, after all, is the primary purpose of reading.

Teaching phonics and phonemic awareness in such ways and from the aforementioned principles helps keep letter/sound cues in proper perspective, but only when children spend substantially more time daily in listening to books read aloud (live, and on tape); in reading independently or with a partner (even if they still read the pictures more than the words); in discussing the literature they have heard and read; in reading classroom messages, signs, directions, and other informational print; in composing and writing together with the teacher, as a group; and in writing independently. Teaching phonics first and only, as some people urge, is a good way of separating children who *can* do isolated phonics from those who *can't*, but it is not a good way to teach children to read, since reading is much more than attacking words. Phonics first and only can be particularly difficult and limiting for children whose prior experiences with books have been limited.

Furthermore, we should not assume that children or adults who have difficulty recognizing and/or sounding out words cannot comprehend texts effectively; indeed, even "dyslexic" readers can often comprehend well (Fink, 1995/96; Weaver, 1994c), because of the redundancy of language and the knowledge they bring to texts. To deny them access to whole and meaningful texts until they can "do" phonemic awareness and phonics well is inexcusable—a point to which I shall return.

In summary, research suggests, then, that our best plan may be to teach phonics and phonemic awareness in the context of reading and writing, to all children; provide tutoring within and/or outside the classroom for children who need more individualized and/or more direct help with letter/sound relationships and/or decoding; and probably to discontinue such help for children who have benefitted little from a year's daily individualized tutoring, while increasing the emphasis on developing strategies for deriving meaning. The limitations of extended tutoring in phonological matters is suggested not only by experimental research, but by anecdotes such as the one about Erica in the next section.

The Potential Harm from Assessment and Diagnosis

My concern about the possible overemphasis on phonics and skills in recent documents purporting to promote a "balanced" approach to reading leads naturally to a concern about an undue emphasis on children's achievement of arbitrary performance standards and the continual attempt to discover (that is, to "diagnose") reading difficulties in children. These concerns arise particularly from California's *Every Child a Reader* and from Texas Governor Bush's reading initiative paper (January 1996). Unlike the committee that prepared the California report, Governor Bush did not use the term "performance standards," but he said that the Texas Education Agency will make available a diagnostic tool for teachers to use, perhaps as early as kindergarten. "Diagnose the problems so you can cure them," he says.

On the one hand, we do need to assess children's current abilities and needs and work to meet those needs. But on the other hand, we can always find problems when that's what we look for. Given the history of reading instruction, I fear that looking for problems and then trying to remediate them will result in an *un*balanced reading program for some children, wherein they are kept busy doing skills work and have little opportunity to engage in the meaningful reading and writing that will, in fact, do the most to help them become better readers (Anderson, Hiebert, Scott, & Wilkinson, 1985; Tunnel & Jacobs, 1989; Krashen, 1993; Fink, 1995/96; McQuillan, forthcoming).

Why do I fear this result? Because that is what we teachers and our educational system as a whole have traditionally done to children who have difficulty with phonics or other so-called reading skills. And that's what politicians and their collaborators seem bent on doing again—with a vengeance.

Let me explain in more detail, using examples of three readers whose competence is undervalued by conventional means of assessment.

Gina

To remind ourselves of the kinds of strategies used by good readers, let us examine some miscues from Gina, a woman in her early forties who, after skating professionally for many years, opened her own skating school in Australia (Marek, 1996).

Like Jay and Anne, the good sixth- and first-grade readers previously discussed, Gina makes miscues because she predicts what is coming next. Many of these miscues remain uncorrected because they fit the context and don't seriously affect meaning. For example:

even
It doesn't seem the waves could ~~ever~~ get that high.

this
He invited me to have a seat and listen to ~~his~~ strange tale.

beginning
Then, suddenly, the boy felt the Zephyr ~~begin~~ to shake.

full of
Then the air was ~~filled with~~ the sound of breaking branches and

ripping sails.

When she has made a miscue that doesn't make sense or sound grammatical in context, Gina tends to correct it:

©
"Yes, Miss, it's very important," I said to the lady on the telephone.

In this case, Gina got all the way to the end of the sentence, realized that what she had said didn't sound right (she had omitted the *to*), returned to *I said*, and read from there through the rest of the sentence to make the sentence grammatical.

Thus Gina's miscues show her using the strategies of effective readers: predicting, monitoring comprehension, and confirming or correcting as needed. Unfortunately, though, she had somehow been perceived as a poor reader—even though teachers commonly ignore such miscues when made by readers they *consider* proficient. Consequently, Gina was convinced that she was a nonreader and indeed that she suffered from undiagnosed dyslexia. While many teachers seem to realize that it's okay for good readers to make miscues, they have often demanded word-perfect reading from the readers they consider less proficient. This, along, with heavy skills instruction, is what convinced Gina that she could not read.

VOWEL DIGRAPH ea

The vowel digraph ea has three sounds: long e, short e, and long a. If a word is unfamiliar, try each of the three sounds. You should then recognize the word. Show the sound of ea on the line after each word. Show the sound of a short e with an unmarked e.

Key: Each ē   Head e   Great ā

1. Treatment ē
2. Steadier a ✓
3. Stealthy ✓
4. Teak ā ✓
5. Greatest ā
6. Wreath ē
7. Dealt e
8. Congeal ē
9. Sheath ✓
10. Creased ā ✓
11. Measles ē
12. Beacon ā ✓
13. Breakneck ā -
14. Heathen e ✓
15. Heavenly e
16. Easel ē
17. Sweat ē ✓
18. Unhealthy e
19. Seasoning ē
20. Chesapeake ✓
21. Streamlined ē
22. Treachery ē ✓
23. Defeated ē
24. Pheasants ē ✓

25. Creaking ē
26. Jealousy ✓
27. Appeal e ✓
28. Decrease ē
29. Beefsteak e
30. Peasant e
31. Peaceable e ✓
32. Reveal
33. Weapon
34. Cleansing
35. Beagle
36. Sneakers
37. Feathery
38. Feat
39. Flea
40. Meanwhile
41. Cease
42. Heavily
43. Pealed
44. Weasel
45. Dread
46. Eatable
47. Increasing
48. Dealer

Finish your work! (-41)

49. Treacherous
50. Headquarters
51. Cleanliness
52. Meant
53. Underneath
54. Breakthrough
55. Repeal
56. Streaked
57. Weathered
58. Meantime
59. Eagerness
60. Eaves
61. Threatened
62. Leased
63. Leash
64. Breakwater
65. Deafen
66. Eastern
67. Retreating
68. Bleachers
69. Deathless
70. Headache
71. Leaky
72. Sneaky

Figure 7 Worksheet required of Jan, a fourth grader

From Dorothy Watson and Paul Crowley, How can we implement a whole language approach? In Constance Weaver, *Reading process and practice: From socio-psycholinguistics to whole language.* Portsmouth, NH: Heinemann, 1988, p. 264. Reprinted with permission.

Jan

There are many other children who can read well but who simply have trouble with phonics exercises and activities. And no wonder, given the nature of some of them. All too often, children's ability to *read* is equated with their ability to do such exercises and activities.

Let me give you an example of why this is counterproductive and inappropriate. Figure 7 shows a worksheet given to a fourth grade class (Watson, 1996). The directions are to show the sound of *ea* on the line after each word, according to the key for marking a long e (as in *each*), a short e (as in *head*), or a long a sound (as in *great*). Fourth grader

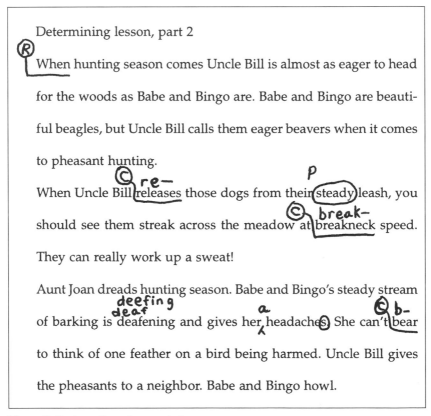

Figure 8 Jan's reading of *ea* words in a passage

From Dorothy Watson and Paul Crowley, How can we implement a whole language approach? In Constance Weaver, *Reading process and practice: From socio-psycholinguistics to whole language*. Portsmouth, NH: Heinemann, 1988, p. 266. Reprinted with permission.

Jan missed 14 out of the first 31 items, which included words she probably didn't even know, such as *sheath, heathen, Chesapeake,* and *treachery.* She didn't even attempt the last 41 items out of the 72. Jan's teacher was concerned at her seeming inability to read *ea* words. But the difficulty was not in *reading ea* words but rather in isolating a sound, sometimes in words she didn't even know.

According to the account by Dorothy Watson, Jan cried herself to sleep the night she got this paper back. Her parents consulted a reading expert, who developed a passage with several *ea* words—a passage based on the knowledge that Jan's father and uncle often went pheasant hunting. In a familiar context, Jan could draw upon her prior knowledge and the context as well as upon her word and phonics knowledge.

Figure 8 shows Jan's miscues on this passage. While she did miscue on some *ea* words, she corrected almost all of them—though not the miscue on *deafening.* In explaining why she said "deefing" when she tried to correct her original miscue, Jan cited the rule "When two vowels go walking, the first one does the talking." (Incidentally, that rule "works" less than 50 percent of the time, according to Clymer, 1963). You may notice that while Jan did omit the word *steady* in the rather unusual and unpredictable phrase *steady leash,* she read the word correctly in the slightly more predictable context of Babe and Bingo's *steady stream of barking.*

You can see, I think, the inappropriateness of assuming that Jan cannot read *ea* words just because she had considerable difficulty with a worksheet. Since Jan was considered a *good* reader, and since someone took the time and trouble to demonstrate that Jan could read common *ea* words in a meaningful context and a conceptually appropriate selection, she was not given remedial *ea* work. But what would have happened if Jan had been considered a poor reader?

Erica

Erica (see Weaver, 1994c) was diagnosed as dyslexic in the first grade. Her teacher noted that she needed improvement in sight vocabulary, word attack skills, and phonics skills; the teacher indicated that Erica had difficulty with short vowel sounds and with visual and auditory discrimination. By the fifth grade, when I first analyzed her reading, Erica had had four years of tutoring by a teacher with training in the Orton-Gillingham approach, though the teaching went beyond strict O-G methodology.

When I met her, Erica was clearly a bright fifth-grader who enjoyed discussing literature and who offered insightful comments into the characters' feelings and motivations. However, both her writing and her reading were rather slow and painful—much less fluent than one would have predicted from her intelligence and liveliness. Each week she attended reading classes with two different tutors.

Because Erica had difficulty identifying words, she had been encouraged to sound out any word she couldn't immediately recognize. When the context was unhelpful or—for whatever reason—she couldn't make use of context, Erica was sometimes unsuccessful in sounding out a word. For example:

On the other hand, she could sound out words successfully when she was also able to use prior knowledge and context:

She was also able to identify "apologize" with ease just two lines after it first occurred, when the context apparently cued her to the meaning:

"You bumped into me. Now you apologize."

So although using phonics alone was difficult if not impossible for Erica, she could successfully combine prior knowledge, context, and letter/sound knowledge to sound out familiar words. She also was strong in predicting, monitoring comprehension, and confirming or correcting. All of these were strengths that had not been recognized through conventional means of assessment, which typically focus on isolated skills.

Two years later, after two more years of skills tutoring, Erica had lost her interest in reading. She was convinced that she had to say or sound out every word, and it was just too much of a struggle. She could read and comprehend much better silently, but silent reading was rarely encouraged. Though not a good reader by conventional standards, she had good reading strategies—but years of skills instruction had made her into an aliterate: that is, someone who can read, but usually chooses not to. As Kenneth Goodman says, "It will not be enough merely to turn troubled readers into reluctant readers" (K. Goodman, 1996b). But that's what an overemphasis on skills has done to *many* readers like Erica, who can comprehend reasonably well but who have difficulty with word identification. The case of Erica serves as a reminder that teachers and support personnel must teach strategies and skills in context and also have the knowledge and wisdom to recognize when tutorial help has reached a point of diminishing returns—in other words, to realize when enough is enough.

From all three examples, we can see that if we measure skills in isolation, we are much more likely to underestimate the reading strengths of children who are, or who are *perceived* to be, less proficient readers. It becomes even more problematic when we then provide more skills instruction for such children while giving them fewer or no opportunities to read and write whole texts.

The importance of reading whole texts even when one's word processing skills are weak is underscored by Fink's research with highly successful adults who had been diagnosed as dyslexic in childhood (see chapter 13). These twelve dyslexics' problems "included a history of difficulty with letter identification, word recognition, phonics, reading fluency, reading speed, spelling, laterality, writing, fine motor control, memory, and learning a foreign language" (chapter 13, p. 387). Yet all had become highly successful in their chosen fields. The twelve included an attorney, a biochemist, a graphic artist, a gynecologist, an immunologist (a Nobel laureate), a neurologist, a physicist, a theater set designer, two businessmen, and two special educators. Though these adults still have difficulty with basic phonological skills which severely limit their ability to sound out unfamiliar words, they nevertheless read extensively in their professional fields—materials that are "highly difficult, specialized, technical, and abstract" (Chall, 1983, p. 100); most of them have also authored books and journal articles in their fields.

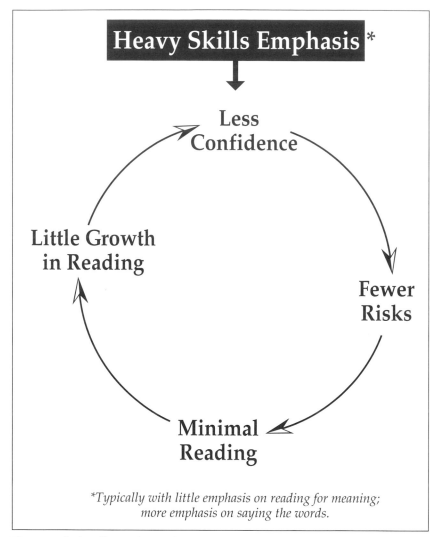

Figure 9 Cycle reflecting heavy skills instruction

How did these adults become such effective readers? Several of them felt profoundly alienated from school, yet all of them read a lot. It was only when they developed and pursued a passionate interest through reading that they finally developed "basic word recognition and fluency." Eleven of the twelve dyslexic readers indicated that they "'finally learned to read' between the ages of 10 and 12" (chapter 13, p. 387). They learned to read by reading.

Is it any wonder that I am concerned, for example, that Texas Governor George Bush (1996) has suggested using $35 million of Goals 2000 money for "reading skill academies"? We might better have academies that promote reading for fun and in pursuit of one's own interests and curiosity.

Effects of Defining Reading as Word Identification

Defining reading first and foremost as word identification has discouraged children from taking risks as readers: they read only easy texts wherein they know most of the words (and therefore have little opportunity to learn new words from reading); sometimes they won't read unless someone is available to help with them words; and, of course, they rarely choose to read, either for pleasure or for information. This vicious cycle is delineated in Figure 9.

As this diagram indicates, heavy skills instruction and overemphasis on getting all the words creates readers with less confidence than readers who have been encouraged to focus on meaning. Because they think of reading as word identification and realize they aren't especially good at identifying most of the words, they take fewer risks as readers, and they tend to do the minimal amount of reading that they can get by with. Unfortunately, however, it's not skills work but the reading of whole, meaningful texts that will do the most to help them improve their reading (e.g., Anderson, et al., 1985; Tunnel & Jacobs, 1989; Krashen, 1993; Fink, 1995–96; McQuillan, forthcoming). Therefore, such readers make relatively little progress compared to classmates who are perceived as good readers and who are at least *allowed* to use good reading strategies, if not actively encouraged or taught to do so.

Using letter/sound knowledge to identify words is critical, but not enough to produce proficient readers. Children who are taught effective reading strategies or at least allowed to *use* their effective strategies unimpeded tend to develop more confidence in themselves, to be more willing to take risks as readers and therefore to read more, and consequently to become more effective readers with larger vocabularies and a greater understanding of concepts and the world (see Figure 10, adapted from Marek & Goodman, 1996).

As the above discussion should suggest, I am especially concerned about the kinds of instruction given to children thought to lack readiness for reading and children thought not to be good readers. Children who have not had books read to them again and again before they come to school have commonly been put in lower so-called "ability" groups, and then given instruction that serves to keep them from becoming highly proficient readers. Research summaries by Patrick Shannon (1985), Robert Hillerich (1985), and Richard Allington and Anne McGill-Franzen (Allington, 1983, 1991, 1994; McGill-Franzen & Allington, 1991) show, for instance, that readers in lower groups have typically

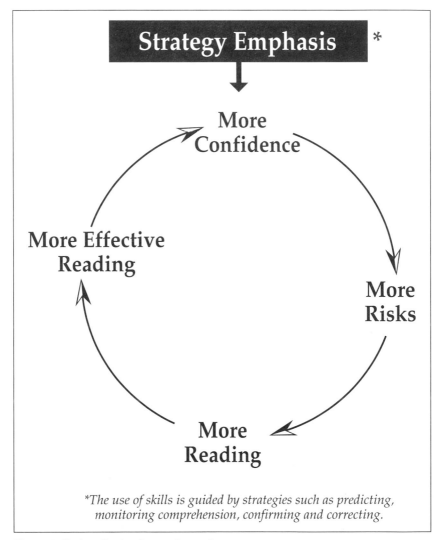

Figure 10 Cycle reflecting instruction and use

Adapted from Ann M. Marek and Yetta M. Goodman, "Revaluing Readers and Reading," in *Retrospective Miscue Analysis: Revaluing Readers and Reading* (Katonah, NY: Richard C. Owen, 1996).

- received much more drill in isolated words than readers in higher groups;
- had lessons focused more on literal recall of text than on drawing inferences, analyzing, evaluating, and so forth;
- been told to "sound out" a problem word, or been given the word, instead of given help in developing strategies for dealing with problem words independently.

In each instance, the kind of instruction typically given to those perceived as poorer readers has been less productive than the instruction given to those perceived as good readers. "In other words, the instruction traditionally offered in different groups [has] literally created different kinds of readers" (Allington & Cunningham, 1996, p. 17). The rich get richer, while the poor get poorer, academically speaking—*all as a result of deliberate educational policy.*

Of course, it is particularly the children with limited literacy experiences in the home and preschool who fall victim to the more limiting kinds of instruction. This, in turn, creates a vicious cycle that goes something like this: Children with few or no book experiences in the home, many of whom are from lower-class families, may have less letter and letter/sound knowledge than other classmates; therefore, they are often put into developmental classes or lower "ability groups." In such groups, they typically receive less effective instruction and have few opportunities to read whole books or write whole texts (often, not more than a paragraph). As a result, they may do well at skills work, but they find it nearly impossible to read whole books, articles, or assignments. Therefore, the academic gap between them and their peers widens, and they receive a less effective education overall. This, in turn, leads to their getting lesser jobs that perpetuate the lower socioeconomic status of their family and their children. As Allington and Cunningham (1996) note, our schools have typically done much better "at sorting and labeling at-risk children than at accelerating their academic development" (p. 1).

Rexford Brown, in *Schools of Thought* (1991), gives an example of a "successful" all-black school district to demonstrate how an exclusive focus on basic skills, even where there is strong community support for education, prevents students from aspiring to or attaining a level of achievement beyond that of their parents. Of course some people find this quite acceptable. For instance, Douglas Carnine, in his remarks to the Governor's Business Council's pre-summit workshop in Texas, said, "Don't get caught on closing the learning gap or you'll create problems for public education" (Governor's Business Council, 1996, p. 59). This sounds like a rationalization for not trying to give lower-class students the kind of education that will make them genuine readers and writers in the fullest sense: a rationalization for promoting word-identification reading but not thoughtful, critical reading. Some politicians may find this attractive as public policy, but for the schools to deliberately settle for or promote less effective education for some children is, I think, unacceptable. We *can* do better. (See, for instance, Allington and Cunningham, *Schools that Work: Where All Children Read and Write*, 1996).

So What Are Some Major Concerns with Documents That Claim to Promote a Balanced Reading Approach?

While I was concerned about the potential implications of California's *Every Child a Reader* (California Reading Task Force, 1995), at least it was abstract in many of its recommendations. I am far more concerned about several of the statements and recommendations in the follow-up document designed to guide classroom teaching: the document titled *A Balanced, Comprehensive Approach to Teaching Reading in Prekindergarten Through Grade Three*, which is a reading program advisory from the California Department of Education (1996). Here are some of the items that concern me, each expressed in the words of the document itself. In responding, I will cross-reference points that have been generously referenced before.

1. *"Research has shown repeatedly that phonemic awareness is a powerful predictor of success in learning to read"* (p. 7). Yes, but this observation depends significantly upon the fact that standardized reading tests for the primary grades focus substantially on letter/sound identification and word identification, so naturally success at "reading" (at taking standardized tests of reading) will correlate highly with phonemic awareness. Other measures might yield different results. Second, the fact that phonemic awareness is a predictor of success in learning to read does *not* mean that phonemic awareness must be developed before children can begin learning to read; it can and will develop in the process of learning to read. This is particularly true when children are encouraged to spell the sounds they hear in words, as they first begin to write. Discussion of letter/sound patterns in reading also helps.

2. *"Phonemic awareness is the most important core and causal factor separating normal and disabled readers (Share and Stanovich, 1995)"* (p. 7). Of course—since we define disabled readers (dyslexic readers, anyway) as those who have difficulties "in single word decoding, usually reflecting insufficient phonological processing abilities"

(Orton Dyslexia Society Research Committee, 1994, p. 4). Instead of defining reading disability on this basis, we might better define it as a reader's inability to orchestrate language cues and strategies to construct meaning from appropriate texts (linguistically appropriate texts for which the reader has sufficient background knowledge). We do not *have* to characterize reading ability in terms of phonological processing or phonemic awareness alone (Weaver, 1994c; Y. Goodman & Marek, 1996).

3. *"Without phonemic awareness, phonics can make no sense"* (p. 7). This is in fact false—at least if we assume that "phonics" includes onsets and rimes. There is a wealth of evidence that children find it easier to hear syllables and the onsets and rimes of syllables than to hear "separate" phonemes. Promoting phonemic awareness first goes against normal development, which progresses from the larger units to the smaller.

4. *"By using this limited set of letters to build as many familiar words as possible, students can be convinced of the utility of phonics and shown that every letter matters"* (p. 11). This, too, goes against the grain developmentally. It's easier to become familiar with some whole words through natural but patterned and predictable texts, and by reading these texts to develop a stock of sight words *and* phonics knowledge—with various kinds of assistance, including explicit attention to letter/sound relationships. Also, this statement seems to reflect a distortion of the research that suggests we see virtually every letter in a word (Rayner & Pollatsek, 1989). Even if this is true (see Krashen's counterargument, forthcoming), it does not necessarily follow that one needs to identify every letter before identifying the word, and indeed there is substantial evidence that word identification may precede the identification of individual letters (Smith, 1988). Forcing children to focus on every letter can have the disabling effect of asking the centipede how it moves its legs.

5. *"Teaching phonics opportunistically by pointing out spelling-sound connections only as they arise does not have the same impact on learning [as a systematic, explicit phonics program]"* (p. 11). This claim is *not* supported by most of the recent comparative research, which compares whole language teaching with skills-intensive teaching, including programs for teaching phonemic awareness and letter/sound relationships prior to guiding children in reading texts. Overall, this research suggests that some explicit attention to letter/sound patterns and relationships is probably helpful, but a

systematic program has not typically produced better learning of phonics. Those who make the above claim are relying on the earlier, mostly pre-1967 research, before whole language (whole-to-part teaching) came into being, or the hotly debated study by Foorman, Francis, Beeler, Winikates, and Fletcher (1997). Or else they are interpreting "opportunistically" to mean rarely.

6. *"When readers skip or fail to understand the words of the text, comprehension suffers"* (p. 14). This is a vast overstatement. Many words are not crucial to understanding a text—and even when we identify and understand all the words, we begin forgetting the exact words within less than a second. Emphasizing correct identification of all the words tends to distract readers from the goal of reading, to construct meaning from texts. Furthermore, it tends to discourage readers from reading.

7. *"A book is said to be at a child's independent level if 95 to 100 percent of the words can be read correctly. . . . Regardless of how well a child already reads, high error rates are negatively correlated with growth; low error rates are positively linked with growth. A text that is too difficult, then, not only serves to undermine a child's confidence and will but also diminishes learning itself"* (p. 17). Are we to assume, in this context, that a book is "too difficult" if the child does not read 95 to 100 percent of the words correctly? Consider, for example, the miscues of Jay, who read the passage about Muriel the horned "toad," and Anne, who read the passage about the circus: neither of them read quite 95 percent of the words correctly in these passages. Extremely high error rates are indeed not so likely to correlate with reading growth, but we must be careful not to withhold books from children just because we think they will have trouble with too many of the words. Children often choose books that are more difficult for them than their teacher or parents would have selected (Krashen, in press), and fortunately so, for reading itself is the best source of most of the vocabulary we learn beyond the primary years (Nagy, Anderson, & Herman, 1987; Nagy & Herman, 1987). Furthermore, children's confidence can be undermined far more readily by the expectation that they read almost every word correctly than by a text with unknown words. We need to promote reading, not inhibit it by unrealistic expectations and demands.

8. *Learning activities for first grade include "providing multiple opportunities first to read decodable text and eventually to read predictable text*

and easy trade books" (p. 21). By decodable text, the authors mean text wherein most of the content words reflect the phonics patterns taught, especially the consonant-vowel-consonant pattern (as in *Nan can fan Dan*). Apparently the authors of the California document are unaware of the considerable body of research showing that such "regular" but unnatural text is more difficult to read than text that includes natural language patterns, including some larger, interesting words (like *elephant, rhinoceros, chocolate, bicycle*). Children find it easier to process patterned texts with repeated lines and only a slight change from page to page. Such patterned books are more appropriate instructional material than the "decodable" texts recommended for practicing phonics.

9. *Interventions for children having difficulty with phonemic awareness and phonics skills should be "more intense than the typical classroom experience, providing personalized assessment-based instruction; more time and practice on selected skills, concepts, and strategies; and smaller adult-student ratios"* (p. 27). Such intervention may indeed be helpful. However:

- assistance with phonics skills may be helpful only up to a point, beyond which it does little to improve even word identification, and much to convince children that reading is not worth the trouble;

- providing more time for independent reading in school is probably much more important than providing more skills assistance (see McQuillan's research, in progress, which shows a strong positive correlation between free reading and reading scores on the National Assessment of Educational Progress, but a substantial negative correlation with skills instruction—or in other words more skills instruction correlates with lesser reading ability, not greater);

- we must be careful not to assume that difficulty in demonstrating phonemic awareness and phonics skills means that a child cannot read well—witness the adult dyslexics in Fink's study, who had become outstanding in their fields (chapter 13); such an assumption could lead to our withholding quality reading material as we have traditionally done, instead of encouraging readers to read books and other texts that interest them;

- providing more time for reading is especially critical for the children who do not have ready access to books at home, yet we could all too easily repeat history and provide more skills work and less actual reading for these children.

10. *"It is crucial that the children of California be provided with the most effective instructional methods and materials possible and then be held to high standards of achievement"* (p. 30). Of course it is important to have high expectations for children, but this statement reminds me of Allington's (1994) observation that our schools have traditionally been much better at sorting and labeling at-risk children than at accelerating their learning, especially their learning to read. Therefore, we must ask: "High standards of achievement in what? Demonstrating phonemic awareness and phonics skills in isolation?" Insistence on diagnosing difficulties, so common in the documents mentioned earlier in this chapter, could all too easily lead to sorting and labeling children rather than to more effective instruction and more and more opportunities to read and write whole texts. We must not let this happen.

Fortunately, this so-called *Balanced, Comprehensive Approach* document (California Department of Education, 1996) is not binding on local educational agencies or other entities. Perhaps this fact will help reduce its influence in California and elsewhere.

Toward a Balanced Reading Program

What, then, can we do to insure a balanced reading program that neither neglects necessary reading skills nor overemphasizes them, placing many children at risk of becoming nonreaders or aliterates? Following are some major recommendations.

1. *See that all children have rich literacy experiences in preschool.* Children who do not speak English natively should attend preschools where their native language is spoken, in addition to English, so that they do not lose the ability to communicate with family and community members who may be monolingual in a language other than English.

2. *Keep meaning the major focus, always:* from the very beginning of reading, when teaching strategies and skills, and when assessing reading ability.

3. *Remember that phonemic awareness, letter/sound knowledge, and word knowledge develop in the process of becoming an independent reader.* Avoid phonics first. Instead, offer alternative models for developing phonemic awareness and phonics knowledge in the classroom—models that reflect what is now known and widely agreed upon regarding the effective teaching of phonics.

4. *See that assessment does not focus on skills apart from their use in deriving meaning from texts.* For example, assess phonics skills through reading and writing, not in isolation.

5. *See that "at risk" readers and those who need extraordinary help with strategies and skills receive additional tutorial help and additional opportunities to engage in individual and assisted reading.* Tutorial help should not take away from the time allotted for individual reading and writing, which also needs to be increased, not reduced.

6. *Develop creative ways to provide this extra time and help for readers who need it.* For example (see Allington & Cunningham, 1996), provide:

   • support from reading buddies, including classmates, older children, aides, senior citizens;

   • instructional aids such as books on tape and high quality multimedia computer programs that engage readers interactively;

   • in-classroom support from other professionals, such as speech/language teachers and reading specialists;

   • support before and/or after school and/or on Saturdays from such specialists (who could be given staggered schedules);

   • library support before and/or after school;

   • supplementary literacy programs and events, such as schoolwide "read-ins."

7. *Invest in long-term professional development for teachers.* Such development should enable teachers to

   • understand the reading process itself;

   • provide children with a rich literacy environment and many opportunities to read and write;

   • teach phonics skills interactively and effectively;

   • demonstrate and guide students in using effective reading strategies and in orchestrating strategies and skills;

   • demonstrate processes used in comprehending texts and guide students in comprehending texts themselves (e.g., in making connections among text elements and in drawing inferences and conclusions, in analyzing and synthesizing and evaluating);

   • assess various factors related to children's reading (especially their strategies for and success at comprehending) and make instructional plans based on such assessments.

In Conclusion

If state boards and departments of education and politicians could do only three things to help more children learn to read more effectively and more deeply, I'd suggest they be these:

- Ensure that all children receive quality pre-school experiences, which include being read to, reading together in shared book experiences, writing collaboratively with guidance, reading and writing themselves as best they can, and using oral language in various ways. Attention can be given to developing phonics knowledge and phonemic awareness through oral language, but such teaching may be most effective and/or efficient when done in conjunction with written texts. Such experiences will give less advantaged children a chance to start kindergarten more in step with their relatively advantaged peers.

- Reduce class size to under twenty, and preferably no more than sixteen in the primary grades, so that teachers can give children the individual attention and support they need.

- Ensure that both preservice and inservice teachers receive modeling and mentoring as they interact with children to teach reading more effectively.

If we want to improve reading instruction significantly, we simply must make a massive investment in teacher education. Teachers need guidance not merely in teaching phonics and phonemic awareness, but in teaching reading strategies and the use of phonics skills within those strategies. Teachers need guidance in helping children develop background knowledge and concepts and in learning to process texts for meaning. Equally important, they need guidance in learning to analyze their students' strengths and needs as readers. Standardized tests do not provide the kinds of information that teachers need. Such tests are good at rank-ordering students and schools, and indeed, that is what they are designed to do (e.g., Wiggins, 1989); however, they don't give any insight into how a reader is processing text and therefore what kinds of help a reader needs. Teachers must be able to collect and analyze a wide range of data in order to plan effective instruction.

I'm becoming increasingly convinced that in educating preservice teachers, we cannot do an adequate job as long as we remain in our college classrooms. It's like trying to teach swimming by focusing first on one component skill and then another, but not yet allowing the would-be swimmer to try to coordinate the needed skills in the water. It's also like trying to teach phonics first, before children have had extensive engagement with texts. Preservice teachers need modeling and mentoring on site, in primary grade classrooms with real kids, and with teachers who themselves are expert at such teaching. Until we have enough faculty and expert classroom teachers to provide such guidance, we will continue to turn out many certified teachers who, in reality, are not adequately prepared to teach reading.

Teachers currently in classrooms likewise need intensive modeling and mentoring. Graduate coursework may be helpful—and indeed, surely ought to be required. But again, such coursework needs to be supplemented by, or to include, sufficient mentoring as teachers try to apply new learning in their actual teaching. The kind of modeling and mentoring that inservice teachers need can be provided by knowledgeable, skilled language arts consultants, teacher educators, or other classroom teachers.

Surely teacher development will be costly. But in the long run, it can be even more costly to society not to invest heavily in the professional development of teachers, both preservice and inservice. No instructional program, no matter how good it is, will adequately meet the needs of all children—or even most children. No program can substitute for knowledgeable teachers. With just a program but not a wealth of knowledge and understanding, teachers will teach the program, but not necessarily the students. With appropriate knowledge and skills, a teacher can adapt the program, supplement it, or even supplant it with teaching procedures that do a better job of meeting children's needs.

In short, there is no quick fix. In order to build a stronger America, we need to invest not in programs, but in teachers and kids.

Notes

1. This paper is a revised and expanded version of a presentation made before the long-range planning committee of the Texas State Board of Education in May, 1996. Some of the material in this chapter is adapted from a fact sheet in the second (1997) printing of Weaver, Gillmeister-Krause, and Vento-Zogby (1996).

2. Some people have difficulty with the idea that it is acceptable not to preserve every word of the text as long as essential meaning is preserved. To encourage them to reconsider this opinion, you might ask them to listen to the following excerpt from Graham Greene's *The Power and the Glory* (1940) as you read it aloud at a normal pace. Tell them in advance that you will want them to write down what they have heard:

> The young men and women walked round and round the plaza in the hot electric night: the men one way, the girls another, never

speaking to each other. In the northern sky the lightning flapped. It was like a religious ceremony which had lost all meaning, but at which they still wore their best clothes.

The passage is too long to retain in short-term memory until all of it has been read, so listeners are not able to remember the entire passage verbatim. Compare your listener's rendition with the original. Usually, the essential meaning is preserved (up to a point, at least) though the words are changed—or the exact words may be retained, but only part way through the passage. Point out to your listener that the exact words of a text begin to fade from memory in less than a second after they are heard or read.

3. Those familiar with various claims about the reading process may realize that that this model is an attempt to rise above many of the current controversies and models, simply by being more abstract. (This is analogous to resolving a paradox by considering the phenomena at a different level.)

Instead of suggesting that miscue research invalidates the claim that good readers read most words on the page, or vice versa, that word-identification research invalidates miscue research (both of which have been claimed in the professional literature), I prefer to offer a model that is sufficiently abstract to accommodate both claims. Similarly, instead of challenging the claim that readers fixate on virtually every word and "see" every letter of a word (a critique offered by Krashen, forthcoming), I have chosen to incorporate this conclusion into the model along with research suggesting that we identify words before identifying or "seeing" their individual letters (F. Smith, McConkie & Zola, 1981; Rayner & Pollatsek, 1989).

While I myself am more persuaded by some bodies of research than by others, my visual model is an attempt to account for such seemingly antithetical observations as these (from Weaver, 1994b, p. 211):

a) Proficient readers automatically "see" the individual letters in most content words and many function words, *even though* their equally automatic use of context makes this unnecessary for identifying most words (McConkie & Zola, 1981; Rayner & Pollatsek, 1989).

b) Proficient readers automatically (and with lightning speed) make use of contextual constraints as they read (Pearson & Stephens, 1994; Goodman, 1967, 1973, 1982), *even though* their equally automatic processing of letter sequences and words makes the use of context unnecessary in identifying familiar words (summarized in Adams, 1990 and in Stanovich, 1991, who includes references to several research studies documenting that the effect of context in identifying words takes place in a few milliseconds).

c) Proficient readers—at least many of them—identify most of the words in a text most of the time, *even though* their primary goal is to construct meaning rather than to identify words.

d) Proficient readers pay most attention to constructing meaning from a text, *even though* they do identify most of the words in the process (Pearson & Stephens, 1994; Goodman, 1967, 1973, 1982).

e) Proficient readers automatically "hear" the words of the text (Paterson & Coltheart, 1987); Banks, Oka, & Shugarman, 1981), *even though* translating written words into spoken words is rarely necessary for getting meaning, and in fact slows down their reading significantly (Tanenhaus, Flanigan, & Seidenberg, 1980).

f) In short, proficient readers make simultaneous (or near simultaneous) and redundant use of all the information available to them, *even though* this is not necessary unless problems arise. It is for this reason that I have called the model a *redundancy* model of reading.

4. The constructivist model of learning represented in Figure 6 is an attempt to capture insights such as the following (Weaver, Gillmeister-Krause, & Vento-Zogby, 1996): (1) for us to learn, input from the environment must be comprehensible; (2) input is made comprehensible by the mind interacting with the environment; (3) directive instruction may also help make input comprehensible. Such a model seems increasingly to underlie researchers' concepts of how phonics should be taught—even if they advocate teaching phonics systematically.

Works Cited

Adams, M. J. (1990). *Beginning to read: Thinking and learning about print.* Cambridge: MIT Press.

Adams, M. J., & Bruck, M. (1995). Resolving the "Great debate." *American Educator, 19* (2), 7, 10–20.

Allington, R. L. (1983). The reading instruction provided readers of differing reading abilities. *The Elementary School Journal, 83,* 548–99.

Allington, R. L. (1991). The legacy of "slow it down and make it more concrete." In J. Zutell & S. McCormick (Eds.), *Learner factors/teacher factors: Issues in literacy research and instruction* (pp. 19–29). Chicago: National Reading Conference.

Allington, R. L. (1994). The schools we have. The schools we need. *The Reading Teacher, 48,* 14–29.

Allington, R. L., & Cunningham, P. M. (1996). *Schools that work: Where all children read and write.* New York: Harper Collins College Publishers.

Allington, R. L., & Walmsley, S. A. (Eds.). (1995). *No quick fix: Rethinking literacy programs in American elementary schools.* New York: Teachers College Press.

Anderson, R. C., Hiebert, E. H., Scott, J. A., & Wilkinson, I. A. G. (1985). *Becoming a nation of readers: The report of the commission on reading.* Champaign, IL: Center for the Study of Reading, University of Illinois.

Ayres, L. R. (1993). *The efficacy of three training conditions on phonological awareness of kindergarten children and the longitudinal effect of each on later reading acquisition.* Unpublished dissertation, Oakland University, Rochester, Michigan.

Baddeley, A. D., & Lewis, V. (1981). Inner active processes in reading: The inner voice, the inner ear, and the inner eye. In C. A. Perfetti & A. M. Lesgold (Eds.), *Interactive processes in reading* (pp. 107–29). Hillsdale, NJ: Erlbaum.

Ball, E., & Blachman, B. (1991). Does phoneme awareness training in kindergarten make a difference in early word recognition and developmental spelling? *Reading Research Quarterly, 26,* 49–66.

Banks, W. P., Oka, E., & Shugarman, S. (1981). Internal speech: Does recoding come before lexical access? In O. J. L. Tzeng & H. Singer (Eds.), *Perception of print: Reading research in experimental psychology* (pp. 137–70). Hillsdale, NJ: Erlbaum.

Barr, Jene. (1949). *Little circus dog.* Chicago: Albert Whitman.

Barshinger, J. (1995). *A national Delphi study of desired factors for whole-language classroom environments.* Unpublished dissertation, Northern Illinois University, DeKalb.

Beck, I. L., & Juel, C. (1995). The role of decoding in learning to read. *American Educator, 19* (2), 8, 21–25, 39–42.

Boder, E. (1973). Developmental dyslexia: A diagnostic approach based on three atypical reading-spelling patterns. *Developmental Medicine and Child Neurology, 15,* 663–87.

Bond, D. L., & Dykstra, R. (1967). The cooperative research program in first-grade reading instruction. *Reading Research Quarterly, 2,* 5–142.

Bradley, L., & Bryant, P. E. (1983). Categorizing sounds and learning to read—a causal connection. *Nature, 301,* 419–521.

Bradley, L., & Bryant, P. E. (1985). *Rhyme and reason in reading and spelling.* I.A.R.L.D. Monographs No. 1. Ann Arbor: University of Michigan Press.

Brown, J., Goodman, K. S., & Marek, A. M. (1996). *Studies in miscue analysis: An annotated bibliography.* Newark, DE: International Reading Association.

Brown, R. G. (1991). *Schools of thought.* San Francisco: Jossey-Bass.

Bush, George W. (1996). The governor's reading initiative: A Governor George W. Bush Public Education Initiative. Overview plus a paper presented at the mid-winter Texas Education Association conference, January 31, 1996, Austin, TX.

Byrne, B., & Fielding-Barnsley, R. (1991). Evaluation of a program to teach phonemic awareness to young children. *Journal of Educational Psychology, 83,* 451–55.

California Department of Education. (1996). *A balanced, comprehensive approach to teaching reading in prekindergarten through grade three.* Sacramento: California Department of Education.

California Reading Task Force. (1995). *Every child a reader.* Sacramento: California Department of Education.

Calkins, L. M. (1980). When children want to punctuate: Basic skills belong in context. *Language Arts, 57,* 567–73.

Carbo, M. (1988). Debunking the great phonics myth. *Phi Delta Kappan, 70,* 226–40.

Chall, J. (1967/1983). *Learning to read: The great debate.* New York: McGraw-Hill.

Chomsky, C. (1978). After decoding: What? *Language Arts, 53,* 288–96, 314.

Clarke, L.K. (1988). Invented versus traditional spelling in first graders' writings: Effects on learning to spell and read. *Research in the Teaching of English, 22,* 281–309.

Clay, M. M. (1987). Learning to be learning disabled. *New Zealand Journal of Educational Studies, 22,* 155–73.

Clymer, T. L. (1963). The utility of phonic generalizations in the primary grades. *The Reading Teacher, 16,* 252–58.

Cunningham, A. E. (1990). Explicit versus implicit instruction in phonemic awareness. *Journal of Experimental Child Psychology, 50,* 429–44.

Cunningham, P. M. (1995). *Phonics they use: Words for reading and writing* (2nd ed.). New York: HarperCollins College Publishing.

Dahl, K. L., & Freppon, P. A. (1991). Literacy learning in whole-language classrooms: An analysis of low socioeconomic urban children learning to read and write in kindergarten. In J. Zutell & S. McCormick (Eds.), *Learner factors/teacher factors: Issues in literacy research and instruction* (pp. 149–58). Chicago: National Reading Conference.

Dahl, K. L., & Freppon, P. A. (1992). *Learning to read and write in inner-city schools: A comparison of children's sense-making in skills-based and whole language classrooms*. Final Report to the Office of Educational Research and Improvement. Washington, DC: U. S. Department of Education. (Grant No. G 008720229)

Dahl, K. L., & Freppon, P. A. (1994). A comparison of innercity children's interpretations of reading and writing instruction in the early grades in skills-based and whole language classrooms. *Reading Research Quarterly, 30*, 50–74.

DiStefano, P., & Killion, J. (1984). Assessing writing skills through a process approach. *English Education, 16*, 203–7.

Eeds, M., & Wells, D. (1989). Grand conversations: An exploration of meaning construction in literature study groups. *Research in the Teaching of English, 23*, 4–29.

Ehri, L. C. (1991). Development of the ability to read words. In R. Barr, M. Kamil, P. Mosenthal, & P. D. Pearson (Eds.), *Handbook of reading research*, (Vol. 2, pp. 383–417). New York: Longman.

Ehri, L. C. (1994). Development of the ability to read words: Update. In R. Ruddell, M. Ruddell, & H. Singer (Eds.), *Theoretical models and processes of reading* (4th ed., pp. 323–58). Newark, DE: International Reading Association.

Ehri, L. C. (1995). Phases of development in reading words. *Journal of Research in Reading, 18*, 116–25.

Ehri, L. C., & Robbins, C. (1992). Beginners need some decoding skill to read words by analogy. *Reading Research Quarterly, 27*, 13–26.

Elbro, C. (1990). *Differences in dyslexia: A study of reading strategies and deficits in a linguistic perspective*. Copenhagen: Munksgaard International Publishers.

Fink, R. (1995/96). Successful dyslexics: A constructionist study of passionate interest reading. *Journal of Adolescent and Adult Literacy, 39*, 268–80.

Foorman, B. R. (1995). Research on "The great debate": Code-oriented versus whole language approaches to reading instruction. *School Psychology Review, 24*, 376–92.

Foorman, B. R., Francis, D. J., Beeler, T., Winikates, D., & Fletcher, J. M. (1997). Early interventions for children with reading problems: Study designs and preliminary findings. *Learning Disabilities: A Multi-Disciplinary Journal, 8*, 63–71.

Fountas, I. C., & Pinnell, G. S. (1996). *Guided reading: Good first teaching for all children*. Portsmouth, NH: Heinemann.

Fox, B., & Routh, D. K. (1980). Phonemic analysis and severe reading disability in children. *Journal of Psycholinguistic Research, 9*, 115–19.

Freppon, P. A. (1988). *An investigation of children's concepts of the purpose and nature of reading in different instructional settings.* Unpublished doctoral dissertation, University of Cincinnati, Ohio.

Freppon, P. A. (1991). Children's concepts of the nature and purpose of reading in different instructional settings. *Journal of Reading Behavior, 23,* 139–63.

Freppon, P. A. (1995). Low-income children's literacy interpretations in a skills-based and a whole-language classroom. *Journal of Reading Behavior, 27,* 505–33.

Freppon, P. A., & Dahl, K. L. (1991). Learning about phonics in a whole language classroom. *Language Arts, 68,* 190–97.

Gibson, E. J. (1985). Trends in perceptual development. In H. Singer & R. B. Ruddell (Eds.), *Theoretical models and processes of reading* (3rd ed., pp. 144–73). Newark, DE: International Reading Association.

Glushko, R. J. (1979). The organization and activation of orthographic knowledge in reading aloud. *Journal of Experimental Psychology: Human Perception and Performance, 5,* 674–91.

Goldstein, D. M. (1976). Cognitive-linguistic functioning and learning to read in preschoolers. *Journal of Educational Psychology, 68,* 680–88.

Goodman, K. S. (1967). Reading: A psycholinguistic guessing game. *Journal of the Reading Specialist, 6,* 126–35.

Goodman, K. S. (1973). *Theoretically based studies of patterns of miscues in oral reading performance.* Detroit: Wayne State University. (ED 079 708)

Goodman, K. S. (1996a). *On reading: A common-sense look at the nature of language and the science of reading.* Portsmouth, NH: Heinemann.

Goodman, K. S. (1996b). Principles of revaluing. In Y. M. Goodman & A. M. Marek (Eds.), *Retrospective miscue analysis: Revaluing readers and reading* (pp. 13–20). Katonah, NY: Richard C. Owen.

Goodman, Y. M., & Marek, A. M. (Eds.) (1996). *Retrospective miscue analysis: Revaluing readers and reading.* Katonah, NY: Richard C. Owen.

Goodman, Y. M., Watson, D. J., & Burke, C. L. (1996). *Reading strategies: Focus on comprehension* (2nd ed.). Katonah, NY: Richard C. Owen.

Governor's Business Council. (1996, April). Partial transcript of a pre-summit workshop on reading, Picking a research based reading program. Houston.

Goswami, U. (1986). Children's use of analogy in learning to read: A developmental study. *Journal of Experimental Psychology, 42,* 73–83.

Goswami, U. (1988). Orthographic analogies and reading development. *Quarterly Journal of Experimental Psychology, 40,* 239–68.

Goswami, U. (1993). Toward an interactive analogy model of reading development: Decoding vowel graphemes in beginning reading. *Journal of Experimental Child Psychology, 56,* 443–75.

Goswami, U., & Bryant, P. (1990). *Phonological skills and learning to read.* Hove, East Sussex: Lawrence Erlbaum.

Green, G. (1940). *The power and the glory.* New York: Viking Press.

Griffith, P. L., & Olson, M. W. (1992). Phonemic awareness helps beginning readers break the code. *The Reading Teacher, 45,* 516–25.

Gunderson, L., & Shapiro, J. (1988). Whole language instruction: Writing in 1st grade. *The Reading Teacher, 41,* 430–37.

Gunning, T. (1988). *Decoding behavior of good and poor second grade students.* Paper presented at the annual meeting of the International Reading Association, Toronto.

Gunning, T. (1995). Word building: A strategic approach to the teaching of phonics. *The Reading Teacher, 48,* 484–88.

Haskell, D. W., et al. (1992). Effects of three orthographic/phonological units on first-grade reading. *Remedial and Special Education, 13,* 40–49.

Hillerich, R. L. (1995). Let's pretend. *Michigan Journal of Reading, 18,* 15–18, 20.

Hoffman, P. R., & Norris, J. A. (1994). Whole language and collaboration work: Evidence from at-risk kindergartners. *Journal of Childhood Communication Disorders, 16,* 41–48.

Honig, B. (1995). The role of skills in a comprehensive reading program: The necessity for a balanced approach. Paper presented to the State Board of Education of Texas, December 27, Austin.

Honig, B. (1995). *Teaching our children to read: The role of skills in a comprehensive reading program.* Thousand Oaks, CA: Corwin Press.

Iverson, S., & Tunmer, W. (1993). Phonological processing skills and the reading recovery program. *Journal of Educational Psychology, 85,* 112–26.

Juel, C. (1988). Learning to read and write: A longitudinal study of 54 children from first through fourth grades. *Journal of Educational Psychology, 80,* 437–47.

Juel, C. (1994). *Learning to read and write in one elementary school.* New York: Springer-Verlag.

Juel, C., Griffith, P. L., & Gough, P. B. (1986). Acquisition of literacy: A longitudinal study of children in first and second grade. *Journal of Educational Psychology, 78,* 243–55.

Juel, C., & Roper/Schneider, D. (1985). The influence of basal readers on first grade reading. *Reading Research Quarterly, 22,* 134–52.

Just, M., & Carpenter, P. (1980). A theory of reading: From eye fixations to comprehension. *Psychological Review, 87,* 329–54.

Kasten, W. C., & Clarke, B. K. (1989). *Reading/writing readiness for preschool and kindergarten children: A whole language approach.* Sanibel: Florida Educational Research and Development Council. (ED 312 041)

Kirtley, C., Bryant, P., MacLean, M., & Bradley, L. (1989). Rhyme, rime and the onset of reading. *Journal of Experimental Psychology, 48,* 224–45.

Knapp, M. S., and associates. (1995). *Teaching for meaning in high-poverty classrooms.* New York: Teachers College Press.

Krashen, S. D. (1993). *The power of reading: Insights from the research.* Englewood, CO: Libraries Unlimited.

Krashen, S. D. (1996a). *Every person a reader: An alternative to the California task force report on reading.* Culver City, CA: Language Education Associates.

Krashen, S. D. (1996b). Is free reading always easy reading? *California English,* (Spring), 23.

Krashen, S. D. (In progress.) Eye fixation research.

Kucer, S. B. (1985). Predictability and readability: The same rose with different names? In M. Douglass (Ed.), *Claremont Reading Conference 49th yearbook* (pp. 229–46). Claremont, CA: Claremont Graduate School.

Laminack, L. (1991). *Learning with Zachary*. Richmond Hill, Ontario: Scholastic Canada.

Lenel, J. C., & Cantor, J. H. (1981). Rhyme recognition and phonemic perception in young children. *Journal of Psycholinguistic Research, 10*, 57–68.

Lyon, G.R. (1995a). Research initiatives in learning disabilities: Contributions from scientists supported by the National Institute of Child Health and Human Development. *Journal of Child Neurology, 10*, 120–28.

Lyon, G. R. (1995b). Toward a definition of dyslexia. *Annals of Dyslexia, 45*, 3–27.

Lyon, G.R. (1996). The state of research. In S. Cramer & W. Ellis (Eds.), *Learning disabilities: Lifelong issues* (pp. 3-61). Baltimore, MD: Paul Brookes Publishing.

Mann, V. (1986). Phonological awareness: The role of reading experience. *Cognition, 24*, 65–92.

Manning, M., Manning, G., & Long, R. (1989). *Effects of a whole language and a skill-oriented program on the literacy development of inner city primary children.* (ED 324 642)

Marek, A. M. (1996). An accomplished professional: A reader in trouble. In Y. M. Goodman & A. M. Marek (Eds.), *Retrospective miscue analysis: Revaluing readers and reading* (pp. 51–70). Katonah, NY: Richard C. Owen.

Marek, A. M., & Goodman, Y. M. (1996). Revaluing readers and reading. In Y. M. Goodman & A. M. Marek (Eds.), *Retrospective miscue analysis: Revaluing readers and reading* (pp. 203–7). Katonah, NY: Richard C. Owen.

McConkie, G. W., & Zola, D. (1981). Language constraints and the functional stimulus in reading. In A. M. Lesgold & C. A. Perfetti (Eds.), *Interactive processes in reading* (pp. 155–75). Hillsdale, NJ: Erlbaum.

McGill-Franzen, A., & Allington, R. (1991). The gridlock of low reading achievement: Perspectives on practice and policy. *Remedial and Special Education, 12* (3), 20–30.

McIntyre, E., & Freppon, P. A. (1994). A comparison of children's development of alphabetic knowledge in a skills-based and a whole language classroom. *Research in the Teaching of English, 28*, 391–417.

McQuillan, J. (In progress.) *The effects of print access, skills teaching, and poverty on state-level NAEP reading scores: A path analysis.*

Mills, H., O'Keefe, T., & Stephens, D. (1992). *Looking closely: Exploring the role of phonics in one whole language classroom.* Urbana, IL: National Council of Teachers of English.

Morais, J., Bertelson, P., Carey, L., & Alegria, J. (1986). Literacy training and speech segmentation. *Cognition, 24*, 45–64.

Moustafa, M. (1990). *An interactive/cognitive model of the acquisition of a graphophonemic system by young children.* Unpublished doctoral dissertation, University of Southern California, Los Angeles.

Moustafa, M. (1991). Recoding in whole language reading instruction. *Language Arts, 70*, 483–87.

Moustafa, M. (1995). Children's productive phonological recoding. *Reading Research Quarterly, 30*, 464–76.

Moustafa, M. (In press). Reconceptualizing phonics instruction. In C. Weaver (Ed.),*Practicing What We Know: Informed Reading Instruction.*

Nagy, W. E., Anderson, R. C., & Herman, P. A. (1987). Learning word meanings from context during normal reading. *American Educational Research Journal, 24*, 237–70.

Nagy, W. E., & Herman, P. A. (1987). Breadth and depth of vocabulary knowledge: Implications for acquisition and instruction. In M. McKeown & M. Curtis (Eds.), *The nature of vocabulary acquisition* (pp. 19–35). Hillsdale, NJ: Erlbaum.

Nation, K., & Hulme, C. (1997). Phonemic segmentation, not onset-rime segmentation, predicts early reading and spelling skills. *Reading Research Quarterly, 32*, 154–67.

National Center for Education Statistics. (1996). *NAEP 1994 reading report card for the nation and the states.* Washington: U. S. Department of Education, Office of Educational Research and Improvement.

Nicholson, T. (1991). Do children read words better in context or in lists? A classic study revisited. *Journal of Educational Psychology, 83*, 444–50.

Paterson, F. A. (1996). *Mandating methodology: Promoting the use of phonics through state statutes.* Unpublished manuscript, University of Oklahoma, Department of Educational Leadership and Policy Studies.

Paterson, K. E., & Coleheart, V. (1987). Phonological processes in reading: A tutorial review. In M. Coltheart (Ed.), *Attention and performance XII: The psychology of reading* (pp. 421–47). London: Erlbaum Associates.

Pearson, P. D., & Stephens, D. (1994). Learning about literacy: A 30-year journey. In R. B. Ruddell, M. R. Ruddell, & H. Singer (Eds.), *Theoretical models and processes of reading* (4th ed., pp. 22–42). Newark, DE: International Reading Association.

Perfetti, C. A. (1985). *Reading ability.* New York: Oxford University Press.

Perfetti, C. A., Beck, I., Bell, L. C., & Hughes, C. (1987). Phonemic knowledge and learning to read are reciprocal: A longitudinal study of first grade children. *Merrill-Palmer Quarterly, 33*, 283–319.

Perfetti, C. A., & McCutcheon, D. (1982). Speech processes in reading. In N. Lass (Ed.), *Speech and language: Advances in basic research* (Vol 7, pp. 237–69). New York: Academic Press.

Peterson, M.E., & Haines, L. P. (1992). Orthographic analogy training with kindergarten children: Effects on analogy use, phonemic segmentation, and letter-sound knowledge. *Journal of Reading Behavior, 24*, 109–27.

Porter, W. S. (1936). *The complete works of O. Henry.* Garden City, NY: Doubleday, Doran.

Powell, D., & Hornsby, D. (1993). *Learning phonics and spelling in a whole language classroom.* New York: Scholastic.

Pressley, M. (1994). State-of-the-science primary-grades reading instruction or whole language? *Educational Psychologist, 29*, 211–15.

Rayner, K., & Pollatsek, A. (1989). *The psychology of reading.* Englewood Cliffs, NJ: Prentice Hall.

Rhodes, L. (1979). Comprehension and predictability: An analysis of beginning reading materials. In J. Harste & R. Carey (Eds.), *New perspectives on comprehension* (pp. 100–30). Bloomington, IN: School of Education, Indiana University.

Ribowsky, H. (1985). *The effects of a code emphasis approach and a whole language approach upon emergent literacy of kindergarten children.* Alexandria, VA: ERIC. (ED 269 720)

Richgels, D., Poremba, K. & McGee, L. (1996). Kindergartners talk about print: Phonemic awareness in meaningful contexts. *The Reading Teacher, 49,* 632–42.

Routman, R., & Butler, A. (1995). Why talk about phonics? *School Talk, 1* (2). National Council of Teachers of English.

Santa, C. M. (1976–1977). Spelling patterns and the development of flexible word recognition strategies. *Reading Research Quarterly, 12,* 125–44.

Shannon, P. (1985). Reading instruction and social class. *Language Arts, 62,* 604–13.

Shapiro, J. (1990). Research perspectives on whole-language. In V. Froese (Ed.), *Whole language: Practice and theory* (pp. 313–56). Boston: Allyn & Bacon.

Share, D. L., & Jorm, A. F. (1987). Segmental analysis: Co-requisite to reading, vital for self-teaching, requiring phonological memory. *European Bulletin of Cognitive Psychology, 7,* 509–13.

Share, D. L., & Stanovich, K. E. (1995). Cognitive processes in early reading development: A model of acquisition and individual differences. *Issues in Education: Contributions from Educational Psychology, 1,* 1–35.

Simonds, H. D., & Ammon, P. (1989). Child knowledge and primerese text: Mismatches and miscues. *Research in the Teaching of English, 23,* 380–98.

Smith, F. (1994). *Understanding reading* (5th ed.). Hillsdale, NJ: Erlbaum.

Smith, J. W. A., & Elley, W. B. (1995). *Learning to read in New Zealand.* Katonah, NY: Richard C. Owen.

Snider, V. E. (1995). A primer on phonemic awareness: What it is, why it's important, and how to teach it. *School Psychology Review, 24,* 443–55.

Stahl, S. L. (1992). Saying the "p" word: Nine guidelines for exemplary phonics instruction. *The Reading Teacher, 45,* 618–25.

Stahl, S. A., & Kuhn, M. R. (1995). Does whole language or instruction matched to learning styles help children learn to read? *School Psychology Review, 24,* 393–404.

Stahl, S. A., McKenna, M. C., & Pagnucco, J. R. (1994). The effects of whole-language instruction: An update and a reappraisal. *Educational Psychologist, 29,* 175–85.

Stahl, S. A., & Miller, P. D. (1989). Whole language and language experience approaches for beginning reading: A quantitative research synthesis. *Review of Educational Research, 59,* 87–116.

Stanovich, K. E. (1984). The interactive-compensatory model of reading: A confluence of developmental, experimental, and educational psychology. *Remedial and Special Education, 5,* 11–19.

Stanovich, K. E. (1991). Word recognition: Changing perspectives. In R. Barr, M. L. Kamil, P. B. Mosenthal, & P. D. Pearson (Eds.), *Handbook of reading research* (Vol. 2, pp. 418–52). New York: Longman.

Stanovich, K. E., Cunningham, A. E., & Feeman, D. J. (1984). Intelligence, cognitive skills, and early reading progress. *Reading Research Quarterly, 19,* 278–303.

Stephens, D. (1991). *Research on whole language: Support for a new curriculum.* Katonah, NY: Richard C. Owen.

Stice, C. F., & Bertrand, N. P. (1990). *Whole language and the emergent literacy of at-risk children: A two-year comparative study.* Nashville: Center for Excellence, Basic Skills, Tennessee State University. (ED 324 636)

Tanenhaus, M. K., Flanigan, H., & Seidenberg, M. S. (1980). Orthographic and phonological activation in auditory and visual word recognition. *Memory and Cognition, 8*, 513–20.

Torgeson, J. K., & Hecht, S. A. (1996). Preventing and remediating reading disabilities: Instructional variables that make a difference for special students. In M. F. Graves, P. Van Den Broek, & B. M. Taylor (Eds.), *The first R: Every child's right to read* (pp. 133–59). New York: Teachers College Press.

Traw, R. (1996). Large-scale assessment of skills in a whole language curriculum: Two districts' experiences. *Journal of Educational Research, 89*, 323-39.

Treiman, R. (1985). Onsets and rimes as units of spoken syllables: Evidence from children. *Journal of Experimental Psychology, 39*, 161–81.

Treiman, R., & Baron, J. (1983). Phonemic-analysis training helps children benefit from spelling-sound rules. *Memory and Cognition, 18*, 559–67.

Treiman, R., & Chafetz, J. (1987). Are there onset- and rime-like units in printed words? In M. Coltheart (Ed.), *Attention and performance XII: The psychology of reading* (pp. 281–98). Hillsdale, NJ: Erlbaum.

Tunmer, W. E., & Nesdale, A. R. (1985). Phonemic segmentation skill and beginning reading. *Journal of Educational Psychology, 4*, 417–27.

Turner, R. L. (1989). The "great" debate: Can both Carbo and Chall be right? *Phi Delta Kappan, 71*, 276–83.

Tunnell, M. O., & Jacobs, J. S. (1989). Using "real" books: Research findings on literature based reading instruction. *The Reading Teacher, 42*, 470–77.

Vellutino, F. R., & Denckla, M. B. (1991). Cognitive and neuropsychological foundations of word identification in poor and normally developing readers. In R. Barr, M. L. Kamil, P. B. Mosenthal, & P. D. Pearson (Eds.), *Handbook of reading research* (Vol. 2, pp. 571–608). New York: Longman.

Vellutino, F. R., & Scanlon, D. M. (1987). Phonological coding, phonological awareness, and reading ability: Evidence from a longitudinal and experimental study. *Merrill-Palmer Quarterly, 33*, 321–63.

Vellutino, F. R., et al. (1996). Cognitive profiles of difficult-to-remediate and readily remediated poor readers: Early intervention as a vehicle for distinguishing between cognitive and experiential deficits as basic causes of specific reading disability. *Journal of Educational Psychology, 88*, 601–38.

Wagstaff, J. (No date.) *Phonics that work! New strategies for the reading/writing classroom.* New York: Scholastic.

Watson, D. (1996). *Making a difference: Selected writings of Dorothy Watson* (Ed. by S. Wilde). Portsmouth, NH: Heinemann.

Weaver, C. (1994a). *Phonics in whole language classrooms.* (ED 372 375)

Weaver, C. (1994b). *Reading process and practice: From socio-psycholinguistics to whole language* (2nd ed.). Portsmouth, NH: Heinemann.

Weaver, C. (1994c). Reconceptualizing reading and dyslexia. *Journal of Childhood Communication Disorders, 16* (1), 23–35.

Weaver, C. (In press). Understanding and helping Jaime with reading and with language: A psycholinguistic and constructivist perspective. In E. R. Silliman, L. C. Wilkinson, & L. P. Hoffman, *Children's journeys through school: Assessing and building competence and development in language and literacy.* San Diego: Singular Publishing Group.

Weaver, C. Gillmeister-Krause, L., & Vento-Zogby, G. (1996). *Creating support for effective literacy education.* Portsmouth, NH: Heinemann.

Wiggins, G. (1989). A true test: Toward more authentic and equitable assessment. *Phi Delta Kappan, 70,* 703–13.

Wimmer, H., Landerl, K., Linortner, R., & Hummer, P. (1991). The relationship of phonemic awareness to reading acquisition: More consequence than precondition but still important. *Cognition, 40,* 219–49.

Winick, D. (1997). Edited transcript from *Critical Balances: Early Instruction for Lifelong Reading.* Houston, May 16, 1997. <http://www.readingonline.org/critical/houston/>

Yopp, H. (1992). Developing phonemic awareness in young children. *The Reading Teacher, 45,* 696–703.

II The Reading Process

2 Learning about Literacy: A 30-Year Journey

P. David Pearson
University of Illinois at Urbana-Champaign

Diane Stephens
University of Hawaii

Pearson and Stephens document changing conceptions of the reading process over the past three decades by chronicling what they, and many others, have learned about reading from linguistics, psychology, sociology, literary theory, and other disciplines. Around 1960 reading was thought of as a rather straightforward perceptual process of translating letters into sounds. This changed, however, with the rise to prominence later in the 1960s of work derived from structural linguistics. Especially important have been the insights from psycholinguists, who studied the implications of transformational-generative grammar for language comprehension, language acquisition, and reading. Pearson and Stephens document the contributions of psycholinguistics, notably in the work of Kenneth Goodman and Frank Smith, to reading theory and pedagogical theory. They further demonstrate the importance of cognitive psychology, which, for example, postulated the concept of schemas that enable us to make sense of the world and of what we read.

Sociolinguistics, which began as a discipline in the late 1960s and early 1970s, has also produced important new insights, such as an understanding of the relationships between dialect, oral reading, and comprehension, and a broadening of the concept of context to include the place and situation in which reading takes place. Pearson and Stephens conclude their intellectual history by discussing the contributions made to reading theory by Louise Rosenblatt's transactional theory, and by semiotics.

A section on "Asking New Questions" extends the historical analysis to present questions of learning, teaching, and pedagogy; a final section, "Finding Answers," expresses the authors' recent understanding that many questions related to teaching are political questions: "Each time we ask and answer 'For/to whom?,' 'When?', 'Under what conditions?', and 'To what end?', we are asking questions that are not just pedagogical but political." Pearson and Stephens conclude that "in the 1990s, it is no longer enough to 'teach reading'; rather, we must ask ourselves hard questions about the politics of literacy. . . ." And, I would add, we must ask ourselves hard questions about the politics of instruction in reading and literacy.

Originally published in C. Gordon, G. D. Labercane, and W. R. McEachern (Eds.), *Elementary Reading Instruction: Process and Practice*. Ginn Press, 1992. Reprinted with permission of the authors.

The two of us have been teaching long enough to have witnessed many changes in the way that teachers in our profession think about the teaching and learning of reading. And we are delighted to have been asked to write the opening chapter for a book *[Elementary Reading Instruction]* that will introduce you to some of the most interesting yet problematic issues in our field. In this chapter, we will set the stage for what will come in the rest of this book by talking not so much about reading per se, but about what we have learned about reading from other disciplines such as linguistics, psychology, sociology, and literary theory. We want to accomplish this task in a somewhat unusual but, we hope, interesting way. Instead of talking about each discipline in turn, we will take you on a guided historical tour of our encounters with these disciplines in our own teaching careers. We take you down these historical paths because we think you will better appreciate their impact if you can see how they influenced the field of reading as you see it today and how they influenced our thinking as teachers. Even though the theoretical way station where we have stopped in the 1990s is intellectually more comfortable and more accommodating than our earlier theoretical way stations, we have learned much from each intellectual stopover. We think that you will too.

The Way Things Were

In the mid-1960s, we tended to view reading as a pretty straightforward perceptual process. Readers, we thought, accomplished their task by translating graphic symbols (letters) on a printed page into an oral code (sounds corresponding to those letters). After that they "listened" to the sounds and to the words they had produced in the translation process. Comprehension of written material was nothing more than comprehension of speech produced by the reader. In this simple view of reading, there was no difference between oral and written language comprehension. But reading was not really viewed as a language process. Instead it was thought of as a perceptual process that, when accompanied by a translation process, produced a linguistic code which was treated by the brain as a language process.

Think for the moment about the implications of this view for teaching and learning reading. Clearly the major implication was that the primary concern of teachers should be to make sure that children could discriminate among the visual symbols they encountered on the printed page and that they could translate them into a verbal code. Given this view, it is not hard to see why the prevailing methods of teaching beginning reading in this era were phonics and whole-word instruction. In both of these approaches, whether the unit of focus is a letter or a word, the basic task for the student is to translate from the written to the oral code. This view of reading was quite consistent with another prevailing instructional emphasis during this period—skills. If phonics knowledge was what children needed to learn in order to perform the translation process, then decomposing phonics into separable bits of knowledge (letter-to-sound or, in the case of spelling, sound-to-letter correspondences), each of which could be presented, practiced, and tested independently, was the route to helping them acquire that knowledge.

The Journey Begins

Somewhere in the middle to late 1960s, scholars from many different fields of inquiry began to study the reading process: it would become an interdisciplinary quest from which the field of reading would never return. The first to take reading under their wings were the linguists, who wanted to convince us that reading was a language process closely allied to its sibling language processes of writing, speaking, and listening. Then came the psychologists and the sociologists and the psycholinguists and the sociolinguists and the philosophers and the political theorists and the critical theorists. It is not altogether clear why reading has attracted such interest from people in other fields. Our best explanation is that it is because reading is considered by so many to be a key to success in other scholastic endeavors. It is commonplace to hear citizens from all walks of life make statements of this ilk: "If you can't read, you'll never be able to learn things by yourself."

The Linguistic Perspective

In 1963, Charles Fries published a book entitled *Linguistics and Reading*. In it, he outlined what he thought the teaching of reading would look like if it were viewed from the perspective of linguistics. In the same decade, several other important books and articles (e.g., Thomas, 1965;

Wardhaugh, 1969) appeared, each carrying essentially the same message: if we examine reading (sometimes writing was included) from the perspective of the modern science of linguistics, we will have different models and methods of teaching reading.

One of the important insights typically put forward by linguists was that all literate societies try to represent key features of their oral language in their written language. So, for example, we have letters to represent the basic units of sound, usually referred to as *phonemes*. And we have spaces between words to represent juncture. Juncture is the property of sound that permits us to discriminate between *I scream* and *ice cream* or *my skis* and *mice keys* And we have special typographical features, such as <u>underlining</u>, *italics*, **boldface type,** ALL CAPS, and **<u>*COMBINATIONS OF ALL FOUR*</u>** to represent the linguistic property of *stress*. The property of stress, which tells the listener of a sentence what to pay clearest attention to (what the news is), is captured by the distinctions between these sentences (stress indicated by boldface type):

1. **Chris** won the award. (Chris, not someone else, won it!)

2. Chris **won** the award. (She won it, she did not steal it, nor was it given to her!)

3. Chris won the **award.** (Not the game, not the contest, not the money, but the award!)

Another important insight that we gained from linguists was that we do not have to represent in the written language (what linguists call the orthography) things that will be easily inferred from the normal processes of language, be they written or oral. So, for example, even though the past tense marker *-ed* is pronounced in three different ways (/əd/ as in *padded*, /d/ as in *nabbed*, and /t/ as in *capped)*, there is no need to mark its pronunciations with three different spellings because we will, in the natural process of pronouncing words in our language, provide the variation appropriate to the situation. In other words, we will not read /nabəd/ or /nabt/ when we see *nabbed* because our knowledge of and experience with our oral language will predispose us toward a contextually appropriate pronunciation. And, in fact, as readers, we gain an advantage when the past tense marker is nearly always spelled the same way in the sense that the correspondence between spelling *(ed)* and meaning (think past tense) is highly consistent irrespective of the particular phonological context (/əd/, /d/, or /t/) in which it occurs.

A third important insight, though it is not an insight whose influence is limited to the nature and role of written language, came to us from linguistics during this period. It was during this era that transformational-generative grammars replaced conventional structural linguistics as the dominant paradigm within the field. Noam Chomsky published two revolutionary treatises during this period. With the publication of two books—*Syntactic Structures* in 1957 and *Aspects of the Theory of Syntax* in 1965—Chomsky revolutionized the field of linguistics and paved the way for equally dramatic changes in the way that psychologists thought about and studied the processes of language comprehension and language acquisition. What Chomsky did was to provide a characterization of the nature of language and language development that completely undermined the behaviorist accounts of language comprehension and acquisition that had dominated both linguistics and psychology during the previous 50 years. Language comprehension could not be explained by stringing together the meanings of adjacent words, Chomsky contended. If linear processing was really the nature of language comprehension, how could we ever explain how it is, in example 4, that people know perfectly well that *warrior* and *felt* are related as subject and verb within a single sentence into which other clauses have been embedded.

4. The pensive warrior, weary of bearing the burden of his family's woes and angry with people in the audience whose blank stares belied a fundamental jealousy, truly felt that he had earned the award.

Chomsky also provided the basis for a nativist view about language acquisition—a view that holds that humans come to the world "wired" to acquire the language of the community into which they are born. He and others (see, especially, McNeill, 1966) drew this inference from two basic and contrasting facts about language: (a) language is incredibly complex and (b) language is acquired easily and naturally by children living in an environment in which they are simply exposed to (rather than taught!) the language of their community before they get to school. Only a view that children are equipped with some special cognitive apparatus for inferring complex rules could explain this remarkable feat.

Since our prevailing views of both reading comprehension and reading acquisition were derived from the same behavioristic language assumptions that Chomsky and his peers had attacked, if not destroyed, many people in the field of reading began to question whether those prevailing views would hold up when we applied similar perspectives and criticisms to analyses of written language comprehension and acquisition.

The Psycholinguistic Perspective

During the decade after the publication of *Syntactic Structures* a new field of inquiry, psycholinguistics, evolved. In its first several years of existence, the field devoted itself to determining whether the views of linguistic competence and language acquisition that had been set forth by Chomsky and his colleagues could serve as psychological models of language performance. There were two major lines of research. One group of researchers studied the implications of these new linguistic theories for language comprehension; the second, for language acquisition. Most notable among the comprehension efforts was the development of the derivational theory of complexity. It held that the number of grammatical transformations (a grammatical transformation involves some basic structural change in a sentence—e.g., changing a sentence from active voice to passive voice, or switching the order of clauses in a complex sentence) that were needed to get from the surface structure of a sentence (the surface form is the way that a sentence would appear in speech or writing) to its underlying deep structure (the deep structure is the hypothesized form in which a sentence would be encoded in our memory) was an index of the difficulty that we, as language users, would experience trying to understand the sentence. So, for example, the derivational theory of complexity would predict that sentence 5 would be harder to understand than sentence 6 because sentence 6 is closer to the deep structure of the idea, as loosely expressed in statement 7.

> 5. Before he became an arsonologist, Smithers was plagued by memories of the explosion.
> 6. Smithers' plaguing memories of the explosion influenced his decision to become an arsonologist.
> 7. Smithers remembered the explosion. This caused him to study arson. He became an arsonologist.

While that effort waned after about a decade because of conceptual changes within linguistics and because of research findings that contradicted the simple elegance of the derivational theory of complexity, the field of psycholinguistics and the disposition of psychologists to study language with more complex theoretical tools had been firmly established and remains with us even today.

The language acquisition group (see Brown, 1970) established that language learning was a rule-governed process. In contrast to earlier views, these psycholinguists found that children did not imitate written language; rather, as members of a language community, they were participants in language and invented for themselves rules about how oral language works. This insight allowed researchers to explain such constructions as "I eated my dinner" and "I gots two foots." Children inferred, in the first case, that the past tense was formed by adding /əd/ and, in the second, that to make the verb agree with a plural object (foots), it was necessary to make it plural also. They also inferred that the plural of a noun was formed by adding /s/. This insight, that children's oral language learning was rule-governed, revolutionized our ideas about language learning. Chomsky had argued that children were innately predisposed to learn language; Brown and his colleagues detailed the process through which children managed this rather amazing feat. Their work showed conclusively that children were active learners who inferred rules and tested them out. Much as Goodman would later show with written language, "mistakes" in oral language could be used to understand the rule systems that children were inventing for themselves. In addition, this research by psycholinguists also detailed the regular, stage-like process of language acquisition. Children began using one-word utterances to communicate meaning and, over time and with sufficient exposure and practice, moved to two-word utterances, to three-word sentences with subjects, verbs, and direct objects, and on and on to ever greater complexity. Perhaps most amazingly, children became proficient users of oral language in a relatively short period of time (most children were quite proficient users of oral language long before they started kindergarten), and they managed to do this without direct instruction (e.g., a parent saying to a child, "Today we will learn the letter *b*. Say /buh/.").

This work had a major impact on the thinking of reading educators. It occurred to several of us in the field that it might be useful to adopt something like a nativist framework in studying the acquisition of reading. And we began to ask questions like, what would the teaching of reading and writing look like if we assumed that children can learn to read and write in much the same way as they learn to talk? What would happen if we assumed that children were members of a community in which reading and writing are valued activities that serve important communication functions? What if we assumed that the most important factors in learning to read and write were having genuine reasons for communicating in these media and having access to a database in which there was so much print and talk about print that students could discover the patterns and regularities on their own, much as they do when they discover the patterns and regularities of oral language. While much of the seminal work involved in putting these assumptions to empirical tests would wait for a couple of decades (e.g., Harste, Burke, & Woodward, 1984), the seeds of doubt were firmly planted by the middle 1960s.

Two influential individuals, Kenneth S. Goodman and Frank Smith, led the reading field in asking and addressing these kinds of questions. In 1965, Goodman published an article entitled "A Linguistic Study of Cues and Miscues in Reading," in which he demonstrated that the errors children made while reading orally were better viewed as windows into the inner workings of their comprehension processes than as mistakes to be eradicated. He found, for example, that when students read words in story contexts as opposed to reading them in unrelated word lists, they were able to read many more words, implying that using context aided comprehension and word identification. He also found that the mistakes that they did make while reading in context revealed that they were trying valiantly to make sense of what they read. Goodman was so taken with this sense-making disposition that he decided to eschew the term *oral reading error* in favor of a new term, *miscue*. In another seminal piece, "Reading: A Psycholinguistic Guessing Game," Goodman (1967) laid out the elements of language that he thought that readers employed as they constructed meaning for the texts they encountered. In reading, he conjectured, readers use three cue systems to make sense of text: syntactic cues, semantic cues, and graphophonemic cues. Word order, he argued, provides syntactic cues for the reader. In sentence 8, the reader would use syntactic cues to predict the type of word (a noun) that would come next in the sentence.

8. A boy and his dog went skipping down the _____.

Goodman also argued that readers use meaning (semantic) cues to predict. In the sentence above, the reader would not only have predicted a noun, but also would have predicted a particular kind of noun—something on which one could skip: a street, a path, a trail, a road, a sidewalk. Lastly, Goodman believed, readers use graphophonemic cues—knowledge of sound-symbol relationships. Encountering the *s* would narrow the list of predicted possibilities to *street* and *sidewalk,* while the subsequent letter *i* would enable readers to confirm that the word was *sidewalk.* By attending to all of these cue sources. Goodman contended, readers could reduce their uncertainty about unknown words or meanings, thus rendering both the word-identification and comprehension processes more manageable. Indeed, Goodman saw no reason, in discussing reading, to distinguish between a word-identification and a comprehension phase. Readers are naturally motivated to make sense of the texts they encounter in reading, and phenomena like letter identification and word identification are better viewed as epiphenomena, as seamless parts of the same overall process of rendering texts sensible.

Smith's revolutionary ideas were first presented in 1971 in a book entitled *Understanding Reading*. In this seminal text, Smith argued that reading was not something one was taught, but rather was something one *learned* to do. Smith believed that there were no special prerequisites to learning to read, indeed, that reading was simply making sense of one particular type of information in our environment. As such, reading was what one learned to do as a consequence of belonging to a literate society. One learned to read from reading. The implication, which Smith made explicit, was that the "function of teachers is not so much to *teach* reading as to help children read" (p. 3).

Smith also advanced the argument that reading was only incidentally visual. By that, Smith meant that being able to see was necessary but not sufficient to achieve understanding. He identified four sources of information—orthographic, syntactic, semantic, and visual—all of which he claimed were somewhat redundant, and argued that skilled readers would make use of prior knowledge, the other three sources, and therefore rely minimally on visual information. Indeed, Smith felt that it was important for readers to use the other sources so that they could minimize their dependence on the amount of information to which they attended as they read. Readers who focused too heavily on visual information would lose sight of meaning.

Third, Smith advanced the idea that reading was a matter of making informed predictions. He argued that good readers were readers who set reasonable criterion levels for making predictions—that is, they were willing to take risks as readers.

Smith's fourth major contribution to reading theory was his belief that reading, all knowing, was a constructive process, that individuals made sense of what they encountered based on what they already knew. Even perception, he contended, was a decision-making, predictive process based on prior knowledge.

The psycholinguistic perspective had a number of influences on the field of reading. First, it encouraged us to value literacy experiences that focused on making meaning. This meant that many classroom activities—particularly worksheets and games that focused on enabling skills such as specific letter-sound correspondences, syllabification activities, structural analysis skills, specific comprehension activities, or study skills—were devalued.

Second, it helped us to value texts, especially those designed for use with beginning, or emerging, readers, in which authors relied sufficiently on natural language patterns, thus making it possible for emerging readers to use their knowledge of language to predict words and meanings. This meant that texts that relied on high-frequency words in short, choppy sentences (what we have come to call "basalese"), as in example 9, or those based upon the systematic application of some phonics element, as in example 10, were correspondingly devalued.

9. Run, John, run.	10. Nat can bat.
Run to Dad.	Nat can bat with the fat bat.
Dad will run.	The cat has the fat bat.
Run, Dad.	The rat has the fat bat.
Run, John.	Nat has the fat bat.
See them run.	Bat the bat, Nat.

Third, the psycholinguistic perspective helped us understand the reading process and appreciate children's efforts as readers. Errors became generative rather than negative. They were no longer things to be corrected: instead they were windows into the workings of the child's mind, allowing both the teacher and the child to understand more about the reading process and reading strategies. Understanding miscues also helped educators focus on comprehension and appreciate risk taking; at the same time, it led us to question the value of perfect pronunciation and recitation.

Fourth, psycholinguists gave us a means (miscue analysis) and a theory (reading as a constructive process) that were remarkably distinct from previous ideas about reading. The perspective made explicit links between oral and written language acquisition and helped us view reading as language rather than perception. In a sense, psycholinguistics continued the changes and traditions begun by the linguistic perspective; however, within the reading field, its influence was deeper and broader than its academic predecessor.

Most important, psycholinguistics affected our views of teaching and learning in a fundamental way. We began to rethink our ideas about what needed to be taught. We began to rethink the relationship between teaching and learning. So, instead of asking, "What can I teach this child so that she will eventually become a reader?" we began to ask, "What can I do to help this child as a reader?" Some teachers began to welcome all children into what Smith (1988) referred to as "The Literacy Club" (pp. 214–316) as an alternative to teaching children so-called prerequisite skills.

The Journey Continues

The cognitive psychology perspective

If psycholinguistics enabled psychologists to reexamine their assumptions about language learning and understanding by placing greater emphasis on the active, intentional role of language users, its immediate historical successor, cognitive psychology, allowed psychologists to extend constructs such as human purpose, intention, and motivation to a greater range of psychological phenomena, including perception, attention, comprehension, learning, memory, and executive control of all cognitive processes.

We cannot emphasize too strongly the dramatic nature of the paradigm shift that occurred within those branches of psychology concerned with human intellectual processes, largely as a result of these two movements, psycholinguistics and cognitive psychology. The previous half-century, from roughly the teens through the fifties, had been dominated by a behaviorist perspective in psychology that shunned speculation about the inner workings of the mind. Just show us the surface-level outcomes of the processes, as indexed by overt, observable behaviors. Leave the speculation to the philosophers. That was the contextual background against which both psycholinguistics and cognitive psychology served as dialectical antagonists.

The most notable change within psychology was that it became fashionable for psychologists, perhaps for the first time since the early part of the century (e.g., Huey, 1908; Thorndike, 1917), to study reading. And in the decade of the 1970s, works by psychologists flooded the literature on basic processes in reading. One group focused on text comprehension by trying to ferret out how it is that readers come to understand the underlying structure of texts. So we had many researchers, most notably Nancy Stein (e.g., Stein & Glenn, 1979) and David Rumelhart (1975) offering us story grammars—structural accounts of the nature of narratives, complete with predictions about how those structures impede and enhance human story comprehension. And we had others who chose to focus not on the narrative but on the expository tradition in text. The most important early work here was completed by Walter Kintsch (1974) and Bonnie Meyer (1975). Like their colleagues interested in story comprehension, they believed that structural accounts of the nature of expository (informational) texts would provide valid and useful models for human text comprehension. And in a sense, both of these efforts worked. Story grammars did account for story comprehension. Analyses of the structural relations among ideas in an informational piece did account for text comprehension. But what neither text-analysis tradition really tackled was the relationship between the knowledge of the world that readers bring to text and comprehension of those texts. In other words, by focusing on the structural rather than the ideational, or content, characteristics of texts, they failed to get to the heart of comprehension. That task, as it turned out, fell to one of the 1970s' most popular and influential movements, schema theory.

Schema theory (Anderson & Pearson, 1984; Rumelhart, 1980) is a theory about the structure of human knowledge as it is represented in memory. In our memory, schemata are like little containers into which we deposit particular experiences that we have. So, if we see a chair, we store that visual experience in our chair schema. If we go to a restaurant, we store that experience in our restaurant schema. If we attend a party, our party schema. . . . And schema theory does a nice job of explaining not only how and where we store things, but also how we establish relations between one schema and another in our minds schemata and particular things stored in a particular schema can serve a role in other schemata. So a particular chair representation that sits quietly in a chair schema might fill the slot for weapon in a murder schema when reading a mystery novel.

Schema theory does an admirable job of explaining reading comprehension, which probably, more than any of its other features, accounts for its popularity within the reading field. Put simply, probably too simply, comprehension of text occurs when we are able to find slots within particular schemata to place all the elements we encounter in a text. To say that we have "accounted for" a text is to say that we have found a "schema" home for each of the ideas in the text.

But schema theory also explains learning. We learn when something goes awry with comprehension and we have to make some structural change in our existing array of schemata to account for that anomaly. Some very minor learning occurs, according to David Rumelhart, even in the most straightforward act of comprehension. His contention is that every encounter with a new example of a well-established schema, say a chair, changes the schema ever so slightly. In other words, our schema for chair will never be the same after that new experience. Put differently, experience guarantees a dynamic quality for all our schemata. Rumelhart (1980) labeled this modest learning process *accretion*. A second level of learning is called *tuning*. In tuning, new encounters require adjustments, some minor and some substantial, in the structure of our schemata. So, if Jane Johnson's experience with dogs includes only terriers, toy poodles, and cocker spaniels, she may set a restriction on the range of sizes that dogs can come in. If she encounters a wolfhound, a husky and a collie, and learns that all three are dogs, she will have to alter the structure of her dog schema to allow for a greater range of sizes. Clearly, this is the most common kind of learning that all of us experience in life. It is captured in the reaction, "Hmm, I didn't know that," accompanied by an inner conviction to alter our knowledge structure. The third kind of learning, *restructuring*, occurs less frequently. It is what happens when our worlds get turned upside down. A common everyday example occurs when we come to terms with evidence that the earth revolves around the sun, and not vice versa. It is not just that fact that has to be changed. The discovery, more accurately the *acceptance* of the discovery, requires lots of other facts, relations, and schemata to be altered and rearranged.

It is not hard to see why schema theory was so appealing to theoreticians, researchers, and practitioners when it arrived on the scene in the 1970s. In a sense, it provides a rich and detailed theoretical account of the everyday intuition that we understand and learn what is new in terms of what we already know. It also accounts for another everyday intuition about why we, as humans, so often disagree about our interpretation of an event, a story, an article, a movie, or a TV show. We disagree because we approach the phenomenon with varied background experiences and knowledge. It accounts for a third everyday intuition that might be called the "It's all Greek to me" experience: sometimes we just do not have enough background knowledge to understand a new experience or text.

While these insights may not sound earthshaking, for the field of reading and for education more generally, they were. Examined in light of existing practices in the 1970s, they continued the revolutionary spirit of the linguistic and psycholinguistic perspectives. Schema theory encouraged us to ask,

- What is it that my children already know? And how can I use that to help them deal with these new ideas that I would like them to know?

rather than,

- What is it that they do not know? And how can I get that into their heads?

More specifically with respect to reading comprehension, schema theory encouraged us to examine texts from the perspective of the knowledge and cultural backgrounds of our students in order to evaluate the likely connections that they would be able to make between ideas that are in the text and the schema that they would bring to the reading task. Schema theory, like the psycholinguistic perspective, also promoted a constructivist view of comprehension, a view that says that all readers, be they 5 or 55 or 105, have to construct a coherent model of reading for the texts they read. Given its emphasis on the central role of prior knowledge, schema theory could not hold otherwise. The most important consequence of this constructivist perspective is that there is inherent ambiguity about where meaning resides. Does it reside in the text? In the author's mind as he/she sets pen to paper? In the mind of each reader as he/she builds a model of meaning unique to his/her experience and reading? In the interaction between reader and text?

Sociolinguistic Perspective

Sociolinguistics as a discipline developed in parallel with psycholinguistics. Beginning with the work of Labov (1972) and Baratz and Shuy (1969), sociolinguists had important lessons for those of us in literacy. Mainly these lessons focused on issues of dialect and reading. What the sociolinguists were finding in their research was that dialects were not ill-formed or half-formed variations of standard English. Instead, each dialect constituted a well developed linguistic system in its own right, complete with rules for variations from standard English and a path of language development for its speakers. In other words, speakers of dialects expressed linguistic *differences,* not linguistic *deficits.* The goal of schooling was not, and should not be, to eradicate the dialect in the process of making each individual a speaker of standard English. Instead, sociolinguists told us, we should find ways to accommodate the children's use of the dialect while they are learning to read and write. Several proposals for achieving this accommodation were tried and evaluated. The first was to write special readers for dialect speakers. In the early 1960s, several examples of black dialect readers appeared and, almost as rapidly, disappeared from major urban districts. They failed primarily because African American parents did not want their children learning with "special" materials; they wanted their children to be exposed to mainstream materials that were used by other children. The second equally unsuccessful strategy was to delay instruction in reading and writing until the oral language became more standardized. Teachers who tried this technique soon found out just how resistant and persistent, early language learning can be. The third, and most successful, approach to dialect accommodation involved nothing more than recognizing that a child who translates a standard English text into a dialect is performing a remarkable feat of translation rather than making reading errors. So, an African American child who says /pos/ when he sees *post* is simply applying a rule of Black English, which requires a consonant cluster in ending position to be reduced to the sound of the first consonant. Unfortunately for children who speak a dialect, we, as a field, did not take the early lessons of the sociolinguists to heart. Even today, we can find schools in which children are scolded for using the oral language that they have spent their whole lives learning. Even today, we find children whose dialect translations are treated as if they were oral reading errors.

Sociolinguistics also helped us rethink the notion of context. Prior to the advent of the sociolinguistic perspective, when educators talked about context in reading, they typically meant the print that surrounded particular words on a page. You were told, for example, that if the meaning of a word was not clear, context clues would help. To teach these context clues, students completed worksheets designed to draw their attention to particular types of context clues. Sentence 11 might be used to help students understand that the entire sentence might help them identify the unknown word, while sentence 12 might be used to show students how appositives, in this case in parentheses, could provide context clues.

11. Plowing his field one day late in spring, the farmer was struck by the *incongruity* of ice at the side of the road; he did not expect to see ice at this time of the year.

12. The derivational theory of complexity held that the number of grammatical *transformations* (a basic structural change in a sentence, e.g., changing a sentence from active voice to passive voice or switching the order of clauses in a complex sentence) that were needed to get from the *surface structure* of a sentence (the way that a sentence would appear in speech or writing) to its underlying *deep structure* (the hypothesized form in which a sentence would be encoded in our memory) was an index of the difficulty that we, as language users, would experience trying to understand the sentence.

In the 1980s, and primarily because of the work of sociolinguists, the meaning of the word *context* expanded to include not only what was on the page, but what Bloome and Green (1984) referred to as the instructional, noninstructional, and home and community contexts of literacy. From a sociolinguistic perspective, reading always occurred in a context, a context that was shaped by the literacy event at the same time as it shaped the event. Language then helped us learn what there was to know at the same time as it was changed by the knowing. The sociolinguistic version of knowledge and language as constructed processes was consistent with the constructivist views emerging from cognitive psychology and from psycholinguists and served to help advance the constructivist notion to an even broader set of contexts.

In addition to demonstrating the importance of these contexts on reading (and of reading on these contexts), sociolinguists also began to demonstrate that reading itself was a social process. Here, as in other fields, parallels were drawn between oral and written language. Michael Halliday (1973), for example, had identified seven social functions served by oral language and argued that these functions played a major role in language development. He theorized that children learned to talk because it served some function for them; for example, it allowed them to get needs met, to establish communication, to ask questions. Sociolinguistic research on written language suggested that written language too was a social process that served a function for the user. Perhaps most notably, Shirley Brice Heath (1983) conducted research in two relatively poor Piedmont communities, Roadville and Trackton, and demonstrated the considerable differences between communities relative to the way oral and written language were acquired. She contrasted those perspectives with the predominately white middle-class expectations of school and in so doing, helped us all to understand that literacy, like all behavior, was inherently social and that behaviors were learned ways of being and could only be interpreted in light of those ways.

The work of Gordon Wells (1986) also had a major impact on the field during this time. He studied preschool children's literacy experiences, documenting how often children were read to and how frequently they talked about books with others; he compared their preschool experiences with their subsequent school experiences. His 10-year study helped the field clearly understand the relationship between prior literacy experiences and school success; those children who had had the most exposure to books as preschoolers were the children who were most successful in school. Wells found that the reverse was also true— children who had had the least exposure to written texts had the most trouble academically.

Over all, perhaps the most significant impact of the sociolinguistic perspective was that it heightened our consciousness about language as a social and therefore cultural construction. Suddenly, or so it seemed, reading was a part of a bigger and more complex world than it ever had been before. Sociolinguists helped us understand the role of language in school settings, showing us, for example, that often success in reading was not so much an indication of reading "ability" per se, but of the success the individual experienced in learning how to use language appropriately in educational settings and how well the child learned to "do school." They contrasted the functions that language serves in school with the functions it serves outside of school and helped us rethink the role of language within the classroom. They also helped us understand about the role of community and brought into the foreground learning as a social process. Consequently, many educators began to rethink the competitive atmosphere of classrooms and of school labels and made changes within schools so that children could learn from and with each other. In addition, by studying the community outside of school, sociolinguists made us conscious of social, political, and cultural differences; as a result, we began to rethink our judgments of language and behavior. We saw that any judgment call we made, rather than reflecting the "right" way, simply reflected "our" way—the way we as teachers thought and talked and behaved because of the cultural situation in which we lived outside as well as inside of school.

With these contributions from sociolinguists, it was becoming more and more apparent that reading was not only not context free but that it was embedded in and not separable from multiple contexts.

Asking New Questions

As we hope this brief history makes clear, what we know about reading, how we think about reading, even what we call reading has changed considerably over the last 30 years. Reading, once the sole domain of educators, has become transdisciplinary. The knowledge base that has grown out of the once separate fields of psychology, sociology, linguistics, and literary theory has been created by and/or shared with educators. Indeed, many individuals now identify themselves as educators and as cognitive psychologists, psycholinguists, sociolinguists, literary theorists, and even sociopsycholinguists. "Reading" is no longer solely thought of as simply something one does or teaches, but rather is understood as a complex, orchestrated, constructive process through which individuals make meaning. Reading, so defined, is acknowledged as linguistic, cognitive, social, and political.

This reconceptualization of reading has led us to even newer journeys, journeys that are just now beginning, at least for many mainstream reading educators. Some of the journeys involve redirecting roads that, while already traveled, have not taken us as far as we want to go. For example, in response to challenges raised about the static nature of schemata as presented in the early versions of schema theory (e.g., Rumelhart, 1980), Rand Spiro and his colleagues (e.g., Spiro et al., 1987) have advanced cognitive flexibility theory as a way of explaining learning in more dynamic domains, domains they refer to as "ill-structured domains." This theory is being used to explain such complex, diverse, and dynamic events as learning to read, learning to teach, and learning to diagnose medical problems.

Other journeys involve taking paths that, while available for decades, have not been well traveled. Many educators, for example, are just now rereading (perhaps reading for the first time) Rosenblatt's 1976 edition of her 1938 text, *Literature as Exploration*, and her more recent *The Reader, the Text, the Poem* (1978). In her work, she argues that meaning is something that resides neither in the head of the reader (as some had previously argued) nor on the printed page (as others had argued). Instead, Rosenblatt contends, meaning is created in the transaction between reader and document. This meaning, which she refers to as the poem, resides above the reader-text plane. Meaning is therefore neither subject, nor object, but transaction.

The newest journeys being taken by reading educators are along the paths of semiotics (a branch of philosophy devoted to the study of signs and symbols; Eco, 1979), poststructuralism (a field that will undoubtedly question the commonly accepted view of readers as meaning constructors; Foucault, 1980) and critical theory (a philosophical perspective that situates the present in the past as it challenges us to rethink our future; Giroux, 1991).

While both Spiro and Rosenblatt ask us to rethink our current ideas about text and comprehension (Spiro does it by invoking Wittgenstein's metaphor of "criss-crossing" the landscape from multiple directions: Rosenblatt does it with the metaphor of the poem), the semioticians further challenge our ideas about text by suggesting that everything we perceive is a potential text and that each of these texts has unlimited meaning possibilities. The poststructuralists, meanwhile, nudge our ideas about the construction of meaning, deconstructing a text to show the complex relationship between language and culture. They point out, for example, that many of the words we use for the mind suggest that we envision it as a container with limited storage capacity. They ask us to consider what would happen if we shifted our metaphor to something like space, or time, something which could never be "filled." Meanwhile, the critical theorists are beginning to raise our political consciousness, showing how the present came to be as a result of political decisions that were made in the past. For example, women entered teaching because they were seen as having the right temperament to work with children; however, once in schools as teachers, they were asked to abandon that temperament and instead unaffectedly transmit knowledge into the minds (containers again) of children (Shannon, 1989). Similarly, they urged us to consider the political implications of our current decision making and to tie those decisions to our ideas about the kind of society we wish to create.

However, despite these kinds of new questions, and despite differences that exist across and between these multiple perspectives (and, we would add, across and between reading educators), what we have learned over the last 30 years has led to a number of beliefs that we currently hold in common. We agree that reading is a constructive and multiple contextualized process. As a consequence, we no longer think of literacy as an independent, isolated event. Instead, literacy events are seen as being shaped by the multiple contexts in which they are enacted. We agree that it matters whether the audience for your writing is a particular individual who is going to receive your letter in the mail or a teacher who is going to grade your punctuation. It matters whether you are reading a book because you chose it or because it was an assignment for the whole class. Similarly, it matters, when you are studying a topic, whether you developed the questions or they were handed to you on a ditto. Even place matters. Reading a novel, at your own leisure and pace, curled up on a pillow in a reading corner evokes a different stance than if the novel is being read, chapter by assigned chapter, within a specified time period while sitting squarely in a tablet armchair. It matters whether there are characters, settings, and problems in those novels that permit particular readers to identify with the cultural markers in the text versus repeatedly reading about characters whose lives and experiences bear no resemblance to the lives, needs, or aspirations of those readers. It matters whether the norms in classroom discussions privilege single versus multiple interpretations. In the one case, we see recitations in which a single voice dominates the discussion; in the other, we see conversations among multiple voices.

Because we share a basic constructivist perspective on knowledge and learning, we share a set of standards for curriculum. We want students to understand the role of reading in the construction of knowledge, and so we provide opportunities for them to use reading and writing to learn. To do so, we help them develop questions that they want answered and help them find ways to find their own answers. This happens across the curriculum, not just during reading or language arts period. We want students to value and choose reading, and so we read to them and provide time for them to read by themselves and with others. We want them to learn from and with each other, and to understand that knowledge is socially constructed, and so we provide time for students to work with, and learn from, each other. We want them to understand the relationships and insights that can be gained by looking at the world through the lens of different cultures, so we encourage multiple interpretations and celebrate diversity. We want them to learn about reading and learning, and so we talk with them about the process—helping them to name what they do so that they can be informed by their own reflections.

But we debate, however, about the order and nature of these experiences. We debate the role of the teacher. Should the teacher "prepare the environment" in the spirit of Maria Montessori so that students have the opportunity to learn what the teacher considers important? Or should the classroom be more open? More structured? How much should the teacher's voice be a part of the conversation? How little? Is good teaching a matter of being highly visible in the classroom? Or of being nearly invisible? What does "supporting learning" look like? How can we see it? Learn how to do it? Teach within its boundaries?

We debate what should be learned. In studying a topic, should all students learn the same thing? At the same time? Is it "all right" if students learn different things? At different times? Should students always/never study the same topic? Are there really core things that everyone should learn, core topics everyone should study? If so, who decides what those are and how they should be learned? What about process? How much do students need to know about knowing? About reading? About writing? And what are we teaching for? Do we choose content that will help students change the world or that which will help them accept and find success within the status quo?

We debate the role of the students. How much voice should they have? How should they bring their lives, their multiple realities, into the classroom? Do we need to build background or accept it? Should the backgrounds/experiences of all have equal value in our classroom? Equal time? Equal influence? Should students be cocreators of curriculum? Coevaluators of progress? Of grades? Just how active should students be? Is our responsibility primarily to them as individuals? As a group? Or to the content? What is their responsibility to us?

We debate the role of the reading material. Should students all read the same text? If so, which texts and in what order? Who chooses the materials our students read? Who should choose? What should be the criteria for choosing? Should texts be the primary source of learning, or one of many? And what are students supposed to "get" out of texts? Particular answers? New questions? Both? Neither?

We debate assessment, sometimes arguing against assessment and for evaluation and almost always arguing about tests. What should get tested, why, and by whom? How should test results be used? Should *test, assessment,* and *evaluation* be synonymous terms? Do we want to foreground the growth of the individual or compare the individual with the group? What does it mean to be accountable? To whom should we be accountable? To the students? To their parents? To the broader community? To all? And if we try to be accountable to all of these constituencies, do we end up working against ourselves and/or our students? How can accountability best be addressed? Do we need several systems? Just one? None? Is accountability the same as responsibility? As trustworthiness? Just what is it that we want to hold schools/teachers/students responsible for? What would count as evidence that we are doing a good job?

We debate the structure of school itself. Who should be making these kinds of decisions about teaching, learning, students, text, curriculum, and assessment? Students? Teachers? Teachers and students together? Principals? Central office staff? School boards? Publishers? Legislators?

Just who is in charge and who should be? How do those rules get established? Should they be changed? If so, how? These kinds of questions have arisen because we now understand a great deal about the reading/learning process, and we wonder if, in the process of developing a "science" of education and educational research, we have contrived a way of "doing school" that bears little resemblance to the real learning and teaching that motivated human societies to create schools in the first place.

These kinds of questions have arisen because we now understand that much of what we have learned in school in the past privileged one kind of knowing (e.g., that written by what are now critically referred to as "dead white men") and that other kinds of knowing have been slighted, indeed, even ignored, and we wonder whether we should try to right past wrongs and how we would go about doing so.

These kinds of questions have arisen because, as a society, we believe that better tomorrows are built by knowledgeable, reflective, literate people, and because we hold schools responsible for providing students with opportunities to learn what it feels like to be knowledgeable, reflective, and literate.

Finding Answers

As we all begin the task of answering these kinds of questions for ourselves, it is important for each of us to keep in mind that it is not only the questions that are new and challenging. What is also new, what is surfacing now and has not surfaced before, is a realization that these and all questions are, at heart, questions of power and control. They are political questions and, in turn, our answers are also political. Each time we ask and answer, "What works?" or "What matters?", we are simultaneously asking, "For/to whom?", "When? ", "Under what conditions?", and "To what end?"

Perhaps the field is facing no greater challenge than the challenge that has come about because of our political awareness. We now know, and are selfconsciously aware, that every time we make a decision to honor one voice in the conversation, it is also a decision to silence another voice. This cuts across each and every question raised earlier and across all the questions we will think of later.

In both K–12 and university-level classrooms, it means that when we decide to lecture, we privilege our voice and silence those of our students. It also means that if we choose the other extreme, if we choose a curriculum that consists of projects initiated solely by students, we run the risk of silencing our voices. It means that when we order textbooks, we are denying choice, and when we allow students to read whatever they want, we are limiting their access to certain knowledge bases. In one extreme, we devalue the contribution that students can make in the other, we devalue the contribution of experience and expertise. In both K–12 and university classrooms, it means that when we present students, through experiences, texts, and lectures, with the dominant perspective, with what is seen and understood by the so-called majority, by those who operate within the power code, we are silencing multiple and divergent perspectives. We are choosing to hold students accountable for seeing the world through our eyes. If we do not, if we equally value all perspectives and privilege none, we run the risk of denying students access to the power code. By so doing, we limit the possibilities for new and better tomorrows. With the best of intentions, we perpetuate the status quo of both individuals and our society.

These concerns may seem lofty and abstract but they are real and concrete. Each time we pick up a book to read to the class, we are making a decision about what voices will be heard, about what perspectives will be honored. And so too are we making those decisions when we choose topics to study, make seating charts, refer or not refer students to special education, count answers right or wrong on tests, call on some students and not others, send a child to detention, or plan reading groups and assignments.

Similarly, those decisions are being made about us. When committees and administrators decide what books we can use, what tests we will give, how we will use those results, what counts for promotion, the are making political decisions, decisions to privilege some voices and ignore others. And when we choose to follow or challenge those mandates, we are making political decisions, decisions about the power we have or want to have in our classrooms, over and with our students.

We believe that this new-found political consciousness has the power to alter, and we hope to improve, what we do in the name of school. We have learned a great deal over the past 30 years; among our insights is the recognition that knowledge alone is not enough to make schools better. What is needed is a continuing self-consciousness about the decisions we make, about the kinds of futures we want for ourselves, our students, our educational system, our community. It has taken us the last 30 years to understand that literacy is woven into everything we do, to recognize and accept that literacy offers the possibility of empowerment but does not guarantee it. Our choice now is to decide how to use our new information and our new political self-consciousness. We need to make informed, careful decisions about the role literacy will play in our lives and about the role we want literacy to have in the lives of our students. In the 1990s, it is no longer enough to "teach reading"; rather, we must ask ourselves hard questions about the politics of literacy, of the doors that literacy can open and those we can close, and we must somehow learn to live with the tension that comes from knowing that there is no longer one right answer to any question worth asking.

References

Anderson, R.C., & Pearson, P.D. (1984). A schema-theoretic view of basic processes in reading comprehension. In P.D. Pearson (Ed.), *Handbook of reading research* (pp. 255–91). White Plains, NY: Longman.

Baratz, J., & Shuy, R. (1969). *Teaching black children to read.* Washington, DC: Center for Applied Linguistics.

Bloome, D., & Green, J. (1984). Directions in the sociolinguistic study of reading. In P.D. Pearson (Ed.), *Handbook of reading research* (pp. 395–452). White Plains, NY: Longman.

Brown, R. (1970). *Psycholinguistics.* New York: Macmillan.

Chomsky, N. (1957). *Syntactic structures.* The Hague: Mouton.

Chomsky, N. (1965). *Aspects of the theory of syntax.* Cambridge, MA: MIT Press.

Eco, U. (1979). *The role of the reader: Explorations in semiotics of text.* Bloomington, IN: Indiana University Press.

Foucault, M. (1980). *Power/knowledge: Selected interviews and other writings, 1972–1977.* New York: Random House.

Fries, C.C. (1963). *Linguistics and reading.* New York: Holt, Rinehart.

Giroux, H. (Ed.), (1991). *Modernism, post-modernism, and feminism: Rethinking the boundaries of educational discourse.* Albany, NY: State University of New York Press.

Goodman, K.S. (1965). A linguistic study of cues and miscues in reading. *Elementary English, 42,* 639–43.

Goodman, K.S. (1967). Rending: A psycholinguistic guessing game. *Journal of the Reading Specialist, 4,* 126–135.

Halliday, M.A.K. (1973). *Explorations in the functions of language.* London: Edward Arnold.

Harste, J.C., Burke, C., & Woodward, V. (1984). *Language stories and literacy lessons.* Portsmouth, NH: Heinemann.

Heath, S.B. (1983). *Ways with words.* New York: Cambridge University Press.

Huey, E.B. (1908). *The psychology and pedagogy of reading.* New York: Macmillan.

Kintsch, W. (1974). *The representation of meaning in memory.* Hillsdale, NJ: Erlbaum.

Labov, W. (1972). *Language of the inner city.* Philadelphia, PA: University of Pennsylvania Press.

McNeill, D. (1966). Developmental psycholinguistics. In F. Smith & G.A. Miller (Eds.), *The genesis of language* (pp. 15–84). Cambridge, MA: MIT Press.

Meyer, B.J.F. (1975). *The organization of prose and its effects on memory.* Amsterdam: North Holland Publishing.

Rosenblatt, L.M. (1976). *Literature as exploration* (3rd ed.). New York: Modern Language Association. (Original work published 1938)

Rosenblatt, L.M. (1978). *The reader, the text, the poem: The transactional theory of the literary work.* Carbondale, IL: Southern Illinois University Press.

Rumelhart, D. (1975). Notes on a schema for stories. In D.G. Bobrow & A.M. Collins (Eds.), *Representation and understanding Studies in cognitive psychology* pp. 211–36). New York: Academic.

Rumelhart, D. (1980). Schemata: The building blocks of cognition. In R.J. Spiro, B.C. Bruce, & W.F. Brewer (Eds.), *Theoretical issues in reading comprehension* (pp. 33–58). Hillsdale, NJ: Erlbaum.

Shannon, P. (1989). The struggle for control of literacy lessons. *Language Arts, 66,* 625–34.

Smith, F. (1971). *Understanding reading: A psycholinguistic analysis of reading and learning to read.* New York: Holt, Rinehart.

Smith, F. (1988). *Understanding reading: A psycholinguistic analysis of reading and learning to read.* Hillsdale, NJ: Erlbaum.

Spiro, R.J., Vispoel, W., Schmitz, W., Samarapungavan, A., & Boerger, A. (1987). Knowledge acquisition for application: Cognitive flexibility and transfer in complex content domains. In B.C. Britton & S. Glynn (Eds.), *Executive control processes in reading.* Hillsdale, NJ: Erlbaum.

Stein, N., & Glenn, C.G. (1979). An analysis of story comprehension in elementary school children. In R. Freedle (Ed.), *New directions in discourse processing* (Vol. II, pp. 53–120). Norwood, NJ: Ablex.

Thomas, O. (1965). *Transformational grammar for the teacher of English.* New York: Holt, Rinehart.

Thorndike, E.L. (1917). Reading as reasoning: A study of mistakes in paragraph reading. *Journal of Educational Psychology, 8,* 323–32.

Wardhaugh, R. (1969). The teaching of phonics and comprehension: A linguistic evaluation. In K.S. Goodman & J. Fleming (Eds.), *Psycholinguistics and the teaching of reading* (pp. 79–90). Newark, DE: International Reading Association.

Wells, G. (1986). *The meaning makers.* Portsmouth, NH: Heinemann.

3 To Err Is Human: Learning about Language Processes by Analyzing Miscues

Yetta M. Goodman
Kenneth S. Goodman
University of Arizona

Starting from the premise that everything humans do, they do imperfectly, Goodman and Goodman explain the term "miscue" as the unexpected responses of children and adults reading orally. Ken Goodman originally chose the term because of the negative connotation of the term "error"; he wanted to emphasize that unexpected responses reflect readers' linguistic or conceptual cognitive structures. The authors illustrate how miscues reflect readers' strategies, and particularly how the important strategy of prediction leads readers to make miscues. A child who at first might not be thought to be an effective reader is viewed quite differently when we see how her miscues reflect good reading strategies, how she learns from the text, and, more generally, when we learn to see "the dynamic transaction between a reader and written language." Readers are intuitive grammarians who integrate all the language cueing systems (grammatical, graphophonic, semantic, and pragmatic) as they use strategies for constructing meaning from texts. A section on schema-forming and schema-driven miscues explains how readers' prior knowledge and experiences affect both their understanding of texts and their miscues. In the following section, Goodman and Goodman suggest that a single process of making sense underlies both oral and silent reading, though of course there are differences too. The authors conclude by arguing that reading research that focuses on "isolated sounds, letters, word parts, words, and even sentences" severely distorts the reading process and our understanding of it. Miscues analysis research, however, does provide insight into that process.

Originally published in R.B. Ruddell, M.R. Ruddell, and H. Singer (Eds.), *Theoretical Models and Processes of Reading* (4th ed.). International Reading Association, 1997. Reprinted with permission.

Everything people do, they do imperfectly. This is not a flaw but an asset. If we always performed perfectly, we could not maintain the tentativeness and flexibility that characterize human learning and the ways we interact with our environment and with one another. This model of imperfection causes us as researchers not to worry about why people fall short of perfection; rather, we are concerned with why people do what they do and with what we can learn about language processes from observing such phenomena.

The power of language users to fill knowledge gaps with missing elements, to infer unstated meanings and underlying structures, and to deal with novel experiences, novel thoughts, and novel emotions derives from the ability to predict, to guess, to make choices, to take risks, to go beyond observable data. We must have the capability of being wrong lest the limits on our functioning be too narrowly constrained. Unlike the computer, people do not exhibit specifically programmed, totally dependable responses time after time. We are tentative, we act impulsively, we make mistakes, and we tolerate our own deviations and the mistakes of others.

If you doubt that perfection in human behavior is the exception rather than the norm, consider how intensely a performer of any kind—athletic, actor, musician, writer, reader—must practice to achieve anything approaching error-free performance. If you doubt our view of how people deal with mistakes, think about the proofreader who skips over errors in a text or the native North Americans who deliberately insert flaws in handicrafts to remind themselves that the crafts are the work of human hands.

Miscues: Unexpected Responses

For more than 25 years we have studied the reading process by analyzing the miscues (or unexpected responses) of children and adults orally reading written texts. Ken Goodman coined this use of the word *miscue* because of the negative connotation and history of the term *error*. The term miscue reveals that miscues are unexpected responses cued by readers' linguistic or conceptual cognitive structures.

We started with the assumption that everything that happens during reading is caused, that a person's unexpected responses are produced in the same way and from the same knowledge, experience, and intellectual processes as expected responses. Reading aloud involves continuous oral response by the reader, which allows for comparisons between expected and observed responses. Such comparisons reveal the reader's knowledge, experience, and intellectual processes. Oral readers are engaged in comprehending written language while they produce oral responses. Because an oral response is generated while meaning is being constructed, it not only is a form of linguistic performance but also provides a powerful means of examining readers' process and underlying competence.

Miscue analysis requires several conditions. The written material must be new to the readers and complete with a beginning, middle, and end. The text needs to be long and challenging enough to produce sufficient numbers of miscues for patterns to appear. In addition, readers receive no help and are not interrupted. At most, if readers hesitate for more than 30 seconds, they are urged to guess, and only if hesitation continues are they told to keep reading even if it means skipping a word or phrase. Except that it takes place orally and not silently, the reading during miscue analysis requires as normal a situation as possible.

Depending on the purpose of miscue analysis research, readers often have been provided with more than one reading task. Various fiction and nonfiction reading materials have been used, including stories and articles from basal readers, textbooks, trade books, and magazines. Readers have been drawn from elementary, secondary, and adult populations and from a wide range of proficiency and racial, linguistic, and national backgrounds. Studies have been conducted in many languages other than English and in various writing systems (Goodman, Brown, & Marek, 1993).

Betsy's oral reading of the folktale "The Man Who Kept House" (from McInnes, Gerrard, & Ryckman, 1964, pp. 282–283) is used throughout for examples (Goodman, Watson, & Burke, 1987). The story has 68 sentences, 711 words. Betsy, a 9-year-old from Toronto, was selected by her teacher as representative of students with reading difficulties. Betsy read the story hesitantly, although in most places she read with appropriate expression. Below are the first 14 sentences (s1–s14) from the story, with the actual printed text on the left and the transcript of Betsy's oral reading on the right.

Text	*Transcript*
s1 Once upon a time there was a woodman who thought that no one worked as hard as he did.	Once upon a time there was a woodman. He threw . . . who thought that no one worked as hard as he did.
s2 One evening when he came home from work, he said to his wife, "What do you do all day while I am away cutting wood?"	One evening when he . . . when he came home from work, he said to his wife, "I want you do all day . . . what do you do all day when I am always cutting wood?"

s3	"I keep house," replied the wife, "and keeping house is hard work. "	"I keep . . . I keep house," replied the wife, "and keeping . . . and keeping . . . and keeping house is and work."
s4	"Hard work!" said the husband.	"Hard work!" said the husband.
s5	"You don't know what hard work is!	"You don't know what hard work is!
s6	You should try cutting wood!"	You should try cutting wood!"
s7	"I'd be glad to," said the wife.	"I'll be glad to," said the wife.
s8	"Why don't you do my work some day?	"Why don't you. . . . Why don't you do my work so . . . some day?
s9	I'll stay home and keep house," said the woodman.	I'll start house and keeping house," said the woodman.
s10	"If you stay home to do my work, you'll have to make butter, carry water from the well, wash the clothes, clean the house, and look after the baby," said the wife.	"If you start house. . . . If you start home to do my work, well you'll have to make bread, carry . . . carry water from the well, wash the clothes, clean the house, and look after the baby," said the wife.
s11	"I can do all that," replied the husband.	"I can do that. . . . I can do all that," replied the husband.
s12	"We'll do it tomorrow!"	"Well you do it tomorrow!"
s13	So the next morning the wife went off to the forest.	So the next day the wife went off to the forest.
s14	The husband stayed home and began to do his wife's job.	The husband stayed home and began to do his work.

Betsy's performance reveals her language knowledge. These examples are not unusual; what Betsy does is done by other readers. She processes graphophonic information: most of her miscues show a graphic and phonic relationship between the expected and the observed response. She processes syntactic information: she substitutes noun for noun, verb for verb, noun phrase for noun phrase, verb phrase for verb phrase. She transforms phrases, clauses, and sentences: she omits an intensifier, changes a dependent clause to an independent clause, shifts a *wh* question sentence to a declarative sentence. She draws on her conceptual and linguistic background and struggles toward meaning by regressing, correcting, and reprocessing as necessary. She predicts appropriate structures and monitors her own success based on the degree to which she is making sense. She develops and uses psychosociolinguistic strategies as she reads. There is nothing random about her miscues.

Reading Miscues and Comprehension

Since we understand that the brain is the organ of human information processing, that it is not a prisoner of the senses but controls the sensory organs and selectively uses their input, we should not be surprised that what is said in oral reading is not what the eye has seen but what the brain has generated for the mouth to report. The text is what the brain responds to; the oral output reflects the underlying competence and the psychosociolinguistic processes that have generated it. When expected and observed responses match, we get little insight into this process. When they do not match and a miscue results, researchers have a window on the reading process.

We have come to believe that the strategies readers use when miscues occur are the same as when there are no miscues. Except for s3, s8, and s9, all of Betsy's miscues produced fully acceptable sentences or were self-corrected. By analyzing whether miscues are semantically acceptable with regard to the whole text or are acceptable only with regard to the prior portion of text, it is possible to infer the strategies readers actively engage in. s2 provides a powerful example. Betsy reads, *I want you do all day*, hesitates, reads slowly, and eventually—after a 23-second pause—reconsiders, probably rereads silently, and self-corrects the initial clause in this sentence. The verb *said* in the sentence portion prior to her miscue and her knowledge about what husbands might say when they come home from work allowed her to predict *I want you*. . . . After she self-corrects the first part of the dialogue, she reads, *when I am always cutting wood* for *while I am away cutting wood* with confidence and continues her reading. These two substitution miscues (*when* for *while* and *always* for *away*) produce a clause that fits with the meaning of the rest of the story. The more proficient the reader, the greater the proportion of semantically acceptable miscues or miscues acceptable with the prior portion of the text that are self-corrected (Goodman & Burke, 1973).

In s12 Betsy produces, *Well you do it tomorrow* instead of *We'll do it tomorrow.* Although it seems that Betsy simply substitutes *well* for *we'll* and inserts *you,* the miscues are shown to be more complex when we examine how the phrase and clauses are affected by the miscues. Betsy substitutes an interjection prior to the subject *you* to substitute for the noun and the beginning of the verb phrase represented by the contraction *we'll.* In addition, Betsy shifts intonation to indicate that the wife rather than the husband is talking. Apparently Betsy predicted that the wife was going to speak to maintain the pattern of husband-wife conversation that is established by the author in the previous sections (s2 and s11). Although the author's intended meaning is changed, the sentence is semantically acceptable within the story.

A reader's predicting and confirming strategies are evident in miscues that are acceptable with the text portion prior to the miscues. Such miscues often occur at pivotal points in sentences, such as junctures between clauses or phrases. At such points the author may select from a variety of linguistic structures to compose the text; the reader has similar options but may predict a structure that is different than the author's. Consider these examples from Betsy's reading:

Text	*Transcript*
s38 "I'll light a fire in the fireplace and the porridge will be ready in a few minutes.	"I'll light a fire in the fireplace and I'll . . . and the porridge will be ready in a flash . . . a few minutes."
s48 Then he was afraid that she would fall off.	Then he was afraid that the . . . that she would fall off.

Betsy's predication of *I'll* instead of *the* in the second clause of the first example is logical. Since *and* often connects two parallel items, it is not an unreasonable prediction that the second clause will begin with the subject of the first. However, when *I'll* does not fit with the second clause, Betsy confidently disconfirms her prediction and immediately self-corrects. The miscue substitution of *the* for *she* in the second example is also at a pivotal point in the sentence. Whenever an author uses a pronoun to refer to a previously stated noun phrase, a reader may revert to the original noun phrase. The reverse phenomenon also occurs. When the author chooses a noun for which the referent has been established earlier, the reader may use that pronoun. Choosing a noun for which the referent has been established earlier, the reader may use that pronoun. Betsy was probably predicting *the cow* that *she* refers to. These miscues clearly show that Betsy is an active language user as she reads. Ken Goodman has done studies on the control readers have over determiners and pronouns in relation to the cohesion of text (Goodman, 1983; Goodman & Gespass, 1983).

The idea that miscues often occur at specific pivotal points in any text is important enough to provide an example from another reader. An Appalachian reader, while reading the sentence "By the time I got out and over to where they were," inserted *of the water* between *out* and *and*. In the previous paragraph the male character is in the water. The author and the reader have similar options at this point in the grammatical structure. The prepositional phrase *of the water* is understood by the reader though not stated by the author and therefore may be omitted or inserted without changing the meaning. In this case, the reader makes explicit what the author left implicit.

Miscues that result in semantically acceptable structures are confirmed as acceptable to readers and, therefore, are less likely to be corrected than those that are not acceptable or acceptable only with the immediately preceding text. Miscues at pivotal points in the text are often acceptable with regard to the preceding text. Of the ten semantically acceptable miscues that Betsy produced in the first excerpt, she corrected only one (*all* in s11). However, of the six miscues that were acceptable only with the prior portion of the text, she corrected four. Such correction strategies tend to occur when the reader believes they are most needed—when a prediction has been disconfirmed by subsequent language cues.

Insights are gained into the reader's construction of meaning and the process of comprehension when we ask questions such as "Why did the reader make this miscue? Does it make sense in the context of this story or article?" Through such examination, it is possible to see the pattern of comprehending strategies a reader engages in.

We contrast comprehending—what the reader does to understand during the reading of a text—with comprehension—what the reader understands at the end of the reading. Open-ended retellings that always follow the reading during miscue analysis are an index of comprehension. They add to the profile of comprehending, which shows the reader's concern for meaning as expressed through the reading miscues. Retellings also provide an opportunity for the researcher or teacher to gain insight into how concepts and language are actively used and developed throughout a reading event.

Although the concept of retelling is common to present-day research, in the early sixties when we first used this concept, many questioned the term and the appropriateness of its use in reading research. Rather than asking direct questions that would give cues to the reader about what is significant in the story, we asked for unaided retelling. Information on the readers' understanding of the text emerges from the organization they use in retelling the story, from whether they use the author's language or their own, and from the conceptions or misconceptions they reveal. Here is the first segment of Betsy's retelling:

> Um . . . it was about this woodman and um . . . when he . . . he thought that he um . . . he had harder work to do than his wife. So he went home and he told his wife, "What have you been doing all day." And then his wife told him. And then, um . . . and then, he thought that it was easy work. And . . . so . . . so his wife, so his wife, so she um . . . so the wife said, "Well so you have to keep," no . . . the husband says that you have to go to the woods and cut . . . and have to go out in the forest and cut wood and I'll stay home. And the next day they did that.

By comparing our interpretation of the story with Betsy's retelling and her miscues, we are able to analyze how much learning has occurred during Betsy and the author's transaction. For example, although the story frequently uses *woodman* and *to cut wood, forest,* the noun used to refer to setting, is used twice. Not only does Betsy provide evidence in her retelling that she knows that *woods* and *forest* are synonymous, she also indicates that she knows the author's choice is *forest.* The maze she works through suggests her search for the author's language. Her oral language mazes are evidence of her intentions and self-correction patterns. Betsy seems to believe that the teacher is looking for the author's language rather than her own. Additional evidence of Betsy's concern to reproduce the author's language is seen in her use of *woodman* and *husband.* In the story, the woodman is referred to as *woodman* and *husband* eight times each and as *man* four times; the wife is referred to only as *wife.* Otherwise pronouns are used to refer to the husband and wife. In the retelling, Betsy uses *husband* and *woodman* six times and *man* only once; she called the wife only *wife.* Betsy always uses appropriate pronouns in referring to the husband and wife. However, when cow was the referent, she substituted *he* for *she* twice. (What does Betsy know about the sex of cattle?)

The linguistic and conceptual schematic background a reader brings to reading not only shows in miscues but is implicit in the developing conceptions or misconceptions revealed through the reader's retelling. Betsy adds to her conceptual base and builds her control of language as she reads this story, but her ability to do both is limited by what she brings to the task. In the story, the husband has to make butter in a churn. Betsy makes miscues whenever butter-making is mentioned. For example, in s10 she substituted *bread* for butter. (Breadmaking is much more common than butter-making as a home activity for North American children.) The next time *butter* appears, in s15, she reads it as expected. However, in s18, *Soon the cream will turn into butter,* Betsy reads *buttermilk* for *butter*. Other references to butter-making include the words *churn* or *cream*. Betsy reads *cream* as expected each time it appears in the text but produces miscues for *churn*. She pauses about 10 seconds at the first appearance of *churn* and finally says it with exaggerated articulation. However, the next two times *churn* appears, Betsy reads *cream*.

Text	Transcript
s25 . . . he saw a big pig inside, with its nose in the churn.	. . . he saw a big pig inside, with its nose in the cream.
s28 It bumped into the churn, knocking it over.	It jumped . . . it bumped into the cream, knocking it over.
s29 The cream splashed all over the room.	The cream shado [nonword miscue] . . . splashed all over the room.

In the retelling Betsy provides evidence that her miscues are conceptually based and not mere confusions:

> And the husband was sitting down and he poured some buttermilk and um . . . in a jar. And, and he was making buttermilk, and then he um . . . heard the baby crying. So he looked all around in the room and um. . . . And then he saw a big, a big, um . . . pig. Um . . . he saw a big pig inside the house. So, he told him to get out and he, the pig, started racing around and um . . . he di . . . he um . . . bumped into the buttermilk and then the buttermilk fell down and then the pig, um . . . went out.

Betsy, who is growing up in a metropolis, knows little about how butter is made in churns. She knows that there is a relationship between cream and butter, although she does not know the details of that relationship. According to her teacher, she has also taken part in a traditional primary school activity in which sweet cream is poured into a jar, closed up, and shaken until butter and buttermilk are produced. Although Betsy's miscues and retelling suggest that she has only some knowledge about butter-making, the concept is peripheral to comprehending the story. All that she needs to know is that butter-making is one of the wife's many chores that can cause the woodman trouble.

For a long time, teachers have been confused about how a reader can know something in one context but not know it in another. Such confusion comes from the belief that reading is word recognition; on the contrary, words in different syntactic and semantic contexts become different entities for readers, and Betsy's response to the structure *keep house* is good evidence for this. In s3, where the clauses *I keep house* and *and keeping house* occur the first time, Betsy reads the expected responses but repeats each several times before getting the words right, suggesting that she is grappling with their meanings. In s9 she reads *start house and keeping house* for *stay home and keep house*, and she reads the first phrase in s10 as *If you start home to do my work.* The structure *keep house* is a complex one. To a 9-year-old, *keep* is a verb that means being able to hold on to or take care of something small. *Keeping house* is no longer a common idiom in American or Canadian English. *Stay home* adds complexity to *keep house.* Used with different verbs and different function words, *home* and *house* are sometimes synonyms and sometimes not. The transitive and intransitive nature of *keep* and *stay* as well as the infinitive structure *to keep* and *to stay* add to the complexity of the verb phrases.

In her search for meaning and her transaction with the published text, Betsy continues to develop strategies to handle these complex problems. In s14 she produces *stayed home;* however, in s35 she encounters *keeping house* again and reads, *perhaps keeping house . . . home and . . . is . . . hard work.* She is exploring the concept and grammaticality of *keeping house.* She first reads the expected response and then abandons it. In the story *home* appears seven times and *house* ten times. Betsy reads them correctly in every context except in the patterns *staying home* and *keeping house.* Yet as she continues to work on these phrases throughout her reading she finally is able to handle the structures and either self-corrects successfully or produces a semantically acceptable sentence. Thus Betsy's miscues and retelling reveal the dynamic transaction between a reader and written language.

Through careful observation and evaluation, miscue analysis provides evidence of the ways in which the published text teaches the reader (Meek, 1988). Through continuous transactions with the text, Betsy develops as a reader. Our analysis also provides evidence for the published text as a mediator. Betsy is in a continuing zone of proximal development as she works at making sense of this text (Vygotsky, 1978). Because the text is a complete one it mediates Betsy's development.

The Reader: An Intuitive Grammarian

Reading is not simply knowing sounds, words, sentences, and the abstract parts of language that can be studied by linguists. Reading, like listening, consists of processing language and constructing meaning. The reader brings a great deal of information to this complex and active process. A large body of research has been concerned with meaning construction and the understanding of reading processes and has provided supporting evidence to many of the principles we have revealed through miscue analysis. However, there is still too little attention paid to the ability of readers to make use of their knowledge of the syntax of their language as they read.

Readers sometimes cope with texts that they do not understand well by manipulating the language. Their miscues demonstrate this. The work of both Chomsky and Halliday has helped us understand the syntactic transformations that occur as readers transact with texts. Such manipulations are often seen when readers correctly answer questions about material they do not understand. For example, we ask readers to read an article entitled "Downhole Heave Compensator" (Kirk, 1974). Most readers claim little comprehension, but they can answer the question "What were the two things destroying the underreamers?" by finding the statement in the text that reads, "We were trying to keep drillships and semisubmersibles from wiping out our underreamers" (p. 88). It is because of such ability to manipulate the syntax of questions that we decided to use open-ended retellings for miscue analysis.

In miscue analysis research, we examine the syntactic nature of the miscues, the points in the text where miscues occur, and the syntactic acceptability of sentences that include miscues. Readers often produce sentences that are syntactically, but not semantically, acceptable. In s10 Betsy finally reads, *If you start home to do my work* for the text phrase *If you stay home to do my work*. Her reading of this phrase is syntactically acceptable in the story but unacceptable semantically since it is important to the story line that the woodman stay home.

We became aware that readers were able to maintain the grammaticality of sentences even if the meaning was not maintained when we examined the phenomenon of nonwords. Such nonsense words give us insight into English-speaking readers' grammatical awareness because sentences with nonwords often retain the grammatical features of English although they lose English meaning. Betsy produces only two nonword miscues among the 75 miscues she produces. In s58 Betsy reads, *As for the cow, she hang between the roof and the gorun* instead of the expected response *She hung between the roof and the ground*. She repeats *and the* prior to *ground* three times and pauses for about ten seconds between each repetition. She seems to be aware that the word *ground* is not a familiar one in this context, but she maintains a noun intonation for the nonword. This allows her to maintain the grammatical sense of the sentence so that later in the story when the text reads *the cow fell to the ground,* she reads it as expected without hesitation.

Use of intonation also provides evidence for the grammatical similarity between the nonword and the text word. Miscues on the different forms of *to* (as the initial part of an infinitive or as a preposition), *two,* and *too* are easy to clarify by paying attention to intonation patterns. Nonwords most often retain similarities not only in number of syllables, word length, and spelling but also in bound morphemes—the smallest units that carry meaning or grammatical information within a word but cannot stand alone (for example, the *ed* in carried). In one of our research studies (Goodman & Burke, 1973), a group of 6th graders read a story that included the following sentences: "Clearly and distinctively Andrew said 'philosophical. '" and "A distinct quiver in his voice." The nonword substitutions for each were different depending on the grammatical function of the word. For *distinctly* readers read nonwords that sounded like *distikily, distintly* and *definely,* while for *distinct* they read *dristic, distink, distet.*

There is abundant evidence in miscues of readers' strong awareness of bound morphemic rules. Our data on readers' word-for-word substitutions, whether nonwords or real words, show that, on average, 80 percent of the observed responses retain the morphemic markings of the text. For example, if the text word is a noninflected form of a verb, the reader will tend to substitute that form; if the word has a prefix, the reader's substitution will tend to include a prefix. Derivational suffixes will be replaced by derivational suffixes, contractional suffixes by contractional suffixes.

Maintaining the syntactic acceptability of the text allows readers to continue reading and at the same time to maintain the cohesion and coherence of the text. Only a small portion of Betsy's substitution miscues do not retain the same grammatical function as the text word. Analysis of the word-for-word substitutions of 4th and 6th graders showed that their miscues retained the identical grammatical function over 73 percent of the time for nouns and verbs (Goodman & Burke, 1973). Function words were the same 67 percent or more of the time, while noun modifiers were retained approximately 60 percent of the time. In addition, an examination of what kinds of grammatical function were used for substitution when they were not identical indicated that nouns, noun modifiers, and function words are substituted for one another to a much greater degree than they are for verbs. Again this suggests the power of grammaticality on reading. Of 501 substitution miscues produced by 4th graders, only three times was a noun substituted for a verb modifier, and 6th graders made such a substitution only once in 424 miscues.

Evidence from miscues occurring at the beginning of sentences also adds insight into readers' awareness of the grammatical constraints of language. Generally, in prose for children few sentences begin with prepositions, intensifiers, adjectives, or singular common nouns without a preceding determiner. When readers produce miscues on the beginning words of sentences that do not retain the grammatical function of the text, we could not find one miscue that represented any of these unexpected grammatical forms. (One day we will do an article called "Miscues Readers Don't Make." Some of the strongest evidence comes from all the things readers could do that they do not.) These patterns are so strong that we have been able to detect manufactured examples in some professional texts. The authors have offered examples of errors readers don't make.

Readers' miscues that cross sentence boundaries also provide insight into the readers' grammatical sophistication. It is not uncommon to hear teachers complain that readers read past periods. Closer examination of this phenomenon suggests that when readers do this they are usually making a logical prediction that is based on a linguistic alternative. Although Betsy does this a few times, we will use an example from a story we used with fourth graders: *He still thought it more fun to pretend to be a great scientist, mixing the strange and the unknown* (Goodman & Goodman, 1978). Many readers predict that *strange* and *unknown* are adjectives and intone the sentence accordingly. This means that their voices are left up in the air, so to speak, in anticipation of a noun. The more proficient readers in the study regress at this point and self-correct by shifting to an end-of-the-sentence intonation pattern. Less proficient readers either do not correct at all and continue reading sounding surprised or try to regress without producing the appropriate intonation pattern.

Interrelations of All the Cueing Systems

Reading involves the interrelationship of all the language systems. All readers use graphic information to various degrees. Our research (Goodman & Burke, 1973) demonstrates that the least proficient readers we studied in the 6th, 8th, and 10th grades use graphic information more than the most proficient readers. Readers also produce substitution miscues similar to the phonemic patterns of text words. An examination of Betsy's word substitution miscues reveals that she pays more attention to the look-alike quality of the words than to their sound-alike quality. Although attention to graphic features occurs more frequently than attention to the phonemic patterns, readers use both systems to show that they call on their knowledge of the graphophonic system. Yet the use of these systems cannot explain why Betsy would produce a substitution such as *day* for *morning* or *job* for *work* (s13 and s14). She is clearly showing her use of the syntactic system and her ability to retain the grammatical function and morphemic constraints of the expected response. But the graphophonic and syntactic systems together do not explain why Betsy could seemingly understand words such as *house, home, ground,* and *cream* in certain contexts but not in others. To understand these aspects of reading, one must examine the interrelationship of all the cueing systems.

The integration of all the language systems (grammatical, graphophonic, semantic, and pragmatic) are necessary in order for reading to take place. Miscue analysis provides evidence that readers integrate cueing systems from the earliest initial attempts at reading. Readers sample and make judgments about which cues from each system will provide the most useful information in making predictions that will get them to meaning. All of the miscue examples we have cited point to the notion that readers monitor their reading and ask themselves, "Does this sound like language?" (syntactically acceptable) and "Does this make sense in this story?" (semantically acceptable). Finally, if they have to return to the text to check things, they look more closely at the print using their graphophonic knowledge to confirm and self-correct as they read.

As readers make use of their knowledge of all the language cues, they predict, make inferences, select significant features, confirm, and constantly work toward constructing a meaningful text. Not only are they constructing meaning, they are constructing themselves as readers.

Schema-Forming and Schema-Driven Miscues

Our analysis of oral reading miscues began with the foundational assumption that reading is a language process parallel to listening. Everything we have observed among readers from beginners to those with great proficiency supports the validity of this assumption. The analysis of miscues, in turn, has been the basis for the development of a theory and model of the reading process (see K.S. Goodman, this volume).

What we have learned about miscues in reading has been applied to aspects of language such as spelling, composition, response to literature, and oral language development. Such research, liberated from the "perfection misconception," has demonstrated the linguistic creativity of humans. Errors children make as they develop oral language have provided insight not only into how the young learn language but into the nature of language—how it develops, grows, and changes (Brown, 1973). Children also invent schemata about the nature of written language as they become writers (Ferreiro & Teberosky, 1982; Goodman & Wilde, 1992). Invented punctuation and spelling are especially good examples of the ways in which children learn to control the relationship between the sound system of their dialects and the conventions of the writing system (Read, 1986; Wilde, 1992). Adults develop the craft of writing through making miscues (Shaughnessy, 1977). Rosenblatt (1978) has long argued for a transactional view of reader response to literature in which all response is seen as a transaction between reader and text that of necessity results in variation among readers as they proceed toward interpretation, evaluation, and criticism. The readers' schemata are vital to the transactions.

What we have learned from the study of oral reading miscues and what we have seen in research on other language processes can help to explain the generation of miscues. The concept of schema is helpful to explore how miscues are necessary to language learning. A schema, as we define the term, is an organized cognitive structure of related knowledge, ideas, emotions, and actions that has been internalized and that guides and controls a person's use of subsequent information and response to experience.

Humans have schemata for everything they know and do. We have linguistic schemata (which we call rules) by which we produce and comprehend language. For example, we know when to expect or produce questions and when a question requires an answer. We have schemata for what language does and how it works. With such schemata, we use language to control the behavior of others. We have conceptual schemata for our ideas, concepts, and knowledge of the world. We may reject a Picasso portrait because it does not meet our expectation or schema of the human face.

Our work has led us to believe that humans also develop overarching schemata for creating new schemata and modifying old ones. These we might call schemata for new schema formation. Chomsky's (1965) concept that the generation of language is controlled by a finite set of transformational rules is a case of a schema for schema formation. The rules determine and limit what syntactic patterns may be accepted as grammatical in a language; these same rules also make it possible for speakers to create new sentences that have never been heard before but will be comprehensible to others.

Conceptual schemata work much the same way, and they are also controlled by overarching schemata. That explains why we often use analogy and metaphor in making connections to well-known words and ideas when we talk about new experiences. An example is the use of the term *docking* for space travel. Conceptual and linguistic schemata are at work simultaneously. The schemata must all be in harmony. If more than one complexity occurs, the result is compounding; the possibility of miscues increases disproportionately.

The earlier discussion about Betsy's miscues relating to the concepts of *to stay home* and *to keep house* is a good example. Her complete retelling after reading, indicates good understanding of these concepts. In order to build this kind of understanding, Betsy has to work hard during her reading. She relates her own limited knowledge of staying home and keeping house to the meanings she is constructing in transaction with the author. She has to develop control over the syntactic and conceptional complexity of *stay home* and *keep house* and add to her understanding of the relationship of *home* and *house*. She keeps selectively using the available graphophonic cues to produce both expected and unexpected responses. It is important to understand the complexity of thinking that Betsy has to use and that her miscues reflect. Much of children's language learning can be explained in terms of developing control over language schemata. With growing linguistic and conceptual schemata, children use language to predict, process, and monitor expression and comprehension.

Now let's reconsider a concept from miscue analysis: miscues are produced by the same process and in response to the same cues as expected responses. Putting that together with what we have just said about schema formation and use, we can consider miscues from the perspective of two schema processes: *schema-forming* or *schema-driven* miscues. And since schemata can be forming while we use our existing schemata, both processes can go on at the same time.

Piaget's (1977) concepts of assimilation and accommodation are pertinent here. A schema-forming miscue may be seen as a struggle toward accommodation, while a schema-driven miscue shows assimilation at work. Further, the effect of the miscue on subsequent language processing or intent may result in a disequilibrium, which may lead to reprocessing—that is, self-correction. Schemata may need to be abandoned, modified, or reformed as miscues are corrected.

A *schema-forming* miscue reflects the developmental process of building the rule systems of language and concepts, learning to apply those language rule systems, and delimiting them. For example, Susie responds to the printed name Corn Flakes on a box of cereal by pointing to each line of print successively while drawing out the word *ceeerrreeeeuuuull* until she finishes moving her finger. Although she has not yet developed the concept that English print is alphabetic, she shows through her unexpected response that she is developing a schema concerning a relationship between the length of print and the length of oral utterance.

The young child's development of the rules of past tense, number, and gender are reflected in the miscues children make in oral language (Brown, 1973). Rebecca, age 3, provides a good example when she says to her aunt, who is waiting to read her a story, "I'll come and get you in a few whiles." She shows her control of the schema for pluralization (*few* takes a plural) but she has taken *while,* which functions as a noun in the idiom *wait a little while* and has made it a count noun (*a few whiles*).

In the view of some scholars, a subject's production of language is dependent on whether the subject is dealing with old or new information. A schema-forming miscue is likely to involve new information, either linguistic or conceptual, which may not be easily assimilated. A schema-driven miscue may involve either old (given) information or new information in a predictable context. Furthermore, the schema, as well as the information, may be old or new.

A *schema-driven* miscue is one that results from the use of existing schemata to produce or comprehend language. In our research the concept of prediction has become important. Texts are hard or easy in proportion to how predictable they are for readers. They may use their existing schema to predict and comprehend, but sometimes the organization of the knowledge—that is, the schema on which the predictions are made—is so strong that it overrides the text and miscues occur. In the initial paragraph of a story that many adolescents and adults have read for us, the phrase *the headlamps of the car* occurs. The majority read *headlights* rather than *headlamps.* Many of those who do read *headlamps* indicate that they expected *headlights* and had to reread to accept *headlamps.*

Language variations also show evidence of schema-driven miscues. We shift dialects and registers when we move from formal written language to more informal styles or from one regional dialect to another. Tommy was overheard saying to his mother, a Texan, "Mom, Dad wants to know where the bucket is" and then to his father, a midwesterner, "Here's the pail, Dad." Tommy had learned to switch codes depending on the situation, and his schema-driven responses were appropriate to each parent. Understanding that dialect miscues are driven by schema may help teachers and researchers see them in proper perspective. A rural African American 4th grader in Port Gibson, Mississippi, was reading a story that included the line *the ducks walked in single file.* At this point in the story, mother duck was leading her babies in a proud and haughty manner. The child reading that line produced *the ducks walk signifying.*

The malapropisms that we all exhibit are also evidence of schema-driven miscues at work. We try to use schemata for word formation beyond word-formation limits. These result in miscues in listening as well as speaking. TV's Archie Bunker was upset because of the *alteration* he had had with a boisterous customer. We can't help relating the concept of schema-driven miscues to Tannen's (1990) work on conversations between men and women and among different ethnic groups. "I make sense of seemingly senseless misunderstandings that haunt our relationships and show that a man and a woman can interpret the same conversation differently, even when there is no apparent misunderstanding," she writes (p. 13). By understanding the reasons that underlie our misunderstandings perhaps we can form schemata that will help us "prevent or relieve some of the frustration" (p. 13).

In many cases it is not easy to separate miscues into schema-forming or schema-driven processes since they often occur simultaneously. At any particular point in time, it is fairly easy to explain the schemata that drive the miscues that occur. Schema formation, on the other hand, is less likely to occur at a single point and be easily discernible in a single miscue. The study of children's writing development allows us one way to observe the process of schema formation. It also reveals how both schema-forming and schema-driven miscues can occur in concert. An example from a story that Jennifer wrote in the 1st grade illustrates invented spelling that is driven by her linguistic schemata. Jennifer produced past-tense verbs about 20 times. Each reflected her invented phonic rules (and her awareness of the phonological rules of her own speech) since each had the letter *d* or *t* at the end, representing the appropriate phoneme. These spelling miscues included *rapt* (wrapped) and *yeld* (yelled). Her phonic schemata at this point led her to invent consistent spellings of single letters for single sounds. But a year later her spelling represented an awareness of the interrelationship of both the morphophonemic rules (past tense taking one of three forms depending on the preceding consonants) and the orthographic rule that spelling is not determined by sound in a simple one-to-one manner. Of 28 regular past-tense verbs in a story she wrote in the 2nd grade, 25 were spelled conventionally. Jennifer was in a classroom where a lot of writing was encouraged but there was no direct teaching of spelling. During this year, she continually reformed her schemata and moved toward socially conventional ones.

Readers' miscues often can be driven by conceptual schemata, but at the same time readers can be forming new schemata. This is often revealed through the retelling as well as the miscues. In our research, we have had children read a story that has a significant concept represented by an unfamiliar but high-frequency word. One such word was *typical*. Although the children who read this story often reproduced oral substitutions for *typical* in the text (such as *tropical, type-ical,* and *topical*), they usually were able to explain the meaning of the word as it developed in the reading of the text. One Texas youngster said, "Oh, yeah, *tropical* means ordinary, just like all kinds of other babies. But, you know, it could also be a big storm."

Sometimes a new word represents a concept well known to the reader. In this case the reader must assimilate the new term to the old concept. Bilingual students often face this when they begin to read in a second language. We studied Arabic immigrant students who produced miscues on the word *plow* in a story they were reading, substituting *palow, pull, pole, polo, plew,* and *blow,* among other words and nonwords (Goodman & Goodman, 1978). However, they all were able to provide evidence that they had a "plowing" schema. One reader's example is representative: "Well, it's a thing with two handles and something pointing down. You got to pull it. But they don't push it with a camel. They push it with a cow. When the cow moves, the one who's pushing it got to go push on it so it goes deeper in the underground." In such a context we see both schema-driving and schema-forming processes taking place in a dynamic way. These 4th grade Arabic readers are new to English. They use their developing knowledge of English to produce unexpected responses to the word *plow* and their knowledge about plowing to show understanding of the concept (schema-driven). At the same time, they add new knowledge as they encounter the English word for the concept (schema-forming). The example also indicates that the reader rejected the story element that a camel was used to pull a plow as implausible because of his conceptual schema.

We hope that our discussion of the role miscues play in language learning communicates to teachers and researchers that miscues are the positive effects of linguistic and conceptual processes rather than the failure to communicate or comprehend. If a language user loses meaning, she or he is likely to produce a miscue. If the language user chooses a syntactic schema different from the author's, a miscue will likely result. If a reader or listener interprets in a way different from the meaning intended by the speaker or author, a miscue will result. Miscues reflect readers' abilities to liberate themselves from detailed attention to print as they leap toward meaning. Readers make use of their linguistic and conceptual schemata to reverse, substitute, insert, omit, rearrange, paraphrase, and transform. They do this not only with letters and single words, but with two-word sequences, phrases, clauses, and sentences. Their own experiences, values, conceptual structures, expectations, dialects, and lifestyles are integral to the process. The meanings they construct can never be a simple reconstruction of the author's conceptual structures because they are dependent on the reader's schemata.

Risk-taking has been recognized as a significant aspect of both language learning and proficient language use. In risk-taking there is a necessary balance between tentativeness and self-confidence. Miscues reflect the degree to which existing schemata fit the existing circumstance and the level of confidence of the language user. In speaking a second language, speakers often show great tentativeness, consciously groping for control of developing schemata. As their confidence grows so does their risk-taking, and their miscues show the influence either of schemata for the first language (schema-driven) or of their developing schemata for the second language (schema-forming). An example of the former cautious type is this sentence from a native Spanish-speaking adult who is asking his English teacher for advice: "Ms. Buck, please, I hope I do not molest you." This oral miscue is driven by the speaker's schema for the Spanish *molestar* (to bother). In her response to the student, the teacher will provide information that will help the student form a schema to provide semantic limits for the English *molest.*

Oral and Silent Reading

We need to say a word about the relationship between oral and silent reading since much of miscue analysis research uses oral reading. The basic mode of reading is silent. Oral reading is special since it requires production of an oral representation concurrently with comprehending. The functions of oral reading are limited. It is a performing art used by teachers, entertainers, politicians, and religious leaders. We have already explained why we use oral reading in miscue analysis. But a basic question remains: Are oral and silent reading similar enough to justify generalizing from studies of oral reading miscues to theories and models of silent reading?

In our view, a single process underlies all reading. The language cueing systems and the strategies of oral and silent reading are essentially the same. The miscues we find in oral reading occur in silent reading as well. We have some research evidence of that. Studies of nonidentical fillers of cloze blanks (responses that do not match the deleted words) show remarkable correspondence to oral reading miscues and indicate that the processes of oral and silent reading are much the same (Anderson, 1982; Cambourne & Rousch, 1979; Chapman, 1981). Still, there are dissimilarities between oral and silent reading. First, oral reading is limited to the speed at which speech can be produced: therefore, it need not be as efficient as rapid silent reading. Next, superficial misarticulations such as *hangaber* for *hamburger* occur in oral reading but are not part of silent reading. Also, oral readers, conscious of their audience, read passages differently from when they read silently. Examples are production of nonword substitutions, persistence with several attempts at problem spots, overt regression to correct miscues already mentally corrected, and deliberate adjustments in ensuing text to cover miscues so that listeners will not notice them. Furthermore, oral readers may take fewer risks than silent readers. This can be seen in the deliberate omission of unfamiliar words, reluctance to attempt correction even though meaning is disrupted, and avoidance of overtly making corrections that have taken place silently to avoid calling attention to miscues. Finally, relatively proficient readers, particularly adults, may become so concerned with superficial fluency that they short-circuit the basic concern for meaning. Professional oral readers (newscasters, for example) seem to suffer from this malady. With these reservations noted, we believe that making sense is the same in oral and silent reading; in construction of meaning, miscues must occur in both.

Parts and Wholes

Too much research on language and language learning is still concerned with isolated sounds, letters, word parts, words, and even sentences. Such fragmentation, although it simplifies research design and the complexity of the phenomena under study, seriously distorts processes, tasks, cue values, interactions, and realities. Many years ago, Kintsch (1974) wrote as follows:

> Psycholinguistics is changing in character. . . . The 1950s were still dominated by the nonsense syllables . . . the 1960s were characterized by the use of word lists, while the present decade is witnessing a shift to even more complex learning materials. At present, we have reached the point where lists of sentences are being substituted for word lists in studies of recall recognition. Hopefully, this will not be the endpoint of this development, and we shall soon see psychologists handle effectively the problems posed by the analysis of connected text (p. 2).

Through miscue analysis we have learned that, other things being equal, short language sequences are harder to comprehend than are long ones. Sentences are easier than words, paragraphs easier than sentences, pages easier than paragraphs, and stories easier than pages. We see two reasons for this. First, it takes some familiarity with the style and general semantic thrust of a text's language for the reader to make successful predictions. Style is largely a matter of an author's syntactic preferences; the semantic context develops over the entire text. Short texts provide limited cues for readers to build a sense of either style or meaning. Second, the disruptive effect of particular miscues on meaning is much greater in short texts. Longer texts offer redundant opportunities to recover and self-correct. This suggests why findings from studies of words, sentences, and short passages produce different results from those that involve whole texts. It also raises a major question about using standardized tests, which employ words, phrases, sentences, and short texts to assess reading proficiency.

Sooner or later all attempts to understand language—its development and its function as the medium of human communication—must confront linguistic reality. Theories, models, grammars, and research paradigms must predict and explain what people do when they use language and what makes it possible for them to do so. Researchers have contrived ingenious ways to make a small bit of linguistic or psycholinguistic reality available for examination. But then what they see is often out of focus, distorted by the design. Miscue analysis research makes fully available the reality of the miscues language users produce as they participate in real speech and literacy events. Huey (1908) said: "And so to completely analyze what we do when we read would almost be the acme of a psychologist's achievements, for it would be to describe very many of the most intricate workings of the human mind, as well as to unravel the tangled story of the most remarkable specific performance that civilization has learned in all its history" (p. 6). To this we add that miscues are the windows on language processes at work.

References

Anderson, J. (1982, July). *The writer, the reader, the text.* Paper presented at the 19th annual UKRA Reading Conference. Newcastle-upon-Tyne, UK.

Brown, R. (1973). *A first language: The early stages.* Cambridge, MA: Harvard University Press.

Cambourne, B. & Rousch, P. (1979). *A psycholinguistic model of the reading process as it relates to proficient, average, and low-ability readers* (Tech. Rep.). Wagga Wagga, NSW, Australia: Riverina College of Advanced English, Sturt University.

Chapman, J. (1981). The reader and the text. In J. Chapman (Ed.), *The reader and the text.* London: Heinemann.

Chomsky, N. (1965). *Aspects of the theory of syntax.* Cambridge, MA: MIT Press.

Ferreiro, E. & Teberosky, A. (1982). *Literacy before schooling.* Portsmouth, NH: Heinemann.

Goodman, K.S. (1983, July). *Text features as they relate to miscues: Determiners* (Occasional Paper No. 8). Tucson, AZ: Program in Language and Literacy, College of Education, University of Arizona.

Goodman, K.S., Brown, J., & Marek, A. (1993). *Annotated chronological bibliography of miscue analysis* (Occasional Paper No. 16). Tucson, AZ: Program in Language and Literacy, College of Education, University of Arizona.

Goodman, K.S. & Burke, C.L. (1973, April). *Theoretically based studies of patterns of miscues in oral reading performance* (Project No. 9-0375). Washington, DC: U.S. Office of Education.

Goodman, K.S. & Gespass, S. (1983, March). *Text features as they relate to miscues: Pronouns* (Occasional Paper No. 7). Tucson, AZ: Program in Language and Literacy, College of Education, University of Arizona.

Goodman, K.S. & Goodman, Y.M. (1978). *Reading of American children whose language is a stable rural dialect of English or a language other than English* (Final Report, Project NIE-C-00-3-0087). Washington DC: U.S. Department of Health, Education and Welfare, National Institute of Education.

Goodman, Y.M., Watson, D., & Burke, C. (1987). *Reading miscue inventory: Alternative procedures.* New York: Richard C. Owen.

Goodman, Y.M. & Wilde, S. (1992). *Literacy events in a community of young writers.* New York: Teachers College Press.

Huey, E.B. (1908). *The psychology and pedagogy of reading.* New York: Macmillan.

Kintsch, W. (1974). *The representation of meaning in memory.* Hillsdale, NJ: Erlbaum.

Kirk, S. (1974, June). Downhole heave compensator: A tool designed by hindsight. *Drilling-DCW,* 88.

McInnes, J., Gerrard, M., & Ryckman, J. (Series Eds.). (1964). *Magic and make believe* (Basal Program). Don Mills, Ont.: Thomas Nelson.

Meek, M. (1988). *How texts teach what readers learn.* Exeter, UK: Thimble.

Piaget, J. (1977). *The development of thought: Equilibration of cognitive structures.* New York: Viking.

Read, C. (1986). *Children's creative spelling.* London: Routledge & Kegan Paul.

Rosenblatt, L. (1978). *The reader, the text, the poem.* Carbondale, IL: Southern Illinois University Press.

Shaughnessy, M. (1977). *Errors and expectations.* New York: Oxford University Press.

Tannen, D. (1990). *You just don't understand: Women and men in conversation.* New York: Morrow.

Vygotsky, L. (1978). *Mind in society.* Cambridge, MA: Harvard University Press.

Wilde, S. (1992). *You kan red this! Spelling and punctuation for whole language classrooms, K-6.* Portsmouth, NH: Heinemann.

III New Perspectives on Phonological Awareness and Phonics

4 Considering the Research on Phonological Awareness and Phonics

Constance Weaver
Western Michigan University

This chapter provides an overview of key research questions surrounding much of the work presented in this section. Researchers have, in some cases, tentatively concluded that phonemic awareness *can* be taught, but significant limitations and underlying assumptions need to be recognized—especially in the current climate, where a few key studies carry weight and influence they were not intended to sustain. Significant questions need to be posed and addressed before the conclusion is drawn that research points definitively toward direct instruction in phonological awareness as the best or the only method of helping children develop phonics knowledge. As Weaver argues, the real question—How do educators help children become truly literate individuals?—can sometimes be obscured in research that is not explicit about its own limits and exclusions.

Essays in other sections of this volume touch upon the development of concepts relating to the perception of sounds and letters and the relationship between the sound (phonological) system and the orthographic (spelling) system of our language. These concepts include phonological awareness (awareness of various units of sound, such as syllables, onsets and rimes, and phonemes); awareness of onsets (the initial consonant[s] in a syllable) and rimes (the vowel of the syllable, plus any consonants that may follow); phonemic awareness (awareness of the *separate* sounds in words); the alphabetic principle (that sounds and sound patterns are represented by letters); and the teaching of phonics (letter/sound patterns and correspondences).

These concepts are further illustrated in the introduction to this volume and in many of the articles. A great deal of research has focused recently upon just one of these concepts, phonemic awareness. Because the aim of this book is to offer research beyond that being widely disseminated and touted these days, none of the studies focusing specifically or primarily on phonemic awareness have been included (but see

Weaver's summary of some of the experimental research in chapter 11).
Nor have studies that focus on teaching phonological awarness and/or
phonics to students who have been diagnosed as dyslexic.

Despite these exclusions, it is important to note that researchers have
discovered that there is a strong correlation between phonemic awareness and the scores on standardized tests of reading, particularly in the
first grade. Therefore, some researchers have set out to investigate
whether phonemic awareness can be taught and, if so, whether such
teaching correlates with higher test scores. Superficially, the answer
seems to be yes—but there is much more to it than that.

For example, the test scores may not be very much higher, even
after extensive and intensive teaching. Gaskins, Ehri, Cress, O'Hara,
and Donnelly (Dec. 1996/Jan. 1997) report on instruction with first
graders who seemed unable to segment spoken words into phonemes
and who had little awareness of letter/sound relationships other
than in the initial positions of words. The investigators describe an
extensive and intensive program of teaching phonemic awareness
and phonics, a program lasting over much of a school year. For comparison, the investigators administered to these first graders the same
reading and spelling tests that had been administered to the previous year's first graders: the Wide Range Achievement Test (WRAT)
word-reading and spelling tests.

Statistical tests showed that the group that received the intensive
instruction in hearing sounds and matching letters and sounds made
statistically significant greater gains in reading words than the previous year's class. However, the mean performances differed by only
six words: 57 words read correctly in the spring by the previous year's
class, and 63 words read correctly in the spring by the children in the
phonics-intensive program. The difference turned out to be statistically significant, but is it educationally significant enough to warrant
the enormous amount of instructional time it required—particularly
in light of evidence that reading itself does wonders to improve reading? (See, for instance, the research summarized by Tunnell & Jacobs
in chapter 12).

Another example is the research undertaken by Foorman, Francis,
Beeler, Winikates, and Fletcher (1997). The particular study in question included 209 first graders and 166 second graders who were
receiving Chapter 1 services for "at risk" students. In the regular
classroom, the children received one of three different kinds of treatments: direct instruction in phonological and particularly phonemic
awareness, letter/sound correspondences, blending, shared reading
of Big Books, and other activities from the Open Court program; a

program that embedded phonics into authentic reading and writing activities and emphasized phonemic awareness and spelling patterns; or whole language teaching that emphasized authentic reading and writing (classrooms wherein the researchers have not yet reported how much time and attention were given to phonemic awareness and phonics in the context of reading and writing). These instructional programs were complemented by tutorial assistance of various kinds (for more details, see Weaver's summary on experimental research in chapter 11).

In May, the direct instruction group had significantly higher scores than either of the other groups on the Woodcock Johnson-Revised Basic Reading (Letter-Word Identification and Word Attack) and on its Broad Reading test (letter/word identification and passage comprehension). The greatest differences occurred on the Basic Reading test: the direct instruction group scored at the 44th percentile, the embedded phonics group at the 32nd percentile, the whole language group at the 27th percentile, and the standard curriculum group at the 17th percentile. On the Formal Reading Inventory (FRI: Wiederholt, 1986), which tests narrative and expository reading comprehension through multiple choice questions, the groups did not differ, on the average.

At first, results like this seem to offer a strong argument for direct instruction of phonological awareness and phonics skills. On the other hand, we note that the groups were not significantly different in comprehension, at least not on the one independent test of comprehension. What we are left wondering about are issues like this:

- How appropriate are standardized tests as measures of reading ability, perhaps especially at grade one? (A substantial body of research challenges their appropriateness and comprehensiveness.)
- Do children develop phonemic awareness and phonics knowledge from learning to read? And if so, does this occur just as readily (or more so) among heterogenous groups of students as it does among students who have been taught phonemic awareness and phonics before reading patterned and other simple texts? (There is not much research on these questions, but from what research there is, the answer seems to be yes; see, for example, Weaver's summaries of experimental research in chapter 11.)
- What about the children's development of effective strategies for processing text to derive meaning? (The brief passages on first grade comprehension tests do not tell us much about children's ability to process text for meaning, much less about their reading strategies.)

- What about the development of children's attitude toward reading and their concept of themselves as readers, and writers? (See Dahl & Freppon, chapter 10.)

- What about children's development of an understanding of story; the ability to discuss story elements, compare stories and story elements, illustrators, and authors; and their ability to critique the stories they read? In short, what about children's development as literate individuals?

- What about the development of groups with varying kinds of instruction over time, in such factors as decoding ability, reading strategies, attitudes about reading and themselves as readers, and development of literacy as more broadly conceptualized?

- For example, will the children who were not in the direct instruction classrooms catch up with letter and word identification and word attack skills, while maintaining at least an equal ability to process texts for meaning? (There is very little longitudinal research, but most of the existing comparative research studies suggest that children in whole language classrooms develop as good a grasp of the alphabetic principle and phonics skills as children in skills-intensive classrooms, and maintain it over two or three years. See research by Dahl & Freppon, chapter 10, and the research summarized in Weaver's discussion of experimental research; also see the article by McIntyre & Freppon, chapter 7).

- Can children who have difficulty with phonological processing and recognition of letter/sound patterns be helped by intensive work in these areas? (The answer seems to be that most can.)

- Will children who persist in having difficulties with decoding skills over time nevertheless find it possible to overcome those difficulties through massive reading and/or to read for meaning effectively, despite continued word identification problems? (See chapters 12, 13, and 14.)

These and other questions should help us realize the limitations of the studies that deal exclusively, or almost exclusively, with matters relating to phonological awarness and phonics.

Why, then, include this section of research in this book? Primarily for four reasons: (1) to showcase some interesting, relevant studies that are not widely known; (2) to emphaze the point that the widely cited research on phonemic awarness by no means deals with the entire spectrum of related issues; (3) to emphasize the point that no one study seems to have sufficiently investigated the relationships and interrelationships among sound-related and letter/sound-related factors; and (4) to encourage longitudinal research that will encompass not only more of these relationships but focus on the interplay between these factors and the development of reading strategies and the ability to comprehend texts, affective factors that are critical to becoming literate, and children's progress toward becoming an independent and avid readers, and writers.

To underscore the limitations of all the research studies focusing on phonological and phonics issues, let me mention some of what the studies described in the following section of *Reconsidering a Balanced Approach to Reading* do and do not tell us:

1. Moustafa's article (chapter 5) and the study reported in her dissertation suggest that being able to recognize words is more helpful in decoding unfamiliar words than knowledge of letter/sound correspondences. However, it does not compare instructional procedures, such as the effects of teaching words versus teaching phonics on children's ability to decode unfamiliar (nonsense) words. Other studies are needed to assess that and also to assess, for example, the possibility that one strategy for reading unfamiliar words works better initially but another strategy works better later, or that one strategy works better for some children but another strategy works better for others.

2. Peterson and Haines's study (chapter 6) demonstrates that teaching children letter/sound rime analogies in words (e.g., The same -*all* in *ball* and *fall*) as well as the initial consonant differences, *b-* and *f-*) can promote the ability to segment words into onsets and rimes and phonemes, and to make letter/sound connections. On the other hand, it does not document how the children read the test words: seemingly on sight, in letter/sound chunks, or by blending individual letters. This might have been an interesting and valuable aspect or extension of the study.

3. McIntyre and Freppon's study (chapter 7) found that children in a skills-based classroom and a whole language classroom both learned the alphabetic principle and letter/sound relationships, and the pattern of acquisition was similar in the two kinds of classrooms, across the two years of the study. On the other hand, these researchers did not examine the development of phonemic awareness separate from phonics knowledge, as some other studies have done, nor did they relate the development of phonics knowledge to the use of phonics knowledge in actual reading and writing (as Dahl and Freppon do in chapter 10).

4. Ayres's research (chapter 8) demonstrates that direct teaching of phonological awareness seems to promote such awareness better than indirect teaching alone, but that such direct teaching seems to be most effective when children have already had extensive experiences with literature. Her dissertation study (1993) also found that certain measures of children's ability to segment words into phonemes correlated more strongly with standardized test scores than measures that focused more on recognition of onsets and rimes. Furthermore, her study suggested not only that phonological awareness promotes learning to read, but that learning to read promotes phonological awareness. However, it did not explicitly investigate this reciprocal relationship.

Like all good researchers, the authors of these articles discuss other limitations of their studies, too (at least in the original studies, such as their dissertations). For instance, Ayres points out that,

> Based upon contemporary constructs of the nature of reading, standardized tests provide a limited glimpse of student achievement. While one of the hallmarks of a standardized test is the timed structure of each subtest, the time constraints often penalize careful young readers. This is particularly true at the first grade level when fluency is not well established. This narrow definition, in addition to the constraints placed upon six-year-old children by the rigid format of standardized tests, represents a limitation to the study. (1993, p. 158)

These limitations apply to other quantitative studies and measures as well.

In short, each of these studies, like the others mentioned or even discussed elsewhere in this book, addresses only one or two pieces of the puzzle surrounding the development of phonological and phonics knowledge. And as other articles clearly indicate, the use of such knowledge involves, by itself, only one of the three major cueing systems that proficient readers use in reading: semantic, syntactic, and grapho/phonemic (letter/sound). Therefore, it would be extremely unwise for us to take any one study on phonological awareness or phonics, or even the entire gamut of studies, as telling us how we should teach reading and develop literacy. We need a more rounded research picture for that—a picture suggested in Weaver's "balanced reading" article and filled out by many of the other articles in this volume. An attempt to summarize much of what we have learned from various kinds of research about reading and learning/teaching to read can be found in Weaver's summary of some of the experimental research in chapter 11. Of course this summary too is subject to revision as we learn more about reading, learning to read, and teaching others to read.

Works Cited

Foorman, B.R., Francis, D.J., Beeler, T., Winikates, D., & Fletcher, J.M. (1997). Early interventions for children with reading problems: Study designs and preliminary findings. *Learning Disabilities: A Multi-Disciplinary Journal, 8,* 63–71.

Gaskins, I.W., Ehri, L.C., Cress, C., O'Hara, C., & Donnelly, K. (Dec. 1996/Jan. 1997). Procedures for word learning: Making discoveries about words. *The Reading Teacher, 50,* 312–27.

5 Reconceptualizing Phonics Instruction

Margaret Moustafa
California State University, Los Angeles

No theory, no matter how battered, is ever abandoned until a successor is provided. We know that children have difficulty segmenting spoken words into phonemes. We know that struggling readers given extensive instruction in letter-phoneme correspondences to the exclusion of working with authentic texts do not become better readers. Yet traditional, parts-to-whole, letter-phoneme instruction continues because we have lacked a successor theory of how children learning to read an alphabetic script acquire a letter-sound system.

New discoveries in linguistics have led to a successor theory: onset-rime analogy. Onset-rime analogy theory may be summarized as follows: (1) In onset-rime languages such as English, the psychological units of spoken syllables are onsets and rimes. Onsets are any consonants before the vowel in a syllable; rimes are the vowel and any consonants after it in a syllable. (2) Young children are competent at dividing spoken words into onsets and rimes but not into phonemes, when onsets or rimes consist of more than one phoneme. That is, they can analyze the spoken word *smiles* into /sm/ and /ilz/ but have difficulty analyzing it into /s/, /m/, /i/, /l/, and /z/. (3) Children just beginning to read use analogy between known and unknown print words to figure out how to pronounce unknown print words, and they make such analogies at the onset-rime level rather than at the phonemic level. (4) The more print words children recognize, the better position they are in to make analogies between known and unknown print words to pronounce unknown print words. (5) Children's knowledge of print words better explains their ability to pronounce unknown print words than their knowledge of letter-phoneme correspondences.

Moustafa reexamines the written code to which children apply their phonological and cognitive processes when learning to read in English. Further, she argues that letter-sound correspondences in English are not based on abstract rules but are socially constructed representations where given letters and letter strings have multiple possible pronunciations even within one dialect. Finally, whole-to-parts phonics instruction is described as a theoretically grounded alternative to traditional parts-to-whole phonics instruction.

We know that young children have difficulty segmenting spoken words into phonemes (Liberman, Shankweiler, Fischer, & Carter, 1974; Treiman, 1983, 1985). We know that phonics rules are inconsistent (Bailey, 1967; Burmeister, 1968; Clymer, 1963; Emans, 1967). We know that letter-phoneme correspondences are not a few, simple, one-to-one, letter-phoneme correspondences but an elaborate network of more than two hundred letter-phoneme and letter-digraph correspondences (Berdiansky, Cronnell, & Koehler, 1969; Venezky, 1967). We know that when struggling readers are given extensive phonics instruction to the exclusion of working with authentic texts, they do *not* become better readers (Allington, 1980, 1983). We know that early readers in authentic whole language classrooms acquire word-identification skills and letter-sound correspondences better than children in phonics-emphasis classrooms (Freppon, 1991; Kasten & Clarke, 1989; Klesius, Griffith, & Zielonka, 1991; Mullis, Campbell, & Farstrup, 1993; Reutzel & Cooter, 1990; Ribowsky, 1985).

Yet traditional, parts-to-whole phonics instruction is not only alive and well in theory and practice, it is currently experiencing an orchestrated revival. We see it in the popularity of Adams's book (1990), *Beginning to Read*. We see it in the promotion of phonemic awareness. We see it in California's 1995 Reading Task Force report, *Every Child a Reader*. We see it in the 1995 passage of a California law requiring teachers to teach phonics. We see it in a multitude of newspaper articles across the country proclaiming the success of phonics instruction.

What is happening? The assumption that children learn to read alphabetic script by learning the sounds of letters is deeply rooted in Western culture. It can be traced back at least as far as Socrates (Venezky, 1967). It enjoys wide public support. Most people in the United States believe they learned to read through being taught the sounds of letters. The assumption that children learn to read by learning the sounds of letters is part of our cultural belief system.

Implicit in virtually every discussion about teaching children letter-sound correspondences are two assumptions: (1) that knowledge of letter-phoneme correspondences enables readers to pronounce print they have never seen before without help from other readers and (2) that such knowledge is amenable to direct instruction. Typically, when children are having difficulty learning to read, their knowledge of letter-phoneme correspondences is blamed and it is thought that if only we teach them phonics (i.e., letter-phoneme correspondences) they will be able to read. In other words, the problem lies with either the child or the instruction.

Historically, traditional phonics instruction has been the only explanation of how children learning to read an alphabetic script learn to pronounce unfamiliar print words. Although researchers from various orientations agree that the first print words children learn to recognize are learned as unanalyzed wholes (e.g., Ehri, 1994; Goodman & Goodman, 1979; Gough & Hillinger, 1980; Perfetti, 1985), words learned as unanalyzed wholes have not traditionally been considered a source of learning to pronounce unfamiliar print.

Three decades ago Goodman (1965) demonstrated that children have another way to figure out unfamiliar print words besides letter-sound correspondences or being told by another reader. He showed that they also use their knowledge of the world and the language represented in the text to figure out unfamiliar print words. Goodman asked primary-grade children to read words in lists and then to read stories that contained the same words. The average first graders got almost two-thirds of the words they missed on the list right in the story. The average second and third graders had a 75 percent and 82 percent gain respectively in the story over the list.

Could the children in Goodman's study have read the words better in the stories because they saw the words for a second time in the stories? To some extent, but not entirely. Nicholson, Lillas, and Rzoska (1988) gave six- and eight-year-old good readers (children reading a year or more above their grade level) and six- and eight-year-old poor readers (children reading a year or more below their grade level) stories and words in lists, in counterbalanced order. One-half of the children—including both good and poor readers—read the story first and the list second; the other half read the list first and the story second. Nicholson and his associates found that the early readers, the children reading at a second-grade level or below, read 43 percent to 52 percent of the words they missed in the list right in the stories. Only the more proficient readers, the children reading at a fourth-grade level or above, did as well on the lists as in the stories. The more proficient readers had become like us: fluent readers who can pronounce print words equally well in isolation and in context.

Goodman's findings have withstood the test of replication studies. Experimental studies have consistently found that early readers use context (Stanovich, 1991, p. 431) and that they read words in the context of stories better than out of such context (Nicholson, 1991). *If early readers used only letter-sound correspondences to figure out print words, they would read words in stories the same as they read them in lists.*

From other studies (e.g., Kucer, 1985; Rhodes, 1979; Ruddell, 1965; Tatham, 1970), we also know that early readers are better able to use their knowledge of the world and the language represented in the text to figure out unfamiliar print words when the language of the text is familiar to them than when the language is unnatural or unfamiliar. That is, children can read text with familiar language such as "Catch me, catch me, if you can" more easily than text with regular but unnatural language such as that found in "decodable" text (e.g., "Nan can fan Dan.").

Discoveries such as these, along with the discoveries of problems in phonics instruction cited at the beginning of this paper, led to a downplaying of phonics instruction for a time, in theory if not in practice. But these discoveries, as valuable as they are, have not provided a replacement theory for traditional parts-to-whole phonics instruction. For one thing, even in the context of stories, early readers frequently do not figure out unfamiliar words. For another thing, these discoveries do not explain how, as children become more experienced readers, they pronounce print words correctly that do not exist in their spoken vocabulary. Finally, these discoveries do not explain how children *acquire* letter-sound correspondences. Nature abhors a vacuum. Thus, despite the known problems of traditional phonics instruction, traditional phonics instruction still stands—correct or incorrect—as the most complete explanation for how children learn to pronounce unfamiliar print.

Kuhn (1962) surveyed the evolution of scientific thinking in the physical sciences for the last two thousand years and found that no theory, no matter how battered, is ever abandoned unless a successor is already provided. Phonics instruction has been battered by the research cited in the beginning of this paper, but no successor theory for how children pronounce unfamiliar print has been provided . . . until now.

Now new discoveries in linguistics have led to a successor theory. In the following pages I will explain the successor theory, compare it to the traditional theory, re-examine the written code in English, and describe phonics instruction that is compatible with the findings presented in this paper. I will begin by briefly discussing the new discoveries in linguistics. Get ready for some surprises.

The Psychological Units of Spoken Syllables: Onsets and Rimes

Traditionally, we have divided spoken syllables into phonemes. The word *smiles*, for example, consists of five phonemes: /s/, /m/, /i/, /l/, and /z/. Now the discovery of onsets and rimes has given us another way to view spoken syllables. Onsets are any consonants before a vowel in a syllable; rimes are the vowel and any consonants after it in a syllable (Halle & Vergnaud, 1980; MacKay, 1972). In *smiles* the onset is /sm/ and the rime is /ilz/. In some words, such as *do* and *baby*, each onset and rime consists of a single phoneme. In these words it is immaterial whether we speak of phonemes or of onsets and rimes. However, in most syllables, in most words, there is more than one phoneme in either the onset or the rime, or in both the onset and the rime.

Linguists call onsets and rimes the psychological units of a syllable. MacKay discovered them when he analyzed slips of the tongue such as "With this wing I thee red." Several researchers have shown that young children are competent at analyzing spoken words into onsets and rimes but not into phonemes when onsets or rimes consist of more than one phoneme. That is, they can mentally analyze the word *smiles* into /sm/ and /ilz/, but not into /s/, /m/, /i/, /l/, and /z/.

Treiman (1983, 1985) found that eight-year-old, English-speaking children are able to split syllables presented to them orally between their onsets and rimes but have difficulty splitting them anywhere else, even with training. She suggests that *children first learn to analyze spoken syllables into onsets and rimes and later learn to analyze onsets and rimes into their constituent phonemes.*

Goswami and Bryant (1990) reanalyzed an experiment by Calfee (1977) and showed that five- and six-year-old, English-speaking children can manipulate onsets and rimes without being taught to do so. Calfee told the children "When I say *greet*, you say *eat*; when I say *ties*, you say *eyes*." Although Calfee was not studying onsets and rimes, he was, in effect, asking the children to delete the onsets in the words he gave them and pronounce the remaining rimes. Calfee found that the children did very well on this task. In fact, they were right in over 90 percent of the practice tries. They were able to manipulate onsets and rimes without being taught to do so. Thus, Goswami and Bryant suggest that *the phonological ability children bring to learning to read is their ability to manipulate onsets and rimes.*

The fact that young children can split spoken words into onsets and rimes more easily than into phonemes (when phonemes are parts of onsets or rimes) raises the possibility that children use onsets and rimes rather than phonemes to pronounce new print words. A reanalysis of a study by Wylie and Durrell (1970) indicates just that. Wylie and Durrell showed sets of letter sequences which represent rimes such as *-ack*, *-eck*, *-ick*, *-ock*, and *-uck* to children at the end of first grade and gave the children instructions such as "Circle the one that says *ock*" and "Circle the one that has an /o/ in it." They found that the children were significantly more successful at identifying letter sequences representing rimes (e.g., *-ock*) than in identifying letters representing single phonemes that are parts of rimes (e.g., *o* in *-ock*).

These research findings suggest that (1) reading instruction predicated on the assumption that young children learn to pronounce unfamiliar print using phonemes is developmentally inappropriate, and (2) young children use their knowledge of onsets and rimes rather than a knowledge of phonemes to pronounce unfamiliar print.

The Replacement Theory: Onset-Rime Analogy

Traditional instruction in letter-sound correspondences has also assumed that children need to be taught letter-sound correspondences. Again, recent research offers another perspective. Goswami (1986, 1988), studying kindergarten-, first-, and second-grade-aged children, showed that children use analogy between known print words and unknown print words to figure out how to pronounce unknown print words. She showed children pairs of print words containing the same letter sequences, such as *beak* and *peak*. She told each child what one word was and asked the child what the other word was. She found that the children who had begun to read were able to use the print words she pronounced for them to figure out how to pronounce the other print word when they did not already know it; the children who had not begun to read were not able to do so. Consistent with onset-rime research findings, Goswami (1986, 1988) and Goswami and Mead (1992) found that children make significantly more analogies between words with analogous rimes (e.g., *beak* and *peak)* than between words with analogous phonemes (e.g., *beak* and *bean*) when the phoneme in question is a part of a rime (e.g., the phoneme /e/ in the rimes /ek/ and /en/).

When Goswami showed the children two analogous print words and told them how to pronounce one of the words, the children needed more information than Goswami supplied to pronounce the second word. That is, if Goswami pronounced *beak* for the children and then asked them to pronounce *peak,* the children still needed to know that *p* represents /p/ to pronounce it. According to the rule-making principle described below, another set of print words the children recognize, such as *pat* and *bat,* or *pat* and *pit,* could have led to the formation of a rule that *p-* represents /p/ and enabled them to pronounce *peak* once Goswami pronounced *beak* for them.

Goswami (1986, 1988) found among children who had begun to read no development in their ability to use analogy when she provided the basis for analogy. Early readers were able to make analogies as well as more advanced readers when Goswami told the children one of the print words. Consequently, she suggests that "analogy is a relatively primitive strategy most frequently used in the early stages of learning to read" (1988, pp. 246–47).

Goswami posits that it is not the ability to make analogies that develops but the number of print words from which children can make analogies (1986, p. 82). She suggests that the more print words children recognize the better position they are in to make analogies. My research described later in this paper supports Goswami's suggestion. Among the first-grade children I studied, I found that the more print words children were able to pronounce, the more analogous unfamiliar print words they were able to pronounce (Moustafa, 1990, 1995).

Building on Treiman's work (1983, 1985), Goswami posits that "development proceeds from the initial recognition of whole words to a stage of lexical analogy in which large sub-word units are extracted, and only then to a stage in which finer-grained analysis of words in grapheme-phoneme units becomes possible" (1988, p. 265). She suggests that children extract rules about a letter-sound system through the process of making analogies between print words. For example, the kind of comparison involved in making an analogy between *beak* and *peak* could lead to the formation of a rule that -*eak* is pronounced /ek/ (1986, p. 82).

Glushko (1981) studied proficient adult readers using analogy. He suggests that when readers learn to recognize a print word, they remember the letters and the pronunciation together. Then when they recognize parts of familiar words in unfamiliar words, they remember the pronunciation of the letters. Ehri (1980) has shown that second-grade children remember letters and their pronunciations together when letters are parts of meaningful words. The findings of Treiman (1983, 1985), Wylie and Durrell (1970), Goswami (1986, 1988), and Goswami and Mead (1992) suggest that, for children who speak languages that have onsets and rimes, the units of speech remembered along with the letters are at least as large as onsets and rimes.

The process of making analogies is strikingly similar to the process children use to learn spoken language. Linguists have found that young children acquire the ability to create spoken messages they have not heard before by first learning spoken messages as unanalyzed wholes through social interaction (e.g., *liedown*). Then, as they acquire more and more unanalyzed wholes (e.g., *liedown*, *sitdown*, *getup*, and *getdown*), they are in a position to compare similar unanalyzed wholes, figure out their parts, and recombine the parts to produce original messages. For example, once children have learned that *liedown* and *sitdown* consist of *lie down* and *sit down* and that *getup* and *getdown* consist of *get up* and *get down*, they can recombine the parts to say *sit up* without having heard it before. Wong Fillmore (1976) first discovered the process in five-, six-, and seven-year-old, Spanish-speaking children learning

English through social interaction with English speakers. Peters (1977, 1983), Bowerman (1982), and others have found that two-year-olds use the same process in learning their first language.

Both the process of learning to pronounce unfamiliar print words described by Goswami and the process of learning to speak a language described by Wong Fillmore, Peters, Bowerman, and others move from acquiring unanalyzed speech wholes in a sociolinguistic context to recognizing similar parts in unanalyzed wholes and recombining parts. In both processes the unanalyzed wholes are acquired through interaction with a person or persons who are more experienced with the code. In both processes rules are thought to be abstracted by the learner through experience with similar unanalyzed wholes.

The similarity between the processes suggests that the cognitive process that underlies the acquisition of spoken language also underlies learning to pronounce unfamiliar print. If it does, learning to pronounce unfamiliar print words using a letter-sound system could be spontaneous as children learn to recognize more and more print words as unanalyzed wholes. The findings of Tunmer and Nesdale (1985) are consistent with this possibility. Tunmer and Nesdale studied six first-grade classes, three that had no direct instruction in phonics and three that emphasized traditional phonics instruction. Tunmer asked the children to pronounce novel print words (pronounceable words they made up) and analogous conventional print words. They found a greater correlation between the children's ability to pronounce the novel words and their ability to pronounce the conventional words than between the children's ability to pronounce the novel words and their instruction. While the children's ability to pronounce the conventional words accounted for 77 percent of the children's correct pronunciations of the novel words (r = .88), the children's instruction accounted for only 17 percent of the children's correct pronunciations of the novel words (r = .41).

In summary, these research findings suggest that as children learn to recognize whole print words, they remember the letters and the pronunciations together. Then, as they learn to recognize more and more print words, they encounter print words with like letters or letter strings representing like onsets (e.g., *smiles* and *small*) or like rimes (e.g., *part* and *cart*) and begin to figure out the parts of the words (e.g., *sm*- is pronounced /sm/, and -*art* is pronounced /art/). Finally, as they encounter unfamiliar print words with similar letter strings (e.g., *smart*) they make analogies between familiar and unfamiliar print words to pronounce the unfamiliar words. The process is a whole-to-parts process rather than a parts-to-whole process.

Traditional Theory vs. Onset-Rime Analogy

In perhaps the most referenced book of the decade on reading, *Beginning to Read*, Adams (1990) reports on a large body of research that shows a positive correlation between children's knowledge of letter-phoneme correspondences and children's ability to read. Perhaps because we have traditionally assumed that children learn to read by being taught letter-phoneme correspondences, this body of research has been interpreted as support for traditional letter-phoneme instruction. But is it?

Correlation does not establish cause and effect. Goswami (1988), Smith (1988), and others claim that letter-phoneme correspondences are acquired as a *consequence* of learning to read. The body of correlational research Adams reports on can just as legitimately be used to support the claim that a knowledge of letter-phoneme correspondences is a consequence of learning to read.

Is knowledge of letter-phoneme correspondences a prerequisite to being able to figure out unfamiliar words? One way to investigate the question is to use comparative research rather than correlational research. I am aware of four studies that compare children's knowledge of letter-phoneme correspondences and their knowledge of onset-rime analogy with their ability to pronounce unfamiliar print words: Ehri and Robbins's (1992), Bruck and Treiman's (1992), Nation and Hulme's (1997), and my own (Moustafa, 1990, 1995).

The findings of the first three studies support the traditional theory. However, there are problems with the designs of these studies. Ehri and Robbins argue that children need some knowledge of letter-phoneme correspondences in order to pronounce unfamiliar print via analogy, but the phonemes they use in their argument (e.g., the /f/ in *feel*) are single-phoneme onsets. Since single-phoneme onsets are both phonemes and onsets, the argument rests on the level of analysis employed by the researchers rather than a difference in actual speech sounds.

Bruck and Treiman (1992) instructed some first-grade children in letter-phoneme correspondences and some other first-grade children in analogy. They found the children who received instruction in letter-phoneme correspondences could pronounce new print words better than children who received instruction in analogy. However, they excluded from their study children who could pronounce more than six words in the Woodcock-Johnson word list. Recall that what develops is not the ability to make analogies but the number of print words from which children can make analogies (Goswami, 1986; Moustafa, 1995). As a result, Bruck and Treiman's method of selecting children for their study assured that the children in their study would be constrained in their ability to use analogy to pronounce unfamiliar print words because they lacked the basis for making analogies: a developing body of print words they recognized. Bruck and Treiman's finding that children who have not begun to read do not use analogy is consistent with Goswami's finding.

Nation and Hulme (1997) argue that onset-rime segmentation does not predict early reading and that phonemic segmentation does. There are two problems with this argument. First, the theory is not that onset-rime segmentation predicts early reading but that onset-rime segmentation is more available to early readers than phoneme segmentation for learning speech-print connections when there is more than one phoneme in an onset or rime. Second, by saying that phonemic segmentation predicts early reading, Nation and Hulme attribute causation to correlational research. Correlation does not establish causation.

In my work (Moustafa, 1990, 1995), I found that children's knowledge of analogous print words explained children's pronunciation of unfamiliar print words significantly better than their knowledge of letter-phoneme correspondence (p < .001). I showed seventy-five first-grade children common print words (e.g., *green, black, hat, new),* analogous novel words (e.g., *grack* from *green* and *black; hew* from *hat* and *new),* and the constituent letters and digraphs of the novel words. If the children could correctly pronounce a novel word and both of its analogous common words, I credited onset-rime analogy. If the children could correctly pronounce a novel word and all its constituent letters and digraphs, I credited the children's knowledge of letter-phoneme correspondences. If both explanations could be credited, I credited both explanations.

As shown in Table 1, the children's knowledge of letter-phoneme correspondences accounted for 64 percent of the correct pronunciations of the novel words but their knowledge of analogous print words accounted for 95 percent of the correct pronunciations within the corpus of print words in the study. The correct pronunciations that were not accounted for by the print words in the study could be accounted for by other words the children recognized. For example, one child pronounced *grack* and the analogous word *green* correctly but she did not recognize the analogous word *black.* (Recall that *grack* was created by taking the *gr-* from *green* and the *-ack* from *black.*) However, when I showed her the word *back,* a word not in the study, she was able to pronounce *back.* Hence, the child could have been making analogies between *green* and *back* to pronounce *grack.*

Table 1

Explanations for How Children Correctly Pronounced Unfamiliar Print Words

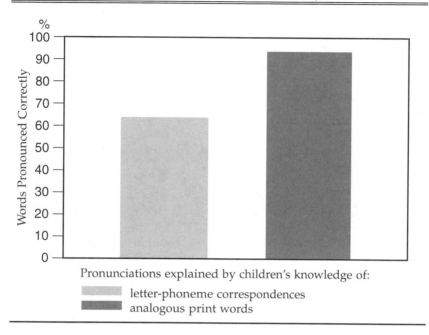

The children's knowledge of analogous print words not only accounted for more correct pronunciations than their knowledge of letter-phoneme correspondences, it also accounted for every correct pronunciation that the children's knowledge of letter-phoneme correspondences accounted for. This overlap suggests that while it appears children are blending sounds of letters to pronounce unfamiliar words, they are actually using analogy with familiar words to pronounce unfamiliar words.

Let us explore this point further. In part of my study (Moustafa, 1990), I showed the children novel print words and asked them to (1) say the print words, (2) circle the parts of the words, (3) say the sounds of the parts, and then (4) say the print words again. Sometimes the children could not pronounce the novel print words correctly before they identified the parts and the sounds but they could pronounce the same words correctly after they identified the parts and the sounds. At first glance, the children appeared to be using letter-phoneme correspondences to identify the words. However, a closer inspection of the evidence suggests otherwise. In half the cases the children did not correctly identify all the sounds of the letters and digraphs; in all the cases the children correctly identified all the common words used to create the novel words. *Clearly onset-rime analogy explains children's correct pronunciations of unfamiliar words better than their knowledge of letter-phoneme correspondences does.*

At the time Adams wrote *Beginning to Read*, Treiman's work on children's understanding of onsets and rimes versus phonemes was new. Goswami had barely published her work in children's use of analogy. Comparative research had not been done between traditional letter-phoneme instruction and onset-rime analogy. The full implications of onset-rime analogy were not understood. Adams reported on Treiman's and Goswami's work, but it was too soon to integrate the implications of their work into the book's conclusions.

In *Beginning to Read* Adams did, however, say that research on onsets and rimes and on analogy held promise for the future. She was right. They have ushered in a new understanding of how children learn to pronounce unfamiliar print. We now know that *in learning to pronounce unfamiliar print words via the letter-sound system, children initially acquire print words as unanalyzed wholes*; that children make analogies between familiar and unfamiliar print words to pronounce unfamiliar print words; and that children's knowledge of how to pronounce print words accounts for their ability to pronounce unfamiliar print words better than their knowledge of letter-phoneme correspondences does.

The next question we need to ask is, What instructional strategies best foster children's use of analogy between familiar and unfamiliar print words in pronouncing unfamiliar print words? However, before we take up this question, we need to turn from examining children's phonological and cognitive processes to examining the written code to which children apply these processes when learning to read in English.

The Written Code: Multiple Possibilities

Traditionally we have talked of phonics rules and exceptions to the rules, or regular words and irregular words, or phonics generalizations. Phonics rules were first challenged when Clymer (1963) tested forty-five of the most clearly stated phonics rules in four widely used reading programs and discovered the rules were not very reliable. Only half of the thirty-one rules for vowels worked at least 60 percent of the time, and the most reliable rules often applied to infrequent letter-sound patterns. Clymer's work stood the test of replication studies (e.g., Bailey, 1967; Burmeister, 1968; Emans, 1967).

Berdiansky, Cronnell, and Koehler (1969), building on the work of Venezky (1967), attempted to construct more reliable rules by analyzing a corpus of over 6,000 one- and two-syllable words within the comprehension vocabulary of six- to nine-year-olds. Among the words they analyzed, Berdiansky and her associates found sixty-nine letters and digraphs related to thirty-eight phonemes in 211 different ways. Among these 211 correspondences they found 166 letter-phoneme rules that could be applied to ten or more words—106 rules for vowels and sixty for consonants.

The implications of this discovery are staggering. If a reading program taught one rule a week, nine months a year, every year, for four years, kindergarten through third grade, with no time for reviewing, testing, and reteaching, it would cover only 144 rules.

But more importantly, even if children were to learn all 166 rules that apply to ten or more one- and two-syllable words, how would they know which ones to use when they encountered a letter or letter string with multiple possible pronunciations? In my Midwestern dialect, the letter *o* is pronounced one way in *so, go,* and *no* and another way in *do* and *to.* The digraph *ow* is pronounced one way in *cow, how, now, wow,* and *meow* and another way in *mow, tow, grow, know, show, snow, stow,* and *throw,* and two different ways in *bow,* depending on the meaning (e.g., *took a deep bow* and *shot the arrow with the bow*). No doubt some of the letter-phoneme correspondences in my dialect differ from some of the letter-phoneme correspondences in your dialect.

Adams (1990) and Wylie and Durrell (1970) have suggested that letter-rime correspondences are more stable than letter-phoneme correspondences. However, in my Midwestern dialect, the letter string *-eak* is pronounced one way in *beak, leak, peak, weak, creak, freak, sneak, speak,* and *streak* and another way in *break* and *steak.* The letter string *-one* is pronounced one way in *bone, cone, lone, tone, zone, drone, phone, shone,* and *stone,* another way in *gone,* another way in *done, none, honey,* and *money,* and still another way in *one.* The letter string *-ood* is pronounced one way in *good, hood, wood,* and *stood,* another way in *food, mood,* and *brood,* and still another way in *blood* and *flood.* Moreover, whether the letter *o* is described as representing a phoneme or a rime, it is still pronounced one way in *so, go,* and *no* and another way in *do* and *to.* Whether the digraph *ow* is described as representing a phoneme or a rime, it is still pronounced one way in *cow, how, now, wow,* and *meow* and another way in *mow, tow, grow, know, show, snow, stow,* and *throw,* and two different ways in *bow.*

These multiple possible pronunciations of given letters and letter strings are an inescapable consequence of the fact that, as a culture, we use standardized spelling. Until the nineteenth century spelling was not standardized, and consistency in spelling was not viewed as important. In the seventeenth century *catt, catte, kat, katt,* and *katte* were all acceptable spellings of *cat.* Shakespeare, one of the great writers of all times, signed his will with two different spellings of his name (Cummings, 1988, p. 21; cited in Goodman, 1993, p. 41). Standardized spelling evolved over time through consensus and is arbitrary. *Standardized spelling is not a principled, natural phenomenon but a social convention.*

Standardizing spelling once helped typesetters but it now also helps readers. Spelling that is standardized across dialects is accessible to a wider range of people than multiple spellings which reflect the pronunciation of various dialects. Speakers of Bostonian, Southern, and Midwestern U.S. dialects can all read the *Los Angeles Times.* Moreover, standardized spelling enables readers to read familiar print words more efficiently than nonstandardized spelling, even when the nonstandardized spelling is "phonically correct" for a given dialect. To illustrate, read the following three sentences.

New York is a nice city. Shikago iz a nise sidee tue. I like Chicago.

Unless you have read these sentences before, you probably read the second sentence slower than the first and last sentences, even though (if you speak my dialect) *Chicago* is pronounced /shikago/, *is* is pronounced /iz/, and *nise, sidee,* and *tue* are phonically possible renditions of *nice, city,* and *too.* Once a given spelling becomes familiar, it is easily recognized and does not need to be "figured out" each time it is encountered. Read the passage about New York and "Shikago" a few more times and see how much easier it becomes to read the sentence about Shikago.

Given the arbitrariness of standardized English spelling, both within and across dialects, *a search for reliable letter-sound rules or generalizations is not only futile, it is mistaken.* It is more appropriate to speak not of letter-sound rules or generalizations but of *multiple possible pronunciations of letters and letter strings.* In the process of figuring out how to pronounce an unfamiliar print word, a reader can just as legitimately evoke one possible pronunciation of a letter or letter string by analogy to one word as another possible pronunciation by analogy to another word.

As a result, onset-rime analogy does not, by itself, help readers solve the problem of the inconsistencies in the English letter-sound system when encountering unfamiliar print words. How, then, would a reader know which analogy to make when encountering an unfamiliar print word? The only way I can think of is that readers who are focused on making meaning in the reading process use their knowledge of spoken words and the context as well as their knowledge of letter-sound correspondences to decide on appropriate pronunciations of ambiguous letters and letter strings. In the case of unfamiliar print words in readers' spoken vocabulary, readers' knowledge of spoken language can serve as a check on inappropriate analogies and encourage them to look for alternate pronunciations which make sense. In the case of words not in a reader's spoken vocabulary, a reader may or may not make an appropriate analogy.

Proponents of traditional phonics instruction suggest that children need phonics instruction to spell correctly. However, less than half of the 166 letter-phoneme rules that Berdiansky, Cronnell, and Koehler (1969) developed for readers worked when Cronnell reversed them for spellers (Adams, 1990). What if the unit of analysis is letter-onset and letter-rime rather than letter-phoneme? Then can writers use analogy between familiar and unfamiliar print words to spell unfamiliar print words? That is, can writers use their knowledge of how to spell a word with a given onset or rime to spell another word with the same onset or rime? To some extent but not entirely. Knowing how to spell *cat* can help writers spell *can* and *coat* by analogy to *cat* but not *king* and *keep*. Knowing how to spell *make* can help speakers of my dialect spell *bake, cake, fake, rake, take, brake*, and *stake* by analogy to *make*, but not *ache, break*, and *steak* which have the same rime as *make*—and whether *brake* or *break* and *stake* or *steak* is the appropriate spelling depends on meaning. Knowing how to spell *fun* can help speakers of my dialect spell *bun, gun, run*, and *sun* by analogy to *fun*, but not *done, son, won*, or *one* which have the same rime as *fun*—and whether *sun* or *son* is the appropriate spelling depends on meaning. Knowing how to spell *blue* can help speakers of my dialect spell *due, sue, clue, flue*, and *true* but not *dew, few, new, blew, drew, flew, grew, knew*, and *stew*, or *to, too*, and *two*, or *shoe*, or *view*, or *flu* which have the same rime as *blue*—and whether *blue* or *blew*, and *due, do*, or *dew*, and *to, too*, or *two*, and *flue, flew*, or *flu* are the appropriate spellings depends on meaning.

This is not to say there are limitless possibilities in letter-sound correspondences. The word *cake* cannot be represented as *ckae*. Nor is it to say there are not patterns. The words *bake, cake, make*, and *fake* share a common letter-rime pattern. It is to say, however, *that there are often multiple possible patterns to represent the same onset and the same rime, and the appropriate pattern to use when spelling is determined by social custom, not an abstract rule.* Whether *fun* is spelled *fun* or *phun* (as in *phone*), whether *cake* is spelled *cake* or *ceak* (as in *break*), whether *blue* is spelled *blue* or *blew* (as in *new*) or *blo* (as in *to*) or *bloo* (as in *too*) or *bloe* (as in *shoe*) or *bliew* (as in *view*) or *blu* (as in flu) is an arbitrary decision driven by convention. Through extensive experience with print, we literate adults have become so comfortable with these conventions that conventional spellings feel "right" and unconventional spellings feel "wrong." Still, the particular spelling of a rime in any given word is nothing more than convention.

There are two additional reasons that phonics instruction does not necessarily help in spelling. First, many words are not pronounced the way they are written. For example, in my Midwestern dialect, I say "wader" for *water*, "famly" for *family*, and "camra" for *camera*. Also, many spellings represent meaning rather than pronunciation. For example, a regular past-tense verb ending is represented by *-ed* whether it is pronounced /t/ as in *kicked* or /d/ as in *called*, and the first syllables in *breakfast* and *knowledge* reflect their meanings, not their pronunciations.

Again, onset-rime analogy, by itself, does not help writers solve the problem of the inconsistencies in the English letter-sound system when trying to spell unfamiliar print words. Writers, like readers, must choose between multiple possibilities, only this time their choices are guided by their knowledge of spoken language to some extent and their visual memory to a large extent. Writers who make spelling decisions by using analogy to similar-sounding words can write messages which can be read by others. However, they will not necessarily write with standardized spelling. For example, if a child trying to write "The sky is blue" in his or her first draft reasons that *hi* and *sky* end in the same sound and *blue* and *to* end in the same sound, the spelling could be "The ski is blo." *Therefore, when helping children acquire standardized spelling* as they revise their drafts for publication, *it may be misleading to ask them to sound out words they are trying to spell. It might be better to ask "Can you remember what it looks like?"*

If letter-rime correspondences are inconsistent, what have we gained from onset-rime analogy theory? A lot. We have gained new insights into phonological and cognitive processes children employ in learning to read an alphabetic script. What we have *not* gained is a simple letter-sound system . . . nor should we expect to, given that we have, and benefit from, standardized spelling. The fact that there are multiple possible ways to pronounce the same letter or letter string suggests that children need to acquire many print words in order to be in a position to make analogies with various possible pronunciations of the same letter or letter string. The arbitrariness and complexity of the English letter-sound system suggests that children who are having difficulty with the letter-sound system do not lack a knowledge of the "rules" but lack extensive experience with a complex, arbitrary orthographic system.

Whole-to-Parts Phonics Instruction

Now let us return to the question, What instructional strategies best foster children's use of analogy between familiar and unfamiliar print words to pronounce unfamiliar print words? Again recall that what develops is not the ability to make analogies but the number of print words from which children can make analogies (Goswami, 1986; Moustafa, 1995). Recall also that early readers read print words in the context of familiar language better than out of context or in the context of unfamiliar or unnatural language (Goodman, 1965; Kucer, 1985; Nicholson, 1991; Nicholson, Lillas, & Rzoska, 1988; Rhodes, 1979; Ruddell, 1965; Tatham, 1970). From this research, it follows that *the best way to help early readers acquire a body of print words from which they can make analogies is to help them read and write text with familiar language.* This can be done through instructional techniques such as shared reading, the Language Experience Approach, and free voluntary reading.

For example, a teacher working with emergent and early readers can use shared reading to teach phonics by first reading a predictable story *to* the children while pointing to the words in full view of the children, then reading the story *with* the children while continuing to point while reading, and finally, when the children are very familiar with the language of the story, inviting the children to read it *by* themselves, alone or to student partners. Once the children are able to read the story by themselves with one-to-one matching of spoken words and print words, the teacher can ask children to choose their favorite words in the story. The teacher can then, in front of the children, write each word the children suggest on a separate piece of paper; highlight a letter or letters representing an onset or a rime in the word to be studied; say to the children "This/These letter(s) say(s) [sound];" and then, collaboratively with the children, put the words on the classroom wall, grouping them with other words that contain like letters or letter strings where the words come from previously studied stories. As words come up with like letters and letter strings which represent different onsets (e.g., *c-* in *cat* and *cents*) and rimes (e.g., *-ood* in *good* and *food*), the teacher and children can collaboratively regroup the words into subsets of letter strings which represent different onsets or rimes. These phonics lessons are brief but build over time as more and more stories are read *to*, *with*, and *by* children. In this way *instruction proceeds from whole text to whole word and lastly to parts of words.*

I call these phonics lessons whole-to-parts phonics lessons to distinguish them from traditional, decontexualized, parts-to-whole phonics lessons. Like traditional phonics instruction, whole-to-parts phonics instruction is explicit, systematic, and extensive. However, whole-to-parts phonics instruction has several advantages over traditional phonics instruction: the words being studied arise out of contexts which are meaningful to the children and hence they are more memorable; the instruction is compatible with how we now know children acquire a letter-sound system; and, the lessons are time-efficient, inexpensive, and easy to implement. For a more in-depth description of whole-to-parts phonics instruction, see my chapter in this book's companion volume, *Practicing What We Know: Informed Reading Instruction* (Weaver, 1998).

Reconceptualizing Phonics Instruction

Onset-rime analogy has given us new understandings of phonological and cognitive processes young children employ in learning to read English, an onset-rime language with an alphabetic script. We have learned that young English-speaking children learning how to read English script are competent at analyzing spoken words into onsets and rimes but not into phonemes when onsets or rimes consist of more than one phoneme (Treiman, 1983, 1985). That is, they can analyze the spoken word *stop* into /st/ and /op/ but not into /s/, /t/, /o/, and /p/. We have learned that children just beginning to read remember the pronunciations of letters and letter strings which represent onsets and rimes better than they remember the pronunciations of letters which represent phonemes when phonemes are parts of onsets or rimes (Goswami, 1986, 1988; Goswami & Mead, 1992; Wylie & Durrell, 1970). We have learned that rather than using letter-phoneme rules to figure out new print words as we literate adults have traditionally thought they do, children use their knowledge of letter-onset and letter-rime correspondences in familiar print words to figure out the pronunciation of unfamiliar print words (Goswami, 1986; 1988; Goswami & Mead, 1992; Moustafa, 1995). We have learned that the more print words children recognize, the better they are able to figure out how to pronounce unfamiliar print words (Goswami, 1986; Moustafa, 1995). These discoveries, combined with the discoveries that children read print in text with familiar language better than print in isolation or with unfamiliar or unnatural language (Goodman, 1965; Kucer, 1985; Nicholson, 1991; Nicholson, Lillas, & Rzoska, 1988; Rhodes, 1979; Ruddell, 1965; Tatham, 1970), suggest that the most appropriate instruction to support children's acquisition of the English letter-sound system is instruction which helps them read using text with familiar language.

In our examination of English letter-sound correspondences above, we saw that given letters and letter strings can be pronounced in multiple possible ways (e.g., in my Midwestern dialect the letter string *-ood* is pronounced one way in *good*, another way in *food*, and still another way in *blood*); that in spelling there are multiple possible ways to represent given onsets and rimes (e.g., in my dialect the rime /ak/ is written one way in *bake*, another way in *break* and still another way in *ache*); and that the "correct" way is decided by social convention, not by abstract rules. This multiplicity points to the need for readers to use their knowledge of spoken language to figure out an appropriate pronunciation for given letters and letter strings, and for writers to use their knowledge of spoken language to some extent and their visual memory to a large extent to figure out the appropriate letters and letter strings to use in order to spell conventionally. It also points to a need for children who are learning to read to have extensive experiences with a wide variety of texts with familiar language. As children acquire more and more print words as they learn to read more and more stories through activities such as those described above, they will encounter multiple pronunciations of given letters and letter strings and be in a better position to use their knowledge of spoken language to select appropriate pronunciations when making analogies between familiar and unfamiliar print words.

Finally, this paper has outlined whole-to-parts phonics instruction, wherein teachers of early readers first read a story with familiar language *to* and *with* children and then invite the children to read the story *by* themselves. Finally, after the children have learned to recognize the print words in the story as unanalyzed wholes using their knowledge of spoken language to guide them, the teacher underlines or highlights letters or letter strings representing onsets or rimes in words to be studied and discusses the sounds represented by the letters or letter strings with the children. In this way, instruction, like learning, proceeds from whole to parts and is grounded in meaningful language.

The research reviewed in this paper has focused on the role of words learned as unanalyzed wholes acquired in the context of familiar language in acquiring a letter-sound system. *Yet, children's knowledge of print words is but one of many factors which influence children's ability to figure out unfamiliar print. Perhaps the most important of the other factors is the extent of children's experiences with print.* Some children come to school more familiar than others with book language and the purposes and pleasures of print from having stories read to them in their preschool years; this experience can account for variations in the rate of learning to read (Feitelson, Kita, & Goldstein, 1986; Heath, 1982; Wells, 1986). The language of print differs from spoken language. For example, on the playground we talk about someone being *mean*; in the story of Cinderella we say Cinderella had a *cruel* stepmother.

In face-to-face communication we use contractions (e.g., *I'm* or *he's*); in books we usually use uncontracted forms (e.g., *I am* or *he is*). Children who are familiar with the language, purposes, and pleasures of print through extensive, pleasurable experiences in being read to have background knowledge that they can bring to learning to read that children who have not been well read to do not yet have.

When we see children struggling to learn to read in school, it is important to ask what these children know about literacy and whether they have been well read to in their preschool years, and to begin reading to them as soon and as often as possible when they have not been well read to. As children who have not been well read to in their preschool years have more and more meaningful, pleasurable experiences of being read to in school, they will be better able to use their knowledge of print language to acquire unanalyzed whole words in the context of stories and thereby acquire letter-sound knowledge.

The strength that virtually all children bring to learning to read is their knowledge of language. Children use language to acquire their first unanalyzed whole print words. They use language to figure out the parts of whole print words. They use language to figure out print they have not encountered before. Powerful reading instruction builds children's knowledge of language and the world, *and* builds *on* their knowledge of language and the world. Out of such an instructional program children will eventually become literate adults who, like us, can and do use literacy for their own purposes and pleasures.

References

Adams, M. (1990). *Beginning to read: Thinking and learning about print.* Cambridge: MIT Press.

Allington, R. L. (1980). Poor readers don't get to read much in reading groups. *Language Arts, 57,* 872–76.

Allington, R. L. (1983). The reading instruction provided readers of different reading abilities. *The Elementary School Journal, 83,* 95–107.

Bailey, M. H. (1967). The utility of phonic generalizations in grades one through six. *The Reading Teacher, 20,* 413–18.

Berdiansky, B., Cronnell, B., & Koehler, J. (1969). *Spelling-sound relations and primary form-class descriptions for speech-comprehension vocabularies of 6–9 year-olds.* (Technical Report No. 15.) Los Alamitos, CA: Southwest Regional Laboratory for Educational Research and Development. (Summarized in Smith, 1988.)

Bowerman, M. (1982). Reorganizational processes in lexical and syntactic development. In E. Wanner & L. R. Gleitman (Eds.), *Language acquisition: The state of the art* (pp. 319–46). New York: Cambridge University Press.

Bruck, M., & Treiman, L. (1992). Learning to pronounce words: The limitations of analogies. *Reading Research Quarterly, 27,* 374–88.

Burmeister, L. E. (1968). Usefulness of phonic generalizations. *The Reading Teacher, 21,* 349–56.

Calfee, R. (1977). Assessment of individual reading skills: Basic research and practical applications. In A. S. Reber & D. L. Scarborough (Eds.), *Toward a psychology of reading* (pp. 289–23). New York: Erlbaum.

California Reading Task Force (1995). *Every child a reader.* Sacramento, CA: California Department of Education.

Clymer, T. (1963). The utility of phonic generalizations in the primary grades. *The Reading Teacher, 16,* 252–58.

Cummings, D.W. (1988). *American English spelling: An informal description.* Baltimore, MD: The Johns Hopkins University Press.

Cunningham, P. (1995). *Phonics they use: Words for reading and writing.* New York: Harper Collins.

Ehri, L. C. (1980). The development of orthographic images. In U. Frith (Ed.), *Cognitive processes in spelling* (pp. 311–38). London: Academic.

Ehri, L. C. (1994). Development of the ability to read words: Update. In Ruddell, R. B., Ruddell, M. R, and Singer, H. (Eds.), *Theoretical models and processes of reading* (pp. 323–58). Newark, DE: International Reading Association.

Ehri, L.C., & Robbins, C. (1992). Beginners need some decoding skill to read words by analogy. *Reading Research Quarterly, 27,* 13–26.

Emans, R. (1967). The usefulness of phonic generalizations above the primary grades. *The Reading Teacher, 20,* 419–25.

Feitelson, D., Kita, B., & Goldstein, Z. (1986). Effects of listening to series stories on first graders' comprehension of use of language. *Research in the Teaching of English, 20,* 339–56.

Freppon, P.A. (1991). Children's concepts of the nature and purpose of reading in different instructional settings. *Journal of Reading Behavior, 23,* 2, 139–63.

Glushko, R. J. (1981). Principles for pronouncing print: The psychology of phonography. In A.M. Lesgold & C.A. Perfetti (Eds.), *Interactive processes in reading* (pp. 61–84). Hillsdale, NJ: Erlbaum.

Goodman, K. (1993). *Phonics phacts.* Portsmouth, NH: Heinemann.

Goodman, K. (1965). A linguistic study of cues and miscues in reading. *Elementary English, 42,* 639–43.

Goodman, K., & Goodman, Y. (1979). Learning to read is natural. In L. B. Resnick & P.A. Weaver (Eds.), *Theory and practice of early reading* (Vol. 1, pp. 137–54). Hillsdale, NJ: Erlbaum.

Goswami, U. (1986). Children's use of analogy in learning to read: A developmental study. *Journal of Experimental Child Psychology, 42,* 73–83.

Goswami, U. (1988). Orthographic analogies and reading development. *The Quarterly Journal of Experimental Psychology, 40A,* 239–68.

Goswami, U., & Bryant, P. (1990). *Phonological skills and learning to read.* Hillsdale, NJ: Erlbaum.

Goswami, U., & Mead, F. (1992). Onset and rime awareness and analogies in reading. *Reading Research Quarterly, 27,* 153–62.

Gough, P. B., & Hillinger, M. L. (1980). Learning to read: An unnatural act. *Bulletin of the Orton Society, 30,* 180–96.

Halle, M., & Vergnaud, J. (1980). Three dimensional phonology. *Journal of Linguistic Research, 1,* 83–105.

Heath, S. B. (1982). What no bedtime story means: Narrative skills at home and school. *Language in Society, 11,* 49–76.

Kasten, W. C., & Clarke, B. K. (1989). *Reading/writing readiness for preschool and kindergarten children: A whole language approach.* Sanibel: Florida Educational Research and Development Council. (ED 312 041)

Klesius, J. P., Griffith, P. L., & Zielonka, P. (1991). A whole language and traditional instruction comparison: Overall effectiveness and development of the alphabetic principle. *Reading Research and Instruction, 30,* 47–61.

Kucer, S. (1985). Predictability and readability: The same rose with different names? In M. Douglas (Ed.), *Claremont reading conference forty-ninth yearbook* (pp. 229–46). Claremont, CA: Claremont Graduate School.

Kuhn, T. (1962). *The structure of scientific revolutions.* Chicago, IL: University of Chicago.

Liberman, I., Shankweiler, D., Fischer, F., & Carter, B. (1974). Explicit syllable and phoneme segmentation in the young child. *Journal of Experimental Child Psychology, 18,* 201–12.

MacKay, D. G. (1972). The structure of words and syllables: Evidence from errors in speech. *Cognitive Psychology, 3,* 210–27.

Moustafa, M. (1990). *An interactive/cognitive model of the acquisition of a graphophonemic system by young children.* Unpublished doctoral dissertation, University of Southern California, Los Angeles.

Moustafa, M. (1995). Children's productive phonological recoding. *Reading Research Quarterly, 30,* 3, 464–76.

Mullis, I., Campbell, J., & Farstrup, A. (1993). *NAEP 1992 reading report card for the nation and the states,* Report No. 23–STO6. Washington, D.C.: National Center for Education Statistics.

Nation, K., & Hulme, C. (1997). Phonemic segmentation, not onset-rime segmentation, predicts early reading and spelling skills. *Reading Research Quarterly, 32,* 154-67.

Nicholson, T. (1991). Do children read words better in context or in lists? A classic study revisited. *Journal of Educational Psychology, 83,* 444–50.

Nicholson, T., Lillas, C., & Rzoska, M. (1988). Have we been misled by miscues? *The Reading Teacher, 42,* 6–10.

Perfetti, C.A. (1985). *Reading ability.* New York: Oxford University Press.

Peters, A. (1977). Language learning strategies: Does the whole equal the sum of the parts? *Language, 53,* 560–73.

Peters, A. (1983). *The units of language acquisition.* New York: Cambridge University Press.

Reutzel, D., & Cooter, R. (1990). Whole language: Comparative effects on first-grade reading achievement. *Journal of Educational Research, 83,* 252–57.

Rhodes, L. K. (1979). Comprehension and predictability: An analysis of beginning reading materials. In J. Harste & R. Carey (Eds.), *New perspectives on comprehension* (pp. 100–30). Bloomington, IN: School of Education, Indiana University.

Ribowsky, H. (1985). *The effects of a code emphasis approach and a whole language approach upon emergent literacy of kindergarten children.* (ED 269 720)

Ruddell, R. (1965). The effect of oral and written patterns of language structure on reading comprehension. *The Reading Teacher, 18,* 270–75.

Smith, F. (1988). *Understanding reading.* (4th ed.) Hillsdale, NJ: Erlbaum.

Stanovich, K. E. (1991). Word recognition: Changing perspectives. In R. Barr, M. L. Kamil, P. Mosenthal, & P. D. Pearson (Eds.), *Handbook of reading research* (Vol. 2, pp. 418–52). Hillsdale, NJ: Erlbaum.

Tatham, S. (1970). Reading comprehension of materials written with select oral language patterns: A study at grades two and four. *Reading Research Quarterly, 5,* 402–26.

Treiman, R. (1983). The structure of spoken syllables: Evidence from novel word games. *Cognition, 15,* 49–74.

Treiman, R. (1985). Onsets and rimes as units of spoken syllables: Evidence from children. *Journal of Experimental Child Psychology, 39,* 161–81.

Tunmer, W. E., & Nesdale, A. R. (1985). Phonemic segmentation skill and beginning reading. *Journal of Educational Psychology, 77,* 417–27.

Venezky, R. L. (1967). English orthography: Its graphical structure and its relation to sound. *Reading Research Quarterly, 2,* 75–105.

Wells, G. (1986). *The meaning makers.* Portsmouth, NH: Heinemann.

Wong Fillmore, L. (1976). *Cognitive and social strategies in second language acquisition.* Unpublished doctoral dissertation, Stanford University, Stanford, CA.

Wylie, R., & Durrell, D. (1970). Teaching vowels through phonograms. *Elementary English, 47,* 787–91.

6 Orthographic Analogy Training with Kindergarten Children: Effects on Analogy Use, Phonemic Segmentation, and Letter-Sound Knowledge

Margareth E. Peterson
Leonard P. Haines
University of Saskatchewan

This study investigates the effects of teaching children analogies in letter patterns, based on onset and rime units. For example, the first word in a pair was shown to child: *ball*, for instance. The child was then shown that the letters *-all* stayed together to make the sound "all." Then, the word *fall* was placed below it, and the child was told that it said "fall." The trainer would point out that the last three letters of the words were the same and sounded the same, but the first letter sounded different. Subsequent procedures were designed to reinforce the separation of these words into their differing onsets and initial letters, *b-* and *f-*, and their common rime and the remaining letters, *-all*.

Peterson and Haines reasoned that the process of reading instruction would most strongly facilitate segmentation skill if the natural units of children's speech and the orthographic units used in the introduction of reading were closely matched. Thus, they hypothesized that breaking words into onsets and rimes and their corresponding letters might help children deduce letter-sound correspondences, especially since the onsets were also single phonemes. Part of the research that encouraged this hypothesis had demonstrated that although phonemic segmentation training by itself has a positive effect on reading, the greatest benefit occurs when the categorization of sounds is taught in combination with the letters representing those sounds (Bradley & Bryant, 1985).

The first part of this study demonstrates a significant correlation between the ability to read words by analogy and segmentation ability, but does not address the issue of causation. Over the course of the month, the experimental group showed the greatest increases in segmentation skill, but the control group showed nearly as much gain overall. With letter-sound knowledge, there were no significant increases for the control group, whereas the differences were significant for all experimental subgroups. In the test of word recognition by analogy, the gains of the experimental group are consistently greater than the gains of the control group.

Peterson and Haines conclude that the pattern of development in letter-sound knowledge also suggests that segmentation ability based on the ability to detect onsets and rimes is necessary in order for children to extract letter-sound knowledge by analogy: "The pattern of results suggests a complex interactive effect whereby facilitation of sound segmentation ability, letter-sound knowledge, and reading by analogy have occurred in a kind of mutual synergy."

Originally published in *Journal of Reading Behavior, 24*(1),(1992), 109–27. Copyright National Reading Conference, 1992. Reprinted with permission.

It is generally believed that phonological awareness is both an important skill as children move into reading and a necessary component of skilled reading. There is, however, considerable debate about the nature of the relationship. Phonological skills have been shown to be predictive of subsequent progress in reading acquisition and have also been considered causally related (Bradley & Bryant, 1983, 1985; Stanovich, Cunningham, & Cramer, 1984). Some have maintained that phonological skills are a by-product of experience with print, and usually acquired within the context of reading (Ehri, 1984; Morais, Bertelson, Cary, & Alegria, 1986; Read, Zhang, Nie, & Ding, 1986). Still others have argued for a complex, interactive relationship (Perfetti, Beck, Bell, & Hughes 1987; Treiman, 1987). Perfetti et al. (1987), on the basis of a series of partial time-lagged correlations, concluded that more primitive skills such as synthesis stand in a nonreciprocal causative relationship to reading, whereas phoneme awareness was considered to hold a more reciprocal relationship.

Two sets of findings seem firmly established. First, phonological awareness is developmental in nature. Children's acquisition of awareness of the phonological structure of speech occurs in the order of words to syllables to phonemes (Liberman, Shankweiler, Fischer, & Carter, 1974; Rozin & Gleitman, 1977; Leong & Haines, 1978). Second, phonological awareness takes different forms. Some forms are acquired with ease at an early age; other forms seem to emerge as a result of certain learning conditions. Whereas awareness of rhyme seems to occur almost spontaneously in even very young children (Bradley & Bryant, 1985), the ability to attend to phonemes is difficult to acquire and only seems to evolve when circumstances require it; for example, during exposure to an alphabetic script (Morais, Cary, Alegria, & Bertelson, 1979; Read, Zhang, Nie, & Ding, 1986).

Much of the early research on the relationship between reading and phonological awareness did not consider intrasyllabic units. For example, Liberman and her colleagues (Liberman, Shankweiler, Fischer, & Carter, 1974) and Leong and Haines (1978) studied young children's ability to analyze words into syllables and phonemes. Recent phonological theory has advanced the position that the syllable is more than a series of phonemes (Treiman, 1983). Treiman (1987) suggested that if the relationship between phonological awareness and reading is to be better understood, our conception of phonological awareness must be expanded to include sub-syllabic units.

The syllable is believed to have an internal organization consisting of the onset (the syllable's initial consonant or consonant cluster) and the rime (the vowel and any consonants that come after it) (Halle & Vergnaud, 1980). Pursuing this notion, Treiman produced psychological evidence for subsyllabic units by demonstrating that children and adults prefer to divide spoken syllables into onset and rime units (Treiman, 1983, 1985). She also found that children analyze syllables into onsets and rimes before they analyze rimes or multiple-phoneme onsets into their component phonemes.

That the rime plays a prominent role in children's language development is, perhaps, manifested by their facility with rhyme, a skill children develop at a very young age (Bradley & Bryant, 1985). The relationship between rime units and words that rhyme is obvious—words that rhyme share the same rime unit. As well, there is increasing evidence that children's early knowledge of nursery rhymes is strongly connected with later reading success (Bryant, Bradley, MacLean, & Crossland, 1989), suggesting that the onset and rime may be functional units for beginning reading instruction.

Bryant and Goswami (1987) reasoned that children's awareness of rhyme contributes to later reading success because it helps children categorize common spelling patterns. That is, if children know how to read *light*, they can use their knowledge of rhyme to read *fight*. Goswami's (1986, 1988) study of the role of orthographic analogies in reading development indicated that children do make such inferences. She trained children to read a word such as *beak* and then tested their ability to read new words that shared either the first three letters *(bean)*, the last three letters *(peak)*, or shared letters not in sequence *(bask)*. Goswami discovered that beginning readers were able to make use of analogies to read unknown words. She noted a progression in children's analogy use, with ending analogies being easiest. Even non-readers were able to make ending analogies. On the basis that ending analogies are words that rhyme, Goswami linked children's use of analogies to the research showing that a child's phonological awareness facilitates subsequent reading ability. She posited that the link between rhyming skill and reading might be that children's experience with rhyme facilitates word recognition by analogy. Through analogies, children extract large subword units from which knowledge of spelling-sound relationships might be deduced.

Another study (Bryant, MacLean, Bradley, & Crossland, 1990) suggested that children's early knowledge of nursery rhymes plays a strong role in the development of children's awareness of phonemes. Using data from a 3-year longitudinal study, Bryant and his colleagues showed that children's knowledge of nursery rhymes predicted their success in reading and spelling 2 to 3 years later. A path analysis indicated a strong path from nursery rhyme knowledge to rhyme and phoneme detection. In turn, the paths from rhyme detection and phoneme detection to reading were strong although the direct path from nursery rhyme knowledge to reading was weak and nonsignificant. Thus, these researchers concluded that nursery rhymes contributed to rhyme detection, which, in turn, led to phoneme detection and, finally, success in reading. However, their study was based on correlational analyses and does not delineate how knowledge of nursery rhymes might lead to phoneme detection.

We hypothesized that orthographic analogies based on onset and rime units (words that rhyme) might be importantly related to children's letter-sound knowledge because such analogies might help children deduce letter-sound correspondences. Baron (1977) pointed to the problems inherent in teaching grapheme-phoneme rules outside the context of words. It is extremely difficult to produce many phonemes in isolation. Pronouncing a string of phonemes slowly adds two extra phonemes (e.g., "bat" becomes "buh-ah-tuh") (Liberman, Shankweiler, Liberman, Fowler, & Fischer, 1977). We reasoned that when children are introduced to print, they not only use their knowledge of rhyme to group words with common spelling patterns; they also isolate the initial phoneme, or onset, and make the letter-sound connection. That children can isolate single phonemes if those phonemes form the onset of the word they hear was demonstrated by Kirtley, Bryant, MacLean, and Bradley (1989). Thus, in recognizing that the last three letters have the same sound in both *cold* and *bold*, children might then deduce the sound associated with the letter *c* in this context.

A second question derived from these studies was whether analogy training based on the onset and rime units of speech would facilitate segmentation ability. Because children's segmentation ability has been shown to be predictive of later reading acquisition, some have advocated segmentation training prior to reading instruction (Elkonin, 1973; Lundberg, Frost, & Petersen, 1988; Rozin & Gleitman, 1977; Williams, 1980). The rationale is that young children must recognize the phoneme in speech in order to make the letter-sound correspondences required in learning to read. Elkonin used blank markers to help children conceptualize the component sounds of words. He believed that letters would only confuse prereaders. He introduced letters only when children showed proficiency in segmentation tasks. Hohn and Ehri (1983) showed that using letters to teach segmentation did not confuse beginning readers. In their study, children learned to segment as quickly when training was accompanied by letters as they did when training was accompanied by blank tokens. On a posttest, they discovered that the letter-trained children segmented the sounds they had practiced in training more effectively than did the non-letter subjects. They suggested that letter-training "enabled learners to acquire a visual sound-symbolizing system that they could use to distinguish and represent the separate phonemes in memory" (p. 760). More recent evidence confirms their position. Although segmentation training alone has a positive effect on reading, the greatest benefit occurs when sound categorization is taught in combination with the letters representing those sounds (Bradley & Bryant, 1985).

Morais and his co-workers (Morais, Alegria, & Content, 1987) also maintained that segmentation skill can be developed in the context of reading. They do not dispute that segmentation ability can be stimulated in prereading activities. Rather, they are concerned that "children showing low segmental ability are at risk of being unjustly considered as too immature to begin learning to read and write" (p. 433). Entrance into a reading program may be unnecessarily delayed.

This issue regarding the context in which phonological skills emerge prompted us to investigate the conditions under which reading instruction will stimulate segmentation skill. We reasoned that the process of reading instruction would most strongly facilitate segmentation skill if the natural units of children's speech and the orthographic units used in the introduction of reading were closely matched. Onset and rime units meet that requirement. We asked another related question: Would proficiency in the detection of onset and rime lead young children to awareness of smaller components such as the phoneme?

Method

Subjects

Forty-eight children just completing their eighth month of kindergarten were selected randomly from six regular kindergarten classrooms in two schools in the Saskatoon Public School District. The kindergarten classes, which operate on a half-day basis, are primarily activity-based but introduce the children to beginning literacy systematically throughout the kindergarten year. When the study began, the ages of the children ranged from 64 months to 76 months, with an average age of 70 months. One child was absent at the time of posttesting and was, therefore, dropped from the study, leaving 47 children.

To ensure that the children be of average ability or better and at a preliminary reading level, the *Peabody Picture Vocabulary Test-Revised* (PPVT-R) (Dunn & Dunn, 1981), and the Letter Identification and Word Identification subtests of the *Woodcock Reading Mastery Test-Revised* (WRMT-R) (Woodcock, 1987) were administered. Children whose PPVT-R scores were more than 1 SD below the mean (scaled score below 85), whose word identification score exceeded 14, or whose letter identification score exceeded 38 were not included in the study. Children were also pretested on all of the words being used for the Word Recognition by Analogy pretest. These words were presented for reading in randomized order interspersed with filler words from a revised Dolch preprimer list (Johnson, 1971). The *Test of Awareness of Language Segments* (TALS) (Sawyer, 1987), a measure of the ability to segment sentences into words and words into phonemes, was administered to determine segmentation skill and placement into either a high, middle, or low segmentation group. Sixteen children were chosen for each segmentation group. High segmenters were those children with a TALS score between 25 and 36; children with a TALS score between 14 to 23 were assigned to the middle segmenter group; children scoring between 0 and 11 on the TALS were placed in the low segmenter group.

To establish experimental and control groups equivalent on segmentation ability, the TALS scores were rank ordered. To ensure that any advantage for existing segmentation ability would accrue to the control group, children with odd numbers were assigned to the control group ($M = 18.04$, $SD = 9.98$) and the remainder became the experimental group ($M = 17.58$, $SD = 10.11$).

Materials

Segmentation ability. Segmentation ability was measured using the TALS (Sawyer, 1987) and the Identifying Phonemes in Spoken Words subtest of the *Durrell Analysis of Reading Difficulty* (Durrell & Catterson, 1980). The TALS tasks were chosen to provide for measurement of a range of segmentation ability. Two subtests were used from the TALS: "Sentences-to-Words" and "Words-to-Sounds." In the "Sentences-to-Words," the examiner presents a sentence orally and the child is asked to use blocks to mark the words in the sentence. In the "Words-to-Sounds," the examiner presents a word orally and the child is asked to use the blocks to show the different sounds in that word. Durrell's "Identifying Phonemes in Spoken Words" subtest was chosen because it requires the child to divide spoken words into onset and rime units. The examiner presents a word orally and the child is asked to give the first sound of that word.

Letter-sound knowledge. The Supplementary Letter checklist of the WRMT-R was used to test knowledge of letter sounds. The child was asked to give the sound of alphabetic letters presented in lower case. The number of sounds produced correctly was recorded.

Word recognition by analogy. The word recognition by analogy test, adapted from Goswami (1986), is presented in Appendix A. Because age of acquisition (AOA) of spoken words affects word retrieval and children's reading accuracy (Coltheart, Laxon, & Keating, 1988), clue words chosen had ratings of less than 3 on the Gilhooly and Logie (1980) acquisition ratings. These words were then cross-checked for frequency in print. In order to present words that the child was most likely to be familiar with in speech but not in print, words chosen had a frequency count in print of less than 100 (Carroll, Davies, & Richman, 1971).

Children were sequentially presented with 10 clue words and asked to read 3 test words that were analogous to each clue word under three conditions: an ending analogy condition, a beginning analogy condition, and a 2-letter analogy condition. No instruction about how to use the clue word was given. The examiner simply said "This word says cold." Placing the analogous word directly below the clue word, the examiner asked, "What does this word say." Each test word was removed once the child had attempted to read it so that only one test word was visible at a time. Presentation of analogy word types was randomized to control for order effects.

Procedure

Before the training sessions began, we administered pretests of letter-sound knowledge, segmentation skill, and word recognition by analogy. There were no significant differences between the experimental and control groups on any of these measures. Once pretesting was completed, the children in the experimental group were given a series of orthographic analogy training sessions, whereas the control group remained in the regular kindergarten curriculum.

Each child was seen individually in a quiet room in their school. Training took place in 15-minute sessions for a maximum of seven sessions over a one-month period. Across these sessions, 10 different rime units were introduced. The orthographic analogies used for training were based on onset and rime units of speech (Appendix B). The initial words presented for each rime unit were of early acquisition (AOA less than 3). Because we were testing children's ability to deduce letter-sound correspondences, letter-sounds were never presented as isolated units. Where individual letters were given, only letter-names were used. The general training procedures were as follows.

The first word was placed on an easel. The child was told "This word is ball." After the child repeated the word, the child was shown that the three letters *all* stayed together to make the sound "all"; the *b* made the word say "ball." The child was asked to tell what *all* said, and what the word was when the *b* was placed in front of *all*. Then the word *fall* was placed directly below the word *ball* so that the orthographic similarity was easily detected. The children were told that this new word said "fall." We made explicit to the child that in *fall* and *ball* the last three letters were the same and they also sounded the same. But, the first letter made the words sound different. The children were again asked to give the sound of *all*. The letters *f* and *b* were physically removed from the easel, leaving *all* in place. The *b* and *f* were then alternately placed in front of the *all* and we modelled the resulting pronunciation. Finally, the children were asked to alternately place *b* and *f* in front of *all* and name the resulting word. Four other rhyming words were individually placed on the easel directly below the initial word. The child's attention was drawn to the new onset and the new word made by that onset. Each word was pronounced for the child and then the child was asked to read the new word made with the new onset.

At the end of the training period, the letter-sound knowledge, segmentation ability, and word recognition by analogy tasks were administered to all children as posttests.

Results

The analysis of our data was carried out in two stages. We first examined the ability of the children to read words by analogy prior to any training, then went on to analyze the effects of the analogy training upon segmentation ability, letter-sound knowledge, and ability to read words by analogy.

Orthographic analogies

The data for the experimental and control groups, combined in our analysis of ability to use analogies prior to training and presented in Table 1, were subjected to a Segmentation ability × Analogy type analysis of variance with the last factor repeated. Consistent with our hypothesis, ability to perform the segmentation tasks was predictive of the children's ability to read words by analogy, as reflected in a significant main effect for Segmentation ability [$F(2, 45) = 8.68, p < .001$]. The main effect of Analogy type also reached significance [$F(2, 90) = 15.12, p < .001$], indicating that the number of words read by analogy depended on whether analogies occurred in the beginning positions, ending positions, or involved two letters in common.

The interpretation of these main effects must be qualified by a significant interaction [$F(4, 90) = 3.89, p < .01$]. A simple effects analysis of this interaction (Keppel, 1982) indicated that position was a significant factor for high [$F(2, 30) = 10.15, p < .01$] and middle segmenters [$F(2, 30) = 3.57, p < .05$], but not low segmenters [$F(2, 30) = 3.25, p > .05$]. Simple comparisons showed that high segmenters' performance on ending analogies was significantly better than on beginning analogies [$F(1, 90) = 17.65, p < .001$] and two-letter analogies [$F(1, 90) = 35.59, p < .001$]. There was no significant difference between beginning and two-letter analogies [$F(1, 90) = 3.11, p > .05$]. The middle segmenter group performed significantly better on ending compared with two-letter analogies [$F(1, 90) = 6.93, p < .01$]; no other comparison was significant. Scheffé multiple comparisons further highlight these results. For ending analogies, high segmenters performed better than middle segmenters, but middle and low segmenters did not differ significantly. For beginning and two-letter analogies, high segmenters exceeded low segmenters, but there was no significant difference between high and middle segmenters, nor between middle and low segmenters.

Table 1

Pretraining Mean Number (and Standard Deviation) of Correct Analogies for Analogy Groups as a Function of Analogy Type

Segmentation Ability	Analogy Type			
	Ending	Beginning	Two-letter	Total
High	3.38 (2.68)	1.88 (2.13)	1.25 (1.95)	6.50 (5.93)
Middle	1.19 (1.60)	0.94 (2.32)	0.25 (0.78)	2.38 (4.40)
Low	0.31 (0.60)	0.00 (0.00)	0.00 (0.00)	0.31 (0.60)

These results confirm Goswami's (1986, 1988) findings that children in the preliminary stages of reading acquisition are able to read words by analogy. The ability to do so relates directly to the child's skill at solving segmentation tasks, with high segmenters particularly proficient at making analogies in ending positions relative to all other conditions.

Our findings in this part of the study do not clarify the issue of causation. That is, it is not clear whether the ability to read some words by analogy, along with other early reading skills, has stimulated segmentation skill, or whether segmentation skill has brought about the ability to read words by analogy. The pattern of results favor the explanation that analogies are easiest to perform when shared letters occur at the ends of words because this kind of orthographic analogy corresponds to onset-rime units in speech. Accordingly, an advantage is conferred by the sharing of natural units in speech and print. This pattern seems to be particularly salient and productive for children who display more advanced segmentation ability.

Analogy training

Segmentation skill. The pretest and posttest scores of onset-rime segmentation as measured by the Durrell task (Table 2) were analyzed first. As presented in Table 2 and depicted in Figure 1, control and experimental groups showed an increase in performance. However,

Table 2

Mean Scores on Pretests and Posttests

Test	Segmentation Ability	Control		Experimental	
		Pre	Post	Pre	Post
Durrell [25]	High	20.00 (4.28)	21.43 (2.99)	21.38 (1.60)	23.25 (0.71)
	Middle	17.13 (3.87)	19.00 (4.90)	19.25 (4.09)	21.88 (3.64)
	Low	6.38 (5.71)	8.25 (5.90)	12.38 (7.89)	19.25 (3.54)
TALS [36]	High	29.14 (2.12)	30.14 (3.58)	28.75 (2.25)	31.38 (2.88)
	Middle	19.13 (3.00)	20.25 (3.01)	18.50 (3.30)	25.00 (3.85)
	Low	6.00 (3.16)	8.25 (2.77)	5.50 (3.16)	10.38 (4.31)
Letter-sound [26]	High	18.43 (4.58)	19.57 (4.35)	18.63 (3.62)	21.38 (2.83)
	Middle	11.00 (4.90)	11.50 (6.30)	11.88 (4.40)	17.13 (4.52)
	Low	3.25 (2.87)	4.25 (3.58)	7.75 (4.40)	9.75 (5.97)
Analogies [30]	High	3.86 (4.30)	5.86 (5.98)	9.13 (6.62)	14.50 (5.68)
	Middle	1.75 (2.71)	2.63 (3.16)	3.00 (5.76)	9.13 (7.38)
	Low	0.13 (0.35)	0.00 (0.00)	0.50 (0.76)	2.13 (2.48)

Note: Square brackets contain the maximum obtainable score. Round brackets provide the standard deviations.

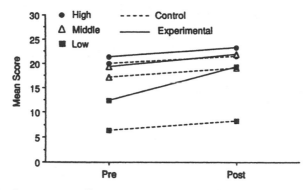

Figure 1. Analogy training effects on onset-rime (Durrell).

the experimental group showed the greatest increases. To test the significance of these observations, the data were submitted to a $2 \times 3 \times 2$ (Training × Segmentation × Time) ANOVA with repeated measures on Time (pre/post). The results indicated significant main effects for Training [$F(1, 41) = 12.24$, $p < .001$], Segmentation [$F(1, 41) = 25.36$, $p < .001$], and Time [$F(1, 41) = 26.26$, $p < .001$]. The significant Training × Segmentation interaction [$F(2, 41) = 3.28$, $p < .05$] was subjected to a simple main effects analysis. This analysis indicated that the interaction was mainly attributable to a significant effect for low segmenters [$F(1, 41) = 17.12$, $p < .001$] but not for the other two groups. A simple comparison of pre- and postscores for low segmenters indicated that the postscore gain was highly significant for experimental low segmenters, [$F(1, 41) = 27.80$, $p < .001$] but was not significant for control low segmenters [$F(1, 41) = 2.06$, $p > .05$].

To examine further the performance of the low experimental group, a Scheffé multiple comparison of their pre- and posttraining scores was also conducted.

Whereas there is a significant difference between middle and low segmenters before training, after training this significant difference disappeared.

Table 2 and Figure 2 present the training effects on segmentation ability as measured by TALS. Each of the experimental groups showed improvement on the posttests with the largest gains apparent in the middle segmenter group. A $2 \times 3 \times 2$ (Training × Segmentation × Time) ANOVA with repeated measures on Time (pre/post) was conducted. This revealed significant effects for Segmentation [$F(1, 41) = 262.67$, $p < .001$], Time [$F(1, 41) = 41.62$, $p < .001$], and a significant Training × Time interaction [$F(1, 41) = 11.42$, $p < .01$]. A simple effects analysis of

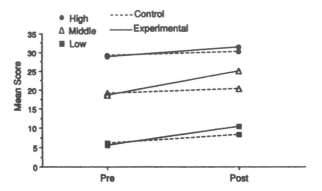

Figure 2. Analogy training effects on segmentation (TALS).

the Training × Time interaction established a significant improvement for the experimental group [$F(1, 23) = 36.50, p = .001$] and for the control group [$F(1, 22) = 6.44, p < .05$]. A simple comparison of pre- and posttraining scores of the experimental group revealed a significant comparison for all of the Experimental segmentation levels [High, $F(1, 41) = 5.24, p < .05$; Middle, $F(1, 41) = 32, p < .001$; Low, $F(1, 41) = 18.04, p < .001$], but none of the Control segmentation levels [High and Middle segmenters, $F(1, 41) = < 1$; Low, $F(1, 41) = 3.84, p > .05$].

A Scheffé multiple comparison on pre- and posttest scores was also conducted. This revealed that there was a significant difference between the Experimental middle and both the Experimental high and Control high groups on pretraining scores. On posttraining scores, the significant difference between the Experimental middle and Control high groups disappeared.

Letter-Sound knowledge

The effects of the analogy training on letter-sound knowledge are presented in Table 2 and Figure 3. A 2 × 3 × 2 (Training × Segmentation × Time) ANOVA with repeated measures on Time (pre- and posttest scores) was conducted to determine effects of training on letter-sound knowledge. Posttraining scores on lettersound knowledge were significantly different from pretraining scores [$F(1, 41) = 41.46, p < .001$]. The main effect for Training was significant [$F(1, 41) = 5.93, p < .05$] as was the main effect for Segmentation ($F = 36.12, p < .001$). There was also a Training × Time interaction [$F(1, 41) = 14.04, p < .01$]. A simple effects analysis clarified this interaction, revealing a significant effect for the control group [$F(1, 22) = 5.58, p < .05$] but a much greater effect for the experimental group ($F(1, 23) = 33.09, p < .001$). Simple com-

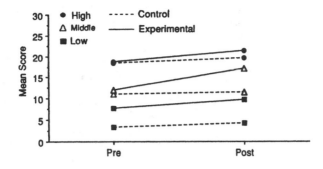

Figure 3. Analogy training effects on letter-sound knowledge.

parisons of pretraining with posttraining scores established that there were no significant comparisons for any of the control subgroups whereas comparisons were significant for all experimental subgroups [High, $F(1, 41) = 12.05, p < .01$; Middle, $F(1, 41) = 43.92, p < .001$); Low, $F(1, 41) = 6.37, p < .05$].

From Figure 3, it is apparent that Middle segmenters benefitted most from training. A Scheffé multiple comparison was conducted on the pre-training and again on the posttraining scores of the experimental group. The results showed that prior to training the performance of high segmenters was significantly different from the performance of middle segmenters. After training, that difference is no longer significant.

Word recognition by analogy

The mean number of words read correctly before and after training is given in Table 2 and illustrated in Figure 4. The gains of the experimental group are consistently greater than the gains of the control group. A $2 \times 3 \times 2$ (Training × Segmentation × Time) ANOVA with repeated measures on Time (pre- and posttraining scores) revealed significant Training [$F(1, 41) = 10.24, p < .01$], Segmentation [$F(1, 41) = 12.18, p < .001$], and Time effects [$F(1, 41) = 56.93, p < .001$]. There were also significant Training × Time [$F(2, 41) = 24.32, p < .001$] and Segmentation × Time [$F(2, 41) = 7.40, p < .01$] interactions. A simple effects analysis of the significant Training × Time interaction showed a significant effect for the control group [$F(1, 22) = 5.58, p < .05$]. However, this effect was far exceeded by the significant effect for the experimental group [$F(1, 23) = 38.03, p < .001$]. A simple comparison of pre- and post-training scores of the control group revealed a significant comparison for control high segmenters only [$F(1, 41) = 5.55, p < .05$].

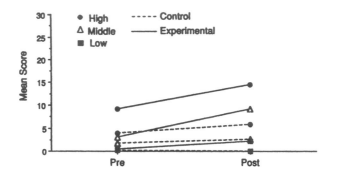

Figure 4. Analogy training effects on analogy reading.

In contrast, the simple comparison for experimental high segmenters was more significant [$F(1, 41) = 40.05, p < .001$]. Although a Scheffé multiple comparison showed no significant difference between high experimentals and controls before training, this difference was significant after training. The simple comparison was also significant for experimental middle segmenters [$F(1, 41) = 52.19, p < .001$] but not for experimental low segmenters [$F(1, 41) = 3.70, p > .051$].

Discussion

In summing up this study and its implications, we can begin by looking at the patterns of influence of the analogy training across the different measures for each segmentation group separately and relative to each other. First, the low segmenter group showed virtually no ability to use analogies to read unknown words prior to the analogy training. The analogy training did not significantly improve these children's ability to read words by analogy. However, even though segmentation ability was not directly trained, analogy training with print resulted in improvement in segmentation ability. The more basic onset-rime task showed a highly significant improvement for this group. TALS segmentation and letter-sound knowledge each showed significant but smaller effects.

The analogy training showed a somewhat different influence upon middle and high segmenters. The middle group's greatest improvement occurred in their ability to perform the word reading by analogy task and in their letter-sound knowledge. They also made significant and simultaneous gains in the TALS segmentation task. The high segmenter group showed a training effect similar to the middle segmenters. Ability to read new words by analogy improved markedly for these children. On the segmentation measures, onset-rime showed no gain, most likely due to a ceiling effect, whereas the TALS improved slightly but significantly. Letter-sound knowledge also made a small but significant improvement.

A progression in the acquisition of segmentation ability is evident in these findings. For low segmenters, the onset-rime segmentation was influenced most, followed by the more complex phonemic segmentation measured by the TALS. Middle segmenters, who were already proficient in onset-rime, showed considerable improvement in the TALS and in letter-sound knowledge. High segmenters showed a similar pattern moderated by ceiling effects. These findings concur with Treiman's research in demonstrating that onset and rime units play an important role in the progression of segmentation ability. Children's awareness of rime, as represented by the Durrell task, occurred before more sophisticated skills such as phoneme detection and letter-sound knowledge. The pattern in the development of letter-sound knowledge also points to the conclusion that segmentation ability based on onset and rime detection is necessary in order for children to extract letter-sound knowledge by analogy. As children learned to detach the onset from the rime, progress in letter-sound knowledge was evidenced.

The pattern of results suggests a complex interactive effect whereby facilitation of sound segmentation ability, letter-sound knowledge, and reading by analogy have occurred in a kind of mutual synergy. Our findings seem to be consistent with Perfetti's (1984) conclusion that "a child learning to read is helped by the early emergence of some levels of phonemic awareness and that deeper levels of phonemic awareness may be a consequence of learning to read" (p. 51). The present research indicates that onset-rime segmentation is one level of phonemic awareness whose early emergence can facilitate beginning reading. In the pre-training analogy test, it was evident that children who were more able to perform onset-rime segmentation were better able to read words by analogy. The way in which early emergence of onset-rime segmentation may help children learn to read is also evidenced in the performance of the control high segmenters whose performance on analogies showed a significant increase even without analogy training. The training, however, increased levels of phonemic awareness among the children in the experimental group, demonstrating that experience with print cultivates further phonemic awareness.

Our results support the interpretation that there is some critical threshold level of segmentation skill. When segmentation ability has reached this critical level, letter-sound knowledge and reading by analogy are mutually facilitative in an interactive sense. Children who had not yet reached this critical level did not show such mutual facilitation effects. Rather, the analogy training seemed to foster segmentation skills and letter-sound knowledge which both appear to be prerequisite to ability to read words by analogy.

These findings shed some light on why rhymes play a role in children's awareness of phonemes (Bryant, MacLean, Bradley, & Crossland, 1990). The theoretical framework provided by Ehri and her coworkers can assist in the interpretation. Ehri and Wilce (1980) stated:

> Readers need to be able to analyze words into sounds so as to recognize what segments there are to be symbolized in print. Likewise, when they look at the printed form of words, they need to be able to justify the presence of letters by finding sounds in the word for them to symbolize. (p. 380)

The onset and rime training in this study built on children's existing language base by introducing the printed word in segments that corresponded to sounds in speech children already recognized as separable units. Guiding the children through the process of mapping the recognizable onset in speech to the corresponding letter in print enabled them to attach a visual image to the sound that could then be stored in memory as a distinguishable and separate phoneme. Thus, the analogy training can be viewed as facilitating a bilateral mapping between natural units of speech and corresponding segments of orthography. However, for those children yet unable to perform onset-rime segmentation, the training does not operate in a bilateral fashion, but acts as a symbolizing system to facilitate the acquisition of onset-rime segmentation. Mutual facilitation between orthographic segments and corresponding speech segments then becomes evident in concurrent gains in segmentation and letter-sound knowledge.

Limitations

In reflecting upon what the results of this study reveal about the role of analogies in reading acquisition, the nature of the tasks and of the stimuli used in the study must be considered. The monosyllabic words of three or four letters chosen as stimuli represent simple onset-rime structures appropriate for the beginning readers in this study. The extent to which the findings generalize to classes of words with multisyllabic structure and more complex onsets and rimes should be investigated. It would also be instructive to explore the power of the training procedure used in this study by contrasting it with a treatment technique that highlights the phoneme in other ways.

Limitations related to aspects of group selection and assignment to control or experimental conditions should also be considered. Although they were randomly selected from their classrooms, the children in this study were not randomly assigned to experimental and control groups. The intention was to create groups equated on the crucial factor of pre-training segmentation ability, and this was accomplished. However, the subgroups were not equated on the other pretest measures, and initial differences could have influenced the outcomes. An alternative approach would have been to assign the subjects randomly to the treatment groups and adjust statistically for differences in the pretest scores.

It is important to examine the question of the extent to which the training effects are sustained over time. The training period in this study was limited in duration and there were no time-lagged follow-up measures to determine the stability of the outcomes. Systematic exploration of different training periods and how these influence the training effects would be valuable.

The literacy instruction in the classrooms could be a factor in the children's acquisition of some of the skills measured in the study. Experimental and control groups contained children from each classroom, thus minimizing any systematic bias based on the instruction being provided by specific teachers. However, it is possible that the training effects measured in this study may have resulted from an interaction between the experimental treatment and literacy instruction provided in the classroom during the study.

A further issue is whether the training effects in this study generalize to authentic reading situations. A logical extension would involve examining if and how analogies can be activated while the child is in the process of reading continuous text. Certainly the meaning focus and temporal processes of the reading act would place a more complex set of demands on the analogy strategy than was required during the teaching procedures used in our study.

Instructional implications

In conclusion, the present study affirms the results of research showing that analogy training specifically based on onset-rime units is an effective method to assist children as they move into reading. Such training appears to be useful not just for those children who are "ready for it" by being the most advanced in their group. All children in our study benefited, albeit in different ways. The potentially "at-risk" children, our low segmenter groups, did not improve in word reading but did respond with improved sound segmentation ability, a skill that appears to be a precursor to reading by analogy. Although we recognize that letter-sound knowledge and segmentation skill can be taught in other ways, the onset and rime approach builds on a beginning reader's existing language base. We have demonstrated an advantage of this approach—children with weak segmentation ability can improve their skills in the context of reading while children with more developed segmentation ability can progress in other reading skills.

It remains to be considered how the kind of training described in this study could be delivered within the classroom context. We hesitate to suggest that children receive direct instruction in reading words by analogy through importation of these techniques. Rather, we envision the teacher guiding the child through the kind of scaffolding strategies described by Bruner (1978) within the zone of proximal development as outlined by Vygotsky (1978). Careful and contextual demonstration and modelling by the teacher of the kinds of contrasts and correspondences used in this study could best lead the child to an understanding with support of what they cannot accomplish unsupported. When used at opportune times, with opportune materials, in natural settings, the careful calibrated "nudges" of the observant, child-aware teacher could assist the learner to acquire the analogy strategy as one ingredient in the complex repertoire of knowledge, skills, and strategies that combine to promote literacy acquisition.

References

Baron, J. (1977). Mechanisms for pronouncing printed words: Use and acquisition. In D. LaBerge & S. J. Samuels (Eds.), *Basic processes in reading: Perception and comprehension* (pp. 175–216). Hillsdale, NJ: Erlbaum.

Bradley, L., & Bryant, P. E. (1983). Categorizing sounds and learning to read—a causal connection. *Nature, 301,* 419–21.

Bradley, L., & Bryant, P. E. (1985). *Rhyme and reason in reading and spelling,* Ann Arbor, MI: University of Michigan Press.

Bruner, J. (1978). The role of dialogue in language acquisition. In A. Sinclair, R. Jarvella, & W. Levelt (Eds.), *The child's conception of language* (pp. 240–56). New York: Springer-Verlag.

Bryant, P., Bradley, L., MacLean, L., & Crossland, J. (1989). Nursery rhymes, phonological skills and reading. *Journal of Child Language, 16,* 407–28.

Bryant, P., & Goswami, U. (1987). Beyond grapheme-phoneme correspondences. *European Bulletin of Cognitive Psychology, 7,* 439–43.

Bryant, P., MacLean, L., Bradley, L., & Crossland, J. (1990). Rhyme and alliteration, phoneme detection, and learning to read. *Developmental Psychology, 26,* 429–38.

Carroll, J. B., Davies, P., & Richman, B. (1971). *The American heritage word frequency book.* New York: Houghton Mifflin.

Coltheart, V., Laxon, V., & Keating, C. (1988). Effects of word imageability and age of acquisition on children's reading. *British Journal of Psychology, 79,* 1–11.

Dunn, L., & Dunn, L. (1981). *Peabody picture vocabulary test-revised.* Circle Pines, MN: American Guidance Service.

Durrell, D. D., & Catterson, J. H. (1980). *Durrell analysis of reading difficulty,* San Antonio, TX: Psychological Corporation.

Ehri, L. C. (1984). How orthography alters spoken language competencies in children learning to read and spell. In J. Downing & R. Valtin (Eds.), *Language awareness and learning to read* (pp. 119–47). New York: Springer-Verlag.

Ehri L. C., & Wilce, L. S. (1980). The influence of orthography on readers' conceptualization of the phonemic structure of words. *Applied Psycholinguistics, 1,* 371–85.

Elkonin, D. B. (1973). USSR. In Downing, J. (Ed.), *Comparative reading* (pp. 551–79). New York: Macmillan.

Gilhooly, K. J., & Logie, R. H. (1980). Methods and designs: Age of acquisition, imagery, concreteness, familiarity, and ambiguity measures for 1,944 words. *Behavior Research Methods and Instrumentation, 12,* 395–427.

Goswami, U. (1986). Children's use of analogy in learning to read: A developmental study. *Journal of Experimental Psychology, 42,* 73–83.

Goswami, U. (1988). Orthographic analogies and reading development. *The Quarterly Journal of Experimental Psychology, 40,* 239–68.

Halle, M., & Vergnaud, J-R, (1980). Three dimensional phonology. *Journal of Linguistic Research, 1,* 83–105.

Hohn, W. E., & Ehri, L. (1983). Do alphabet letters help pre-readers acquire phoneme segmentation skill? *Journal of Educational Psychology, 75,* 752–62.

Johnson, D. D. (1971). The Dolch list re-examined. *The Reading Teacher, 24,* 455–56.

Keppel, G. (1982). *Design and analysis: A researcher's handbook.* Englewood Cliffs, NJ: Prentice-Hall.

Kirtley, C., Bryant, P., MacLean, M., & Bradley, L. (1989). Rhyme, rime and the onset of reading. *Journal of Experimental Psychology, 48,* 224–45.

Leong, C. K., & Haines, C. F. (1978). Beginning readers' awareness of words and sentences. *Journal of Reading Behavior, 10,* 393–407.

Liberman, I., Shankweiler, D., Fischer, F. W., & Carter, B. (1974). Explicit syllable and phoneme segmentation in the young child. *Journal of Experimental Child Psychology, 18,* 201–12.

Liberman, I., Shankweiler, D., Liberman, A., Fowler, C., & Fischer, F. (1977). Phonetic segmentation and recoding in the beginning reader. In A. S. Reber & D. L. Scarborough (Eds.), *Toward a psychology of reading: Proceedings of the CUNY Conference* (pp. 207–25). Hillsdale, NJ: Erlbaum.

Lundberg, I., Frost, J., Petersen, O. (1988). Effects of an extensive program for stimulating phonological awareness in preschool children. *Reading Research Quarterly, 23,* 263–84.

Morais, J., Alegria, J., & Content, A. (1987). The relationship between segmental analysis and alphabetic literacy: An interactive view. *European Bulletin of Cognitive Psychology, 7*, 415–38.

Morais, J., Bertelson, P., Cary, L., & Alegria, J. (1986). Literacy training and speech segmentation. *Cognition, 24*, 45–64.

Morais, J., Cary, L., Alegria, J., & Bertelson, P. (1979). Does awareness of speech as a sequence of phones arise spontaneously? *Cognition, 7*, 323–31.

Perfetti, C. (1984). Reading acquisition and beyond: Decoding includes cognition. *American Journal of Education, 93*, 40–60.

Perfetti, C., Beck, I., Bell, L., & Hughes, C. (1987). Phonemic knowledge and learning to read are reciprocal: A longitudinal study of first grade children. *Merrill Palmer Quarterly, 33*, 283–319.

Read, C., Zhang, Y., Nie, H., & Ding, B. (1986). The ability to manipulate speech sounds depend on knowing alphabetic writing. *Cognition, 24*, 31–44.

Rozin, P., & Gleitman, L. R. (1977). The structure and acquisition of reading II: The reading process and the acquisition of the alphabetic principle. In A. S. Reber & D. L. Scarborough (Eds.), *Toward a psychology of reading: Proceedings of the CUNY Conference* (pp. 55–141). Hillsdale, NJ: Erlbaum.

Sawyer, D. J. (1987). *Test of awareness of language segments.* Rockville, MD: Aspen.

Stanovich, K., Cunningham, A., & Cramer, B. (1984). Assessing phonological awareness in kindergarten children: Issues of task comparability. *Journal of Experimental Child Psychology, 38*, 175–90.

Treiman, R. (1983). The structure of spoken syllables: Evidence from novel word games. *Cognition, 15*, 49–74.

Treiman, R. (1985). Onsets and rimes as units of spoken syllables: Evidence from children. *Journal of Experimental Child Psychology, 39*, 161–81.

Treiman R. (1987). On the relationship between phonological awareness and literacy. *European Bulletin of Cognitive Psychology, 7*, 524–29.

Vygotsky, L. S. (1978). *Mind in society.* Cambridge, MA: Harvard University Press.

Williams, J. P. (1980). Teaching decoding with an emphasis on phoneme analysis and phoneme blending. *Journal of Educational Psychology, 72*, 1–15.

Woodcock, R. W. (1987). *Woodcock reading mastery tests-revised.* Toronto: Psycan.

Author Notes

This research was partially supported by a University Graduate Scholarship to the first author from the University of Saskatchewan.

Appendix A

Analogy Testing Word List

Clue Word	Analogous Words		
cold [1.83]	bold (12)	colt (29)	cone (18)
coat [1.97]	goat (66)	coal (63)	foam (5)
rain [2.11]	pain (14)	rail (24)	aims (1)
fork [2.25]	cork (11)	fort (25)	torn (30)
band [2.36]	sand (135)	bans (0)	ants[b]
dark[a]	bark (40)	dart (5)	army (47)
room [2.44]	boom (8)	root (76)	mood (10)
heat [2.78]	beat (80)	heal (2)	team (80)
lamp [2.83]	camp (52)	lamb (14)	hams (4)
peep [2.89]	beep (1)	peel (4)	weed (10)

Note. AOA is presented in square brackets; frequency is presented in round brackets.
[a] Gilhooly and Logie give no AOA for dark. However, darkness has a mean AOA of 2.42.
[b] Carroll, Davis, and Richman give no frequency count for ants. The frequency count for ant is 78; the frequency count for ant's is 7.

Appendix B

Analogy Training Words

dad [1.25]	mad (31)	lad (24)	gad (0)	tad (0)	fad (0)
ball [1.50]	fall (129)	wall (106)	mall (1)	hall (59)	gall (0)
face [1.66]	dace (0)	race (92)	lace (16)	pace (17)	mace (0)
dog [1.89]	log (56)	fog (41)	cog (0)	hog (4)	jog (0)
ring [2.08]	king (188)	ting (2)	wing (32)	ping (0)	ding (4)
cake [2.14]	rake (13)	sake (1)	bake (16)	fake (0)	wake (19)
book [2.14]	rook (0)	cook (45)	good (1)	hook (20)	nook (0)
pet [2.19]	net (26)	bet (24)	met (80)	jet (62)	wet (133)
jump [2.22]	bump (19)	sump (0)	lump (12)	pump (11)	hump (4)
kick [2.28]	sick (76)	nick (20)	wick (5)	hick (0)	tick (10)

Note. AOA is presented in square brackets; Frequency is presented in round brackets.

7 A Comparison of Children's Development of Alphabetic Knowledge in a Skills-Based and a Whole Language Classroom

Ellen McIntyre
University of Louisville

Penny A. Freppon
University of Cincinnati

This study examines how six low-income children developed alphabetic knowledge in two different instructional settings, a skills-based classroom and a whole language classroom. As McIntyre and Freppon explain, all the children learned alphabetic concepts and skills needed for reading and writing, and the pattern of acquisition was similar across the two-year period in the two different instructional settings. Indeed, it appears that the variation may have been greater from individual to individual than between instructional approaches, one more bit of evidence that the instructional approach itself may not make a tremendous difference in the learning of phonics and the use of phonics knowledge to read and write. The researchers mention that the notable difference between classrooms is not the alphabetic knowledge acquired, "but in what else the children were doing" that supported their learning. In contrast to the skills-based classroom, the whole language classroom enabled children to learn through the reading and writing of actual texts.

McIntyre and Freppon conclude with some very interesting observations: (1) that children do need to have alphabetic knowledge before they can orchestrate the many concepts and skills needed for independent reading and writing; (2) that alphabetic knowledge can be developed successfully in very different instructional contexts; (3) that teaching phonics explicitly doesn't always mean using particular instructional sequences or teaching phonics in isolation; and (4) that "phonics instruction does not have to be random or eclectic, but can be carefully planned and well thought through in whole language."

This study presents the results of a two-year naturalistic case study of how six children in two different instructional settings acquired alphabetic knowledge as they developed as readers and writers. In this study, alphabetic knowledge included knowledge of the graphemic and phonemic nature of written language, grapheme/phoneme correspondences, and use of graphophonics as a tool for reading and writing. This longitudinal study examined these children's development as it occurred in both skills-based and whole language classrooms. We begin by briefly framing this study within the historical debate on phonics instruction and previous research on children's development of alphabetic knowledge. After describing our approach and results, we discuss what our study may mean to the fields of beginning literacy development and instruction.

Theoretical Framework

The debate over phonics in beginning literacy instruction has been one of the most controversial in the field of literacy. Chall's (1967) landmark review of research on the comparable effects of phonics-oriented versus other beginning reading instructional programs led to the strong conclusion that phonics instruction was necessary for beginning reading. The "Great Debate" resulted in an increase in the teaching of phonics in American schools and the learning of alphabetic knowledge through a rigorous curricular scope and sequence.

More recent comparisons of phonics-focused and meaning-focused instruction have also shown that programs including systematic, sequential phonics instruction lead to higher word reading achievement and spelling (e.g., Adams, 1990; Ball & Blachman, 1991; Ehri, 1991; Juel, 1991; Mason, 1980; Yopp, 1992). Many have concluded there is little harm and much value in systematic, sequential phonics programs, the central component of which is teaching correspondences between letters or groups of letters and their pronunciations (e.g., Adams). Juel has speculated that these phonics programs are useful in beginning reading chiefly because they provide a strategy for looking at sound patterns in words. Indeed, some suggest it might simply be that "directness" helps children attend to words and letter sounds and makes the difference in children's acquisition of alphabetic knowledge (McIntyre, 1992; Resnick, 1979).

On the other hand, some theories of language learning and pyscholinguistic research have called into question the necessity of systematic, sequential phonics instruction. Studies have shown that many children can and do obtain alphabetic understandings without this kind of phonics instruction. Studies of early readers (Bissex, 1980; Sulzby, 1985) and studies of learners in whole language classrooms (Freppon, 1991; McIntyre, 1990; Mills, O'Keefe, & Stephens, 1992; Morrow, 1992; Winsor, 1990) indicate that some children construct this necessary information through their own exploration with print and interactions with others. Juel (1991) has shown that phonemic awareness increases through exposure to printed words, and many researchers (Adams, 1990; Gunderson & Shapiro, 1988; Sulzby & Teale, 1991) have suggested that more advanced phonemic awareness can come with opportunities to invent spellings and to read in emergent ways. Even whole-word trained readers often acquire decoding skill eventually (Ehri, 1991).

Children's acquisition of alphabetic knowledge

Studies of emergent and beginning reading suggest that children acquire some levels of graphophonic understanding before they read or write conventionally (Adams, 1990; Biemiller, 1970; Ferriero & Teberosky, 1983; Gibson, 1972; Gough & Hillinger, 1980; Mason, 1980; Sulzby, 1985). Children move globally and recursively through stages of knowledge about print and reading. First, children learn broad concepts about print, such as the pragmatic, semantic, and syntactic nature of print, after which they spend some time "glued to the print" in what appears to be a period of sound/symbol study. Finally, children are able to "orchestrate" information in order to read new text. For example, Biemiller found that children's earliest reading attempts were characterized by context-dependent "errors" that were unrelated to the graphemes on the page. Later in their development, children's errors were graphically similar to those on the page, but they often disrupted comprehension. Finally, children were able to "put it all together," and their errors were contextually appropriate and graphically similar. The development of these skills occurs in a continual, seamless manner, not in discrete stages.

In her study of young children's story re-enactments, Sulzby (1985) found similar, though more detailed, stages. One emergent reading strategy all children demonstrated before they read conventionally was reading "aspectually." For many children this meant they focused on sound/symbol relations and the task of decoding (often unsuccessfully) such that their renditions of favorite storybooks showed an exclusive focus on phonics. Additional studies (Bissex, 1980; Freppon

& Dahl, 1991; McIntyre, 1990) suggest that at some point in their development toward conventional literacy, all children lend conscious analytic attention to sounds and symbols regardless of whether they are comprehending.

Studies of children's emergent writing (Bissex, 1980; Daiute, 1990; Dyson, 1991; Hubbard, 1990; Sulzby, 1992; Sulzby & Teale, 1991) and invented spelling (Gentry, 1987; Goswami & Meade, 1992; Gunderson & Shapiro, 1988; Henderson & Beers, 1980; Read, 1971) also contribute to our understanding of children's acquisition of alphabetic knowledge. Children's drawings, scribbles, letter strings, copying, and labeling are natural and important parts of becoming conventionally literate. Children often write for functional purposes by first using strings of letters, or "deviant" spellings that have no sound/symbol correspondences. When children begin to incorporate sounds, they first map the most salient sounds, with vowels being the last phonemic entities to be perceived (Ehri, 1991). Over time, children let go of more and more of the emergent forms and adopt those of more conventional text.

One comparison study (Dahl & Freppon, in press) showed differences in the application of phonics knowledge in mid-first grade by children in skills-based and whole language classrooms. The children in the whole language classrooms used their alphabetic knowledge more frequently and for more varied purposes than did the children in skills-based classrooms, reflecting the writing experiences and peer interactions that were a regular part of the curriculum.

Although these studies have helped us understand the acquisition of alphabetic knowledge, they do not clarify the knotty question of how children's day-to-day experiences in classrooms affect their development. The present study shows *how* children acquired alphabetic knowledge in two different types of instructional settings, one with a code emphasis and the other with a meaning emphasis. The question we investigated was:

What was the pattern of acquisition and use of alphabetic knowledge of six children as they developed as readers and writers in skills-based and whole language settings?

Method

This study of children's acquisition of alphabetic knowledge in different instructional settings draws on two larger naturalistic studies that examined how low-income, urban children made sense of classroom instruction in the early grades. The first study investigated children's literacy learning in what are identified here as skills-based classrooms, classrooms with code-focused beginning literacy instruction (Purcell-

Gates & Dahl, 1991). The second study replicated the first using what are identified here as whole language classrooms, classrooms with meaning-focused beginning literacy instruction (Dahl & Freppon, in press). There were several classrooms for each type.

Participants

The six children addressed in this report were part of the two larger studies mentioned above. In those studies, children from each of the two types of classrooms were randomly selected and observed from among those who qualified for the federal free and reduced lunch program. The literacy knowledge of these children was assessed at the beginning of kindergarten and the end of first grade. The written knowledge tapped at the beginning and end of the study included: 1) *intentionality,* defined by asking "Does the child understand that written language carries meaning, that is, is intentional?" 2) *story structure knowledge*—an implicit schema for macrostructure elements of fictional narrative, 3) *written narrative register*—an implicit schema for sentence level features typical of written language, 4) *alphabetic principle*—understanding of ways English written language maps onto oral language or understanding of a grapheme-phoneme relationship, 5) *concepts of writing-reflection* of ways children conceptualize writing as a system (i.e., With the directive to write anything they can, do they draw borders on the paper, draw pictures, write letters, or write words?), 6) *Concepts About Print*—Clay's (1979) test measuring understanding of conventions for reading or writing English. For details on how these assessments were given and analyzed, see Purcell-Gates (1989).

For the current study, we report the data gathered from observations of three of the randomly selected children from each of the two types of classrooms matched on the basis of their pre- and post-measures. None of these six children demonstrated alphabetic knowledge at the beginning of kindergarten, and all learned how to read and write (albeit at different levels of proficiency) by the end of first grade. (We purposely did not choose one child in the whole language group who had alphabetic knowledge at the beginning of kindergarten, nor did we choose a child who was referred to special education.) These children represented the range of experience and learning of the randomly-selected children in each site, from most experienced, to less experienced, to least experienced. Thus, our selection, occurring after observations were completed, was based on comparable beginning of kindergarten and end of first-grade achievement for three matched pairs of children at three levels of achievement. The children we selected from the larger group of children we observed are described below.[1]

Audrey and Charlie: Most Experienced Learners

Audrey (from the skills-based group) and Charlie (from the whole language group) quickly and easily became able students in kindergarten, and they continued to perform at the "top" of their classes. Audrey was pro-active and a diligent worker. She was in the "top" reading group in first grade and was frequently singled out as the "best reader in the class." Charlie was skilled, pro-active, and well-motivated, and in first grade he quickly became one of the most proficient readers.

Mary Ann and Jason: Less Experienced Learners

Mary Ann (from the skills-based group) and Jason (from the whole language group) both fell into the "average" group of learners, according to the assessment procedures of the larger study. Mary Ann was in the "middle" reading group in first grade and has been referred to as a "passive" learner (Purcell-Gates & Dahl, 1991) because she did what she was told in school, but little else, as far as literacy activities. In the early part of kindergarten, Jason seemed to shy away from literacy interactions, but later he became more active. Throughout first grade he said he loved to read and had clear preferences for some books.

Rodney and Ann: The Least Experienced Learners

Rodney (from the skills-based group) and Ann (from the whole language group) were least experienced with literacy activities prior to school, according to our assessments. Rodney began school a happy and motivated learner. He appeared to love story time, but about mid-year, he seemed to struggle to understand instruction and directions. In first grade he was in the middle reading group, but had difficulty there. Ann appeared to love school from the beginning and participated enthusiastically. She seemed to love story time and often looked on as other children read. Ann was motivated to write, but often struggled to do so.

Settings: skills-based and whole language

In both skills-based settings the teachers, Ms. Burke (kindergarten) and Ms. Hinton (first grade), were experienced practitioners who believed in the curriculum and instruction they provided the children. In particular, they believed children should have systematic and sequential phonics instruction as planned and set forth in a published series and that children learn to read from basal stories or other texts tailored to that plan or sequence with respect to new vocabulary. They believed children must first learn a set of sight words and some decoding strategies before actually learning to read. The first-grade teacher believed young children could write, and beginning in January of that year, she provided topics for the children to write about and picture dictionaries for them to use for spelling.

A typical morning in the skills-based first grade usually began with a short independent reading time during which children could silently read texts of their choice. Following independent reading time, Ms. Hinton always conducted whole class reading instruction from the "most advanced" level basal reader, sight word drill and other skill work from the chalkboard or ditto sheets. She regularly taught graphophonic relations to the whole class during these skill lessons using a formal phonics program. Then for about 90 minutes daily, with small groups (based on achievement level) Ms. Hinton conducted reading instruction on the meanings of basal stories, reading for fluency, and decoding unknown words. She often stopped briefly to work with individual children on decoding words during this time. The other children worked at their desks on worksheets dealing with word analysis, phonics, and sight words, or they copied from the board to practice handwriting. The children were expected to complete their work independently. Those children who finished their seatwork could read books, work puzzles, draw, or play language games.

The whole language teachers, Ms. Slimson (kindergarten) and Ms. Headway (first grade) believed that children learn to read and write through meaningful interactions with literate others and good books. The teachers were experienced and understood whole language theory. They read storybooks to children several times a day (to the whole class, small groups, and to individual children). Writing and reading instruction were integrated (e.g., children were encouraged to write about their reading). In first grade the teacher led a structured writing workshop allowing children to write on topics of their choice, alone or in small groups, and helping children during individual conferences. Both the kindergarten and first-grade teachers regularly called children's attention to the graphophonic aspects of written language within the context of reading stories or writing texts. They did this during whole class lessons and briefly with individual children. For example, the kindergarten teacher often asked children to read chorally with her from big books; she then asked the children about the beginning sounds and symbols of the titles of the books. One of the goals of the first-grade teacher was to teach children to use decoding as a strategy for ascertaining unknown words. She taught these skills both incidently and in planned, explicit ways to the whole class under the assumption that children would take from instruction as they could. She also worked with the children who seemed developmentally ready to understand

and use these skills. Thus, there was explicit phonics instruction using literature during reading lessons.

A typical morning in the whole language first grade usually included a meeting to accomplish daily routines such as job assignments, distribution of materials, lunch orders, and discussion of the calendar. Ms. Headway often taught letter/sound relations during this time. For example, she would ask, "Will the person whose name starts with /rrr/ take the lunch count today?" while directing children's attention to Robert's name on the job chart. After read aloud time, Ms. Headway often demonstrated the writing process by writing something, such as the "news" of the day. She frequently called children's attention to the sounds of words as she wrote corresponding letters. Later in the morning during "workshop" time children were encouraged to write by using what they knew of the phonemic nature of language. Their emergent products were always accepted and valued, and children were often helped to spell inventively by the teacher or their peers.

Reading was taught to the whole class using literature. Ms. Headway also used this time to draw children's attention to the alphabetic system and occasionally explicitly taught them about word "families" such as *rag, tag,* and *bag.* In the spring of the year, Ms. Headway also taught the children in small groups, focusing her attention on teaching a variety of reading strategies while the other children read or wrote independently or with a peer, listened to stories on tape, or participated in dramatic play. The teacher's primary focus was on meaning, and skill instruction always occurred in the context of reading, writing, and talking about texts the children enjoyed. Although at times the teachers in both kindergarten and whole language classrooms helped individual children decode or encode, it was always directly connected to understanding a whole text.

Table 1 summarizes the participants in the study and the instructional settings. Table 2 summarizes the instructional procedures, with specific attention to the teaching of alphabetic concepts and skills, in each of the two settings.

Procedures

We observed the teachers, the larger group of children from which the six children in this study were drawn, and their classmates primarily in the morning twice weekly from October of their kindergarten year through the end of first grade. We chose a nonparticipant observer stance and consciously decided to affect the instructional and learning processes as little as possible. Data gathering involved close, systematic, and persistent observation. To document instruction, in our field notes

Table 1

Study Participants

Children	Setting	Experience
Audrey	Skills-based	Most
Charlie	Whole language	Most
Mary Ann	Skills-based	Less
Jason	Whole language	Less
Rodney	Skills-based	Least
Ann	Whole language	Least

Teachers	Setting	Year
Ms. Burke	Skills-based	Kindergarten
Ms. Slimson	Whole language	Kindergarten
Ms. Hinton	Skills-based	First grade
Ms. Headway	Whole language	First grade

we recorded what the teacher and children were doing, (e.g., the teacher works with small reading group, while Rodney completes seatwork; or teacher reads a book to three children, while Ann writes a story with Ashley). We sat physically close to the observed child, recorded what the child and his or her teacher said and did, noted the child's interaction with others, and documented what materials the child used. The observed child wore a remote microphone to enable us to record exact language use. Anyone who came within the range of the microphone was tape-recorded. Therefore, when the teacher or other children interacted with the observed child, we transcribed his or her words. When the teachers asked the observed child questions or tried to help him or her, this was also captured. We also photocopied the children's written work and most texts they read. Finally, we interviewed the teachers informally throughout the school years about their beliefs and practices. In addition, we conducted and tape-recorded formal interviews.

Analysis

The goal of the analysis was to identify each observed child's knowledge and use of the alphabetic system across contexts during both years of school. We examined field notes, transcribed audio-tapes, and coded for talk and action related to each child's use of the system. When children read, wrote, talked, interacted with others, or evidenced any use of alphabetic knowledge in any way, these instances were marked on field notes. Then, using categories derived from the data, yet informed by the collective work of Adams (1990), Sulzby (1985; 1992), Henderson and Beers (1980), Gentry (1987), and Read (1971), we

Table 2

Summary of Instructional Practices

SKILLS-BASED

Approximately one book read aloud daily in kindergarten
Reading readiness program in kindergarten
One letter a week taught in kindergarten
Daily workbooks and worksheets (on letter/sound recognition and matching)
    in kindergarten
Sight words and decoding taught isolation in late kindergarten
Approximately one book read aloud daily in first grade
Basals as primary tool in first grade (whole class and small group)
Seatwork on phonics, other word attack skills and sight words through work
    sheets and oral drill in first grade
Daily phonics instruction with basal words and sentences in first grade
Some self-directed reading time for those who finished seatwork in first grade
Short daily independent reading in first grade
Journal writing with assigned topics and accurate spelling in late first grade

WHOLE LANGUAGE

Several books read aloud daily in kindergarten
Self-selected reading time in kindergarten
Daily writing time (often connected to literature) in kindergarten
Daily News of the Day, choral reading with Big Books, read aloud time, with
    attention to letter/sound relations in kindergarten
Invented spelling encouraged in kindergarten
Several books read aloud daily in first grade
Self-selected reading time in first grade
Writing workshop in first grade (with emphasis on revision and editing as well
    as on writing on self-selected topics)
Lessons on reading and writing (in large groups, small groups, and with indi
    viduals) with attention to letter/sound relations
Invented spelling encouraged
Decoding taught explicitly as a strategy for word identification (incidentally and
    in a planned way for some children)

developed a coding system. These coding categories included: graphemic knowledge, phonemic knowledge, knowledge of sound/symbol correspondences, experimentation with (attention to) sound/symbol correspondences, effective use of sound/symbol correspondences, emergent reading behavior, emergent writing behavior, and level of invented spelling. Each of these categories are defined in the Results section of this paper.

Researchers coded data together and separately, and they refined, elaborated, and added to the existing codes (based on what was shown in the data). Every field note instance of knowledge or use of the alphabetic system, along with the children's emergent reading and writing behaviors, and the contexts in which they occurred, were transferred to data sheets that included the alphabetic knowledge code, the child's reading behavior, the text, writing behavior, and a space for elaborations of the codes. These data sheets were then read and color-coded for ways children showed and used their knowledge of the alphabetic system. The categories of actions were examined by time and by child: The child's first certain instance of demonstrated alphabetic knowledge (using conservative judgments of inclusion in each of the categories) were noted. Finally, the categories were described using examples from transcribed tapes and field notes. Table 3 summarizes the procedures.

Table 3

Data Collection and Analysis Procedures

DATA COLLECTION

1. Two observations weekly for two years of literacy instruction
2. Sample observations of entire school day
3. Primarily nonparticipatory observations
4. Field notes on focal child and instruction
5. Audiotape recording of all focal child's talk and instruction within tape's range
6. Probes of children about their work
7. Collection of reading and writing texts and documents
8. Informal and formal interviews with classroom teachers

DATA ANALYSIS

1. Field notes, transcripts, probes, and interviews incorporated into field note data
2. Instruction and literacy behaviors coded
3. Behaviors related to alphabetic knowledge coded
4. Literacy behaviors and alphabetic knowledge (informed by the work of Adams, 1990; Gentry, 1987; Henderson & Beers, 1980; Read, 1971; Sulzby, 1985; 1992) entered onto data sheets that include name, date, context, reading and writing behaviors, level of invented spelling
5. Data sheets reviewed and coded for different ways children showed their knowledge and use of the alphabetic system
6. Progression of alphabetic knowledge by each individual child (through examining the kinds of texts read and written the ways they used alphabetic knowledge, peer and teacher interactions, and the time frame in which these occurred)
7. Categories that formed the pattern of development explicated in this article with each child's first evidence of the alphabetic knowledge of that category used as the example

Results

The six children that we matched in pairs on the basis of comparable achievement at the end of first grade had all learned alphabetic concepts and skills during their first two years of school, although at different rates of proficiency acquisition. The children's knowledge of the alphabetic system was demonstrated in several different ways during their first two years of school. All 6 children exhibited largely the same chronological acquisition pattern regardless of instructional setting. The sophistication of knowledge and rate of acquisition of alphabetic awareness were also very similar by case study, as shown by the dates in which the children first exhibited a particular behavior or concept (see Table 4).

The differences found in this two-year study were not in how fast or how well children learned the alphabetic system, but in what the children did with their new knowledge. Children in the skills-based group, for the most part, exhibited alphabetic knowledge when they decoded isolated words or individual words in basal sentences. Audrey, the most proficient learner, also used her alphabetic knowledge to do some writing across the two years. In contrast, all 3 children in the whole language group used their alphabetic knowledge to read literature and to write extensively on self-selected topics daily during kindergarten and first grade. The differences resulted from the children's instructional settings, primarily due to the differences in texts the children read and wrote and the differences in interactions with their teachers and peers. The pattern of development and discussion of the concepts and skills the children exhibited are described below.

The pattern of alphabetic knowledge acquisition

The acquisition of alphabetic knowledge is presented chronologically, according to when all or most of the children's *first* documented understanding or use of knowledge occurred. Thus, the categories show the acquisition pattern across instructional settings. Differences in texts children read and wrote, and interaction patterns, are noted in the examples, marked either skills-based or whole language. The examples are selected to represent each child and both instructional settings equally while still using a typical example that reflected all children. Although the knowledge and skill acquisition categories are depicted through three examples, all 6 children's first examples are dated in Table 4.

Children's development of alphabetic knowledge was captured in five broad categories of behaviors that included their development of: 1) *sound sense*, 2) *sound/symbol sense*, 3) *experimentation with the alphabetic*

Table 4

Date of Demonstration of Each Child's Acquisition of an Alphabetic Knowledge or Skill

Knowledge/Skill	Audrey (SB	Charlie (WL)	Mary Ann (SB)	Jason (WL)	Rodney (SB)	Ann (WL)
Sound sense	K - Mar	K -Jan	K - Mar	K - Jan	K - May	K - Feb
Sound/symbol sense	K - Jan	K - Feb	FG - Sep	K - Feb	FG - Oct	K - Feb
Experimentation:						
oral	K - Apr	Not clear	FG - Dec	K - Apr	FG - Oct	K - May
reading	K - Dec	FG - Sep	FG - Jan	K - Apr	FG - Mar	FG - Jan
writing	FG - Nov	K - Mar	Not clear	K - Feb	FG - Jan	FG - Feb
Effective use of alphabetic knowledge with help:	FG - Sep	K - Mar	FG - Jan	FG - Sep	FG - Mar	FG - Oct
reading	FG - Dec	FG - Dec	FG - Feb	FG - Mar	FG - May	FG - May
writing	FG - Jan	FG - Sep	Not clear	FG - Oct	FG - Apr	FG - Apr

system for reading or writing, 4) *successful use of the alphabetic system with help,* and 5) *successful use of the alphabetic information independently.* Within these categories, further differentiation of developmental patterns are described in each section.

Sound Sense. All 6 children in this study demonstrated the ability to hear matching sounds in words during their kindergarten year, with Audrey's and Charlie's acquisition documented months before Rodney's and Ann's. The children showed awareness that certain words have the same sounds as others, such as in rhyme or beginning alliteration, or simply that the orally recalled letter 'm' "goes with" /m/. Students revealed their knowledge in recognition activities (such as by matching a picture of a hat with a horse) or in production tasks (when providing a rhyming word for a given word).

In the skills-based classrooms, recognition of similar sounds was most often exhibited during oral drill of beginning sound matches or when the lesson focused on the recognition of rhyming words. In the kindergarten whole language classroom, this knowledge was often exhibited during story time when the teacher, Ms. Slimson, explicitly pointed out and asked about sounds of words and their corresponding symbols or when the children wrote. Children usually responded to story time and writing sessions by echoing sounds under their breath or by answering the teachers' questions about similar sounds and their letters.

The following examples depict children in both settings.

> *Example:*
> Audrey looks at the chart that exhibits rhyming words and says, "corn-horn, hen-pen, cat-hat, rug-bug." (Skills-based, K:1/14)

> *Example:*
> Mary Ann is asked to produce the letter that "goes with" the word 'seal,' she cannot do it, but she does say, "Saw? See? /ssss/?" (Skills-based, K:3/15)

> *Example:*
> Charlie is asked by the researcher to tell about his work, and upon showing his product he says, "It starts like snake." (Whole Language, K:1/24)

According to Adams (1990), one of the first signs of alphabetic knowledge acquisition is to hear matching sounds in words. Adams explains that recognition of rhymes and phonemes is a prerequisite to learning and using the alphabetic system, with recognition of rhymes developing early and easily. Interestingly, all 6 children demonstrated this awareness early in their development and before their use of sounds and symbols to read or write.

The notable difference in these examples is not the knowledge the children acquired, but in what else the children were doing. In the skills-based classroom, children acquired sound sense primarily through completing teacher-assigned worksheets, while the children's work in the whole language classroom reflected their personal agenda. The children in the whole language classrooms acquired critical alphabetic understandings through doing work that was functional. This point becomes increasingly obvious the closer the children come to conventional literacy.

Sound/Symbol Sense. In kindergarten, all 6 children learned that sounds correspond to symbols in written language. Some demonstrated this knowledge when trying to complete a worksheet (e.g., a child asks, "What goes with /k/?"), while others used the information to begin to identify words or write. The concept that letters correspond to sounds was emphasized during instruction in both instructional settings. In the skills-based classrooms, this knowledge was primarily exhibited in whole-class oral drill activities of letter/sound correspondences. In kindergarten the teacher usually did not refer to the written grapheme, only the oral name. In the whole language classrooms sound/symbol correspondence knowledge was exhibited most often as children wrote, even when their typical writing strategy was to write a string of random letters, copy, or write what they knew by heart (e.g., a child might work on one sound, then finish her text with random letters). Sound/symbol knowledge was also shown during story time in the kindergarten and first grade year as the teachers asked questions about letters that match sounds in the books read.

> *Example:*
> Ms. Burke reviews the work sheet the children are to work on independently. She asks the class, "What sound does 'h' make?" Audrey responds in unison with some of the others, "/huh huh/."
> "L?" continues the teacher.
> "/Llll/," Audrey says.
> "M?" asks Ms. Burke.
> Audrey responds "/mmm/." (Skills-based, K:1/26)

> *Example:*
> During a whole class lesson on beginning sounds, Ms. Hinton asks Mary Ann, "What sound does 'h' make?" Mary Ann says, "/huh huh huh/." (Skills-based, F:9/9)

> *Example:*
> Ann is at the table writing when a child asks, "How do you write 'Freddy?' Ann responds, "I hear a 'E' in Freddy. 'E.'" (Whole Language, K:2/14)

Children learned both the phonemic nature of words (as in Ann's example) and that letters correspond to sounds (as in Audrey's and Mary Ann's examples) early in their development. Quite understandably, the skills-based group learned correspondences separate from learning words (that was how they were taught) through doing worksheets and oral drill. In contrast, the whole language group learned letter/sound relations along with recognition of beginning sounds of words, usually during story reading episodes.

For all 6 children, the use of *beginning* sounds of words to identify them or to write came at the same time or soon after they began learning sound/symbol correspondences. The children often used the beginning sounds to write or to decode with little or no regard for the rest of the printed word. Sometimes children used the beginning sounds appropriately but were not successful in identifying words or conventionally spelling them.

In the skills-based kindergarten classroom the emphasis was on learning the beginning sounds of words orally (e.g., the teacher was heard saying, "M like in /m m mother/") and learning printed words by sight (mostly through flash cards of number and color words). Most printed words and all phonics related to word reading was taught only in first grade. Audrey, however, was able to use her alphabetic skill to ascertain the "sight" words, as the next example shows.

In the whole language group, children used the beginning sounds of letters most often during writing time in both kindergarten and first grade. These children also began to use beginning sounds when reading familiar books.

Example:
Ms. Burke directs the children's attention to the ditto page that has several color words on it (for sight word practice). She tells the children to find the word 'blue' and color in the corresponding box. Audrey scans all the words, mouthing the beginning sounds of each. She finds blue and mouths "/bl bl bl/," then colors the box. She finishes the page in this way, correctly coloring the boxes. (Skills-based, K:3/11)

Example:
During the reading aloud of a basal sentence in first grade, Mary Ann miscues by reading 'turtle' for 'that.' She looks hard at the words and says, "/t t t turtle/." (Skills-based, F:10/26)

Example:
Jason begins his story about getting new shoes on his birthday. He says to himself, slowly and distinctly, "In my birthday . . . ," and he carefully makes an 'N,' then an 'F' beside it. He turns to Charlie and announces he can't make an 'M.' After help, he continues

sounding out his message and he writes 'birthday' as 'bd.' (Whole Language, K:2/12).

The children's focus on the beginning sounds of words confirms much of the research synthesized by Adams (1990) indicating that children more easily identify initial consonant sounds than endings or vowels. Clearly, both instructional settings emphasized beginning sounds, and beginning sounds are more informative about words than endings sounds. Awareness and use of beginning sounds of words is a natural developmental step for children to take in acquiring alphabetic knowledge because of the "psychological reality" of onsets and rimes of words (Adams, 1990, p. 312). As was typical with other concepts developed, the children in the skills-based classroom most often demonstrated their knowledge through their work on dittos or reading of the basal. In contrast, children in the whole language classrooms demonstrated their knowledge through obtaining and giving help as they read self-selected books and wrote their own texts.

Experimentation with the Alphabetic System. Most of the children chose to "play with" the sounds of language. This occurred without an apparent function other than to experiment. For example, after a lesson on rhyming words one day, Rodney humorously said to a classmate who was leaving, "Bye Jon Bon," indicating his recognition of rhyme and his tendency to "play with" language. With some of the children, experimentation of the alphabetic system also occurred when they attempted to read or write.

In the skills-based classroom, the oral experimentation was evident as the three children were often observed mumbling sounds under their breaths as the teacher sounded out words or another child read. However, these children rarely experimented with the alphabetic system when reading or writing. This may have been due to their instructional context, a context that called for accuracy when reading or writing.

In the whole language classrooms, oral experimentation with sounds occurred nearly year-round during both years. However, it occurred most extensively as children began to catch on to the system. This was evident during story time as their teacher talked about sounds and during writing time as they talked about (but not necessarily used) the sounds in words. The children in the whole language classrooms also experimented with the alphabetic system when reading and writing. In writing, they used sound/symbol relations for part of their texts, and integrated random letters, copying, writing what they knew automatically, or drawing to communicate their meanings. Thus, their written

texts were not yet readable to others, even though they had some command of the code. The examples include an oral, reading, and writing
occurrence of experimentation.

> *Example:*
> After Ms. Hinton explains the directions for completing the work-
> sheet, she reminds the children they could figure out words by
> looking at the first letter and thinking about the sound that goes
> with it, "like 'm' goes /m/," she says. Rodney responds by saying
> to himself, /m . . . m . . . m . . . monkey/." (Skills-based, F:10/13)

> *Example:*
> Ms. Slimson holds the book *You Can* in front of Jason and says,
> "Look at the title, what does it say? Read it with me. . . You Can."
> Jason very deliberately reads "you /c ca n/," emphasizing the
> sounds as he studies the print. (Whole language, K:4/2)

> *Example:*
> Early in first grade, Jason experiments with the code, using some
> of it functionally, but using random letters as well. One day he
> writes 'tBL iLDere tailspin snac tdll' and reads it as, "I like to play
> T-ball. I like Derek. We like to watch Tailspin. We like to watch
> snakes down in Kentucky. We like turtles." He writes this story by
> using the code, copying text, and getting help from his teacher and
> peers to spell the word 'tailspin.' (Whole language, F:10/8)

This behavior shows the development of metacognitive understandings about the alphabetic code. It differs from learning "sound
sense" and "sound/symbol sense" in that it is self-initiated, and children at this stage now appear conscious of their knowledge and use of
sounds and/or symbols. All 6 children appeared to "study" the print
to some extent, regardless of instructional context, exhibiting this behavior under their breaths. These actions contribute to the research on
children's development toward conventional reading and writing. Children often go through a period in which they lend conscious attention
to sounds and sound/symbol relations of words, exhibiting their
graphophonic knowledge before they actually read or write conventionally to communicate (Sulzby, 1985).

The children's experimentation with the alphabetic system to write
was illustrative of Gentry's (1987) "deviant" or "pre-phenomic"
stages of spelling development. Although there was some evidence
of the code in use, all salient sounds were not yet mapped, and these
children appeared to write random strings of letters with
sound/symbol mapping, possibly also using what they knew about
the visual "look" of a word.

Later in the school year, these interactions with the code moved to
a period of extensive experimentation with the alphabetic system to

read. The six children went through a period of overusing alphabetic knowledge when they "read," such that their renditions of texts sounded like unsuccessful attempts at decoding. This action occurred with children in both classroom settings and with many different kinds of texts, including those the children had previously "read" from memory.

Example:
Mary Ann reads the first page of a basal text during the morning silent reading time. For the sentence that reads, "'Mrs. Lee, see what I have!' said Meg," Mary Ann reads, "/may. . . may. . . as / see /this. . . i . . . i . . . o/ Meg." (Skills-based, F:1/17)

Example:
Rodney reads a favorite book during morning silent reading. He had previously read the pictures and read from memory, but in this instance, he focuses closely on the sound/symbol relations. His rendition includes, "Ed was /boo . . . d- do . . . is . . . ee . . . es. . . es/ let's . . . let's play mong-ster Eddie /s/ said Alice." (Skills-based, F:3/1)

Example:
Jason reads *Rudolph* a picture book of the popular song that Jason knew by heart, focusing on the code when he reads. He reads, ". . . and if you /eh v er/ saw him you would /ee v en/ say it glows." (Whole language, F:12/10)

This reading behavior is characteristic of "aspectual" reading (Sulzby, 1985) that occurs when children focus on one aspect of written language to the exclusion of other aspects as they emerge as readers. Despite the differences in instruction, these six children acquired this strategy in a similar developmental chronology.

Successful Use of the Alphabetic System with Help. This action involved children's effective use of the code for reading or writing with help from their teacher or a peer.

In the skills-based classroom, this kind of interaction occurred only in first grade and usually happened during whole class instruction when children read aloud individually from a chart or the blackboard. The teacher's goal was to help students learn to decode and to learn sight words from the basal texts. In the whole language classrooms, the teachers also often helped children to read by using the code as a word-getting strategy, usually in a one-on-one situation as the child read a self-selected book. It also frequently occurred when the teachers helped the children write by sounding the words for them as they wrote words they wanted.

Example:
Ms. Hinton directs Mary Ann's attention to the second sentence on the board (She got a red rose.) and asks her to read it. Mary Ann begins, "She gets-"
Ms. Hinton interrupts, "How many vowels in that word?"
"One."
"So the 'O' says . . . " Mary Ann is silent, so Ms. Hinton says, "/ah/. 'G' says /guh/, 'o' says /ah/, so'g-o' says . . . "
"Go," Mary Ann answers.
"Not this time, you told me the 'o' says . . . "/ah/."
"Put the 'g' in front of /ah/," Ms. Hinton prompts.
Mary Ann is silent, so Ms. Hinton provides the sound, "/gah/."
Mary Ann says, "Got."
"Right, keep going."
Mary Ann continues reading the sentence, "She got a red . . .
"How many vowels in the word?"
"Two."
Ms. Hinton prompts, "'R-o' says . . ."
"/r . . . roe/."
"Good, put the 's' on it."
" / rose /. Rose. "
"Very good, now read it aloud."
Mary Ann rereads the sentence, "She got a red rose."
    (Skills-based, F:1/11)

Example:
Ms. Slimson gets out the predictable Big Book, *The Ghost*, and points to the word 'see' and asks, "What is the first letter?"
Charlie says, " 'S'."
Ms. Slimson continues, "and after that is what?"
Charlie says, "'E'."
"Look at the letter and figure it out . . . /sss/ . . ."
Charlie says, "I know it! I know it. See! See!"
    (Whole language, K:3/22)

Example:
Ms. Headway looks on as Ann and Pam look at *Witches in the Wind*. She reads to them, "Witches in the . . . "
Both children say, "sky."
"What's it start with Ann? Look at the sounds here,"
Ms. Headway says as she points to the word 'wind.'
"Witch," Ann tries.
"Witches in the *wind*," her teacher says, "Oh, you are looking. Good job, you are pointing to the words." (Whole language, F:10/31)

Although the children had alphabetic knowledge at this period in their development, they could not use it without help. In the skills-based classroom help occurred with basal texts, whereas in the whole language classroom children were helped to read texts of their choosing.

In both settings, the teachers tried to get children to focus on words and to use decoding as a strategy when they read.

Successful, Independent Use of the Alphabetic System. As the children moved toward conventional writing, they began to consistently and systematically use sound/symbol relations to spell. The children followed patterns of Read (1971) and Gentry's (1987) developmental stages of spelling. At this point in their development, they usually communicated by using phonemic or transitional spelling (Gentry) and were considered conventional writers, defined as the point at which the text is readable to another conventionally literate person (Sulzby, 1992).

In the skills-based classrooms, successful use of graphophonics to write was less evident, likely due to the children's understanding that they were to spell conventionally. In the whole language classroom, effective use of the code occurred soon after the children's experimental phase.

> *Example:*
> Audrey's first documented effective use of the code to write is in January when she writes, in response to a prompt, 'Mr. Fig is my bast cariter in Mr. Fig book. He is so fat but I sil like him. He is so friandle. He is so nis in the book,' for Mr. Fig is my best character in *Mr. Fig* book. He is so fat but I still like him. He is so friendly. He is so nice in the book. (Skills-based, F:1/25)

> *Example:*
> Charlie begins using the code systematically such that others can read his texts in early first grade. He writes 'I ws writing my wirs bk house,' for "I was riding my horse back home." (Whole language, F:9/17)

> *Example:*
> Jason begins to use the code systematically in October of first grade. He writes a story one day, using the code as his primary strategy. He writes, 'I lic Brian Hyasnis we pla on the plagrn wy r gog t pajr toda I lic Brian' for "I like Brian, He is nice. We play on the playground. We are going to pictures today. I like Brian." (Whole language, F:10/10)

Most of the children became conventional writers before they became conventional readers. Gunderson and Shapiro (1988) suggest that children learn the code most effectively when they write, especially when there is a need to communicate in ways others can understand. Successful use of the alphabetic system to read was evident at the same time or soon after children's use of the system to write. By the end of first grade, all six children used decoding as a tool for comprehending texts, even quite lengthy texts. All the children read individual words by sight, and some read books from memory and sight, before they began to use the code to read. Orchestration of alphabetic knowledge to read was documented only when children either miscued or decoded in ways that made obvious their use of sound/symbol relations.

In the skills-based first grade, examples were captured most often with trade books, rather than their often-read basals, because their oral reading of basals was often accurate, making it difficult to observe graphophonic strategies. In the whole language first grade, children read many books every day, so they exhibited more graphophonic miscues, indicating their use of alphabetic knowledge. Examples document the children's first successful use of graphophonics to read whole text.

Example:
Audrey reads *There's an Alligator Under My Bed.* On pages six and seven the text says, 'But they never saw it. It was up to me. I just had to do something about that alligator.' Audrey reads, "But they /nav/ . . . /n-niv er/ never . . . /s/ . . . /so/ it . . . /seel/ seed it. It was up to me. I just had to do some . . . things . . . /a boat/ . . . (glances at picture that shows a board used as a plank for the bed) . . . a-board that alligator." (Skills-based F:12/8)

Example:
Rodney reads *A Monster is Coming,* his favorite book, using decoding as a strategy. He reads, "Eddie was bored. There was /nut/ . . . nothing to do. He had /k . . . k . . . k/ come—Rodney continues, sounding out the very predictable words he had previously read simply by looking at the pictures, such as 'nose,' 'legs,' 'feet,' and 'hands.' (Skills-based, F:5/11)

Example:
Ann reads *Two Little Dogs,* using decoding as a strategy and self-correcting miscues. "They saw a /buh buh/ big, big dog," she reads. After she finishes, she reads the entire book again fluently and accurately, substituting 'the' for 'they,' then self-correcting. (Whole language, F:5/10)

When examining each child's behaviors, the individuality of the learners is evident. For example, Jason acquired knowledge of sounds and symbols by February of kindergarten, and this knowledge was metacognitive, shown by his experimentation with sounds and symbols as he wrote. Audrey, on the other hand, learned sounds and symbols early in kindergarten, but did not show a metacognitive understanding until well into first grade. Also, Charlie's and Mary Ann's knowledge was not always apparent, simply because they did not verbalize this kind of information as much as did the other children; hence, they received "not clear" notations for some of the behaviors. Each of the six children in this study learned to orchestrate alphabetic knowledge with knowledge of stories, syntax, and the process of reading by the end of first grade, with Audrey and Charlie reading more complex texts than Rodney and Ann.

Discussion

The six children in this study gradually increased their alphabetic knowledge and use, becoming more knowledgeable about the code before they could read or write conventionally. Although experimentation with the code (to spell inventively or read aspectually, for example) appeared early on, the children acquired some alphabetic knowledge before they read and wrote conventionally. Certainly, their experiences with print enabled them to become more sophisticated users of the code, but for these six children reading and writing particular texts and the teachers' instructional interactions did not make much difference in whether they acquired alphabetic knowledge and skill.

The differences in rates of learning and depth of the individual children's alphabetic knowledge by the end of first grade had to do with each child's developing knowledge and prior experiences. This helps explain why Audrey and Charlie (the most experienced learners in each setting) moved to conventional writing and reading before Rodney and Ann. The children's acquisition pattern confirms research that suggests some alphabetic knowledge is essential to becoming conventionally literate. As the children developed more sophisticated uses of alphabetic knowledge, they moved through the emergent literacy stages documented by other researchers (Adams, 1990; Biemiller, 1970; Ferriero & Teberosky, 1983; Gentry, 1987; Read, 1971; Sulzby, 1985). These researchers have shown that children are able to "orchestrate" the many necessary concepts and skills for conventional reading and writing only after they have alphabetic knowledge. This study confirms that finding. Importantly, while the children in the whole language setting showed their knowledge more frequently, the overall pattern of acquisition across the two years was similar, regardless of the kind of instruction children received, as long as they received some instruction on the code. A discussion of this developmental progression follows.

Developmental progression

All 6 children moved from highly contextualized readings and writings to more differentiated behaviors in which they used alphabetic knowledge regardless of their instructional setting. They first gained a sense of rhyme, alliteration, and rhythm in language, and soon after, they began to associate sounds with symbols. In both instructional settings, children learned these concepts early in their schooling, similar to what is shown by studies of children who learn to read at home (Bissex, 1980; Sulzby, 1985). It seems these concepts are learned through interactions with texts and others (Freppon & Dahl, 1991; Mills, O'Keefe, & Stephens, 1992; Reid, 1993; Schickedanz, 1990).

Most of the children spent time focused on sound/symbol relations as they wrote, and all six children spent time in sound/symbol "study" as they read in emergent ways. This "experimentation" may explain why some children have been found to have less trouble decoding nonsense syllables than familiar, meaningful words (Adams, 1990). It seems the children were further refining their alphabetic knowledge during this period, as indicated by their later moves toward more conventional literacy behaviors. The children gained metacognitive understandings (Sulzby & Teale, 1991; Yaden & Templeton, 1986) from this experimentation. These understandings appeared earlier and more frequently in the whole language classrooms, possibly because children's experimentation (and talk) were supported. This also helps explain why, in the Dahl and Freppon study (in press), children who received whole language instruction were using alphabetic knowledge more frequently in mid-first grade than children in the skills-based classrooms. However, all 6 children eventually indicated their metacognitive understandings.

All 6 learners focused on words and word-getting as they emerged as readers, confirming that word identification, in concert with other aspects of literacy, is indeed an important part of literacy acquisition (Adams, 1990; Ehri, 1991; Lomax & McGee, 1987; Stanovich, 1991). All the children also moved through a period in which they could successfully use alphabetic knowledge with some kind of help. In the skills-based classrooms, the teachers helped the children decode so as to ascertain unknown words and successfully read basal sentences. The children in the whole language classrooms were often "scaffolded" in one-on-one situations in which they were attempting to read or write whole texts. These scaffoldings look much like those shown by Vygotsky (1978). This indicated that when children were in this period, they were in the "zone of proximal development" (p. 78), in which they were able to learn with and through teachers and peers in ways that enabled them to use the knowledge independently later.

The six children in both instructional settings engaged in talk and action that revealed learning of concepts and skills that were not part of the primary instructional focus of those classrooms. The three children in the accuracy-focused, skills-based classrooms wrote by way of invented spelling, art, and talk even though these were not sanctioned activities. These children also read in unconventional "aspectual" ways during independent reading time. The three children in the whole language classroom learned rhyming words and other forms of alliteration, the sounds that matched symbols, and how to use beginning sounds to ascertain words, even though they did not experience traditional practice in systematic and sequential phonics. Although meaning-making was always the overall goal of the whole language teachers, the teachers helped children focus on the code when they worked with the children individually or in small groups. The difference was that the help occurred as children needed it, not because they were following a specific curricular scope and sequence. These learners also focused on sounds and symbols to the exclusion of meaning even when the curriculum remained meaning-focused.

Conclusions

This study contributes to our understanding of how children develop alphabetic knowledge and the effect their instruction has on their learning. It points to several common features in the instructional programs for these six children: time for reading self-selected texts, at least some writing, and explicit phonics instruction. However, while it supports Chall's conclusion that phonics instruction is a necessary ingredient in beginning reading instruction, it suggests that such instruction can successfully take place in very different instructional contexts. Although all four teachers directly taught about sounds and symbols and their relations every day, instruction was contextualized differently. Being explicit did not always mean using specific instructional sequences or teaching phonics in isolation. Thus, it helps move the "Great Debate" along by suggesting it might be better not to categorize instruction as either/or (phonics or meaning-focused).

   This study shows that students can learn alphabetic knowledge in whole language classrooms. Phonics instruction does not have to be random or eclectic, but can be carefully planned and well thought through in whole language. The two whole language classrooms were well grounded in whole language philosophy during both years. They both provided the kinds of learning opportunities typical of this curriculum. These two teachers should be seen as individual instantiations of whole language. Despite what some may believe about the place of phonics in whole language instruction, each teacher valued the graphophonic cueing system, and her teaching reflected this. Phonics instruction was an integral part of the daily classroom interactions. These two teachers deliberately and explicitly provided this instruction to the whole class, to small groups, and to individuals.

However, the results of this study cannot be generalized. Our analysis may not have identified all that the children knew or did not know about the alphabetic nature of language. The pattern of alphabetic knowledge acquisition shown in this study is also limited by what the children did not show. Nor do we know—because these six children were selected on the basis of similar achievement to enable us to compare their developmental patterns—whether one approach might have been more beneficial than the other to a larger number of children in these classes.

Future research will contribute to increased knowledge about children's development of alphabetic understanding. We need more naturalistic and longitudinal studies of children's development in different instructional settings, particularly with children who have few literacy experiences outside of school. The following questions require further study: What lies beneath the labels of various instructional approaches that truly benefits children? How do teachers meet the individual needs of a diverse group of children in different instructional settings? Why do some children not learn alphabetic concepts or skills, or seem not to orchestrate this knowledge to read and write? What are the long-term outcomes from different instructional settings?

Note

1. Altogether, 12 randomly selected children from each of the three sites in the original, skills-based study (N = 36) and 12 children from each of the two sites in the follow-up whole language study (N = 24) were assessed on the measures. The children in this study were selected from these groups.

References

Adams, M.J. (1990). *Beginning to read: Thinking and learning about print.* Cambridge, MA: The MIT Press.

Ball, E.W., & Blachman, B.A. (1991). Does phoneme segmentation training in kindergarten make a difference in early word recognition and developmental spelling? *Reading Research Quarterly, 26,* 49–66.

Biemiller, A. (1970). The development of the use of graphic and contextual information as children learn to read. *Reading Research Quarterly, 6,* 77–96.

Bissex, G.L. (1980). *GNYS at work: A child learns to read and write.* Cambridge, MA: Harvard University Press.

Chall, J. (1967). *Learning to read: The great debate.* New York: McGraw-Hill.

Clay, M. M. (1979). *Early detection of reading difficulties.* Portsmouth, NH: Heinemann.

Dahl, K.L., & Freppon, P.A. (in press). A comparison of inner-city children's interpretation of reading and writing instruction in the early grades in skills-based and whole language settings. *Reading Research Quarterly.*

Daiute, C. (1990). The role of play in writing development. *Research in the Teaching of English, 24,* 4–47.

Dyson, A.H. (1991). Viewpoints: The word and the world—reconceptualizing written language development, or do rainbows mean a lot to little girls? *Research in the Teaching of English, 25,* 97–123.

Ehri, L.C. (1991). The development of the ability to read words. In R. Barr, M.L. Kamil, P. Mosenthal, & P.D. Pearson (Eds.), *Handbook of reading research: Vol. II* (pp. 383–417). New York: Longman.

Ferriero, E., & Teberosky, A. (1983). *Literacy before schooling.* Exeter, NH: Heinemann.

Freppon, P.A. (1991). Children's concepts of the nature and purpose of reading in different instructional settings. *Journal of Reading Behavior: A Journal of Literacy, 23,* 139–67.

Freppon, P.A., & Dahl, K.L. (1991). Learning about phonics in a whole language classroom. *Language Arts, 68,* 190–98.

Gentry, R. (1987). *Spel is a four letter word.* Portsmouth, NH: Heinemann.

Gibson, E.J. (1972). Reading for some purpose. In J.F. Kavanaugh & I.G. Mattingly (Eds.), *Language by ear and by eye* (pp. 3–19). Cambridge, MA: MIT Press.

Goswami, U., & Meade, F. (1992). Onset and rime awareness and analogies in reading. *Reading Research Quarterly, 27,* 152–63.

Gough, P.B., & Hillinger, M.L. (1980). Learning to read: An unnatural act. *Bulletin of the Orton Society, 30,* 180–96.

Gunderson, L., & Shapiro, J. (1988). Whole language instruction: Writing in first grade. *The Reading Teacher, 40,* 430–37.

Henderson, E.H., & Beers, J.W. (1980). *Developmental and cognitive aspects of learning to spell: A reflection of word knowledge.* Newark, DE: International Reading Association.

Hubbard, R. (1990). There's more than black and white in literacy's palette: Children's use of color. *Language Arts, 67,* 492–500.

Juel, C. (1991). Beginning reading. In R. Barr, M.L. Kamil, P. Mosenthal, & P.D. Pearson (Eds.), *Handbook of reading research: Vol. II* (pp. 759–88). New York: Longman.

Lomax, R.G., & McGee, L.M. (1987). Young children's concepts about print and reading: Toward a model of word-reading acquisition. *Reading Research Quarterly, 22,* 237–56.

Mason, J. (1980). When do children begin to read: An exploration of four-year-old children's letter and word reading competencies. *Reading Research Quarterly, 2,* 203–28.

McIntyre, E. (1990). Young children's reading strategies as they read self-selected books in school. *Early Childhood Research Quarterly, 5,* 265–77.

McIntyre, E. (1992). Individual literacy instruction for young low-SES learners in traditional urban classrooms. *Reading Research and Instruction, 31,* 53–63.

Mills, H., O'Keefe, T., & Stephens, D. (1992). *Looking closely: Phonics in a whole language classroom.* Portsmouth, NH: Heinemann.

Morrow, L. (1992). The impact of a literature-based program on literacy achievement, use of literature, and attitudes of children from minority backgrounds. *Reading Research Quarterly, 27*, 250–75.

Purcell-Gates, V. (1989). Written language knowledge held by low-SES inner-city children upon entering kindergarten. In S. McCormick & J. Zutell (Eds.), *Cognitive and social perspectives for literacy research and instruction: Thirty-eighth yearbook of the National Reading Conference* (pp. 95-106). Chicago: National Reading Conference.

Purcell-Gates, V., & Dahl, K.L. (1991). Low-SES children's success and failure at literacy learning in skills-based classrooms. *Journal of Reading Behavior, 23*, 1–34.

Read, C. (1971). Pre-school children's knowledge of English phonology. *Harvard Educational Review, 41*, 1–34.

Reid, K. (1993). Another vision of 'visions and revisions.' *Remedial and Special Education, 14*, 14–16.

Resnick, L.B. (1979). Theories and prescriptions for early reading instruction. In L.B. Resnick & P.A. Weaver, (Eds.), *Theory and practice of early reading: Vol. II* (pp. 321–38). Hillsdale, NJ: Erlbaum.

Schickedanz, J. (1990). *Adam's righting revolutions: One child's literacy development from infancy through grade one.* New York: Heinemann.

Stanovich, K.E. (1991). Word recognition: Changing perspectives. In R. Barr, M.L. Kamil, P. Mosenthal, & P.D. Pearson (Eds.), *Handbook of reading research: Vol. II* (pp. 418–52). New York: Longman.

Sulzby, E. (1985). Children's emergent reading of favorite storybooks: A developmental study. *Reading Research Quarterly, 20*, 451–58.

Sulzby, E. (1992). Transitions from emergent to conventional writing. *Language Arts, 69*, 290–97.

Sulzby, E., & Teale, W. (1991). Emergent literacy. In R. Barr, M.L. Kamil, P. Mosenthal, & P.D. Pearson (Eds.) *Handbook of reading research: Vol. II* (pp. 727–58). New York: Longman.

Yaden, D.B., & Templeton, S. (Eds.). (1986). *Metalinguistic awareness and beginning literacy.* Portsmouth, NH: Heinemann.

Vygotsky, L.V. (1978). *Mind in society: The development of higher psychological processes.* Cambridge, MA: Harvard University Press.

Winsor, P.J.T. (1990, November). *Developing phonemic awareness: Knowledge and practice in holistic instruction.* Paper presented at the National Reading Conference, Miami, FL.

Yopp, H.K. (1992). Developing phonemic awareness in young children. *The Reading Teacher, 45*, 696–707.

8 Phonological Awareness Training of Kindergarten Children: Three Treatments and Their Effects

Linda R. Ayres
Oakland University

A major purpose of Ayres's (1993) study was to combine literature-based, child-centered pedagogy with the concepts of phonemic awareness training that had emerged from quantitative research, so that teachers could teach phonemic awareness in the classroom without compromising their pedagogical or theoretical beliefs about learning. To this end, she investigated the efficacy of three training conditions upon the phonological awareness of kindergarten children, and the possible effects on reading achievement at the end of first grade. This article is based upon her dissertation, which in 1995 was named Outstanding Dissertation of the Year by the International Reading Association.

The children in the experimental groups received an experimental treatment for 20 minutes a day for ten weeks, during the first half of their kindergarten year. During the second half of the year, the treatment conditions were reversed, so that each group received a second, different experimental treatment. This enabled Ayres to investigate not merely the question of which experimental treatment was most successful, but which combinations and in what order.

Treatment Group A received direct instruction in phonological awareness, using puppets, oral language stories, games, and songs. Treatment Group B was taught through an indirect, literature-based approach. Attention to rhyme and alliteration derived from text and involved book-making and writing activities to emphasize those phonological characteristics. Treatment Group AB combined the direct approach of Treatment A with the indirect approach of Treatment B: essentially, the puppets interacted with literature to deliver lessons in phonological awareness. For all three groups, invented spelling was instructed mainly at a writing center. Treatment Group X served as a comparison group. This group was given an alternate treatment for 20 minutes a day in an area unrelated to phonological awareness training, but nevertheless worthy of instructional time: story mapping and retelling after shared reading, facilitated by a felt board and cutouts. Treatment Group Y was the control group. The children in this group received no instruction in phonological awareness other than that in the regular district kindergarten program, where they were routinely exposed to a variety of literacy experiences, including interaction with letter names and letter sounds (1993, pp. 41–42; p. 154).

During the first treatment period, all but one of the treatment groups showed growth in phonological awareness: Treatment A appears to have had the greatest effect on children's ability to segment; Treatment B indicated a significant effect on rhyming, beginning and ending phonemes; and Treatment X also showed a significant effect when compared with the control group. The second treatment period saw the effect of Treatment A remaining strong, and treatment B was significantly more effective than Treatment AB when tested on segmentation of sounds.

The design of the study allowed Ayres to examine the effect of treatment sequence as well as individual treatment effect. Specifically, since each group received two treatments, each in a different order, it was possible to ask: "Is phonological awareness training more effective when it is delivered during the first half of the kindergarten year, or are children more receptive to such instruction after they have been exposed to a more broad based literacy curriculum?" Results of this study clearly indicate that the type and sequence of training has a measurable effect on phonological awareness. Direct instruction produced the most significant effect during both training conditions; however, the effect was greatest when delivered during the second portion of the year, after the children had participated in a variety of experiences with literature. Overall, two treatment sequence groups were especially effective: B (indirect/literature-based instruction) followed by AB (direct and indirect instruction); and X (story mapping and retelling) followed by A (direct instruction). Ayres concludes that "The most important implication from this study is that training in phonological awareness is both possible and advantageous for children" (1993, p. 153). She observes that "The most effective means of instruction seems to begin with literature as a foundation for the direct instruction that will come later in the year" (1993, p. 144), when it appears to be more effective.

Based upon these results, Ayres has developed a kindergarten phonological awareness training program, *The Phonological Zoo*© (1993). The program consists of nine months of lessons in phonological awareness training, and is based upon literature selections chosen for their rhyme and alliteration patterns and text features. *The Phonological Zoo*© is divided into three phases of instruction. Phase One focuses on activities designed to build nursery rhyme knowledge and familiarity with folk tales. Phase Two deals with rhyming, and Phase Three addresses alliteration, segmentation, and sound/letter correspondence.

Apart from the pedagogical aspects of this study, three other results also prove especially interesting. First, the children in the story mapping and retelling group also showed a substantial gain in phonological awareness during the first training period, indicating that indirect effects on specific language skills are possible when children attend closely to the structure of stories and are engaged in discussion. Second, the control group, which had no specific training in phonological awareness, showed the least gains on phonological awareness measures (p. 131, p. 138). Yet, the reading achievement measures taken at the end of the first grade (California Achievement Test's subtests on word reading, word analysis, vocabulary, and comprehension) showed no significant differences between the control group and the treatment groups (p. 146). More precisely, the control group's performance was lower on all the reading subtests than Sequence Group X,A (one of the most effective sequence groups), but on the comprehension subtest the control group outperformed Sequence Groups A,X and AB,B (the two weakest sequence groups).

The third interesting result of this study concerns the multiple regression analyses following posttesting at the end of first grade, which suggests that children who have developed phonological awareness may read differently than those who have not. The latter rely more on whole word visual cues than upon letter/sound information, and their reading achievement depends more upon cognitive ability than upon word attack strategy. Direct instruction appears to provide an important skill such that children are able to achieve reading success regardless of their cognitive ability (p. 149). This has important implications for educators, who are dedicated to developing children's reading ability, in spite of intelligence level.

On a different note, from the unexpected gains made by the control group, Ayres concludes that "students whose phonological awareness is less than completely developed are nevertheless capable of making progress in reading" (p. 150). These data lead to the conjecture that phonological awareness and reading are linked in a facilitative relationship, in which phonological awareness enables children to make progress more quickly than children without such skills.

Taking the various kinds of data together, this study indicates that there is "more of a reciprocal relationship between phonological awareness and reading" rather than a unidirectional relationship, in which phonological awareness would be considered a prerequisite to reading (1993, p. 150). Further, Ayres (1993, p. 151) notes Ehri's (1979) caution: that "if a skill is facilitative, as phonological awareness appears to be, the effect may last only temporarily." The controls will "catch up," as they did in Ayres's study. What we need, of course (as Ayres writes), are studies that would follow the children's reading progress and achievement for another few years—and studies that would measure a wider range of factors relevant to the development of reading, writing, and literacy.

Most children enter kindergarten filled with anticipation that they will soon discover the secrets of reading and writing. Fortunately for most of these children, literacy acquisition will progress with little to no difficulty. But for some the road will not be smooth. Some children may not yet have the "literacy tools" to access the crucial secrets of literacy. One of these secrets is the alphabetic script, and one of the tools is phonological awareness.

Research over the past two decades has repeatedly implicated phonological awareness as a crucial factor in reading acquisition (Bradley & Bryant, 1978, 1983, 1985; Bryant & Bradley, 1985; Fox & Routh, 1976; Liberman, 1973; Mann, 1984; Maclean, Bradley, & Bryant, 1988; Rozin & Gleitman, 1977; Share, Jorm, Maclean, & Mathews, 1984; Stanovich, Cunningham, & Cramer, 1984; Stanovich, Cunningham, & Feeman, 1984; Treiman & Baron, 1981; Tunmer & Nesdale, 1985; Vellutino & Scanlon, 1987; Williams, 1980). A substantial amount of evidence indicates that the relationship is significant (Calfee, Lindamood, & Lindamood, 1973; Fox & Routh, 1980; Helfgott, 1976; Stanovich, Cunningham, & Cramer, 1984), and remains robust, independent of IQ and family background (Bradley & Bryant, 1985; Goldstein, 1976; Torneus, 1984; Zifcak, 1981). The strength of this relationship allows performance on phonemic segmentation or blending tasks to be viewed as a precursor of subsequent success in reading acquisition (Blachman, 1984b; Bradley & Bryant, 1985; Juel, Griffith, & Gough, 1986; Lundberg, Olofsson, & Wall, 1980; Mann & Liberman, 1984; Share et al., 1984).

This study addresses the emergence of phonological awareness in young children and its predictive capacity to later reading development. It investigates the effect of three treatment conditions designed to enhance phonological awareness of prereaders in the context of the kindergarten classroom.

Phonological awareness refers to an individual's awareness of and access to the sounds of language (Mattingly, 1972). It involves the conscious or unconscious understanding of units of sound (words, syllables, the onsets and rimes of syllables, and individual phonemes) and the ability to separate, combine and manipulate them. Successful use of phonological awareness skills in reading implies a firm grasp of the alphabetic principal as a visual representation, or written version, of our spoken language. This understanding is crucial if one is to make sense of our alphabetic orthography (Adams, 1990), which ascribes a systematic and predictable relationship between sounds and letters. For many children who experience difficulty learning to read, however, the system is not logical or even apparent. They are unable to make sense of the alphabetic system because they are unaware of the sound system that underlies it. Their lack of phonemic awareness (awareness of the "separate" sounds in words) and its relation to our alphabetic script may be the area most determinant of their reading success (Adams, 1990).

Research on reading acquisition indicates that children who experience early success in reading also demonstrate high levels of phonological awareness, which serves to facilitate the reading process (Stanovich, Cunningham, & Cramer 1984). Although its development is clearly a vital component in the reading process, researchers hold differing views regarding the nature of the relationship between phonological awareness and reading.

Some view phonological awareness as a prerequisite to reading (Bradley & Bryant, 1985; Fox & Routh, 1976; Golinkoff, 1978; Jorm & Share, 1983; Liberman, 1973; Lundberg & Olofsson, 1980; Rozin & Gleitman, 1977; Treiman & Baron, 1983; Tunmer & Nesdale, 1985; Williams, 1980). This view holds that without the knowledge that words have constituent sounds, and that letters map to those sounds, it is impossible to make progress in reading. It is a necessary, but not sufficient skill for reading acquisition (Tunmer & Nesdale, 1985).

In contrast, some view phonological awareness as a consequence of learning to read (Ehri & Wilce, 1980; Morais, Carey, Alegria & Bertelson, 1979). A skill is a consequence of reading if it would inevitably be acquired as a result of learning to read (Tunmer & Nesdale, 1985). In this view, the process of learning to read is necessary and sufficient for acquiring the skill.

Other researchers consider phonological awareness important as a facilitative, but not a necessary skill in learning to read (Goldstein, 1976). Since it is not a necessary ingredient, it should be possible to find readers who do not possess this skill (Tunmer & Nesdale, 1985). Studies viewing phonological awareness as a facilitator are those in which the subjects achieved quicker success by virtue of training in the skill, yet the controls made progress too (Ehri, 1979).

A final view of phonological awareness considers that it is necessary to reading acquisition, but in concert with one or more other necessary correlates (Tunmer, Herriman, & Nesdale, 1988), such as cognitive ability. With each study added to the literature, evidence is presented that inevitably supports one theory of the relationship while simultaneously contradicting another. It is an area that has generated lively debate in the research community, and has left elementary teachers profoundly confused.

Yet, even in the presence of such debate and confusion, the identification of phonological skill as highly implicated in reading progress is widely recognized. Given the importance of phonological awareness in the reading process, impatient questions plague all who are interested in literacy development. Is it possible to provide instruction for children who exhibit little awareness of the phonological structure of their language? Can a successful training program be implemented that will reduce the risks of reading failure for those children? If so, at what age would the most benefit from training be derived, and through which methods would it be accomplished most successfully? Importantly, could an effective training program be delivered within the constraints of a typical kindergarten classroom setting with regard to class size and instructional approach? These applied research questions are particularly important to the widespread implementation of research findings, which often require modification to be field applicable.

The concept of emergent literacy suggests that the foundations of literacy develop from a child's early experiences with print prior to the onset of formal reading instruction (Teale, 1989). From experiences such as storybook reading, rhyming and other oral language games, and observations of adult literacy models, children construct understandings about the operations of oral and written language, as well as about its functions and uses. Instruction in phonological awareness may not be effective for children who have not first experienced such a background of literacy enjoyment and exploration. Therefore, the question of when to instruct is an important one.

A second important question with regard to instruction in phonological awareness concerns pedagogy. Sulzby and Teale (1991) caution that empirically based training methods, used for research purposes in short term studies, are not necessarily ideal methods for implementation in the day-to-day curriculum. Early experiences with literacy instruction help to shape children's opinions and attitudes toward literacy that can have far-reaching influence on life choices. Therefore, classroom activities for young children must be captivating enough to hold the imagination, engaging enough to sustain active involvement for a period of time, and stimulating enough to motivate further literacy exploration.

Several studies have shown positive results after training children in phonological awareness (Ball & Blachman, 1991; Bradley & Bryant, 1983, 1985; Content, Kolinsky, Morais, & Bertelson, 1986; Fox & Routh, 1976; Hohn & Ehri, 1983; Marsh & Mineo, 1977; Treiman & Baron, 1983; Rosner, 1974; Williams, 1980; Zurova, 1973). Most have taken place, however, in one-to-one or small group situations between the experimenter and subject. Content, Kolinsky, Morais, and Bertelson, for example, report training through corrective feedback in individual testing situations (1986). Rosner provides an individual assignment of phonological training to each child based upon the needs shown during individual testing (Rosner, 1974). Kindergarten children were trained individually by Hohn and Ehri (1983), while preschoolers received individual training in studies by Fox and Routh (1976), Marsh and Mineo (1977), Trieman and Baron (1983), and Zurova (1973). Ball and Blachman (1991) trained kindergarten children in small groups of five. Williams (1980) reports successful results from training carried out in a typical classroom setting of special education students. Clearly, there have been few reported training studies expressly designed for use in classroom situations typical of today's kindergartens, yet results of these and other studies strongly indicate such a need.

This study addressed that need by investigating the effect of three treatment conditions designed to enhance phonological awareness of prereaders in the context of the kindergarten classroom. Treatments were conceived from a perspective congruent with current developmental practice, an issue of theoretical as well as pedagogical importance (Sulzby & Teale, 1991). They were based upon nursery rhymes, books, and stories which emphasized specific phonological features of words. Activities involved songs, games, puppets, dances, and writing. Thus, training occurred within an activity and literature-based context geared to the developmental level of kindergarten children. In addition, each treatment was delivered to whole classes of children, rather than to small groups within the class, which is typical of past training procedures.

Study Design

With intact classrooms as treatment groups, this study was developed in a quasi-experimental, non-equivalent control group design. The study includes two categorical variables. The first categorical variable was treatment, which had five levels including three treatment groups, a comparison group, and a control group. The second categorical variable was testing occasions, which had four levels of variables, including pretest, transition test, posttest, and delayed posttest occasions. Each of the treatment groups (Group A, Group B, and Group AB) received a different form of training in phonological awareness skills of rhyming, alliteration, and segmentation. The fourth group (Group X) received an alternate treatment, which consisted of instruction in story mapping and retelling, which are important components of reading instruction not overtly related to phonological awareness. All experimental groups received 20 minutes of daily instruction from explicit daily lesson plans which helped to ensure treatment fidelity and prevent experimenter bias. A fifth group (Group Y) served as a control group, and received no literacy treatment specific to this research study, although the children were involved in daily reading, writing and oral language activities included in the district kindergarten curriculum.

The three treatment groups and one comparison group were instructed by two teachers in separate buildings, each with morning and afternoon classes of kindergarten children. To anticipate and allow for teacher factors which posed a threat to the study's internal validity, the treatments were repeated in a subsequent ten-week training period, with treatments prescribed to alternative groups. Table 1 shows teacher assignment to treatment group per training period. Specific materials were used in Treatment A; therefore, Treatments A and AB were paired in a single teacher's classroom during each training period. This helped to ensure treatment fidelity and obviate contamination to Treatments B and X.

The design of the study allowed each treatment group to receive a different treatment during the second ten-week training period. By the completion of both ten-week training periods, each group had received phonological awareness training through a direct approach (Treatment A or AB) and through an indirect approach (Treatment B or Treatment AB). Thus, each treatment group is indicated by the sequence of training: Group A,X—direct instruction followed by alternate treatment; Group AB, B—combined direct and indirect instruction followed by indirect instruction; Group B, AB—indirect instruction followed by combined direct and indirect instruction; Group X,A—alternate treatment followed by direct instruction; and Group Y—no intervention. This counterbalanced design allowed the investigation of sequence of treatment effect as well as treatment effect alone. It also provided information regarding kindergarten children's receptivity to direct and indirect instruction at different times of the year.

Table 1

Treatment conditions by training period

		Training Period 1	Training Period 2
Teacher 1	AM class:	Treatment A	Treatment B
	PM class:	Treatment AB	Treatment X
Teacher 2	AM class:	Treatment X	Treatment AB
	PM class:	Treatment B	Treatment A

Four research questions were explored and addressed by related research hypotheses.

Question one

What is the level and variation of phonological awareness demonstrated by kindergarten children prior to the onset of formal reading instruction?

Hypothesis One. The population mean of kindergarten children will be significantly greater than chance on measures of phonological awareness prior to the onset of reading instruction.

The examination of this hypothesis provided information on both the presence of phonological awareness skills in kindergarten aged children prior to formal reading instruction, and our ability to measure that awareness.

Question two

Will various forms of training result in significantly different performance on phonological awareness measures?

Hypothesis Two (a). The mean scores on phonological awareness measures at transition testing will be significantly higher for the treatment groups combined (Groups A + B + AB) than for the control groups combined (Groups X + Y).

Based upon the success of training in previous studies (Ball & Blachman, 1991; Bradley & Bryant, 1985; Goldstein, 1976; Fox & Routh, 1976) all training groups, regardless of treatment condition, were expected to show gains in phonological awareness. Conversely, the comparison group and the control group were not expected to show appreciable gains in the absence of training. Therefore, the training groups as a whole should have significantly higher scores than the control groups as a whole.

Hypothesis Two (b) There will be a significant difference between the mean scores of the Comparison Group (Group X), and the Control Group (Group Y) on measures of phonological awareness taken at transition and posttesting.

Neither the control group nor the comparison group received training in phonological awareness. Both groups, however, were expected to show some gains in phonological awareness due to the literacy based, but non-treatment related instructional experiences they encountered in the normal kindergarten curriculum. Since their experience in phonological awareness was similar, their gains were expected to be similar. Differences that result may be due to the alternative treatment the comparison group received, which were intended to offset extraneous variables that may affect the performance of the control group.

Hypothesis Two (c). There will be significant differences between the mean scores of the treatment groups (Groups A, B, and AB) on phonological measures taken at transition and posttesting.

Based upon evidence from previous studies on phonological awareness training (Ball & Blachman, 1991; Bradley & Bryant, 1985), direct instruction that includes manipulation of sound-symbol characters (letters) results in significant gains on posttest measures. Treatment A includes plastic, magnetic letters as well as other alphabet manipulables as direct instruction components. Therefore, Group A was expected to show significantly higher scores than Group B, which received indirect instruction that did not include manipulables. Given the effectiveness of direct instruction in phonological awareness, direct instruction coupled with a literature component was expected to provide a more effective instructional approach than direct instruction alone. Group AB coupled direct instruction with a literature base, which was expected to result in significantly greater gains on phonological awareness measures.

Question three

Will the type and sequence of training have an effect on phonological awareness measures taken at the end of the second training period and subsequent reading achievement?

Hypothesis Three. There will be significant differences between treatment sequence groups (Group A,X) (Group AB,B) (Group B,AB) (Group X,A) on posttest measures of phonological awareness and reading achievement measured one year later.

Due to the counterbalanced design of the study, each treatment group received a different treatment during the second ten-week training period. By the completion of both training periods, each group had received phonological awareness training through a direct approach (Treatment A and Treatment AB) and through an indirect approach (Treatment B and Treatment AB). Because all treatment groups had received both direct and indirect training in phonological awareness, their reading achievement scores at the end of the following year were not expected to show significant differences based upon treatment alone. However, differences in scores may be due to the unique sequence of treatment each training group experiences.

Question four

What is the relationship between phonological awareness measures of kindergarten children and reading acquisition measured one year later?

Hypothesis Four (a) There will be a significant correlation between phonological awareness as measured in kindergarten, and reading acquisition measured one year later.

Considerable evidence shows that a strong relationship exists between children's phonological awareness and the facility of reading acquisition. Scores from transition and posttest phonological awareness measures will be subjected to correlational analyses to determine the strength of the relationship.

Hypothesis Four (b) The relationship between phonological awareness and reading acquisition will be specific; there will be significantly less correlation between phonological awareness as measured through sound categorization tests of kindergarten children and mathematical ability measured one year later, compared to the correlation between phonological awareness and reading achievement measured one year later.

To determine that gains in phonological awareness relate specifically to the language areas of reading and spelling, rather than to all areas of academic skill, it is necessary to correlate those gains with something other than reading or spelling. Mathematics is an academic area expected to show little relation to changes in phonological awareness. Mathematic measures were taken at the end of subjects' first grade year using the same standardized test used to collect reading achievement data. Those scores were used to test this hypothesis.

Method

Subjects

Participants in this study (N = 113) were attending half-day, public school kindergarten, in a predominantly white, middle class, economically and ethnically diverse, suburban U.S. school district, with an approximate enrollment of 10,000 students. Eight children were dropped from the study due to reassignment to other kindergarten classes, or movement from the geographical area. At the end of treatment, 105 subjects remained. The mean age at the time of pretesting was 5.4 years, with a range of 4.8 years to 6.4 years. Simple regression analyses revealed no significant differences between treatment groups in age, $F(4,104) = .92$, $p > .05$, or gender, $F(4, 104) = .67$, $p > .05$.

Dependent variables

Phonological awareness measures

The following measures of phonological awareness were administered and used as dependent variables.

Word Recognition Test (Clay, 1979). Children were asked to identify and pronounce any of the following words that they could recognize: mother, here, me, am, with, car, children, help, not, too, meet, away, are, shouted, I. Children received a score from 1 to 15.

Oddity Test (Bradley & Bryant (1978). The examiner voiced four monosyllabic words, with three sharing a common sound. The child's task was to identify the "odd word out," the word that did not fit with the other three. The test contains three series of patterns to assess recognition of beginning, middle, and ending phoneme. Each series consists of ten sets of four words. Two practice trials in each series were given to the children prior to the test. Following is the beginning phoneme series as an example. Practice trials - 1) rot, rod, rock, *box*; 2) lick, lid, *miss*, lip. Test patterns - 1) bud, bun, bus, *rug*; 2) peg, pen, *well*, pet; 3) *leap*, mean, meal, meat; 4) roof, room, *food*, root; 5) pip, pin, *hill*, pig; 6) kid, kick, kiss, *fill*; 7) crack, crab, crag, *trap*; 8) ham, *tap*, had, hat; 9) lot, *mop*, lock, log; 10) slim, *flip*, slick, slip. Scores ranged from 0 to 30.

Memory Test (Bradley & Bryant (1978). The Oddity test involves memory as well as phonological categorization skill. To allow for that ability to be factored out later, a memory test was administered following the Oddity test. The same words were presented to the children. Their task was to merely repeat the words in the order given. Scores ranged from 0 to 30.

Supply Initial Consonant Test (Stanovich et al., 1984). Examiner presented the subject a pair of monosyllabic words identical in medial and final sound. The initial phoneme, however, had been removed from the second word. Subjects were asked to identify the missing sound from the second word. For instance, the examiner would say, "Say the word 'cat.' Now say 'at.' What sound do you hear in 'cat' that is missing in 'at?' " Subjects were then given 10 pairs of words. For example, meal—eel, fill—ill, sit—it. Scores ranged from one to ten.

Yopp-Singer Phoneme Segmentation Test (Yopp, 1987). Examiner pronounced a monosyllabic word. The subject was to repeat each sound in the word in order, thus breaking the word into its constituent sounds. Three practice trials preceded the 22 item test. Practice trials: ride, go, man. Word list: dog, keep, fine, no, she, wave, grew, that, red, me, sat, lay, race, zoo, three, job, in, ice, at, top, by, do. Scores ranged from 1 to 22.

Reading achievement measures

Subjects' performance on reading achievement measures was used to determine the longitudinal effect of the Training Periods, and to establish the relationship between phonological awareness and later reading acquisition. Reading achievement was measured in May of the year following the end of treatment through the measures listed below. *Word Analysis subtest of the California Achievement Test (CAT/5) Level 11, Form A(1992).* This test measured the students' ability to recognize portions of words representing vowel sounds, beginning and ending consonant sounds, consonant blends and digraph sounds. It also measured students' ability to recognize five sight words: again, walk, know, when, and how. It was administered orally in approximately 16 minutes. A maximum of 28 points was possible.

Vocabulary subtest of the California Achievement Test (CAT/5) Level 11, Form A. This test measured the students' ability to decode and recognize the meaning of words, tapping an understanding of synonyms, word categories, and definitions. Word meaning was assessed in isolation, phrases, and in sentences. The subtest took approximately 25 minutes, and a maximum of 30 points was possible.

Comprehension subtest of the California Achievement Test (CAT/5) Level 11, Form A. This subtest measures the students' understanding of sentences and short passages. The items require students to extract details, analyze characters, identify main ideas, and interpret events. The first ten items assessed students' listening comprehension, while the remaining 24 items required students to read short passages and answer questions. Students were given approximately 35 minutes to complete this portion of the test. A maximum of 34 points was possible.

Dictation Test (Clay, 1979). This measured students' ability to ascribe letters to sounds as perceived from a dictated sentence. Subjects were asked to write the following sentence: "The bus is coming. It will stop here to let me get on." The test was group administered in approximately 10 minutes. One point was given for every sound represented by the student. Scores ranged from 1 to 37.

Dependent variable: math achievement

Math Computation subtest of the California Achievement Test (CAT/5) Level 11, Form A. This test measured the students' ability to perform addition and subtraction of whole numbers. It was administered in approximately 30 minutes, and consisted of 28 items.

Procedure

Pretesting

Seven examiners, all certified classroom teachers, were trained by the investigator to administer the pretest, transition test, and posttest tasks. Following standard procedures, examiners collected pretest data from all subjects prior to the first ten-week training period in September, 1991. Pretest measures included a group administered Invented Spelling Test (Mann, 1987). Although this test was administered on all testing occasions, it was inappropriate for use as a dependent measure in the study due to the difficulty of group administration.

Children were tested individually on each of the remaining dependent measures in the following order: Oddity Tests of beginning, middle, and ending phonemes (Bradley & Bryant, 1978), Memory Test (Bradley & Bryant, 1978), and a Word Recognition Test (Clay, 1979). Due to the subjects' young age and their overall limited performance on the tests just mentioned, the Yopp-Singer Test and Supply Initial Consonant Test, both more difficult phonological awareness measures, were not administered as pretests. Interrater reliability on all pretest measures was .98.

Experimenter teacher training

Experimenter teachers and their principals attended a 5-hour initial training session in August, 1991. Materials and daily lesson plans for each treatment group were provided. Bi-weekly meetings were held throughout the course of the study to discuss ongoing treatment procedures and upcoming plans.

First intervention: training period I

The first ten-week training period began on September 23, 1991 following pretesting of subjects. Each treatment of phonological awareness training differed in materials and technique and was driven by specific daily lesson plans which the teachers rigorously followed.

Treatment Group A: This group received direct instruction in phonological awareness and phoneme-grapheme relationships built around original stories written for this treatment, puppets, magnetic plastic letters, songs, and word games. Rhyme, alliteration and segmentation were directly instructed by puppets who repeatedly drew the children's attention to those phonological features in words, stories and songs. See Appendix A for detailed plans and sequence of instruction. Invented spelling was instructed at a writing center, which was equipped with letter stamps, letter tiles for use with Elkonin-like boxes (Elkonin, 1973), letters with kinesthetic properties, writing implements and paper of various types and colors.

Treatment Group B: This group received indirect instruction through a literature-based approach. Specific literature selections were chosen for each lesson, which was instructed according to the prescribed lesson plans. Attention to rhyme and alliteration stemmed from the text and incorporated extension activities to highlight the phonological features of words present in each literature selection. Instruction revolved around poems and books written with rhyme and alliteration, and all-class as well as individual bookmaking and extension activities. Invented spelling was instructed at a writing center, which was equipped with writing implements and paper of various types and colors.

Treatment Group AB: This group was instructed in an approach that combined the literature based instruction of Group B and the direct instruction of Group A. Instruction for this group revolved around poems and books written in rhyme and alliteration, similar to those used for Group B. Literature selections were chosen for each lesson and were instructed according to prescribed lesson plans. In addition, the puppets, magnetic plastic letters, songs, and word games used in Group A interacted with the text, thereby merging both approaches. Invented spelling was instructed at a writing center, which was equipped with letter stamps, letter tiles for use with Elkonin-like boxes, letters with kinesthetic properties, writing implements and paper of various types and colors.

Treatment Group X: This group, the comparison group, was instructed in story mapping and retelling of familiar folk tales, which were read in a shared reading approach. The retelling of each folk tale was facilitated with felt board cutouts.

Treatment Group Y: This was the control group, which received no instruction in phonological awareness other than that present in the district kindergarten curriculum.

Transition testing

The first ten-week intervention period was completed on November 27, 1991. Following the first intervention, subjects' phonological awareness levels were assessed by the same 7 examiners who administered the pretests. In addition to measuring the effect of Training Period I, these transition measures served as covariates of the posttest measures, which followed Training Period II. Transition testing was conducted during the two weeks between December 2, 1991 and December 13, 1991.

Transition test measures included Invented Spelling (Mann, 1987), Oddity Tests of beginning, middle, and ending phonemes (Bradley & Bryant, 1978), Memory Test (Bradley & Bryant, 1978), Yopp-Singer Phoneme Segmentation Test (Yopp, 1987), and Supply Initial Consonant Test (Stanovich, Cunningham, & Cramer, 1984). Interrater reliability was .98.

Second intervention: training period II

Following transition testing of subjects, the second training period began on January 6, 1992 and was completed 10 weeks later, on March 20, 1992. Teachers used materials and lesson plans identical to those used in Training Period I; however treatments were prescribed to alternate classes per design, as shown in Table 1.

Posttesting

Following the second intervention, subjects' phonological awareness levels were assessed by the same 7 examiners who administered the pretests and transition tests. Posttesting was conducted during the three weeks between March 23, 1992 and April 10, 1992. Posttest measures were identical to Transition test measures.

Delayed posttesting

At the end of subjects' first grade year, delayed posttest measures were collected using the Word Recognition, Vocabulary, Comprehension, and Mathematics subtests of the California Achievement Test (CAT/5). These tests were given by district paraprofessionals trained in standardized test administration. In addition, students were given a Dictation Test by the investigator, and subjects' first grade classroom teachers were asked to complete a Teacher Perception Questionnaire. Interrater reliability was .98.

Treatment of the Data

Subjects' mean scores and standard deviations on pretest measures were computed and Multiple Regression Correlation Analysis was performed as a means of determining differences in treatment group that existed prior to training. Subjects' mean scores and standard deviations were computed on transition test measures, and Multiple Regression Correlation Analysis was performed as a means of determining significant differences on dependent measures by treatment group. Of equal importance, by regressing, or removing the pretest scores from the analysis, the procedure adjusted the transition test results for differences that may have existed in treatment groups prior to training. Planned comparisons were then performed to determine significant differences related to research hypotheses.

Similarly, following posttest data collection in March, subjects' mean scores and standard deviations were computed, and Multiple Regression Correlation Analysis was performed as a means of determining significant differences on dependent measures by treatment group during this second training period. Planned comparisons were performed to determine significant differences related to research hypotheses.

During the second treatment period, however, the identity of the treatment groups assumed an added dimension. Each treatment group received a second treatment during the second ten-week training period (refer to Table 2 and Table 3). These sequence groups were treated as a dependent variable through Multiple Regression Correlation Analysis. Results indicated whether the sequence of treatment conditions caused significant differences among groups. For instance, Treatment B may be more effective when it succeeds Treatment AB (Group AB,B). Or conversely, Treatment AB may be more effective when it follows Treatment B (Group B,AB). Results of Group A,X will indicate lasting effects of Treatment A, and Group X,A will indicate if it is more advantageous to postpone phonological awareness training until the second half of kindergarten.

At the end of the subjects' first grade year, reading achievement data were collected. Group means were computed and analyzed for comparison through Multiple Regression Correlation Analysis and planned comparisons. Correlation matrixes were computed with all of the dependent variables entered for analysis to determine the relationship between each of the phonological awareness and reading achievement measures.

The relationship among the measures was also examined by forced stepwise multiple regression analyses. The predictor variables were chronological age, Math Computation, Memory (a control measure given with the Oddity test), and Phonological Awareness. Math computation was entered in place of IQ, as a measure of non-verbal cognitive ability. The criterion variables were Word Recognition, Vocabulary, Comprehension, Dictation, and Combined Reading, the latter being a combination of all achievement measures collapsed into one score. Results of these analyses revealed the amount of variance that can be attributed to phonological awareness after age, non-verbal cognitive ability, and memory have been factored out.

Considerations of the Analysis

Assumptions of normality and linearity

Multiple Regression/Correlation procedure is based on two assumptions: normally distributed dependent measures and a linear relationship among covariates and treatment conditions (Cohen & Cohen, 1983). To ensure that the normality assumption was met normalized z-scores as well as raw scores were analyzed. Significance levels of both are reported. The linearity assumption can be verified by testing for a significant interaction among treatments of covariate vectors in the MRC analysis (Keppel, 1973; Cohen & Cohen, 1983). When an interaction was detected the Johnson-Neyman technique was employed (Huitema, 1980). The purpose of the Johnson-Neyman technique is to determine areas of non-significance and significance associated with the interaction of X and Y (Huitma, 1980). Scores that fall within the determined region of non-significance indicate no significant differences in treatment effect between X and Y. Scores that fall above the range of non-significance indicate that treatment Y has a significant effect; and scores that fall below the range of non-significance indicate that treatment X has a significant effect. In Training Period I, the regression slope of Group AB was negative, causing interaction between all other slopes. This indicates that treatments were differentially effective for students with differing pretest scores. The Johnson-Neyman procedure was followed for comparisons on Total Oddity, Supply Initial Consonant, and Total Phonological Awareness Measures.

Planned comparisons and familywise error rate

This study examined 8 planned comparisons, with degrees of freedom $(a-1) = 4$, in the analyses relating to Training Condition I and Training Condition II. The analyses relating to Sequence Group examined 10 planned comparisons, also with 4 degrees of freedom. Clearly, both analyses exceed the assumed limit of comparisons if treatment source degrees of freedom is the accepted benchmark. Caution suggests that some measure of correction should be employed to reduce the risk of familywise error since a prudent standard for the number of planned comparisons appears to rest somewhere slightly above or below the degrees of freedom associated with the treatment source of variance (Keppel, 1973).

One method of correction suggested by Keppel is the Modified Bonferroni Test (1973). In a study with five treatment conditions and eight planned comparisons, such as the Training Condition analyses reported here, the corrected rejection probability is a = .025, rather than a = .05. Similarly, with five treatment conditions and ten planned comparisons, such as the Sequence Group analyses in this study, the corrected rejection probability is α = .020.

There is a conflict in assuming a more stringent a level in interpreting planned comparisons (Keppel, 1973) . That conflict occurs in instances when significance is indicated at an uncorrected a level, but not at the a level corrected for familywise error. In this study, that range of ambiguity would be between a = .025 and α = .05 for the first two sets of analyses, and between α = .020 and α = .05 for the third set of analyses. Rather than rejecting the null hypothesis for values falling within that range, Keppel suggests that the researcher take no formal action, opting to suspend judgment instead. Since the null hypothesis has not been rejected, the decision contributes nothing to familywise error, yet it clearly indicates comparisons that may have potential interest for further research (1973).

Comparisons reported here are measured by the more conservative standards of α = .025 and α = .020, which reflect a correction for familywise error appropriate to the number of comparisons in each analysis. The uncorrected level of significance is also reported, accompanied by a "suspend judgment" notation (†). Significance levels throughout the study appear as follows: p > .05 = accept null hypothesis; p < .05† = suspend judgment; p < .025* = corrected for FW error, highest criterion for rejection of null hypothesis; and p < . 01** = reject null hypothesis.

Results

This study has two major components: a training component, which is divided into two ten-week training periods; and a longitudinal component, which measures the effect of training one year later.

Results of the training component are reported in three sets of analyses. Training Period I and Training Period II report effects of treatment separately and examine the merits of each. Differences between Sequence Groups follow, with results suggesting a preferable order of treatment. The longitudinal component is reported in two sets of analyses. The first set reports data related to the longitudinal effects of training, and the second reports data regarding the relationship of phonological awareness and reading acquisition.

Means, adjusted means, and standard deviations for all pretest, transition test, and posttest variables appear in Table 2. In this, as well as subsequent covariate analyses reported, the manner of the coding effects was such that Group Y formed a reference group.

Table 2

Means, adjusted means, and standard deviations on pretest, transition test, and posttest measures by treatment group

Measure	Group A, X			Group B, AB			Group AB, B			Group X, A			Group Y		
	M	Adj M	(SD)	M	Adj M	(SD)	M	Adj M	(SD)	M	Adj M	(SD)	M	Adj M	(SD)
Pretest															
Oddity	8.31		(4.76)	6.32		(3.50)	7.95		(2.01)	5.32		(4.20)	6.82		(2.86)
Memory Word Rec	1.19		(3.27)	1.36		(3.97)	.25		(1.12)	.08		(.40)	.14		(.64)
Trans Test															
Oddity	10.06	10.50	(5.54)	11.64	15.21	(6.11)	9.50	9.66	(3.89)	9.76	9.92	(4.28)	8.46	8.46	(4.95)
Memory Sup In Cons	3.75	5.77	(4.68)	3.05	4.91	(3.71)	2.10	2.57	(3.92)	2.60	4.30	(3.62)	1.32	1.32	(2.70)
Yopp-Singer	6.69	11.80	(9.10)	2.27	4.10	(4.54)	1.60	1.83	(4.43)	2.04	4.20	(4.43)	.73	.73	(2.98)
Total PA	20.50	28.07	(17.61)	16.96	24.20	(10.95)	13.20	14.06	(7.30)	14.40	20.74	(9.54)	10.50	10.50	(9.02)
Posttest															
Oddity	10.94	10.17	(6.46)	13.09	13.13	(7.38)	10.85	10.48	(5.60)	9.56	7.68	(4.94)	10.32	10.32	(5.66)
Memory Sup In Cons	4.31	4.65	(4.66)	5.91	8.19	(4.54)	4.35	5.54	(3.89)	6.40	9.39	(4.21)	2.77	2.77	(3.22)
Yopp-Sing	6.31	5.61	(9.41)	8.23	12.75	(8.28)	2.45	1.70	(5.45)	5.00	6.47	(7.46)	2.55	2.55	(3.84)
Total PA	21.56	17.81	(17.85)	27.23	32.57	(17.10)	17.65	7.05	(11.98)	20.96	22.51	(13.53)	15.64	15.64	(9.62)

Note: Group A = direct instruction; Group B = indirect instruction; Group AB = combination direct + indirect; Group X = Story Map + retelling; Group Y = control; Group A, X = direct instruction in Training Condition I followed by Story + retelling in Training Condition II.

Thus, the adjusted mean of the control group is always equal to the actual mean because of groupwise status as a reference group. Pretest scores were used to determine differences in treatment group that existed prior to training. No significant differences were found on the Word Recognition Test $F(4, 105) = 1.52$, $p > .05$ or the Oddity Test $F(4, 105) = .53$, $p > .05$. These non-significant group differences are important to note as they provide evidence of group equivalence prior to the treatments, which increase the internal validity of inferences about treatment effects.

Variation of phonological awareness

Pretest scores were also used to evaluate Hypothesis One, which concerns the level and variation of phonological awareness measurable in kindergarten children before formal reading instruction has commenced. To examine this hypothesis, one-group, two-tailed t-tests were performed on subjects' Pretest Oddity scores. Separate t-tests were performed on each of the three sub-tests: beginning phoneme, middle phoneme, and ending phoneme. Each test had 10 items with 4 possible responses for each item. Chance level was set at 2.5, which is the expected number of correct responses based on random guesses on all items.

None of the t-tests revealed levels of phonological awareness greater than chance. The sample mean for the beginning phoneme was 2.24. The test yield, $t(1, 104) = -1.49$, $p = .14$, which is consistent with a sample drawn from a population having a mean of 2.5. The sample mean for the middle phoneme was 2.49, which approached, but did not exceed the chance level. The test yield, $t(1, 104) = -.03$, $p = .97$, is again consistent with a sample drawn from a population having a mean of 2.5. The sample mean for the ending phoneme was the lowest of the three subtests at 2.07. The test yield, $t(1, 104) = -3.281$, $p = .001$ indicates a level significantly lower than chance. The fact that the sample mean of each subtest fell below 2.5 indicates that the Oddity Test is reflecting random variation for this group at pretest.

In order to examine the pretest responses more closely in terms of hypothesis one (Horowitz, 1974), a binomial test of individual scores was employed. An individual score of 6 or more, as indicated by the binomial, would be significantly greater than the level of chance ($p < .05$). Five of the sample of children reached this level on the beginning phoneme portion of the Oddity Test. The remainder of the 105 subjects scored 5 or below. On this first test, only a few of the children demonstrated significant levels of phonological awareness, while the majority of the children did not.

Similar binomial tests on the middle and ending phoneme indicated similar results. This indicates that subjects entering kindergarten had minimal levels of phonological awareness as measured on the tests employed. However, these results may be spurious due to the substantial amount of children who scored 0 on the Oddity subtests (20% = beginning phoneme; 12% = middle phoneme; and 15% = ending phoneme). In many cases, a score of 0 reflects a fifth response to the four item test: a shrug, a lack of verbal response, or a refusal to complete the test. Since this fifth response was not anticipated, and therefore not recorded by examiners, it is difficult to assess its frequency; however, it represents a possible compromise to the validity of the t-tests.

Training component

The remaining analyses in the training component are directed by Hypothesis Two (a), Two (b), Two (c) and Hypothesis Three, which examine the effect of three treatment conditions, contrasting each with the control and comparisons groups as well as to each other.

The following planned comparisons were examined for significant differences: treatment groups combined (A + B + AB) versus control groups combined (X + Y); comparison group (X) versus control group (Y); treatment groups versus control group (A vs. Y), (B vs. Y), and (AB vs. Y); and treatment group versus treatment group (A vs. B), (A vs. AB), and (B vs. AB).

The data were analyzed through hierarchical multiple regression, with transition test scores as the dependent variable, treatment group as the independent variable, and pretest Oddity scores as the covariate. The test for linearity indicated an interaction between the treatment groups and the covariate in all analyses except Yopp-Singer. Simple regressions by treatment group indicated the negative regression slope of Treatment Group AB to be the cause of the interaction. After removing Group AB and performing a further test of linearity among the remaining groups, results showed no interaction, and planned comparisons could then be determined with Analysis of Covariance. Comparisons involving Group AB were completed on raw scores using the Johnson-Neyman technique. Those comparisons are signified in each table as JN, and results are discussed as differential effects.

Effects of training period I

Table 3 indicates significant differences in treatment effect for Training Period I.

Table 3

Significant differences in treatment effect on raw and normalized scores on Transition measures at the conclusion of Training Period I

Comparison	Oddity Test		Supply Initial Consonant		Yopp-Singer		Total PA Measures	
	raw	norm	raw	norm	raw	norm	raw	norm
Overall Comparisons								
A+B+AB vs. X+Y	n/s	n/s	n/s	n/s	n/s	n/s	n/s	n/s
X vs. Y	$F_{(1,47)}=4.10$†	$F_{(1,47)}=4.31$†	n/s	n/s	n/s	n/s	$F_{(1,47)}=5.23$**	$F_{(1,47)}=5.45$*
Control Comparisons								
A vs. Y	n/s	n/s	n/s	n/s	$F_{(1,38)}=10.27$**	$F_{(1,38)}=11.45$**	$F_{(1,38)}=5.93$**	$F_{(1,38)}=6.07$*
B vs. Y	$F_{(1,44)}=8.15$**	$F_{(1,44)}=7.36$**	n/s	n/s	n/s	$F_{(1,44)}=4.14$†	$F_{(1,44)}=6.59$*	$F_{(1,44)}=9.13$*
AB vs. Y	JN $F_{(1,44)}=7.31$** when pretest scores are <7.6	—	JN $F_{(1,44)}=7.31$** when pretest scores are <8.0	—	n/s	n/s	JN $F_{(1,44)}=7.31$** when pretest scores are <7.9	—
Treatment Comparisons								
A vs. B	$F_{(1,38)}=5.15$†	n/s	n/s	n/s	$F_{(1,38)}=4.19$†	n/s	n/s	n/s
A vs. AB	JN $F_{(1,36)}=7.56$** when pretest scores are <7.5	—	JN $F_{(1,36)}=7.56$** when pretest scores are <6.3	—	$F_{(1,36)}=9.12$**	$F_{(1,36)}=6.30$*	JN $F_{(1,36)}=7.56$** when pretest scores are <6.0	n/s
B vs. AB	JN $F_{(1,42)}=7.31$** when pretest scores are <5.2	—	JN $F_{(1,42)}=7.31$** when pretest scores are <6.6	—	n/s	n/s	JN $F_{(1,42)}=7.31$** when pretest scores are <5.9	n/s

Note: Total Oddity pretest scores were used as the covariate on all Transition Test measures

n/s = non-significance   JN = Johnson Neyman technique   † = suspend judgment a.05   *p = Critical Value $_{FW}$ a.025   **p = a.01

From the analyses of Training Period I, Treatment A appeared to be significantly more effective than the control group on Yopp-Singer, $F(1, 38) = 11.45$, and on Total PA Measures, $F(1, 38) = 6.07$. Treatment A was also significantly different than Treatment AB on Yopp-Singer $F(1, 36) = 6.30$. In addition, Johnson-Neyman results indicated a differential effect between A and AB as shown in Table 3. It appears that students who scored lower on the pretest benefited more by Treatment AB than students who scored higher on the pretest; and students who scored higher on the pretest benefited more by Treatment A.

Two additional treatments showed significantly different results. Treatment B showed a significantly greater effect than the control group on Oddity $F(1, 44) = 7.36$, and Total PA, $F(1, 44) = 9.13$. Treatment X showed a significant effect when compared with the control group on Total PA, $F(1, 47) = 5.45$. Normalized scores are reported here.

Effects of training period II

The data gathered at posttesting was analyzed with posttest scores as the dependent variable, treatment group as the independent variable, and respective transition test scores as the covariate. The test for linearity revealed no interaction between the treatment groups and the covariate, therefore, planned comparisons were determined with Analysis of Covariance. Table 4 indicates significant differences in treatment effect.

From the analysis of the data from Training Period II, Treatment A shows significantly greater effect than the control group on Supply Initial Consonant, $F(1,47)=5.45$. In addition, Treatment B is significantly more effective than Treatment AB on Yopp-Singer, $F(1,42)=7.97$.

Treatment sequence

Hypothesis Three (a) extends the analysis to include both training periods as it examines the sequence of treatment and the effect of each on phonological awareness acquisition. As in previous analyses, the data gathered at posttesting were analyzed through hierarchical multiple regression, with posttest scores as the dependent variable, treatment group as the independent variable, and Pretest Oddity Test scores as the covariate. The test for linearity revealed no interaction between the treatment groups and the covariate, therefore planned comparisons were determined with Analysis of Covariance. With five treatment conditions and ten planned comparisons, the significance level was set at .020 (Keppel, 1973).

Table 4

Significant differences in treatment effect on raw and normalized scores on Posttest measures at the conclusion of Training Period II

Comparison	Oddity Test		Supply Initial Consonant		Yopp-Singer		Total PA Measures	
	raw	norm	raw	norm	raw	norm	raw	norm
Overall Comparisons								
A+B+AB vs. X+Y	n/s	n/s	$F(1,104)=6.89^{**}$	$F(1,104)=5.90^{*}$	n/s	n/s	$F(1,104)=4.28†$	n/s
X vs. Y	n/s	n/s	n/s	n/s	n/s	n/s	n/s	n/s
Control Comparisons								
A vs. Y	n/s	n/s	$F(1,47)=7.58^{**}$	$F(1,47)=5.45^{>}$	n/s	n/s	n/s	n/s
B vs. Y	n/s	n/s	n/s	n/s	n/s	n/s	n/s	n/s
AB vs. Y	n/s	n/s	$F(1,42)=4.10†$	n/s	$F(1,44)=6.39^{*}$	n/s	n/s	n/s
Treatment Comparisons								
A vs. B	n/s	n/s	n/s	n/s	n/s	n/s	n/s	n/s
A vs. AB	n/s	n/s	n/s	n/s	n/s	n/s	n/s	n/s
B vs. AB	n/s	n/s	n/s	n/s	$F(1,42)=8.33^{**}$	$F(1,42)=7.97^{**}$	$F(1,42)=4.17†$	n/s

Note: Transition test scores were used as the covariate for each individual Posttest measure

n/s = non-significance   † = suspend judgment a.05   *p = Critical Value $_{FW}$ a.025   **p = a.01

The first set of comparisons examined each sequence group in relation to the control: A,X versus Y; AB,B versus Y; B,AB versus Y; and X,A versus Y. The second set of comparisons examined sequence groups as they relate to each other in effect: A,X versus X,A; AB,B versus B,AB; A,X versus B,AB; A,X versus AB,B; AB,B versus X,A; and B,AB versus X,A. Table 5 indicates significant differences in sequence effect on all dependent measures.

From the analysis relating to the effects of sequence treatment, two sequence groups appear to be significantly different than the Control Group on one or more phonological measures: Treatment B,AB and Treatment X,A. Treatment B,AB showed significant effect on Yopp-Singer, $F(1, 44) = 8.20$, and on Total PA, $F(1, 44) = 6.43$. Treatment X,A showed significant effect on Supply Initial Consonant, $F(1, 47) = 11.49$. In addition, both Treatments were significantly more effective than other treatment conditions. Treatment X,A showed greater effect than Treatment A,X on Supply Initial Consonant, $F(1, 41) = 6.32$ and a greater effect than Treatment AB,B on Supply Initial Consonant, $F(1, 45) = 5.06$ and Yopp-Singer, $F(1, 45) = 5.87$. Treatment B,AB appeared to be significantly more effective than Treatment AB,B on Yopp-Singer, $F(1, 47) = 13.84$.

Longitudinal component

To examine the longitudinal effects of phonological awareness training, the following measures were administered one year after the end of treatment: Dictation Test (Clay, 1979), an invented spelling assessment of phonological awareness; and the Word Recognition, Vocabulary, and Comprehension subtests of the California Reading Achievement Test (CAT/5), Level 11, Form A. The Math Application subtest was also administered for use in comparative analyses.

During the year between posttesting and delayed posttesting, 13 subjects moved from the school district, and therefore left the study. The Dictation Test was group administered and scored by the investigator in the subjects' first grade classrooms. The subtests of the California Achievement Test were administered in small group settings, keeping the order of administration static: Word Analysis, Vocabulary, Comprehension, and Math Computation. A split-half correlation for each subtest was calculated and corrected for attenuation using the Spearman-Brown formula to provide an estimate of internal consistency (Ferguson, 1971). The corrected reliability estimate for subjects in this study was .85 on the Word Recognition subtest, .90 on the Vocabulary subtest, .82 on the Comprehension subtest, and .82 on the Math Computation subtest.

Table 5

Significant differences in sequence effect on raw and normalized scores on Posttest measures at the conclusion of Training Period II

Comparison	Oddity Test		Supply Initial Consonant		Yopp-Singer		Total PA Measures	
	raw	norm	raw	norm	raw	norm	raw	norm
Control comparisons								
A,X vs. Y	n/s	n/s	n/s	n/s	n/s	n/s	n/s	n/s
AB,B vs. Y	n/s	n/s	n/s	n/s	n/s	n/s	n/s	n/s
B,AB vs. Y	n/s	n/s	$F_{(1,44)}=8.01**$	$F_{(1,44)}=5.46†$	$F_{(1,44)}=9.70**$	$F_{(1,44)}=8.20**$	$F_{(1,44)}=11.54**$	$F_{(1,44)}=6.43**$
X,A vs. Y	n/s	n/s	$F_{(1,47)}=13.34**$	$F_{(1,47)}=11.49**$	n/s	n/s	$F_{(1,47)}=5.26†$	n/s
Sequence Comparisons								
A,X vs. X,A	n/s	n/s	$F_{(1,41)}=6.29*$	$F_{(1,41)}=6.32*$	n/s	n/s	n/s	n/s
AB,B vs. B,AB	$F_{(1,42)}=4.60†$	n/s	n/s	n/s	$F_{(1,42)}=12.31**$	$F_{(1,42)}=13.84**$	$F_{(1,42)}=11.21**$	$F_{(1,42)}=5.41†$
A,X vs. B,AB	n/s	n/s	n/s	n/s	n/s	$F_{(1,38)}=4.39†$	$F_{(1,38)}=5.56†$	n/s
A,X vs. AB,B	n/s	n/s	n/s	n/s	n/s	n/s	n/s	n/s
AB,B vs. X,A	n/s	n/s	$F_{(1,45)}=6.45*$	$F_{(1,45)}=5.06*$	$F_{(1,45)}=5.46*$	$F_{(1,45)}=5.87*$	$F_{(1,45)}=5.10†$	n/s
B,AB vs. X,A	n/s	n/s	n/s	n/s	n/s	n/s	n/s	n/s

Note: Total Oddity pretest scores were used as the covariate

n/s = non-significance   † = suspend judgment a.05   *p = Critical Value $_{FW}$ a.025   **p = a.01

Effects of training

The data gathered at delayed posttesting was analyzed through hierarchical multiple regression, with reading achievement scores as the dependent variable, treatment group as the independent variable, and Pretest Oddity Test scores as the regressor. Means and standard deviations of Delayed Posttest Reading Achievement measures are reported in Table 6. As in previous analyses reported here, the manner of the coding effects was such that Group Y formed a reference group. Thus, the adjusted mean of the control group is always equal to the actual mean because of groupwise status as a reference group.

The test for linearity revealed interactions between the treatment groups and the covariate on the following dependent variables: Dictation, Comprehension, and Combined Reading. Simple regressions by treatment group indicated the negative regression slope of Treatment Group AB,B to be the cause of the interaction. This indicates that treatments were differentially effective for students with differing pretest scores. After removing Group AB,B and performing a further test of linearity among the remaining groups, results showed no interaction, and planned comparisons were determined with Analysis of Covariance. Comparisons involving Group AB,B were completed using the Johnson-Neyman technique. There were no significant differences between treatment groups, other than the differential effect of Treatment AB. Although the means of Group B,AB and Group X,A remain higher than other groups on all measures and the results fell within the suspend-judgment region, the differences were not sufficient to yield statistical significance. It should be remembered, however, that significance levels for this set of analyses were set at the conservative level of .020 to reduce the rate of family-wise error. Comparisons that fall within the range of .020 and .05 would therefore be indicated as having potential for further research.

Relationship of phonological awareness to reading acquisition

Intercorrelations of pretest, transition test, posttest, and delayed posttest dependent variables, shown in Table 7, were examined to ascertain the nature and strength of the relationship among them.

While most phonological measures correlate significantly with each other, a few do not. The pretest Oddity test shows non-significant relationships with Transition Yopp-Singer ($r = .18$), Transition Supply Initial Consonant ($r = .12$), and Posttest Supply Initial Consonant ($r = .16$). The correlation between Transition Yopp-Singer and Posttest Oddity ($r = .26$), and Posttest Supply Initial Consonant ($r = .25$) are weaker than the other relationships indicated.

Table 6 Means (and standard deviations) for Delayed Post Test reading, dictation, and math by treatment group

TrGp	CAT WR	CAT Voc	CAT Comp	CAT Tot Rdg	Dictation	Comb Rdg	Math
A,X	18.86 (5.96)	17.29 (8.93)	18.47 (6.38)	54.71 (19.24)	29.14 (12.40)	83.86 (27.61)	14.57 (4.33)
B,AB	19.90 (4.20)	20.25 (7.14)	21.30 (6.30)	61.45 (16.31)	32.95 (5.77)	94.40 (20.69)	16.75 (4.15)
AB,B	17.87 (5.77)	17.07 (5.99)	16.47 (5.04)	51.40 (15.33)	30.93 (10.23)	82.33 (23.46)	11.07 (5.15)
X,A	19.81 (5.56)	19.05 (6.84)	22.48 (6.68)	61.33 (17.01)	30.52 (9.77)	91.86 (24.85)	16.48 (4.67)
Y	19.64 (3.80	17.77 (6.17)	22.23 (4.86)	59.64 (13.25)	28.59 (8.71)	88.23 (19.28)	18.18 (3.66)

Table 7 Intercorrelations between phonological awareness measures and achievement measures

		1	2	3	4	5	6	7	8	9	10	11	12	13	14	15	16	17
1	Pre Oddity	1.00																
2	Tr YS	.18	1.00															
3	Tr SIC	.12	.48	1.00														
4	Tr Oddity	.27	.32	.32	1.00													
5	Tr Tot PA	.22	.72	.76	.75	1.00												
6	Post YS	.28	.40	.54	.46	.62	1.00											
7	Post SIC	.16	.25	.36	.30	.39	.52	1.00										
8	Post Oddity	.27	.26	.53	.54	.59	.58	.35	1.00									
9	Post Tot PA	.29	.39	.58	.50	.64	.86	.78	.76	1.00								
10	Wd Recog	.14	.18	.37	.34	.42	.50	.34	.41	.53	1.00							
11	Vocabulary	.14	.15	.38	.41	.43	.54	.40	.39	.55	.60	1.00						
12	Comp	.05	.11	.34	.32	.33	.53	.35	.45	.55	.59	.65	1.00					
13	Math	-.01	.08	.29	.21	.27	.36	.11	.24	.29	.49	.32	.47	1.00				
14	Dictation	.09	.16	.27	.21	.29	.32	.27	.27	.38	.61	.43	.34	.16	1.00			
15	Tchr Per	.32	.20	.43	.33	.41	.49	.39	.44	.55	.64	.54	.51	.36	.62	1.00		
16	Tot Read	.14	.19	.43	.42	.47	.62	.43	.49	.64	.83	.887	.87	.49	.55	.67	1.00	
17	Comb Rdg	.13	.21	.41	.38	.45	.55	.40	.45	.60	.84	.76	.73	.40	.82	.74	.92	1.00

Correlations greater than .21 are significant at the .05 level.
Correlations greater than .27 are significant at the .01 level.

When correlations between phonological awareness measures are viewed by testing occasion, a clearer pattern is observable. Table 8 displays the relationship between phonological awareness measures taken at pretest, transition test, and posttest occasions and reading achievement at the end of the following year.

To determine that gains in phonological awareness relate specifically to the language areas of reading and spelling, rather than to all areas of academic skill, it is necessary to correlate those gains with something other than reading or spelling. Mathematics is an academic area that would be expected to show little relation to changes in phonological awareness. Hypothesis Four(b) directs this set of analyses, as it examines the specificity of the relationship between phonological awareness and reading.

Mathematics group means from measures taken at the end of subjects' first grade year were computed and entered as a dependent variable in a correlation matrix along with reading achievement.

A test of significance between dependent correlations (Cohen & Cohen, 1983) revealed significance in all cases. That is, on the dependent variable Post Total Oddity, $r_{xy} - r_{vy}$ is significant at the $p < .01$ level; on the dependent variable Yopp-Singer, $r_{xy} - r_{vy}$ is significant at the $p < .01$ level; on the dependent variable Supply Initial Consonant, $r_{xy} - r_{vy}$ is significant at the $p < .01$ level; and on the dependent variable Post Total PA, $r_{xy} - r_{vy}$ is significant at the $p < .01$ level. From these data, phonological awareness clearly appears to be specific to the language area of reading.

Although the differences between $r_{xy} - r_{vy}$ were significant on all dependent variables measured, another set of analyses was performed to further define the specificity of phonological awareness to reading. The relationships among the measures, for each treatment group, were also examined by forced stepwise multiple regression analyses, with selected dependent variables entered into the equation in a fixed order. The purpose of this analysis was to study the unique influence phonological awareness had on reading achievement after other important influences had been factored out. Those other influences, predictor variables, were chronological age, math computation ability, and memory. Subjects' scores on these variables were entered in that order, leaving the post-total phonological awareness measures to be entered last. In this way, it was possible to discern the amount of variance in reading attributable to phonological awareness after other influences had been removed. Math Computation was entered in place of IQ, as a measure of non-verbal cognitive ability.

Table 8

Correlations between Total Phonological Awareness measures at pretest, transition test, and posttest occasions, and reading achievement measures by Treatment Group.

	Word Rec	Vocabulary	Comp	Dictation	Comb Read	Math
Group A,X						
Pre	.09	.08	.03	.00	.06	.06
Trans	.68	.56	.67	.45	.77	.67
Post	.81	.64	.63	.46	.83	.63

Correlations greater than .51 are significant at the .05 level.
Correlations greater than .64 are significant at the .01 level.

	Word Rec	Vocabulary	Comp	Dictation	Comb Read	Math
Group B,AB						
Pre	.08	.33	.26	.05	.21	.25
Trans	.39	.61	.52	.55	.60	.40
Post	.43	.55	.66	.39	.57	.37

Correlations greater than .43 are significant at the .05 level.
Correlations greater than .55 are significant at the .01 level.

	Word Rec	Vocabulary	Comp	Dictation	Comb Read	Math
Group AB,B						
Pre	−.40	−.49	−.34	−.59	−.58	-.06
Trans	.50	.17	.03	.27	.29	.19
Post	.49	.46	.68	.40	.54	.51

Correlations greater than .50 are significant at the .05 level.
Correlations greater than .62 are significant at the .01 level.

	Word Rec	Vocabulary	Comp	Dictation	Comb Read	Math
Group X,A						
Pre	.46	.26	.16	.52	.45	.16
Trans	.30	.37	.24	.31	.36	.27
Post	.55	.58	.46	.53	.62	−.01

Correlations greater than .42 are significant at the .05 level.
Correlations greater than .54 are significant at the .01 level.

	Word Rec	Vocabulary	Comp	Dictation	Comb Read	Math
Group Y						
Pre	.18	.47	.37	−.09	.20	−.03
Trans	.43	.56	.55	.10	.44	.53
Post	.45	.57	.62	.16	.49	.35

Correlations greater than .41 are significant at the .05 level.
Correlations greater than .53 are significant al the .01 level.

	Word Rec	Vocabulary	Comp	Dictation	Comb Read	Math
All Groups						
Pre	.14	.14	.05	.09	.13	−.01
Trans	.42	.43	.33	.29	.45	.27
Post	.53	.55	.55	.38	.60	.29

Correlations greater than .21 are significant at the .05 level.
Correlations greater than .27 are significant at the .01 level.

The first variable entered was age, which accounted for little variance in all groups (less than 7%) except in Group A,X. Interestingly, its influence on this group was substantial: Vocabulary (14% of the variance), Comprehension (22% of the variance), Dictation (13% of the variance). It was even significant in two instances: Word Recognition (35% of the variance, $p < .05$), and Combined Reading (35% of the variance, $p < .05$). The influence of memory was slight, accounting for less than 8% in all but the two lowest achieving groups: Group A,X (20% of the variance in Comprehension) and Group AB,B (12% of the variance in Vocabulary, 57% of the variance in Dictation, and 36% of the variance in Combined Reading). Cognitive ability accounted for a substantial amount of variance in all groups. The one striking exception, however, is its lack of influence on Group X,A. For this group, cognitive ability accounts for only 6% of the variance in Word Recognition, 1% of the variance in Vocabulary and Comprehension, 3% in Dictation, and 2% in Combined Reading.

The influence of the final entry, phonological awareness, is substantial for all treatment groups. It is most pronounced in Group X,A where it accounts for 51% of the variance in Vocabulary. These correlational analyses

Table 9

Unique task composite variance attributable to phonological awareness on all criterion variables by treatment group after age, math and memory effects are partialed out.

Tr Group	Step			Criterion Variables							
Group A, X		1.		2.		3.		4.		5.	
		R^2	R^2Inc		R^2	R^2Inc	R^2	R^2Inc	R^2	R^2Inc	R^2
R^2Inc	1.	.35	.35**	.14	.14	.22	.22	.13	.13	.35	.35
	2.	.47	.13	.16	.03	.32	.09	.14	.01	.40	.05
	3.	.49	.02	.18	.02	.52	.20*	.15	.01	.42	.01
	4.	.73	.24**	.48	.3`*	.61	.09	.37	.21	.77	.35**

Tr Group	Step			Criterion Variables							
Group B,AB		1.		2.		3.		4.		5.	
		R^2	R^2Inc		R^2	R^2Inc	R^2	R^2Inc	R^2	R^2Inc	R^2
R^2Inc	1.	.02	.02	.02	.02	.01	.01	.03	.03	.01	.01
	2.	.56	.53**	.48	.46**	.30	.30*	.53	.50**	.59	.58**
	3.	.56	.00	.48	.00	.30	.00	.56	.03	.60	.01
	4.	.59	.03	.60	.11*	.55	.25**	.58	.02	.70	.10*

Table 9 *continued*

Tr Group Group AB,B R²Inc	Step	1. R²	R²Inc	2. R²	R²Inc	3. R²	R²Inc	4. R²	R²Inc	5. R²	R²Inc
	1.	.02	.02	.00	.00	.00	.00	.00	.00	.00	.00
	2.	.43	.41**	.12	.12	.51	.51**	.01	.01	.13	.13
	3.	.31	−.12	.24	.12	.56	.05	.58	.57	.49	.36**
	4.	.41	.11	.23	−.01	.66	.10	.61	.03	.55	.06

Tr Group Group X,A R²Inc	Step	1. R²	R²Inc	2. R²	R²Inc	3. R²	R²Inc	4. R²	R²Inc	5. R²	R²Inc
	1.	.01	.01	.02	.02	.00	.00	.07	.07	.05	.05
	2.	.08	.06	.03	.01	.01	01.	.11	.03	.06	.02
	3.	.10	.02	.04	.01	.05	.94	.18	.08	.12	.06
	4.	.46	.36**	.54	.51**	.24	.19*	.37	.19*	.49	.37**

Tr Group Group Y R²Inc	Step	1. R²	R²Inc	2. R²	R²Inc	3. R²	R²Inc	4. R²	R²Inc	5. R²	R²Inc
	1.	.02	.02	−.48	.00	.06	.06	.01	.01	.02	.02
	2.	.36	.34**	.28	.00	.19	.13	.32	.31**	.42	.39**
	3.	.37	.01	.29	.00	.23	.04	.40	.08	.46	.04
	4.	.45	.08	.44	.16*	.48	.25**	.40	.00	.53	.07

Tr Group All Groups	Step	1. R²	R²Inc	2. R²	R²Inc	3. R²	R²Inc	4. R²	R²Inc	5. R²	R²Inc
	1.	.01	.01	.01	.01	.03	.03	.00	.00	.01	.01
	2.	.24	.23**	.11	.09**	.23	.20**	.03	.03	.17	.15**
	3.	.24	.00	.11	.00	.24	.00	.03	.00	.17	.00
	4.	.40	.16**	.34	.23**	.42	.18**	.15	.12**	.42	.25**

*p<.05, **<.01

Criterion Variables
1 = CAT Word Recognition Subtest
2 = CAT Vocabulary Subtest
3 = CAT Comprehension Subtest
4 = Dictation Test
5 = Combined Reading

Predictor Variables
Step 1 = Age
Step 2 = Math
Step 3 = Memory
Step 4 = PhonAware

illustrate the sound relationship between phonological awareness and reading. Further, they provide additional evidence that the phonological awareness levels of prereading children are accurate predictors of later reading achievement. The strongest predictors of reading achievement appear to be the scores on the Post Yopp-Singer test, taken at the end of kindergarten. Transition Supply Initial Consonant scores and Transition Oddity scores, taken in the middle of the kindergarten year, appear to be less robust, but nevertheless moderate predictors of reading achievement. Pretest Oddity scores seem to have limited predictive capacity to first grade reading achievement, although they correlate significantly with Transition Oddity and Posttest Yopp Singer and Oddity scores.

Correlational analyses also provided evidence of the specific nature of the relationship between phonological awareness and reading. The correlation of scores between phonological awareness and reading is far more robust than the correlation between phonological awareness and math. This indicates that a child's awareness of the sound structure of the language has a greater impact upon reading achievement than upon achievement in math.

Discussion

It is clear that phonological awareness training of prereaders during their first semester in kindergarten has a measurable effect on their ability to perceive rhyme and alliteration. It is also clear that training influences young kindergarten children's ability to segment sounds as measured on the Yopp-Singer and Supply Initial Consonant Tests. These findings support conclusions drawn from previous training studies (Ball & Blachman, 1991; Bradley & Bryant, 1985).

The type of training appears to make a difference. Two treatments investigated in this study emerge as equally compelling in phonological awareness instruction for children in the first months of kindergarten. Treatment A, direct instruction, was more effective in instructing children in segmentation, whereas Treatment B, indirect instruction, seems to have more impact on children's ability to detect rhyming and alliteration patterns. That is not surprising since Treatment B is based on literature selections chosen for the rhyming and alliteration patterns contained in the text. Finally, although Treatment X, story-mapping and retelling, was originally designed as a comparison/control treatment, its effect was significantly different from the control group. In contrast, Treatment AB, combination direct + indirect, does not appear to impart the type of instruction beneficial to children of this age and at this early stage of their kindergarten experience.

The results of Training Period II are somewhat different from those in the first training period. It appears that all of the treatments combined outperformed the comparison and control groups combined on the Supply Initial Consonant Test. When contrasted with the singular lack of effect on the same measure in Training Period I, these results seem to imply that children of this age are more receptive to instruction in phonological awareness in general. The subjects' mean age at the beginning of the second training period was 5.6, compared with a mean age of 5.4 at the beginning of the first training period. In addition, the children had experienced four months of kindergarten curriculum, which provided them with a recent background of literacy experience at the start of the second training period. This may have provided a more fertile environment for instruction in phonological awareness. Stahl and Miller's (1989) discussion of stages of reading development and the prevailing construct of emergent literacy (Sulzby & Teale, 1991) lend support to this observation.

In both training periods, Treatment A differed significantly from the control group on the Supply Initial Consonant Test, suggesting that direct instruction has a greater effect upon children's ability to segment phonemes from words, when compared with instruction provided through the district curriculum.

Just as the effect of Treatment A remains strong in both training periods, it is interesting to note a change in the effectiveness of Treatment AB, which occurs during this second training period. It was concluded from Training Period I that this treatment was not effective for children during the first semester of their kindergarten year. In contrast, the results of Training Condition II cautiously suggests the opposite, provided the treatment is delivered during the second semester of their kindergarten year. Results indicate that Treatment AB was significantly more effective than Treatment B on Yopp-Singer. In addition, the analysis on raw score data show that Treatment AB differs significantly from the control group on Yopp-Singer; however, the null hypothesis was rejected with reservation due to lack of support from normalized data. In addition, the effect of Treatment AB on Supply Initial Consonant was strong enough only to suspend judgment with reservation, indicating again that normalized scores did not support raw score data. Though these two comparisons are not statistically significant, they provide more than a suggestion that time of instructional delivery is as important as instructional content when dealing with young children.

The sequence of training is an important consideration when working with young children. Analysis of sequence treatment data, as indicated in Table 5, show two sequence groups unmistakably emerging as significantly more effective than the control: Treatment B,AB and Treatment X,A. Both treatments show the greatest effect on the Yopp-Singer and Supply Initial Consonant tests of phoneme segmentation. These results are encouraging when viewed with the current literature on the robust relationship between phonemic segmentation and later reading ability (Mann, 1986; Stanovich, Cunningham, & Cramer, 1984; Perfetti, Beck, Bell & Hughes, 1987; Share, Jorm, Maclean, & Matthews, 1984; Treiman & Baron, 1983). Vellutino (1988) reports in his longitudinal study of kindergarten children that "the most important finding (of the study) is that the tests which were most highly and most reliably correlated with oral reading ability were those which depended heavily on phonemic segmentation ability" (p. 81).

Treatments X,A and B,AB provide an effective method of enhancing phonemic segmentation for children at an early, prereading age. The similar pattern of these two sequence treatments strongly suggests a preferred order of instruction. Direct instruction seems to be most effective when it is delivered during the second portion of the year, after a variety of experiences with literature have been experienced by the children. Kindergarten children appear to receive and retain instruction in phonological awareness when a foundation of literacy is laid during the first portion of the school year.

When training in phonological awareness is a consistent part of the kindergarten curriculum, with explicit attention given to segmentation, delivered at an appropriate time, children's phonological awareness is measurably enhanced.

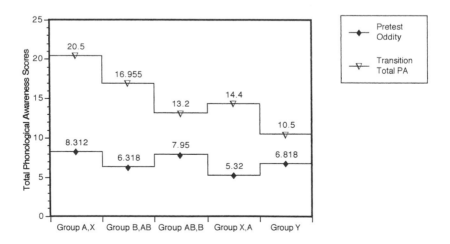

Figure 1 Training condition I: gains on total phonological measures by treatment group

It had been predicted from Hypothesis Three(b) that reading achievement measures would be significantly different between treatment sequence groups one year after training. Table 6 indicates that the treatment means of Groups B,AB and X,A, which had both shown the greatest effect during training, remained the highest on

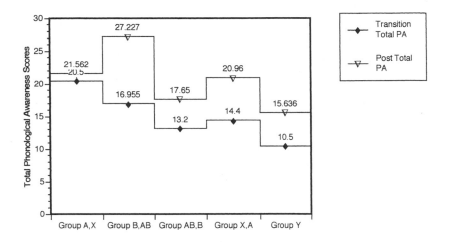

Figure 2 Training condition II: gains on total phonological measures by treatment group

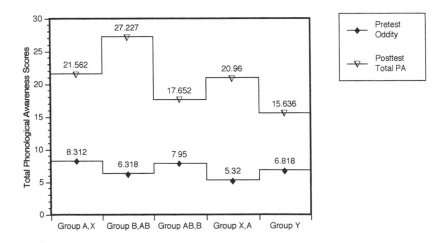

Figure 3 Growth by sequence group

all reading achievement measures at the end of first grade. However, the advantages they gained from treatment, although remaining strong, did not result in significant differences when compared with the control group. Although scores of the control group were lower than Group X,A on all subtests, they approached that of the other groups, and results did not show significant effect on any measure. When interpreting these results it is worth noting the conservative α level employed in this study in all tests of significance. In addition, numerous other factors served to influence the findings, for example limited length of initial treatment, effects of subsequent instruction in both kindergarten and first grade, choice of measures to assess dependent variables, subjects' home factors, and complexity of classroom contexts.

The correlational data shed additional light on the relationship between phonological awareness and reading. The generally weak correlation of pretest and reading achievement scores shown in Table 7 may be due to the task requirements of the Oddity Test, which was difficult for young kindergarten children. Although it is considered a discerning measure, it could be that the Oddity Test alone does not give an accurate portrayal of phonological awareness when administered to kindergarten students early in the year. If used as a pretest, perhaps an appropriate complementary measure for the Oddity Test would be a simpler task, such as a rhyme choice or rhyme supply task.

When it is administered in December, however, or midway through the year, the Oddity Test gives a more accurate measure of phonological awareness ($r = .38$). This test and the Supply Initial Consonant Test ($r = .41$) were the measures most highly correlated to reading. Similarly, in May the Yopp-Singer test ($r = .55$) was the best predictor. This is consistent with previous studies (Bradley & Bryant, 1985; Liberman, Shankweiler, Fischer, & Carter, 1974; Lundberg, Olofsson, & Wall, 1980; Mann, 1984; Mann & Liberman, 1984; Stanovich, Cunningham, & Cramer, 1984; Vellutino,1987) that indicate that segmentation, such as that required on the Supply Initial Consonant and the Yopp-Singer tests, is a powerful predictor of reading achievement.

The specificity of the relationship between phonological awareness and reading is supported in this study. All tests for differences between dependent correlation of phonological awareness and reading or math measures were significant at the .01 level. Clearly, from these data the linguistic skills involved in segmenting and blending are more closely related to reading ability than to mathematical reasoning ability.

The stepwise MRC analyses further helped define this relationship. These results illustrate the amount of variance on each criterion variable that can be uniquely attributed to phonological awareness. Table 9 clearly shows that on every subtest of reading achievement, the variance explained for All Groups by phonological awareness was significant at the .01 level. The Word Recognition subtest indicates $R^2 = .40$, R^2 increase = .16, F = 24.73; the Vocabulary subtest indicates $R^2 = .34$, R^2 increase = .23, F = 31.75; the Comprehension subtest indicates $R^2 = .42$, R^2 increase = .18, F = 28.82; the Dictation test indicates $R^2 = .15$, R^2 increase = .12, F = 12.68; and Combined Reading, $R^2 = .42$, R^2 increase = .25, F = 39.85. These results further emphasize the unique and specific relationship of phonological awareness and reading achievement.

Closer examination of these results by treatment group reveals a striking difference in scores between groups. The amount of variance on reading achievement measures that can be explained by phonological awareness in the control group is limited when compared with Groups X,A and A,X, which received direct instruction in phonological awareness during the training year. In addition to showing the most amount of variance attributable to phonological awareness, Groups X,A and A,X show the least amount of variance attributable to math, which was entered into the regression analyses as a measure of non-verbal cognitive ability. This suggests that the reading performance of Groups X,A and A,X was not as contingent upon general cognitive abilities as it was upon phonological awareness. This may indicate that children with less cognitive ability can nevertheless achieve reading success if they are provided direct instruction in phonological awareness, similar to that in Treatment A. Without effective training in phonological awareness, successful reading achievement appears to depend upon cognitive ability more than learned skill.

These results further indicate that the manner in which the children in each group approach the reading task may differ considerably. Direct Instruction appears to provide children with a skill more powerful than non-verbal cognitive ability. Juel, Griffith, and Gough (1986) reach a similar conclusion in their longitudinal study of first and second grade children. They suggest that children who have not developed a systematic phonological system, but who have achieved at least average reading comprehension levels at the end of first grade, are reading "in a qualitatively different manner than their peers who have good spelling-sound knowledge" (Juel, Hillinger, & Gough, 1986). These children have a greater reliance upon whole word visual cues than letter-sound information.

Further examination of the study's treatment conditions is necessary to determine the consistency of the effects reported here. A greater number of teachers delivering each treatment would lend more reliability to the results. In addition, the type of first grade instruction received by the subjects following the initial year of intervention is an important factor that should be pursued and analyzed in future longitudinal studies, as should an alternate standardized measure of reading achievement at the end of first grade. Another important issue to explore is at-home reading and literacy background of subjects, both prior to and following intervention.

Conclusions

This study demonstrates that phonological awareness can be measured in kindergarten children prior to the onset of formal reading instruction, and that they are responsive to training in phonological awareness, even with relatively short periods of intervention.

This study further suggests that Direct Instruction is more effective than Indirect Instruction; and it is most effective when delivered during the second half of the kindergarten year following an initial treatment of literacy building, in which the children encounter a variety of experiences with oral and written language. When training in phonological awareness is delivered at an appropriate time, with explicit attention given to segmentation, children's phonological awareness is measurably enhanced.

The variance in reading attributed to phonological awareness is greater for students whose instruction is delivered directly. Further, the variance in reading attributed to cognitive ability for those children appears to be less. This indicates that when trained in phonological awareness using the direct instruction methods of Treatment A, children's reading is more reliant upon their use of those skills than upon their general intelligence. By extension, it can be concluded that training in phonological awareness increases children's chances for successful reading, regardless of cognitive ability. Further observation of these subjects and their groupwise performance is necessary in order to be more definitive on this point.

The controlled nature of the study provided evidence that suggests an absence of productive attention to the phonological aspects of language development in the typical kindergarten curriculum. The children in the control group showed little growth in phonological awareness other than what might be expected due to maturation and exposure to a literacy based program. Certainly, children in traditional classrooms are exposed to the alphabet and letter-sound relationships; however, all too often they are given worksheets, such as alphabet dot-to-dot and phonics picture-letter-matching. These kinds of activities are neither appropriate nor instructive in the foundational linguistic skills for which they are prescribed. Instruction in phonological awareness must involve the sound system, with countless opportunities to hear stories, to repeat phrases, to invent similar sounding patterns, and to play with sounds in a manner that focuses children's awareness of the language upon syllables and phonemes. Children must become re-aware of, with conscious attention given to, the very aspects of their language that they have learned so proficiently up to that point. When children are given systematic, consistent training in phonological awareness that focuses on the speech patterns and sounds of our language, their levels of phonological awareness are significantly enhanced. However, the appropriateness of the training is dependent upon the degree to which it addresses the phonological structure of the language in word play and sound categorization, before connecting those speech patterns and sounds with their visual representations. The oral aspects of phonological awareness training place it deeper in the linguistic system than the typical "phonics" instruction tends to reach (Adams, 1990).

Finally, this study has provided an effective means of training kindergarten children in phonological awareness that has direct and immediate classroom applicability to teachers in the field. The training procedures used in this study are research based, but modified in ways that clearly capture the attention of the children, who frequently continued singing the songs or playing the games well after their lessons had finished. The instruction used in this study could easily be incorporated into an existing kindergarten program, which would provide a firm foundation of phonological awareness for all children prior to formal reading instruction (Ayres, 1993). The instructional techniques of these training procedures are pedagogically sound and appropriate to young children's physical and cognitive development. Further, the literature-based, activity-oriented nature of each treatment successfully merges the seemingly conflicting philosophies of phonological awareness instruction and whole language, which is critical in today's educational climate.

Although this study falls short of being conclusive regarding the role of phonological awareness in reading acquisition, the results reported here extend previous research that implicates phonological awareness as a crucial, enabling factor in learning to read. It has demonstrated that early training in phonological awareness is both possible and efficacious, while it has provided insight into the nature and sequence of training. Finally, this study has provided an effective means of training kindergarten children in phonological awareness that merges the prevailing constructs of reading acquisition and offers a unique approach with direct classroom applicability.

Works Cited

Adams, M. (1990). *Beginning to read: thinking and learning about print.* Cambridge, MA: MIT Press.

Ayres, L. (1993a). *The efficacy of three training conditions on phonological awareness of kindergarten children and the longitudinal effect of each on later reading acquisition.* Unpublished doctoral dissertation, Oakland University.

Ayres, L. (1993b). *The phonological zoo: A language awareness training program for young children.* Walled Lake, MI: Walled Lake.

Ball, E. & Blachman, B. (1991). Does phoneme awareness training in kindergarten make a difference in early word recognition and developmental spelling? *Reading Research Quarterly, 26,* 49–66.

Bertelson, P. (1986). The onset of literacy: Liminal remarks. *Cognition, 24,* 1–30.

Blank, M., & Sheldon, F. (1971). Story recall in kindergarten children: Effect of method of presentation on psycholinguistic performance. *Child Development, 42,* 299–312.

Borg, W., & Gall, M. (1989). *Educational Research.* New York: Longman.

Bradley, L., & Bryant, P. E. (1978). Difficulties in auditory organization as a possible cause of reading backwardness. *Nature, 271,* 746–47.

Bradley, L., & Bryant, P. E. (1979). The independence of reading and spelling in backward and normal readers. *Developmental Medicine and Child Neurology, 21,* 504–14.

Bradley, L., & Bryant, P.E. (1983). Categorising sounds and learning to read—a causal connection *Nature, 301,* 419–21.

Bradley, L., & Bryant, P.E. (1985). *Rhyme and reason in reading and spelling.* Ann Arbor: University of Michigan Press.

Brown, A. (1975). Recognition, reconstruction and recall of narrative sequences of preoperational children. *Child Development, 46,* 155–56.

Brown, H., & Cambourne, B. (1987). *Read and retell.* Portsmouth, NH: Heinemann.

Bryant, P.E., & Bradley, L. (1985). *Children's reading problems.* Oxford: Blackwell.

California achievement test (CAT/5). (1993). Monterey, CA: Macmillan/McGraw-Hill School Publishing Co.

Calfee, R., Lindamood, P., & Lindamood, C. (1973). Acoustic-phonetic skills and reading—kindergarten through twelfth grade. *Journal of Educational Psychology, 64,* 293–98.

Chomsky, C. (1972). Stages in language development and reading. *Harvard Educational Review, 42,* 1–33.

Clay, M. (1979). *The early detection of reading difficulties,* (3rd ed.). Portsmouth, NH: Heinemann.

Cohen, J., & Cohen, P. (1983). *Applied multiple regression/correlation analysis for the behavioral sciences.* Hillsdale, NJ: Erlbaum.

Content, A., Kolinsky, R., Morais, J., & Bertelson, P. (1986). Phonetic segmentation in prereaders: Effect of corrective information. *Journal of Experimental Child Psychology, 42,* 49–72.

Crowder, R. G. (1982). *The psychology of reading.* New York: Oxford University Press.

Doctor, E. A., & Coltheart, M. (1980). Children's use of phonological encoding when reading for meaning. *Memory and Cognition, 8,* 195–209.

Downing, J. (1979). *Reading and reasoning.* New York: Springer-Verlag.

Ehri, L. C. (1979). Linguistic insight: Threshold of reading acquisition. In T. Waller & G. E. MacKinnon (Eds.), *Reading research: Advances in theory and practice* (pp. 63–114). New York: Academic Press.

Ehri, L. C., & Wilce, I. S. (1980). The influence of orthography on readers' conceptualization of the phonemic structure of words. *Applied Psycholinguistics, 1,* 371–85.

Elkonin, D.B. (1973). U.S.S.R. In J. Downing (Ed.), *Comparative reading.* New York: Macmillan.

Ferguson, George A. (1971). *Statistical analysis in psychology and education.* New York: McGraw-Hill.

Fox, B., & Routh, D.K. (1975). Analyzing spoken language into words, syllables and phonemes: A developmental study. *Journal of Psycholinguistic Research, 4,* 331–42.

Fox, B., & Routh, D. K. (1976). Phonemic analysis and synthesis as word-attack skills. *Journal of Educational Psychology, 68,* 70–74.

Fox, B., & Routh, D.K. (1980). Phonemic analysis and severe reading disability in children. *Journal of Psycholinguistic Research, 9,* 115–19.

Fuller, R. (1974). Breaking down the IQ walls: Severely retarded people can learn to read. *Psychology Today,* October, 97–102.

Gleitman, L. R., & Rozin, P. (1977). The structure and acquisition of reading I: Relations between orthographies and the structure of language. In A. S. Reber & D. L. Scarborough (Eds.), *Toward a psychology of reading.* Hillsdale: Erlbaum.

Goldstein, D. M. (1976). Cognitive-linguistic functioning and learning to read in preschoolers. *Journal of Educational Psychology, 68,* 680–88.

Golinkoff, R. M. (1978). Phonemic awareness skills and reading achievement. In F. B. Murray and J. J Pikulski (Eds.), *The acquisition of reading.* Baltimore: University Park Press.

Gough, P. B., & Hillinger, M. L. (1980). Learning to read: An unnatural act. *Bulletin of the Orton Society, 30,* 179–96.

Hohn, W., & Ehri, L. (1983). Do alphabet letters help prereaders acquire phonemic segmentation skills? *Journal of Educational Psychology, 75,* 752–62.

Horowitz, L. (1974). *Elements of statistics for psychology and education.* New York: McGraw-Hill.

Huitema, B. (1980). *The analysis of covariance and alternatives.* New York: Wiley & Sons.

Jorm, A. F., & Share, D. L. (1983). Phonological recoding and reading acquisition. *Applied Psycholinguistics, 4,* 103–47.

Juel, C., Griffith, P., & Gough, P. (1986). Acquisition of literacy: A longitudinal study of children in first and second grade. *Journal of Educational Psychology, 78,* 243–55.

Keppel, G. (1973). *Design and analysis: A researcher's handbook.* New Jersey: Prentice-Hall.

Keppel, G., & Zedeck, S. (1989). *Data analysis for research designs.* New York: W. H. Freeman and Co.

Knafle, J.D. (1973). Auditory perception of rhyming in kindergarten children. *Journal of Speech and Hearing Research, 16,* 482–87.

Knafle, J.D. (1974). Children's discrimination of rhyme. *Journal of Speech and Hearing Research, 17,* 367–72.

Lehr, S. (1988). Child's developing sense of theme as a response to literature. *Reading Research Quarterly, 23,* 337–57.

Lenel, J.C., & Cantor, J. H. (1981). Rhyme recognition and phonemic perception in young children. *Journal of Psycholinguistic Research, 10,* 57–68.

Liberman, I. Y. (1973). Segmentation of the spoken word and reading acquisition. *Bulletin of the Orton Society, 23,* 65–77.

Liberman, I. Y., Rubin, H,, Duques, S. L., & Carlisle, J. (1985). Linguistic skills and spelling proficiency in kindergartners and adult poor spellers. In D. B. Gray & J. F. Kavanaugh (Eds.), *Biobehavioral measures of dyslexia* (pp. 163–76). Parkton, MD: York Press.

Liberman, I. Y., & Shankweiler, D. (1979). Speech, the alphabet and teaching to read. In L. Resnick and P. Weaver (Eds.), *Theory and practice of early reading.* Hillsdale, NJ: Erlbaum.

Liberman, I. Y., & Shankweiler, D. (1985). Phonology and the problems of learning to read and write. *Remedial and Special Education, 6,* 8–17.

Liberman, I. Y., Shankweiler, D., Fischer, F. W., & Carter, B. (1974). Explicit syllable and phoneme segmentation in the young child. *Journal of Experimental Child Psychology, 18,* 201–12.

Liberman, I., Shankweiler, D., Liberman, A.M., Fowler, C., & Fischer, F. W. (1977). Phonetic segmentation and recoding in the beginning reader. In A.S. Reber & D.L. Scarborough (Ed.), *Toward a psychology of reading* (pp. 207–26). New York: Erlbaum.

Lundberg, I. (1978). Aspects of linguistic awareness related to reading. In A. Sinclair, R. J. Jarvella, and W. J. M. Levelt (Eds.), *The child's conception of language.* Berlin: Springer-Verlag.

Lundberg, I., Olofsson, A. & Wall, S. (1980). Reading and spelling skills in the first school years predicted from phonemic awareness skills in kindergarten. *Scandinavian Journal of Psychology, 21,* 159–73.

Maclean, M., Bryant, P., & Bradley. (1987). Rhymes, nursery rhymes, and reading in early childhood. *Merrill-Palmer Quarterly, 33* (3), 255–81.

Mandler, J., & Johnson, M. (1977). Remembrance of things parsed: Story structure and recall. *Cognitive Psychology, 9,* 111–51.

Mann, V. A. (1984). Longitudinal prediction and prevention of early reading difficulty. *Annals of Dyslexia, 34,* 117–36.

Mann, V. A. (1986a). Why some children encounter reading problems. In J. K. Torgesen & B. Y. L. Wong (Eds.), *Psychological and educational perspectives on learning disabilities* (pp. 133–59). Orlando, FL: Academic Press.

Mann, V. A. (1986b). Phonological awareness: The role of reading experience. *Cognition, 24,* 65–92.

Mann, V. A. (1991). Phonological awareness and early reading ability: One perspective. In D. J. Sawyer & B. J. Fox (Eds.), *Phonological awareness in reading, the evolution of current perspectives* (pp. 191–215). New York: Springer-Verlag.

Mann, V., Tobin, P., & Wilson. (1987). Measuring phonological awareness through the invented spelling of kindergarten children. *Merrill-Palmer Quarterly, 33* (3), 365–91.

Mann, V., & Brady, S. (1988). Reading disability: The role of language deficiencies. *Journal of Consulting and Clinical Psychology, 56,* 811–16.

Mann, V., & Ditunno, P. (1990). Phonological deficiencies: Effective predictors of future reading problems. In G. Th. Pavlidis (Ed.), *Perspectives on dyslexia* (Vol. 2). New York: Wiley and Sons.

Mann, V., & Liberman, I. (1984). Phonological awareness and verbal short-term memory. *Journal of Learning Disabilities, 17,* 592–99.

Marsh, G., & Mineo, R. (1977). Training preschool children to recognize phonemes in words. *Journal of Educational Psychology, 69,* 748–53.

Mattingly, I. G. (1972). Reading, the linguistic process and linguistic awareness. In J. F. Kavanaugh & I. G. Mattingly (Eds.), *Language by ear and by eye: The relationship between speech and reading* (pp. 133–47). Cambridge, MA: MIT Press.

Morais, J., Cary, L., Alegria, J., & Bertelson, P. (1979). Does awareness of speech as a sequence of phones arise spontaneously? *Cognition, 7,* 323–31.

Morrow, L. (1985). Reading and retelling stories: Strategies for emergent readers. *Reading Teacher, 38* (9), 870–75.

Morrow, L. (1985). Retelling stories: A strategy for improving young children's comprehension concept of story structure and oral language complexity. *Elementary School Journal, 85* (5), 647–61.

Nesdale, A., Herriman, M., & Tunmer, W. (1984). Phonological awareness in children. In W. E. Tunmer, C. Pratt, & M. L. Herriman (Eds.), *Metalinguistic awareness in children.* New York: Springer-Verlag.

Nesdale, A., Herriman, M., & Tunmer, W. (1980). The development of phonological awareness. In C. Pratt and R. Grieve (Eds.), *Language awareness in children. Vol. 7. Education research and perspectives.* Nedlands: University of Western Australia.

Olofsson, A., & Lundberg, I. (1983). Can phonemic awareness be trained in kindergarten? *Scandinavian Journal of Psychology, 24,* 35–44.

Olofsson, A., & Lundberg, I. (1985). Evaluation of long term effects of phonemic awareness training in kindergarten: Illustrations of some methodological problems in evaluation research. *Scandinavian Journal of Psychology, 26,* 21–34.

Perfetti, C. A., Beck, I., Bell, L., & Hughes, C. (1987). Phonemic knowledge and learning to read are reciprocal: A longitudinal study of first grade children. *Merrill-Palmer Quarterly, 33,* 283–319.

Read, C. (1971). Preschool children's knowledge of English phonology. *Harvard Education Review, 41,* 1–34.

Read, C. (1978). Children's awareness of language, with emphasis on sound systems. In A. Sinclair, R. J. Jarvella, and W. J. M Levelt (Eds.), *The child's conception of language.* Berlin: Springer Verlag.

Read, C., Yun-Fei, A., Hong-Yin, N., & Bao-Qing, D. (1986). The ability to manipulate speech sounds depends on knowing alphabetic writing. *Cognition, 24,* 31–44.

Rosner, J. (1974). Auditory analysis training with prereaders. *The Reading Teacher, 27,* 379–84.

Rosner, J., & Simon, D. (1971). The auditory analysis test: An initial report. *Journal of Learning Disabilities, 4,* 384–92.

Rozin, P., & Gleitman, L. R. (1977). The structure and acquisition of reading II: The reading process and the acquisition of the alphabetic principled. In A. S. Reber & D. L. Scarborough (Eds.), *Toward a psychology of reading.* Hillsdale, NJ: Erlbaum.

Rumelhart, D. (1975). Notes on a schema for stories. In D. Bobrow & A. Collins (Eds.), *Representation and understanding: Studies in cognitive science.* New York: Academic Press.

Share, D. L., Jorm, A. F., MacLean, R., & Mathews, R. (1984). Sources of individual differences in reading acquisition. *Journal of Educational Psychology, 76,* 1309–24.

Skjelfjord, V. (1976). Teaching children to segment spoken words as an aid in learning to read. *Journal of Learning Disabilities, 9,* 297–306.

Snowling, M., & Perin, D. (1982). The development of phoneme segmentation skills in young children. In J. Sloboda and D. A. Rogers (Eds.), *The acquisition of symbolic skills.* New York: Plenum Press.

Stahl, S., & Miller, P. (1989). Whole language and language experience approaches for beginning reading: A quantitative research synthesis. *Review of Educational Research, Vol. 59,* No. 1, 87–116.

Stanovich, K. E., Cunningham, A., & Cramer, B. (1984). Assessing phonological awareness in kindergarten children: Issues of task comparability. *Journal of Experimental Child Psychology, 38,* 175–90.

Stanovich, K.E., Cunningham, A.E., Feeman, D.J., (1984). Intelligence, cognitive skills, and early reading progress. *Reading Research Quarterly, 19,* 3, 279–303.

Sulzby, E., & Teale, W. (1991). Emergent literacy. In R. Barr, M. Kamil, P. Mosenthal, and P.D. Pearson (Eds.), *Handbook of reading research: Vol. II. New York: Longman.*

Thorndyke, P. (1977). Cognitive structures in comprehension and memory of narrative discourse. *Cognitive Psychology, 9,* 77–110.

Torneus, M. (1984). Phonological awareness and reading: A chicken and egg problem? *Journal of Educational Psychology, 76,* 1346–58.

Treiman, R., & Baron, J. (1981). Segmental analysis ability: Development and relation to reading ability. In T. G. Waller & G. E. MacKinnon (Eds.), *Reading research: Advances in theory and practice, Vol. 3,* (pp.159–98). New York: Academic Press.

Treiman, R., & Baron, J. (1983). Phonemic-analysis training helps children benefit from spelling-sound rules. *Memory and Cognition, II,* 382–89.

Tunmer W., & Nesdale, A. (1985). Phonemic segmentation skill and beginning reading. *Journal of Educational Psychology, 77,* 417–27.

Tunmer, W., Herriman, M., & Nesdale, A. (1988). Metalinguistic abilities and beginning reading. *Reading Research Quarterly, 23,* 134–58.

Tunmer, W.E., & Nesdale, A.R. (1985). Phonemic segmentation skill and beginning reading. *Journal of Educational Psychology, 77,* 417–27.

Vellutino, F., & Scanlon, D. (1987). Phonological coding, phonological awareness, and reading ability: Evidence from a longitudinal and experimental study. *Merrill-Palmer Quarterly, 33* (3), 321–63.

Wagner, Richard K. (1988). Causal relations between the development of phonological processing abilities and the acquisition of reading skills: A meta-analysis. *Merrill-Palmer Quarterly, 34* (3), 261–79.

Wagner, R. K., & Torgesen, J. K. (1987). The nature of phonological processing and its causal role in the acquisition of reading skills. *Psychological Bulletin, 101,* 192–212.

Whaley, J. (1981a). Readers expectations for story structure. *Reading Research Quarterly, 17,* 90–114.

Whaley, J. (1981b). Story grammars and reading instruction. *Reading Teacher, 34,* 762–71.

Williams, J. (1980). Teaching decoding with an emphasis on phoneme analysis and phoneme blending. *Journal of Educational Psychology, 72,* 1–15.

Yopp, H. (1985). Phoneme segmentation ability: A prerequisite for phonics and sight word achievement in beginning reading? In J. Niles & L. A. Harris (Eds.), *Issues in literacy: A research perspective. Thirty-fourth yearbook of the National Reading Conference* (pp. 330–36). Rochester, NY: National Reading Conference.

Yopp, Hallie K. (1988). The validity and reliability of phonemic awareness tests. *Reading Research Quarterly, 23,* 159–77.

Zhurova, L. Y. (1973). The development of analysis of words into their sounds by preschool children. In C. A. Ferguson and D. I. Slobin (Eds.), *Studies of child language development.* New York: Holt, Rinehart, and Winston.

Zifcak, M. (1981). Phonological awareness and reading acquisition. *Contemporary Educational Psychology, 6,* 117–26.

IV Becoming Literate

9 Literacy Learning in a Whole Language Classroom: Reading Concepts and Reading Strategies First Graders Know and Use

Penny Freppon
University of Cincinnati

Ellen McIntyre
University of Louisville

The authors of this chapter begin by noting some significant differences between whole language classrooms and traditional ones, including the fact that "traditional word perfect oral reading is not emphasized in reading instruction." This and other unconventional literacy behaviors naturally arouse concern. In this report, based on year-long observation and documentation, the authors seek to determine whether the literacy behaviors encouraged in whole language classrooms actually move children toward independent, conventional reading, or to undesirable strategies and inappropriate concepts of reading.

Freppon and McIntyre describe in detail the children's reading concepts and strategies in the autumn and winter of first grade. In the spring of first grade, the authors used three specific measures to explore the reading behaviors and strategies of some "average" readers: interviews with the children; samples of oral reading that were analyzed; and altered, "incomprehensible" passages to determine the children's concepts of the purpose and nature of reading. The researchers conclude that "These children's beginning reading strategies and explorations with print lead to conventional, independent reading. Further, they appear to foster desirable concepts about the nature and purpose of reading. . . . Moreover, they understood and used phonics in reading and read stories using well-balanced, conventional strategies." The article ends with various suggestions, including the recommendation that whole language teachers monitor children's emergent explorations with print carefully, "since the timeline for learning to read and the need for specific instruction varies with individual children."

Originally published in *Reading* (1993), copyright by the UK Reading Association. Reprinted with permission.

Reading instruction in whole language classrooms differs significantly from the traditional experience (Bergeron, 1990; McGee & Richgels, 1990). For example, whole language classroom environments encourage the self-selection of reading materials of various genres and levels of difficulty, independent reading, shared reading, and reading for extended periods of time. Because of these rather significant differences in instruction, young children's beginning reading behaviours are quite visible in the whole language setting. Importantly, in whole language classrooms, traditional word perfect oral reading is not emphasized in reading instruction. Rather, children frequently participate in reading in a variety of ways such as reading pictures with text-like language, inventing text, and combining several similar reading actions (McIntyre, 1990). Observations of these unconventional reading behaviours understandably arouse teachers' and parents' curiosity and may cause concern. Do such reading behaviours move children toward independent, conventional reading? Or, do such behaviours lead to undesirable strategies and inappropriate concepts of reading? To date, research provides little empirical evidence that addresses these questions. This article provides important information about first-graders' reading concepts and strategies as they evolved during the school year in a whole language classroom.

The Teacher, the Children, and the Classroom

On a September morning first-grade teacher, Marianne, settles herself on the floor among the children she called together for a small group book demonstration. She begins by holding up a copy of Goss and Harste's (1985) *It Didn't Frighten Me!* and says, "I wanted to share this book with you." Marianne stops to invite a few more children, who have stopped to watch, into the group and then reads the title. Lynne interrupts her teacher to ask if the word *didn't* from the title of the book is a compound word.

"Not a compound word, it's a contraction. A contraction means two words put together to make a shorter word that means the same thing. Didn't means did not." When Marianne turns back to the book, Julia announces, "I predict it's gonna have beautiful pictures!"

As she opens the book most of the children respond in chorus, "It does!" "It reminds me of *King Bidgood's in the Bathtub*," someone says. Marianne and the children then engage in a brief discussion of other books that seem similar to this one. Then she reads the title, author, and illustrator and begins to read the text, "One pitch black, very dark night, right after mother turned off the light. . . ." Marianne finishes the entire book while pointing to the words. As she reads she encourages the children to join in with the repetitive, predictable sections. Most of them do. When the story is finished, Marianne gives copies of the book to each of the children and says, "Now you can read it." She then settles herself with a notebook, in which she records her observations of children's reading. Her records document a variety of reading strategies.

One child, Tommy, carefully examines the pictures on each page, turning the pages slowly. Maria reads loudly by looking at the pictures and chanting, "One pitch black night, right after mom turned out the light . . ." Kimberly points to the words as she reads mechanically, making sure she reads every word exactly as printed, "One . . . pitch . . . black . . . very dark . . . night. . . ." Chet casually flips through his copy. However, his primary behaviour is to lean over to look at Julia's book and listen as she reads.

This description of a reading group's interactions in a whole language classroom illustrates the kind of instruction that occurred regularly in support of children at a variety of developmental levels of learning to read. It also shows the variety of concepts and strategies young children have about reading as they emerge as literate individuals.

Marianne is an experienced whole language teacher who organizes her instruction on the assumption that literacy develops through interactions with more proficient language users. Her beliefs about literacy learning are revealed through her instructional actions. She views her role as one who facilitates children's *transactions* with text (Harste, Woodward, & Burke, 1982).

Each morning this classroom begins with a "class meeting" that includes, among other things, taking the register, lunch count, sharing time, and storybook readings. During this time, Marianne introduces many new books of various genres. The children are invited to make predictions about the content of the books based on cues from the cover, title page, and dedication page. During the readings, the children are encouraged to make further predictions, ask questions, or briefly share events from their own lives that connect with the events in the texts. After each reading, Marianne encourages the children to read that particular book sometime during the day.

After the class meeting, for approximately 60 to 90 minutes, the children either read or write in a "workshop" environment. To begin the workshop, Marianne asks each individual child to share his or her plans for the morning with the group. Children know they are expected to spend the morning reading and/or writing on topics of their choice. Standing up to share their plans with the group helps children focus and use the time efficiently. Once they begin working, Marianne takes a few minutes to observe and record what individual children are doing with their time. Then she typically calls a heterogeneous group of children together for small group reading, book chats, or a skill lesson such as matching voice to print.

At the beginning of the first-grade year, the small group reading time usually involves demonstration of a book with a highly predictable pattern (Holdaway, 1979). Marianne often uses big books with large print in order to help all children follow along. She usually points to words as she reads and encourages the children to join in the reading when they can. Children participate in various ways. Their ways of interacting with print help reveal their different developmental levels of learning to read. Because she often has multiple copies of predictable storybooks, Marianne asks the children to "read" the books as soon as she finishes the demonstration. This allows her to view closely the children's reading strategies and discern their emerging understandings about reading. Book chats are structured times to share favourite books. Most often children do not read during this small group time, but talk about the books they chose to bring to the group. These sharing times allow children to hear about a variety of books, and help them develop a critical stance toward literature.

Skill lessons occur during the beginning of the school year. These lessons usually involve "think alouds" about reading strategies. For example, one day Marianne demonstrated how to choose a book by slowly and deliberately browsing through an assortment of books, commenting on them and making predictions about their content. Another day Marianne thumbed through a book while commenting on the illustrations and asking questions about the story. At other times, she discusses how she works out unknown words in a story. This teacher modelling occurs to demonstrate how readers construct meaning through interactions with print.

After the reading/writing workshop time, Marianne gathers the children together to share how their morning went. Children discuss the books they read or the texts they wrote. This time allows for closure and provides time for Marianne to record and evaluate the children's reading and writing processes as well as their productions.

Young Children's Reading Strategies and Concepts in the Autumn and Winter of First Grade

From the first day of school through the middle part of February of first grade, we conducted a study to examine children's behaviours as they learned to read within this whole language classroom. The study took place in the "library" or reading centre. This area housed a variety of types of texts including wordless books, picture books, short novels, anthologies of poetry, nonfiction books, magazines, reference books. There was also a set of tape-recorded books with headphones and tape recorders. The library had several pillows, two small rocking chairs, and a cupboard fixed up to be a cozy corner where two or three children could read together.

The children who spent time in the library were carefully observed twice weekly and their actions were recorded in field notes. Reading behaviours were audio-taped and all the books they chose to read were recorded. Emergent reading attempts were compared to the actual texts in the books in order to document categories of reading strategies. The researchers found that as children read in this setting, their strategies often looked quite unconventional.

Some of the children read entire books using only one kind of reading strategy, while others used a variety of strategies to read one text. Several factors influenced children's reading behaviours. These factors included the children's familiarity with the books read, and the kind or type of text, and stage of reading development. For example, when children were very familiar with the text or the book was highly predictable, they were more likely to read from memory. For example, when children read Martin's highly repetitious *Brown Bear, Brown Bear,* they read in a chanting, sing-song manner. Sometimes, even when they did not have the text memorized, children incorporated text-like language into their reading. The following example of Billy's reading in *Clifford the Big Red Dog,* a story he knew fairly well but had not memorized, helps show this behaviour. Billy read, "If I throw a stick he brings it back" for the text, *I throw a stick, and he brings it back to me.*

When children were unfamiliar with stories, they often still read the pictures with text-like language. That is, the text they produced sounded like "book language." For example, when Dusty read the first line of Sendak's *Where the Wild Things Are,* instead of reading *"The night Max wore his wolf suit and made mischief of one kind and another,"* he read, "In the morning the boy went to California." At other times, the children's reading interactions were talk about the pictures and their language was almost completely in oral register.

About November of the first-grade year, many of the children began to focus primarily on the print as they read, often reading from memory, but also reading by skipping words, slowly sounding out words, and even skipping whole pages to search for words they knew. During this time, children seemed to read without concern for the meaning of the story. They seemed instead to be tackling surface-level print concepts. For example, Maria read "he . . . had . . . to . . . a hat" for the text *His head will have to have a hat*. Sulzby (1985) calls this strategy "reading aspectually" and describes it as a time in children's emergent reading development when they focus on only one aspect of print to the exclusion of all other aspects. This strategy occurred most often when there were few lines of text on the page or the book had controlled language (as in scheme books). Possibly this occurred because the text seemed manageable to the children. This early reading behaviour fell away as the children gained confidence and became more skilled in reading.

Many times children employed more than one strategy as they read a book. For instance, when Daniel read *Clifford, The Big Red Dog,* he read part of it from memory (the book had been read to the class several times), and part of it by focusing on the letter/sound relations to figure out unknown words. Daniel consistently used the letter/sound strategy on the last few pages of the book that contained only one sentence per page.

The results of this study suggest that as children emerge as readers in a whole language classroom, they exhibit many varied reading behaviours. As stated, children's familiarity with the books they read, the type of text they read, and their individual development in learning to read influence their behaviours. Further, the classroom environment played a role in that the wide variety of texts and extended period of reading time allowed children to use varied strategies and flexible reading behaviours.

Young Children's Reading Concepts and Strategies in the Spring of First Grade

In the early spring we decided to take a closer look at the reading concepts and strategies of some "average" readers. This investigation helped address the outcomes of children's use of unconventional beginning reading strategies. The children participating in this study were selected because they represented the majority of the children in this first-grade whole language classroom. The teacher and the researcher worked together to identify "average" readers using standardized tests, school records, and the teacher's observations and insights. The children's reading behaviours were explored in three ways. Data gathering took place in several sessions, during which the children talked with the researcher about reading and they read stories to the researcher in a quiet place at school.

One way to discover what children know about reading is to see what they have to say. Reading interviews provided a way to do this.

Children were asked structured questions about reading and about themselves as readers. For example, they were asked what they did when they came to words they didn't know.

Oral reading samples were also recorded. The children were given two stories to read. They were asked to read the way they would if they were reading by themselves. These reading samples were analyzed and the errors children made given close attention. This provided a way to see what children did when they read and to check to see if actual reading actions were similar to children's talk about reading. For example, if the child discussed various reading strategies in the interview, the oral reading sample provided actual evidence of strategy use.

In addition, children were given Canney and Winograd's (1979) altered passages. The goal of this activity was to gain access to the children's reading concepts. This test consists of five short passages of print, four of which are altered in ways to make them incomprehensible. For instance, one line of print was *"Children go to ready are got."* When students were given these passages the researcher said, *"Some people say they can read this and some people say they can't, what do you think? Is this something a person can or is this something a person can't read?"* Children were given opportunities to express what they thought about these passages and to read them if they wished. Their responses such as "You can read it but it doesn't make sense!" helped reveal their understanding of the purpose and nature of reading.

The following section provides a discussion of the outcomes of these three measures and shows representative examples taken from the interviews, the children's oral reading, and their responses to altered passages. Combining these three areas of information helped compose portraits of these learners and the reading concepts and strategies the children knew and used.

The interview data indicated that the children viewed reading as a process of making sense of text. When asked direct questions about the nature of reading the vast majority of children said the most important thing about reading was understanding the story. The interview results also revealed that the children were very much aware of their own reading strategies and how they learned to read as the samples below show.

Researcher: What do you do when you come to a word you don't know?

Nickie: *Well, sometimes I just skip it and come back. Or I can read it over at the start.*

Researcher: How do you know if you read a word wrong?

Sam: *See, you can see if it sounds like a story.*

Researcher: Is learning to read hard?

Michael: *Well no, you just see these words all the time when somebody reads to you and you decide you want to learn them and that's how you get better and better.*

The interviews also showed that the children viewed reading as functional and useful in their everyday lives. When asked if they could read without a book the children responded with rich descriptions about how they used reading outside of school.

Researcher: Can you read if you don't have a book?

Ella: *Sometimes I read the soup labels so I know what I want. And sometimes my brother (laughing) wants Italian dressing and he gets another!*

Researcher: Can you read if you don't have a book?

Mark: *Yeah, you can read stuff on peoples' shirts and you can read stuff on TV. Like if someone is talking in French you can read the stuff on the bottom. It's just like TV is a book!*

The results on oral reading showed that these children use balanced strategies. That is, they often use all three cueing systems—meaning, syntax, and letter/sound relations or phonics—when they made substitutions. The children also reread to keep the flow of fluent reading going. Combined self-corrected miscues, intonation, and rereading behaviours revealed significant self-monitoring in these first graders. In all the analysis of oral reading samples indicated that children actually used the varied strategies they talked about in their interviews. Moreover, it documented that these children had important knowledge about reading and used it to read effectively. Oral reading samples provided evidence of conventional reading behaviours that were guided by an underlying belief that reading is essentially a sense making process.

The children rejected the passages of incomprehensible print over 90% of the time by saying it could not be read or by making important semantic distinctions. Often these distinctions were made when a child said, *"Well, maybe someone could say the words, but it just doesn't make sense!"* Interestingly, many children laughed at the passages. And they quizzed the researcher by asking, *"Is this something you just typed up?"* They also invited the researcher to share the joke as they read. For example, a child slapped his leg, giggled, and said, *"Listen to this!"* as he reread the passage directly to the researcher.

The findings of all three measures used to access children's reading concepts and strategies were consistent. Results indicated that children's reading knowledge and skills were grounded in the belief that reading must make sense. Findings also supported the claim that these children had sound, conventional reading strategies by the spring of their first-grade year.

Conclusions and Discussion

At the beginning and mid-term of first grade, children participating in these studies frequently engaged in a variety of unconventional reading behaviours (McIntyre, 1990). At first glance these appear to be haphazard. Use of reading strategies such as mixing *real* reading and memory reading or telling a story from the pictures might be viewed as an indication of regression in children's knowledge or as a signal for some form of instructional intervention. However, the findings of these two studies indicate that these reading behaviours did not indicate a problem or the need for intervention.

These children's beginning reading strategies and explorations with print lead to conventional, independent reading. Further, they appear to foster desirable concepts about the nature and purpose of reading. The children spent time engaged in a variety of emergent reading behaviours during the autumn and winter of first grade and by spring came to hold concepts of reading as a meaning-based process. Moreover, they understood and used phonics in reading and read stories using well-balanced, conventional strategies.

This information is important to teachers, parents, and researchers concerned about children's early reading. In particular, the results presented here are of interest to teachers interested in whole language. Previous research suggests that the beginning reading behaviours described in this article occur during times of transition in gaining expertise and organizing knowledge (Kamberelis & Sulzby, 1988). This lends strength to the claim that as children learn to read they must integrate existing concepts and strategies with new information. This is a dynamic process with complex cognitive demands. It is reasonable to infer that when children cope with new information about reading they often focus on certain strategies to the exclusion of others for a period of time, e.g., saying only the words they know in a story until they attain new understandings and skills. The findings of the two studies reported here suggest that children experience various transition periods as they become conventional readers. Importantly these transition periods appear to cause no harm and may be a contributing supportive factor in literacy acquisition.

Teachers interested in carrying out whole language instruction are, of course, concerned with children's progress toward conventional and independent reading. This research indicates that emergent reading strategies such as those described here during autumn and winter of first grade are part of learning to read conventionally. The findings presented in this article are also supported in other studies (Ferriero & Teberosky, 1982; Kamberelis & Sulzby, 1988; Sulzby, 1985).

Whole language educators are encouraged to monitor children's explorations with print carefully since the timeline for learning to read and the need for specific instruction varies with individual children. Teachers are also encouraged to share their understandings of research conducted in whole language classrooms with parents and administrators. It is important for parents to understand that children's developmental learning patterns become more visible when their reading experiences are not confined to traditional round robin oral reading. Children's early explorations with print play an important role in learning about the nature and purpose of reading. Parents need to understand how reading skills emerge and be shown that acceptance of unconventional behaviours, reading errors, and the child's approximations to adult-like reading is important to supporting reading growth. Because it is crucial that reading instruction be closely aligned with children's emerging knowledge and skills, teachers and researchers need to work together to investigate the transaction between children's understandings and instructional efforts to support their learning.

References

Bergeron, B.S. (1990) What does the term whole language mean? Constructing a definition from the literature. *Journal of Reading Behavior, 22,* 301–29.

Bridwell, N. (1963) *Clifford the big red dog.* New York: Scholastic Books.

Canney, G. & Winograd, P. (1979) *Schemata for reading and reading comprehension performance.* (Tech. Rep. No 120). Urbana, IL: University of Illinois. Center for the Study of Reading, (ERIC Document Reproduction Services No. ED 169 520).

Ferreiro, E. & Teberosky, A. (1982) *Literacy Before Schooling.* Portsmouth: Heinemann.

Freppon, P.A. (1991) Children's concepts of the purpose and nature of reading in different instructional settings. *Journal of Reading Behavior, 23,* pp. 139–63.

Harste, J.C., Woodward, V.A. & Burke, C.L. (1989) Examining our assumptions: A transactional view of literacy and learning. *Research in the Teaching of English, 20,* 458–81.

Holdaway, D. (1979) *The foundation of literacy.* Exeter, NH: Heinemann.

Kamberelis, G. & Sulzby, E. (1988) Transitional knowledge in emergent literacy. In J.E. Readence & R.S. Baldwin (Eds.), *Dialogues in literacy research: Thirty-seventh Yearbook of the National Reading Conference* (pp. 95–106). Chicago, IL: National Reading Conference.

Martin, B. (1967) *Brown bear, brown bear, what do you see?* New York: Holt, Rinehart, & Winston.

McGee, L.M. & Richgels, D.J. (1990) *Literacy's beginnings.* Needham Heights, MA: Allen and Bacon.

Goss, J.L. & Harste, J.C. (1985) *It didn't frighten me!* Worthington, OH: Willowship Press.

McIntyre, E. (1990) Young children's reading strategies as they read self-selected books in school. *Early Childhood Research Quarterly, 5,* 265–78.

Sendak, M. (1963) *Where the wild things are.* New York: Harper.

Sulzby, E. (1985) Children's emergent reading of favorite storybooks: A developmental study. *Reading Research Quarterly, 20,* 458–81.

10 A Comparison of Innercity Children's Interpretations of Reading and Writing Instruction in the Early Grades in Skills-based and Whole Language Classrooms

Karin L. Dahl
The Ohio State University

Penny Freppon
University of Cincinnati

This comparison derives from two separate studies: an investigation of sense-making in skills-based classrooms (Dahl, Purcell-Gates, & McIntyre, 1989) and a study of learner interpretations of reading and writing instruction in whole language classrooms (Dahl & Freppon, 1992). Both original studies were ethnographic in nature, with multiple data sources that were preserved in the comparison.

Dahl and Freppon explain their theoretical perspectives: Within each study, children's learning is viewed as transactive, that is, within classroom reading and writing contexts that are sociolinguistic. The skills-based curriculum reflected the assumption "that written language is learned through teacher-directed lessons and practiced as discrete skills that are taught sequentially.... In contrast, the whole language perspective is based on the idea that written language is learned primarily in meaning-centered and functional ways, and reading and writing are learned from whole to part by engagement in the processes themselves."

Dahl and Freppon characterize the interpretations that learners made of their instruction in reading and writing. First, most of the focal learners in both kinds of classrooms were concerned about accuracy. Second, the children in both groups progressed toward understanding of letter-sound relations (phonics), but among the first graders, it was mostly those in the whole language classrooms who used letter-sound knowledge to read conventionally and to self-correct in reading. Third, while learners in both kinds of classrooms demonstrated enjoyment of literature, there were considerable differences in how children viewed trade books; only the children in the whole language classrooms were much inclined to spontaneously talk about story elements, make connections between and among books, or take a critical stance toward books, suggesting how authors might have improved them. Fourth, children in both classrooms developed various ways of coping when they experienced difficulty in reading and writing; when working on their own, passivity seemed to be the most pervasive coping strategy among the children in skills-based classrooms. Fifth, there were substantial differences between the two groups with regard to "sense of self as reader/writer and persistence." The sense of self and the persistence exhibited by the learners in the whole language classrooms were exhibited only by the most proficient readers and writers in the skills-based classrooms.

The cross-study comparison involved several quantitative measures as well: an assessment of the children's understanding of intentionality, concepts about print, alphabetic principle, story structure, written narrative register, and concepts of writing. On the pretests, the children in the whole language kindergartens scored slightly lower on every measure but one. On the posttests, the whole language children scored significantly higher on the assessment of written narrative register, but the differences on the other measures were not significant. A third comparison involved reading processes and writing events. Dahl and Freppon describe these in some detail, illustrating with vignettes from various learners.

Some of the authors' findings, particularly those from the quantitative measures, indicate a number of similarities in learning outcomes. On the other hand, many other findings indicate that the children made different sense of reading and writing, depending at least in part upon the instructional situations and procedures. One notable comparison involved letter/sound knowledge. The quantitative measures showed children in both kinds of classrooms to be about equal in their acquisition of letter/sound knowledge. Yet the qualitative measures showed children using that knowledge differently. The children in the whole language classrooms made more extensive use of their letter/sound knowledge in both reading and writing.

Dahl and Freppon draw another significant contrast from the data:

> Children as sense makers in these two studies seemed to exemplify the distinction between literacy skills and literate behaviors. Some of the children in skills-based classrooms did not weave together the "cloth of literacy" (Purcell-Gates & Dahl, 1991, p. 21), nor move beyond their role as answer makers. Generally, they participated in reading and writing events, completed their work and learned literacy skills, but did not get involved personally nor see reading and writing as going beyond something for school. The children in whole language classrooms also learned skills and engaged in literate behaviors. Importantly, some degree of literate behavior was demonstrated by children of all levels of proficiency in these classrooms.

In the long run, the authors surmise, it may be the personal engagement in literacy, or lack thereof, that makes the critical difference for these innercity students: "The prognosis for children who are engrossed in books at the first-grade level and who think of themselves as readers and writers and are mindful of their strengths and weaknesses appears hopeful. It suggests at least the possibility that these children may continue to choose to read in the grades ahead and that they might sustain their roles as writers. In contrast, those who in first grade have already disengaged from literacy instruction appear to have begun the pattern of turning away from school." (Dahl, 1992)

Originally published in *Reading Research Quarterly,(30)*1, (1995), 50–74. Copyright 1995 by the International Reading Association. Reprinted with permission.

This cross-curricular comparison was initiated to shed light on two issues: first, how innercity children in the United States make sense of and interpret their beginning reading and writing instruction in the early grades of school, and second, how learners' interpretations may differ when they experience skills-based or whole language classroom programs. The comparison, therefore, addresses the consequences of differing literacy curricula as they are evident in children's interpretations. We have chosen skills-based and whole language curricula because they are widely used and draw on sharply contrasting notions of teaching and learning. Our focus on innercity children grows from the concern that these children are often particularly vulnerable to the vicissitudes of instruction. We find the research documenting the pervasive failure of this group in literacy learning particularly troubling and see the need for research that explores the effects of curricula as documented from the learner's perspective.

Previous research on innercity children has addressed sociological issues (Ogbu, 1985), family contexts (Taylor & Dorsey-Gaines, 1988), and the influence of instructional factors such as materials, grouping arrangements, and social contexts (Au, 1991; Bloome & Green, 1984). More recent studies have addressed children's sense making within specific curricula (Dahl, 1992; Dahl, Freppon, & McIntyre, 1993; Freppon, 1991, 1993; Oldfather & Dahl, 1994; Purcell-Gates & Dahl, 1991), but have not made extended comparisons across curricula.

While patterns of failure among American innercity children in learning to read and write in the early grades have been well documented (McGill-Franzen & Allington, 1991; Smith-Burke, 1989), few studies have sought children's interpretations of their initial school experiences in reading and writing. Child-centered interpretations of learning to read and write are particularly important in the context of current debates about differing instructional approaches. In order to provide productive instructional contexts for beginning readers and writers in innercity schools, educators must know how these children experience skills-based and whole language programs and what consequences may arise.

This cross-curricular comparison was a two-step process; each curriculum was investigated separately, and then the overall comparison was conducted. The two studies involved were an investigation of sense making in skills-based classrooms (Dahl, Purcell-Gates, & McIntyre, 1989) and a study of learner interpretations in whole language classrooms (Dahl & Freppon, 1992). Both studies were designed as ethnographies so that emergent designs and multiple data sources could be used to generate detailed and layered descriptions of children's learning. We wanted to examine the knowledge being acquired by learners (their hypotheses) and to investigate how children's opportunities, interactions, and processes of learning led to the construction of particular models of sense making. The cross-curricular comparison was an ethnology, a comparative analysis of multiple entities (Goetz & LeCompte, 1984). It was conducted by tracing a group of students through a series of comparable data in the skills-based and whole language settings. (See Griffin, Cole, & Newman, 1982, for a discussion of "tracer units.") The thick description, original contexts, and interpretations of each study were preserved in the comparative analysis (Brown, 1990). The focus was on similarities and differences of innercity children's experiences and knowledge, their sense making, across these contrasting literacy curricula.

Theoretical perspectives

Within each study, children's learning was viewed as transactive. Descriptions of learning events accounted for ways that learner knowledge and patterns of action, social and cultural contexts, and programs of instruction were shaped and transformed in relation to each other. Viewing language learning through a transactional lens meant accounting for the learner's actions and behaviors during instruction as well as accounting for the ways each learner's linguistic-experiential reservoir, background, and stance influenced those actions (Rosenblatt, 1989).

Within this transactive frame, we utilized two main theoretical perspectives. The first of these was the view that classroom reading and writing contexts are socio-psycholinguistic. Learning about reading and writing and engaging in both processes occur in dynamic contexts (Broome & Green, 1984; Dyson, 1991). The sense learners make depends on social and cultural classroom contexts (Green & Meyer, 1991) and the children's own evolving understandings of written language (Dahl, 1993; Meyers, 1992). Meanings are shaped by transactions among these and other factors (Rosenblatt, 1985). Classroom milieu, the child's individual stance toward literacy (Bussis, Chittenden, Amarel, & Klausner, 1985; Purcell-Gates & Dahl, 1991), development in literacy learning (Clay, 1975; Sulzby, 1985), and the dynamics within specific learning events shape and influence knowledge construction and motivation (Dahl & Freppon, 1991).

The second strand centered on the theoretical differences between the instructional approaches involved in this comparison. The skills-based curriculum is based on the idea that written language is learned through teacher-directed lessons and practiced as discrete skills that are taught sequentially. It uses specific reading and writing tasks as vehicles for skill acquisition and emphasizes a standard of accuracy and neatness as children engage in reading and writing (Knapp & Shields, 1990). Materials, usually in the form of basal readers, worksheets, and writing workbooks, are viewed as instruments for learning specific skills, and the curriculum is centered on the development of reading and writing proficiency (DeFord, 1984). In the skills-based classroom, the role of the student is to learn and integrate specific skills, participate in instruction, and engage in assigned skill practice. The teacher is responsible for structuring learner activities, providing instruction, and monitoring learner progress.

In contrast, the whole language perspective is based on the idea that written language is learned primarily in meaning-centered and functional ways, and reading and writing are learned from whole to part by engagement in the processes themselves (Edelsky, 1991; Goodman, 1986). Whole language classrooms include a variety of printed materials (trade books, catalogs, student-authored works, etc.), and students regularly write about self-selected topics in sustained writing periods. Through daily choices of reading materials and writing topics the student plays a significant role in shaping his or her own learning. The teacher "leads from behind" (Newman, 1985), demonstrating reading and writing behaviors, instructing directly, and supporting children's efforts to learn. Thus, the curriculum is primarily learner centered and driven by a view of children as active language learners (Halliday, 1978; Holdaway, 1979; Wells, 1986).

Review of related research

Research in three general areas informed this comparison. The first was a group of studies adopting the situated/sociocultural perspective in the study of children's literacy learning. A second included both emergent literacy explanations of reading and writing development and documentation of sociocultural influences on the success or failure of low socioeconomic status (SES) children in school. The final area of related literature was research exploring instructional dimensions that influence children's literacy learning.

Situated/sociocultural perspective. In their British study Edwards and Mercer (1987) investigated ways that knowledge is transmitted and received in elementary classrooms. Their research was based on the premise that human thought, understandings, and knowledge construction are intrinsically social and cultural. In *Common Knowledge* (1987), these researchers describe how the process of education, investigated primarily through the analysis of classroom discourse, imparts different kinds of knowledge. Much of what children learn in classrooms is not the intended aim of instruction but rather other, "hidden agenda" knowledge rooted in the philosophy of instruction itself. Thus, most instruction aimed at transmitting general or decontextualized knowledge inevitably also imparts common knowledge that is embedded in the talk and actions of everyday classroom life.

In the United States, researchers have used ethnographic perspectives to explore routine classroom events that influence young children's sense making (Cochran-Smith, 1984; Dyson, 1989, 1991; Rowe, 1989). Cochran-Smith (1984) documented how contextualized story reading events helped children learn unique language strategies needed to interpret stories. These language strategies were conveyed through teacher/student social interactions during read-alouds. In her investigation of children's writing, Dyson (1991) described how the child's interest, ordinary classroom interactions, and the larger social world influenced writing. Similarly, research analyzing preschool children's social interactions at the writing table (Rowe, 1989) documented the social dimensions of learning and their influence as children posed, tested, and revised their hypotheses about literacy. Children learned the roles of author and audience as they interacted with each other and with their teachers. These investigations demonstrate the importance of understanding the social and cultural milieu of classrooms as contexts shaping literacy development.

In the 1990s, ethnographic investigations continued to explore additional dimensions of children's literacy learning in instructional settings. For example, Kantor, Miller, and Fernie (1992) adopted a situated perspective that acknowledged the importance of classroom social and cultural life. These researchers studied the ways literacy was integral in various classroom contexts. For example, at the art table children focused on merging media and print, while in the block area literacy served to facilitate play and friendship in structuring "rights" and "rules." Results indicated that varying classroom contexts shaped the nature of literacy events and outcomes. A related study by Neuman and Roskos (1992) revealed the influence of classroom environment and documented the effects of literacy objects in the classroom. The presence of books and writing materials merged with and shaped the talk and actions related to literacy in preschoolers' play. The study showed that inclusion of literacy objects in classroom environments increased the quantity and quality of children's literacy activity during play. These studies, in general, underscore the influence of social contexts and classroom structures on early literacy development in schools.

Emergent literacy explanations. Research addressing emergent literacy has documented that young learners are aware of written language in their environment and begin their journeys as readers and writers by participating in home literacy events (Holdaway, 1979). The amount and nature of these early experiences affects later success in learning to read and write (Harste, Burke, & Woodward, 1981; Teale, 1986). Events that help children learn that print helps "get things done" (Teale & Sulzby, 1986, p. 28) and early storybook routines shape children's interpretations of literate activity (Gibson, 1989; Harste, Burke, & Woodward, 1983; Heath, 1983; Taylor, 1983; Teale, 1984; Wells, 1986).

Sociocultural mores about literacy permeate these emergent literacy experiences (Ferriero & Teberosky, 1982; Heath, 1982; Schieffelin & Cochran-Smith, 1984). Societal orientations inform children about the ways oral and written language are used in their community and shape interpretations of school-based literacy instruction (Delpit, 1986, 1988). When the expectations of schooling are in conflict with these sociocultural mores, learners experience difficulty and often reject or fail to identify with school-based concepts (Taylor & Dorsey-Gaines, 1988). The literature on at-risk populations indicates that cultural conflicts affect school success (Donmoyer & Kos, 1993; Jordan, Tharp, & Baird-Vogt, 1992; Mitchell, 1992). Intervention programs and attempts to balance schools racially have not reversed the overall pattern that low-SES children often fail to achieve satisfactory progress in reading and writing (Ogbu, 1985; Pelligrini, 1991; Trueba, 1988). Recurring analyses of Chapter 1 programs and special remedial reading efforts often document the failure of such programs to close the gap between these learners and their grade-level counterparts (McGill-Franzen & Allington, 1991). Thus, while this body of research has enriched our understanding of early literacy development, there remains a need to investigate low-SES children's interpretations of beginning reading and writing in school.

Instructional dimensions. Classic studies of reading instruction have contributed to our understanding of the influence of different kinds of instruction on literacy learning (Bond & Dykstra, 1967; DeLawter, 1970;

MacKinnon, 1959). These investigations have focused primarily on the outcomes of reading skills under specific instructional conditions. For example, MacKinnon's (1959) work investigated reading improvement when children read with a tutor and with peers. More recent studies have examined cultural factors and literacy acquisition (Au, 1991) and children's sense making under differing classroom conditions (Freppon, 1991). Freppon's comparative study focused on children's interpretations in skills-based and whole language classrooms but was limited to average readers and their concepts about the purpose and nature of reading. While these studies have described instructional differences and specific outcomes, we have yet to document children's interpretations of instruction in depth and over time in order to more fully understand what learners experience in contrasting curricula.

The current investigation, as a cross-curricular comparison, extends this body of research in a number of ways; it documents learner activity and interpretations of reading and writing across 2 years of schooling in classes with the same curriculum (skills-based or whole language), and it provides a basis for comparison of literacy learning across these years. Thus, this study extends knowledge gained from in-depth classroom studies. It provides a comprehensive account of the learner's perspective, documents and compares learner hypotheses across skills-based and whole language curricula, and draws conclusions about innercity children's success and failure in learning to read and write in these contrasting settings. The focus is on the consequences of each curriculum as seen from the perspective of the children and on the similarities and differences in children's experiences across these two instructional environments.

Method

Sites

The cross-study comparison involved eight classrooms in two midwest cities. The schools were matched across studies using three socioeconomic indicators. Each school contained a majority of children from urban families with low income levels, most families received public assistance, and the schools' mobility rates were high. Of the three schools involved in the skills-based study (Dahl, Purcell-Gates, & McIntyre, 1989) only two could be matched with comparable whole language sites. Thus, the comparison did not include one skills-based site included in the report of the original study (Purcell-Gates & Dahl, 1991). The elementary school populations in the cross-study comparison were representative of the racial and cultural mix typical of urban low-income populations in the midwest; that is, they included African American and White Appalachian students. At both the kindergarten and first-grade levels there were two skills-based classrooms and two whole language classrooms.

A critical aspect of the cross-study comparison was whether the skills-based and whole language classrooms selected for the study were reasonable exemplars. Three indicators were used to validate the class-room sites: teacher interviews, classroom observations, and teacher self-report data using the Theoretical Orientations to Reading Profile (DeFord, 1985). Within each study the specific classroom instructional programs were described in terms of their materials, activities, teaching routines, and learner roles.

Skills-based instruction. The skills-based kindergartens included traditional reading readiness programs with extensive emphasis on letter-sound relations; the first-grade programs used a newly adopted traditional basal program with ancillary workbooks and dittos provided by the central administration. First-grade teachers carried out instruction in small-group sessions, while the remaining students completed seatwork assignments. Learners copied and filled in missing words for sentences written on the chalkboard, and they occasionally wrote in journals and writing workbooks. In first grade, children took part in whole-group choral reading and skill recitation lessons with the teacher. They also participated in small-group round robin reading on a daily basis and had the opportunity to select trade books from a small class-room selection when their work was complete. Teachers followed the skill sequence in the basal program and met deadlines for unit completion established by the district. Storybook reading by the teachers was separate from reading instruction and was often followed by discussion primarily aimed at recall of specific story events or characters.

Whole language instruction. The whole language classrooms utilized extended periods of self-selected independent reading and writing, and teachers worked with individual learners or small groups. The reading materials included a wide variety of children's literature and extensive classroom libraries. Instruction in first grade was carried out with whole-group sessions using extended storybook reading and included teacher demonstrations of reading strategies and skills. The writing program embraced writing workshop routines and used children's literature to suggest story themes and evoke topics. Teachers demonstrated and discussed composing processes and conducted conferences about writing skills with children. Learners engaged in daily writing about self-selected topics and also wrote in journals and shared their writing in whole-class sessions. Most first graders wrote stories that were published within the classroom. Student-authored books and whole-class collaborations were part of the classroom reading materials. Writing and reading share sessions with the whole class were included in the daily schedule.

Informants

In each study a gender-balanced sample of 12 learners in each school site was randomly selected from the classroom pool of kindergarten children who qualified for the federally funded free or reduced lunch program. Since there were two skills-based sites and two whole language sites, this pool provided 24 learners from each study. These 48 children were assessed initially for their knowledge of written language. From this initial sample of learners, the focal learners for each site were randomly selected. Since mobility rates for the schools were relatively high, the initial sample served as a reserve of learners that could be substituted if focal learners moved away early in the study.

Across both studies the focal learners represented similar numbers of urban children who were African American or White Appalachian. Of the eight focal learners in the skills-based study, four were African American children and three were White Appalachian. One White Appalachian learner moved away midstudy. Mobility rates were projected to be particularly high for the whole language study; thus six focal learners were selected in each of the two sites. There were six African American children and six White Appalachian children. All of these focal learners remained to the end of first grade.

Procedures

The process for conducting this investigation involved first executing each study separately and then carrying out the cross-curricular comparison. Step One focused on students' sense making or interpretations within each curriculum and documented their opportunities and processes of learning. Step Two involved data analysis procedures for the cross-case comparison. This comparative analysis entailed tracing the focal learners through their actions and activities over time in order to examine what students learned and how instructional opportunities and patterns influenced this learning. Procedures for this comparative analysis are described in the data analysis section.

Qualitative and quantitative data collection processes in Step One were implemented in similar ways in each investigation to ensure comparability. In each study, one researcher was assigned to each school and engaged in data collection for the 2-year period. The initial task was to gain familiarity with students and classroom routines and then begin initial assessment of written language knowledge for the full sample of eligible learners. After the assessment was complete, the focal learners were closely observed across the 2-year period and, along with the children in the initial sample, assessed for written language knowledge at the end of first grade. Thus, the weekly observation of focal learners was bounded by pre- and posttests administered at the beginning and end of the study.

Qualitative procedures for documenting learner activity. In each study the researchers generated field notes in twice-weekly classroom visits across the span of 2 years. One focal learner was followed closely in each observation. That learner wore a remote microphone interfaced with an audiotape recorder so that spontaneous utterances could be captured as the 2-hour observation period progressed. Particular attention was paid to learner statements and actions that indicated evolving hypotheses about reading and writing. The emphasis within these research efforts was documentation of the learner's experience as it could be substantiated in talk, reading/writing behaviors, and overt actions. The researchers shadowed focal learners and, where appropriate, probed by asking routine questions such as "What are you doing now?" or, "Tell me about that." The researcher also kept a record of instruction, learner behaviors, and the contexts in which each event occurred. Original field notes were elaborated and typed along with partial transcripts produced from audiotape recordings. Thus, the outcome of each observation was an extended set of field notes in which transcripts of learner talk, oral reading samples, and learner actions were integrated. Copies of all learner papers (writing samples, ditto sheets) were also included. These elaborated accounts and artifacts were subsequently coded by the research team for learner behaviors and strategies, then analyzed for sense-making patterns.

In both studies, the researchers functioned as participant observers but kept to the observer end of the continuum as nearly as possible, rather than intervening in learning events. The point of these observations was to determine what happens without greatly altering the classroom settings or taking a teaching role during instructional events.

Quantitative assessment of written language knowledge. In each curriculum, learners from the sample of eligible low-SES children (24 in each study) completed an array of six tasks assessing various aspects of written language knowledge. These tasks were administered at the beginning of kindergarten and the end of first grade. Both normed measures and measures unique to this study were used. Our underlying notion was that written language exists as a whole and is composed of various domains that may be examined at different levels. The domains selected were identified as ones related to success in learning to read and write in school (Dahl, Purcell-Gates, & McIntyre, 1989); they formed a picture of each learner's schemata about written language. These assessments included measures of intentionality, alphabetic principle, story structure, concepts about print, written narrative register, and concepts of writing. Table 1 provides a description of each task and describes procedures for task administration.

The six tasks were administered in three sessions spaced over a 3-week period. The intentionality task was first for all learners, and subsequent task order was counterbalanced across learners.

Data analysis

A variety of data analysis procedures were utilized in the two ethnographies and the cross-curricular comparison. Table 2 presents an overview of the two-step process and outlines both qualitative and quantitative data analysis procedures for each major task.

As shown in Table 2, Step One focused on both qualitative and quantitative procedures to determine learner interpretations of reading and writing. Step Two procedures focused on comparisons of data by tracing a group of students through a series of comparable events in the skills-based and whole language settings (Griffin, Cole, & Newman, 1982). In order to understand how children's sense making might differ by instructional contexts, it was necessary to examine the knowledge acquired within each approach. The similarities and differences in measures of written language knowledge for learners in the two curricula were analyzed. Further comparisons were made of learners' reading processes and writing experiences. In these analyses teachers and their actions were not under investigation. Rather, the focus was on comparing children's interpretations of reading and writing as they evolved in the skills-based and whole language classrooms.

Pattern generation across qualitative sources. In each study, coding systems were established that captured categories emerging from field note data. These codes represented both learner behaviors and the context in which they occurred. Coded data were then aggregated to determine patterns of learner behavior and evolving learner hypotheses about reading and writing within each study. Data narratives written for each focal learner further documented learner hypotheses, and grids that summarized learner sense-making patterns were generated to facilitate comparison across learners. The Appendix displays a sample grid prepared for a focal learner in first grade.

Table 1

Summary of written language knowledge assessments

Task	Description	Procedures
Intentionality	Accesses schema for written language as a system with accessible meaning	• Present printed sentence and ask child if there is anything on the paper. Probe to capture child's responses.
Concepts about print	Standardized test (Clay, 1979), taps major book reading and print concepts	• Follow established procedures using the Stones form.
Alphabetic principle	Accesses knowledge of letter-sound relations and alphabetic principle	• Present familiar environmental print in contextualized and decontextualized events. • Ask child to write 10 dictated spelling words. • Ask child to write anything s/he can and to tell about the writing.
Story structure	Accesses schema for the macrostructure of written narratives	• Read a story to the child. Take a short break to prevent rehearsal effects. Ask child to retell story. • Engage the child in puppet play. Prompt the child to "tell me a story" during the course of play.
Written narrative register	Accesses knowledge of syntactic and lexical features found in storybooks using the difference score between an oral language sample and a written language sample	• Ask the child to tell all about an event such as a birthday party or family outing. • Familiarize the child with a wordless picture book. Ask the child to pretend to read the story to a doll. Encourage the child to make it "sound like a real book story."
Concepts of writing	Accesses the child's concepts about writing as a system using the written artifact generated under the "Alphabetic principle" procedure	• Ask child to tell about his/her writing.

Table 2

Summary of data analysis procedures

Step	Task	Data collected	Analyses conducted
Step One: Analysis of data for each study conducted separately	Task #1 (Qualitative): Document evolving learner hypotheses and interpretations of reading/writing in each study.	• Field notes across kindergarten and first grade for each study • Transcripts of learner talk • Written artifacts	• Code data (codes emerge from each data set). • Determine patterns for each focal learner. • Summarize data patterns for half-year periods. • Reduce data narratives to grids for each learner. • Aggregate learner patterns across sites. • Determine major patterns for each study.
	Task #2 (Quantitative): Document change in written language knowledge for focal learners in each study through pre/post comparison.	Pre- and postdata for each focal learner in each study on the following six measures: • Intentionality • Concepts about print • Alphabetic principle • Story structure • Written narrative register • Concepts of writing	• Score pre/post measures and analyze with ANOVA with repeated measures across focal learners within each study.

Step	Task	Data collected	Analyses conducted
Step Two: Comparison of data across studies	Task #3 (Qualitative): Compare learner interpretations of reading/ writing across skills-based and whole language settings.	• Field notes/transcript accounts of focal learner actions and utterances • Data narratives and grids	• Write global hypotheses and substantiation. • Compare across data sets using tracer units.
	Task #4 (Quantitative): Compare change in written language knowledge scores across skills-based and whole language settings.	• Six tasks measuring pre and post knowledge of written language for learners in each study	• Analyze between-group scores with a 2(Group) x 2(Time) mixed measure ANOVA with repeated measures.
	Task #5 (Combined): Compare reading processes of represent- ative focal learners across studies.	• Reading samples from the midpoint of first grade in two contexts, self-selected trade books and teacher- selected texts	• Compare miscue and strategy patterns across contexts and across studies by proficiency levels.
	Task #6 (Combined): Compare writing events across studies and describe kind of writing produced.	• Kindergarten and first-grade writing data for two time samples (Nov. and Feb.) in both studies—includes all writing samples and related field notes	• Identify kind of writing, amount, and task. Compare across studies.

When comparisons were made across curricular settings, the grids for each focal learner from each of the sites for each half year were aligned, and successive reviews were made for patterns of behavior across several learners. Specific tracer units were used for comparison: talk and action during reading and writing, interactions during instruction, and patterns of activity during independent work. Researchers' hypotheses about similarities and differences across learners in skills-based and whole language classrooms were written by each member of the research team. Subsequently, the researchers read and reread all of the team members' hypotheses and generated a list of tentative findings for the cross-study comparison. The team reviewed substantiating data in field notes for disputed areas and compiled further documentation when clarification was needed. The tentative findings representing similarities and differences in children's reading and writing patterns were also critiqued by outside consultants in a 2-day project review. Attention was paid in this audit to the soundness of research claims and protection against bias.

Analysis of written language knowledge assessments. Scoring procedures for the six written language tasks were drawn from the body of research supporting each task and from the range of children's responses within this study. Table 3 summarizes the scoring procedures and indicates the specific point levels within each task.

As indicated in Table 3, differential weightings were assigned to some items within specific tasks.

In the intentionality task, the salient dimension was the extent of children's understanding of print as meaningful and functional (Harste, Burke, & Woodward, 1983). Thus, the scoring range represented how close each learner came to stating that written language carries meaning. The scale was developed from children's responses in this study as they were questioned about a sentence printed on a piece of paper.

In the story structure task, weighted scores were assigned for various components of the macrostructure of story according to their relative significance among specific story elements (Stein, 1979, 1982; Stein & Glenn, 1975, 1979; Whaley, 1981). *Setting* (character, place, time) and *reaction* (the response of the character to the problem) were assigned 2 points and *beginning, attempt, outcome,* and *ending* were each assigned 1.

The alphabetic principle and concepts of writing scoring represented increments of knowledge and sophistication indicated in children's responses. On the basis of current research, conventional spellings demonstrating visual, phonetic, and nasal sound strategies were scored higher on the scale than use of one letter to represent a word (Gentry, 1982, 1987; Read, 1971). Stories or groups of related sentences were scored higher on the scale than single words or phrases (Clay, 1975, Dyson, 1991; Harste, Burke, & Woodward, 1983; Sulzby, 1992).

Table 3

Analysis and scoring procedures of written language knowledge assessments

Task	Scoring process	Scoring rubric
Intentionality	Range of scores 1–5	1=No evidence of the concept of intentionality 2=Response limited to view related to school factors 3=Child sees purpose of writing as labeling or naming 4=Child identifies writing as something serving broader purpose 5=Strong evidence of concept that written language carries meaning
Concepts about print	Scored using Clay's (1979) protocol for Stones	N/A
Alphabetic principle	Scoring scale applied to all three measures with the most frequently occurring level used, range of scores 1–8 points	1=No evidence of letter-sound knowledge (scribbles, pictures) 2=Single letter represents word (P for "pink," semiphonetic) 3=Two letters represents a word (PK for "pink," semiphonetic) 4=Maps all sounds heard (DA for "day," phonetic) 5=Maps letter-sounds based on articulation, no nasal articulation (SG for "song," phonetic) 6=Maps letter-sounds based on articulation, includes vowels (PLEY for "play," phonetic) 7=Conventional spelling demonstrated; shows visual, phonetic, and nasal sound strategies 8=Majority of words spelled conventionally
Story structure	Range of scores 0–8 points, all elements scored	2 pts.=Setting 2 pts.=Reaction involving response of character(s) to formation of a goal 1 pt. =Beginning or precipitating event of an episode 1 pt. =Response of the character to the problem 1 pt. =Outcome or stated success or failure of the attempt 1 pt. =Ending—providing a consequence
Written narrative register	Scored using Purcell-Gates (1988) protocol	N/A
Concepts of writing	Range of scores 1–7, each artifact scored	1=Drawing: line borders, picturelike marks 2=Scribbles: writinglike marks, scribbles, shapes 3=Letter/number forms: scribbles with letters, letterlike, numberlike forms 4=Letters mixed: pictures with embedded print, letters with numbers 5=Letters: Ungrouped letters, letter strings 6=Words: Pseudowords, words 7=Words/sentences: Extensive word writing, sentences, or stories

Two tasks, written narrative register and concepts about print, were scored according to their prescribed procedures (Clay, 1979; Purcell-Gates, 1988).

Once scoring was complete for all tasks, pre- and posttest results for each study were analyzed for within-group and between-group findings. While the number of students tested in each curriculum was the same at the beginning of kindergarten, patterns of student mobility within these innercity sites reduced the numbers of students tested at the end of first grade. In the skills-based curriculum the initial sample of 24 changed to 15, and in the whole language sample the change was from 24 to 21.

The statistical procedure for cross-curricular comparison was a two-factor hierarchical arrangement augmented by a within-group variable. This one-between/one-within-groups design with provision for unequal Ns (Kennedy & Bush, 1985, pp. 521–31) used a repeated measures analysis. The between-groups variable was the skills-based or whole language treatment, and the within-groups variable was the array of six pre- and posttests (intentionality, story structure, alphabetic principle, concepts about print, written narrative register, and concepts of writing). For each measure, a group (skills-based vs. whole language) × time (pretest, posttest) mixed model analysis of variance (ANOVA) with repeated measures was computed using a $p<.05$ alpha level. Subjects with missing data (due to task refusal) were eliminated from that specific dependent variable only.

This design was chosen because it provided for two specific characteristics of the cross-curricular comparison. First, there was no random assignment of learners to treatments; instead, learners came from intact skills-based or whole language classrooms. Second, teachers differed in spite of careful selection procedures. While teachers were chosen as excellent exemplars of their particular curriculum and had comparable time periods in which to carry out their instruction, there was some variation across teachers. The design we used was appropriate for intact classrooms when they comprised levels of the nested variable (Kennedy & Bush, 1985, p. 522), and it made provision for teacher variation by nesting teachers within the treatment variable.

Analysis of reading processes and writing events. As part of the cross-curricular comparison, analyses were conducted to examine and compare reading processes and writing events across studies. After both studies were concluded, a subsample of six first-grade focal learners, three skills based and three whole language, were selected for a direct comparison of actions during the reading process. These children represented a range of reading experience and ability. The group included a proficient reader, an average reader, and a less-experienced reader from the skills-based and whole language classrooms. Criteria for learner selection were based on triangulated data from field notes, miscue analysis of actual reading samples, and teacher judgment. The sampling of learner reading behaviors was carried out with reading samples from the midpoint of first grade to the end of that year. The classrooms from which these six children were selected included opportunities both to read self-selected trade books and to participate in small-group reading lessons with the teacher. Thus, two contexts, independent reading of self-selected trade books and teacher-directed reading of texts selected by the teacher, were compared across skills-based and whole language first grades. Analysis of reading processes entailed identifying patterns from miscue and strategy data in reading samples across contexts and comparing these patterns across studies by levels of proficiency.

Comparative analysis of writing events that focal learners experienced was also conducted at the conclusion of both studies. The kindergarten and first-grade writing artifacts from November and February, time samples that captured representative periods of instruction and learner activity, were reviewed. The purpose was to describe the writing tasks and generally the kind of writing that focal learners produced during these periods. Field note descriptions of learner behaviors during writing events also were collected for each of the focal learners during these periods. Analysis of writing events entailed tabulating types of writing artifacts for focal learners within the sampled time periods and determining patterns in learner actions and responses to writing activities.

Results

The findings from this cross-curricular comparison spanned three general areas: patterns of learner sense making, written language knowledge measures, and contrasts among reading processes and writing events.

Qualitative findings: Patterns of learner sense making

The qualitative findings focused on interpretations that learners made of their instructional experiences. In the skills-based and whole language investigations, patterns of behavior were taken as indicators of learner hypotheses about reading and writing. Thus, common patterns across the data grids of the majority of focal learners were taken as learner interpretations of a particular curriculum. Comparison across the two studies revealed five areas in which there were prominent patterns.

Pattern 1: Interest in accuracy. In both studies most focal learners were concerned about accuracy. Comparisons of children's talk and actions across the two groups revealed an interest in "getting it right." In kindergarten, children erased repeatedly when learning to form letters and spell words. They asked each other about letter forms, erased, worked on writing that did not measure up to their standards, and tried again. In first grade they tried to accurately map letters and speech sounds and searched for correctly spelled words by looking through books or using available environmental print. These accuracy-focused behaviors sometimes occurred in whole language groups in spite of the teacher's advice to "get your ideas down" or the direction to spell words as they sounded. In both studies these behaviors were evident in learners with various levels of expertise in reading and writing. It appeared that learners began school with some focus on accuracy and sustained that interest in both curricula.

The concern of focal learners in both studies with accuracy was of particular interest because these two instructional settings differed greatly in their demand for production of correct written language responses. One of the main tenets of the whole language philosophy is acceptance of errors as potentially productive in the learning process. In contrast, the skills-based curriculum is aimed at mastery of specific skills or subskills through practice, and correct responses were highly valued in the skills-based curriculum.

Pattern 2: Phonics growth. While a general progression toward understanding of letter-sound relations occurred among children in both studies, cross-curricular analysis of reading and writing behaviors for January, February, and March of first grade indicated differing strategies for using letter-sound knowledge. Table 4 presents the range of phonics strategies in reading and writing that were recorded in field notes about focal learners during these months. Examples are provided in parentheses to clarify specific strategies. Use of specific strategies is indicated with an x under each focal learner's number. As would be expected, some learners used more than one strategy during this period.

The patterns of strategy use in phonics indicate some areas of similarity. During this period both skills-based and whole language learners used strategies that showed they were gaining awareness of phonics and experimenting with letter-sound relations. The differences were evident in the cluster of whole language learners (8 of the 12 focal learners) using strategies that demonstrated application of their letter-sound knowledge. One skills-based focal learner demonstrated application of letter-sound relations through her conventional reading and use of transitional spellings.

Table 4 *Comparison of phonics strategies in mid first grade*

Category	Strategy	Whole language learners												Skills-based learners						
		1	2	3	4	5	6	7	8	9	10	11	12	13	14	15	16	17	18	19
Gaining awareness of letter-sound relations	Copies words to complete writing tasks																X	X		X
	Makes series of guesses to identify unknown word in reading (*BL-, BLO, BLAY, BLOK, PLAY, PLOK for "plate"*)																	X		X
	Writes single letter for salient sound in a word, context: teacher support (*D* for "these;" *ICP* for "I saw pigs")	X				X	X													
	Represents some phonemes with appropriate letter (*GT* for "cheetah")						X		X	X										
Experimentation with letter-sound relations	Sounds out words in reading by exaggerating sounds (*FA LA GUH for "flag"*)														X		X			
	Represents some phonemes in word with appropriate letters. (*CLSRME* for "classroom;" *WI* for "why")			X					X							X			X	
	Produces a nonsense word in reading by using graphophonic cues										X							X	X	X
	Miscues with matching for the word's beginning sound (*RED* for "rose," *ME* for "many")							X					X	X	X	X				

| | Strategy | Whole language learners | | | | | | | | | | | | Skills-based learners | | | | | | |
		1	2	3	4	5	6	7	8	9	10	11	12	13	14	15	16	17	18	19
Application of letter-sound relations	Uses letter-sound relations to self-correct in reading (*SHIVER* corrected to "shouted")		X					X	X				X							
	Produces transitional spelling for unknown words (*HED UNDR THE HAYSAK* for "hid under the haystack")		X					X			X	X	X	X						
	Produces conventional spelling				X															
	Reads conventionally using well-organized graphophonemic knowledge				X				X		X	X		X			X			

Note Whole language learners 1=Addie, 2=Ann, 3=Carrie, 4=Charlie, 5=Doughs, 6=Eustice, 7=Isaac, 8=Jason, 9=Maury, 10=Shemeka, 11=Tare, 12=Willie; skills-based learners: 13=Audrey, 14=Ellen, 15=Eric, 16=Janice, 17=May Ann, 18=Maya, 19=Rodney.

These differences in application of phonics knowledge seemed to reflect the writing experiences in each curriculum and the contexts for phonics practice. Children in whole language classrooms experimented with letter-sound relations during daily writing experiences. These writing periods included individual teacher conferences and frequent peer interactions where coaching on letter-sound relations took place. There also were teacher demonstrations of writing processes in which letter-sound mapping was explained (Freppon & Dahl, 1991).

The letter-sound practice in skills-based classrooms was conducted for the most part as seatwork. There were teacher demonstrations of sounding out with the whole group but rarely were these episodes connected to the reading or writing of connected text. Instead, they were part of separate skill instruction. Learners dependent on the curriculum and learners who were inclined to be more passive approached phonics skill lessons as part of their daily paperwork. Their perspective appeared to be that it needed to be completed to please the teacher. Often these children did not put their phonics skills to use when reading.

Pattern 3: Response to literature. Learners in both studies demonstrated enjoyment of literature. Almost all focal learners were attentive during storytime and listened with rapt attention as stories were read. Storybooks clearly were a source of pleasure and interest within each curriculum.

The cross-study analysis of children's responses to literature, however, revealed considerable differences in hypotheses children held about trade books. These differences were related to two areas: (a) the nature and amount of experience that children had with trade books, and (b) the insights that children demonstrated about books.

The role that children's literature played in the skills-based sites was relatively small. Learners in these classrooms listened to storybooks read by their teacher and occasionally explored some trade books after completing their work. For the most part, basal readers and skill worksheets served as the primary reading materials in these classrooms. Even when trade books were available, focal learners tended to stay with their basal materials.

The participation structures during storybook reading were restricted in skills-based classrooms. Teachers preferred that children listen to stories quietly and save their comments until the story's end. Teachers asked children comprehension questions about each story, and children commented about favorite events during story discussions.

A representative storybook lesson occurred when the teacher read *What Mary Jo Shared* (Udry, 1966) while the children listened. This story involved a little girl's quest for something unique to take to school to share. As the story unfolded the little girl considered various animals, such as grasshoppers and even an imaginary pet elephant. At the end of the story the teacher asked if anyone could really have an elephant for a pet. There were several opinions, but Eric was adamant and began vigorously shaking his head yes. He announced, "I keep it outside." The teacher asked, "What would you feed it?" and Eric turned to the page in the book that told what elephants ate. This exchange formed the pattern for successive questions about what children would do and what the book said. Learners, including Eric, were adept at finding information that the book offered and adding their opinions.

The role that children's literature played in the whole language classrooms was somewhat different. Trade books were a central vehicle for literacy instruction. Each day children listened and interacted as several books were read by their teacher. Further, learner-chosen trade books were read by children independently each day in first grade, and many books were incorporated into daily writing experiences. Isaac, for example, was a learner who used familiar books to prompt writing topics. He wrote personal versions of many storybooks, changing the plot or adding a personal twist to the language.

Participation structures during storybook reading with the teacher varied across the two whole language sites, but generally learners in these classrooms were encouraged to participate actively during storybook sessions. Children made predictions, commented on illustrations, asked questions about the story, stated opinions, responded to wordings and letter-sound relations, and acted out story events.

A typical storybook session occurred, for example, when the teacher read a predictable book entitled *Oh No* (Faulkner, 1991). The plot involved a series of mishaps, each resulting in a spot appearing somewhere. The recurring phrase *Oh no* was part of each episode. Children listened and looked at the words and pictures. Midway through the story their comments were particularly revealing.

Teacher   [reading and pointing to the words] *There's a spot on my skirt. There's a spot on my pants, cause I fell in the dirt.*
Chris: It looks like mud.
Teacher: Would it make sense if it says mud?
Children: Yes.
Isaac: It's D . . . dirt.
Terry: If you don't know what the words say, you can look at the pictures and see if the pictures tell.
Teacher: Look at the words and the pictures. [nods] That's good. Here's another one. *There's a spot on my sweater.*

Chris: It doesn't look like a sweater. [pause] It doesn't look like a spot.

Teacher: Does it look like a shirt?

Children: [all at once] Yes. Well maybe. No.

Teacher: So we have to look at the words to figure it out.

Kira: But sweater and shirt start with the same.

Teacher: Same letter.

Cindy: They should put tee shirt because that's what it looks like.

Teacher: So you don't think this makes sense. But it says—

Terry: But down there they put sweater.

Teacher: Shirt starts with *SH*, shhhhh.

Maury: Just like *The Shrinking Shirt.*

Willie: And *Jump Frog Jump* [when the protagonist says "shh."]

Teacher: *There's a spot on my tie. There's a spot on my chin from this blueberry pie. Oh no!*

Willie: On that page it's just one word, and on the other one it tells where it came from.

Teacher: That's right. It doesn't tell where the spot on the tie came from.

LaWanda: It could say, "From the hot dog he ate."

Teacher: [doubling back] *There's a spot on my chin from this blueberry pie.*

Kira: Every time I see that it makes me want to eat.

Teacher: *There's a spot on my shorts* [children all reading along]. *There's a spot on my knee.*

Doug: That don't look like knee.

Kira: It sounds like a E for knee.

Teacher: There are Es in it.

Sandy: Two Es.

Teacher: *There's a spot on my dress everybody can see. Oh no!*

Isaac: Look, it's kind of a pattern with the pattern [Oh no] and the letters too. First it says *S* then *D* then *S.*

Shemeka: [exasperated] It would make sense if they said where the spot came from and then on the next page tell where it came, before—and then said "Oh no."

Teacher: So you want "Oh no" on every page?

[Shemeka nods in agreement.]

Teacher: *There's a spot on my spoon—*

Terry: Probably from not washing good.

Charlie: From somebody eating with it.

Teacher: *There's a spot on my bowl. There's a spot on my cup and it looks like a hole. Oh no.*

Sara: [commenting about the illustration] You know what they
               should do; they should make water coming out.
Isaac: It looks like a clock. Turn it [the page] back.
[The teacher turns back so the illustration can be scrutinized, then
resumes reading.]
Teacher: *There's a spot on my hand. There's a spot on my face. . . .*
Chris: Oh! Oh! I know, I know.
Willie: I know what that's gonna be.
Maury: She's got chicken pops.
Teacher: [reviewing] *There's a spot on my face.*
Tara: "Oh no" on the next page.
Willie: That's gonna be spots everywhere 'cause she got the spots
               off her plate.
Isaac: Turn it back to the spoon. It looks like a spot.
Maury: I got the chicken pops right now!

In this segment of storybook interaction, it was clear that learners
were engaged in figuring out how the story worked. They attended to
pattern and thought about story language, sound-symbol relations,
and illustrations. They critiqued the story and related their own experiences to its events. The teacher stopped the story as requested, supported children's efforts to clarify, and listened to volunteered ideas.

When the two representative vignettes about storybook read-alouds
were compared, differences in learner opportunities were evident. In the
skills-based example, *What Mary Jo Shared*, the learners' responses were
elicited at the end of the story only and guided by the teacher's questions.
Children participated by using story information to support their opinions. In the whole language example, the discussion took place throughout the story reading event. It was based on learner observations and
included teacher responses and questions. The opportunity to construct
meaning was present throughout the whole language read-aloud lesson.

Interacting with storybooks in these ways clearly contributed to
what these children knew about stories and how they responded to
trade books. Data analyses revealed that children in whole language
classrooms demonstrated a range of insights from their experiences.
These patterns were not evident among learners in skills-based classrooms. Three categories of interpretation were evident: learning storybook language, gathering intertextual knowledge, and adopting a
critical stance.

Learning storybook language was evident in children's writing. Their
written stories included dedication pages, illustrations, dots to indicate
continuing events, and formulaic endings. Patterns of action indicated
children were learning about written language from reading and lis-

tening to trade books. The following story written in October of first grade by Isaac demonstrated this influence.

The Scary Hairy Spider

When me and Ricky was playing outside, we saw a spider and
    Ricky picked up the spider.
I said, "Ooo gross!"
And I said, "Ricky put that spider down or you will get bit and . . . if
    you get bit, don't come to me!"
And . . . if you come I will not help you.
And if you ask me twice, I still won't help you.

The End

The story was written in book form, with each line on a separate page. It included illustrations and a title page and was typical of many stories written about daily experiences but shaped by structures and language patterns found in books.

Gathering intertextual knowledge was demonstrated by whole language children in first grade as they spontaneously talked about characters, events, and plot arrangements across stories. Children appeared to be building a story world that included a repertoire of story elements. The following comments were characteristic of this learner pattern:

"Oh that reminds me of the butcher, the baker, and the candlestick
    maker."
"You have to look for the cat. It's like *Each Peach Pear Plum,*"
    [Ahlberg & Ahlberg, 1985].
"That looks like a Eric Carle book."

Learners appeared to have a memory for books and used their intertextual knowledge as they participated in story events. In contrast, no pattern of intertextual insights was present in the skills-based study. Learners' attention was directed toward other matters when stories were read by the teacher, and their spontaneous utterances did not include these connections.

Adopting a critical stance was shown as children in whole language classrooms made suggestions about how professional authors could improve their stories. Children criticized story endings and talked about what would improve the illustrations. In skills-based classrooms children talked about story events and answered comprehension questions. There were few critical comments about stories.

Pattern 4: Coping strategies of learners experiencing difficulty. In both skills-based and whole language classrooms the least proficient readers and writers developed various ways of dealing with teacher expectations and instructional demands. While the patterns of behavior and strategies for coping were similar in some ways for children in the two studies, the cross-study contrasts were significant.

The similarities in behavior patterns were most evident in teacher/student conferences at the individual level. When skills-based teachers gave one-on-one help to learners experiencing difficulty, the children could focus on the lesson and increase their learning efforts. Outcomes of one-on-one interactions in skills-based classrooms often resulted in children getting the correct answer or showing they understood. Similarly, in whole language classrooms, one-on-one teacher/student interactions were productive for learners experiencing difficulty. In this context, learners responded positively and increased their efforts to accomplish the expected task.

The greatest difference in coping behaviors across studies occurred when these same learners worked on their own. Interestingly, passivity appeared to be the most pervasive coping strategy for learners experiencing difficulty in skills-based classrooms. Their strategies also included bluffing their way through reading lessons by reading paralinguistically and copying from others without efforts to produce meaning on their own. Field observations showed that learners sat and stared for periods of time, marked randomly on worksheets just to finish them, and waited for or asked for help. Their behaviors indicated they weren't making sense of what they were doing. One learner acted out somewhat aggressively, but in general the coping behaviors of children experiencing difficulty in the skills-based study seemed aimed at just getting through the assigned reading or writing activity. Rather than "taking on the task" of reading, they tended to avoid it and found ways to get by in the classroom (Purcell-Gates & Dahl, 1991).

One exception to this pattern was a skills-based learner who coped by creating opportunities for individual instruction. Creating a "school for one", (Dahl, Purcell-Gates, & McIntyre, 1989) entailed one of two strategies, either acting out sufficiently to be required to stay after school or interrupting small-group instruction by holding up the workbook, looking baffled, and asking, "What I pose a do?" in a loud voice. Both strategies produced private sessions with the teacher in which personal instruction was given and the learner's questions answered.

The coping behaviors of comparable children from whole language classrooms were shaped by the social contexts in their classrooms. Learners often interacted with their peers when they didn't know what to do. Within the periods of extended independent reading or writing, they tended to tag along with other learners. In doing so they seemed to establish their own support systems. For example, in group reading situations they actively listened to other children and picked up phrases and sentences, saying them along with others. When a struggling learner copied from children's papers during writing, there also was an attempt to write independently by simply adding letters, drawing, or talking about words or letters that could be added. These peer interactions indicated some attempt to carry on the activity meaningfully.

In writing, the least proficient learners in the whole language first grades developed some avoidance behaviors. These children sometimes moved around the room and interacted socially with peers. They also set up elaborate clerical duties such as getting word cards for others, becoming the illustrator in collaborative book writing, sharpening pencils, setting up supplies (paper, pencils, and crayons), and helping or organizing other helpers in writing tasks. They stalled and avoided the act of writing, often altering their behavior only in one-on-one sessions with the teacher.

Pattern 5: Sense of self as reader/writer and persistence. Among the patterns reflecting the learners' interpretations, two trends were particularly prominent in whole language classrooms. Whole language learners demonstrated in nearly every classroom observation a perception of themselves as readers and writers. Further, these learners sustained their attention in literacy episodes and persisted when engaged in reading/writing tasks.

Focal learners in whole language classrooms, particularly in the first-grade year, frequently made impromptu statements about themselves as readers and writers. Rather than focusing primarily on the acts of reading and writing, these children were interested in themselves and their progress. They frequently talked about what they knew how to do, what they were going to do next, and what they saw as a challenge or difficult task. These statements occurred spontaneously within the context of independent reading or writing time. Many remarks about self were made to no one in particular; others were part of the talk among learners as children engaged in reading and writing. The following statements are representative:

> "I can read the whole book."
> "I got that book at home, I already know it."
> "Me and him wrote four books."
> "I can read . . . just not out loud."
> "I can spell that without even looking."
> "When I was in kindergarten, I couldn't write or spell a thing."
> "I'm a gonna write, I'm a gonna draw, I'm a gonna do one more
>   page."
> "I'll read it all by myself, I don't need any help."

Within the whole language classrooms this pattern was evident in children who read proficiently as well as in those who struggled with reading and writing, though less proficient readers and writers made more statements about what they were "gonna do" than about what they knew.

Analysis of field notes in whole language classrooms indicated that these statements were often connected with a second pattern of behavior, *persistence*. Consistently, whole language learners moved from reading one book to reading another, sustaining the act of reading across the independent reading period. Learners also read books collaboratively, talking about the pictures, commenting about the story, and reading in turns. These learners appeared to be engrossed in their reading and usually sustained their attention and effort. Sometimes learners kept reading during teachers' signals to put books away, and a few continued reading as the rest of the class began a new activity or lined up for lunch.

The pattern of persistence was evident in writing as some learners worked on the same story day after day or initiated an elaborate writing project and worked on it continuously with the support of friends throughout a given writing period. For example, Eustice, one of the least proficient writers in first grade, began a six-part book about his family. Each separate section addressed a different family member, and the project, spanning three consecutive writing periods with extensive teacher support, was characterized by Eustice excitedly arranging the book's sections in piles on his writing desk, wrestling with what to write about each person, and asking excitedly "Can I publish it?" over and over.

The skills-based classrooms also contained these patterns of sense of self and persistence, but the patterns were restricted to the most proficient readers and writers. Maya, for example, commented "I'm writing without even looking at the board." The pattern was evident in writing events also. For example, Audrey, being assigned to copy a group of sentences from the board and add an illustration, generated an original story. As she added speech bubbles for the characters she elaborated, "There's a red light and there's a stop sign and there's how fast you should be going. And the rain started raining and it come down splash and she said, 'Ha Jan and Pam.'" Audrey persisted with this story well past the lesson. The remote mike picked up Audrey talking through the story again later in the day, this time discussing Jan and Pam with another child (Dahl, Freppon, & McIntyre, 1994).

The frequency of these remarks and episodes differed across studies. Even for the most proficient readers and writers there were only a few scattered utterances captured in the first grade year in skills-based sites, whereas such utterances were frequent in whole language classrooms, occurring in nearly every classroom visit in the first-grade year. In the skills-based sites the less proficient readers and writers sometimes made spontaneous statements during their work, but the statements were focused on task rather than self.

> "Dag, I wrote this on the wrong one."
> "I [know] what I pose to do, but what I pose to do first?"
> "I'm pasting my fox next to the *b*, where are you pasting yours?"
> (Purcell-Gates & Dahl, 1991)

Learners in skills-based classrooms, for the most part, were engaged in teacher-directed or teacher-assigned tasks and tended to complete them diligently. Their independent reading tended to be brief, and the prevailing pattern was to abandon books after reading a page or two. The most proficient learners, however, did reread basal stories on their own and tended to sustain that activity.

Quantitative findings: Written language knowledge assessments

The pretest results in both studies showed that these randomly selected children held a very restricted view of written language (Dahl & Freppon, 1991; Purcell-Gates, 1989). When the skills-based pretest results were compared to those of the whole language study, it was clear that children in the two whole language kindergartens scored slightly lower on every measure but one. Learners in both studies tended to view written language as something for school and were generally unfamiliar with print as a way to convey meaning. Learner grasp of print conventions, the alphabetic principle, and concepts of writing indicated little familiarity with written language. Pretest data on story structure and written narrative register showed that learners were unfamiliar with the language of storybooks and the macrostructure of written stories. At the end of the first-grade year learners in both investigations demonstrated considerable improvement.

Of particular interest in this cross-curricular comparison was whether there were significant differences in the quantitative measures when the skills-based and whole language posttest data were compared. A 2 (Group) × 2 (Time) mixed measures ANOVA with repeated measures was carried out on all six of the written language measures. Tables 5 and 6 present these data.

A significant Group × Time interaction was obtained for written narrative register only [$F(1,2) = 27.95$, $p < .05$] with the whole language group scoring higher on the posttest than the skills-based group. The effect size was .07 (Hedges, 1982). Significance was not obtained on any of the other five outcome measures.

Contrasts in reading processes and writing events across studies

The analysis of reading processes involved a proficient reader, an average reader, and a less experienced reader from each curriculum. Each was selected as representative of the given proficiency level within the curriculum. Three findings were evident from the comparison of reading samples for the selected learners at each level of proficiency.

First, the reading behaviors of the selected skills-based learners differed across teacher-directed and independent reading contexts. The skills-based learners used strategies independently that they did not use with the teacher. A finer grained analysis of these patterns is included in McIntyre (1992). In contrast, the selected whole language learners read in similar ways in both contexts.

A second finding was that the whole language learners at each proficiency level demonstrated greater breadth strategically in both teacher-directed and independent contexts. Generally, the strategies of the skills-based learners were to identify known sight words, try to use letter-sound relations, and wait to be told an unknown word. The whole language learners generally used picture clues, skipped unknown words, reread and self-corrected, used letter-sound relations, asked for help, and commented about the story.

Table 5

Means and standard deviations obtained on outcome measures

	Skills-based		Whole language	
	Pretest	**Posttest**	**Pretest**	**Posttest**
Intentionality	2.71	4.43	2.29	4.86
(1–5)	(1.68)	(1.22)	(1.35)	(0.65)
Concepts about print	7.27	16.60	6.43	18.52
(0–24)	(4.30)	(4.69)	(3.88)	(2.77)
Alphabetic principle	1.13	4.60	1.05	4.48
(1–8)	(0.35)	(1.45)	(0.22)	(1.63)
Story structure	3.29	4.57	3.62	5.43
(1–8)	(1.59)	(1.83)	(1.75)	(1.33)
Written narrative	23.92	43.00	19.58	63.42
register* (0–102)	(18.52)	(16.95)	(13.43)	(18.20
Concepts of writing	3.71	5.93	3.49	6.43
(1–7)	(1.92)	(1.21)	(1.88)	(0.51)

Note: The scores under each measure are the possible range, except for written narrative register, which is the actual range. Standard deviations are in parentheses. * Significant Group × Time interaction ($p<.05$) was obtained.

Third, the levels of engagement, as shown by patterns of learner persistence, effort, and interest in reading, were different across studies among learners who were average or less experienced readers. In the skills-based study, these two clusters of children did not demonstrate involvement by staying with reading tasks independently. Their whole language counterparts, in contrast, were persistent in their reading and highly active as they read independently.

Descriptions from these comparisons at each proficiency level are presented in the sections that follow. The contrasts include miscue data and evidence of reading strategies from reading samples during the mid and latter part of first grade as documented in teacher-directed and independent contexts.

Proficient readers: Audrey and Charlie. Audrey was the most proficient reader in her skills-based (SB) classroom. She read accurately and fluently in a word-calling manner in teacher-directed contexts, often waiting to be told an unknown word and sometimes sounding words out. Audrey's independent reading involved more strategies. Sometimes she read parts of a story conventionally, then switched to a focus on letter-sound cues. She seemed to experiment or play with the text when reading alone. Consistently, she was actively engaged in reading and performed as a persistent reader in both teacher-directed and independent contexts.

Charlie, in a whole language (WL) classroom, alternated between oral and silent reading. His oral reading substitutions in both teacher-directed and independent contexts indicated that he used all three cuing systems as well as picture clues. Charlie commented while reading and discussed the story line with himself. He worked on unknown words and said occasionally, "I don't know this one." He used letter-sound cues and rereading to figure out words.

Table 6

ANOVA table for written narrative register

Source	DF	SS	MS	F
Between				
A Group	1	956.47	956.47	3.91
B/A Teachers within Group	2	489.04	244.52	
Within				
C Time	1	15297.07	15297.07	171.93
AC Group × Time	1	2486.88	2486.88	27.95*
BC/A	2	177.94	88.97	

* $p < .05$

Average readers: Mary Jane and Jason. In teacher-directed lessons Mary Jane (SB) simply stopped reading when she came to an unknown word. She read only the words she knew and relied on the teacher to supply unknown words. Teacher encouragement led to the inclusion of some letter-sound cues, though these were rarely employed in independent reading. Working alone, Mary Jane did not tend to remain engaged in reading.

Jason (WL) used a wide range of strategies such as skipping, rereading, and picture clues across contexts. Miscue data indicated that he used story meaning and sentence structure to identify unfamiliar words and that sometimes his substitutions showed an overreliance on phonics. Jason stayed with a story when it was difficult and sometimes commented about what he was reading.

Less experienced readers: Rodney and Ann. Rodney (SB) demonstrated a limited range of skills when reading with the teacher. He guessed at words using his repertoire of sight words *(was? it? is?)* and used picture clues, though often without success. His independent reading often consisted of talking about the story and using picture prompts. By the end of first grade his independent reading had declined, and Rodney tended to avoid reading in any context.

Ann (WL) used several strategies to get unknown words across contexts: rereading, letter-sound mapping, and using picture cues. Miscue analysis indicated an overreliance on phonics using the beginning sound only. Ann often talked about the story, and her independent reading behaviors indicated an active and engaged stance.

Comparison of writing tasks across studies

Analysis of writing tasks and products indicated that focal learners in skills-based classrooms, for the most part, produced written answers on assigned worksheets as their writing activity in kindergarten. Of these, most tasks involved circling letters that corresponded to beginning sounds of pictured items (e.g., *t* for *tub*) and identifying whole words that corresponded to pictures or color names.

In the whole language kindergartens, writing involved exploration. Learners produced letter strings, usually with accompanying drawings and sometimes with meaning assigned after the work was complete. Children copied environmental print, often adding illustrations, and some writing artifacts included invented spelling.

The contrasts between curricula were more pronounced in first grade. In skills-based classrooms, writing was primarily for sight word and specific skill practice. Children copied sight words from the board, either lists or sentences, and participated in workbook activities that called for copying the correct word or sentence or circling a sight word and its matching picture. Learners worked on making their writing neat and on spelling each word correctly.

While learners routinely completed this writing as "paperwork," there also was some interest in composing. A writing event from the November samples captured this phenomenon. The writing task was to use words written on the board (*rowboat, motorboat,* and *sailboat*) to write a sentence in the *Think and Write* workbook. The workbook page provided places for children to draw and write. The teacher's directions were, "Write a sentence about a boat. You could name the boat. If you need help spelling, raise your hand.[11]

Jamie, a first grader in the skills-based study, began by drawing. After his rowboat picture was complete, he wrote *CAN BOAT* on the lines provided under the picture square. Next, he said "Go" and wrote *GO.* Looking determined, Jamie read his sentence so far under his breath, wrote *TWO* and then reread the sentence again, this time pointing to each word. Continuing the effort, Jamie frowned for a moment, then said "the" and wrote it. He looked at the sentence, sort of scanning it and added an S to the word boat. His text read *CAN BOATS GO TWO THE.* Jamie then paused thoughtfully and raised his hand to request the word *river.* The episode ended as Jamie said the word he needed over and over.

Writing in this instance was focused at the sentence level, and the assigned topic was related to a basal story. Jamie was engaged in writing his intended meaning and carefully monitored his work.

A comparable writing event in whole language classrooms occurred in the same time period involving Willie, also a first grader. During the writing workshop period, Willie wrote a spinoff story for the book *The Chocolate Cake,* which he had read earlier. He copied the title and used the book's format. Looking at the book, Willie wrote:

> *DTA SAID M-M-M-M-M* [Dad]
> *GRONDMA SAID M-M-M-M-M* [Grandma]
> *MYAAT SAID M-M-M-M-M* [my aunt]
> *BODY SAID M-M-M-M-M* [baby]

As he slowly said each person's name, Willie looked to the side and listened to the sounds, then he wrote the letters. Next, he copied the repeated phrase from the first page of the book. He arranged one sentence to a page, placing the sentences at the bottom as if illustrations would follow. Willie reread his four pages, then smiled and added the last *WILLIE SAID M-M-M-M.*

In this event there was an effort to map letters and sounds and a supporting text to structure the project. There was no revision after rereading.

In general, when writing tasks and products were compared, the differences reflected the function that writing served in each curriculum. In the skills-based classrooms, the learners completed teacher-assigned writing tasks designed to provide practice in skills. In the whole language classrooms, the writing periods were centered on learner-generated topics and learner exploration of written language. Children often received help from their peers and from the teacher.

The kinds of writing produced differed markedly across curricula. In first grade the children in whole language classrooms primarily produced work at the sentence, paragraph, and story levels. First graders in skills-based classrooms also produced some stories, but for the most part they worked on completing workbook assignments or on text written by the teacher on the board. Many writing tasks included sentence completion, fill in the blanks, and sentence or sight word copying with choices that learners could make among words.

Comparison of learning opportunities

While the focus in this cross-curricular comparison was on learner interpretations of beginning reading and writing instruction, contrasts in learning opportunities were evident. In the sections on phonics growth, response to literature, and writing tasks, we described learner patterns of behavior that related to each curriculum. In Table 7 we summarize the learning opportunities in these three areas.

While we recognize that a comprehensive account of differing learning opportunities across curricula is beyond the scope of this article, some distinctions can be drawn from our field note accounts. The two vignettes that follow are representative of reading instruction in skills-based and whole language first-grade classrooms and serve to illustrate differences in learning opportunities during teacher-directed lessons.

Reading vignette—Skills-based. In one skills-based classroom, the teacher introduced the basal story "The Yellow Monster," which told about a yellow bulldozer that some children had discovered. She talked briefly to the small group about the author, explained what the word *author* meant, and then read an abstract of the story. She added, "So during the story you should be thinking about . . . what IS the monster." The children then began to read the story aloud one by one as others followed along, some pointing to the words as they listened. The teacher urged children to focus carefully on words. "Look at the word . . . what's the word?" she said repeatedly. The children not reading aloud said the word to themselves when the teacher stopped a reader. For example, Shirika read some words incorrectly during her turn. The teacher intervened, "Look at the word, that is not what it says. Put your finger under

Table 7 *Learning opportunities across curricula*

Aspect of literacy	Curriculum	Learning opportunities
Phonics growth	Skills-based	Letter-sound relations were addressed in skill lessons. Teachers showed how to sound out words, and learners sounded out words as they read aloud. Worksheets about phonics were required as seatwork. Boardwork asked learners to copy words grouped by letter-sound patterns.
	Whole language	Teachers demonstrated sounding out during whole-group instruction with big books. In reading lessons letter-sound relations were one of the cuing systems that learners used to figure out words. Writing workshops included help for individual learners grappling with what letters to write for their intended meaning. Peers provided letter-sound information during daily writing.
Response to literature	Skills-based	Children listened to stories read aloud and responded to the teacher's questions. Children read trade books of their choice when their seatwork was completed or during morning lunch-count routines.
	Whole language	Tradebooks were the primary reading material, and learners read books of their choice independently. Read-alouds with the teacher included children's talk during the story. Information was provided about authors, illustrations, genre, and connections across literary works.
Writing tasks and products	Skills-based	Writing tasks were assigned and generally addressed specific skills in the basal program. Learners copied sentences using basal sight words. During boardwork they completed sentences by choosing from word choices that were generated by class members. They worked on specific writing lessons in the *Think and Write* workbook. There were some periods where writing journals were used.
	Whole language	Daily writing workshop periods included sustained writing about self-selected topics. Teachers provided individual conferences during writing workshops. They also demonstrated using letter-sound knowledge to spell words. Learners used trade books to prompt topics and word choices. They copied from books. Peers suggested ideas to one another and worked together on spelling. Learners wrote stories and read them to others.

the sentence *it likes to dig* The next word is *follow.*" Shirika repeated *follow.* During their turns, each of the five children in the group read three or four story sentences. Maya took her turn:

> Maya: *"Here is the monster," said Nina.*
> *"Don't go too near it."*
> *"Oh, I know what that is," said Linda.*
> *"This monster is big and yellow. It's a helping monster," said Tom.*
> Teacher: Said who?
> Maya: Tim.
> Teacher: O.K.

The story continued with the next reader and the next until it ended with teacher talk about reading carefully rather than rushing and saying the wrong word. "When you come across a word that you don't know, I want you to take the time to figure out what it is. Sound out the word or ask someone," she urged. Learners were then instructed to reread the story, practice the words and think about them on their own.

Reading vignette—Whole language. The whole language teacher and a small group of children looked through their copies of a new paperback, and they talked about what they liked from their initial scanning. They discussed what the story was going to be about after looking at the pictures and noting some of the words. Then one child simply began to read aloud, and others joined in. The teacher moved in and out of the children's parallel oral reading (reading so the children's voices predominated). When children faltered, the teacher asked questions, prompted with the sound that matched the beginning of the word, or asked about the picture. She also asked children to talk about the story, make predictions, and clarify what they thought. The teacher asked, "How do you know?" and "Why do you think that?" as children told their ideas. Midway through the story the teacher asked learners to "read with my finger" and pointed to one particular sentence, encouraging children to reread it with her. Children read the sentence but stumbled on the word *gate.* They talked about how they figured out the word (the various cueing systems they used). The teacher asked children to discuss the developing story in light of its beginning and then invited them to finish on their own. She said, "I'll let you find out what other trouble they get into." After children finished reading on their own, some were asked to do rechecks (rereadings) to clear up parts where they had trouble.

Reflection. In these two vignettes the learning opportunities differed markedly. Learners in the skills-based lesson had the opportunity to focus sharply on words, take their reading turn, listen to others, and practice reading the story on their own. Their attention was directed to the point of the lesson, and they received consistent coaching from their teacher as they read. In contrast, the whole language lesson was more diverse. Learners received various kinds of assistance, they were encouraged to use multiple cuing systems, and each reader read nearly all of the story. There was an opportunity to think about how to read and construct a sense of the story.

When data from Table 7 reporting learning opportunities in phonics, response to literature, and writing tasks are considered along with the reading instructional patterns illustrated in the vignettes, several contrasts are evident. The skills-based curriculum placed children, for the most part, in teacher-directed contexts where they engaged in reading or writing practice and interpreted or made sense of concepts from the instructional program. There was a focus on specific skills and practice opportunities assigned by the teacher. In contrast, the whole language curriculum engaged learners in sustained periods of reading and writing. Planned lessons took place in teacher-directed contexts, there was direct skill instruction focused on strategies, and learner choice was pervasive. Further, individual conferences provided contexts for instruction and support for independent reading and writing efforts.

Conclusions and Discussion

This cross-curricular comparison had two goals: It sought to capture learners' interpretations of beginning reading and writing instruction across the first 2 years of schooling in skills-based and whole language classrooms, and it structured a comparison across these two contrasting literacy curricula. The point was to make visible the similarities and differences across curricula in the children's interpretations of reading and writing and to extend our understanding of these curricula for innercity children.

The results presented a somewhat paradoxical picture. On the one hand, some findings, particularly those from quantitative measures, indicated a number of similarities in learning outcomes as measured by the tasks assessing written language knowledge. The cross-curricular comparison also documented that children made progress in both approaches. Given the controversy about direct or indirect instruction, especially for minority children (Delpit, 1986, 1988), and the "great debate" about phonics, these findings were of particular interest.

On the other hand, many of the findings demonstrated that learners made different senses of reading and writing in light of their experiences. The significant difference in written narrative register was taken to reflect curricular differences. Whole language learners generated significantly more syntactic and lexical features of story language, and they experienced extended exposure to and interaction with storybooks. In contrast, skills-based classrooms offered less emphasis on literature experiences.

The findings about letter-sound relations suggested that we have been asking the wrong questions. The important issue was not how children were taught in school-based settings, but rather what sense they could make. Unquestionably, phonics learning varied among focal learners in both studies. The essential difference was in the application learners made of their letter-sound knowledge and whether it was meaningful to them in terms of their understanding of written language knowledge. Children in one-on-one conferences with the teacher in both curricula seemed able to focus on letter-sound relations with teacher support. In independent writing contexts in the whole language classrooms children also learned to look twice at letters and sounds and tended to apply letter-sound relations more often during reading and writing episodes.

Finally, the cross-curricular comparison indicated distinctive differences in the affective domain (Turner, 1991). Learners in whole language classrooms expressed extensive interest in themselves as literacy learners. Moreover, their talk and actions revealed an understanding of their strengths and weaknesses as readers and writers. The linked patterns of sense of self as reader/writer and persistence indicated the establishment of a "disposition for learning" and provided evidence of learner ownership and a positive attitude toward literacy. In the skills-based study these two patterns were evident only among the most proficient readers and writers. This learner pattern was considered important in light of the vexing problem of patterns of failure that often characterize innercity learners in public schooling.

The paradox of differing findings from qualitative and quantitative data merits some explanation. In this comparison qualitative and quantitative data sources were considered as multiple perspectives revealing various kinds of information. The qualitative data tapped learner utterances and patterns of action over time and thus yielded data that revealed learner interpretations of reading and writing. The quantitative measures, in contrast, served as pre/post samples and indicated students' written language knowledge in specific domains. Because the sampling and focus differed in some areas across qualitative and quantitative data, the respective findings also differed. For example, data about attitudes toward reading and writing were prominent in the qualitative data but not sampled in the specific quantitative tasks. Similarly, data about accuracy in reading and writing events, responses to literature, and coping strategies of learners were evident in qualitative data, but not assessed in quantitative tasks.

There were three areas where qualitative and quantitative data converged in focus. First, in the area of written narrative register (knowledge of the language of storybooks), the qualitative and quantitative findings were in agreement and favored whole language. Second, in phonics knowledge, the qualitative and quantitative findings were at odds. Qualitative data indicated more application of letter-sound knowledge in daily writing events in whole language classrooms, but this difference was not supported in the quantitative alphabetic principle findings. Third, in writing production there was a difference in qualitative and quantitative findings. The former indicated greater sustained writing experiences for whole language learners, yet the quantitative task assessing writing showed no significant difference in the kinds of writing learners produced.

The disagreement in alphabetic principle findings suggests that, as assessed in these tasks, the two curricula may not differ widely in the phonics knowledge that learners gain. The difference was in what learners in differing curricula did with their phonics knowledge. Finally, in the area of writing production, the differences between qualitative and quantitative findings reflected learner interpretations of the writing task. Whole language learners responded to the writing task as a prompt for knowledge display. They produced lists of words or lists of sentences instead of their usual stories. The testing context and the task prompt appeared to shape learner interpretations about what the task required.

On a more general level, this cross-curricular comparison indicated differences in children's fundamental understandings about what literacy was for. The distinction between literacy skills and literate behaviors is central to understanding the contrasting outcomes documented in this comparison. Literacy skills are the concepts and behaviors that learners use as they read and write. They are elements of proficient reading and writing that are taught and practiced in most school-based settings. Literate behaviors are somewhat broader; they include learners reflecting on their own literate activity and using oral language to interact with written language by reacting to a story, explaining a piece of writing, or describing a favorite book to another person (Heath & Hoffman, 1986). Literate behaviors also include taking on the tasks of reading and writing, valuing one's own experience and personal language and connecting them with written language, and communicating about written language experiences. When learners see their own experience as valid knowledge and use reading and writing for their own purposes, the journey toward literate behaviors is soundly under way.

Children as sense makers in these two studies seemed to exemplify the distinction between literacy skills and literate behaviors. Some of the children in skills-based classrooms did not weave together the "cloth of literacy" (Purcell-Gates & Dahl, 1991, p. 21) nor move beyond their role as answer makers. Generally, they participated in reading and writing events, completed their work and learned literacy skills, but did not get involved personally nor see reading and writing as going beyond something for school. The children in whole language class-rooms also learned skills and engaged in literate behaviors. Importantly, some degree of literate behavior was demonstrated by children of all levels of proficiency in these classrooms.

Learners who demonstrated the disposition for learning took on the task of reading and writing for their own purposes. The majority of chil-dren in whole language classrooms and the most proficient readers in the skills-based sites demonstrated this pattern of engagement and ownership. Thus, the greatest difference appeared to be not what was being taught, but what children were learning—about themselves, about reading and writing, about school.

Limitations

The comparison of these two studies was restricted to urban, low-SES children learning to read and write in skills-based and whole language kindergarten and first-grade settings. No standardized measure of phonemic awareness was used in the array of quantitative measures that were part of the pre/post comparison. Thus, claims about phonics growth are limited to patterns that were documented in field notes of classroom observations. Comparative studies are generally limited by the extent to which the data being compared are parallel. This current study compared the outcomes of four years of research in eight class-rooms in two very different instructional settings. Thus, it is important to clarify some potentially troubling issues that arise in any compara-tive study and particularly in one of this duration and complexity.

The current research project was guided by some overarching prin-ciples. First, children's knowledge construction was identified through patterns of learner talk and action. Researchers focused on the learn-ers' perspectives, and codes and categories emerged from the actual learner behaviors in all eight classrooms. What these learners said and did in consistent ways over time formed the basis of sense-making cat-egories. Second, the instructional contexts of the skills-based and whole language classrooms clearly acted to shape children's behaviors in var-ious ways. Students' talk and actions can only be made manifest within the bounds of behavior considered acceptable in any classroom. The theoretical differences between the skills-based and whole language curricula, subsequent teacher and student reading and writing behaviors, and classroom rules of conduct determined to a large extent the written language interactions that could be observed in these studies. Third, we combined this understanding with careful and rigorous analysis of children's observable actions across both instructional contexts. The reported similarities and differences between skills-based and whole language groups were grounded in what these children, from highly similar low-SES populations and cultural groups, did to make sense of written language in these contrasting curricula.

Implications

The contrasts in learner sense making across studies reinforced the notion that we must consider the learner's perspective and individual differences in reading and writing development in order to understand children's reading and writing behaviors. Beyond documenting classroom curricula and their consequences, we need to know what children believe, what events and contexts shape their thinking, and how instruction can better fit children's evolving knowledge and skills.

In the final analysis, acquiring the disposition for learning may be the most critical occurrence in the early grades. The innercity learners in our study have many years of schooling ahead of them. The prognosis for children who are engrossed in books at the first-grade level and who think of themselves as readers and writers and are mindful of their strengths and weaknesses appears hopeful. It suggests at least the possibility that these children may continue to choose to read in the grades ahead and that they might sustain their roles as writers. In contrast, those who in first grade have already disengaged from literacy instruction appear to have begun the pattern of turning away from school (Dahl, 1992). The contrasts in this cross-curricular comparison tell us that learners are making sense of themselves in terms of their experiences in the early grades and that these early learner perceptions may establish patterns with far-reaching consequences.

Directions for future research

Future studies that compare across curricula might focus on some of the issues raised in this investigation. The area of phonemic awareness could be investigated across curricula in terms of instructional interactions and learner interpretations. The contrasting learning opportunities in skills-based and whole language classrooms should be investigated in detail. Finally, cross-curricular comparisons need to extend to the upper grades, where investigations of sustained instruction across 2 or more years in whole language and/or traditional basal programs have rarely been conducted with primary focus on learner interpretations.

References

Ahlberg, J., & Ahlberg, A. (1985) *Each peach pear plum*. New York: Scholastic.

Au, K. (1991). *Cultural responsiveness and the literacy development of minority students*. Paper presented at the annual meeting of the National Reading Conference, Palm Springs, CA.

Bloome, D., & Green, J. (1984). Directions in the sociolinguistic study of reading. In P.D. Pearson (Ed.), *Handbook of reading research* (Vol. 1, pp. 395–422). New York: Longman.

Bond, G.L., & Dykstra, R. (1967). The cooperative research program in first-grade reading instruction. *Reading Research Quarterly, 2,* 5–142.

Brown M.J.M. (1990). *An ethnology of innovative educational projects in Georgia*. Paper presented at the annual meeting of the American Evaluation Association, Washington, DC.

Bussis, A.M., Chittenden, E.A., Amarel, M., & Klausner, E. (1985). *Inquiry into meaning*. Hillsdale, NJ: Erlbaum.

Clay, M.M. (1975) *What did I write?* Portsmouth, NH: Heinemann.

Clay, M.M. (1979). *Stones: The concepts about print test*. Portsmouth, NH: Heinemann.

Cochran-Smith, M. (1984). *The making of a reader*. Norwood, NJ: Ablex.

Dahl, K. (1992). Ellen, a deferring learner. In R. Donmoyer & R. Kos (Eds.), *At-risk learners: Policies, programs, and practices* (pp. 89–102). Albany, NY: State University of New York Press.

Dahl, K. (1993). Children's spontaneous utterances during reading and writing instruction in whole language first grade classrooms. *Journal of Reading Behavior: A Journal of Literacy, 25*(3), 279–94.

Dahl, K.L. & Freppon, P.A. (1991). Literacy learning in whole language classrooms: An analysis of low socioeconomic urban children learning to read and write in kindergarten. In J. Zutell & S. McCormick (Eds.) *Learner factors/teacher factors: Issues in literacy research and instruction* (40th Yearbook of the National Reading Conference, pp. 149–58). Chicago: National Reading Conference.

Dahl, K. & Freppon, P. (1992). *Literacy learning: An analysis of low-SES urban learners in kindergarten and first grade*. (Grant No. R117E00134). Washington, DC: Office of Educational Research and Improvement, U.S. Department of Education.

Dahl, K.L., Freppon, P.A. & McIntyre, E. (1994). *Composing experiences of low-SES emergent writers in skills-based and whole language urban classrooms*. Manuscript submitted for publication.

Dahl, K.L., Purcell-Gates, V., & McIntyre, E. (1989). *Ways that inner-city children make sense of traditional reading and writing instruction in the early grades* (Grant No. G008720229). Washington, DC: Office of Educational Research and Improvement, U.S. Department of Education.

Deford, D.E. (1984). Classroom contexts for literacy learning. In T. Raphael (Ed.), *The contexts of school-based literacy* (pp. 161–80). New York: Random House.

Deford, D.E. (1985). Validating the construct of theoretical orientation in reading instruction. *Reading Research Quarterly, 20,* 351–67.

Delawter, J.A. (1970). *Oral reading errors of second grade children exposed to two different reading approaches.* Unpublished doctoral dissertation, Columbia University, New York.

Delpit, L.D. (1986). Skills and other dilemmas of a progressive black educator. *Harvard Educational Review, 56,* 379–85.

Delpit, L.D. (1988). The silenced dialogue: Power and pedagogy in educating other people's children. *Harvard Educational Review, 58,* 280–98.

Donmoyer, R., & Kos, R. (1993). At-risk students: Insights from/about research. In R. Donmoyer & R. Kos (Eds.), *At-risk students: Portraits, policies, programs, and practices* (pp. 7–36). Albany, NY: SUNY Press.

Dyson, A.H. (1989). *Multiple worlds of child writers: Friends learning to write.* New York: Teachers College Press.

Dyson, A.H. (1991, February). Viewpoints: The word and the world—reconceptualizing written language development or do rainbows mean a lot to little girls? *Research in the Teaching of English, 25*(1), 97–123.

Edelsky, C. (1991). *With literacy and justice for all: Rethinking the social in language and education.* New York: Falmer Press.

Edwards, E., & Mercer, N. (1987). *Common knowledge.* New York: Methuen.

Faulkner, K. (1991). *Oh no.* New York: S & S Trade.

Ferriero, E., & Teberosky, A. (1982). *Literacy before schooling.* Exeter, NH: Heinemann.

Freppon, P.A. (1991). Children's concepts of the nature and purpose of reading and writing in different instructional settings. *Journal of Reading Behavior: A Journal of Literacy, 23,* 139–63.

Freppon, P.A. (1993). *Making sense of reading and writing in urban classrooms: Understanding at-risk children's knowledge construction in different curricula* (Grant No. R117E1026191). Washington, DC: Office of Educational Research and Improvement, U.S. Department of Education.

Freppon, P.A., & Dahl, K.L. (1991). Learning about phonics in a whole language classroom. *Language Arts, 69,* 192–200.

Gentry, J.R. (1982). An analysis of developmental spelling in GYNS AT WRK. *The Reading Teacher, 36,* 192–200.

Gentry, J.R. (1987). *Spel is a four-letter word.* Portsmouth, NH: Heinemann.

Gibson, L. (1989). *Literacy learning in the early years through children's eyes.* New York: Teachers College Press.

Goetz, J.P., & Lecompte, M.D. (1984). *Ethnography and qualitative design in educational research.* New York: Academic Press.

Goodman, K. (1986). *What's whole in whole language?* Portsmouth, NH: Heinemann.

Green, J., & Meyer, L. (1991). The embeddedness of reading in classroom life: Reading as a situated process. In C. Baker & A. Luke (Eds.), *The critical sociology of reading pedagogy* (pp. 141–60). The Netherlands: John Benjamins.

Griffin, P., Cole, M., & Newman, D. (1982). Locating tasks in psychology and education. *Discourse Processes, 5,* 111–25.

Halliday, M.A.K. (1978). *Language as a social semiotic: The social interpretation of language and meaning.* Baltimore, MD: University Park Press.

Harste, J., Burke, C., & Woodward, V.A. (1981). *Children, their language and their world: Initial encounters with print* (Grant No. NIE-G-790132). Washington, DC: National Institute of Education.

Harste, J., Burke, C., & Woodward, V.A. (1983). *The young child as writer-reader, and informant* (Grant No. NIE-G-80-0121). Washington, DC: National Institute of Education.

Heath, S.B. (1982). What no bedtime story means: Narrative skills at home and school. *Language in Society, 11,* 49–76.

Heath, S.B. (1983). *Ways with words: Language, life, and work in communities and classrooms.* New York: Cambridge University Press.

Heath, S.B., & Hoffman, D.M. (1986). *Inside learners: Interactive reading in the elementary classroom* [Videotape]. Palo Alto, CA: Stanford University.

Hedges, L.V. (1982). Estimation of effect size from a series of independent experiments. *Psychological Bulletin, 92*(2), 490–99.

Holdaway, D. (1979). *The foundations of literacy.* Portsmouth, NH: Heinemann.

Jordan, C., Tharp, R.G., & Baird-Vogt, L. (1992). Just open the door: Cultural compatibility. In M. Saravia-Shore & S.F. Arvizu (Eds.), *Cross-cultural literacy* (pp. 3–18). New York: Garland.

Kantor, R., Miller, S.M., & Fernie, D.E. (1992). Diverse paths to literacy in a preschool classroom: A sociocultural perspective. *Reading Research Quarterly, 27,* 185–201.

Kennedy, J., & Bush, A.J. (1985). *An introduction to the design and analysis of experiments in behavioral research* (pp. 521–31). Lanham, MD: University Press of America.

Knapp, M.S., & Shields, P.M. (1990). Reconceiving academic instruction for children of poverty. *Phi Delta Kappan, 71,* 752–58.

MacKinnon, A.R. (1959). *How do children learn to read?* Toronto: Coop Clark.

McGill-Franzen, A., & Allington, R.L. (1991, May/June). The gridlock of low reading achievement: Perspectives on practice and policy. *Remedial and Special Education, 12*(3), 20–30.

McIntyre, E. (1992). Young children's reading behaviors in various classroom contexts. *Journal of Reading Behavior: A Journal of Literacy, 24*(3) 339–91.

Meyers, J. (1992). The social contexts of school and personal literacy. *Reading Research Quarterly, 27,* 297–333.

Mitchell, V. (1992). African-American students in exemplary urban high schools: The interaction of school practices and student actions. In M. Saravia-Shore & S.F. Arvizu (Eds.), *Cross-cultural literacy* (pp. 19–36). New York: Garland.

Neuman, S.B., & Roskos, K. (1992). Literacy objects as cultural tools: Effects on children's literacy behaviors in play. *Reading Research Quarterly, 27,* 203–25.

Newman, J. (1985). Insights from recent reading and writing research and their implications for developing whole language curriculum. In J. Newman (Ed.), *Whole language: Theory in use* (pp. 7–36). Portsmouth, NH: Heinemann.

Ogbu, J.H., (1985, October). *Opportunity structure, cultural boundaries, and literacy.* Paper presented at the Language, Literacy, and Culture: Issues of Society and Schooling seminar, Stanford University, Palo Alto, CA.

Oldfather, P., & Dahl, K. (1994). Toward a social constructivist reconceptualization of intrinsic motivation for literacy learning. *Journal of Reading Behavior: A Journal of Literacy, 26*(2), 139–58.

Pellegrini, A. (1991). A critique of the concept of at risk as applied to emergent literacy. *Language Arts, 68,* 380–85.

Purcell-Gates, V. (1988). Lexical and syntactic knowledge of written narrative held by well-read-to kindergartners and second graders. *Research in the Teaching of English, 22,* 128–60.

Purcell-Gates, V. (1989). Written language knowledge held by low-SES, inner-city children entering kindergarten. In S. McCormick & J. Zutell (Eds.), *Cognitive and social perspectives for literacy research and instruction* (39th Yearbook of the National Reading Conference, pp. 95–105). Chicago: National Reading Conference.

Purcell-Gates, V., & Dahl, K. (1991). Low-SES children's success and failure at early literacy in skills-based classrooms. *Journal of Reading Behavior: A Journal of Literacy, 23*(1), 1–34.

Read, C. (1971). Pre-school children's knowledge of English phonology. *Harvard Educational Review, 41,* 1–34.

Rosenblatt, L. (1985). Viewpoints: Transaction versus interaction—A terminological rescue operation. *Research in the Teaching of English, 19,* 96–106.

Rosenblatt, L. (1989). Writing and reading: The transactional theory. In J. Mason (Ed.), *Reading and writing connections* (pp. 153–76). Needham Heights, MA: Allyn & Bacon.

Rowe, D.W. (1989). Author/audience interaction in the preschool: The role of social interaction in literacy lessons. *Journal of Reading Behavior: A Journal of Literacy, 21,* 311–49.

Schieffelin, B.B., & Cochran-Smith, M. (1984). Learning to read culturally. In H. Goelman, A. Oberg, & F. Smith (Eds.), *Awakening to literacy* (pp. 3–23). London: Heinemann.

Smith-Burke, M.T. (1989). Political and economic dimensions of literacy: Challenges for the 1990's. In S. McCormick & J. Zutell (Eds.), *Cognitive and social perspectives for literacy research and instruction* (39th Yearbook of the National Reading Conference, pp. 19–34). Chicago: National Reading Conference.

Stein, N.L. (1979). *The concept of story: A developmental psycholinguistic analysis.* Paper presented at the annual meeting of the American Educational Research Association. San Francisco, CA.

Stein, N. (1982). The definition of a story. *Journal of Pragmatics, 6,* 487–507.

Stein, N.L., & Glenn, C.G. (1975). *A developmental study of children s recall of story material.* Paper presented at the meeting of the Society for Research in Child Development, Denver, CO.

Stein, N.L., & Glenn, C.G. (1979). An analysis of story comprehension in elementary school children. In R.O. Freedle (Ed.), _Discourse processing: Advances in research and theory_ (Vol. 2, pp. 53–120). Norwood, NJ: Ablex.

Sulzby, E. (1985). Children's emergent reading of favorite storybooks: A developmental study. _Reading Research Quarterly, 20,_ 458–81.

Sulzby, E. (1992). Transitions from emergent to conventional writing. _Language Arts, 69,_ 290–97.

Taylor, D. (1983). _Family literacy: Young children's learning to read and write._ Portsmouth, NH: Heinemann.

Taylor, D., & Dorsey-Gaines, C. (1988). _Growing up literate: Learning from inner-city families._ Portsmouth, NH: Heinemann.

Teale, W.H. (1984). Reading to young children: Its significance for literacy development. In H. Goelman, A. Oberg, & F. Smith (Eds.), _Awakening to literacy_ (pp. 110–21). London: Heinemann.

Teale, W.H. (1986). Home background and young children's literacy development. In W.H. Teale & E. Sulzby (Eds.), _Emergent literacy: Writing and reading._ Norwood, NJ: Ablex.

Teale, W.H., & Sulzby, E. (1986). Introduction: Emergent literacy as a perspective for examining how young children become writers and readers. In W.H. Teale & E. Sulzby (Eds.), _Emergent literacy: Writing and reading._ Norwood, NJ: Ablex.

Trueba, H. (1988). Culturally-based explanations of minority students' academic achievement. _Anthropology and Education Quarterly 19,_ 270–87.

Turner, J. (1991). _First graders' intrinsic motivation for literacy in basal instruction and whole language classrooms._ Paper presented at the annual meeting of the National Reading Conference, Palm Springs, CA.

Udry, J.M. (1966). _What Mary Jo shared._ Chicago: Albert Whitman.

Wells, G. (1986). _The meaning makers._ Portsmouth, NH: Heinemann.

Whaley, J. (1981). Story grammars and reading instruction. _The Reading Teacher, 34,_ 762–71.

Appendix

Sample grid of learner patterns

Grids summarize learner patterns of activity in reading and writing as documented in field notes. They include notations about activity during instructional periods, information about stance, and dates of important vignettes.

Name: Willie
Time interval: Jan.–May of first grade
Curriculum: Whole language

Reading activity:

Reads whole books with teacher, discusses gist. Frequent near-conventional reading. Miscues show balance of cuing systems, many strategies. Close monitoring of own reading. Self-corrects. Begins to vary strategies in independent reading—sometimes telling a story for pages with extensive text, then reading conventionally pages with a small number of sentences. Often reads collaboratively with friend, alternating pages.

Writing activity:

Writes books with partner, suggests words, writes some sentences, talks about what could come next in story. Sustained writing every period from February on. Writes about personal experience. Composing behavior includes saying words and phrases as he writes them, rereading, asking for spelling, completing the written piece.

Instruction periods (whole group):

Reads along with the teacher. Continually interrupts story reading with comments about patterns or statements connecting prior knowledge with story.

Stance:

Active, interested in reading and writing. Sustains independent work, often deeply engrossed.

Vignettes:

January 16 Sustained reading with teacher, whole book.
March 6 Revision conference with teacher, adds quotation marks.

11 Experimental Research: On Phonemic Awareness and on Whole Language

Constance Weaver
Western Michigan University

After warning readers about some of the limitations and common misinterpretations of experimental research, Weaver proceeds to discuss two bodies of research: one focusing primarily on phonemic awareness and its effects, and the other focusing on whole language teaching and its effects, compared with the teaching in skills-intensive classrooms.

The phonemic awareness research is discussed under four headings: research that merely claims a correlation between phonemic awareness and scores on standardized tests of reading; research that is interpreted to mean that phonemic awareness is a prerequisite to learning to read, or at least a facilitator (necessary but not sufficient condition) in learning to read; research that is interpreted as showing that phonemic awareness is a consequence of learning to read; and research suggesting a reciprocal relationship: that phonemic awareness helps in learning to read, but that learning to read also develops phonemic awareness. Weaver concludes that almost all of the studies can be interpreted as supporting, or at least not contradicting, the hypothesis that phonemic awareness and learning to read facilitate one another. This discussion is followed by a list of concerns about this particular body of research.

A second section summarizes a growing body of experimental research that has typically been ignored by phonics advocates and the public. From 1985 onward, such research has compared the traditional teaching of isolated reading and writing skills to the development of literacy in classrooms considered to be "literature-based" or "whole language." The latter might be called "skills-in-context" classrooms where the teachers help children develop reading and writing skills as they read whole texts and write together and independently. Weaver's generalizations about such research are drawn only from research studies that include standardized tests or subtests, along with an array of other measures. From the research available in 1994, Weaver makes the following observations. Overall, in comparison with children in skills-intensive and/or phonics-intensive primary grade classrooms, the children in the whole language, skills-in-context classrooms typically

- do at least as well on standardized measures, including measures of phonics knowledge;
- use their phonics more effectively;
- read for meaning better, rather than just to identify words;
- develop more strategies for dealing with problems in reading, such as problem words;
- write longer pieces with more sophisticated vocabulary;
- develop vocabulary, spelling, grammar, and punctuation skills as well as or better than children in more traditional classrooms;
- develop a better sense of themselves as readers and greater independence as readers and writers.

Weaver discusses in substantial detail the various studies that have given rise to these generalizations. Some of these studies were conducted over two years (one for three years) and focused on at-risk children. Concerns about this body of research are also raised.

The chapter ends with a list of generalizations that might reasonably be drawn from research on reading and learning to read, particularly the bodies of research discussed in this article. Finally, Weaver discusses concerns that have led to a renewed emphasis on teaching phonics and phonemic awareness, followed by a brief discussion of certain unproductive or downright harmful teaching and assessment practices from the past and present that we should not repeat or perpetuate.

The section on whole language research is adapted from Weaver's *Reading Process and Practice: From Socio-Psycholinguistics to Whole Langage,* 2nd ed. (pp. 310-323, 355-357). Copyright Heinemann, 1994. Reprinted with permission.

Experimental research is often quantitative in nature, with standardized tests as the measure of the effectiveness of the experimental treatment. Such studies, mostly focusing on phonemic awareness, are discussed in the first section of this chapter. Other experimental research may use qualitative measures, such as interviews and observations, but this data may be quantified, too, according to certain predetermined criteria. Such are the studies comparing whole language with skills-intensive classrooms in the second section, though these studies also included standardized tests as measures of effectiveness.

Experimental research, with its experimental and control groups, its independent and dependent variables, its careful assignment of research subjects to experimental and control groups (in much of the current research), and its often elaborate research design, is often thought to be "objective," by which people seem to mean it proves things, it gives "the truth" about them. The public in general tends to regard experimental research as "scientific." However, science itself, particularly the "hard" sciences, has moved beyond this assumption. A mind-expanding event occurred in 1905, when Albert Einstein discovered that light has the properties of a particle. This would not have been so exciting a finding if Thomas Young had not discovered, in 1803, that light has the properties of a wave. Both are true because the observed properties of light depend upon how the researcher chooses to measure it (Zukav, 1979). In other words, so-called objective reality is necessarily affected by the observer's assumptions, research design, methodology, and perceptions. This accounts, at least in part, for the sometimes contradictory conclusions from different experimental studies.

Concerns about These Bodies of Experimental Research and Their Interpretation

Many educators believe that experimental research is no more reliable than naturalistic, observational research. There are many reasons for their concerns—many reasons, other than contradictory results, why we should not take such research as necessarily demonstrating "the truth" about educational phenomena. The following are some general concerns about experimental research studies and the reporting and interpretation of them:

1. The Pygmalion Effect, according to which experimental subjects rise to the expectation that they will do better than controls. For example, the teachers in the experimental groups might teach especially well, knowing the probable biases of the investigator(s).

2. Statistical significance often masks small differences that are not necessarily educationally significant. Research summaries often report only the direction of the difference and its statistical significance, not the magnitude of the difference. Slight differences, even if statistically significant, may not be worth the time needed to teach the skill in question.

3. Often, equally plausible alternative hypotheses are not considered within the same study. For example, a study may assess the effects of teaching phonemic awareness on learning to read, or vice versa—but not both. When only one reasonable causal relationship is assessed in a given study, the results may suggest a unidirectional relationship when, in fact, a multidirectional relationship is more complete.

4. Correlation and "predictive value" are often taken as, or confused with, causation. For example, Juel, Griffith, and Gough (1986) conclude with what they had expected to find: that "although exposure to print would aid growth in phonemic awareness, it would do little to increase cipher knowledge until a prerequisite amount of phonemic awareness is attained" (p. 249). They also in effect concluded that synthetic phonics instruction does not adequately develop phonemic awareness or the decoding skill it is designed to promote, for some children. Because they view some phonemic awareness as a prerequisite to decoding skill, the investigators therefore recommend oral phonemic awareness training "for entering first-grade children with poor phonemic awareness" (p. 249). They do not consider the possibility that greater print exposure might substantially increase both phonemic awareness and cipher knowledge, the possibility that more or different kinds of phonological training might have the same effect, or the possibility that phonemic awareness training may not be of much help either. This is the potential difficulty with correlational research: it is all too easy for the investigators or others to draw conclusions about causal relationships that are not warranted by that particular data.

5. Such studies usually report only aggregate scores, not individual differences. But individual differences become highly significant in the classroom. When one kind of instruction is reported as better than another, what often gets lost is the fact that even the more effective approach does not work, for many children. No instruction is magic, and the authors of research articles need to remind their readers of that.

Research Studies Focusing Primarily on Phonemic Awareness

As commonly defined, phonemic awareness is one aspect of phonological awareness. The broader term, *phonological awareness*, refers to awareness of sound units in language, such as syllables, the onsets and rimes within syllables (which figure into alliteration and rhyme), and the individual phonemes. The *onset* consists of any consonant(s) that may precede the vowel in a syllable—for example, the /t/ in *tip*, the /ch/ (a single sound) in *chip*, and the /tr/ in *trip*. The *rime* is the vowel of a syllable, plus any consonant(s) that might follow—for example, the /ip/ in *tip*, the /ips/ in *tips*, the /ants/ in *chants*, and the /alkt/ in *walked*. *Phonemes* are what we have learned to think of as the separate sounds in words, even though they are not very easily separable from the stream of speech. For example, *trips* consists of five phonemes, /t/, /r/, /i/, /p/, /s/. *Phonemic awareness*, then, is awareness of these "separate" sounds, the sounds we commonly associate with letters of the alphabet. Most of the research studies dealing with phonemic awareness use measures that require not just the practical ability to hear differences in phonemes within words that themselves are within sentences and meaningful contexts (e.g., in order to distinguish *tan* from *van*, in *He got a tan at the beach*). In addition, such studies require the ability to analyze words into their phonemes and sometimes to manipulate those phonemes.

At first, the research on phonemic awareness focused on the correlation between phonemic awareness and standardized test scores. That is, the research showed that a high degree of phonemic awareness is commonly associated with high scores on standardized tests in kindergarten and first grade, whereas low phonemic awareness is commonly associated with lower standardized test scores. Examples will be discussed below as *correlational* studies. Other researchers claim their research shows phonemic awareness to be a necessary *prerequisite* to learning to read, or at least a necessary but not sufficient cause or *facilitator*. At the other extreme, some research suggests that phonemic awareness is a *consequence* of learning to read. Other studies and investigators suggest a *reciprocal* role: that phonemic awareness facilitates learning to read, but that reading also promotes phonemic awareness— and that learning to read is possible without fully mastering phonological awareness (for an example of the latter, see Fink, chapter 13). Only some of the most widely cited studies will be discussed in detail below, since there are quite a few. The division into kinds of studies is a modification of Ehri's (1979) categories.

Correlation

One of the more comprehensive studies showing a correlation between phonemic awareness and reading comprehension is that undertaken by Stanovich, Cunningham, and Feeman (1984). Their study was particularly designed to assess the validity of the claim made by Arthur Jensen (1981) about a high correlation between intelligence and reading comprehension. The study in question demonstrates a much lower correlation, but our major concern here is other aspects of the study, particularly those involving the reading of the first graders in the study.

With the first graders, the investigators examined the relationships between four important determiners of reading comprehension ability, as measured by a standardized test: decoding speed, listening comprehension, phonological awareness, and general intelligence. The several measures included two very different tests of general intelligence; tests of listening comprehension; the Reading Survey test of the Metropolitan Achievement Test, which assesses reading comprehension but does not directly test word decoding; a test of decoding speed, using 20 real words and 20 pseudowords; and tests of "phonological awareness," all of which assess phonemic awareness in particular. The investigators undertook a series of grouped hierarchical multiple regression analyses, factor analysis, and path analysis. The different analyses produced related results, leading to the overall conclusion that general intelligence is not a particularly good predictor of reading comprehension ability. However, "there is evidence for the importance of three relatively independent abilities in predicting early reading progress" (p. 295): verbal (oral) comprehension ability, phonological (phonemic) awareness, and speed of decoding, which emerged as a separate predictor, independent of phonological awareness.

Stanovich, Cunningham, and Feeman also point out that these relatively independent factors contributing to reading comprehension "support multiple-factor theories of individual differences in reading ability" (p. 295; see also p. 297). See also Share, Jorm, Maclean, & Matthews (1984), whose research led to the surprising conclusion, among others, that peer ability in phonemic segmentation is as good a predictor of individual reading achievement as the child's own ability (p. 1317).

The title of an article by Nation and Hulme (1997) suggests the essential point of their research study: "Phonemic segmentation, not onset-rime segmentation, predicts early reading and spelling skills." This study involved 25 children from each of three grade levels in the United Kingdom: Year 1 (approximately equivalent to first grade), Year 3, and Year 4. All of the children had had "a traditional mixture of whole language and phonics reading instruction" (p. 158). Various measures were used to assess children's phonological awareness, including, specifically, their phonemic awareness. Reading ability was measured using the British Ability Scales, a standardized test of single-word reading ability. The ability to segment words into phonemes increased with age, as did the ability to categorize alliteration at the beginnings of words and rhyme at the ends of words. Nevertheless, the ability to segment spoken nonwords into onset-rime units did not increase with age and did not correlate significantly with increased ability to read words. The researchers note that onset-rime segmentation was difficult for all the ages tested, a finding that differs from the research-based suggestion of Goswami and Bryant (1990) that awareness of onsets and rimes develops early and naturally. Such differences in research results can often be accounted for by the use of research measures that make different demands upon children, a point that should be kept in mind in reading all these research summaries. In any case, Nation and Hulme found that phonemic segmentation ability was an excellent predictor of the ability to read and spell single words—much more so than the measured ability to segment nonwords into onsets and rimes (p. 164), which showed almost no correlation at all with this ability.

Mann, Tobin, and Wilson (1987) investigated whether children's pre-conventional spellings could predict later reading ability. Such early spellings often reflect finer sound distinctions than those captured in phonemic analysis and thus seem to reflect an ability to hear the small-est phonological features of spoken words. The investigators concluded from their study that the phonological accuracy of kindergarten spellings can predict first grade reading ability, as measured by the word identification and word attack subtests of the Woodcock Reading Mastery Tests (Woodcock, 1973). Indeed, there was even some evidence that kindergartners' phonological spellings presaged reading ability at the end of second grade (presumably as measured in the same ways). Or in other words, children's phonological spellings, like phonemic awareness, correlate with certain aspects of reading—at least with word reading and word attack.

Prerequisite/facilitator

The studies in this section conclude either that some phonemic aware-ness is a prerequisite to decoding skill and therefore to learning to read (e.g., Juel, Griffith, and Gough, 1986), or that phonemic aware-ness is a necessary though not sufficient condition for learning to read (e.g., Tunmer & Nesdale, 1985).

A study by Juel, Griffith, and Gough (1986) was undertaken to test a simple model of early literacy acquisition. This study defines the set of spelling/sound correspondence rules of the language as its *ortho-graphic cipher* (p. 244), and argues that "phonemic awareness could not possibly lead to decoding or spelling without some experience with print" (p. 245). However, this study also claims "that until some pre-requisite amount of phonemic awareness is attained, exposure to print will do little to increase knowledge of the cipher" (p. 245).

On what evidence do Juel, Griffith, and Gough base this claim? The study involved 80 children, from their first- through second-grade years. The children were placed in one of two basal reading series, which was supplemented with a synthetic phonics program developed by the local school district, for twenty to thirty minutes in each read-ing period. The teachers were provided with a script for teaching these lessons. The research involved a large battery of tests, including six subtests of phonemic awareness; the Bryant Test of Basic Decoding Skills, consisting of 50 nonsense words to assess cipher knowledge (Bryant, 1975); the reading comprehension subtest of the IOWA, to assess reading comprehension; and the spelling and reading subtests of the Wide Range Achievement Test, which require the child to spell words and to pronounce individual words (WRAT; Jastak, Bijou, & Jastak, 1978). Other tests assessed spelling, writing, oral language, and listening comprehension.

The researchers found that phonemic awareness and listening comprehension appeared to strongly affect end-of-year performance in spelling, word recognition, writing, and reading comprehension in first grade, and also to a lesser extent in the second grade (p. 249). At the end of first grade, a high phonemic awareness group had a mean score of 27.9. In contrast, the group of children who had low phonemic awareness typically did very poorly on the Bryant decoding test (a mean score of 3.7). The authors note, in fact, that "Despite having been exposed to large amounts of print and a year of phonics instruction, many children with poor phonemic awareness could not read a single nonsense word at the end of first grade." From such results, Juel, Griffith, and Gough conclude that "children will not acquire spelling-sound correspondence knowledge until a prerequisite amount of phonemic awareness has been attained," (p. 254), though exposure to print is necessary too (p. 244). Further, they conclude what they expected to find: that "although exposure to print would aid growth in phonemic awareness, it would do little to increase cipher knowledge until a prerequisite amount of phonemic awareness is attained" (p. 249). They also in effect conclude that synthetic phonics instruction does not adequately develop phonemic awareness or the decoding skill it is designed to promote, for some children. Because they view some phonemic awareness as a prerequisite to decoding skill, the investigators therefore recommend oral phonemic awareness training "for entering first-grade children with poor phonemic awareness" (p. 249).

Tunmer and Nesdale's study (1985) compared children in two "psycholinguistic" first-grade classrooms where there was "no incidental or formal instruction in phonological recoding skills" with classrooms where the instruction was eclectic and included a heavy emphasis on phonological recoding skills (recoding letters into sounds, written words into spoken words). The decoding of real words and the decoding of pseudowords were highly correlated with one another and also with reading comprehension. Furthermore, all three variables correlated significantly with the method of instruction: the children in the eclectic classrooms were typically those who scored highest, and the differences were quite substantial. On the other hand, there was almost no correlation between the two different instructional methods and the phonemic segmentation ability that the children exhibited (p. 425). That is, the method of instruction seemed to make little difference in the children's ability to segment phonemes.

A particularly interesting finding from the Tunmer and Nesdale study is the following: All 22 of the students who passed the decoding test (with both real words and nonsense words) passed the test requiring segmentation of words into individual phonemes. However, none of the 24 students who failed the phonemic segmentation test passed the decoding test (p. 423). This is taken as supporting the argument of Juel, Griffith, and Gough (1986), that phonemic awareness precedes decoding ability. However, all it necessarily demonstrates is a correlation between the two, not a causal relationship.

Other studies have undertaken to train children in phonemic awareness and see if the experimental groups score better on various measures than the control groups. Fox and Routh (1976) concluded that children are receptive to training in blending only after they have developed some minimum ability to segment phonemes. Working with prereaders, the Olofsson and Lundberg study (1983) suggested that segmentation and blending may be best learned in highly structured phonological training programs (which did not necessarily involve any reading). In a landmark study, Bradley and Bryant (1985) investigated 400 children between the ages of four and five, over a four-year period. The group that categorized pictures by the sounds they had in common and received training in rhyming and alliteration using magnetic plastic letters performed substantially better than the groups with less or no phonological training, on tests of reading and spelling that were administered during the last phase of the study. Working with the magnetic letters corresponding to the sounds seems to be what made the biggest difference between the most successful group and the one that had only oral training. Ball and Blachman (1991) obtained similar results: the group that received training in both phonemic segmentation and name/letter sound correspondences did better than the other two groups on later measures of reading

Torgeson and Hecht (1996) review several interesting research studies and their conclusions in a study they undertook to investigate the effects of different tutorial strategies on "dyslexic" children whose slowness in developing word reading skills seems to result from difficulty in processing the phonological features of language. Before describing their study-in-progress, the authors make some important observations. They note, for instance, that a significant number of children with lesser phonological abilities do not profit from traditional training in phonological awareness or from synthetic phonics instruction that emphasizes sounding out words by blending the sounds of individual phonemes (pp. 142–144). Other statements are also important:

- It is not clear whether successful intensive remediation of alphabetic reading skills eventually leads to normalization of reading comprehension in dyslexic children without additional instruction specifically devoted to reading comprehension skills. (p. 143)

- It is clear that programs likely to be successful with children who have phonological processing problems must provide some form of explicit and direct instruction in "phonics" to help these children acquire better alphabetic reading skills. However, whether this instruction should follow traditional synthetic methods that provide much decontextualized practice in sounding out both words and nonwords, or whether the phonics instruction should be embedded within the context of whole-word reading, is a question of instructional emphasis that remains open for research. (p. 145)

- Finally, it is clear that children must be taught to use whatever alphabetic decoding skills they have in the service of getting meaning from text. Whether to focus relatively more time on building autonomous alphabetic decoding skills or to work toward earlier integration of phonics and context-based skills in decoding new words is an important question that also remains open. (p. 145)

These statements are worth citing because the six-year study by Torgeson and Hecht currently underway is funded by the National Institute for Child Health and Development (NICHD), an organization being credited with having funded research that shows we should be teaching reading by phonics first and only, to all children. Obviously, however, these researchers make no such claim from their ongoing work.

The first of their studies within the larger project is to determine what kind of instructional program has the greatest immediate impact "on word-level reading skills and long-term impact on fluency and comprehension skills" among children who have been diagnosed as having particularly weak phonological skills, as documented especially by letter naming and phoneme elision tasks. The study initially involved 200 kindergarten children. The children were randomly assigned to one of four treatment conditions: "(1) a group receiving implicit phonological awareness training plus phonics instruction embedded within real word reading and spelling activities; (2) a group receiving explicit oral and phonological awareness training plus synthetic phonics instruction (PASP); (3) a regular classroom support group receiving individual instruction to support the goals of the regular classroom reading program (RCS), and (4) a no treatment control group" (p. 146). Children in each treatment group received 80 minutes of one-on-one supplemental teaching each week for two-and-a-half years.

After this instructional period, the group receiving oral phonological awareness training plus synthetic phonics scored substantially higher than any other group on a measure of word attack skills (p. 151), and very slightly higher than the other treatment groups on all measures except passage comprehension, as measured by the Woodcock Reading Mastery Test–Revised. Of these differences, the only statistically significant one was between this phonological awareness/synthetic phonics group and the control group that had no additional tutoring. On the other hand, all three treatment groups clustered close together on all measures except word attack, and there was a substantial difference between each of the treatment groups and the control that received no additional tutoring. Furthermore, some children were much better able to take advantage of the one-on-one instruction in first grade than in kindergarten. Thus, while the authors approve of alterations to the general kindergarten curriculum that would promote phonological awareness as an oral language skill, they by no means argue for phonics first and only. Indeed, their research could be taken as supporting a conclusion from Ayres's research (1993, and chapter 8), that children are better able to take advantage of direct instruction in phonological awareness after they already have had reading instruction that focuses on the meaning of texts.

In a study reported by Vellutino and colleagues (1996), the investigators were interested in seeing whether the number of children labeled reading impaired/disabled could be substantially reduced by providing tutoring in phonological skills. Thus, the study evaluated a large group of children from kindergarten through fourth grade. In the middle of the first-grade year, subsamples of poor and "normal" readers were selected for in-depth study. Poor readers were randomly assigned to either a tutored group or a nontutored "contrast" group. The tutored group received daily tutoring for 30 minutes a day for between one and two school semesters, depending on progress. The results reported in this particular article are mainly from measures administered individually in kindergarten through second grade to the poor readers who received individual tutoring. "In each session, portions of time were devoted to helping the child develop a sight vocabulary, helping him or her to acquire phoneme awareness, attuning him or her to the alphabetic principle, and facilitating phonetic decoding and writing skills" (p. 610). These were considered important because a majority of children and adults labeled reading disabled have difficulty with phonological processing. However, time was also spent in fostering the deliberate use of a variety of strategies for word identification, not just phonics—and the amount of time spent with different kinds of instruction was adjusted to the individual child's needs. In addition, about half of the 30 minutes was usually spent in reading connected text. The authors found that with such tutoring, most of these children (more than 85 percent of those tutored) scored within the average or above average ranges on standardized tests of reading achievement, after one semester of tutoring. In terms of the total school populations, then, fewer than 3 percent did not achieve average or above average levels after a semester's tutoring. This is substantially fewer than those commonly labeled reading disabled (around 9 percent).

Foorman, Francis, Beeler, Winikates, and Fletcher (1997) report on a study providing early intervention for children receiving Chapter 1 services. The study included 209 first graders and 166 second graders. In their regular classroom, students received either (1) direct instruction in phonological awareness from the Open Court program (1995), which included phonemic awareness activities, letter/sound correspondences, blending, shared reading of Big Books, and other activities; (2) embedded phonics based on a classroom version of Hiebert, Colt, Catto, and Gary's (1992) restructured Chapter 1 program, which emphasized phonemic awareness and spelling patterns; or (3) whole language. Writing, spelling, and phonics instruction were to occur in context in the whole language classrooms, but the preliminary report (Foorman et al., 1997) does not indicate how much time was spent on phonics in the whole language classrooms, or specifically how it was taught. In addition to regular classroom teaching, the children received tutorial help either one-on-one or in groups of three. For the direct instruction and embedded phonics students, the Chapter 1 tutorial either matched the classroom method or was what the school district called reading empowerment, based on the work of Marie Clay (1985, 1993). The whole language students all received reading empowerment. In May, the direct instruction group had significantly higher scores than either of the other methods on the Woodcock-Johnson-Revised Basic Reading (Letter-Word Identification and Word Attack) and on its Broad Reading test (letter/word identification and passage comprehension). The greatest differences occured on the Basic Reading Skills test: the direct instruction group scored at the 44th percentile, the embedded phonics group at the 32nd percentile, the whole language group at the 27th percentile, and the standard curriculum group at the 17th percentile. On the Formal Reading Inventory (FRI: Wiederholt, 1986), which tests narrative and expository reading comprehension through multiple-choice questions, the groups did not differ, on average.

In a less formal study than the preceding ones, Gaskins, Ehri, Cress, O'Hara, and Donnelly (1996) investigated the effects of explicitly teaching children to analyze words into their constitutent phonemes on thirteen first-grade children, eight of whom were repeating first grade and five of whom were deemed to be at risk of reading failure. Teachers at this school had been teaching children to read unfamiliar print words by analogy with key sight words that were phonically regular. This worked for many children but not for all. Observation and reflection suggested that the children had not analyzed the key words into constituent parts, especially the phonemes. According to Ehri's model of sight word learning (1991, 1994, 1995), children begin reading sight words by remembering some distinctive, purely visual cue(s), such as the double l's in yellow. Next comes a partial alphabetic phase in which they remember limited matches between salient letters and sounds, often the beginning and ending letter/sounds. This is followed by a full alphabetic phase in which children remember matches between *all* letters and sounds. According to Ehri's model, this third phase is important for children to retain sight words in memory well enough to use them to read unfamiliar print words by analogy with larger chunks of letters and sounds, such as onsets, rimes, and syllables

Those involved in this project did not exactly test this model; rather, they taught children to analyze the key words into constituent sounds, to match letters and sounds, to talk about letters and sounds (to become reflective; to develop metacognitive awareness), and to spell the key words; every day they also read texts that contained words with familiar spelling patterns. In an attempt to determine the success of their word analysis program in comparison with the analogy training they had used the previous year, the investigators compared the groups of children's scores on the Wide Range Achievement Test (WRAT) word-reading and spelling tests. In the spring, the 13 children in the enhanced word-learning program read 63 words correctly; the 13 children in the previous class had read 57 words correctly the previous year. This difference was statistically significant (not likely to have occured by chance), though small. The mean spelling performances also favored the group in the enhanced program, but the differences were not statistically significant.

It is critical to note that while all of these studies and others suggest that phonemic awareness has a positive effect on reading achievement as measured by standardized tests, none of the researchers suggest or claim that phonemic awareness and decoding skill are all that is needed in learning to read. And as discussed below, there is even research which suggests the opposite: that phonemic awareness can be a consequence of learning to read. So the studies in this section do not necessarily suggest that reading *doesn't* promote phonemic awareness; that is simply something that was not investigated.

Consequence

The Tunmer and Nesdale (1985) study discussed above can be interpreted as providing support for the idea that phonemic awareness is more a result of learning to read than a cause. They compared three classes in which the students had no incidental or formal instruction in phonological recoding (blending) with three eclectic classes that included a heavy emphasis on phonological recoding. The investigators had the children pronounce both real words and pseudowords. Their results indicated a greater correlation between the children's ability to pronounce the pseudowords and their ability to pronounce the conventional words than between their ability to pronounce the pseudowords and their instruction. In other words, the heavy emphasis on phonological recoding in half the classrooms did not seem to develop phonemic awareness better than the no-phonics situation.

Furthermore, "while the children's ability to pronounce the conventional words accounted for 77 percent of the children's correct pronunciations of the novel [pseudo] words ($r = .88$), the children's instruction accounted for only 16 percent of the children's correct pronunciations of the novel [pseudo] words ($r = .41$)" (Moustafa, chapter 5). These aspects of the Tunmer and Nesdale (1985) study thus support the idea that the more words children can read, the more likely they are to be able to decode unfamiliar print words (up to a point, of course). Or to put it differently, this research supports the argument that phonemic awareness is at least partly a consequence of learning to read.

A key question then becomes, how/why does knowing more print words make it easier to decode unfamiliar print words? Goswami (1986, 1988), in studying kindergarten, first-, and second-grade children, demonstrated that children use analogy with known print words to help them figure out unknown print words. More specifically, of course, they use analogy with the *parts* of known print words to figure out unknown words. In other words, they decode unfamiliar print words by pronouncing familiar and pronounceable letter/sound *chunks*. These chunks are typically syllables, parts of syllables—namely onsets and rimes—or other pronounceable chunks (Gunning 1995 describes several studies wherein children and adults used pronounceable word parts to decode words). Or, as Goswami puts it, "development proceeds from the initial recognition of whole words to a stage of lexical analogy in which large sub-word units are extracted, and only then to a stage in which finer-grained analysis of words in grapheme-phoneme units becomes possible" (1988, p. 255). In other words, recognition of letter/sound correspondences, and probably phonemic awareness as well, develop as a consequence of learning to read.

As Goswami (1993) points out, the idea that analogy may be an important strategy in early reading has been supported by classroom studies in which children are trained to decode words using rime analogies (e.g., Peterson and Haines, 1992; White and Cunningham, 1990; Gaskins et al., 1996).

From Moustafa's research (1990, 1995, and chapter 5) it appears that onsets and rimes are particularly important chunks in reading by analogy. Furthermore, it appears that children use onset-rime chunks more than single phoneme knowledge to read unfamiliar print words. In Moustafa's study with 75 first graders, the children's knowledge of letter/phoneme correspondences could account for 64 percent of the correct pseudowords used in the study. However, their recognition of actual words accounted for 95 percent of the correct pronunciations of the pseudowords. Or in other words, when children appear to be blending the individual sounds of letters together to pronounce unfamiliar words, they may actually be using parts of familiar words to pronounce unfamiliar word parts, by analogy. *And knowledge of whole words seems to be an even better predictor of decoding skill than knowledge of letter/sound correspondences, which of necessity includes phonemic awareness.*

Although not directly addressing the question of whether phonemic awareness is at least partly a consequence of learning to read, Moustafa's research could be taken as supporting that possibility. So can several other studies. For example, Morais, Carey, Alegria, and Bertelson (1979) showed that illiterate adults were not aware of separate phonemes but could do phonemic segmentation after they learned to read. Mann (1986) found evidence of the effect of reading experience on Japanese children's awareness of phonemes as well as evidence of the reverse relationship, while Wimmer, Landerl, Linortner, and Hummer titled their research article "The relationship of phonemic awareness to reading acquisition: More consequence than precondition but still important" (1991).

Reciprocal

Most of the research on the development of phonemic awareness—and decoding ability—suggests that there is a reciprocal relationship between these phonological skills and reading itself. Even when the research and/or the researchers suggested that one or both of these skills are prerequisite to learning to read, the data is usually not incompatible with the view that there is a reciprocal relationship. Similarly, the research and researchers suggesting that phonemic awareness and/or decoding ability are a consequence of learning to read do not indicate that these phonological skills are *only* a consequence of learning to read, and not learned in any other way. Thus most of the research discussed so far can be taken as supporting, or at least not contradicting, the view that phonemic awareness and decoding facilitate learning to read *and* vice versa.

Interestingly, Adams and Bruck (1995) report the following, which also suggests reciprocal relationships: "that developing phonemic awareness in concert with letters and sounds is better than presenting letters and sounds alone (Ball & Blachman 1991), and that developing phonemic awareness with letters is more effective than developing phonemic awareness alone (Bradley & Bryant 1983; Byrne & Fielding-Barnesley 1991; Cunningham 1990)" (p. 16). This alone begins to suggest a reciprocal relationship between phonemic awareness (oral perception of "separate" speech sounds), letter/sound knowledge, and reading itself: that each facilitates the other.

Though Juel, Griffith, and Gough (1986) suggest that some phonemic awareness is a necessary prerequisite to developing decoding skill, they also argue that some experience with print is necessary too for developing decoding and spelling skills (p. 245). They also indicate that "exposure to print no doubt influences phonemic awareness, but it is not viewed [by them] as a *primary* shaper of phonemic awareness."

Other studies and other investigators more strongly suggest a reciprocal relationship between phonemic awareness and the reading of texts—that is, that each facilitates the other. Perfetti, Beck, Bell, and Hughes (1987) is one example. At the outset, they point out that reading is easier than phonemic segmentation, and that some research indicates that phonemic awareness benefits from learning to read (p. 285). On the other hand, there is a strong correlation between reading success and phonemic awareness, and substantial indication that training in phonemic segmentation can positively affect reading success (p. 285). "This, then, is the problem we addressed with the present study: On the one hand, phonemic awareness is logically important for learning to read. On the other hand, explicit phonemic awareness may be a more advanced cognitive skill than word reading, at least some primitive forms of reading. Our proposal for addressing this problem is that learning to read and phonemic awareness develop in tandem, in a reciprocal mutually supporting relationship. A corollary to this major premise is that phonemic awareness is not a unitary ability, but a constellation of abilities" (p. 284).

The investigators report on the 82 first-grade students in the study, two groups taught by a basal reader system that did not include direct phonics instruction and one taught by systematic direct code instruction; the latter included direct instruction in letter/sound correspondences and blending. The basal group assigned to a reading readiness workbook consistently did less well on various measures than the regular basal group or the direct instruction group. The investigators used three tasks to assess phonemic knowledge: a synthesis task that required blending of sounds to form a word, and two other tasks requiring phonemic analysis. At the end of the school year, two measures of the children's reading were used: the child's score on the Wide Range Achievement Test (WRAT) and the progress made by each student through the reading curriculum. The interesting differences occured between the direct instruction phonics group and the regular basal group (henceforth referred to as simply the "basal" group in this discussion).

By the fourth assessment period, the children in the direct code group scored slightly better than the basal group on all three measures of phonemic knowledge, and the direct code group was the only one wherein all the children reached the 75 percent criterion performance that the investigators set for the tasks (pp. 294, 293); three of the children in the basal group did not reach criterion. On the other hand, 42 percent of the basal group had reached criterion on the synthesis (blending) task by the second assessment point, while only 24 percent of the direct instruction group had reached criterion—despite the fact that the direct phonics group had been taught to blend sounds from isolated letters between the first and second assessments. The basal group also got off to a faster start with the phonemic awareness tasks, and their ultimate achievement was slightly higher, too. With data such as this, as well as the conclusions from other research, Perfetti, Beck, Bell and Hughes (1987) themselves conclude that "There is increasing reason to conclude that phonemic knowledge and learning to read develop in mutual support" (p. 317).

A major purpose of Ayres's (1993a) award-winning study was to combine literature-based, child-centered instruction with the concepts of phonemic awareness training that had emerged from quantitative research, so that teachers could teach phonemic awareness in the classroom without compromising their pedagogical or theoretical beliefs about learning. To this end, she investigated the efficacy of three training conditions upon the phonological awareness of kindergarten children, and the possible effects on reading achievement at the end of first grade. Most previous studies training children in phonological awareness had worked with the children in small groups; Ayres wanted to determine whether phonemic awareness could be successfully taught to entire classes of kindergartners and, if so, what might be particularly effective methods. The children were enrolled in half-day kindergarten programs designed to prepare and extend foundations of literacy. One hundred five (105) students completed the training study in the kindergarten year, while 92 remained in the study throughout the first grade. The children in all the experimental groups came from backgrounds not likely to be literacy-rich (p. 133). The children in the control group came from homes with a higher average income and other factors more likely to promote literacy at home (p. 159).

The children in the experimental groups received an experimental treatment for 20 minutes a day for ten weeks, in the fall of their kindergarten year. Each experimental group then received a different treatment in the winter. This enabled Ayres to investigate not merely which of the experimental treatments was most successful, but which combinations and in what order. Treatment group A received direct instruction in phonological awareness, using puppets, oral language stories, games, and songs. Treatment Group B was taught phonological awareness through an indirect, literature-based approach. Attention to rhyme and alliteration derived from texts and involved book-making and writing activities to emphasize the phonological characteristics. Treatment Group AB combined the direct approach of Treatment A with the indirect approach of Treatment B: essentially, the puppets interacted with literature to deliver lessons in phonological awareness. For all three groups, invented spelling was instructed mainly at a writing center. Treatment group X served as a comparison group. This group received an alternate treatment for 20 minutes a day: story mapping and retelling after shared reading, facilitated by a felt board and cutouts. Treatment group Y was the control group; they received no instruction in phonological awareness other than that in the regular district kindergarten program, where they were routinely exposed to a variety of literacy experiences, including interaction with letter names and letter sounds (1993a, pp. 41-42; p. 154).

During the first treatment period, all but one of the treatment groups showed growth in phonological awareness: Treatment A appears to have had the greatest effect on children's ability to segment; Treatment B indicated a significant effect on rhyming and on identifying beginning and ending phonemes; and Treatment X also showed a significant effect when compared with the control group. The second treatment period saw the effect of Treatment A remaining strong, while treatment B was significantly more effective than Treatment AB when tested on segmentation of sounds.

The design of the study allowed Ayres to examine the effect of treatment sequence as well as individual treatment effect. Specifically, since each group received two treatments, each in a different order, it was possible to ask: "Is phonological awareness training more effective when it is delivered during the first half of the kindergarten year, or are children more receptive to such instruction after they have been exposed to a more broad based literacy curriculum?" Results of this study clearly indicate that the type and sequence of training had a measurable effect on phonological awareness. Direct instruction produced the most significant effect during both training conditions; however, the effect was greatest when delivered during the second portion of the year, after the children had participated in a variety of experiences with literature. Overall, two treatment sequence groups were especially effective: B (indirect/literature based instruction) followed by AB (direct and indirect instruction); and X (story mapping and retelling) followed by A (direct instruction). Ayres concludes that "The most important implication from this study is that training in phonological awareness is both possible and advantageous for children" (Ayres, 1993a, p. 153). She observes that "The most effective means of instruction seems to begin with literature as a foundation for the direct instruction that will come later in the year" (1993a, p. 144), when it appears to be more effective. (Based upon these results, Ayres has developed a kindergarten phonological awareness training program, The Phonological Zoo© (1993b), which is divided into three phases of instruction: Phase One focuses on activities designed to build nursery rhyme knowledge and familiarity with folk tales; Phase Two deals with rhyming; and Phase Three addresses alliteration, segmentation, and sound/letter correspondence.)

Two other results from Ayres's study also prove especially interesting. To some researchers, what will seem particularly important is what Ayres concludes from certain multiple regression analyses following post-testing at the end of first grade, which suggest that children who have developed substantial phonological awareness may rely more upon letter/sound information than children who have not. The latter rely more on whole word visual cues than upon letter/sound information, and their reading achievement depends more upon cognitive ability than upon word attack strategy. Direct instruction appears to provide an important skill such that children can achieve reading success regardless of their cognitive ability (1993a, p. 149).

To other researchers, a somewhat different cluster of results may seem equally or more important. First, the children in the story mapping and retelling group showed a substantial gain in phonemic awareness during the first ten weeks, along with the children in groups that were specifically taught phonological awareness. Second, two of the phonological awareness treatment groups did not show any significant differences from the control group on measures of phonological awareness (Treatment A followed by X, and AB followed by B, as shown by Table 5 in chapter 8). Second, though the control group with no training in phonological awareness showed the least gains on phonemic awareness (1993a, p. 131, p. 138), nevertheless the reading achievement measures taken at the end of the first grade (California Achievement Test's subtests on word reading, word analysis, vocabulary, and comprehension) showed no significant differences between the control group and the treatment groups (1993a, p. 146). On the measure of reading comprehension, the best of the treatment combinations (Treatment X followed by A) did about the same as the control group; the others scored lower. Overall on the combined reading measures, the B, AB group scored highest, followed by the control group.

From the unexpected gains made by the control group, Ayres concludes that "students whose phonological awareness is less than completely developed are nevertheless capable of making progress in reading" (1993a, p. 150). This data leads to the conjecture that phonological awareness and reading are linked in a mutually facilitative relationship. That is, phonological awareness facilitates learning to read but learning to read also seems to facilitate phonological awareness.

Taking the various kinds of data together, this study indicates that there is "more of a reciprocal relationship between phonological awareness and reading" rather than a unidirectional relationship, in which phonological awareness would be considered a prerequisite to learning to read (p. 150). Furthermore, Ayres (1993a, p. 151) notes Ehri's (1979) caution that "if a skill is facilitative, as phonemic phonological awareness appears to be, the effect may last only temporarily." The controls will "catch up," as they did in Ayres's study. What we need, of course (as Ayres writes), are studies that would follow the children's reading progress and achievement for another few years—and studies that would measure a wider range of factors relevant to the development of reading, writing, and literacy.

Specific concerns about the research on phonemic awareness

1. Typically the measures of "reading achievement" used are just standardized tests (and in fact, "reading achievement" can be taken to mean scores on standardized tests). This means that the studies usually do not tell us how the reader is progressing in other aspects of reading and literacy development, such as the use of reading and spelling and writing strategies, or the ability to retell what has been read, or interest in reading and writing. It's possible that while advances are being made in some areas, such as phonemic awareness and word reading, the children might be less advanced in other characteristics important to becoming a reader—characteristics which they may or may not develop, in time.

2. The nature of standardized tests is problematic for reading assessment in other ways, too. Such tests often contain subtests dealing with word analysis (especially phonics) and isolated word identification; indeed, even the comprehension passages rely heavily upon word identification because the texts are short and don't include the redundancy that characterizes normal texts. Since the subtests are timed, any child who reads words slowly will score lower than faster readers (Ayers, 1993). So the tests assess the reading of words more than inferencing and other aspects of comprehension and assess decoding speed even more than reading skill.

3. In phonemic awareness training studies, the investigators often worked with the children in small groups (as noted in Ayres, 1993). Thus such studies cannot be taken as evidence that whole class instruction will have the same effects.

4. Tasks for assessing phonemic awareness often differ substantially from one another and may require considerably more than just awareness of phonemes or ability to isolate the phonemes in words. As Tunmer and Nesdale put it (1985, p. 417), "The degree to which phonological [phonemic] awareness is related to reading achievement may therefore depend on the type of task used to measure phonological awareness." Or to put it another way, the various studies are not necessarily equally valid as measures of phonemic awareness.

5. Training in phonemic awareness and phonics doesn't *necessarily* transfer to real reading. Therefore, the studies that don't investigate

the effects on actual reading are not as complete as we really need. Without examining how children read and how they deal with unfamiliar print words, we have little idea of whether or how they are using their phonemic awareness knowledge. (However, some researchers note that children who have developed phonemic awareness training seem to attend more to letters and sounds than children who haven't.)

6. Interpreters of such research sometimes overlook the forest for the trees. For example, it would be easy to emphasize the very slight but not statistically significant difference between the phonological awareness plus synthetic phonics group in Torgeson and Hecht's study (1996) and ignore the much more substantial and statistically significant difference between the control group and *all* the groups that received extensive individual tutoring, regardless of the nature of that tutoring. Of course, this is the fault not of the researchers but those interpreting it. The problem would not be mentioned here if it were not for the fact that this kind of distortion is running rampant these days.

7. There has not been much research, certainly not enough research, on the extent to which learning to read facilitates or causes phonemic awareness (as noted, for example, in Wagner and Torgesen, 1987), or the extent to which focusing on onsets and rimes in conjunction with reading facilitates phonemic awareness and/or the ability to read unknown print words (see chapters 5 and 6). Taken as a whole, these studies are still limited in what they reveal about the development of phonological knowledge in general and its multiple relationships to reading.

Comparative Research on the Effects and Effectiveness of Whole Language Teaching

There are basically three kinds of research supporting whole language learning and teaching: (1) research on language acquisition and emergent literacy, the reading process, and learning itself, which gave rise to whole language practices in the first place; (2) naturalistic research documenting the success of whole language with individual children and classes; and (3) experimental research comparing whole language with more traditional alternatives in the classroom. This section is concerned with the third kind, comparative experimental research. (For summaries of research studies, see Smith &

Elley, 1995; Krashen, 1993; Stephens, 1991; Shapiro, 1990; Heald-Taylor, 1989; Tunnell & Jacobs, 1989; Rhodes & Shanklin, 1989; and Weaver, 1988.)

A primary criterion for inclusion in this review was the requirement that the studies include both standardized test measures and a variety of other measures. All the located studies involved children in preschool, kindergarten, grade one, or grade two. Three studies involved two grade levels and one involved three grade levels; one study and another cluster of studies were longitudinal studies involving children deemed to be at risk of educational failure. These various studies are described in detail, followed by a list of some patterns that seem to emerge from these and other studies.

W. Elley, 1991

Elley, W. B. (1991). Acquiring literacy in a second language: The effect
of book-based programs. *Language Learning, 41*(3), 375–411.

Elley reviews nine studies of the acquisition of English as a second language, most of which were undertaken in the South Pacific and Southeast Asia, including his own earlier study (Elley & Manguhbai, 1983). Typically these studies compared the results of programs based on structured systematic instruction with "book flood" programs, which exposed children to large numbers of high-interest story books. In other words, the studies compared the effects of a direct instruction approach with an indirect approach that might be characterized as "whole language" or "natural" language learning. These studies all involved elementary school students.

What I've considered the direct instruction approach typically involved principles articulated by structural linguists (e.g., Bloomfield, 1942) and audiolingual methodology: practice on a carefully sequenced set of grammatical structures, through imitation, repetition, and reinforcement. The book flood studies reflected typical whole language principles, and usually involved either sustained silent reading of an extensive number of picture books; the Shared Book Experience (Holdaway, 1979), including reading, discussion, and related activities; or a combination of these, which in one instance also included a modified language experience approach.

From these combined studies, the following patterns emerged:

1. Students in the book flood programs did better on almost all standardized measures of reading, including not only comprehension skills but also word identification and phonics skills.

2. Usually favoring the book flood students were differences in measures of oral and written language and vocabulary (e.g., listening comprehension, written story completion), and sometimes differences in other aspects of school achievement as well (see also Elley, 1989).

3. More surprisingly, students in the book flood programs often did better on tests of the grammatical structures explicitly taught in the audiolingual program. Elley notes that this interpretation "was supported by an incidental study in which knowledge and use of English in natural settings was found to be largely unaffected by deliberate instruction in them" (1991, p. 389).

4. Students in Shared Book Experience programs typically showed greater gains on various tests than students in silent reading programs. (Perhaps this result suggests the value of oral reading and discussion, probably including the discussion of letter/sound relationships within the Shared Book Experience.)

5. Students in the book flood programs typically had a more positive attitude toward books and reading. (One wonders if these programs also affected children's attitudes toward English as a second language.)

Elley summarizes, in part, as follows:[11] That pupils showed equally large gains in the discrete-point tests of grammatical structures and vocabulary as they did in the more integrative measures of reading, listening, and writing is particularly damaging for those who argue that structures and vocabulary should be deliberately taught" (1991, p. 402). If more of the comparisons had included tests of decoding skills, perhaps the same conclusion could be drawn for the direct teaching of phonics.

In short, Elley's comparison of these several studies offers powerful evidence for whole language advocates' assertion that language and literacy are acquired gradually, through opportunities to use the language and to engage in literacy events in meaningful contexts.

W. C. Kasten and B. K. Clarke, 1989

Kasten, W. C., & Clarke, B. K. (1989). *Reading/writing readiness for preschool and kindergarten children: A whole language approach.* Sanibel: Florida Educational Research and Development Council. ED 312 041

This year-long study involved children in two preschools and two kindergarten classes in two southwest Florida communities, one school at each level serving as a control and one implementing certain strategies associated with a whole language philosophy of learning. The latter will be referred to here as whole language classrooms and students, even though only the literacy activities were necessarily whole language in orientation. The "business as usual" curriculum in the control classrooms seemed to proceed from common assumptions such as these (Kasten & Clarke, p. 73):

1. Children need to achieve a level of readiness for learning to read that includes extensive experience with letters of the alphabet and the sounds these letters represent. This occurs prior to learning to write.

2. Children are not ready or capable of writing connected text until a certain number of words can be spelled conventionally, and the prerequisite to writing is the ability to copy and formulate letters.

3. Authentic learning is limited to the learning or work produced by individuals who "do their own work," and learning is the result of what the teacher teaches.

Kasten and Clarke offer an extended anecdote that clarifies the nature of instruction stemming from such assumptions. The anecdote is from a private, well-funded, highly regarded preschool with an experienced, capable, highly regarded teacher:

> Ms. R. cheerfully welcomes her students and introduces us to them, reminding them of our names. Children gather in the carpeted area of the room around their teacher who is seated in a chair next to an easel. After some social conversation with the group, Ms. R. introduces the "special guest," who is a puppet named "Goofy Ghost." She announces they will talk about the letter G this day. The teacher elaborates that Goofy wears glasses and plays a guitar. She develops a story orally, preparing them to participate on a given signal with repeating phrases including "/g/ - /g/ - /g/ - /goo/," and "Goofy, good grief!" On the easel is paper with pockets which hold teacher prepared cards.
>
> As the story is completed, the teacher reviews "G" words with the children, and praises them at the end. She asks the children to give themselves a pat on the back, reviews the "G" words again, and they say "/g/ - /g/ - /g/ - /g/" a few more times. At the end, all children stand up to stretch, and are directed to pretend they are watering cans, and to make /g/ sound like water gushing from the watering cans with "/g/ - /g/ - /g/" noises.
>
> Next, the teacher initiates a guessing game with questions to "fill in the blank" orally, such as "Something Mommy puts on your mashed potatoes is . . .," and "You like to chew a stick of. . . ." (pp. 74–75).

The preschoolers are then asked to do some "writing": to copy the design Mrs. R. shows them on a flash card (circle, vertical line, etc.). She reminds them to "do their own work" and not look at anybody else's paper.

The instruction in the whole language preschool and kindergarten was significantly different, reflecting such assumptions as these (Kasten & Clarke, p. 72):

1. Children can write what they want to say before their knowledge of letter/sound relationships is perfect, and before they can spell conventionally.

2. Children can learn to read as they learn to speak, in a holistic, social context in which functions and purposes for reading are evident.

3. Children learn valuable lessons by collaborating with each other, and their learning can be enhanced by what they learn from each other.

In the following anecdote from a whole language preschool class, the paraprofessional teacher and all eight students are members of minority groups from very low socioeconomic neighborhoods. The anecdote illustrates the second and third of the above principles (Kasten & Clarke, pp. 67-68):

> The teacher presents a DLM book and, before she can ask the title, children call out "Three Dogs at the Door." Together the children count aloud the dogs on the cover, discuss the author, Roach Van Allen (1986), and discuss what an "illustrator" means. The children curl at the teacher's feet in an organized formation. The teacher uses a pointer as the class reads chorally. The teacher points out that the word "mad" looks different from the word "disgusted." The teacher asks individuals to act out how they might look if they felt "disgusted." All eight children say "disgusted," making appropriate facial expressions as they do.
>
> The children are extremely attentive, with all eyes on the book. They act out the next interesting word which is "upset," the same way they did with the word "disgusted." The teacher discusses with them how they can use these words when they have those feelings, labeling them for the children as "emotion words." They continue reading and come to the word "irritated." They discuss differences between "irritated," "mad," "upset," and "disgusted."
>
> Teacher and children continue discussing the emotion words. The teacher then flips back through the text to each emotion word and asks which, of the ones they discussed, this one is. Each time some children guess correctly, and seem to be using initial letters to assist in their guesses of "disgusted," "furious," etc.

Since the children are not yet tired of shared reading, they go on to read *I'm the King of the Mountain* (Cowley, 1984b) together, using song and with the children chiming in on the repeated pattern "I'm the king of the mountain: I'm the king of the mountain.[11] Finally, the children have the opportunity to choose books to read by themselves, in pairs, or to the teacher.

This anecdote nicely illustrates not only whole language principles of learning, but some of the procedures used in the whole language preschool and kindergarten classes. Shared reading experiences with predictable or patterned language books were to be used with the children at least twice a day, for a minimum of fifteen minutes each time. The teachers were asked to use a pointer to follow along with the text during the shared reading experiences. They were encouraged to extend the shared reading experiences through dramatization of the story, to use the text to teach concepts and skills, and to do "anything else their creativity might invent." The second aspect of the whole language program involved giving children an opportunity to write at least once a week: not to practice letter formation or to copy letters or someone else's text, but to compose—by writing using their own spellings or giving oral dictation to an adult (Kasten & Clarke, p. 34). While these were the minimum criteria defining the whole language category, more time reading and writing—perhaps considerably more time—may have been spent in these classrooms.

The children were tested using several instruments: a Book Handling Test developed by Y. M. Goodman and B. Altwerger (included in Y. M. Goodman, Altwerger, & Marek, 1989) and a story Retelling Inventory based on the retelling portion of the Reading Miscue Inventory (Y. M. Goodman, Watson, & Burke, 1987), both used with all of the students; the six subtests of the Metropolitan Early School Inventory—Preliteracy (ESI), used as a posttest with preschoolers and both pretest and posttest with the kindergartners; and the Metropolitan Readiness Test (MRT), the latter used as a pretest and posttest only for the kindergartners. As Kasten and Clarke point out, the MRT attempts to assess traditional "readiness" skills, including letter knowledge, initial sounds, ending sounds, the sounds of consonant clusters, and so forth (1989, p.30).

For the preschoolers, many of the differences between groups were not statistically significant. On the tests and subtests that were statistically significant, all the results favored the experimental, whole language classroom. The whole language children showed significantly more development than their comparison peers in the ESI subtest How You Read, on the story Retelling Inventory, and on the Book Handling Test.

For the kindergartners, all the differences except those on two sub-tests of the ESI (What You Read, and Name Writing) were statistically significant, favoring the children in the whole language classroom. Differences were particularly noticeable on subtest E of the ESI, Message Writing. When requested to produce some written message, the control students tended to inform the researchers that they couldn't write, while all of the experimental subjects produced some written message when asked to do so (Kasten & Clarke, p. 64). The whole language kindergartners performed significantly better than their counterparts on all subtests of the Metropolitan Readiness Test, including tests of beginning consonant sounds, letter/sound correspondences, and sounds and clusters of sounds in initial and final positions of words. They could also locate patterns in words or parts of words, and visually match items. In addition, they had a better command of the terminology associated with reading (letter, word, etc.).

However, these test results do not reveal the most significant differences between the control classes and the whole language classes. The investigators' field notes demonstrated that children in the whole language classes were clearly "falling in love with books": "The children frequently chose books over toys during free choice play times, even sometimes asking permission to take the books outside. These groups could be observed 'playing' at shared reading experiences, one student acting as the teacher, with a pointer in hand, and those playing 'student' reading in unison or taking turns reading. On other occasions, one child might sit alone, even with a less familiar book, and pretend to read by formulating a logical story to accompany the illustrations" (Kasten & Clarke, p. 70).

Clearly, these children perceived themselves as readers. They also came to perceive themselves as writers and began to write when asked to do so by the investigators, even if their writings were scribbled or unrecognizable. These behaviors and perceptions differed markedly from those of the control groups. While the whole language children demonstrated superiority in their development of literacy skills, as measured by various tests, their superior development in taking on the behaviors and attitudes of literate individuals was even more evident.

H. Ribowsky, 1985

Ribowsky, H. (1985). *The effects of a code emphasis approach and a whole language approach upon emergent literacy of kindergarten children.* Alexandria, VA: Educational Document Reproduction Service, ED 269 720. (Report developed more fully in Ribowsky's unpublished doctoral dissertation [same title], New York University, New York, 1986).

Though more limited in scope, Ribowsky's study focuses on measures of phonics knowledge.

The year-long study compared the effects of two approaches upon the emergent literacy of fifty-three girls in two kindergarten classes within an all girls' parochial school in the Northeast. The code emphasis classroom used a highly structured, teacher-directed program (Lippincott's *Beginning to Read, Write, and Listen* program). Consisting of twenty-four letter books, each with a teacher's guide, the program focuses mainly on hearing and analyzing phonemes and learning letter/sound correspondences. The whole language classroom used Holdaway's Shared Book Experience (Holdaway, 1979, pp. 72-73).

In order to be fair to both approaches, Ribowsky employed different kinds of measures to assess the children's literacy development: Y. M. Goodman and Alterwerger's assessment of book handling knowledge (included in Y. M. Goodman, Altwerger, & Marek, 1989), the five principal subtests of the Test of Language Development— Primary; and the letter recognition and phoneme/grapheme subtests of the Metropolitan Achievement Test. The tests of letter recognition and phoneme/grapheme correspondence (consonants only) were administered only as posttests, since they were considered too difficult for beginning kindergartners.

Children in the whole language classrooms scored significantly better on all measures of growth and achievement, including the tests of letter recognition and letter/sound knowledge.

L. K. Clarke, 1988

Clarke, L. K. (1988). Invented versus traditional spelling in first graders' writings: Effects on learning to spell and read. *Research in the Teaching of English, 22,* 281–309.

This study compared the spelling development and certain aspects of the reading achievement of first-grade children in classrooms with contrasting approaches to spelling. The teachers in all the classrooms held writing sessions that totaled eighty to a hundred minutes a week, but two of the teachers encouraged traditional ("correct") spellings only, while the other two teachers encouraged children to construct or "invent" spellings of words they did not know. Each teacher used a basal reading program, taught letter sounds (generally in isolation), and taught the identification of initial letters and sounds as an important aid to reading words. Various oral drills and worksheets were used to reinforce the phonics skills.

In October, the students engaged in various pretests. Among other things, they were asked to print as many words as they could, and to read a list of high-frequency words from the Boder Word Recognition Inventory (Boder, 1973). Various aspects of children's writing behaviors were also recorded, including their strategies for spelling. Their written productions were also analyzed.

Differences between the traditional and the inventive spellers included the following:

1. Using invented spelling, more children were able to write independently in the early months, and their productions were significantly longer overall and contained a significantly greater variety of words and a significantly smaller percentage of correct spellings than the children encouraged to use only traditional spelling. (The investigator does not indicate which group could actually spell more words correctly.)

2. On the posttests, children using invented spelling scored significantly higher in two of the three spelling tasks than children using traditional spelling. These tests were the spelling subtest of the Wide Range Achievement Test, Level 1, and a list of low-frequency regularly spelled words (from Baron & Treiman, 1980).

3. Children using invented spelling also had significantly greater scores on three different word recognition tests: the untimed word analysis subtest of the Durrell Word Recognition test; the reading of a word list adapted from Baron and Treiman (1980); and the word attack subtest (on nonsense words) of the Woodcock Reading Mastery tests. Flash word recognition and reading comprehension showed only slight differences between the groups, though those slight differences also favored the inventive spellers.

4. Initially low-achieving children accounted for most of the gain in spelling and reading that resulted from using invented spelling.

The researcher summarizes as follows:

> The superior spelling and phonic analysis skill of children using invented spelling suggested that they benefited from the practice of matching sound segments of words to letters as they wrote and from using their own sound sequence analysis. These differences were major considering that both groups were using basal readers which promote a reliance on processing words by their visual cues rather than by phonic analysis. . . .
>
> Also, encouraging children to use invented spelling may induce them to shift from processing words visually toward using phonetic cue processing earlier than would otherwise occur when using a basal reading program. (Clarke, 1988, p. 307)

Of course, as the investigator notes, some of the most significant benefits of encouraging invented spelling lie in promoting independence, confidence, and more writing. And the children who benefit the most may be those initially found to be low-achieving, by traditional and standardized measures.

P. A. Freppon, 1988

Freppon, P. A. (1988). An investigation of children's concepts of the purpose and nature of reading in different instructional settings. Unpublished doctoral dissertation, University of Cincinnati, Ohio. This study is reported in a 1991 article by Freppon: Children's concepts of the nature and purpose of reading in different instructional settings, *Journal of Reading Behavior, 23*(2), 139–163.

Freppon compared the literacy development of students in two "skills-based" first-grade classrooms with those in two "literature-based" classrooms. She contrasts what the skills-based teachers typically did with what the literature-based teachers did:

> The skill-based teachers: (a) established ability grouping and round-robin oral reading with an emphasis on reading correctly; (b) emphasized drill and practice on discrete skills such as short vowels, blends, and vocabulary words; (c) used a reading basal series exclusively for instruction; (d) required daily completion of skill (word and phonics)-oriented worksheets and workbooks; and (e) followed a traditional, systematic and sequenced curriculum in teaching phonics and vocabulary.
>
> The literature-based teachers: (a) used book demonstrations and modeled reading strategies such as making connections between their own lives and the events in the text when reading to and with children; (b) promoted children's approximations to conventional reading and did not emphasize *word perfect* reading; (c) structured cooperative reading events such as choral and partner reading; (d) emphasized reading for meaning (requiring children to think about what was going on in the story, discussing sense making, directly commenting on making connections with prior knowledge during reading interactions); and (e) taught children to use specific reading strategies including meaning, predicting, skipping words, rereading *(and getting ready to say* the *word)*, guessing, and using graphophonic information. (1991, pp. 143–144)

The following are some of Freppon's conclusions, with contributing evidence:

1. Students in the literature-based group seemed to have a better sense of what sounds like language. Evidence? Of the literature-based group, 97 percent rejected words in scrambled sentence

order as not being languagelike, while only 42 percent of the skills-based group rejected such sentences.

2. Students in the literature-based group seemed to have a stronger sense that reading involves constructing meaning, not merely getting the words right. Evidence? Of the students in the literature-based group, 92 percent said that understanding the story or both understanding and getting the words right are important in reading, while only 50 percent of the skills-based group mentioned meaning or emphasized both as important.

3. Students in the literature-based group reported using more strategies in reading, and were more often observed to do so; also, they more often discussed using meaning to self-monitor.

4. Though children in both groups said they were good readers, those in the literature-based group said they were good readers because they read a lot of books, while children in the skills group said they were good readers because they knew a lot of words.

5. Students in the literature-based group were more successful in using grapho/phonemic cues in conjunction with prior knowledge and other language cues in order to construct meaning. Though the skills group attempted to sound out words more than twice as often, the literature group was more successful in doing so: a 53 percent success rate compared with a 32 percent success rate for the skills group. Also, the literature group more often showed a balanced use of language cueing systems in their substitutions of one word for another.

In short, students in the literature-based group seemed to be making greater progress toward becoming literate.

K. L. Dahl and P. A. Freppon, 1992

Dahl, K. L., & Freppon, P. A. (1992). *Learning to read and write in inner-city schools: A comparison of children's sense-making in skills-based and whole language classrooms.* Final Report to the Office of Educational Research and Improvement. U.S. Department of Education, Grant Award No. R117E00134.

Part of the data described here is reported in two more accessible articles, in addition to the references cited in the discussion below:

Freppon, P. A. (1991). Children's concepts of the nature and purpose of reading in different instructional settings. *Journal of Reading Behavior, 23*(2), 139–163.

Dahl, K. L., & Freppon, P. A. 1991. Literacy learning in whole-language classrooms: An analysis of low socioeconomic urban children learning to read and write in kindergarten. In J. Zutell & S. McCormick (Eds.), *Learner Factors / Teacher Factors: Issues in Literacy Research and Instruction*, pp. 149–158. Chicago, IL: National Reading Conference.

Two studies were involved in this comparison: an investigation of children's sense-making in skills-based classrooms (Dahl, Purcell-Gates, & McIntyre, 1989) and a similar study in whole language classrooms (Dahl & Freppon, 1991). Both studies were ethnographic, spanning a two-year period from kindergarten through first grade, and both studies documented children's evolving hypotheses about reading and writing. The school populations "were representative of the racial and cultural mix typical of the urban low-income populations in the midwest—African American and white Appalachian" (Dahl & Freppon, 1992). The learners at each site were randomly selected from among those who qualified for the federally funded lunch program. Seven learners remained through the two-year skills-based study; twelve completed the whole language study. The "focal learners" were racially balanced in each study (four African American and three Appalachian white in the skills-based study; six of each ethnic background in the whole language study).

At the beginning of kindergarten and at the end of first grade, all learners in both studies completed six kinds of tasks assessing various aspects of written language knowledge: (1) an "Intentionality" task designed to determine to what extent the children understood that written language is a symbol system conveying meaning; (2) Marie Clay's (1979) Concepts About Print test; (3) three tasks designed to determine children's knowledge of the alphabetic principle and their knowledge of letter/sound relations; (4) two tasks designed to determine children's understanding of how written narratives are structured; (5) a task requiring children to pretend to read a wordless storybook to a doll, in order to determine the children's "Written Narrative Register" (Purcell-Gates, 1988); and, (6) a writing task designed to elicit children's concepts of writing. The researchers describe most of these tasks in detail.

Upon entering kindergarten, the children in both studies had a very limited understanding of written language. The children in the whole language kindergartens scored slightly lower on every pretest measure except one. Two years later, children in the skills-based classrooms showed statistically significant gains on all measures except one (the Written Narrative Register); those in the whole language classrooms showed statistically significant gains on all six measures. With five of the six assessment measures (all except Story Structure), the whole language children had lower pretest scores than the skills-based children. However, the whole language children scored higher on all six of the posttest measures (Dahl & Freppon, 1992, p. 24). Two of these six differences were statistically significant: the tests of written register and concepts of writing.

Interestingly, the skills-based group was knowledgeable about intentionality (writing as conveying meaning), though this was not explicitly emphasized during instruction. Similarly, the whole language group had comparable (in fact, slightly higher) scores on the tests of alphabetic principle and letter/sound relations, though these are taught less directly and less extensively in whole language classrooms. Furthermore, a much greater proportion of the whole language learners consistently applied their knowledge of letter/sound relations effectively by the end of first grade (Dahl & Freppon, 1992, p. 36).

The more interesting and significant differences between children in the two kinds of classrooms were qualitative, not quantitative. For example:

1. In the whole language classrooms, children's ongoing talk as they participated in reading and writing demonstrated that they perceived themselves as readers and writers, even if they were relatively less proficient readers and writers than their classmates. Regardless of their proficiency or degree of success, all the whole language children tended to persist in reading and writing activities. In the skills-based classrooms, these patterns were restricted to just the most proficient readers and writers.

2. Children in the whole language classrooms participated actively in the reading and discussion of literature, related new books to previously read texts, and developed a critical stance toward trade books. The curriculum in the skills-based classrooms did not encourage these behaviors in students.

3. In skills-based classrooms, passivity appeared to be the most frequent coping strategy for learners having difficulty. In whole language classrooms, those having difficulty tended to draw upon other learners for support: by saving the phrases and sentences that others could read, by copying what they wrote, and so forth. The less proficient literacy learners in whole language classrooms still attempted to remain engaged in literacy activities with their peers.

4. In reading, whole language students at each level of proficiency demonstrated a greater variety of reading strategies and more active engagement in reading.

5. By the end of first grade, a considerably larger proportion of the whole language children were writing sentences and stories.

In summary, the children in the whole language classrooms demonstrated slightly greater gains on quantitative measures of literacy skills, including knowledge of the alphabetic principle and of letter/sound relations. The greatest differences, however, occurred in the range and depth of attitudes and behaviors characteristic of literate individuals. The authors conclude that "a number of instructional elements and practices were productive for low-SES inner-city children. These included extensive experience with children's literature, writing opportunities with self-selected topics, social contexts where learners could work together, and one-on-one teacher conferences" (Dahl & Freppon, 1992, p. 71). Only the last of these was found in the skills-based classrooms.

P. A. Freppon, 1993

Freppon, P. A. (1993). Making sense of reading and writing in urban classrooms: Understanding at-risk children's knowledge construction in different curricula. Final Report to the Office of Educational Research and Improvement, U.S. Department of Education, Grant Award No. R117E102361-91.

This study built upon the previously described study of Dahl and Freppon (1992). The same children participated in this follow-up study, now as second graders. One question the investigator wanted to address is the frequently asked question, "Do children with experience in a whole language curriculum, particularly in the early grades, have the skills necessary for success in a traditional, skills-based curriculum?" Another research question was the extent to which students maintained the literacy abilities, behaviors, and attitudes they had developed through kindergarten and first grade.

One group of eight children from the original whole language group in Dahl and Freppon (1992) made a transition to a skills-based second grade (the Transition Group), while the other group of nine continued in a whole language classroom in second grade (the Continuing Group). All participating children were given pretests and posttests. Eight focal children, four in each group, were closely followed. Data gathering included written artifacts, reading samples, field notes, and audio and video tapes.

At the end of second grade, there was little difference between groups on the standardized tests, and little difference in their gain from pretest to posttest. Findings from the reading and writing interviews revealed several areas of decline in the Transition Group while the Continuing Group generally remained stable or gained in some areas. For example: the Transition Group, now in a skills-based second grade, showed 37 percent less identification of items to be read beyond school, while the Continuing Group, still in a whole language classroom, showed 33 percent more identification of items to read beyond school. The Transition Group showed a 30 percent decrease in responses reflecting megacognitive or strategic knowledge, while the Continuing Group showed a 30 percent increase. The Transition Group showed a 32 percent increase in statements that writing was difficult, a 38 percent increase in preference for writing with others, and stability in citing the story and surface features as important in writing. The Continuing Group showed no increase in statements that writing was difficult, stability in preference for writing with others, and a 30 percent or greater increase in citing the story and surface features as important in writing (pp. 24–25).

The focal children in the Transition Group concentrated primarily on "getting through" assignments. Persistence in self-selected reading and writing declined in the Transition Group, among all but the most academically proficient child within that focal group. In contrast, the focal children in the Continuing Group maintained talk and action demonstrating a sense of themselves as readers and writers and persisted in self-selected reading and writing during second grade, regardless of their academic proficiency.

The investigator concluded that the children in the Transition Group had the literacy skills necessary for success in the skills-based second grade classroom, but that some of the children showed a loss of motivation for literacy experiences that was not experienced bv the students who continued in a whole language classroom (p. 85).

C. F. Stice and N. P. Bertrand, 1990

Stice. C. F., & Bertrand, N. P. (1990). *Whole language and the emergent literacy of at-risk children: A two-year comparative study*. Nashville: Center of Excellence: Basic Skills, Tennessee State University, ED 324 636.

Stice and Bertrand begin by observing, "Too often poor and minority children are not becoming sufficiently literate to allow the achievement of social and economic parity" (p. 3). They cited Neisser (1986) as demonstrating that neither the traditional approaches to literacy instruction (phonics/skills or traditional basal) nor the decoding, subskills approaches (or behavioral/mastery learning) have proved successful in the case of poor, minority children. Their study focused on the effects of a whole language approach to the literacy development of at-risk first- and second-graders, in comparison with a traditional skills approach.

The study involved fifty children, averaging five each in five whole language classrooms, grades 1 and 2, and their counterparts from traditional skills classrooms. The study included both rural and inner-city children who were deemed to be "at risk," according to typical factors.

Several quantitative and qualitative measures were used to compare the two groups, including scores on the reading portion of the Stanford Achievement Test (Primary I and II), responses to a Concepts About Print survey, analysis of an oral reading and retelling, writing samples, and individual interviews.

On the Stanford Achievement Test, the whole language children showed slightly greater gains than the traditionally taught children, but the gains were too slight to be statistically significant. While the children in the whole language groups scored lower on the Concepts About Print test to begin with, they scored significantly higher on the posttest. The children in whole language classrooms did as well on traditional spelling as their counterparts, while also using more invented spellings. Whole language children offered significantly longer, more complete versions of the stories they retold, suggesting that their comprehension might have been better. They also corrected more of their miscues.

Data from the reading and writing interviews revealed several interesting trends, similar to those in the Freppon study and the Dahl and Freppon study previously cited:

1. The children in the whole language classrooms were more aware of alternative strategies for dealing with problems, such as problems with particular words. For example, when asked, "When you are reading and you come to something you don't know, what do you do?" the whole language children suggested six strategies, while the children in traditional classrooms suggested only three.

2. The whole language children appeared to feel better about themselves as readers and writers. When asked, "Who do you know who is a good reader?" 82 percent of the kindergartners in the whole language classrooms said "Me," but only 5 percent of the kindergartners in the traditional classrooms mentioned themselves. During the first-grade year, when the children were asked directly, "Are you a good reader?" 70 percent of the whole

language children said yes, but only 33 percent of the traditional children said yes.

3. The whole language children appeared to focus more on meaning and the communicative nature of language. For example, when asked, "What makes a good reader?" they reported that good readers read a great deal and that they can read any book in the room. The children in the traditional classrooms tended to focus on words and surface correctness; they reported that good readers read big words, they know all the words, and they don't miss any words.

4. The children in the whole language classrooms seemed to be developing greater independence in both reading and writing. The children in traditional classrooms seemed to be more dependent on the teacher when their initial strategy failed.

Again, the standardized test scores of the children in the whole language classrooms were slightly (though not significantly) better than the scores of children in the traditional classrooms. The other measures discussed suggest, however, that they are far ahead of their counterparts in developing the understanding, strategies, and attitudes of readers, writers, and thinkers.

Whole language versus traditional classrooms: Tentative conclusions from the research

In contrast to the whole language and literature-based classrooms in these studies, the other classrooms have been characterized as traditional and skills-based, teaching skills in isolation. In two of these studies, the skills-based classrooms were characterized particularly by programs teaching phonics in isolation from literature and authentic writing; these were Ribowsky (1985) and Kasten & Clarke (1989). All of these studies used a variety of measures in addition to standardized tests. The following patterns seem to emerge from these studies and others referenced below:

- Children in whole language classrooms typically do as well or better on standardized reading tests and subtests (though the differences are seldom statistically significant).

For example, the whole language kindergartners in Ribowsky's study (1985) scored better on all measures of growth and achievement, including the tests of letter recognition and letter/sound knowledge. In the Kasten and Clarke study (1989), the whole language kindergartners performed significantly better than their counterparts on all subtests of the

Metropolitan Readiness Test, including tests of beginning consonant sounds, letter/sound correspondences, and sounds and clusters of sounds in initial and final positions of words. In the Manning, Manning, and Long study (1989), children in the whole language classroom did better on the Stanford Achievement Test's subtest on word parts, even though only the children in the skills classroom had explicitly studied word parts.

- Children in whole language classrooms seem to develop greater ability to use phonics knowledge effectively than children in more traditional classrooms where skills are practiced in isolation.

For example, in Freppon's study (1988, 1991), the skills group attempted to sound out words more than twice as often as the others, but the literature-based group was more successful in doing so: a 53 percent success rate compared with a 32 percent success rate for the skills group. Apparently the literature-based children were more successful because they made better use of phonics in conjunction with other information and cues. (For another relevant study, see also Cunningham, 1990).

- Children in whole language classrooms seem to develop vocabulary, spelling, grammar, and punctuation skills as well as or better than children in more traditional classrooms.

For example, see Elley's 1991 summary of studies on learning English as a second language; also Clarke, 1988, on spelling; and Stice & Bertrand, 1990, which included spelling. In addition, see Calkins, 1980; Gunderson & Shapiro, 1988; and Smith & Elley, 1995. Di Stefano & Killion (1984) is also relevant.

- Children in whole language classrooms seem more inclined and able to read for meaning rather than just to identify words.

For example, when asked "What makes a good reader?", the children in Stice and Bertrand's study (1990) reported that good readers read a great deal and that they can read any book in the room. The children in the traditional classrooms tended to focus on words and surface correctness; they reported that good readers read big words, they know all the words, and they don't miss any words. In a study by Manning, Manning, and Long (1989; not discussed in detail here), children in the whole language classroom were more likely to read for meaning, read with greater comprehension, and read with greater accuracy (not counting the errors that resulted in no meaning loss).

- Children in whole language classrooms seem to develop more strategies for dealing with problems in reading.

For example, the children in the whole language classrooms in Stice and Bertrand's study (1990) typically described six strategies for dealing with problem words, while the children in traditional classrooms described only three.

- Children in whole language classrooms seem to develop greater facility in writing.

For example, in the Dahl and Freppon study (1992), a considerably larger proportion of the children in the whole language classrooms were writing sentences and stories by the end of first grade. The children in the whole language classrooms in the Kasten and Clarke study (1989) were similarly much more advanced as writers by the end of their kindergarten year.

- Children in whole language classrooms seem to develop a stronger sense of themselves as readers and writers.

Take, for example, the Stice and Bertrand study (1990). When asked "Who do you know who is a good reader?", 82 percent of the kindergartners in the whole language classrooms mentioned themselves, but only 5 percent of the kindergartners in the traditional classrooms said "Me." During the first-grade year, when the children were asked directly "Are you a good reader?", 70 percent of the whole language children said yes, but only 33 percent of the traditional-classroom children said yes.

- Children in whole language classrooms also seem to develop greater independence as readers and writers.

In the Dahl and Freppon study (1992), for instance, passivity seemed to be the most frequent coping strategy for learners having difficulty in the skills-based classrooms. But in whole language classrooms, those having difficulty tended to draw upon other learners for support: by saying the phrases and sentences that others could read, by copying what they wrote, and so forth. That is, these less proficient literacy learners still attempted to remain engaged in literacy activities with their peers. They didn't just give up.

These research results corroborate conclusions from more naturalistic research; they do not stand alone in support of whole language. Furthermore, other comparative studies have generated similar results (see the summaries in Stephens, 1991; Shapiro, 1990; Tunnel & Jacobs, 1989).

From these various studies, it appears that children in whole language classrooms develop reading skills at least as well as children in skills-oriented classrooms, and that they get off to a significantly better start at developing the attitudes, values, and behaviors of literate individuals—to becoming not only competent but eager readers and writers.

Specific concerns about the research on whole language classrooms

Some of the following concerns deal not so much with the research itself, but with the difficulty of comparing it with other research.

1. A major concern with the research comparing whole language with skills-oriented classrooms is that there is still only a small body of research that uses a variety of measures, including standardized tests.

2. Furthermore, the studies have often involved only a small number of classrooms and sometimes only a small number of students chosen as representative from those classrooms. This has enabled researchers to uncover and document individual differences, but generalization must be more tentative than in studies involving large numbers of students.

3. Comparing this set of studies with the phonemic awareness studies is difficult, because only a couple compared whole language classrooms with classrooms where phonics was the particular focus of skills work, and phonemic awareness was not the main focus in either of these two studies. Furthermore, these "whole language" studies have not included as much detail as one might expect regarding what aspects of phonemic awareness and phonics were taught in the contrasting classrooms, or how they were taught.

4. Though a couple of the studies have extended over three years (in one form or another), studies extending from kindergarten through grade three might be even better for demonstrating the efficacy of one kind of approach over another.

5. This body of research also does not demonstrate the extent to which learning to read facilitates or causes phonemic awareness, nor the extent to which focusing on onsets and rimes in conjunction with reading facilitates phonemic awareness and/or the ability to read unknown print words (see Moustafa, chapter 5). So too, these studies are limited in what they reveal about the development of phonological knowledge in general and its multiple relationships to reading.

Generalizations That Can Reasonably Be Drawn from "The Research," Broadly Considered

Because of the limitations of experimental research, and especially the difficulty involved in trying not to affect the results, educators are well advised to combine various kinds of research in deciding upon educational practices. Such research on literacy must include experimental research, of course, but also observational research into the nature of learning, the nature of the reading and writing processes themselves, the ways in which literacy is acquired without direct instruction, and so forth. (See, for example, the range of research reviewed in Stephens, 1991.)

Combining research on the reading process (the introductory article and various others in this volume), the development of phonemic awareness and word reading skills, and classroom research on the development of literacy, we can reasonably draw several generalizations:

1. Proficient and experienced readers typically read many words automatically and easily, which can facilitate the processing of text for meaning. They do not need to use context to help them identify very many words, as younger and less proficient readers do.

2. Nevertheless, proficient readers also use context and their prior knowledge and experience to think ahead, as they read; to enable them to identify words by just sampling visual cues, and thereby to read faster; to monitor comprehension; and to notice when there is a need for correction. In the latter instance, they typically try various "fix-it" strategies as needed to maintain the grammar and meaning of sentences and texts.

3. Learning to read involves, at a minimum, developing strategies for making sense of text as well as developing letter/sound knowledge, and using both together, effectively and efficiently.

4. Children as well as adults tend to read unfamiliar print words in pronounceable chunks, not mainly letter-by-letter. They read unfamiliar print words by analogy with the pronounceable parts of familiar print words.

5. Knowledge of whole words, phonemic awareness, and letter/sound correspondences all seem to facilitate each other. They are also all good predictors of decoding skills.

6. Decoding skills alone are often not adequate to get the pronunciation of unfamiliar print words. Decoding skills give only approximate pronunciations for many unknown print words. Readers

must often use their prior knowledge of words (their listening vocabulary) to get the actual word, and context may be helpful too. Also, readers need to check the context to see if the word pronounced makes sense in that context.

7. Most of the time, context alone is even less adequate for getting the exact word, or sometimes even the general meaning. The most proficient readers use everything they know to get words and meaning from texts—not just prior knowledge and context, and not just letter/sound knowledge, but everything together.

8. Phonemic awareness and learning to read facilitate one another. That is, being able to segment words into phonemes helps in learning to read and write, while reading and rereading familiar texts and writing with invented spellings reinforce and promote the development of phonemic awareness. On the one hand, this suggests that we should not teach phonics first or only, or even phonics in isolation; it should be taught in conjunction with and through reading and writing. On the other hand, this also suggests that we should not neglect phonics and phonemic awareness, either.

9. Phonemic awareness is clearly related to decoding skill in particular, but research is divided as to the direction of that influence. Some research suggests that phonemic awareness is prerequisite to decoding, while other research suggests that decoding words in chunks is a precursor to phonemic awareness. Surely each facilitates the other.

10. Children in programs that emphasize phonemic awareness *may* get off to a better start at decoding (using phonics knowledge) than children with more of an initial emphasis on comprehension. Again, however, the evidence is mixed: some studies suggest that children in classrooms that emphasize reading and writing, with phonics taught in context, get off to just as good a start with phonics as children in phonics intensive classrooms. In classrooms where phonics is not taught at all, children often do as well on reading comprehension as those in phonics-intensive classrooms.

11. Children in programs that emphasize reading and writing whole, interesting, authentic texts typically get off to a better start at solving problems with reading and writing, and at becoming confident and independent readers and writers.

12. Reading difficulties are not traceable to just one source. For example, they may be traceable to difficulty with phonological/orthographic processing (using "phonics" knowledge), to trying to read

words with little regard for making sense of the text, to difficulty in drawing inferences, and so forth. Difficulty with phonological processing is said to be the most common cause of reading difficulty and "dyslexia" (Stanovich, 1988; Lyon, 1995; Boder, 1973, etc.), but that is not necessarily true if we define reading in terms of comprehension rather than identifying words.

Moving in New Educational Directions

We currently hear a call for more phonics and the teaching of phonemic awareness. Indeed, the hue and cry in the marketplace sometimes calls for phonics-first or phonics-only in teaching children to read. It's rare that teachers themselves call for that, but some with a sophisticated understanding of reading and learning to read do join in raising concerns such as the following:

1. All too many young children seem to have no strategy for dealing with unknown print words except to look at the picture or skip it.
2. Older readers, too, seem unaware of the strategy of sounding words out in chunks (then testing to see if the word makes sense in context). Or if they're aware of the strategy, they are not very competent in using it.
3. Children who struggle to read words often choose not to read. Poor word identification skills contribute to less reading, which in turn helps maintain a low level of word identification skill— the "Matthew effect" as described by Stanovich (1986).

These concerns are shared even by many individuals who realize that reading is not an exact process, that readers inevitably miscue, and that it is not necessary to get all the words right in order to construct meaning. Whether or not children in the past had better command of these skills is open to debate, but in any case some children may benefit from more attention to phonemic awareness and phonics than they have been receiving—and more attention to the meanings of words, too.

We must not forget, though, that when some educators began teaching less phonics, there were several problems they were trying to avoid or alleviate:

1. Many children were having difficulty doing phonics activities.
2. Much of what was taught as phonics seemed unrelated to actually using phonics knowledge in reading.
3. Most children did little reading in school because so much time was spent on reading skills—including phonics.

4. Many children who had received significantly more phonics instruction than their peers still could not make good use of phonics knowledge in their reading.

5. Many children could read and comprehend fairly well, but were assessed as poor readers—because they could not do phonics activities well, because they did not read fluently and quickly, or both.

6. All too many children seemed to have no strategy for dealing with unknown print words except to sound them out or ask someone (Applebee, Langer, & Mullis, 1988).

7. Many children were using the *strategies* of good readers, but were judged to be poor readers for reasons such as those above.

8. Because of the emphasis placed on reading all the words correctly, many children who were not good at word identification seldom chose to read.

9. Again, because of the emphasis on word identification, many children who were not good at word identification saw themselves as poor readers, despite good ability to comprehend. This, too, contributed to their seldom choosing to read.

10. Children who were judged to be relatively poor readers were typically given more and more skills work—and fewer opportunities to read more than a paragraph or so. This is especially unfortunate, since there is so much evidence that it's not reading activities that make better readers, but reading itself (Anderson, Hiebert, Scott, & Wilkinson, 1985; in this volume, see chapters 13, 14, 17, and 18).

11. To put it even more bluntly, the ability to do phonics and to identify words easily was used as a gatekeeper, on the assumption that "of course" children couldn't read whole books until they had developed better word-reading skills. This, in turn, served to to perpetuate their status as poorer readers.

In the current thrust for teaching more phonics and phonemic awareness, or teaching it more intensively and systematically, we must avoid these errors of the past—and present. We must especially avoid making phonics a gatekeeper, a prerequisite to being allowed to read real books and participate in the world of literacy. Perhaps our greatest challenge as literacy educators is to give children the specific instructional help they need and can benefit from, without keeping them from reading and writing whole, interesting texts because of their lack of phonics or word identification skills.

Works Cited

Adams, M. J., & Bruck, M. (1995). Resolving the "Great debate." *American Educator, 19, 7,* 10–20.

Anderson, R. C., Hiebert, E. H., Scott, J. A., & Wilkinson, I. A. G. (1985). *Becoming a nation of readers: The report of the commission on reading.* Champaign, IL: Center for the Study of Reading, University of Illinois.

Applebee, A. N., Langer, J. A., & Mullis, I. V. S. (1988). *Who reads best? Factors related to reading achievement in grades 3, 7, and 11.* Princeton, NJ: National Assessment of Educational Progress, Educational Testing Service.

Ayres, L. R. (1993a). *The efficacy of three training conditions on phonological awareness of kindergarten children and the longitudinal effect of each on later reading acquisition.* Unpublished dissertation, Oakland University, Rochester, Michigan.

Ayers, L. R. (1993b). *The phonological zoo: A language awareness training program for young children.* Walled Lake, MI: Walled Lake Elementary School.

Ball, E. & Blachman, B. (1991). Does phoneme awareness training in kindergarten make a difference in early word recognition and developmental spelling? *Reading Research Quarterly, 26,* 49–66.

Baron, J. & Treiman, R. (1980). Use of orthography in reading and learning to read. In J. Kavanaugh & R. Venezky (Eds.), *Orthography, reading and dyslexia.* Baltimore: University Park Press.

Bloomfield, L. (1942). Linguistics and reading. *The Elementary English Review, 19,* 125–30, 183–86.

Boder, E. (1973). Developmental dyslexia: A diagnostic approach based on three atypical reading-spelling patterns. *Developmental Medicine and Child Neurology, 15,* 663–87.

Bradley, L. & Bryant, P. E. (1983). Categorising sounds and learning to read—a causal connection. *Nature, 301,* 419–21.

Bradley, L. & Bryant, P. E. (1985). *Rhyme and reason in reading and spelling.* Ann Arbor: University of Michigan Press.

Bryant, N. D. (1975). *Diagnostic test of basic decoding skills.* New York: Teachers College, Columbia University.

Byrne, B. & Fielding-Barnesley, R. (1989). Phonemic awareness and letter knowledge in the child's acquisition of the alphabetic principle. *Journal of Educational Psychology, 81,* 313–21.

Calkins, L. M. (1980). When children want to punctuate: Basic skills belong in context. *Language Arts, 57,* 567–73.

Clarke, L. K. (1988). Invented versus traditional spelling in first graders' writings: Effects on learning to spell and read. *Research in the Teaching of English, 22,* 281–309.

Clay, M. M. (1979). *Stones: The Concepts About Print test.* Portsmouth, NH: Heinemann.

Clay, M. M. (1985). *The early detection of reading difficulties.* Portsmouth, NH: Heinemann.

Clay, M. M. (1987). Learning to be learning disabled. *New Zealand Journal of Educational Studies, 22,* 155–73.

Clay, M. M. (1993). *Reading Recovery: A guidebook for teachers in training.* Portsmouth, NH: Heinemann.

Cowley, J. (1984). *I'm the king of the mountain.* Katonah, NY: Richard C. Owen.

Cunningham, A. E. (1990). Explicit versus implicit instruction in phonemic awareness. *Journal of Experimental Child Psychology, 50,* 429–44.

Dahl, K. L., & Freppon, P. A. (1991). Literacy learning in whole-language classrooms: An analysis of low socioeconomic urban children learning to read and write in kindergarten. In J. Zutell & S. McCormick (Eds.), *Learner factors/teacher factors: Issues in literacy research and instruction* (pp. 149–58). Chicago: National Reading Conference.

Dahl, K. L. & P. A. Freppon. (1992). *Learning to read and write in inner-city schools: A comparison of children's sense-making in skills-based and whole language classrooms.* Final Report to the Office of Educational Research and Improvement. U.S. Department of Education. (Grant Award No. R117E00134.)

Dahl, K. L. & Freppon, P. A. (1994). A comparison of innercity children's interpretations of reading and writing instruction in the early grades in skills-based and whole language classrooms. *Reading Research Quarterly, 30,* 50–74. Reprinted in this volume.

Dahl, K. L., Purcell-Gates, V., & McIntyre, E. (1989). Ways that inner-city children make sense of traditional reading and writing instruction in the early grades. Final report to Office of Educational Research and Improvement. Washington, DC: U. S. Department of Education. (Grant No. R117E00134).

DiStefano, P., & Killion, J. (1984). Assessing writing skills through a process approach. *English Education, 16* (4), 203–07.

Ehri, L. C. (1979). Linguistic insight: Threshold of reading acquisition. In T. Waller & G. E. MacKinnon (Eds.), *Reading research: Advances in theory and practice,* pp. 63–114. New York: Academic Press.

Ehri, L. C. (1991). Development of the ability to read words. In R. Barr, M. Kamil, P. Mosenthal, & P. D. Pearson (Eds.), *Handbook of reading research,* Vol. 2 (pp. 383–417). New York: Longman.

Ehri, L. C. (1994). Development of the ability to read words: Update. In R. Ruddell, M. Ruddell, & H. Singer (Eds.), *Theoretical models and processes of reading* (4th ed., pp. 323–58). Newark, DE: International Reading Association.

Ehri, L. C. (1995). Phases of development in reading words. *Journal of Research in Reading, 18,* 116–25.

Ehri, L. C., & Wilce, I. S. (1980). The influence of orthography on readers' conceptualization of the phonemic structure of words. *Applied Psycholinguistics, 1,* 371–85.

Elley, W. B. (1991). Acquiring literacy in a second language: The effect of book-based programs. *Language Learning, 41*(3), 375–411.

Elley, W. B. & Mangubhai, F. (1983). The impact of reading on second language learning. *Reading Research Quarterly, 19,* 53–67.

Foorman, B. R., Francis, D. J., Beeler, T., Winikates, D., & Fletcher, J. M. (1997). Early interventions for children with reading problems: Study designs and preliminary findings. *Learning Disabilities: A Multi-Disciplinary Journal, 8,* 63–71.

Fountas, I. C. & Pinnell, G. S. (1996). *Guided reading: Good first teaching for all children.* Portsmouth, NH: Heinemann.

Fox, B. & Routh, D. K. (1980). Phonemic analysis and severe reading disability in children. _Journal of Psycholinguistic Research, 9,_ 115–19.

Freppon, P. A. (1988). _An investigation of children's concepts of the purpose and nature of reading in different instructional settings._ Unpublished doctoral dissertation, University of Cincinnati, Ohio.

Freppon, P. A. (1991). Children's concepts of the nature and purpose of reading in different instructional settings. _Journal of Reading Behavior, 23_ (2), 139–63.

Freppon, P. A. (1993). Making sense of reading and writing in urban classrooms: Understanding at-risk children's knowledge construction in different curricula. Final Report to the Office of Educational Research and Improvement. U. S. Department of Education. (Grant Award No. R117E102361-91.)

Freppon, P. A. (1995). Low-income children's literacy interpretations in a skills-based and a whole-language classroom. _Journal of Reading Behavior, 27_ (4), 505–33.

Gaskins, I. W., Ehri, L. C., Cress, C., O'Hara, C., & Donnelly, K. (1996). Procedures for word learning: Making discoveries about words. _The Reading Teacher, 50,_ 312–27.

Gibson, E. J. (1985). Trends in perceptual development. In H. Singer & R. B. Ruddell (Eds.), _Theoretical models and processes of reading_ (3rd ed., pp. 144–73). Newark, DE: International Reading Association.

Goodman, Y. M., Altwerger, B., & Marek, A. (1989). _Print awareness in preschool children: The development of literacy in preschool children, research and review._ Tucson: Program in Language and Literacy, University of Arizona.

Goodman, Y. M., Watson, D. J., & Burke, C. L. (1987). _Reading miscue inventory: Alternative procedures._ Katonah, NY: Richard C. Owen.

Goldstein, D. M. (1976). Cognitive-linguistic functioning and learning to read in preschoolers. _Journal of Educational Psychology, 68,_ 680–88.

Goswami, U. (1986). Children's use of analogy in learning to read: A developmental study. _Journal of Experimental Psychology, 42,_ 73–83.

Goswami, U. (1988). Orthographic analogies and reading development. _Quarterly Journal of Experimental Psychology, 40A,_ 239–68.

Goswami, U. (1993). Toward an interactive analogy model of reading development: Decoding vowel graphemes in beginning reading. _Journal of Experimental Child Psychology, 56,_ 443–75.

Goswami, U. & Bryant, P. E. (1990). _Phonological skills and learning to read._ London: Erlbaum.

Gunderson, L. & Shapiro, J. (1987). Some findings on whole language instruction. _Reading-Canada-Lecture, 5_ (1), 22–26.

Gunderson, L. & Shapiro, J. (1988). Whole language instruction: Writing in 1st grade. _The Reading Teacher, 41,_ 430–37.

Gunning, T. (1988). _Decoding behavior of good and poor second grade students._ Paper presented at the annual meeting of the International Reading Association, Toronto.

Gunning, T. (1995). Word building: A strategic approach to the teaching of phonics. _The Reading Teacher, 48,_ 484–88.

Heald-Taylor, G. (1989). _The administrator's guide to whole language._ Katonah, NY: Richard C. Owen.

Hiebert, E. H., Colt, J. M., Catto, S. L., & Gary, E. C. (1992). Reading and writing of first-grade students in a restructured Chapter 1 program. *American Educational Research Journal, 29,* 545–72.

Holdaway, D. (1979). *The foundations of literacy.* Sydney: Ashton Scholastic. Distributed in the U. S. by Heinemann.

Jastak, J., Bijou, S., & Jastak, S. (1978). *Wide Range Achievement Test.* Wilmington, DE: Jastak Associates.

Jensen, A. (1981). *Straight talk about mental tests.* New York: Free Press.

Juel, C., Griffith, P. L., & Gough, P. B. (1986). Acquisition of literacy: A longitudinal study of children in first and second grade. *Journal of Educational Psychology, 78,* 243–55.

Kasten, W. C., & Clarke, B. K. (1989). *Reading/writing readiness for preschool and kindergarten children: A whole language approach.* Sanibel, Florida: Educational Research and Development Council. (ED 312 041).

Knapp, M. S., and associates. (1995). *Teaching for meaning in high-poverty classrooms.* New York: Teachers College Press.

Krashen, S. D. (1993). *The power of reading: Insights from the research.* Englewood, CO: Libraries Unlimited.

Lyon, R. (1995). Toward a definition of dyslexia. *Annals of Dyslexia, 45,* 3–27.

Mann, V. A. (1986). Phonological awareness: The role of reading experience. *Cognition, 24,* 65–92.

Mann, V. A., Tobin, P., & Wilson, R. (1987). Measuring phonological awareness through the invented spellings of kindergarten children. *Merrill-Palmer Quarterly, 33,* 365–91.

Manning, M., Manning, G., & Long, R. (1989). *Effects of a whole language and a skill-oriented program on the literacy development of inner city primary children.* (ED 324 642.)

Morais, J., Cary, L., Alegria, J., & Bertelson, P. (1979). Does awareness of speech as a sequence of phones arise spontaneously? *Cognition, 7,* 323–31.

Moustafa, M. (1990). *An interactive/cognitive model of the acquisition of a graphophonemic system by young children.* Unpublished doctoral dissertation, University of Southern California, Los Angeles.

Moustafa, M. (1995). Children's productive phonological recoding. *Reading Research Quarterly, 30,* 464–76.

Nation, K. & Hulme, C. (1997). Phonemic segmentation, not onset-rime segmentation, predicts early reading and spelling skills. *Reading Research Quarterly, 32,* 154–67.

Neisser, U. (1986). New answers to an old question. In U. Neisser (Ed.), *The school achievement of minority children: New perspectives.* Hillsdale, NJ: Erlbaum.

Olofsson, A. & Lundberg, I. (1983). Can phonemic awareness be trained in kindergarten? *Scandinavian Journal of Psychology, 24,* 35–44.

Open Court. (1995). *Collections for Young Scholars.* Chicago, IL: Open Court Publishing Company.

Perfetti, C. A., Beck, I., Bell, L. C., & Hughes, C. (1987). Phonemic knowledge and learning to read are reciprocal: A longitudinal study of first grade children. *Merrill-Palmer Quarterly, 33,* 283–319.

Peterson, M. E., & Haines, L. P. (1992). Orthographic analogy training with kindergarten children: Effects on analogy use, phonemic segmentation, and letter-sound knowledge. *Journal of Reading Behavior, 24* (1), 109–27.

Purcell-Gates, V. (1988). Lexical and syntactic knowledge of written narrative held by well-read-to kindergartners and second graders. *Research in the Teaching of English, 22,* 128–60.

Rhodes, L. K. & Shanklin, N.L. (1989). *A research base for whole language.* Denver, CO: LINK.

Ribowsky, H. (1985). *The effects of a code emphasis approach and a whole language approach upon emergent literacy of kindergarten children.* Alexandria, VA.: Educational Document Reproduction Service. (ED 269 720).

Santa, C. M. (1976-1977). Spelling patterns and the development of flexible word recognition strategies. *Reading Research Quarterly, 12,* 125–44.

Shapiro, J. (1990). Research perspectives on whole-language. In V. Froese (Ed.), *Whole-language: Practice and theory.* Cambridge: Allyn & Bacon.

Share, D. L., Jorm, A. F., Maclean, R., & Matthews, R. (1984). Sources of individual differences in reading acquisition. *Journal of Educational Psychology, 76,* 1309–24.

Share, D. L. & Stanovich, K. E. (1995). Cognitive processes in early reading development: A model of acquisition and individual differences. *Issues in Education: Contributions from Educational Psychology, 1,* 1–35.

Smith, J. W. A., & Elley, W. B. (1995). *Learning to read in New Zealand.* Katonah, NY: Richard C. Owen.

Stanovich, K. E. (1988). Explaining the differences between the dyslexic and the garden-variety poor reader: The phonological-core variable-difference model. *Journal of Learning Disabilities, 21,* 590–604.

Stanovich, K. E., Cunningham, A. E., & Feeman, D. J. (1984). Intelligence, cognitive skills, and early reading progress. *Reading Research Quarterly, 19,* 278–303.

Stephens, D. (1992). *Research on whole language: Support for a new curriculum.* Katonah, NY: Richard C. Owen.

Stice, C. F. & Bertrand, N. P. (1990). *Whole language and the emergent literacy of at-risk children: A two-year comparative study.* Nashville: Center of Excellence: Basic Skills, Tennessee State University. (ED 324 636).

Torgeson, J. K. & Hecht, S. A. (1996). Preventing and remediating disabilities: Instructional variables that make a difference for special students. In M. F. Graves, P. Van Den Brock, & B. M. Taylor (Eds.), *The first R: Every child's right to read* (pp. 133–59). New York: Teachers College Press.

Traw, R. (1996). Large-scale assessment of skills in a whole language curriculum: Two districts' experiences. *Journal of Educational Research, 89,* 323–39.

Tunmer, W. E., & Nesdale, A. R. (1985). Phonemic segmentation skill and beginning reading. *Journal of Educational Psychology, 4,* 417–27.

Tunnell, M. O., & Jacobs, J. S. (1989). Using "real" books: Research findings on literature based reading instruction. *The Reading Teacher, 42,* 470–77.

Van Allen, R. (1976). *Language experiences in education.* Boston: Houghton Mifflin.

Vellutino, F. R., & Scanlon, D. M. (1987). Phonological coding, phonological awareness, and reading ability: Evidence from a longitudinal and experimental study. *Merrill-Palmer Quarterly, 33,* 321–63.

Vellutino, F. R., et al. (1996). Cognitive profiles of difficult-to-remediate and readily remediated poor readers: Early intervention as a vehicle for distinguishing between cognitive and experiential deficits as basic causes of specific reading disability. *Journal of Educational Psychology, 88,* 601–38.

Wagner, R. K., & Torgesen, J. K. (1987). The nature of phonological processing and its causal role in the acquisition of reading skills. *Psychological Bulletin, 101,* 192–212.

Wallach, M. A., & Wallach, L. (1979). Helping disadvantaged children learn to read by teaching them phoneme identification skills. In L. A. Resnick & P. A. Weaver (Eds.), *Theory and practice of early reading* (Vol. 3, pp. 197–215). Hillsdale, NJ: Erlbaum.

Weaver, C. (1990). *Understanding whole language: From principles to practice.* Portsmouth, NH: Heinemann.

Weaver, C. (1988/1994). *Reading process and practice: From socio-psycholinguistics to whole language.* Portsmouth, NH: Heinemann.

Weaver, C. (1994). Reconceptualizing reading and dyslexia. *Journal of Childhood Communication Disorders, 16* (1), 23–35.

Weaver, C. (Ed.). (Forthcoming). *Practicing what We know: Informed reading instruction.* Urbana, IL: National Council of Teachers of English.

White, T. G., & Cunningham, P. M. (1990). *Teaching disadvantaged readers to decode by analogy.* Paper presented at the annual meeting of the American Educational Research Association, Boston, MA, April 1990.

Wiederholt, J. L. (1986). *Formal Reading Inventory.* Austin, TX: PRO-ED.

Wimmer, H., Landerl, K., Linortner, R., & Hummer, P. (1991). The relationship of phonemic awareness to reading acquisition: More consequence than precondition but still important. *Cognition, 40,* 219–49.

Woodcock, R. W., & Johnson, M. B. (1973). *Woodcock Reading Mastery Tests.* Circle Pines, MN: American Guidance Services.

Zukav, G. (1979). *The dancing wu-li masters: An overview of the new physics.* New York: Bantam.

12 Using "Real" Books: Research Findings on Literature-Based Reading Instruction

Michael O. Tunnell
James S. Jacobs
Brigham Young University

In the introduction to their article, Tunnell and Jacobs note that "those who use literature-based reading instruction to challenge the basal tradition boast stunning levels of success with all types of students and particularly with disabled and uninterested readers." The authors discuss two kinds of research studies: controlled, experimental studies and studies that simply looked at growth within whole language classrooms employing literature to teach reading. They begin with a range of different studies, then focus on studies of readers in different categories: readers in Shared Book Experience programs and the Reading Recovery program in New Zealand and Ohio; children with limited command of English; readers who have already failed, including older readers; and "stalled" readers. One hallmark of the readers in all of these programs is that they consciously read for meaning, "not symbols or sounds." The authors discuss ten basic elements of literature-based programs, then conclude with a section on other considerations.

How should reading be taught and with what sorts of materials? Basals or trade books? Phonics or sight words or context clues? Do "real" books come later, after a child has mastered decoding skills? Or might the child start with "real" books from the library or book club and learn skills as needed in so-called "natural context?" What are the best ways of leading a child to literacy?

Advocates of basal instruction cite the logic and successful tradition of their method. Basal reading programs have dominated the classroom for decades—95 to 99% of American teachers relied on the basal in 1958 and 80 to 90% still did as of 1980 (Koeller, 1981).

Those who use literature-based reading instruction to challenge the basal tradition boast stunning levels of success with all types of students and particularly with disabled and uninterested readers. Recently the Whole Language movement, which has gained great momentum in the 1980s, has given renewed attention to individualized reading— redefining and refining the process that primarily uses "real" books to teach and foster literacy.

Can reading be taught successfully without the basal? What does the literature in reading instruction indicate about both the success rate and the components of literature-based, Whole Language approaches to building literacy?

A Variety of Studies

A number of controlled studies have directly compared literature-based reading with basal and mastery learning instruction while others have simply looked at growth within Whole Language classrooms employing literature-based reading programs.

A landmark study by Cohen (1968) used a control group of 130 students in 2nd grade who were taught with basal readers and compared them to 155 children in an experimental group using a literature component along with regular instruction. The schools, in New York City, were selected because of academic retardation likely due to low socio-economic backgrounds of the students.

The experimental treatment consisted mainly of reading aloud to children from 50 carefully selected children's trade picture books— books without fixed vocabulary or sentence length—and then following up with meaning related activities. The children were encouraged to read the books anytime.

The experimental group showed significant increases over the control group (on Metropolitan Achievement Tests and A Free Association Vocabulary Test administered in October and June) in word knowledge ($p < .005$), reading comprehension ($p < .01$), vocabulary ($p < .05$) and quality of vocabulary ($p < .05$). When the six lowest classes were compared, the experimental group showed an even more significant increase over the control.

Cohen's study was replicated a few years later by Cullinan, Jaggar, and Strickland (1974), yielding basically the same results.

Another controlled study that warrants a closer look is one conducted by Eldredge and Butterfield (1986), whose initial study involved 1,149 children in 2nd grade in 50 Utah classrooms. They compared a traditional basal approach to 5 other experimental methods, including 2 that used variations of a literature-based program.

Employing a variety of evaluative techniques (an instrument for evaluating phonics skills developed and validated by Eldredge, the Gates-MacGinitie Reading Test, and a Pictorial Self-Concept Scale), the researchers discovered that 14 of 20 significant differences among the instructional methods favored the literature approach teamed with a series of special decoding lessons (also developed by Eldredge) taking no more than 15 minutes daily.

The other literature-based group also placed highly. Eldredge and Butterfield were able to conclude that "the use of children's literature to teach children to read had a positive effect upon students' achievement and attitudes toward reading—much greater than the traditional methods used." (See also Bader, Veatch, & Eldredge, 1987.)

New Zealand and Ohio

Under the auspices of the New Zealand Department of Education, a literature-based, developmental program for 1st graders called the Shared Book Experience was examined closely. Holdaway (1982) explains that "no grade or structured materials were used and all word solving skills were taught in context during real reading. This experimental group proved equal or superior to other experimental and control groups on a variety of measures including Marie Clay's *Diagnostic Survey.*"

So impressed was the Department of Education that it embarked on a countrywide program of inservice in New Zealand, and subsequently, developmental programs such as Shared Book Experience have taken over on a national scale.

The influence of this New Zealand program spread. The Ohio Reading Recovery Program, reported by Boehnlein (1987) to be an American version of New Zealand's Reading Recovery Program, is specifically targeted at beginning readers who indeed have a profile that will make failure likely. Results of a controlled study match those of the New Zealand findings, which are best encapsulated in this remarkable statement: "After an average of 15 to 20 weeks, or 30 to 40 hours of instruction, 90% of the children whose pretest scores were in the lowest 20% of their class catch up to the average of their class or above and *never need remediation again.*"

The Ohio Reading Recovery program confirmed that gains are maintained, and when compared to control groups, the Reading Recovery children "not only made greater gains than the other high risk children who received no help, but they also made greater gains than the children who needed no help." (See also Pinnell, 1986.)

Limited English Speakers

One of the more recent experiments dealing with literature-based reading and children at high risk of failure is the story of a school on New York City's west side (Larrick, 1987). Of these children, 92% came from non-English speaking homes, 96% lived below the poverty level, and 80% spoke no English when entering school. The Open Sesame program was initiated with 225 kindergarten students, providing them an opportunity to read in an unpressured, pleasurable way—using neither basals nor workbooks. Immersion in children's literature and language experience approaches to reading and writing were the major instructional thrusts, and skills were taught primarily in meaningful context as children asked for help in writing.

As the year concluded, all 225 students could read their dictated stories and many of the picture books shown in class. Some were even reading on a 2nd grade level. School officials were so impressed that they made a written commitment to extend the program gradually through 6th grade.

The following year, the spring of 1987, all 350 in 1st grade were happily reading English—60% on or above grade level. In fact, only 3 of the 350 failed to pass district comprehension tests, and those 3 had been in the United States less than 6 months.

White, Vaughan, and Rorie (1986) reported that 1st grade children from a small, economically depressed rural community responded well to reading and writing programs not using a basal. As to the methods employed, "print was something that permeated their day. . . . Books became theirs, in a natural way, in a real way.'"

Though quick to say that the children understood far more about the reading process than could ever be measured by a pencil and paper test, White and her colleagues were also pleased that 20 of the 25 children scored a grade equivalent of 2.0 or better on the spring standardized tests. The other 5 children had scores of 1.6, 1.7, or 1.9, and the lowest percentile ranking was 54th.

Those Who Have Failed

But what about children who have already failed? Chomsky (1978), in a research report aptly titled "When You Still Can't Read in Third Grade:

After Decoding, What?" addresses the plight of the young "stalled" reader, who for better than 1 year has made no progress in reading.

Chomsky worked in a middle class suburban community near Boston with 5 children in 3rd grade who had average IQs and no apparent language or speech problems but who had always been remedial reading students, hated reading, and had made no progress in reading since 1st grade. Abandoning the intensive decoding program, the researcher instead asked the children to listen to tape recorded stories from "real" books, returning to the book often until the story was memorized.

The neurological impress method using natural, enjoyable text proved to be the key to eventual success. Standardized achievement test scores (MAT) after a year of treatment showed that these no-progress children were off and running. Average increase in overall reading scores was 7.5 months (grade equivalent) and in word knowledge was 6.25 months (grade equivalent), a significant increase for children whose former test scores showed no progress.

Even older children who have experienced years of failure with reading and writing have been exposed to literature-based, Whole Language programs with notable success. Fader et al. (1976) flooded secondary classrooms in inner city Detroit with paperbacks, finding great success in raising reading achievement and developing the reading interests of high school students who ordinarily did not read often or well.

But the true proof of their literature-based program was best put to the test with hardcore subjects—students at the W.J. Maxey Boys' Training School in Lake Whitmore, Michigan. Hundreds of paperbacks were provided for W.J. Maxey, along with the time to read them and no obligation to write the usual book reports or summaries. Another midwestern boys' training school was used as a control group.

Though there were no significant differences to be found in control and experimental groups at the onset, by the end of the school year the boys at W.J. Maxey showed significant gains over the control on measures of self esteem, literacy attitudes, anxiety, verbal proficiency, and reading comprehension. In some instances, the control group's scores actually decreased from the year before while the experimental group's surged ahead, even doubling the control group scores.

Stalled Readers

Stalled children also showed marked improvement in a classroom study with 5th graders. With the entire class, Tunnell (1986) employed a literature-based reading/writing program adapted from the program suggested by Eldredge and Butterfield (1986). Eight of the 28 students in his classroom were reading disabled, receiving federally funded Chapter 1 or resource instruction in a pull-out program.

After 7 months of treatment, the standardized tests (SRA) were administered, and the average gain in the overall reading score was a grade equivalent of 1.1. The 8 reading disabled children, who also were virtually stalled in their reading progress, posted an average gain of 1.3 with a comprehension gain of 2.0.

Even more noteworthy was the swing in reading attitudes in all children. A 13 question reading attitude survey was administered to the class in August and again in April. Negative attitudes toward books and reading virtually disappeared as self concept in relation to literacy rose. (See also Tunnell et al., 1988.)

It is important to note that gains in reading skills using a literature-based approach are not limited to students at risk. In the studies by Eldredge, Holdaway, and Tunnell, the average and above average reader made progress equal to and most often better than students in traditional programs, as measured by the typical achievement tests.

Some of the strongest evidence for the broad use of a Whole Language program involving literature comes from Ray Reutzel, an associate professor at Brigham Young University who took a 1 year leave to teach reading to 63 children in 1st grade in nearby Sage Creek Elementary. With a classroom library of 2,000 books, Reutzel taught the elements and skills of reading within the meaningful context of story books.

No basal was used, nor was the state program of worksheets and drill activities, called the Utah Benchmark Skills. The goal prescribed by the state is to have the students pass the Utah Benchmark Skills Test at an 80% level in May. Reutzel's students scored 93% in January, 13 points higher than district expectations and 4 months earlier than the normal testing time.

When the Stanford Achievement Test (SAT) was given in March, group percentiles across all reading categories—word study skills, comprehension, and total reading—were uniformly in the 99th percentile for the 63 children. Individual scores were all above grade level except for 4 children who scored below 1.6. The lowest score was 1.2, and that from a boy who knew only a few letters of the alphabet when entering 1st grade. Even a girl whose IQ tested at 68 came out at grade level. There was not one nonreading 1st grader in the school (Reutzel and Fawson, 1988).

Meaningful Reading

Rasinski and Deford (1985) indicate why literature-based reading approaches may have a profound positive effect on learners. They compared three 1st grade classrooms, each with competent teachers using different approaches to teaching reading: content centered mastery learning, traditional basal, and child centered literature-based approaches. The researchers looked less at achievement than at student conceptions about reading assessed through interviews.

The responses to the basic questions "What is reading?" or "What happens when you read?" were rated by a team of raters in relation to whether they were meaning related (high score of 7) or letter-sound related (low score of 1). Mean scores showed that children from the literature-based program conceived reading to be more of a meaning related activity than did the other children. The mean scores were mastery group: 3.45, basal group: 4.32, literature group: 4.91.

Conclusions indicate that good readers in all three groups tended to define reading as being concerned with meaning while poor readers saw it as a process of converting symbol to sound. Natural texts support reading as a meaning related activity.

That children in classroom situations can be taught to read from "real" books is not a new idea. Thompson (1971) examined 40 studies from 1937 through 1971 that compared the basal approach to reading instruction with the individualized approach. He noted that 24 of the studies favored individualized reading, while only 1 chose the basal as better. (The remaining studies were ties.)

Thompson concluded that "individualized reading programs can facilitate reading achievement to the extent of basal programs, and . . . more often than not . . . have facilitated higher reader achievement than basal programs in controlled studies." (See also Davis and Lucas, 1971.)

Basic Elements of Literature-Based Programs

Though each study mentioned employed its own brand of literature-based reading instruction, several basic premises are found often in the different approaches. Elements of instruction varied depending upon the age of the students, but in some way the following commonalities were overtly employed or subtly implied in all of the literature-based reading programs.

Premises learned from "natural readers"

Advocates of Whole Language tend to believe reading skills can be acquired in much the same manner as learning to speak (Forester, 1977; Holdaway, 1982). Durkin (1961), for example, identified 49 from a pool of 5,103 students in 1st grade who had received no formal reading instruction but entered school reading at a grade equivalent of 1.5 to 4.6.

These 49 "natural readers" had vastly different racial and socioeconomic backgrounds and IQ levels, but there were common factors in the reading models they had at home. Their families had a high regard for reading, children were read to regularly from age 2 forward, and parents answered frequent questions about words and reading.

Durkin concluded that natural readers acquire abilities through experiences with whole texts provided by strong reading models.

Both Clark (1976) and Thorndike (1973) support Durkin's conclusions. Clark's study of young readers in Scotland yielded two basic common factors in natural readers. All were read to from an early age and all had access to books at home or through libraries.

Thorndike, studying reading comprehension in 15 countries, discovered two conditions that prevailed in strong readers. All had been read to from an early age and had come from homes that respected education.

Immersion in natural text at an early age has the same effects on reading as immersion in aural and spoken language has on speech.

Hoskisson (1979) concurred by suggesting that natural readers "solve the problem of learning to read as they construct their knowledge of written language." Therefore, no formal hierarchy of reading skills should be imposed on children, because only the child can determine what can be assimilated and accommodated within that highly personal cognitive structure. Hearing written language is essential to testing these personal hypotheses about written language.

Learning to read naturally begins when parents read to young children and let them handle books, and that process is continued with the teacher reading aloud and including books naturally in the classroom.

Use of natural text

In every study examined, researchers were emphatic about using children's literature written in natural, uncontrolled language.

Goodman (1988) supports this move away from basal reading materials, especially after evaluating the ways in which such programs select, write, or alter the stories they include: "Basals have tended to isolate sounds, letters, and words from the [language] systems. And they have given little attention to the systems and how they relate in natural texts." He maintains that basal materials often produce distorted abstractions, loss of contextual meanings, and loss of grammatical function due to letter-sound relationships taught in isolation or words used out of context.

The process of controlling vocabulary and syntax also causes a loss of style and makes language less natural and less predictable. A closer look at two leading basal series showed Goodman that only about 20% of the texts reproduced were authentic renderings.

It is also interesting to note that the 104 books used with the 2nd grade children in the Eldredge and Butterfield (1986) study were not controlled for vocabulary. In fact, 91% of the books had readability scores above 3rd grade level, and 62% were at a 4th grade level. Despite the lack of vocabulary control, the students made superior progress.

Neurological impress method

In the studies that involved beginning readers, a variation of the neurological impress method was generally employed.

In Chomsky's study, children "read" in the trade book while following along with the recorded version on audio cassette. Eldredge and Butterfield used reading pairs (dyads) or groups of 3 (triads) where poor readers were teamed with average readers. They sat together and read aloud from the same book; while the faster reader touched words as they were read and the slower reader repeated them. Groups changed every few days, and as proficiency was gained the slower reader began to read silently, using the better reader as a word resource.

Even the use of Big Books, as suggested by Holdaway and White, allows for a form of neurological impress. Big Books usually are trade picture books that have been reproduced in a format large enough to be seen from 20 feet away. With Big Books teachers can have their students follow their fluent reading.

Reading aloud

Another characteristic of literature-based programs is that teachers regularly spend time reading aloud to their students. In all of the studies reviewed, reading aloud seemed to be a must. Daily reading aloud from enjoyable trade books has been the key that unlocked literacy growth for many disabled readers. Opportunities for modeling and neurological impress abound during read aloud time. And, of course, being read to is the essential element in the backgrounds of "natural readers."

Sustained silent reading

SSR is the time provided for students and teacher to read materials of their own choosing without interruption. Every study examined for this report included, as a part of its plan, time for children to be alone with books.

Allington (1977) suggests the more words that pass in front of the eyes, the better the reader becomes. The time children spend in independent reading "is associated with gains in reading achievement" (Anderson et al., 1985, p. 119). Opportunity to reread favorites, reread books recorded on audio tape, or to read something new is the best way to give children the practice they need to apply their newly learned skills.

Teacher modeling

Another important element usually only hinted at by the researchers listed in this article is that of teacher modeling. One of Holdaway's three basic requirements of the Shared Book Experience is that teachers need to present new books with wholehearted enjoyment.

According to the same principle, teachers themselves should read during sustained silent reading (McCracken and McCracken, 1978). A prerequisite for this sort of modeling is a teacher who values reading in his/her personal life and also knows and loves the children's books that will be read by the students.

Emphasis on changing attitudes

An affective approach to reading instruction is also a recurring element of literature-based programs. Tunnell's study showed a marked improvement of student attitudes, and other researchers made comments such as that of Larrick (1987): "Best of all, they loved to read."

Fader et al., (1976, p. 236–37) illustrate an extreme shift in attitude and its benefits with the story of Bill, a 13-year-old, 2nd-grade-level reader who was watched busily reading *Jaws*. When Fader asked him if the book was hard, Bill answered "Sure it's hard. But it's worth it."

Self selection of reading materials

Positive attitude toward reading seems to be affected by allowing children to select their own reading materials. Every study examined had a time when students at every age level were encouraged to find and read books of their own choosing.

Though sometimes books were read together (as with Big Books), there was always a large classroom library from which children could choose their own books. Sustained silent reading is unsuccessful unless children are allowed to read books of their own choosing.

Meaning oriented with skills often taught in meaningful context

Most studies reviewed suggested teaching reading skills as they relate directly to the books and writings of the children (Holdaway, Chomsky,

Larrick, Cohen, Boehnlein). Eldredge and Butterfield employed a brief decoding lesson, but they suggest moving quickly into "real" reading so that the lesson can be put into immediate practice.

Process writing and other output activities

In every instance some sort of follow-up output activity accompanied reading experiences. Often the output activities involved writing. Forester, White, Chomsky, Holdaway, Larrick, Fader, and Tunnell all mentioned writing, and usually process writing in particular. In fact, Chomsky (1978) stated that the children who progressed the most achieved in both reading and writing.

Other Considerations

Success of literature-based programs is well documented. Disabled readers are brought into the world of literacy (and not just decoding) using "real" books. When children learn that reading and books are worth their time, then as Fielding, Wilson, and Anderson (1984) point out, they will spend more self-initiated time in books. Children who participate in this self-initiated practice (some children read from 10 to 20 times more than others) make more progress because frequent personal reading improves the "automaticity" of basic reading skills.

Unfortunately, in a study of 5th graders' activities after school, Fielding (1984) and her colleagues discovered that only 2% of free time is spent reading (a daily average of 9.2 minutes). Half the children read only 4 minutes or less each day, and 30% read 2 minutes or less (10% did not read at all).

It is no surprise that television watching consumed most of their after school time (an average of 136.4 minutes daily). Yet, these researchers concluded that "among all the ways children can spend their leisure time, average minutes per day reading books was the best and most consistent predictor of standardized comprehension test performance, size of vocabulary, and gains in reading achievement between 2nd and 5th grade (Fielding, Wilson, & Anderson, 1984, p. 151).

Greaney (1980), reviewing studies concerning leisure reading, discovered that "a number of studies have reported significant relationships between amount of leisure reading and level of pupil attainment." One of the studies Greaney points to was conducted decades ago by LaBrant (1936). This longitudinal study reported that students completing a 6 year free reading program were, 25 years later, reading significantly more than most other groups to which they had been compared. (Also see Connor, 1954; Maxwell, 1977.) In fact, *Becoming a Nation of Readers* (Anderson et al., 1985, p. 82) suggests that "priority should be given to independent reading."

Fielding, Wilson, and Anderson (1984) note that reading books deepens knowledge of forms of written language. Conversely, primary grade basals have fewer plot complications, less character development, and less conflict among and within characters. They lack the richness in vocabulary, sentence structure, and literary form found in children's books. Koeller (1981) notes a study by Blom, Waite, and Zimet (1970) that "analyzed over 1300 stories in 12 basal readers and noted a regressive pull, developmentally," in the material.

Early experiences with the richness and variety of "real" reading materials seems to give children reason to read, teaching them, as Trelease (1985, p. 6) explains, not only "how to read, but to want to read." The affectivity of literature-based, Whole Language programs gives meaning and pleasure to the process, thus making skills instruction at last meaningful—empowering both teachers and students. At least, it is safe to say the basal reader is not the only way to successfully teach children to read.

References

Allington, Richard. "If They Don't Read Much, How They Ever Gonna Get Good?" *Journal of Reading*, vol. 21 (October 1977), pp. 57–61.

Anderson, Richard C., Elfrieda H. Hiebert, Judith A. Scott, & Ian A.G. Wilkinson. *Becoming a Nation of Readers: The Report of the Commission on Reading*. Washington, DC: The National Institute of Education, U.S. Department of Education, 1985.

Bader, Lois A., Jeannette Veatch, & J. Lloyd Eldredge. "Trade Books or Basal Readers?" *Reading Improvement*, vol. 24 (Spring 1987), pp. 62–67.

Blom, Gaston E., Richard R. Waite, & Sara G. Zimet. "Motivational Content Analysis of Primers." In *Basic Studies on Reading*, edited by Harry Levin and Joanna P. Williams. New York, NY: Basic Books, 1970.

Boehnlein, Mary. "Reading Intervention for High Risk First-Graders." Educational Leadership, vol. 44 (March 1987), pp. 32–37.

Chomsky, Carol. "When You Still Can't Read in Third Grade: After Decoding, What?" In *What Research Has to Say about Reading Instruction*, edited by S. Jay Samuels. Newark, DE: International Reading Association, 1978.

Clark, Margaret. *Young Fluent Readers*. London, England: Heinemann, 1976.

Cohen, Dorothy. "The Effect of Literature on Vocabulary and Reading Achievement." *Elementary English*, vol. 45 (February 1968), pp. 209–13, 217.

Connor, D.V. "The Relationship between Reading Achievement and Voluntary Reading of Children." *Educational Review*, vol. 6 (1953/1954), pp. 221–27.

Cullinan, Bernice, Angela Jaggar, & Dorothy Strickland. "Language Expansion for Black Children in the Primary Grades: A Research Report." *Young Children*, vol. 29 (January 1974), pp. 98–112.

Davis, Floyd W., & James S. Lucas. "An Experiment in Individualized Reading." *The Reading Teacher*, vol. 24 (May 1971), pp. 737–43, 747.

Durkin, Dolores. "Children Who Read before Grade One." *The Reading Teacher*, vol. 14 (January 1961), pp. 163–66.

Eldredge, J. Lloyd, & Dennie Butterfield. "Alternatives to Traditional Reading Instruction." *The Reading Teacher*, vol. 40 (October 1986), pp. 32–37.

Fader, Daniel, James Duggins, Tom Finn, & Elton McNeil. *The New Hooked on Books*. New York, NY: Berkeley, 1976.

Fielding, Linda G., Paul T Wilson, & Richard Anderson. "A New Focus on Free Reading: The Role of Trade Books in Reading Instruction." In *The Contexts of School Based Literacy*, edited by Taffy E. Raphael. New York, NY: Random House, 1984.

Forester, Anne D. "What Teachers Can Learn from 'Natural Readers.' " *The Reading Teacher*, vol. 31 (November 1977), pp. 160–66.

Goodman, Ken. "Look What They've Done to Judy Blume!: The 'Basalization' of Children's Literature." *The New Advocate*, vol. 1 (Winter 1988), pp. 29–41.

Greaney, Vincent. "Factors Related to Amount and Type of Leisure Reading." *Reading Research Quarterly*, vol. 15, no. 3 (1980), pp. 337–57.

Holdaway, Don. "Shared Book Experience: Teaching Reading Using Favorite Books." *Theory into Practice*, vol. 21 (Fall 1982), pp. 293–300.

Hoskisson, Kenneth. "Learning to Read Naturally." *Language Arts*, vol. 56 (May 1979), pp. 489–96.

Koeller, Shirley. "25 Years Advocating Children's Literature in the Reading Program." *The Reading Teacher*, vol. 34 (February 1981), pp. 552–56.

LaBrant, Lou L. *An Evaluation of Free Reading in Grades Ten, Eleven, and Twelve*. Columbus, OH: Ohio State University Press, 1936.

Larrick, Nancy. "Illiteracy Starts Too Soon." *Phi Delta Kappan*, vol. 69 (November 1987), pp. 184–89.

Maxwell, James. *Reading Progress from 8 to 15*. Windsor, England: National Foundation for Educational Research, 1977.

McCracken, Robert, & Marlene McCracken. "Modeling Is the Key to Sustained Silent Reading." *The Reading Teacher*, vol. 31, (January 1978), pp. 406–8.

Pinnell, Gay Su. "Reading Recovery in Ohio 1985-86: Final Report." Technical Report, The Ohio State University, Columbus, OH, 1986.

Rasinski, Timothy V., & Diane E. Deford. "Learning within a Classroom Context: First Graders' Conceptions of Literacy." ED 262 393. Arlington, VA: ERIC Document Reproducing Service, 1985.

Reutzel, Ray, & Parker Fawson. "A Professor Returns to the Classroom: Implementing Whole Language." Unpublished manuscript, Brigham Young University, Provo, UT, 1988.

Thompson, Richard A. "Summarizing Research Pertaining to Individualized Reading." ED 065 836. Arlington, VA: ERIC Document Reproducing Service, 1971.

Thorndike, Robert L. "Reading Comprehension, Education in 15 Countries: An Empirical Study," vol. 3, *International Studies in Education*. New York, NY: Holsted-Wiley, 1973.

Trelease, Jim. *The Read-Aloud Handbook*. New York, NY: Viking/Penguin, 1985.

Tunnell, Michael O. "The Natural Act of Reading: An Affective Approach." *The Advocate*, vol. 5 (Winter/Spring 1986), pp. 156–64.

Tunnell, Michael O., James E. Calder, Joseph E. Justen III, & Phillip B. Waldrop. "An Affective Approach to Reading: Effectively Teaching Reading to Mainstreamed Handicapped Children." *The Pointer*, vol. 32 (Spring 1988), pp. 38–40.

White, Jane H., Joseph L. Vaughan, & I. Laverne Rorie. "Picture of a Classroom Where Reading Is for Real." *The Reading Teacher*, vol. 40 (October 1986), pp. 84–86.

13 Successful Dyslexics: A Constructivist Study of Passionate Interest Reading

Rosalie P. Fink
Lesley College, Cambridge, MA

Fink reports in this study on highly successful adults who had been diagnosed as dyslexic in childhood. These twelve dyslexics' problems "included a history of difficulty with letter identification, word recognition, phonics, reading fluency, reading speed, spelling, laterality, writing, fine motor control, memory, and learning a foreign language." Yet all had become highly successful in their chosen fields. The twelve consisted of an attorney, a biochemist, a graphic artist, a gynecologist, an immunologist (a Nobel laureate), a neurologist, a physicist, a theatre set designer, two businessmen, and two special educators. Though these adults still have difficulties with basic phonological skills that severely limit their ability to sound out unfamiliar words, they nevertheless read extensively in their fields—materials that are very difficult, specialized, and abstract. Most of the twelve have authored books and journal articles in their fields.

How did these adults become such effective readers? Several of them felt profoundly alienated from school, yet all of them read a lot. It was only when they developed and pursued a passionate interest through reading that they finally developed "basic word recognition and fluency." Eleven of the twelve dyslexic readers indicated that they had finally "learned to read" between the ages of 10 and 12. They learned to read by reading (in perhaps the very manner that Moustafa suggests in chapter 5).

Dyslexia, or reading disability, is one of several distinct learning disabilities. Recently it has been reconceptualized and redefined:

It is a specific language-based disorder of constitutional origin characterized by difficulties in single word decoding, usually reflecting
insufficient phonological processing abilities. These difficulties in
single word decoding are often unexpected in relation to age and
other cognitive and academic abilities. . . . Dyslexia is manifest by
variable difficulty with different forms of language, often including,
in addition to problems reading, a conspicuous problem with
acquiring proficiency in writing and spelling.
(Orton Dyslexia Society Research Committee, 1994, p. 4)

Central to this new definition (Shaywitz, Fletcher, & Shaywitz,
1994) is a focus on phonological processing problems revealed
through difficulties in learning decoding, spelling, and writing skills.
The new definition maintains the classic notion of an "unexpected"
reading problem or "discrepancy" between the child's potential (often
measured by the Full Scale IQ) and his or her actual reading achievement (often measured by standardized diagnostic reading tests).
Stanovich (1991) recently proposed that listening comprehension be
used instead, arguing that listening comprehension is a better measure of language processing ability because listening is independent
of skill in decoding print. However, for a variety of reasons, listening comprehension as a measure has not gained wide acceptance in
the reading field, and the discrepancy definition remains (Berninger
& Abbott, 1994).

For older children and adults, the new definition of dyslexia no
longer requires quantifying the discrepancy between reading achievement and potential ability. We lack a standardized and reliable test of
phonological processing (Shaywitz et al., 1994), but for older children
and adults, a case history of early and continuing difficulties in reading unfamiliar words, spelling, and writing constitutes "the distinct
diagnostic signature" of dyslexia, especially when occurring together
with slow and laborious reading and writing, hallmarks of reading disability in a compensated dyslexic (Shaywitz et al., 1994, p. 7).

Regarding instruction, a considerable body of research on dyslexia
has focused on the effectiveness of highly structured skills-based teaching approaches (Cox, 1983; Gillingham & Stillman, 1966; Griesbach,
1993). These include systematic phonics instruction (Chall, 1983) and
multisensory methods (i.e., simultaneous instruction in the use and
association of three sensory channels—visual, auditory, and kinesthetic). Hallmarks of multisensory instruction are tracing and copying
as well as seeing a word and naming its letters aloud while writing.
These methods have been used at all levels of instruction.

In addition, bypass approaches, such as the use of tape recorders and
other devices that circumvent reading, are also integral components of

dyslexia instruction, especially at middle school, secondary, and post-secondary levels (Knight, 1986; Morris, 1983; Vogel, 1987).

For a child with developmental dyslexia, Roswell and Natchez (1977) note that "the chances of success are increased through providing reading materials based on the child's interests" (p. 68). Other researchers as well have studied the role of children's interests in promoting reading development; research findings indicate that both good and poor readers perform significantly better on high interest as compared with low interest materials (Asher, 1980; Asher & Markell, 1974; DiSibio & Savitz, 1982; National Assessment of Educational Progress, 1982). Renninger (1992) concludes that the influence of interest "is particularly salient" when students are in the process of developing their reading skills (p. 391).

Recent studies highlight that many individuals diagnosed with dyslexia eventually learn to read well (Gerber & Reiff, 1991; Lefly & Pennington, 1991) However, studies to date have not examined how dyslexics' ability to read is constructed or at what points in time dyslexics' reading development occurs.

In this article I report new findings about how and when in development dyslexics construct reading skills. I describe 12 highly successful dyslexics in the United States who, on average, developed basic fluency between ages 10 and 12 (3 to 4 years later than peers). Despite difficulties with basic, lower level skills, all were avid readers and ultimately achieved the highest level of reading ability, Chall's Stage 5 (shall, 1983). 1 also analyze how these dyslexics developed the ability to read well and suggest an instructional approach for teachers of children and adults with reading difficulties.

Clearly Dyslexic

The rationale for studying reading development in a group of highly successful adult dyslexics was that they might have devised novel strategies that ultimately would prove useful in the education of other children and adults. Individuals were selected for the study based on an academic profile with severe manifestations of characteristics commonly associated with dyslexia. Subjects were identified as being dyslexic through a history of severe, unexpected childhood difficulties learning to read, particularly difficulties in single word decoding. Each individual's profile and characteristics of dyslexia are shown in Table 1.

The classic definition of dyslexia was used according to U.S. Public Law 94-142, which "assumes a gap or discrepancy between a person's

Table 1

Dyslexia profiles of the 12 interviewees

High achieving adult dyslexics

Problem areas	C.B.	B.B.	J.B.	B.J.B.	C.C.	R.D.	G.D.	C.D.	J.J.	R.K.	A.S.	H.S.
Discrepancy between IQ and reading test scores	+	+	+	+	+	+	+	+	+	+	+	+
Spelling	+	+	+	+	+	+	+	+	+	+	+	+
Learning to read	+	+	+	+	+	+	+	+	+	+	+	+
Letter identification	+	+	+		+	+	+	+			+	+
Writing	+	+		+	+	+	+				+	
Speed (reading and writing)	+	+	+		+	+	+	+	+	+	+	+
Memory		+	+	+	+	+	+	+	+		+	
Laterality					+	+		+	+		+	
Diagnosis/remediation		+	+	+	+	+			+		+	
Learning foreign language	+	+	+	+	+	+	+	+	+	+	+	
Fine motor control		+	+	+	+			+			+	
Hyperactivity					+				+			
Familial dyslexia	+	+	+		+	+	+	+		+	+	+

Note. C. B. = C. Bean , B. B. = B. Benacerraf. J.B. = J. Bensinger, B.J.B. = B.J. Bikofsky, C.C. = C. Corduan , R. D. = R. Davis, G.D. = G. Deem, C. D. = C Drake, J.J. = J. Jones. R. K. = R. Knapp, A S. = A. Simons, H.S. = H. Smart. + indicates presence of problem.

achievement in reading and his or her mental ability, all other things
. . . being equal" (Chall & Peterson, 1986, p. 289). These dyslexics'
problems included a history of difficulty with letter identification,
word recognition, phonics, reading fluency, reading speed, spelling,
laterality, writing, fine motor control, memory, and learning a foreign
language. In addition, their profiles showed significant discrepancies
between verbal and performance test scores, a history of familial
dyslexia, and, in some cases, concommitant attention deficit or hyperactivity disorder. Individuals were considered "successful" if they
met three criteria: (a) supported self financially, (b) demonstrated
salient characteristics of Chall's Stage 5 reading ability as adults
(Chall, 1983; Fink, 1992), and (c) exhibited professional competence
recognized by peers in a chosen career.

Among adult dyslexics who eventually learn to read well, characteristics of dyslexia have been found to persist in adulthood (Lefly &
Pennington, 1991). Despite becoming highly skilled readers, each
dyslexic in the current study showed evidence of persistent adult
symptoms of dyslexia (i.e., difficulty with single word decoding of
unfamiliar words, slow reading, dysphonetic spelling, and letter and
word reversals).

Gilligan's Interview Methodology

Gilligan's clinical interview methodology, which entails open-ended
conversations to explore cognitive and affective dimensions of development (Attanucci, 1988) was used. In this methodology, the inter-
viewing researcher establishes a firm connection with the interviewee
and follows not only her/his own research agenda and prepared questions but also the agenda, needs, questions, linguistic patterns, and
cues of the interviewee. Eighteen specific questions guided the interviews, as shown in Table 2.

Each interview was audiotaped and transcribed in its entirety in
order to preserve descriptive detail and ensure accuracy. The in-depth
interviews took from 3 to 8 hours, and biographical data were collected
to verify interview information. When possible, interviews were conducted in the naturalistic setting of each person's workplace, where subjects recollected their reading history in a developmental framework,
school grade by school grade, content area by content area. An attempt
was made to select subjects from diverse professions. Since highly successful dyslexics in disciplines that require sophisticated Stage 5 reading ability are rare, sample size was limited by the unusual attributes
of the population.

Table 2

Learning interview questions used*

1. As a child having trouble learning to read, as a student later on, and as an adult dyslexic today, what special learning strategies have you used to help with reading, studying, and professional tasks? I'm very interested in finding out what learning strategies or tricks you developed that stand out for you as having been particularly useful.

2. I'd like you to tell me about your struggles, obstacles you faced, and learning strategies that worked for you which you feel led to your present success.

3. What is your earliest memory of learning differently from other children?

4. Tell me about preschool (if you attended), kindergarten, and elementary school.

5. What tasks were particularly difficult for you in elementary school, and what specific strategies did you use to master skills such as reading? Writing? Spelling? Learning multiplication tables? Others?

6. How did your early teachers respond to your learning difficulties?

7. Tell me about your family. How did your parents respond to your learning problems?

8. When you were in elementary school, how did other children react to your learning problems?

9. Tell me about your struggles during adolescence. What schools did you attend? Do any courses stand out as having been particularly troublesome?

10. What specific learning strategies did you use to get through English class, social studies, math, science, foreign language?

11. What special services, if any, did you receive during school?

12. What were your experiences with IQ tests and achievement tests? With Scholastic Aptitude Tests and Graduate Record Exams?

13. Tell me about your relationships with your parents, teachers, and other students during middle school and high school. How did you feel about yourself during this period?

14. Were there people who were particularly helpful to you? Tell me about them.

15. Tell me how you decided to go to college. Why did you decide to go? Was it expected in your family? How did you choose your college? What was the application process like for you? Did teachers encourage you or discourage you? Tell me about it.

16. What were your experiences getting through all the required (and other) courses in college? What specific learning strategies did you use during college?

17. Why did you decide to go to graduate school? How did you get through the required courses? Were there particular courses or exams that stand out as having been stumbling blocks? How did you get through them?

18. What particular strategies do you use in your work as a professional today?

*Developed by author.

In addition to the criteria for "successful dyslexic" discussed earlier, five additional criteria were used for sample selection: field of professional expertise, age, socioeconomic level, gender, and level of educational and professional achievement.

The sample included a Nobel laureate, a member of the National Academy of Sciences, and other outstanding professionals (see Table 3).

These dyslexics were highly successful, with expertise in diverse fields that required high levels and huge amounts of reading: immunology, biochemistry, law, gynecology, physics, neurology, theatre set design, graphic arts, special education, and business.

Gilger (1992) has found that accuracy of retrospective self-report data on learning disabled individuals is adequately reliable and, moreover,

Table 3

Professionally successful dyslexics interviewed

Professions	Dyslexics
Attorney	Amy Simons, Assistant State Attorney, Dade County, Miami, FL.
Biochemist	Ronald Davis, National Academy of Sciences member; professor, Stanford University Medical School, Palo Alto, CA.
Business	Jo Jones, Chief Executive Officer, Jones Company, Salem, MA.
	Hilary Smart, President, Aiskem-Mass., Weston, MA.
Graphic artist	George Deem, adjunct professor, University of Pennsylvania, Philadelphia, PA; freelance artist, New York City.
Gynecologist	Robert Knapp, chair, Department of Gynecology, Harvard Medical School, Boston, MA.
Immunologist	Baruj Benacerraf, Nobel laureate; chair, Department of Comparative Pathology, Harvard Medical School, Boston, MA.
Neurologist	Charles Bean, clinical associate professor, Jefferson Hospital, Philadelphia, PA; private practice, Wilmington, DE.
Physicist	James Bensinger, professor, Brandeis University, Waltham, MA.
Special educators	Charles Drake, founder/director, Landmark School, Prides Crossing, MA.
	Barbara J. Bikofsky, reading specialist, Walker School, Needham, MA.
Theatre set designer	Cap Ellen Corduan, technical set director, Walnut Hill School of Performing Arts, Natick, MA.

is higher for normal or high-achieving subjects in the middle-age range. Therefore, subjects were selected who exceeded Gerber and Reiff's definition of "high success" by being in the top echelons of their fields of expertise (1991, p. 34). They ranged in age from 27 to 70 years, with most from 35 to 45 years old. Individuals younger than 27 were not included, using the rationale that high levels of professional success are rarely achieved during one's 20s.

All were white, middle-class U.S. citizens currently living in California, Massachusetts, New York, Delaware, and Florida. They were reared in working-class or middle-class families and as adults earned salaries that placed them in high socioeconomic categories.

Nine dyslexic men and 3 dyslexic women were interviewed in order to reflect the gender imbalance in the reported dyslexic population (about 3 or 4:1 for males:females). Given the outstanding levels of these people's accomplishments, it would have been impossible to conceal the identity of several of them; therefore, they granted permission to use their real names.

All of these dyslexic women and men were college graduates, most from Ivy League (top-rated) institutions. Ten of the 12 had earned graduate degrees, including seven doctorates. The sample included three MDs, two PhDs, one EdD, one JD, two MFAs, one MEd, and two BAs. Although they struggled with learning to read as children, 7 have authored textbooks and scholarly articles and contributed to the canon of new knowledge in their fields. All 12 use higher level reading and writing daily in their current careers. Despite histories of severe dyslexia, all are skilled readers today.

Did these dyslexics compensate effectively because they were more "intelligent" than other dyslexics? Intelligence may constrain or abet an individual's ability to reach Stage 5 reading, and it has long been assumed on theoretical grounds that intelligence places a limit on language ability, which in turn affects reading ability (Carroll, 1977). Since intelligence, language ability, and reading ability are highly correlated, it is difficult to isolate the effects of one ability from that of the others" (Harris & Sipay, 1990, p. 274). Nevertheless Lefly and Pennington (1991) attempted to do just that: to isolate the effects of intelligence and reading ability. They controlled for IQ in their study of "compensated dyslexics" (adult dyslexics who eventually learned to read well), and concluded that IQ did *not* account for differences in levels of compensation among the adult dyslexics studied.

The in-depth interviews reported here, however, reveal other factors that might be involved in compensation.

Avid Readers

I expected to discover extraordinary bypass and compensation strategies. Presumably, continual frustration with basic skills would lead dyslexics to avoid reading. To my surprise, l found that these dyslexics were avid readers. Although they had persistent troubles with basic, lower level skills (letter and word recognition and phonics), they rarely circumvented reading. On the contrary, they sought out books; they did *not* bypass reading in order to learn. As their own voices revealed, each did a lot of reading, sometimes beginning at an early age.

> Ronald Davis (biochemist)
> You'd start reading a lot. Because you like it. [Grade 3 and up]

> Robert Knapp (gynecologist):
> I went to the library and read a lot on my own. [Grade 2 and up]

Even when their basic skills were rudimentary, each of these dyslexics found reading pleasurable, albeit slow going. Nobel laureate Baruj Benacerraf (immunologist) attests to unmistakable pleasure and joy:

> I managed to read with pleasure, even though it took me longer. always enjoyed reading even though it was tedious. . . . I read a lot! Always! I never avoided reading. Never! Never! Reading sufficiently is one of my greatest pleasures! [Grade 2 and up]

Several of these dyslexics felt profoundly alienated from school, yet they read a lot. Physicist James Bensinger, for example, was very depressed as a child because school was a painful place for him, so he shut off school and read.

> So I did a lot of reading. When I finally learned how to read, I read a lot, I just shut off school, . . . but I did a lot of reading, actually. [Grade 5 and up]

As a child, Bensinger often felt sad and discouraged about school because he was failing; frequently he neglected his homework but did his personal reading instead. Reading apparently was a respite for him, an escape from the cruel, humiliating world of school.

Fluency Developed Later

Hampered by persistent, severe difficulties identifying letters of the alphabet and their corresponding sounds, these dyslexics took significantly longer than nondyslexic peers to develop basic word recognition and fluency. There was a consistent pattern of delay in their development. On average, they developed basic fluency, or smoothness in reading connected text, 3 to 4 years later than peers. "Normal" (nondyslexic) children usually become fluent at a basic level between ages 7 and 8 (Chall, 1983). However, 11 of these 12 dyslexics reported that they "finally learned to read" between the ages of 10 and 12.

There was only one exception: Barbara Bikofsky (special educator), who developed basic fluency only in the 12th grade:

> Senior year I finally did better and learned to read. And write. I took English with the hardest teacher . . . and he taught me how.

These dyslexics' own words reflect the importance of basic fluency as a benchmark in their lives.

> Amy Simons (attorney):
> I didn't learn to read, to read very effectively, until I was in fifth grade.

> Bensinger (physicist):
> In fifth grade, I finally learned to read. We finally found a tutor, Mrs. King, who finally taught me how to read . . . it was a big change!

> Benacceraf (immunologist):
> My problems were earlier. . . . And from about 11 or 12, I surmounted it; I surmounted my reading problem.

Some Weak Basic Skills

Despite the fact that they eventually developed basic fluency, all 12 dyslexics grappled with profound problems with letter identification, word recognition, and sound analysis. In all cases, these basic, lower level skills remained weak through childhood and adolescence. Furthermore, 3 of these dyslexics continue as adults to have serious difficulty with the most basic orthographic skill, namely, letter identification. What remains especially problematic for them are look-alike letters, such as *b, d, p, q, m,* and *n,* which are similar except for differences in orientation and direction of letter parts. For example, renowned New York City graphic artist George Deem, who reads complex authors such as Proust, nevertheless continues to have difficulty distinguishing *b* from *d* in new, unfamiliar words.

> Yes, I am still involved with *b* and *d* If there is a word that I don't know, and it has a *b* or a *d* . . . that gets me very mixed up because I have to look at another word to remember that the *d* goes that way and the *b* goes this way.

Others also continue to struggle with severe letter identification problems.

> Cap Ellen Corduan (theatre set designer)
> I'll write *plymood* for *plywood* on the blackboard. . . . I can't even tell the difference (between *m* and *w*). So my students point it out to me, and they kid me.

> Davis (biochemist):
> I still print today. . . . I print everything in capitals to help with letters like *b* and *d*.

Not only did these adults show profound deficits in letter identification, but they also were constrained in basic phonological skills, which severely limited their ability to sound out new, unfamiliar words. Furthermore, as adults they continue to have serious difficulties translating letters into their corresponding sounds. They tend to use phonics, but not very effectively. For example, Charles Bean (neurologist) attempts to sound out new words through phonological analysis; the problem is that he constructs sounds that are unlike "everybody else's."

> Phonics doesn't always work. Even though I'll read phonetically, my phonetic sounds don't always fit with everybody else's.

Bean's personal use of phonics is unreliable. Cognizant of his inaccuracies, he keeps the role of phonics in proper perspective, as his self-analysis suggests.

> I can't break it down phonetically and make sense. . . . Yet it's not important to me; it's the idea that's important to me and not so much the sound. . . .

Bean keeps in mind the ultimate goal of reading: to make sense from print. He relegates phonics to a secondary position because he believes that thinking about the idea is what matters most.

How were these dyslexics able to think about ideas and make sense from print when their basic, lower level reading skills remained so weak? How did they construct meaning (a higher level skill) despite continuing problems with lower level skills such as letter identification, word recognition, and phonics?

Context and Familiar Schema

The key is that they relied on context to a great extent. Each dyslexic independently reported a heavy reliance on context for making meaning. They used context as children and continue as adults to rely heavily on context, both for simple word recognition and for complex meaning making.

Bikofsky (special educator):
I used context a lot to guess at new words.

Benacerraf (immunologist):
Even today, when I can't figure out a word, I guess from the context. Yes, I guess what makes sense.

Corduan (theatre set designer):
I get the gist of the story and. . . I have it pretty much right!

That Corduan reports having it "pretty much right" suggests that she uses metacognitive checking to monitor her understanding and accuracy. In her own estimation, she is usually correct. That is, her reading is usually accurate and reliable, so she can count on being right most of the time. This assessment fits with results from research by Lefley and Pennington (1991), who found that compensated adult dyslexics read unfamiliar words *nearly as accurately* as nondyslexics. But how did these dyslexics' reading become accurate? How did they manage to guess right?

Dyslexics in this study were marginal decoders for whom contextual facilitation of meaning was a key strategy, both during childhood and adulthood. They all relied heavily on context clues, which were more reliable in a familiar schema.

According to schema theory (Rumelhart, 1980), under certain conditions, context-reliant reading is effective and accurate, especially when the reader possesses background knowledge and has a schema for the material. Regardless of particular schema (e.g., narrative structure, historical writing, scientific paper), prior knowledge is a powerful advantage in facilitating reading accuracy and comprehension.

Each schema is a prototype of knowledge and contains its own component schemata (Rumelhart, 1980). A narrative text (a schema) has its own prototypical story grammar (schemata). In Western literary tradition, these include characters, plots, subplots, problems or conflicts, dénouement, and conflict resolution. Prior familiarity with these narrative schemata enables a person to read a new narrative with increasing comprehension and ease at higher and higher levels. The reason is that familiarity with narrative forms enables prediction and fulfillment of expectations. Each additional reading of a new narrative provides reinforcement of skill in using and applying narrative patterns. Consequently, the more narratives a person reads, the more capable the person becomes of reading and understanding future narratives.

Likewise, a person immersed in reading about science develops familiarity with the highly specialized vocabulary as well as the component schemata of a scientific paper. These include (a) introduction (theoretical framework and research questions), (b) methods section (sampling techniques and analytical approaches), (c) results section (data and conclusions), and (d) discussion section (interpretations and implications of the research). A reader's familiarity with these schemata helps to improve ease and accuracy of comprehension while reading scientific material.

Passionate Interests

These dyslexics' stories revealed a common theme: In childhood, each had a passionate personal interest, a burning desire to know more about a discipline that required reading. Spurred by this passionate interest, all read voraciously, seeking and reading everything they could get their hands on about a single intriguing topic. This intense reading about a favorite subject enhanced their depth of background knowledge and, at the same time, enabled them to gain practice, which fostered fluency and increasingly sophisticated reading skills. By reading in depth about a single domain of knowledge, each became a virtual "little expert" about a subject. Schemata of expertise varied from individual to individual. In addition, there was variation in the age when each dyslexic began focused reading in a high interest schema.

Table 4 shows each person's unique schema and age at which focused schematic reading began.

Table 4

Schema/interest area and age as focus began

Dyslexic	Schema area	Age
B.B.	Biography	7
R.D.	Science	8
R.K.	History	7
J.B.	Physics	10
A.S.	Math	10
C.D.	Religion	11
C.C.	History	11
C.B.	Poetry	12
H.S.	Business	12
B.J.B.	Novels	17
J.J.	Business	22
G.D.	Novels	22

Early reading interests eventually developed into high-powered careers for some of these dyslexics. For others, early reading interests developed into stimulating lifelong hobbies. For example, Corduan (theatre set designer) read avidly about U.S. Civil War history.

> I loved history. Not so much European history; I could care less about that. But the history of the United States. I'm a Civil War buff. Mainly 'cause I like Lincoln. So through reading about Lincoln, I've learned other things.

Corduan's focused reading within a discipline of high interest provided the drill and practice that enhanced her fluency. By reading about a narrow topic, she became familiar with its themes, scripts, and vocabulary and could use context effectively to guess at new words and develop her understanding of historical concepts.

Like Corduan, Knapp (gynecologist) also read avidly about Civil War history.

> I went to the library and read a lot on my own . . . I read lots of history books. I always read history books. Beginning in grade school! And even today, I'm a Civil War buff. I love to read about the Civil War. I own all of Carl Sandburg's *Abraham Lincoln*, all six volumes [pointing]. And I've read all six volumes! I've also read this book [pointing again], which I've read cover to cover, *Battles and Leaders of the Civil War*.

For Nobel laureate Benacerraf (immunologist), early reading interests centered mainly on biographies, beginning in elementary school.

> I read a lot, especially about the lives of famous scientists. I had a special dictionary with pictures, and it told about the lives of famous people. Famous scientists and artists, too. I spent many, many hours reading this book as a child.

Davis (biochemist) had an enormous appetite for advanced science books. His hunger for scientific reading began when he was 7 years old and extended through high school, college, graduate school, and beyond. Davis's scientific reading was driven by his intense curiosity to find out how the physical world works.

> You read science for—how things are put together. . . . My interest in chemistry just came from—it started with my interest in airplanes in grade school . . . that quickly converted to propellant systems in seventh and eighth grades. . . . I became fascinated with nitrogen chemistry. So the way to understand that was to start reading chemistry books. So I got organic chemistry textbooks.

At every age and stage of development, Davis read about science. Spurred by his craving for scientific information, he became expert in scientific vocabulary, concepts, and typical text structures despite the fact that he continued to struggle with word recognition and phonics. His prior knowledge from reading about chemistry enabled him to evoke sophisticated chemical schemata that supported his ability to read complex, highly abstract chemistry books. His motivation sprang from his intense desire to know more about the physical world.

For each of these dyslexics, the specificity of interest-driven reading was extremely important. Through focused reading in highly specialized disciplines, they developed deep background knowledge and became conversant with domain-specific vocabulary, concepts, themes, questions, and typical text structures. Schema familiarity provided the scaffold that supported their development of optimal skills.

Salient Characteristics of Stage 5 Reading

Ultimately, these dyslexics developed most of the salient characteristics of Chall's (1983) Stage 5, construction and reconstruction, the highest level of reading development. Stage 5 is characterized by integration of knowledge, synthesis, and the creation of new knowledge. It entails reading materials that are "highly difficult, specialized, technical, and abstract" (p. 100). According to Chall, the sophisticated Stage 5 reader uses reading for his or her own professional and personal purposes; "reading serves to integrate one's own knowledge with that of others, to synthesize it and to create new knowledge. It is rapid and efficient" (p. 87).

As adults, dyslexics in this study demonstrated all of the salient characteristics of Stage 5 except for rapid speed and efficiency, which they lacked. All of them read materials that are highly difficult, specialized, technical, and abstract. Furthermore, most of them write highly creative, complex materials that are technical, specialized, and abstract. They

Table 5

Types of scholarly writing done

Dyslexic	Writing types
B.B. (immunology)	Books, grant proposals, journal articles
R.D. (biochemistry)	Books, grant proposals, journal articles
R.K. (gynecology)	Books, grant proposals, journal articles
C.B. (neurology)	Book, journal articles
G.D. (art)	Book, journal articles
A.S. (law)	Journal articles
J.B. (physics)	Journal articles, grant proposals
B.J.B. (education)	Master's thesis
C.D. (education)	Doctoral dissertation

integrate and synthesize knowledge from other experts with their own knowledge, and they create and contribute new knowledge in their fields of expertise. These dyslexics' impressive scholarly publications and other creative writings provide evidence of their creation of new knowledge, a hallmark of Stage 5. Table 5 illustrates the types of scholarly writing each dyslexic has contributed to her/his field.

Of the 12 dyslexics, 9 have written and published creative scholarly works. Moreover, the other 3 currently write on a daily basis in their professions. For example, Corduan (theatre set designer) writes homework assignments for her high school students, while Jones and Smart (businessmen) write numerous business memos, letters, and promotional materials.

Some of these dyslexics were prolific writers, publishing numerous seminal papers as well as textbooks in their disciplines. Davis (biochemist), for example, is first author of a textbook on bacterial genetics used widely in Europe and the United States. Knapp (gynecologist) wrote *Gynecologic Oncology*, a medical textbook about the diagnosis and treatment of cervical and ovarian cancers. Knapp's 1986 text has been used in medical schools across the United States. Nobel laureate Benacerraf (immunologist) has authored many books and ground-breaking papers.

Benacerraf, Davis, and Knapp all began their high-interest reading in the primary grades, specifically, Grades 2 and 3. Each has written several books, numerous grant proposals, and between 150 and 200 scholarly articles. Through their prolific scholarly writing, these dyslexic authors have clearly made a major impact on their fields.

The Rich Got Richer

In Stanovich's terms (1986), these dyslexics got richer, or better at reading, as a result of practice. They seem to have used the repetition in narrow, discipline-specific text to promote their skill development. The redundant text material itself may have provided the requisite drill and practice that enhanced their reading development at optimal levels. Furthermore, the high interest value of their reading materials seems to have increased the amount of reading they engaged in. The sheer volume of reading apparently provided greater practice of skills.

Instruction Implications

Constructivist researchers have suggested that different children construct reading in different ways by using alternative developmental pathways (Fischer et al., 1993). This notion is gaining acceptance as teachers increasingly show cognizance of complexity in reading development through use of multicomponent diagnostic reading tests devised with the assumption that a student may perform simultaneously at a high and low level on different aspects of reading (Salvia & Ysseldyke, 1988; Sattler, 1990).

What are the implications for instruction? In this study, the cumulative effect of practice spurred by intense personal interest and attention to one domain proved powerful. These learners, hampered by nagging and persistent deficiencies in basic skills, nevertheless effectively constructed meaning in a single high interest domain.

One overarching implication is clear: Teachers should provide captivating materials based on each student's strengths, prior knowledge, skills, and interests. Yet the dyslexia literature to date focuses largely on skills-based systematic phonics methods and bypass approaches. Despite recommendations in classic textbooks that encourage teachers to incorporate students' individual interests in the reading curriculum (Harris & Sipay, 1990; Roswell & Natchez, 1977), considerable literature on garden variety poor readers as well as dyslexics has tended to emphasize repeated skill drills and mastery of graphophonemic subskills and word recognition. However, the finding from this study, that high interest contextual reading was a major literacy strategy for successful dyslexics, emphasizes the need for teachers to incorporate other approaches and utilize students' individual interests in classroom instruction.

Conclusions drawn from this study are limited by the small sample size; clearly, further research is needed. However, it is noteworthy that, for these dyslexics, lower level skill mastery and speed were not prerequisites to higher level skill construction. These dyslexics did not master basic, lower level skills before moving on to higher level skills. On the contrary, they worked simultaneously on constructing both basic and higher level skills. Apparently, skill construction while learning to read does not always proceed forward and upward in a ladderlike, hierarchical sequence. Concurrently, these dyslexics read at both higher and lower cognitive levels and constructed meaning, developing literacy in their own ways; what drove them was a deep intrinsic motivation based on passionate personal interest.

As teachers, we need to consider diverse ways of learning and teaching. Children can learn through a variety of avenues, using a myriad of topics of special interest. As teachers, we need to consider the plethora of interests of the young people we teach. Too often teachers mistakenly assume that a child who has not mastered word recognition is not "ready" for higher level reading/thinking materials. Too often, educators give only lip service to the notions of individual differences and diversity.

Can the interest value of a difficult, challenging book sustain a child despite hurdles and frustrations with basic skills? Based on these dyslexics' stories, the answer is a resounding "yes." For these dyslexics, the power of personal interest was so compelling as to enable them to read extremely challenging materials well above expected readability levels. This finding fits well with Chall's (1983) notion that "a person may function at differing levels at any one time" (p. 84); Chall asserts that, particularly at the higher levels, a person may read at one stage in one area of knowledge, yet another stage in another area of knowledge (p. 83).

Davis (biochemist) exemplifies a dyslexic who functioned simultaneously at differing levels of reading. As a high school freshman he frequently read college and graduate-level technical science texts even though he continued to have difficulty distinguishing between the letters *b* and *d*, a lower level skill.

> I read quite a few college texts when I was a freshman in high school. I started off with a high school chemistry book; very quickly, then, I went to a college text. . . . Sputnik went up in 1957; I was a sophomore then but I knew it was going up 'cause I read all the journals, various aeronautic journals.

Davis's ability to comprehend sophisticated science texts surpassed his reading ability in other domains. When he applied to graduate school, Davis took the Graduate Record Exam in chemistry, which consists of considerable reading of connected text; it is not merely formulaic reading (Graduate Record Exam Chemistry Test, 1990). He scored in the highest (99.9th) percentile on the chemistry test. However, he scored in only the 16th percentile on the English test of the Graduate Record Exam. His cognitive level was extremely high in chemistry (and other sciences), but low in English, history, and subjects in the humanities.

Indeed, at every level of schooling Davis excelled in science, with straight As, yet consistently got low grades in English, history, and foreign languages (Cs, Ds, and Fs, respectively). Driven by piercing curiosity and interest, he transcended ongoing basic skill weaknesses in the realm of science, which he read with enjoyment, gusto, and deep comprehension.

Enjoyment "is not a hedonistic goal, but the energy that propels a person to higher levels of performance" (Csikszentmihalyi, 1991, p. 133). When a book is interesting and children truly enjoy what they are reading, they sometimes become wholly transported by the reading experience. In common parlance we call this "getting lost in a good book." The reader is so completely involved and transformed by the characters and plot of a novel, for example, as to lose awareness of all else around. The child may not even notice a parent's call to dinner despite the fact that the parent is standing in the same room.

Csikszentmihalyi (1991) calls this total immersion stemming from enjoyment while reading "a flow experience," the feeling of being carried away by a current. When a child's concentration while reading is based on enjoyment and interest this intense, the result is a loss of self-consciousness, which can be extremely liberating, both cognitively and emotionally. For a child who ordinarily has difficulty reading and consequently becomes anxious in most reading situations, such a flow experience while reading an interesting book can be extremely significant.

Capitalize on Students' Interests

When selecting books and magazines, teachers should consider the powerful role of enjoyment and tap each student's interests. One way to ascertain individual interests is by using a reading interest inventory, such as the one shown in Table 6. Reading interest inventories can be modified easily to fit each student's age and developmental stage.

Another way to assess interests is by conducting interviews and inquiring about favorite books and passionate hobbies (arts, sports, history, literature, or science). For students who have had little opportunity to read or develop hobbies, teachers can discover dormant interests by asking about favorite movies and television programs. Teachers can take cues about interesting reading materials directly from the media subject that each student finds compelling.

Table 6

A general reading interest inventory

1. What is the best book that was ever read to you?
2. What is the best book that you ever read yourself?
3. What are your favorite hobbies?
4. What after-school activities do you like best?
5. What are some of your favorite movies?
6. What television programs do you like the most?
7. What are your favorite television specials?
8. What school subjects do you find most interesting?
9. What pets, sports, or art activities do you like best?
10. If you could take a trip, where would you go?

Note Inventory adapted from Burns, Roe, & Ross. (1992).

Personal Interests and Whole Language

A reading curriculum driven by passionate personal interests fits well with the philosophy of whole language instruction. As Goodman (1989) explains, a cornerstone of the whole language philosophy is that "content can only be understood and seriously studied when learners are actively involved and interested in learning, are participating in deciding what will be learned, and are relating what they are learning to what they already know" (p. 114). Davis (biochemist), a severe dyslexic who authored books and over 100 articles, echoes Goodman's focus on learners' interests, involvement, background knowledge, and existing skills.

> I think it's very important to capitalize on what skills and interests you . . . [already] have. It may not be in the curriculum, but I think if you can capitalize on anything that you *can* do, that's really excellent!

Davis succeeded and learned to read well by capitalizing on his own interests and skills. I hope the results of this study will encourage teachers to help other students capitalize on *their* passionate interests.

References

Asher, L.P., & Markell, R.A. (1974). Sex differences in comprehension of high- and low-interest reading material. *Journal of Educational Psychology, 66*, 680–87.

Asher, S R. (1980). Topic interest and children's reading comprehension. In R. Spiro, B.C. Bruce, & W.F. Brewer. (Eds.), *Theoretical issues in reading comprehension* (pp. 525–34). Hillsdale, NJ: Erlbaum.

Attanucci, J. (1988). In whose terms: A new perspective on self, role, and relationship. In C. Gilligan, J.V. Ward, & I.M. Taylor, (Eds.), *Mapping the moral domain* (pp. 201–24). Cambridge, MA: Harvard University.

Berninger, V.W., & Abbott, R. D. (1994). Redefining learning disabilities: Moving beyond aptitude-achievement discrepancies to failure to respond to validated treatment protocols. In G.R. Lyon (Ed.), *Frames of reference for the assessment of learning disabilities: New views on measurement issues* (pp. 163–83). Baltimore, MD: Paul H. Brookes.

Burns, P.C. Roe, B.D., & Ross, E.P. (1992). *Teaching reading in today's elementary schools* (5th ed.). Boston: Houghton Mifflin.

Carroll, J.B. (1977). Developmental parameters in reading comprehension. In J.T.. Guthrie (Ed.), *Cognition, curriculum and comprehension* (pp. 1–15). Newark, DE: International Reading Association.

Chall, J.S. (1983). *Stages of reading development*. New York: McGraw-Hill.

Chall, J.S., & Peterson, R.W. (1986). The influence of neuroscience upon educational practice. In S.F. Friedman, K.A. Klivington, & R.W. Peterson (Eds.), *The brain, cognition, and education* (pp. 287–314). Orlando, FL: Academic Press.

Cox, A. R. (1983). Programming for teachers of dyslexics. *Annals of Dyslexia, 33*, 221–33.

Csikszentmihalyi, M. (1991). Literacy and intrinsic motivation. In S.R. Graubard (Ed.), *Literacy: An overview by 14 experts* (pp. 115–40). New York: Noonday Press.

DiSibio, R.A., & Savitz, F.R. (1982, October). *The elementary classroom teacher: A reading facilitator.* Paper presented at the annual meeting of the College Reading Association, Philadelphia, PA.

Fink, R.P. (1992). Successful dyslexics' alternative pathways for reading: A developmental study (Doctoral dissertation, Harvard Graduate School of Education, 1992). *Dissertation Abstracts International*, F4965.

Fischer, K.W., Knight, C.C., & Van Parys, M. (1993). Analyzing diversity in developmental pathways: Methods and concepts. In W. Edelstein & R. Case (Eds.), *Constructivist approaches to development: Contributions to human development* (pp. 33–56). Basel, Switzerland: S. Karger.

Gerber, P.J., & Reiff, H.B. (1991). *Speaking for themselves: Ethnographic interviews with adults with learning disabilities.* Ann Arbor, Ml: University of Michigan.

Gilger, J.W., (1992). Using self-report and parental-report survey data to assess past and present academic achievement in adults and children. *Journal of Applied Developmental Psychology.* 13(2), 235–56.

Gillingham, A., & Stillman, B. (1966). *Remedial training of children with specific disability in reading, spelling, and penmanship* (7th ed.). Cambridge, MA: Educators Publishing Service.

Goodman, Y. (1989). Roots of the whole language movement. *Elementary School Journal*, 90, 113–27.

Griesbach, G. (1993). *Dyslexia: Its history, etiology, and treatment.* (Report No. CS011300). West Bend, WI: ERIC Document Reproduction Service. (No. ED 358 409)

Harris, A.J., & Sipay, E. (1990). *How to increase reading ability: A guide to developmental and remedial methods* (9th ed.). New York: Longman.

Knight, J. (1986). The adult dyslexic in remediation: The ABCs and much more. *Churchill Forum*, 8, 1-4.

Lefly, D.L., & Pennington, B.F. (1991). Spelling errors and reading fluency in compensated adult dyslexics. *Annals of Dyslexia*, 41, 143–62.

Morris, G.H. (1983). Adapting a college preparatory curriculum for dyslexic adolescents: Confronting the problems of what to teach. *Annals of Dyslexia*, 33, 243–50.

National Assessment of Educational Progress. (1982, July). *Reading comprehension of American youth: Do they understand what they read?* Results from the 1979–80 *National Assessment of reading and literature* (Report No. 11-R-02). Denver, CO: Education Commission of the States.

Orton Dyslexia Society Research Committee. (1994). Operational definition of dyslexia. In C. Scruggs (Ed.), *Perspectives*, 20(5), 4.

Renninger, K.A. (1992). Individual interest and development: Implications for theory and practice. In K. Renninger, S. Hidi, & A. Krapp (Eds.), *The role of interest in learning and development* (pp. 361–95). Hillsdale, NJ: Erlbaum.

Roswell, F., & Natchez, G. (1977). *Reading disability: A human approach to evaluation and treatment of reading and writing difficulties*. New York: Basic Books.

Rumelhart, D.E. (1980). Schemata: The building blocks of cognition. In R. Spiro, B. Bruce, & W. Brewer (Eds.), *Theoretical issues in reading comprehension* (pp. 33–58). Hillsdale, NJ: Erlbaum.

Salvia, J., & Ysseldyke, J.E. (1988). *Assessment in special and remedial education* (4th ed.). Boston, MA Houghton Mifflin.

Sattler, J.M. (1990). *Assessment of children* (3rd ed.). San Diego, CA: Author.

Shaywitz, B.A., Fletcher, J.M., & Shaywitz, S.E. (1994). The conceptual framework for learning disabilities and attention deficit/hyperactivity disorder. *Canadian Journal of Special Education, 9*(3), 1–32.

Stanovich, K.E. (1986). Matthew effects in reading: Some consequences of individual differences in the acquisition of literacy. *Reading Research Quarterly, 21*, 360–406.

Stanovich, K.E. (1991). Discrepancy definitions of reading disability: Has intelligence led us astray? *Reading Research Quarterly, 26*, 7–29.

Vogel, S.A. (1987). Issues and concerns in college LD programming. In D.J. Johnson & J.W. Blalock (Eds.), *Adults with learning disabilities: Clinical studies* (pp. 239–75). Orlando, FL: Grune & Stratton.

14 The Case for Late Intervention: Once a Good Reader, Always a Good Reader

Stephen Krashen
University of Southern California

Jeff McQuillan
California State University, Fullerton

Krashen and McQuillan review much of the research demonstrating that children and adults *can* become good readers, even if they do not do so in their early elementary years. The solution? Late intervention focusing on massive free voluntary reading. The authors begin by discussing the case for free reading, and move on to explore evidence that there is no critical period for learning to read, examples of home-schooled children who became successful late readers, evidence from "recovered" dyslexics (see Fink, chapter 13), and Malcolm X as a specific, historical case. Krashen and McQuillan respond to five possible objections to late intervention focusing on massive free voluntary reading. In concluding, they observe that their arguments for late intervention are not arguments against early intervention, but rather evidence that "once a poor reader, always a poor reader" is not necessarily true. People can and do become good readers later, by reading a lot about whatever interests them; the repeated act of reading itself makes them good readers. Thus the title of this piece, "once a good reader, always a good reader."

The usual solutions proposed for the "literacy crisis" include a focus on "skills" and early intervention. Some early intervention programs have produced good results. There is, however, another option that has not yet been seriously considered, one that has considerable research support—late intervention focusing on massive free voluntary reading.

The Case for Free Reading

There is strong evidence that free voluntary reading is effective in developing literacy. Those who read more read better, write better, spell better, and develop better grammatical competence and larger vocabularies (Krashen, 1993). This conclusion holds for first- and second-language acquirers (see, e.g., Elley, 1991; Elley & Mangubhai, 1983). In addition, free reading is pleasant; it is, in fact, a positive addiction (Nell, 1993).

In arguing that free reading is an effective late intervention, we will present evidence showing that there is no "critical period" for learning to read; that, therefore, late intervention is possible; and that free reading has served as an effective late intervention in a number of cases. We will also treat possible objections to this approach.

There Is No Critical Period for Learning to Read

Elley (1992) studied reading ability in thirty-two countries and reported "some advantage for an earlier start, but it can be said that countries which begin instruction in reading at age seven have largely caught up with the five- and six-year-old starters in reading ability by age nine" (p. 37). Consider Table 1, which summarizes the test scores (for nine-year-olds) for four countries that begin reading at age seven.

It is very significant that all of these countries also rank among the highest in economic development and reported a plentiful supply of books in the home and school library, and reported that public libraries and bookstores were available locally. This suggests that a late start is not a problem when children have access to reading materials.

Table 1

Reading in Late-Starting Countries

Country	Age Begin Reading	Score	Rank Among 32 Countries		Books[b]
			Reading	Economic Development[a]	
Finland	7	569	1	5	135
Sweden	7	539	3	2	174
Norway	7	524	7	3	157
Iceland	7	518	8	4	118

Source: Elley (1994).

Note: Mean reading score for all 32 countries was 500.

[a] Indicates rank calculated from GNP, expenditures for education, life expectancy, and other variables.

[b] Indicates average number of books in the home.

Successful Late Readers: Home-Schooled Children

Learning to read late did not prevent many eminent men and women from eventual success. Einstein is reported to have learned to read at age nine, Rodin at age ten, and Woodrow Wilson at age eleven (Schulman, 1986). In addition to these famous cases, there are also several cases of children as old as eleven learning to read without any apparent harm to their eventual literacy development and educational success. These accounts are of home-schooled children who learned to read well after they would have been expected to read in a regular school setting, in one case five years after the equivalent of first grade and with little or no formal instruction.

Of course, this kind of evidence has limitations: Home schoolers are often required only to submit a portfolio-style assessment of their children's progress, and we do not have a precise picture of how much formal instruction took place. It is clear, however, that in some cases there was no formal instruction. Stein (1994) states that her son, K.S., enjoyed being read to but showed no great interest in reading. Having read Smith's *Reading Without Nonsense*, she was committed to allowing him to read when he felt ready. K.S. would identify "very basic stuff—a label here and there," but never read anything else. One day, Stein writes, they were working on a science project together, and K.S. began to read the directions by himself: "He proceeded to read to me, almost effortlessly, a 100-word paragraph which contained words like 'solenoid,' 'nonmagnetic,' 'rectangle,' 'lengthwise,' 'downward,' and 'workable'" (p. 24).

Sheffer (1987) cites the case of A.A., who was designated as having a Specific Learning Disability at the age of eight, halfway through the first grade. She was pulled out of school by her mother, who then "let her totally alone" and "never gave her an assignment or pressures" (p. 4). By the age of ten, she began to read books and comic books.

Mason (1993a) reports that her daughter, K.M., "could not/did not want to read" at the age of eight and a half. Having tried earlier to push her to learn math, and finding that the pressure made her "hate arithmetic," Mason decided not to intervene with her daughter on reading. Then it happened: around her ninth birthday, "she began to read and two months later she could read at the level of her literate friends. Then she extended her reading, and now (age 15) she reads the way very literate adults do" (p. 28).

Mason (1993b) also describes the case of her son, D.M. The summer D.M. was ten, Mason reports that he could read only a word or two. In the fall, he began "to read store signs and notices with a vengeance." Then at night, "sometime past midnight, he read his way through a fat Spiderman annual his older brother Luke gave him for his birthday last year." He also began reading the sports page of the local newspaper. One day, Mason took him to the local science museum, where he began to read aloud "long paragraphs of technical writing discussing 'atmospheric conditions' and 'helium gases in the stratosphere'" (p. 11).

Davies (cited in Sheffer, 1987) states that her son, K.D., also began reading at the age of ten. "From reading only a few words," Davies writes, K.D. "jumped into whole sentences, often containing fairly difficult words," and now reads mainly comic books at age twelve (p. 5).

H.K. (Kerman, 1993) was reading at a "bare Cat in the Hat level" at the age of ten and a half. Her mother reports:

"During the course of the next year, she did learn the basics about reading, although I shall never know how, since she refused instruction as much as always. We continued to read outloud to her, and she rarely read to herself. My main consolation was that she loved books and didn't think badly of herself. At the age of fourteen, she started to read Scott O'Dell's books. The first one took her two months to read. Two months later, she had read four or five of them. Within six months, she was reading full-length adult fantasy novels, almost entirely feminist by such authors as Mercedes Lackey. She reads voraciously now at the age of 16" (p. 27).

Finally, there is the case of W.M. (Mott, 1993), who at eleven and a half, still did not read despite "sit down lessons with phonics and slogging through books word by word" (p. 11). When his mother decided to take "all hands off his learning, he taught himself when he was ready." She reports that at the age of thirteen and a half, he reads at a ninth-grade level.

These cases have several features in common. As noted above, little or no formal instruction was required, even for a child diagnosed as "learning disabled." Second, no pressure was put on the child by his or her parents. Third, all of the children made rapid progress once they began to read of their own volition. Finally, all had the advantage of having access to a great deal of reading material.

Recovered Dyslexics

Fink (1995–96) studied twelve dyslexics who had become "skilled readers" and were very successful. One was a Nobel laureate, and the sample included three M.D.'s, two Ph.D.'s, one Ed.D., one J.D., two M.F.A.'s, one M.Ed., and two B.A.'s. Nine of the twelve have published creative scholarly works. (This does not, of course, imply that all former dyslexics achieve success; Fink deliberately selected highly successful subjects.) All twelve had been raised in working-class or middle-class families. All had developed basic literacy three to four years later than their peers; eleven of the twelve, in fact, reported that they "finally learned to read" between the ages of ten and twelve (p. 273). The one exception did not learn to read until the twelfth grade.

All of these individuals were "avid readers," reported Fink. "Although they had persistent troubles with basic, lower-level skills (letter and word recognition and phonics), they rarely circumvented reading. On the contrary, they sought out books . . . " (p. 272). According to Fink, their stories "revealed a common theme: in childhood, each had a passionate personal interest, a burning desire to know more about a discipline that required reading. Spurred by this passionate interest, all read voraciously, seeking and reading everything they could get their hands on about a single intriguing topic." This "high interest contextual reading" (p. 277) may have been the reason for their literacy progress and success.

Malcolm X

The case of Malcolm X confirms that reading in areas of interest can cause profound literacy development well beyond elementary-school age. As he describes in his autobiography, Malcolm X had early success in school and was president of his seventh-grade class. His life on the streets, however, "erased everything I'd learned in school" (El-Shabbazz, 1964, p. 154). In prison, in his early twenties, he describes his literacy level as very low. The change came in prison: "Many who hear me today somewhere in person, or on television, or those who read something I've said, will think I went to school far beyond the eighth grade. This impression is due entirely to my prison studies" (p. 171).

These prison studies consisted largely of reading: "In every free moment I had, if I was not reading in the library, I was reading on my bunk. You couldn't have gotten me out of books with a wedge . . . " (p. 173).

Malcolm X specifically gives reading the credit: "Not long ago, an English writer telephoned me from London, asking questions. One was, 'What's your alma mater?' I told him, 'Books'" (p. 179).

Objections

There are five possible objections to this simple solution: (1) poor readers simply do not read well enough to read on their own; (2) the gap between good readers and poor readers is too large to make up with free reading—early intervention is thus the only way; (3) poor readers don't like to read; (4) if readers read what they want to read, they will read only junk; (5) as a practical matter, poor readers often do not have access to a great deal of reading material.

Can Poor Readers Read on Their Own?

Juel (1994), in a study of poor and good readers among "lower middle class" students in Austin, Texas, notes that poor readers improve, but feels that their attainments come "too late" (pp. 125–6). This conclusion is based on the assumption that the basal reader is the only path for improvement. If this is true, poor readers are indeed out of luck.

Inspection of Table 2 (from Juel, 1988) reveals that the poor readers in her sample read at the grade 2.6 level by grade 3 and the grade 3.5 level by grade 4. Thus, by grade 3, the poor readers could read well enough to be able to read many interesting texts, such as the Sweet Valley Kids series, written at the second-grade level (see Cho and Krashen, 1994, 1995a, 1995b, for evidence that this series is effective even with adult second-language acquirers), and many comic books (Casper and Archie are written at the second-grade level). At the time of this writing, the most popular author of books for children is R.L. Stine. His Goosebumps series is considered suitable for children ages nine to twelve.[1]

Foorman, Francis, Shaywitz, Shaywitz, and Fletcher (1997), and Francis, Shaywitz, Stuebing, Shaywitz, and Fletcher (1996) present similar findings: Poor readers stayed well behind good readers on tests of reading comprehension between ages eight and fourteen, but the poor readers continued to improve until age twelve, when curves for both groups appeared to begin to flatten, with a plateau reached at around age fifteen (a higher plateau for the good readers). As Francis et al. note, however, their results do not suggest that reading ability cannot be improved after a given age (p. 15), and they reported a great deal of variability in the age of plateau. What is lacking from these reports is whether any of the poor readers ever had a chance to get involved in a great deal of truly interesting, comprehensible reading. Indeed, this possibility is not even suggested as an option.

Table 2

Reading Comprehension in Grades 1 and 4

RC (ITBS)[a]	Poor Readers[b]	Good Readers[c]
Grade 1	K6	2.4
Grade 2	1.7	3.8
Grade 3	2.6	4.8
Grade 4	3.5	5.9

Source: Juel, 1988.

[a] Denotes Reading Comprehension (Iowa Test of Basic Skills).
[b] Includes readers in the bottom quartile, n = 29, 24 in grade 4.
[c] Includes average or good readers, n = 86, 30 in grade 4.

Instead, the usual prescription is early intervention with an emphasis on phonemic awareness.

Can Poor Readers Make Up the Gap?

Juel (1988, 1994) calculated that by grade 4 good readers had read 178,000 words in school (basal), while poor readers had read only 80,000 words. Juel also reported that good readers read more at home. Let us assume that by grade 4 good readers have read about a million words more than poor readers have. It is not difficult to make up this gap: Comic books contain about 2,000 words each; fifty comics thus contain about 100,000 words, about 10 percent of the gap. One Sweet Valley Kids novel contains about 7,000 words; fourteen of them contain 100,000, another 10 percent of the gap. Once these texts are comprehensible, a few "lost weekends" can make up a good part of the gap. Note that reading one comic per day would add about 500,000 words of reading in a year.

Even if the poor reader waited longer, and the gap became as large as ten million words, it could be made up. Progress accelerates once readers can read novel-length works with enjoyment, such as Stephen King's books that probably run over 150,000 words. Anderson, Wilson, and Fielding (1988) reported that some fifth graders read over ten million words per year, just as many readers of this paper did (and still do).

Reluctant Readers

Juel (1988) reported that the poor readers in her sample disliked reading. There is a simple, powerful way of overcoming dislike of reading—providing children with extremely interesting texts. This approach is supported by case histories of reluctant readers who became enthusiastic readers by reading comic books.

Haugaard (1973) relates that her boys were extremely reluctant readers, three boys "who, one after the other, were notoriously unmotivated to read and had to be urged, coaxed, cajoled, threatened and drilled in order to stay in the super slow group in reading" (p. 84). But when her oldest son discovered comic books, things changed:

"He devoured what seemed to be tons of the things. . . . The motivation these comics provided was absolutely phenomenal and a little bit frightening. My son would snatch up a new one and, with feverish and ravenous eyes, start gobbling it wherever he was—in the car on the way home from the market, in the middle of the yard, walking down the street, at the dinner table. All his senses seemed to shut down and he became a simple visual pipeline" (p. 85).

Comics, in this case, were a conduit to other reading: Haugaard's eldest son gave his comics away to one of his younger brothers and went on to science fiction and books on electronics.

Sustained silent reading (SSR) studies confirm that reading itself is a wonderful motivator. Those who participate in SSR read more on their own than those who do not (Greaney & Clarke, 1973; Pfau, 1967; Pilgreen & Krashen, 1993), and McQuillan (1996) also found that free reading in school had long-term effects on adult bilinguals. Greaney and Clarke's study is especially interesting: Sixth-grade boys who participated in an in-school free reading program for eight and one-half months not only did more leisure reading while they were in the program but also were reading more than comparison students six years later.

Reading aloud can interest even the most hard-core reluctant reader. Trelease (1985) tells the following story:

> Assigned at mid-year to teach a sixth-grade class of remedial students, Mrs. (Ann) Hallahan shocked her new students by reading to them on her first day of class. The book was *Where the Red Fern Grows.*
>
> A hardened, street-wise, proud group (mostly boys), they were insulted when she began reading to them. "How come you're reading to us? You think we're babies or something?" they wanted to know. After explaining that she didn't think anything of the kind but only wanted to share a favorite story with them, she continued reading *Where the Red Fern Grows.* Each day she opened the class with the next portion of the story and each day she was greeted with groans. "Not again today! How come nobody else ever made us listen like this?"
>
> Mrs. Hallahan admitted to me later, "I almost lost heart." But she persevered, and after a few weeks (the book contained 212 pages), the tone of the class's morning remarks began to change. "You're going to read to us today, aren't you?" Or "Don't forget the book, Mrs. Hallahan."
>
> "I knew we had a winner," she confessed, "when on Friday, just when we were nearing the end of the book, one of the slowest boys in the class went home after school, got a library card, took out *Where the Red Fern Grows,* finished it himself, and came to school on Monday and told everyone how it ended" (p. 9).

Fat Kids Who Don't Like to Read: What about Incentives?[2]

"Asked about the likely results of Pizza Hut's popular food-for-reading program, educational psychologist John Nichols replied, only half in jest, that it would probably produce 'a lot of fat kids who don't like to read'" (Kohn, 1993, p. 73).

Incentives, such as pizza and other prizes, are widely used to encourage reading in schools. Rohrbeck, Hightower, and Work (1991, cited in Kohn, 1993) report that 81 percent of the elementary school teachers they surveyed use incentives to improve reading. Research on rewarding reading, however, does not provide convincing support for this practice.

Adler (1989) reported no difference in gains in reading between sixth graders who received pizza certificates for each 250 pages read and a comparison group. Niemeyer (1988) showed slight losses in reading achievement for both experimental and control groups in an incentive program for third and fifth graders. Prizes were given based on the number of pages read. Robbins and Thompson (1989) found no significant gains for first, second, and third graders reading over the summer vacation; students received points for small prizes for each book they read. No control group was used. In Robbins and Thompson (1991), both experimental and comparison students (grades 1–6) gained, but there was no difference between the rewarded and nonrewarded students. Scores for rewarded fifth graders actually declined, even though most of the children in the rewarded group rated themselves as "good readers" and were already regular pleasure readers. Carver and Liebert (1995) found that after a six-week, in-library program where incentives were used generously to motivate students to read (sixty Pizza Hut pizzas, tacos, ice cream, and over three hundred fast food coupons for only forty-two students!), students made no gains in reading. (Students had, however, a very limited range of reading material available; their failure to gain may not have been because of the incentives.)[3]

Several studies appear to show that incentives work. In several cases, however, no comparison group was used, and students in the rewarded group engaged in activities known to promote literacy, such as sustained silent reading and hearing stories (Accelerated Learning Systems, 1993; Christmas, 1993; Potter, 1994; Voorhess, 1993). Peak and Dewalt (1994) used a comparison group, but the comparisons had traditional reading instruction, which has been a steady loser when compared to programs that include or focus on free voluntary reading (Krashen, 1993). In Harrop and McCann (1983), the advantage of the rewarded group was very small, and there were methodological problems: Harrop and McCann performed t-tests on post-test scores rather than comparing gain scores or using analysis of covariance (there were substantial differences between the groups on the pretest). In addition, the same teacher taught both sections, which raises the possibility that the comparison students knew about the incentives the experimental group received, possibly leading to a demoralizing effect.

In Griffith, Deloach, and LaBarba (1984), the entire treatment and measurement period was less than twenty minutes. The researchers had three treatment groups: those promised a reward by someone familiar to the student (teacher), those promised a reward by an unfamiliar person (investigator), and a group promised no rewards. After being asked to read a passage from a self-selected book and to give their opinion of it, the students were then left alone for ten minutes at a table with the book, a crossword puzzle, and another game. Those rewarded by the familiar figure spent significantly less time reading the book on their own than the no-reward group. Those rewarded by an unfamiliar person, on the other hand, spent more time reading than the no-reward students. In this rare demonstration of positive effects of rewards, the best we can conclude is that incentives might work with an unfamiliar rewarder, a situation which is of course unlike that of either school or family and difficult to sustain in any setting.

Thus, none of the studies on incentives show any clearly positive effect on reading that can be attributed solely to the use of rewards. There is, in fact, reason to suspect that the use of rewards can backfire. As Kohn (1993) notes, "Consider the popular program that offers free pizza to children for reading a certain number of books. If you were a participant in this program, what sort of books would you be likely to select? Probably short, simple ones . . ." (p. 65).

Will They Read Only Junk?

It is sometimes asserted that "if children are left to 'do their own thing,' there is no guarantee that they will push themselves ahead to progress as readers and writers" (Stahl, McKenna & Pagnucco, 1994, p. 182). Free reading, however, is not always easy reading. Several studies show that the books children select on their own are more difficult than the reading material assigned by teachers (Bader, Veatch, & Eldridge, 1987; Southgate, Arnold, & Johnson, 1981). In addition, if what teachers consider "good" reading is more challenging reading, several studies show that "voluminous reading actually fosters the tendency to do better reading" (Schoonover, 1938, p. 117). In Schoonover's study, most of the reading done by high school students who had participated in a six-year free reading program involved books that experts had classified as "good reading."

As readers mature, they gradually expand their reading interests. LaBrant (1937), in a study of reading interests of high school students, concluded that "the theory that in a free or extensive reading program designed to utilize interest and to serve individual needs there will be fruitless reading of light fiction gains no evidence from this study" (p. 34). In addition, several studies have found a tendency for older teenagers to prefer more nonfiction than younger teenagers, which also suggests that reading interests expand as students mature (Carter & Abrahamson, 1994).

Recent confirmation that "light reading" does not exclude other reading but in fact seems to encourage it comes from Ujiie and Krashen (1996): Boys who were heavy comic book readers in grade 7 were more likely to enjoy reading in general, to read more, and to read more books than boys who read fewer comic books or none at all.

The Access Problem

The major problem facing the poor reader is the lack of access to books and other interesting reading material. There is consistent evidence that children read more when there is more available for them to read (Morrow, 1982; Morrow & Weinstein, 1982), and there is also evidence that poor readers tend to live in print-deprived environments (Constantino, 1995). Consistent with this research are current studies showing a positive relationship between the quality of school libraries and reading achievement (Elley, 1992; Krashen, 1995; Lance, Welborn, & Hamilton-Pennell, 1993; McQuillan, 1996b). The solution is obvious—school libraries that are stocked with many interesting books and magazines to read, that are open and available to students, and that are inviting, comfortable places to sit and read (Trelease & Krashen, 1996).

Conclusion

The kind of late intervention suggested here is the simplest kind of intervention—providing children with lots of good reading material, and the time and place to read.

Our arguments for late intervention are not arguments against early intervention. We are, however, suggesting that early intervention is not the only possibility. (In fact, it is not a possibility at all for many children.) Those who insist that early intervention is the only way assert that once a child is a poor reader, he or she will always be a poor reader. We do not agree with this pessimistic view. Once a child gets interested in reading, and reading material is available, that child can "catch up" easily and it can happen anytime. In other words, "once a good reader, always a good reader." [4]

Notes

1. According to at least one reviewer (Jones, 1993), the Goosebumps series is of acceptable quality: "none of (Goosebumps) will ever make anyone's Best Books list for their literary quality. Yet, they are widely read and, in the context of the genre, well written" (p. 30). And they are very popular: In the May–June, 1995, list of K–12 bestsellers in the U.S., R.L. Stine captured six of the top ten places.

2. Portions of this section are also published in McQuillan, J., "The effects of incentives on reading." *Reading Research and Instruction, 36, 2,* 111–125.

3. The researchers noted that "it proved difficult to attract a large number of children to take a reading test during the summer" (p. 13), despite the chance to gain one hundred free incentive points.

4. Suggested to us by Deborah Krashen (personal communication).

References

Accelerated Learning Systems. (1993). National study of literature-based reading. Wisconsin Rapids, WI: Accelerated Learning Systems.

Adler, J. (1989). *A middle school experiment: Can a token economy improve reading achievement scores?* (ED 312 620)

Anderson, R., Wilson, P., & Fielding, L. (1988). Growth in reading and how children spend their time outside of school. *Reading Research Quarterly 23,* 285–303.

Bader, L., Veatch, J., & Eldridge, J. (1987). Trade books or basal readers? *Reading Improvement, 24,* 62–67.

Carter, B. & Abrahamson, R. (1994). Nonfiction for young adults: From delight to wisdom. *Indiana Media Journal, 17,* 1–16.

Carver, R. & Liebert, R. (1995). The effect of reading library books at different levels of difficulty upon gain in reading ability. *Reading Research Quarterly, 30,* 26–48.

Cho, K. S. & Krashen, S. (1994). Acquisition of vocabulary from the Sweet Valley Kids series: Adult ESL acquisition. *Journal of Reading, 37,* 662–67.

Cho, K.S. & Krashen, S. (1995a). From Sweet Valley Kids to Harlequins in one year. *California English 1, 1* 18–19.

Cho, K.S. & Krashen, S. (1995b). Becoming a dragon: Progress in English as a second language though narrow free voluntary reading. *California Reader 29,* 9–10.

Christmas, J. (1993). *Developing and implementing a plan to improve the reading achievement of second grade students at Woodbine Elementary School.* (ED 359 493)

Constantino, R. (1995). Two small girls, one large disparity. *The Reading Teacher, 48,* 504.

El-Shabbaz, E. (1964). *The autobiography of Malcolm X.* New York: Ballantine Books.

Elley, W. (1991). Acquiring literacy in a second language: The effect of book-based programs. *Language Learning, 41,* 375–411.

Elley, W. (1992). *How in the world do students read?* Hamburg: International Association for the Evaluation of Educational Achievement.

Elley, W. (1994). *The IEA study of reading literacy: Achievement and instruction in thirty-two school systems.* Pergamon Press.

Elley, W. and Mangubhai, F. (1983). The impact of reading on second language learning. *Reading Research Quarterly, 19,* 53–67.

Fink, R. (1995–96). Successful dyslexics: A constructivist study of passionate interest reading. *Journal of Adolescent and Adult Literacy, 39,* 268–80.

Foorman, B., Francis, D., Shaywitz, S., Shaywitz, B., & Fletcher, J. (1997). The case for early reading intervention. In B. Blachman (Ed.) *Foundations of reading acquisition* (pp. 243-64). Mahwah, NJ: Erlbaum.

Francis, D., Shaywtiz, S., Stuebing, K., Shaywitz, B., & Fletcher, J. (1996). Developmental lag versus deficit models of reading disability: A longitudinal, individual growth curve analysis. *Journal of Educational Psychology, 88,* 3–17.

Greaney, V. & Clarke, M. (1973). A longitudinal study of the effects of two reading methods on leisure-time reading habits. In D. Moyle (Ed.) *Reading: What of the future?* (pp. 107–14). London: United Kingdom Reading Association.

Griffith, K. Deloach, L., & LaBarba, R. (1984). The effects of rewarder familiarity and differential reward preference on intrinsic motivation. *Bulletin of Psychonomic Society, 22,* 313–16.

Harrop, A. and McCann, C. (1983). Behavior modifications and reading attainment in the comprehensive school. *Educational Research, 25,* 191–95.

Haugaard, K. (1973). Comic books: A conduit to culture? *The Reading Teacher, 27,* 54–55.

Jones, E. (1993). Have no fear: Scary stories for the middle grades. *Emergency Librarian 21,1,* 30–31.

Juel, C. (1988). Learning to read and write: A longitudinal study of 54 children from first through fourth grades. *Journal of Educational Psychology, 80,* 437–47.

Juel, C. (1994). *Learning to read and write in one elementary school.* New York: Springer Verlag.

Kerman, K. (1993). A mother learns to understand her child. *Growing Without Schooling, 92,* 27.

Kohn, A. (1993). *Punished by rewards.* Boston: Houghton Mifflin.

Krashen, S. (1993). *The power of reading.* Englewood, CO: Libraries Unlimited.

Krashen, S. (1995). School libraries, public libraries, and the NAEP reading scores. *School Library Media Quarterly, 23,* 235–38.

LaBrant, L. (1937). The content of a free reading program. *Educational Research Bulletin, 16,* 29–34.

Lance, K., Welborn, L., Hamilton-Pennell, C. (1993). *The impact of school library media centers on academic achievement.* Englewood, CO: Libraries Unlimited.

McQuillan, J. (1996a). How should heritage languages be taught? The effects of a free voluntary reading program. *Foreign Language Annals, 29,* 56–72.

McQuillan, J. (1996b). S.A.T. verbal scores and library: Predicting high school reading achievement in the United States. *Indiana Media Journal, 18,* (3), 25–30.

Mason, J. (1993a). Without a curriculum. *Growing Without Schooling 94,* 28.

Mason, J. (1993b). Reading at 10. *Growing Without Schooling 91,* 11.

Mott, I. (1993). Reading at 11. *Growing Without Schooling 91,* 11.

Nell, V. (1988). *Lost in a book.* New Haven, Connecticut: Yale University Press.

Niemeyer, K. (1988). *Books and beyond: Reading achievement, reading for pleasure, and television viewing time.* Dissertation Abstracts International-A, 49, 227A.

Morrow, L. (1982). Relationships between literature programs, library corner designs, and children's use of literature. *Journal of Educational Research, 75,* 339–44.

Morrow, L. & Weinstein, C. (1982). Increasing children's use of literature through program and physical changes. *Elementary School Journal, 83,* 131–37.

Peak, J. & Dewalt, M. (1994). Reading achievement: Effects of computerized reading management and enrichment. *ERS Spectrum, 12,* 31–34.

Pfau, D. (1967). Effects of planned recreational reading programs. *Reading Teacher, 21,* 34–39.

Pilgreen, J. & Krashen, S. (1993). Sustained silent reading with English as a second language high school students: Impact on reading comprehension, reading frequency, and reading enjoyment. *School Library Media Quarterly, 22,* 21–23.

Pitts, S. (1986). Read aloud to adult learners? Of course! *Reading Psychology, 7,* 35–42.

Potter, L. (1994). Putting reading first in the middle school: The principal's responsibility. *Reading Improvement, 31,* 243–45.

Robbins, E. & Thompson, L. (1989). *A study of the Indianapolis-Marion County Public Library's Summer Reading Program for Children.* (ED 316 845)

Robbins, E. & Thompson, L. (1991). *A study of the Indianapolis-Marion County Public Library's Summer Reading Program for Children.* (ED 335 647)

Stahl, S., McKenna, M., & Pagnucco, J. (1994). The effects of whole-language instruction: An update and reappraisal. *Educational Psychologist, 29* (4), 175–85.

Schoonover, R. (1938). The case for voluminous reading. *English Journal, 27,* 114–18.

Schulman, S. (1986). Facing the invisible handicap. *Psychology Today, 2,* 58–64.

Sheffer, S. (1987). *Everyone is able: Exploding the myth of learning disabilities.* Boston: Holt Associates.

Smith, F. (1985). *Reading without nonsense.* New York: Teachers College Press.

Southgate, V., Arnold, H., & Johnson, S. (1981). *Extending beginning reading.* London: Heinemann Educational Books.

Stein, C. (1994). Reveals he can read. *Growing Without Schooling, 98,* 24–25.

Trelease, J. (1985). *The read aloud handbook.* New York: Penguin.

Trelease, J. & Krashen, S. (1996). Eating and reading in the school library. *Emergency Librarian 23,* 5–27.

Ujiie, J. & Krashen, S. (1996). Is comic book reading harmful? Comic book reading, school achievement, and pleasure reading among seventh graders. *California School Library Association Journal 19,* 2, 27–28.

V From California to the Nation

15 Every Person a Reader: An Alternative to the California Task Force Report on Reading

Stephen D. Krashen
University of Southern California

Originally published as a monograph by Language Education Associates (Culver City, California), *Every Person a Reader* is Krashen's alternative to the 1995 California Task Force Report on Reading. Although the research cited is sometimes specific to California, Krashen's recommendations are relevant to the rest of the nation. With specific California references removed, those recommendations are:

- School libraries must contain a wide variety of accessible reading materials and be staffed by qualified librarians.
- Schools and districts should encourage free voluntary reading.
- Schools should have quality literature programs.
- Educators need to focus on long-term development and not overemphasize "early intervention."
- "Skills" are helpful in reading only when they help make texts more comprehensible. They should not be the core of a language arts or reading program.
- Educators should promote accuracy in writing through reading and through appropriate supplementation.
- Literacy-related technology should be de-emphasized until school libraries are adequate.
- Language testing should be reduced drastically, with the time saved used for worthwhile literacy activities, and the money saved invested in school libraries.
- Schools need to provide a print-rich environment in the primary and second language for language-minority children.

The need for implementing each recommendation is well documented in Krashen's essay with a wealth of research.

Introduction

Many people feel there is a literacy crisis in California. The perception, fueled by inaccurate reporting by the press, is that large numbers of children in California cannot read at basic levels. The popular view is that this reading failure begins in the early grades, and needs to be addressed with heavy intervention at that level.

There is also the perception that the 1987 English-Language Arts Framework is part of the cause of the problem, because it did not give enough attention to skills instruction.

These perceptions are not correct. It is true is that children in California scored near the bottom of the country on the NAEP Reading test, given to fourth grade children. It is not true, however, that things have gotten worse in California; McQuillan's analysis (McQuillan, 1995) shows no change in standardized test scores in reading for the last ten years, a result that agrees with national reports of reading. Thus, one cannot blame the 1987 English-Language Arts Framework.

It is also not true that a large number of children in California are completely illiterate. Parker (1995) has pointed out that California's relatively poor performance on the NAEP did not mean that our fourth graders can't read. The test results only showed that they don't read very well. Forty-five percent of the California fourth graders who took the test in 1992 could read at basic levels or above (compared to 59% of children throughout the nation).

The problem in California, then, is not a failure of the previous Framework, nor is it the case that our children are illiterate. The solution is thus not necessarily an abandonment of previously articulated philosophies, nor is it a return to the "basics."

The following set of recommendations are intended to address the real crisis, not the one manufactured by the press.

Recommendations

Recommendation 1:

Every school and district must improve their school libraries. School libraries must contain a wide variety of accessible reading materials and be staffed by qualified librarians.

> "The provision of a rich supply of high-interest story books is a much more feasible policy for improving English learning than any pious pronouncements about the urgent need to raise teacher quality . . ." (Mangubhai & Elley, 1982).

- California ranks near last in the United States in fourth grade reading scores; it also ranks near last in school library quality. This is not a coincidence. A number of studies relate school library quality to reading achievement. Of most interest to California is the finding of a strong positive correlation (r = .495) between books per students in school libraries in 41 states and NAEP fourth grade reading scores (Krashen, 1995). As noted earlier, it is California's performance on this test that has promoted the perception that there is a problem in California. It has also been shown that books in high school libraries relate to SAT scores (McQuillan, in press), and that the quality of school libraries is a good predictor of reading scores across individual schools (Lance et al., 1993) and across countries (Elley, 1993).

- The reason for these correlations is clear: Better libraries mean more access to reading, and more reading, especially free voluntary reading, means better literacy development. Studies confirm that children get a large percentage of books from libraries (Krashen, 1993a, Pucci, 1995), and there is an enormous research literature showing that free reading results in improved reading comprehension, writing style, vocabulary development, spelling and grammatical competence (Krashen, 1993a). This research includes a report showing that California eighth graders who read more for pleasure scored higher on the CAP (California Assessment Program) test of English and language arts (Alexander, 1986). In addition, fourth graders who said they did more free reading in school and out of school did better on the NAEP reading test (Mullis, Campbell, and Farstrup, 1993). Note, however, that more instructional time for reading did not result in better reading:

Scores on 1992 NAEP Reading Test

Students' report of time for free reading in school:

	almost every day	at least once a week	less than weekly
USA	223 (55%)	215 (27%)	203 (18%)
California	214 (57%)	201 (25%)	187 (18%)

Free voluntary reading outside of school:

	almost every day	once/twice a week	once/twice a month	never/ hardly ever
USA	223 (43%)	218 (32%)	209 (12%)	199 (13%)
California	212 (45%)	200 (32%)	196 (11%)	190 (12%)

Instructional time for reading:

	30-45 minutes	60 minutes	90 minutes or more
USA	220 (31%)	219 (51%)	216 (18%)
California	212 (20%)	204 (46%)	198 (34%)

- Books in school libraries are not enough. Students must have access to books and the books must be of interest. Correlations between books per student and reading fall dramatically when access is limited and collections are out of date (Krashen and O'Brian, in press). On the other hand, when library hours are increased and books are added to the school libraries, circulation increases (Houle and Montmarquette, 1984). Libraries need to be open more.

- Schools and districts need to increase student awareness of library services and procedures, especially among language minority students. Studies show that these students often know very little about the school library (Constantino, 1994); librarians may expect teachers to provide this information, and teachers may expect librarians to do so. Both teachers and librarians may expect that every student already knows about the library. An important part of access is a library that welcomes all students.

- There is a huge disparity among children in access to books. Affluent children have more books at home, better public libraries, and often go to schools with better school libraries and classroom libraries (Constantino, 1995). In fact, it is probably the case that many children in school today have practically no access to books, and no quiet, comfortable place to read. There is a powerful relationship between free reading and literacy development. Thus, affluent children do well in school at least partly because of the print-rich environment they experience outside of school. School should not simply be a test that privileged children pass. The school library can be an equalizer.

In Elley's study of reading achievement in 32 countries (Elley, 1993), the number of books in the school library was an excellent predictor of reading scores for less economically developed countries, countries in which the school library was probably the major source of books for children. Less developed countries with better libraries were closer to test scores of the affluent countries; suggesting that a good library can make up part of the gap between the rich and less rich in literacy development.

- The following table shows how far behind California is (data from White, 1990):

Books per student

	elementary school	middle school	high school
USA	18 to 1	16 to 1	15 to 1
California	13 to 1	11 to 1	8 to 1

Money spent on the school library (total library media budget; per pupil)

	elementary school	middle school	high school
USA	$ 15.44	$ 15.50	$ 19.22
California	$ 8.48	$ 7.48	$ 8.21

Number of school librarians (1991 data, from Digest of Educational Statistics, 1993)

	Number of librarians	number of students	ratio
USA	49,718	45,923,000	905 to 1
California	1,200	5,514,000	4595 to 1

The recommendation of this task force is to bring California's school libraries to and comfortably beyond the national averages.

- We must focus on the school library; public libraries in California cannot make up the gap. California ranks near last in the country in number of books and serial volumes per capita in its public libraries: The national average is 2.6 while California has 1.9; only seven states are lower (1991 data; Digest of Educational Statistics, 1993, table 409). Citing Gibson's work, McQuillan (1995) notes that book budgets in public libraries in California have been cut by 25% since 1989, and the number of hours public libraries are open has declined 30% since 1987. California now has the worst public library access in the United States, and children's services have been the hardest hit.

- At this time, some prisoners have much better access to books than our school children do in California. The Preston Penal Institution (California Youth Authority) spends $18.40 per year on books per inmate (compared to $8.21 per student spent by California High Schools). The prison has one librarian for a population of 815. California has one librarian for each 5000 students (R. Moore, personal communication; see also Moore, 1993). The solution is not to cut prison library funds, but to increase public school library funding and staffing.

Recommendation 2:

Schools and districts should encourage free voluntary reading.

- As noted earlier, our fourth graders can read. The problem is that they do not read very well. This situation is similar among adults in the United States. Despite claims of a nation-wide literacy crisis, 95% of the adult population can read at a basic level. In fact, literacy has been increasing steadily in the United States for the last 100 years (Stedman and Kaestle, 1987). Because of the increased demands of modern times, however, the low levels of reading many people achieve is not enough.

- The most effective bridge from low levels of reading ability and higher levels is free voluntary reading, or pleasure reading. This is also the kind of reading that is missing from the lives of many students: 23% of our fourth graders read for pleasure only once a month or less (Mullin et al., 1993).

There is no evidence that children who read for pleasure will stick to easy books and never progress: Free reading is not always easy reading. Several studies show that the books children select on their own are more difficult than the reading material assigned by teachers (Southgate, Arnold, and Johnson, 1981; Bader, Veatch, and Eldridge, 1987). In addition, what teachers consider "good" reading is probably more challenging reading, and several studies show that "voluminous reading actually fosters the tendency to do better reading" (Schoonover, 1938, p. 117). In Schoonover's study, most of the reading done by high school students who had participated in a six year free reading program were books that experts had classified as "good reading." Also, as readers mature, they gradually expand their reading interests. LaBrant (1937), in a study of reading interests of high school students, concluded that ". . . the theory that in a free or extensive reading program designed to utilize interest and to serve individual needs there will be fruitless reading of light fiction gains no evidence from this study" (p. 34). The most recent evidence confirming the value of light reading comes from Ujiie and Krashen (in press): middle school boys who did more comic book reading also read more in general, read more books, and reported that they liked reading better than those who did less comic book reading.

- Sustained silent reading (SSR) is a good way to encourage free voluntary reading. Students in SSR programs make very good gains in reading comprehension, as long as the program lasts long enough (Krashen, 1993a), and there is good evidence that sustained silent reading promotes reading outside of school (Pfau, 1967; Greaney and Clarke, 1975, Pilgreen and Krashen, 1993). Greaney and Clarke's study is especially interesting: Sixth-grade boys who participated in an in-school free reading program for eight and one-half months not only did more leisure reading while they were in the program, but were also reading more than comparison students six years later. Reading in SSR should be entirely self-selected, with no book reports or any other kind of accountability. Interesting reading should be provided by the school, and teachers should read while the students are reading.

Free reading can be done across the curriculum. When history teachers recommend historical novels and make them available, both literacy and subject matter learning are helped. As Jago (1994) has noted, "well-told stories make the past come alive. . . . Mark Helprin made me care about the Italian front in the First World War through *A Soldier of the Great War*. Larry McMurty taught me more about cowboys in *Lonesome Dove* than I ever thought I wanted to know. Nadine Gordimer schooled me in apartheid. Everything I know about the past I learned in historical novels." While Jago notes that there is the danger of distortion, there is no doubt that historical novels can be very educational.

Recommendation 3:

California schools should have quality literature programs.

- Not all reading should be free voluntary reading. Literature is the core component of any language arts program. "Literature," in this report, does not mean an exclusive emphasis on the classics. Our goal is to bring children to the point where they can read and appreciate the classics, but this does not imply that we begin with these difficult texts. Rather, the term "literature" here refers to any texts that improve the lives of our students and help them grow.
- Literature is applied philosophy. It includes ethics, how we are supposed to live, and metaphysics, speculations on why we are here. Fiction is a very powerful way of teaching philosophy. Good stories help us reflect on our behavior and our lives.
- Free voluntary reading and literature help and support each other. Students who have read a great deal on their own will find the texts that teachers assign and recommend much easier to understand. In addition, we know a literature program is successful when children read more. An important goal of literature is to encourage more reading, and a wider range of reading among children.

Reading stories aloud to children is an important part of a literature program. There is strong and consistent evidence that reading to children builds language and literacy competence (Elley, 1989; Trelease, 1995; Bus, Ijzendoorn, & Pelligrini, 1995). Reading stories helps directly, by providing comprehensible and interesting texts, thereby helping in the acquisition of the grammar and vocabulary of printed English. Reading stories helps indirectly as well, by stimulating an interest in reading.

- Districts may make broad suggestions concerning the texts that will be covered by teachers in literature classes, but should not require specific texts. For a text to be effectively taught, it must be one that has real meaning to the teacher. Texts must be of interest to both the teacher and the student.

Recommendation 4:

We need to focus on long-term development, and not overemphasize "early intervention."

A student came to a Zen master, and asked him how long it would take to become enlightened under his guidance. "Ten years," the master said. The student then asked how long it would take if he studied very hard. "Twenty years," the master responded. Surprised, the student then asked how long it would take if he worked very very hard, if he did the practices morning, noon, and night, and became the most dedicated student in the Ashram. "In that case, thirty years," the master responded. "Why, " the student asked, "does it take longer if I work harder?" The master responded, "If you have one eye on your goal, you will only have one eye for your task, and your work will suffer."

Well-intentioned programs of early intervention, with an emphasis on getting children to grade level quickly, may have the same effect.

- Grade-level standards are arbitrary standards. While all children may go through a fairly similar developmental path in language, literacy, and cognitive development, they do not go through this path at the same rate.
- Even if we assume that staying at "grade level" is important, gaps in reading level are not difficult to make up when children get to read interesting texts, when they get "hooked on books" (Fader, 1976; Krashen, 1993a). Juel (1994) calculated that by grade four good readers had read 178,000 words in school, while poor readers had read only 80,000 words. Good readers also read much

more at home; let us assume that by grade four they have read over a million words, while poor readers have read nothing at home. Thus, the difference between them is about a million words. It is not difficult to make up this gap: Comic books contain about 2000 words each; 50 comics thus contain about 100,000 words, about 10% of the gap. One Sweet Valley Kids novel contains about 7000 words; 14 of them contain 100,000, another 10% of the gap. (Of course, such texts are not comprehensible for beginning readers, and simpler texts and language experience stories contain fewer words. But once comics and longer books become comprehensible, progress will accelerate if children have access to them and are encouraged to read them.)

There is good evidence that the gap can be closed in this way. McQuillan (f.c.) reported that home schooled children who were allowed to begin to read whenever they wanted to occasionally began very late, but rapidly achieved "grade level" and beyond. Fink (1995–96) studied 12 dyslexics who had become "skilled readers" and very successful. One was a Nobel laureate, and the sample included three MDs, two PhDs, one EdD, one JD, two MFAs, one MEd, and two BAs. All 12 had developed basic literacy three to four years later than their peers, but all became avid readers, reading a great deal in areas they were interested in. Elley (1992), in a study of reading ability in 32 countries reported ". . . some advantage for an earlier start, but it can be said that countries which begin instruction in reading at age seven have largely caught up with the five- and six-year-old starters in reading ability by age nine" (p. 37). Finland, with the best readers in the world, starts reading instruction at age seven. (A recent study claiming that those with early (kindergarten) reading instruction were better readers in senior high school (Hanson and Farrell, 1995) actually showed that this extra investment paid poor dividends. Those who had the extra instruction were only slightly better as seniors, a difference that was statistically significant but educationally insignificant (effect size = .125). Free reading has a much more powerful effect.)

Recommendation 5:

"Skills" are helpful in reading only when they help make texts more comprehensible. They should not be the core of a language arts or reading program.

- "Skills" refers to the direct teaching of aspects of literacy that results in the child's conscious knowledge of words, rules or principles. No method of teaching reading has ever forbidden the teaching of some "skills." They are a very small part of a literacy development program, however. There are several reasons why skills cannot be the central part of the program:

Language is much too complex to learn consciously in its entirety.

Anyone who has studied linguistics knows how complicated the grammatical system of any language is. Linguists tell us that they have not yet adequately described the grammar of English. This means it is impossible to teach and learn directly. Spelling rules are extremely complicated. If we were to program a computer with the most accurate spelling rules we have, it would make mistakes on half the words it tried to spell (Smith, 1994a).

Phonics rules are extremely complicated, and have numerous exceptions. Clymer (1963) documented this, reporting, for example, that the well-known rule "when two vowels go walking the first does the talking" applies to fewer than 50% of the words with two vowels back-to-back in the basal readers of the 1960s. (For studies replicating Clymer's results, see Adams, 1990, p. 258). Smith (1994b) gives an excellent example of the complexity of phonics, pointing out that the /ho/ combination has many different pronunciations, including *hope, hoot, hook, hour, honest, house, honey, hoist, horse,* and *horizon* (p. 136). Smith also points out that even if a child learns the complex rules governing the pronunciation of /ho/, in order to apply them he or she must first look at the entire word: "The way in which a reader pronounces ho depends on what comes after it . . ." (p. 137).

There are too many vocabulary words for anyone to learn one at a time. Estimates of the size of the educated adults' vocabulary range from about 40,000 to 150,000 words, and middle class students pick up about 3000 new words every year. No vocabulary program can teach this many words (Nagy, Herman and Anderson, 1985).

High levels of literacy can be attained without direct instruction.

Many of those who have developed sophisticated writing styles and the ability to utilize complex grammatical constructions tell us they have done so through reading alone. The author Richard Wright comments: "I wanted to write and did not even know the English language. I bought English grammars and found them dull. I felt I was getting a better sense of the language through novels than through grammar" (Wright, 1966, p. 275).

Research has indicated that readers acquire "small, but reliable" amounts of vocabulary knowledge each time they see a new word in context. Given enough reading, this small increment is enough to account for observed growth in vocabulary. According to Anderson,

Wilson and Fielding (1988), the average middle class fifth grader reads about a million words per year, in school and outside of school. Even getting only 5% of the meaning of a new word with each exposure, a million words of reading will result in vocabulary growth of several thousand new words (Nagy et al., 1985). A million words is not a lot, if a good print environment is available.

There is considerable interest in training children in "phonemic awareness" (PA), the ability to segment a word into its consitutent phonemes. This interest is stimulated by findings showing that poor readers have lower phonemic awareness (Juel, 1994), that very young children differ in PA (Chaney, 1992), that PA is a predictor of reading achievement and that PA can be improved by training (Lundberg, Frost & Peterson, 1988; Cunningham, 1990; Ball & Blachman, 1991; Hatcher, Hulme & Ellis, 1994).

It has been established, however, that PA develops on its own; young children become sensitive to rhyme at an early age (Goswami & Bryant, 1990), and there is evidence that awareness of syllables develops early and without instruction (Wimmer, Landerl, Linortner, & Hummer, 1991; Morais, Bertelson, Cary & Alegria, 1986), while the ability to segment phonemes appears to be a consequence of literacy development (Mann, 1986; Read, Yun-Fei, Hong-Yin & Bao-Ging, 1986; Morais, Bertelson, Cary & Alegria, 1986; Perfetti, Beck, Bell, & Hughes, 1987; Winner, Landerl, Linortner, & Hummer, 1991; Lie, 1991). Wagner and Torgesen (1987) found that the strong relationship between PA and subsequent reading ability disappeared when earlier reading ability was controlled (reanalysis of Lundberg, Olafsson & Wall, 1990). Juel's subjects (discussed above), poor readers followed from grades 1 to 4 (Juel, 1994), attained perfect scores on her test of PA by grade three. Finally, control subjects in PA training studies (cited above) made clear progress in PA without any special training.

There is very suggestive evidence that spelling develops without instruction. Cornman (1902) dropped all spelling instruction from an elementary school for three years and found no decline in spelling growth (reanalysis in Krashen & White, 1989). Hamill, Larson and McNutt (1988) observed that children who had had no spelling instruction caught up with instructed children by grades five and six in spelling accuracy. (For additional evidence, see Krashen, 1989).

Much of our phonics knowledge did not come from instruction. Clymer (1963) reported that different phonics programs teach different rules! He examined four different series and found that of 50 vowel rules, only 11 were in all four series. Others have arrived at similar conclusions: "Beyond the most basic of basics and despite its long history and broad use, the various renditions of the phonic method contain little in the way of consensual recommendations as to the best set of grapheme-phoneme pairs to teach explicitly to our students" (Adams, 1990, p. 245). If this is the case, children's knowledge of complex rules could not have come from instruction.

Finally, the 12 dyslexics studied by Fink (1995–96) who became excellent readers still have problems in "basic phonological skills" (p. 273). Clearly, a thorough knowledge of the rules of phonics is not necessary for learning to read.

> Method comparison studies do not show a superiority for skills-based instruction.

Studies claiming to show that systematic phonics instruction is effective actually show that phonics is better than Look-Say (Chall, 1983) or "straight basal" programs (Adams, 1990, p. 42; see also page 46); they do not compare phonics to methods that focus on real reading of comprehensible texts. In more recent studies, "skill-based" approaches have been compared to methods that emphasize hearing stories and real reading. On communicative tests, the "literature-based" approaches are superior, while on form-based tests there is no difference. In Morrow, O'Conner and Smith (1990), "at-risk" kindergarten children received an extra 60 minutes per day of either traditional instruction focussing on learning the alphabet (with some storybook reading) or a literature-based program, focussing on storybook reading (teachers reading to the children), recreational reading and "literature activities" for one academic year (seven months). The experimental class excelled on reading comprehension and story retelling tests, as well as on a test of "concepts about books and print." On traditional standardized tests focussing on skills and reading readiness, there was no significant difference between the groups. Similarly, Hagerty, Hiebert and Owens (1989) compared second, fourth and sixth graders who did a "literature-based" program with comparison students who had a traditional "skills-based" program. The former included reading tradebooks and writing on topics chosen by the students, while the latter consisted of teacher-directed instruction and "filling out teacher-assigned worksheets which provided practice on particular skills or reading assigned textbook passages" (p. 455). Some free reading was allowed. Students in the literature-based classes outperformed those in the skill-based classes on a standardized test of reading comprehension, and there was no difference on a writing test (samples judged on organization, sentence structure, usage, capitalization, punctuation, spelling and format).

As noted above, phonemic awareness can be trained. But students who receive this training benefit mostly in increased performance on tests of phonemic awareness. The impact on tests of reading comprehension is considerably less (Tunmer, Herriman & Nesdale, 1988; see also phonemic awareness training studies cited earlier). Hatcher et al. (1994) reported that pure PA ("phonology only") training resulted in better performance on tests of PA, but did not result in better performance on a test of reading comprehension.

Method comparison studies involving older students have shown a consistent superiority for sustained silent reading over traditional instruction, using traditional measures of reading comprehension and vocabulary. In sustained silent reading, both students and teachers engage in self-selected reading for a few minutes per day. No book reports or other forms of accountability are required. Forty-one studies of sustained silent reading were cited in Krashen (1993a): In 38 out of these 41 studies, sustained silent reading students equalled or outperformed traditionally taught comparison students on tests of reading comprehension. Results were the most positive for longer term studies (longer than seven months). The reason for this is apparent to most teachers who have done SSR: It takes children time to find a book to read.

- Do we need to teach the complex aspects of phonics and phonemic awareness?

Smith (1994b) has hypothesized that "skills" instruction helps when it facilitates meaningful reading. Some knowledge of the more straightforward sound-spelling correspondences is certainly useful, for example. As Smith points out, a child who has some idea of the sound of the letter /h/ will certainly be helped when confronted with a sentence such as "The man is riding on the h—." This knowledge of phonics helps reduce the possible meanings of the unknown word, and combined with context, helps make the text more comprehensible, leading to comprehension and the development of literacy. Smith notes that when children utilize rules of phonics, they rely largely on initial consonants, and it is these correspondences that are the most regular.

There is a point of diminishing returns with phonics, however. Many phonics rules are not useful. As noted earlier, they are very complex, and have numerous exceptions.

Strangely, proponents of the heavy teaching of phonics often cite *Becoming a Nation of Readers* (Anderson, Heibert, Scott and Wilkinson, 1985) as supporting their position. Goodman (1993) and Weaver (1994) point out, however, that Anderson et al. "clearly see phonics

instruction as playing a very limited role in reading development"
(Weaver, 1994, p. 302). Consider the following excerpt from *Becoming
a Nation of Readers:*

> ". . . phonics instruction should aim to teach only the most impor-
> tant and regular of letter-to-sound relationships . . . once the basic
> relationships have been taught, the best way to get children to
> refine and extend their knowledge of letter-sound correspondences
> is through repeated opportunities to read. If this position is cor-
> rect, then much phonics instruction is overly subtle and probably
> unproductive" (p. 38).

Share and Stanovich (1995) claim to disagree with the view presented
here, but a close reading of their conclusions shows surprising agreement. They state that "a minimal level of phonological sensitivity and
letter-sound knowledge skill may enable a child to acquire rudimentary
self-teaching skill" (p. 22). This "partial decoding" ability, with the help
of context, may be enough to help the child identify the word: ". . . most
irregular words, when encountered in natural text, have sufficient letter-sound regularity (mostly consonantal) to permit selection of the correct target among a set of candidate pronunciations. That is, even an
approximate or partial decoding may be adequate for learning irregular words encountered in the course of everyday reading" (p. 23). This
ability to read with only partial decoding ability sets up a self-teaching chain: "If successfully decoded, an item containing unknown or
unfamiliar correspondences will provide the reader with an opportunity to learn new correspondences and thereby expand the power of
his or her self-teaching mechanism" (p. 28). The only substantive difference between the position presented by Smith and that presented by
Share and Stanovich is that Smith suggests that a limited knowledge
of sound-spelling correspondences is helpful, while Share and Stanovich
insist that it is necessary (see also Tunmer & Chapman, 1995). For the
practitioner, there is no difference.

Similar suggestions are made for teaching phonemic awareness.
Spector (1995), an enthusiastic proponent of phonemic awareness training, concludes that "skills that appear to be less important to teach are
those that are more complex, such as phoneme deletion . . ." (p. 42).

- It is often assumed that very early literacy development must be
  skill-based, that children must first "learn to read" before they
  "read to learn." This cannot be true: the brain acquires language
  in one way: by understanding messages. The language acquisition
  device does not suddenly alter its nature at a certain stage. While
  there is definite individual variation in learning strategies and
  styles, there is no individual variation at the fundamental level of

language acquisition. Just as we all have similarly functioning kidneys, similarly functioning livers, and similarly functioning digestive systems, we all have similarly functioning language acquisition devices (Chomsky, 1975).

- Thus, early literacy is developed the same way higher levels of literacy are developed. The process is comprehension of texts, making sense of what is on the page (Smith, 1994b). This does not mean "mere exposure" to texts, and does not mean teachers should do nothing. The task of the teacher is to provide comprehensible texts and to help children understand texts that are not yet comprehensible.

- There are several ways of providing comprehensible texts to beginning readers. As noted earlier (recommendation 3), reading stories aloud to children has strong research support (Trelease, 1995), and stories are made comprehensible when teachers provide background knowledge and appropriate discussion. Story reading helps children acquire the special grammar, vocabulary and discourse style of the written language (Smith, 1994b) and gets children interested in reading on their own. It does not, of course, help children acquire knowledge of sound-spelling correspondences but makes a huge contribution in other ways (Bus, van Ijzendoorn, & Pellegrini, 1995).

- Language experience is an excellent way of providing interesting, comprehensible texts for beginners. Language experience is a method in which children dictate stories to the teacher. These stories then become the reading texts. Informal observations suggest that child-made stories are often the first texts children want to read.

- As noted earlier, some direct teaching of basic phonics can be useful for beginners. When teachers include some work on the alphabet and basic sound-spelling correspondences, this information can help make texts more comprehensible.

Recommendation 6:

Promote accuracy in writing through reading and through appropriate supplementation.

> "Orthography is so absolutely necessary for a man of letters . . . that one false spelling may fix a ridicule upon him for the rest of his life. . . . I know a man of quality who never recovered (from) the ridicule of having spelled wholesome without the *w*." (Chesterfield, 1919, cited by Hodges, 1987).

- Most of our accuracy, our mastery of the conventions of writing, comes from reading. Reading alone, however, may not provide full mastery of all conventions. Those who have read a great deal, for example, can typically spell nearly all the words they write correctly (Krashen, 1993b), but reading alone may not always result in perfect spelling, the standard required by our society. Similarly, even those who are well-read may have a few gaps in their knowledge of grammar and punctuation.

Here is a plan to develop perfect or near-perfect spellers:

- Stage 1: We should first develop good spellers through massive amounts of reading.
- Step 2. To move from good spelling to perfect spelling, teach students how to use a spelling dictionary. The spelling dictionary should be used only after the writers' ideas are fully developed on the page. Checking spelling is thus part of the "editing" stage of the composing process, the stage at which writers are concerned with cosmetics, not the message. The spelling dictionary can be introduced in junior high school.

A similar plan can be used for grammar:

- Step 1: Children first gain a large degree of grammatical competence through massive amounts of reading.
- Step 2. To move to very accurate grammar, teach students how to use a grammar handbook. The grammar handbook should be consulted only after the writers' ideas are fully developed on the page. Checking grammar is thus part of the editing stage of the composing process. The grammar handbook can be introduced in high school.

Of course, to use a grammar handbook requires a clear understanding of grammar, including concepts and terminology. This information, while not the core of language arts instruction, should be included. Students should have enough conscious knowledge of grammar to use the handbook effectively. This kind of knowledge is much easier to teach to older students.

There is never any reason for students to memorize grammatical terminology or grammatical rules. Rather, they should become experts in using the handbook.

- Another reason to include the study of grammar for older students is as linguistics: Linguistics includes the nature of language, linguistic universals, language change, sociolinguistics, and language acquisition. Sentence diagramming, for example, is properly considered linguistics. Research shows that grammar study has very limited value in helping students read and write better (Elley, Barham, Lamb, & Wyllie, 1976, after a three year study, concluded that ". . . English grammar, whether traditional or transformational, has virtually no influence on the language growth of typical secondary students" pp. 17–18). The study of grammar has, however, value as subject matter. Linguistics is a desirable but peripheral part of the language arts program.

Recommendation 7:

Literacy-related technology should be de-emphasized until school libraries are adequate in California.

> "Bureaucrats seem ever able to find thousands of dollars for up-to-date ways of delivering the same old skills at the very time they cite budget deficits as the reason for laying off librarians" (Ohanian, 1994, pp. 142–3).

> "School officials tout new reading programs, avow their concern with reading goals, and cut Library Media Center book budgets or leave them at 1960 levels to purchase microcomputers, software, CD-ROMs, and videodisks" (Miller and Schonz, 1993, p. 27).

- This task force recommends a three year freeze on all technology related to literacy development and library functioning, with the money going instead to books and other reading materials. The reason for this freeze is that there is no compelling evidence that computers are especially useful in helping children learn to read, nor is there convincing evidence that they have increased anyone's reading ability. It has been noted that most of the software offered for literacy development is dreadful:

> "Most reading software is foolish and impudent, an odious endeavor" (Ohanian, 1994, p. 141).

> "The dim-wittedness offered up by much current software in the name of reading comprehension and thinking skills is quite amazing . . ." (Ohanian, 1994, p. 143).

So far, attempts to apply computer technology to literacy development have not produced any clear evidence that the investment is worth it. Computer-based reading management software that tests and then rewards children for reading has not been shown to be any more effective than simply providing children with a supply of quality, interesting books (Krashen, in press). One widely advertised system, Accelerated

Reader, is expensive. The "basic kit" for a school costs $650. The "economy starter kit" contains tests for "up to 1,000 books" as well as a How to Use the Accelerated Reader Video and a "Whole-School Support Plan" (toll-free phone support) at the bargain price of $1,723. This money should go to the school library.

The best-known computer-based reading program is IBM's Write to Read. Thus far, studies evaluating Write to Read have not produced convincing results. It is not even clear that WTR is superior to traditionally taught comparison groups (Krendl & Williams, 1990). Nor is there evidence that computers have a lasting "novelty" effect. In one study (Chu, 1995), first graders reading interactive books off a computer stopped using all the extra features of the computer by the time they reached their fifth book.

There is also little empirical support for the use of computers in school libraries. While Krashen (1995) reported a modest (r = .38) correlation between the amount of software in school libraries and NAEP fourth grade reading scores for 41 states, the contribution of software was not as strong as the contribution of books, as noted earlier (r = .495 between the ratio of books per child in school libraries and reading scores). In addition, the results of several other studies provide no evidence of an impact of computer software in libraries on literacy development (Lance, Welborn, & Hamilton-Pennell, 1993; Krashen & O'Brian, in press; McQuillan, in press).

Probably the only clearly beneficial use of the computer for literacy development is word-processing. The advantages of word-processing are so obvious that experimental support is not necessary: Nearly every experienced writer uses one. Word-processing is helpful because it makes revision much easier, removing the "inauthentic labor" of writing, and revision is the key to coming up with new ideas. Experienced writers know that as they go from draft to draft they discover new ideas and gain new insights (Sommers, 1980).

Word-processors can also be a big help for teachers who use language experience. To take advantage of the word-processor, however, we do not need the latest and best computers or programs. For nearly all school-related purposes, and most professional purposes, we don't need a 486, 386, or even 286: The old Apple II and AppleWriter or the Bank Street Writer will do very well.

Miller and Shontz (1993, 1995) have documented that school library media centers are now spending more on technology than on books and magazines, and concluded that "access to books is being seriously curtailed by the rapidly deteriorating state of school library collections and community unwillingness to fund them" (1993, p. 27).

They calculated that expenditures for books, when adjusted for inflation, have decreased over the last ten years: The average school library media specialist could purchase only about one-third of a book per child in 1991–92, with book collections in school library media centers remaining "stagnant."

There is no question that computers are extremely important, and it is certain that computers will, some day, be widely and expertly used in schools. But books must come first. Quite often, in visiting a school, one finds a computer room, representing an investment of at least $100,000 in computers, software, and related technology, not to mention staff salaries. In most cases, the equipment is under-used, because it is obsolete, and/or ineffective and/or boring. In the same building is a school library with a pathetically small, out-of-date book collection, with policies that make it hard for children to have access to the few books that are there. In addition, such schools frequently serve populations that are not affluent, where there are few books in the home. The school library is, for these children, often the only source of books. Consider how many books we could buy for the price of one computer.

Recommendation 8:

Language testing should be reduced drastically, with the time saved used for worthwhile literacy activities, and the money saved invested in school libraries.

- The problem with language tests is not one of reliability or validity. Standardized language tests are usually very reliable, and are often quite valid: Someone who has a larger vocabulary will usually do better on a standardized vocabulary test than someone with a smaller vocabulary.

- There are three real problems with tests. First, they push teachers and students in the wrong direction. Students study for tests and teachers teach to prepare students for tests and no force will change this. Thus, if there is a vocabulary test to be given at the end of the year, classroom instruction will include direct instruction on vocabulary. But research strongly suggests that vocabulary is more efficiently acquired by reading. In fact, Nagy, Herman and Anderson (1985) concluded that acquiring vocabulary through reading is ten times as efficient, in terms of words learned per minute, than direct vocabulary instruction. Thus, time is much better spent on reading than on vocabulary instruction. The only possible conclusion is that vocabulary tests work against vocabulary acquisition. (Unless we can convince students that they will do better on vocabulary tests by reading a lot, which appears to many to be an indirect path.)

The second problem is that tests take time. The time saved by reducing language testing could go into free reading (sustained silent reading), literature, reading stories to children, and simply allowing children more browsing time in the library, all of which will have a strong impact on literacy development. Ujiie (personal communication) has obtained estimates of how much time is devoted to testing and preparation for tests at one elementary school in California: Administration of the tests themselves consumes about six hours per year, of which four and one-half hours is devoted to testing language arts and reading. Required preparation for the tests (e.g. "benchmark" tests) consumes another 14 hours per year, of which 6.75 hours is devoted to language and reading. This amounts to over 20 hours per year of required time devoted to testing. Some schools do much more than this, devoting 15–20 minutes per day to test preparation. The school Ujiie studied also devoted two full student-free days to test scoring.

Note that sustained silent reading, at 10 minutes per day, takes up about 30 hours per year. Dumping only the minimum testing is equivalent to rescuing 2/3 of a year of SSR! There is no evidence that testing and preparation for tests helps to develop literacy. On the other hand, there is strong evidence that sustained silent reading does. The only possible conclusion is that testing actually hurts literacy development, because it takes time away from real reading.

The third problem is that tests cost money. Ohanian (1994), in a paper originally written in 1985, reported that standardized testing in the USA costs 100 million dollars per year. If we could save 75 million dollars of this expense, this would amount to one thousand dollars for each school library in the United States per year. (This must be an underestimate as 1985 dollars were used in the calculation.)

- Ironically, an excellent way to increase test scores is to decrease testing, and invest the money into the only means possible for building literacy: books.

- The use of expensive, standardized tests is often defended on the grounds that parents want them. This claim is not supported by the research: Shepard and Bliem (1995) reported that elementary school parents say they find talking to the teacher and seeing samples of their child's work more useful than standardized tests, and after seeing samples of performance assessments, preferred them to standardized tests.

Recommendation 9:

Provide a print-rich environment in the primary and second language for language minority children.

- Our goal, of course, is to help limited English proficient children become literate in English. An extremely effective way to do this is to first build literacy in the student's primary language. Here is a simple, three step argument supporting the transfer of literacy from the first to the second language.

  1) As Frank Smith and Kenneth Goodman have argued, we learn to read by reading, by making sense of what we see on the page (see e.g., Goodman, 1982; Smith, 1994b).

  2) If we learn to read by reading, it will be much easier to learn to read in a language we already understand. It is easier to teach English speaking children to read in English than to teach them to read in French, if they don't understand French.

  3) Once we can read, we can read. The ability to read transfers across languages, even when the writing systems are different. There is evidence that reading transfers from Spanish to English (Mortensen, 1984; Buriel & Cardoza, 1988), Chinese to English (Hoover, 1983), Vietnamese to English (Cummins, Swain, Nakajima, Handscombe, Green, & Tran, 1984), Japanese to English (Cummins et al., 1984), and from Turkish to Dutch (Verhoeven, 1991); in other words, those who read well in one language, read well in the second language (as long as length of residence in the country is controlled for, to account for the first language loss that is common).

In addition to the studies cited above, additional support for the transfer hypothesis comes from studies demonstrating the efficacy of bilingual education (Willig, 1985; Krashen & Biber, 1988).

There are other reasons to promote reading in the primary language: In addition to developing first language literacy, which transfers to English literacy, reading in the first language can be an important means of developing knowledge; those who read more, know more. In addition, reading is an excellent way of continuing first language development.

- Where are the books? Not at home

Books are very scarce in the lives of limited English proficient children. Ramirez, Yuen, Ramey and Pasta (1991) investigated the print environment in the homes of limited English proficient children participating in three types of programs in order to determine if the home print environment was a confounding factor in their study of program effectiveness. It was not. Children in all three programs had similar numbers of books in the home. What was remarkable, however, was the paucity of books in the homes of the children in all three programs: the average number of books in the home that were not schoolbooks was only 22 ("immersion" = 20.4 books; early exit = 23; late exit = 24). By way of comparison, it is not unusual for middle-class children to own 50 to 100 books of their own by the time they are adolescents. The Ramirez et al. figure of 22 included all books in the home, not only children's books.

- Where are the books? Not at school

Pucci (1994) studied policies and book holdings in the Los Angeles Unified School District. She noted that in that district, schools could only buy books from a list of approved books. The maximum number of titles approved for Korean was 19 (17 fiction, 2 non-fiction), for Vietnamese 19 (18 fiction), and for Chinese 106 (68 fiction)! Pucci also examined library collections in nine schools that had a significant number of Spanish-speaking students. The table below presents some of her results (names of the schools used are fictitious).

School Libraries: Books in Spanish and English

Number of books/child

School	% Spanish L1	% LEP	Total Books per Child	Spanish Books/ Spanish Speaking Child
Loma	95%	80%	2.3	.60
Estrella	98%	82%	3.6	.80
Alvarado	90%	82%	2.2	.50
Lily Ave.	30%	35%	4.7	.60
86th St.	65%	65%	3.3	1.00
Homer Middle	85%	70%	3.9	.04
Arapahao Middle	92%	70%	3.2	.12
Harbor	55%	50%	25.4	5.50
Cedar	88%	69%	5.3	1.00

from: Pucci, 1994

Clearly, the book holdings in these schools are inadequate: As noted earlier, the national average for elementary school libraries is about 18 books per child (White, 1990), and nine out of ten schools in the table are well below this, and are even well below the California average, which is one of the worst in the United States. (The exception, Harbor, is a small school, with a total enrollment of 375 children.) While the holdings in English are inadequate, the holdings in Spanish are pathetic.

Pucci also reported that access to the few books available was very restricted. Library visits ranged from once a week to once a month, with some teachers never bringing their students to the library. Library time ranged from 30 to 45 minutes, with a portion of that time for browsing and checking books out. In addition, "libraries at all schools have limits as to the number of books children are allowed to check out," with two books the maximum at all elementary schools, except for Alvarado, which allowed only one book! The middle schools allowed only three books per child every two weeks. In most elementary schools, however, children were allowed to check out more books if they returned the ones they had, if they had the opportunity to use the library.

Pucci reported that "At Alvarado the atmosphere about checking out books was particularly tense, and the children's activity was noticeably regimented. Children browse the bookshelves holding a ruler, which they use to mark the place where they remove a book in order to examine it. They are not allowed to walk back to their table with the book. Rather, they must stand near the shelf and look at it there, deciding if they wish to check it out. Once children have chosen their books they go immediately to check them out and then sit quietly at their assigned seats. Many of them start reading, and finish their book before the end of the allotted library time is up. When this happens, they are not allowed to return the book and check out another. In fact, one third grade teacher was overheard strongly advising the children "not to read." (pp. 74–75).

The situation is clear: reading causes literacy development, but these children have little reading material in the home, and little in school. What little there is in school is not easily accessible, and Constantino's research, cited earlier (Recommendation 1) shows that limited English proficient students do not know much about what is available. Here is an analogy: You are placed on a weight gaining/muscle building program. Your diet is one glass of water and a cracker each day. If you don't gain weight and get strong on this diet, it is your fault—you are just not trying hard enough.

Bilingual education is doing well now. But it could do much better if children had adequate access to reading material.

Call to Action

- Make reading a priority by vastly improving school libraries in California.

- Encourage free voluntary reading by providing reading time and more access to good reading material.

- Promote quality literature programs that encourage teachers to use texts that they are enthusiastic about.

- De-emphasize early intervention, and insure long-term progress by providing a print-rich environment for every child. Reaching "grade-level" should not be our concern; our concern should be eventual attainment. Ironically, students will have no trouble reaching standards when we reduce pressure and give them a chance to read for pleasure and interest.

- Limit skills to their true functions: To make texts more comprehensible and to edit writing. There is also some value in teaching about language in the form of linguistics. But nearly all of our accuracy in writing comes from reading and our reading ability comes from actual reading.

- Language testing needs to be reduced a great deal. The money and time saved can be invested in literacy, in practices that we know are effective.

- Despite the clear importance of technology, it cannot be our first priority in language and literacy education.

- The lack of good reading material is especially serious for limited English proficient children, both in the first and second language. This shortage needs to be addressed immediately.

References

Adams, M. 1990. *Beginning to Read: Thinking and Learning about Print.* Cambridge, MA: MIT Press.

Alexander, F. 1986. California Assessment Program: Annual Report. Sacramento: California Department of Education.

Anderson, R., Heibert, E., Scott, J. & Wilkinson, I. 1985. *Becoming a Nation of Readers.* Washington: National Institute of Education.

Anderson, R., Wilson, P., and Fielding, L. 1988. Growth in reading and how children spend their time outside of school. *Reading Research Quarterly 23,* 285–303.

Bader, L., Veatch, J., and Eldridge, J. 1987. Trade books or basal readers? *Reading Improvement 24,* 62–67.

Ball, E. & Blachman, B. 1991. Does phonemic segmentation training in kindergarten make a difference in early word recognition and developmental spelling? *Reading Research Quarterly 26,* 49–66.

Buriel, R. & Cardoza, D. 1988. Sociocultural correlates of achievement among three generations of Mexican American high school seniors. American Educational Research Journal 25, 177–92.

Bus, A., Ijzendoorn, M., & Pellegrini, A. 1995. Joint book reading makes for success in learning to read: A meta-analysis on intergenerational transmission of literacy. Review of Educational Research 65, 1–21.

Chall, J. 1983. Learning to Read: The Great Debate. New York: McGraw Hill. Updated edition.

Chaney, C. 1992. Language development, metalinguistic skills, and print awareness in 3-year-old children. Applied Psycholinguistics 13, 485–514.

Chomsky, N. 1975. Reflections on Language. New York: Pantheon Books.

Chu, M-L. 1995. Reader response to interactive computer books: Examining literary responses in a non-traditional reading setting. Reading Research and Instruction 34, 352.

Clymer, T. 1963. The utility of phonic generalizations in the primary grades. The Reading Teacher 16, 252–58.

Constantino, R. 1994. Immigrant ESL high school students' understanding and use of libraries: Check this out! SCOPE Journal 93, 6–16.

Constantino, R. 1995. Two small girls, one large disparity. The Reading Teacher 48, 504.

Cornman, O. 1902. Spelling in the Elementary School. Boston: Ginn.

Cummins, J., Swain, M., Nakajima, K., Handscombe, J., Green, D., & Tran, C. 1984. Linguistic interdependence among Japanese and Vietnamese immigrant students. In C. Rivera (Ed.) Communicative Competence Approaches to Language Proficiency Assessment: Research and Application. Clevedon, England: Multilingual Matters.

Cunningham, A. 1990. Explicit versus implicit instruction in phonemic awareness. Journal of Experimental Child Psychology 50, 429–44.

Elley, W. 1989. Vocabulary acquisition from listening to stories. Reading Research Quarterly 24, 174–87.

Elley, W. 1992. How in the World do Students Read? Hamburg: International Association of the Evaluation of Educational Achievement.

Elley, W., Barham, I., Lamb, H., & Wyllie, M. 1976. The role of grammar in a secondary school curriculum. Research in the Teaching of English 10, 5–21.

Fader, D. 1976. The New Hooked on Books. New York: Berkley Books.

Fink, R. 1995–96. Successful dyslexics: A constructionist study of passionate interest reading. Journal of Adolescent and Adult Literacy 39, 268–80.

Goodman, K. 1982. Language and Literacy: The Selected Writings of Kenneth S. Goodman. F. Gollasch (Ed.) London: Routledge.

Goodman, K. 1993. Phonics Phacts. Portsmouth, NH: Heinemann.

Goswami, U. & Bryant, P. 1990. Phonological skills and Learning to Read. Hillsdale, NJ: Erlbaum.

Greaney, V. & Clarke, M. 1973. A longitudinal study of the effects of two reading methods on leisure-time reading habits. In D. Moyle (Ed.) Reading: What of the future? (pp. 107–14). London: United Kingdom Reading Association.

Hagerty, P., Heibert, E., & Owens, M. 1989. Students' comprehension, writing, and perceptions in two approaches to literacy instruction. In S. McCormick and J. Zutell (Eds.) Thirty-eighth Yearbook of the National Reading Conference. Chicago: National Reading Conference. pp. 453–59.

Hammill, D., Larson, S., & McNutt, G. 1977. The effect of spelling instruction: A preliminary study. Elementary School Journal 78, 67–72.

Hanson, R. & Farrell, D. 1995. The long term effects on high school seniors of learning to read in kindergarten. Reading Research Quarterly 30, 908–33.

Hatcher, P., Hulme, C., & Ellis, A. 1994. Ameliorating early reading failure by integrating the teaching of reading and phonological skills: The phonological linkage hypothesis. Child Development 65, 41–57.

Hodges, R. 1987. American spelling instruction: Retrospect and prospect. Visible Language 21, 55–75.

Hoover, W. 1983. Language and Literacy Learning in Bilingual Instruction. Austin: Southwest Educational Development Laboratory.

Houle, R. & Montmarquette, C. 1984. An empirical analysis of loans by school libraries. Alberta Journal of Educational Research 30, 104–14.

Jago, C. 1994. Historical novels offer an eye-opening look at the past. The Outlook, October 17, 1994.

Juel, C. 1994. Learning to Read and Write in One Elementary School. New York: Springer-Verlag.

Krashen, S. 1989. We acquire vocabulary and spelling by reading: Additional evidence for the input hypothesis. Modern Language Journal 73, 440–64.

Krashen, S. 1993a. The Power of Reading. Englewood, CO: Libraries Unlimited.

Krashen, S. 1993b. How well do people write? Reading Improvement 30, 9–20.

Krashen, S. 1995. School libraries, public libraries, and NAEP scores. School Library Media Quarterly, 23, 235–37.

Krashen, S. Computerized reading management systems: More effective than what? California Reader. In press.

Krashen, S. & Biber, D. 1988. On Course: Bilingual Education's Success in California. Ontario, CA: California Association for Bilingual Education.

Krashen, S. & White, H. 1991. Is spelling acquired or learned? A re-analysis of Rice (1897) and Cornman (1902). ITL: Review of Applied Linguistics 91–92, 1–48.

Krashen, S. & O'Brian, B. School library collections and reading achievement. Indiana Media Journal. In press.

Krendl, K. & Williams, R. 1990. The importance of being rigorous: Research on Writing to Read. Journal of Computer Based Instruction 17: 81–86.

Lance, K., Wellborn, L., & Hamilton-Pennell, C. 1993. The Impact of School Library Media Centers on Academic Achievement. Englewood, CO: Libraries Unlimited.

LaBrant, L. 1937. The content of a free reading program. Educational Research Bulletin 16, 29–34.

Lie, A. 1991. Effects of a training program for stimulating skills in word analysis in first-grade children. Reading Research Quarterly 26, 234–50.

Lundberg, I., Frost, J., & Peterson, O. 1988. Effects of an extensive program for stimulating phonological awareness in preschool children. Reading Research Quarterly 23, 263–84.

Mangubhai, F. & Elley, W. 1982. The role of reading in promoting ESL. Language Learning and Communication 1, 151–60.

Mann, V. 1986. Phonological awareness: The role of reading experience. Cognition 24, 65–92.

McQuillan, J. 1995. Did whole language fail in California? CommniCATE 1, 4, 1–2.

McQuillan, J. SAT verbal scores and the library: Predicting high school reading achievement in the United States. Indiana Media Journal. In press.

McQuillan, J. The role of age and instruction in learning to read: The case of 'late' readers. Forthcoming.

Miller, M. & Shontz, M. 1993. Expenditures for resources in school library media centers, FY 1991–92. School Library Journal 39, 26–36.

Miller, M. & Shontz, M. 1995. The race for the school library dollar. School Library Journal 41, 22–33.

Moore, R. 1993. California Dreamin.' Emergency Librarian 21, 17.

Morais, J., Bertelson, P., Carey, L., & Alegria, J. 1986. Literacy training and speech segmentation. Cognition 24, 45–64.

Mortensen, E. 1984. Reading achievement of native Spanish-speaking elementary students in bilingual vs. monolingual programs. The Bilingual Review 11, 3–36.

Morrow, L., O'Connor, E., & Smith, J. 1990. Effects of a story reading program on the literacy development of at-risk kindergarten children. Journal of Reading Behavior 22, 255–75.

Mullis, I., Campbell, J., & Farstrup, A. 1993. NAEP 1992: Reading Report Card for the Nation and the States. Washington, DC: US Department of Education.

Nagy, W., Herman, P., & Anderson, R. 1985. Learning words from context. Reading Research Quarterly 20, 233–53.

Ohanian, S. 1994. Who's in Charge? Portsmouth, NH: Boynton/Cook Publishers.

Parker, D. 1995. Politics and pedagogy: The bookends of California's literacy crisis. California Journal of Teacher Research and School Restructuring, August, 1995.

Perfetti, C., Beck, I., Bell, L, & Hughes, C. 1987. Phonemic knowledge and learning to read are reciprocal: A longitudinal study of first grade children. Merrill-Palmer Quarterly 33, 283–319.

Pfau, D. 1967. Effects of planned recreational reading programs. Reading Teacher, 21, 34–39.

Pilgreen, J. & Krashen, S. 1993. Sustained silent reading with English as a second language high school students: Impact on reading comprehension, reading frequency, and reading enjoyment. School Library Media Quarterly, 22, 21–23.

Pucci, S. 1994. Supporting Spanish language literacy: Latino children and free reading resources in schools. Bilingual Research Journal 18, 67–82.

Ramirez, D., Yuen, S., Ramey, D., & Pasta, D. 1991. Final Report: Longitudinal Study of Structured English Immersion Strategy, Early-Exit and Late-Exit Bilingual Education Programs for Language Minority Students, Vol. I. San Mateo, CA: Aguirre International.

Read, C., Yun-Fei, Z., Hong-Yin, N. & Bao-Qing, D. 1986. The ability to manipulate speech sounds depends on knowing alphabetic writing. Cognition 24, 31–44.

Schoonover, R. 1938. The case for voluminous reading. English Journal, 27, 114–18.

Share, D. & Stanovich, K. 1995. Cognitive processes in early reading development: Accommodating individual differences into a model of acquisition. Issues in Education 1, 1–57.

Shepard, L. & Bliem, C. 1995. Parents' thinking about standardized tests and performance assessments. Educational Researcher 24, 25–32.

Smith, F. 1994a. Writing and the Writer. Hillsdale, NJ: Erlbaum. Second Edition.

Smith, F. 1994b. Understanding Reading. Hillsdale, NJ: Erlbaum. Fifth Edition.

Sommers, N. 1980. Revision strategies of student writers and experienced adult writers. College Composition and Communication. 31, 378–88.

Southgate, V., Arnold, H. & Johnson, S. 1981. Extending beginning reading. London: Heinemann Educational Books.

Spector, J. 1995. Phonemic awareness training: Application of principles of direct instruction. Reading and Writing Quarterly 11, 37–51.

Stedman, L. & Kaestle, C. 1987. Literacy and reading performance in the United States, from 1880 to the present. Reading Research Quarterly 22, 59–78.

Trelease, J. 1995. The Read-Aloud Handbook. New York: Penguin.

Tumner, W., Herriman, M., & Nesdale, A. 1988. Metalinguistic abilities and beginning reading. Reading Research Quarterly 23, 134–58.

Tunmer, W. & Chapman, J. 1995. Context use in early reading development: Premature exclusion of a source of individual differences? Issues in Education 1, 97–100.

Ujiie, J. & Krashen, S. Comic book reading, reading enjoyment, and pleasure reading among middle class and chapter I middle school students. Reading Improvement. In press.

United States Department of Education. 1993. Digest of Educational Statistics. Washington, DC: US Department of Education.

Verhoeven, L. 1991. Acquisition of biliteracy. AILA Review 8, 61–74.

Wagner, R. & Torgesen, J. 1987. The nature of phonological processing and its causal role in the acquisition of reading skills. Psychological Bulletin 101, 192–99.

Weaver, C. 1994. Reading Process and Practice. Portsmouth, NH: Heinemann. Second edition.

White, H. 1990. School library collections and services: Ranking the states. School Library Media Quarterly 19, 13–26.

Willig, A. 1985. A meta-analysis of selected studies on the effectiveness of bilingual education. Review of Educational Research 55, 269–317.

Winner, H., Landerl, K., Linortner, R., & Hummer, P. 1991. The relationship of phonemic awareness to reading acquisition: More consequence than precondition but still important. Cognition 40, 219–49.

Wright, R. 1966. Black Boy. New York: Harper and Row.

16 The California Reading Situation: Rhetoric and Reality

Jeff McQuillan
California State University, Fullerton

This chapter begins by explaining why the California reading situation is relevant to the rest of the nation. Turning to the alleged decline in reading in California, McQuillan explains that there is no evidence for the popular claim that reading scores have declined since 1987, when the state officially adopted a literature-based language arts framework. The widely cited NAEP scores for 1992 and 1994 do not demonstrate substantial change, and the CLAS scores (California Learning Assessment System scores) are incapable of doing so, due to changes made in the test from year one to year two. There are no standardized measures, however, that compare pre-1987 scores with scores in the early to-mid-1990s. Thus McQuillan argues that while the NAEP test scores are indeed low, there is no actual evidence to support the claim that reading scores among California's students have declined significantly between 1987 and now.

And what might be some of the causes for such low performance on the NAEP? Citing correlations between children's free reading and their reading achievement, and between school library resources and reading achievement, McQuillan argues that a major cause for a poor showing on the NAEP is the deplorable lack of books in California's libraries and the relative unavailability of books, libraries, and librarians to children. Another factor is the relative poverty of California's children, in part because poverty inhibits the availability of books and other reading materials in the home, since the presence of such materials correlates significantly with reading scores, including scores on the NAEP. McQuillan also notes that the NAEP assessments in 1992 and 1994 provide evidence that whole language and literature-based teaching produces *higher* reading scores than skills teaching, not lower. Thus there is good reason to be concerned about the reading of California's children, but their reading ability has not necessarily declined in recent years, and the alleged causes for California children's low performance appear not to be the real causes. McQuillan points out that it would be a mistake to abandon true whole language teaching, as "the most likely cause of California's low national ranking in reading achievement is not a literature-based curriculum but a lack of reading materials for California's students." This conclusion correlates with an increasingly substantial body of research and is an important lesson for all of us.

Portions of this chapter will appear in the *Claremont Reading Conference Yearbook, 1996*. Reprinted with permission of the Claremont Reading Conference.

While predictions of the historical importance of present events are always risky, it does not appear unwarranted to mark 1995 as something of a watershed year for the teaching of reading in the United States. That was the year when the nation's most populous state, California, took dramatic and highly publicized steps toward a renewed emphasis on phonics and skills in early literacy instruction. The significance of California's policy decisions for the rest of the country cannot be underestimated, as the case of whole language's supposed failure in California has been cited as justification for changes in other states and, indeed, for a new national policy on literacy instruction (e.g., Chen & Colvin, 1996). Understanding what really happened in California is necessary, then, if we are to get an accurate picture of the genesis of the current (and perhaps future) phonics-based reforms in reading instruction.

The reasons for California's dramatic shift in educational policy were agreed upon almost unanimously by government leaders and commissions, the media, and many members of the research community (see, e.g., California Department of Education, 1995a; California Reading Task Force Report [CRTFR], 1995; Fry, 1996; Stewart, 1996). First, California's reading test scores were said to have "plummeted" (Stewart, 1996, p. 23) to record lows over the previous ten-year period; second, this sharp decline was said to be directly attributable to the adoption of a literature-based reading curriculum in the state in 1987 (CRTFR, 1995), which de-emphasized phonics and skills instruction. As I will show, however, there is no empirical data to sustain either of these assertions. The shift in reading policy was based upon false information and faulty assumptions.

California Rhetoric: Declining Test Scores

The move to reform reading instruction in California began with the appointment of a special Reading Task Force in May 1995 by Superintendent of Public Instruction Delaine Eastin. The impetus for the task force was the release of two sets of test scores which have been widely cited as demonstrating that California's reading performance has dropped significantly since 1987. The first set is from the National Assessment of Educational Progress (NAEP), a federally-funded, standardized reading assessment administered every two years by the U.S. Department of Education to a representative sample of fourth-grade students in forty-one states. In both 1992 and 1994, California's fourth graders ranked among the worst of the participating states. The median score for California in 1992 was 202, the fourth lowest of the states and territories for which data was available, while the overall national average was 215 (on a scale of 0-500). In 1994, California dropped slightly to 197, tying for next to last, while the national average was 212 (Campbell, Donahue, Reese, & Phillips, 1996, p. 25). Rank scores are, of course, slightly misleading, since a difference of a few points can cause a state to rise or drop in rank if the states are clustered closely together. But even when this clustering is taken into account, California still did not fare well: in 1992, the state was in the bottom third, and in 1994, in the bottom quarter (Campbell et al., pp. 59-60). Clearly, California was performing relatively poorly compared with the rest of the nation.

But performing poorly is not the same as declining. To show a decline, one must look at scores from both the beginning and the end of the time period in question. Herein lies the problem: state-level NAEP scores are unavailable before 1992, and the tests are not equivalent to any other standardized reading measure. As such, the NAEP data cannot tell us anything about whether scores went up or down after the implementation of the literature-based curriculum.

The second set of data cited to show California's supposed drop, the California Learning Assessment System (CLAS), suffers from the same lack of comparability. The CLAS tests were administered only twice, in the 1992-93 and 1993-94 school years. Like the NAEP scores, they are not comparable to previous test scores and tell us nothing about how California students performed before and after the 1987 Language Arts Framework adoption which called for a literature-based curriculum. (In fact, due to changes made in the test after the first year of its administration, the two years are not even comparable to each other.) Ironically, the 1993-94 results indicated that more than three-fourths of California's students could read at a "basic" level, a rather strong showing in light of the dismal financial conditions of the state's schools discussed below (California Department of Education, 1995a).

When analyzing the NAEP and CLAS scores, it is important to keep in mind what categories such as "basic" and "proficient" mean in terms of reading proficiency. Both examinations are "criterion-referenced" and have established cutoff points for each level of proficiency. These cutoff points were not made in reference to how schoolchildren performed in the past, but rather were determined on the basis of criteria created by a committee of teachers and researchers. These criteria are different for each test and are necessarily arbitrary (Glass, 1978). On the NAEP test, for example, children who score above the basic level in the fourth grade (a score of 208 on a scale of 0-500) can "demonstrate an understanding of the overall meaning of what they read," can "make obvious connections between the text and their own experiences," and can "extend ideas in the text by making simple inferences" (Campbell et al., 1996, p. 42). For the CLAS examination, "basic" was defined as "literal understanding of a reading selection, both as a whole and in its parts" (California Department of Education, 1995b). Not surprisingly, the two definitions produce two different results. On the NAEP test, only 44 percent of California's children read at or above the basic level; on the CLAS test, more than 75 percent do. It should also be clear from these definitions that scoring at the "basic" level does not mean that children cannot recognize words or will stare blankly when confronted with a text.

A third set of data, commercial test score results, has also been cited by some journalists as evidence of a test score decline (Levine, 1996). The scores are taken from a report by the Policy Analysis for California Education (PACE) group (Guthrie et al., 1988) which equated California's performance on the California Achievement Program (CAP) to national percentile ranks during the early and mid-1980s. At first look, these scores seem to make the case for critics of whole language: as shown in Table 1, California scored near the middle throughout most of the previous decade in the PACE analysis, not near the bottom, as it had done in the 1992 and 1994 NAEP assessments. Upon closer inspection, however, it becomes clear that this data does not show that California ranked around the middle of the states before 1987, nor that scores were rising relative to other states over that same period of time,

Table 1

Comparison of California Achievement Program Scores to National Percentile Rankings

	81	82	83	84	85	86	87
CTBS[a] 1973 norms	59	60	62	64	69	71	—
CTBS 1981 norms	—	41	45	46	54	55	55

(source: Guthrie et al., 1988, Table 7.5)
[a] Denotes California Test of Basic Skills.

nor even that more than half of our students were above the national average in the mid-1980s. Let us take each of these claims in turn.

First, commercial tests are not comparable in any way to the NAEP tests from which California's low national ranking is determined. NAEP scores can be compared only with NAEP scores because they are derived from a set of criteria and representative samples particular to that test and are scored according to a statistical procedure very different from that used by most commercial test givers.

Second, national percentile ranks are *not* the same as ranks among the states (such as those that have been used in the NAEP comparisons). A national percentile rank of 50, for example, does not mean that California ranked in the middle of the states. *National* percentile ranks are derived from comparing the median student scores in a state with the scores of all *students* collectively in the country, while *state* ranks are determined by comparing a state's median score with the median scores of other *states*. An example might clarify this difference. Consider the hypothetical distribution shown in Table 2.

Although state B is separated from state A by 19 raw score points and 25 percentile points, the state rank—determined only in relation to where the state's score falls relative to the others—is two. This illustrates that there is no necessary relationship between national percentile ranks and state ranks.

With large, normally distributed national samples such as those used in NAEP, students in most states will tend to fall around the 50th percentile—that is the nature of normal distributions. Yet only one state will rank in first place, and one in last, despite the fact that the students in those first- and last-ranking states may score about average. We can now see why distinguishing between national percentile ranks and state

Table 2

Hypothetical Distribution of State Test Scores, National Percentile Ranks, and State Ranks

State	MeanRaw Score	National Percentile Rank	State Rank
A	230	75	1
B	211	60	2
C	207	55	3
D	205	53	4
E	200	50	5
F	180	42	6

ranks is so important: California's low 1992 NAEP ranking was a *state* rank, not a national percentile rank. California's national percentile rank of 55 from the 1986-87 CTBS reading test means that the average California student scored better than 55% of all students in the country, *not* that California ranked twenty- seventh out of fifty states in the country in reading.

Another example will help illustrate this difference: In the 1994 NAEP fourth-grade reading test, only fourteen of the forty-two states (33%) had average public school scores above the 50th percentile. This is because students are not evenly distributed among the states, *not* because only a third of American schoolchildren scored above average (a statistical impossibility in norm-referenced comparisons). Minnesota, for example, had a state rank of thirteenth in the nation, but scored below the 50th percentile (Campbell et al., 1996).

Third, although the 1980s CAP assessments and 1992 NAEP tests are not comparable, it is interesting to note that when uninflated measures of the CAP scores are used, the national percentile ranks are in fact quite similar. The most reliable percentile rank from the 1980s CAP program is from 1981-82, the year closest to the 1981 renorming of the test. The percentile rank for that year was 41 (Table 1). The state NAEP scores are not reported with a national percentile ranking, but from the information provided in the 1992 NAEP reports (Campbell et al., 1996, Table 2.1, p. 23; National Center for Education Statistics [NCES], 1994), it appears to be in the high 30s, just a few points below the CAP rank. Given the measurement error in both tests, this small difference is unlikely to be statistically significant. In other words, when compared with students nationwide, the average California fourth grader in 1992 probably ranked about the same as fourth graders in the early 1980s, scoring at around the 40th percentile mark.

The CAP scores do not show that California was on average any better in the 1980s than it was in 1992, nor do they show any serious

Table 3

California Achievement Program Raw Scores for 3rd, 6th, 8th, and 12th Grades, 1984–1990

	1984	1985	1986	1987	1988	1989	1990
3rd	268	274	280	282	282	277	275
6th	249	253	260	260	265	262	261
8th	250	240	243	247	252	256	257
12th	236	241	240	246	250	248	251

(source: Guthrie et al., 1993, p. 34)

declines after the implementation of the 1987 Framework. Table 3 shows the raw scores from the CAP until its discontinuation in 1990. There were slight increases and decreases across different grade levels, but overall the scores were very stable. California's third graders, for example, were performing at the same level in 1990 as they were in 1985, which would be unlikely if the 1987 Framework had caused a dramatic decline in test scores.

Despite repeated claims to the contrary, then, there is no evidence that California reading scores have declined markedly over the past ten years; rather, there is sufficient data to suggest that little change in achievement has occurred since the 1987 Framework adoption. This stability of test scores is remarkable in light of the declining financial status of California's schools (discussed below), a decline that has been largely ignored in the debates over reading achievement in the state.

California Reality: Disappearing Books

The second part of the argument used to promote a renewed emphasis on skills instruction is that whole language was the cause of California's (nonexistent) decline and (very real) low national ranking. As noted earlier, it is true that California ranked relatively low among the states. Is a literature-based curriculum or whole language to blame? Another look at the 1992 NAEP data reveals that the answer appears to be no. As part of the assessment, fourth-grade teachers were asked to indicate their methodological approach to reading as "whole language," "literature-based," and/or "phonics." The average scores for each type of approach were then compared, and those children in classrooms with heavy emphasis on phonics clearly fared the worst. Children in classrooms emphasizing whole language (reported by 40 percent of the teachers) had an average score of 220, those in literature-based classrooms (reported by 49 percent of the teachers) had a score of 221, and students in phonics classrooms (reported by 11 percent of the teachers) came in last with an average score of 208 (NCES, 1994, p. 284). Similar patterns were observed in the 1994 NAEP results (Campbell et al., 1996).[1]

If these teacher self-reports are accurate, then there is no evidence in the NAEP data that the use of whole language leads to lower reading scores. The cause of California's problems would seem to lie elsewhere. As it turns out, there are several likely sources for the state's low ranking, almost all of which were completely ignored by the state's political and educational leaders and by the media. Consider the following factors.

California has some of the worst school libraries in the country.

Massive evidence now exists to suggest that greater access to pleasure-reading materials leads children to read more, and that more reading leads to better reading achievement (e.g., Krashen, 1993, 1996; Stanovich & Cunningham, 1992). Specifically, evidence points up the critical role of school libraries in reading performance. Children get anywhere from 30 to 90 percent of their free reading materials from the school and public library (Krashen, 1993), and the impact of library quality on reading scores has been documented in a variety of studies. Lance and his colleagues (Lance, Wellborn, & Hamilton-Pennell, 1993) found in a study of Colorado schools that the quality of the school library had a direct and powerful effect on reading achievement scores, when controlling for the effects of teacher-pupil ratio, overall school spending, and socioeconomic status of the students. On the national level, Krashen (1995) showed that school library quality was the only significant predictor of a state's 1992 NAEP fourth-grade reading score, even when considering median income, per-pupil spending, and the availability of computer software in a school. My study (McQuillan, 1996a) also found that public and school library quality were important indicators of a state's average SAT score. Internationally, Warwick Elley (1992), in a study of over 200,000 students in thirty-two countries, found that school library quality had a significant impact on a country's reading performance, particularly on students who lived in lesser economically developed countries.

Table 4

School Library Quality in California and the United States

Books per Pupil:	Elementary	Middle	High School
U.S.	18:1	16:1	15:1
California	13:1	11:1	8:1
Per Pupil Spending			
U.S.	15.44	15.50	19.22
California	8.48	7.48	8.21
Librarians per Pupil	**Overall**		
U.S.	895:1		
California	5,496:1		

(source: White, 1990; Snyder & Hoffman, 1996)

How does California rank in school library quality? According to the most recent data available (White, 1990), California places last or nearly last in almost every category, including per-pupil spending, books per pupil, and librarians per pupil. Table 4 shows just how far California is behind the national averages in library quality, and the state's rankings are abysmal: forty-fifth in per-pupil expenditures, forty-ninth in books per pupil, and fiftieth in librarians per pupil.

California has one of the worst public library systems in the United States

Public libraries also have an important impact on children's reading achievement. My study (McQuillan, 1996b) found that there is a very strong correlation (r = 0.70) between a state's 1992 NAEP reading score and public library quality in a state. This finding means that nearly *half* of the variance in state NAEP scores can be accounted for merely by knowing the quality of a state's public library system. Mirroring its poor standing on school libraries, California also ranks near the bottom on several measures of public library quality. Chute (1992) reports that, in 1990-91, California ranked thirty-ninth in books and serials held per capita (1.95 versus 2.53 nationally), forty-third in capital outlay per thousand residents ($666 versus $1,912), and fiftieth in hours open to the public per thousand residents (72.09 hours per week).

Not only does California rank relatively poorly now, but the situation has become far *worse* since the late 1980s. As of 1993, Gibson noted that book budgets in the state had been cut 25 percent since 1989, the number of open hours had decreased 30 percent since 1987, and per capita spending had been reduced 36 percent from 1989. Children's services had been hit hardest, Gibson found, with 25 percent of public libraries reporting cutbacks in this area (Gibson, 1993).

California's children are poor and getting poorer

The only place children can find books outside of the school and public library is at home. But if one is poor, then he or she is much less likely to be able to afford many books. This relationship between poverty, access to books at home, and reading achievement is again seen clearly in the NAEP data: in 1992, the correlation between a measure of poverty and a state's NAEP reading score was -0.73; the correlation between books in the home and a state's average reading score, 0.87 (McQuillan, 1996b). Similar results were found in the 1994 assessment (Campbell et al., 1996). A reasonable interpretation of this data is that children in relatively poor states have less access to books in the home, leading to lower reading test scores.

California ranked ninth in the country in the number of children aged five to seventeen who live in poverty (Bureau of the Census, 1995), with the poverty rate rising an incredible 25 percent between 1989 and 1993 (Schmittroth, 1994). According to the most recent figures, one out of every four California students is living in a family with income below the poverty line.[2] Data gathered in the 1992 NAEP assessment confirms these figures: California ranked tenth-highest among participating states in the number of children who participate in free lunch and nutrition programs. Not surprisingly, the NAEP report also found that the state ranks near the bottom in the percentage of homes with more than twenty-five books in the home (NCES, 1994).

The Verdict on Whole Language

Whole language did not fail in California. There is no evidence that state reading test scores declined after the state implemented its literature-based curriculum framework in the late 1980s. Furthermore, there is very little reliable information on just how widely literature-based reading instruction was actually implemented in the state. The 1992 NAEP reading assessment reported that 69 percent of fourth-grade teachers in California said that they placed "heavy emphasis" on whole language practices in their classrooms, the highest percentage in the country. At the same time, 40 percent also said they gave "moderate emphasis" to phonics and 68 percent said they devoted at least some of their class time to decoding skills (NCES, 1994). Fisher and Hiebert (1990), in an analysis of teacher's self-reported labels concerning reading instruction and their observed reading practices, often found little correspondence between what teachers called their instruction (e.g., "whole language" or "phonics") and what went on in their classrooms. We should be cautious, then, in making any strong claims about just how seriously whole language took root in California based on teacher self-reports.

States looking to learn the "lessons of California" in reading instruction should avoid drawing the same faulty conclusions that the state's media and educational establishment have drawn in regards to whole language. The evidence indicates that the most likely cause of California's low national ranking in reading achievement is not a literature-based curriculum but a lack of reading materials for California's students. Before abandoning whole language, policymakers and teachers would be better advised to look at the state of their school and public libraries, making sure that children have books to read.

Acknowledgments

Portions of this chapter will appear in the *Claremont Reading Conference Yearbook, 1996.* Reprinted with permission of the Claremont Reading Conference.

Notes

1. Chall (1996) claims this interpretation of the NAEP scores is incorrect because "phonics is usually taught in grades 1 and 2, and possibly 3, [and] when it is taught in grade 4, it usually means that the students were already functioning below expectancy" (p. 305). In other words, low-scoring students in phonics classrooms are there because they are poor students to begin with. Chall argues that if we looked at the relationship between phonics and test scores in first and second grade, we would see higher scores for the phonics classrooms.

This interpretation is plausible if we looked only at the results nationally by *individual* classroom, as they are reported in Campbell et al. (1996). It is less persuasive, however, when we calculate the correlation between a *state's* NAEP score and a state's use of phonics in grade four, which (r = .59). If Chall were correct, it would mean that there is no meaningful correlation between what teachers of a given state do in reading instruction in fourth grade and what they do in the first three grades. In this case, it would mean that school districts with a strong emphasis on phonics in grade 4 do not necessarily use phonics in similar proportions in lower grades.

That is possible, of course, but not very likely. It seems much more probable that, on the whole, states, districts, and schools that use a lot of phonics in grade 4 also use a lot of phonics in grades 1, 2, and 3. (Imagine if whole language backers used a similar argument in California—that the real problem was that the state's first-, second turns out to also be very negative-, and third-grade teachers were using phonics, and that the emphasis suddenly changed to whole language in grade 4.)

2. Some have argued (Fry, 1996) that socioeconomic factors cannot account for California's low ranking in reading, since the median income for the state's residents in 1992 was above the national average, and both the percentage of people living below the poverty line and the number of persons twenty-five or older with a college education were about the same as the rest of the country. These figures, however, are for the average Californian, not the average California *parent*, who, as the figures above indicate, are indeed poorer than their counterparts in other states.

References

Berliner, D., & Biddle, B. (1995). *The manufactured crisis: Myths, fraud, and the attack on America's public schools.* Reading, MA: Addison-Wesley Publishing.

Bureau of the Census. (1995). *Statistical abstract of the United States.* Washington, D.C.: U.S. Department of Commerce.

California Department of Education. (1995a). *Educators commit to improving reading and math; Latest and last CLAS scores released, Press release RL95-19.* [Online]. Available: Gopher/North America/USA/California/California Department of Education/CLAS/Press Release.

California Department of Education. (1995b). *Minutes of the Reading Task Force, May 8, 1995* [Online]. Available: Gopher/North America/USA/California/California Department of Education/California Department of Education/State Superintendent Reading Task Force/RTF Minutes 5/14/95.

California Reading Task Force Report (CRTFR). (1995). *Every child a reader.* Sacramento, CA: California Department of Education.

Campbell, J., Donahue, P., Reese, C., & Phillips, G. (1996). *NAEP 1994 reading report card for the nation and the states.* Washington, D.C.: U.S. Department of Education.

Chall, J. (1996). American reading achievement: Should we worry? *Research in the Teaching of English, 30,* 303-310.

Chen, E., & Colvin, R.L. *(1996, July 18). Dole sees problems in schools and blames liberals. Los Angeles Times,* pp. A3, A19.

Chute, A. (1992). *Public libraries in the United States, 1990.* Washington, D.C.: U.S. Department of Education.

Elley, W. (1992). *How in the world do students read? The IEA study of reading literacy.* The Hague, Netherlands: International Associations for the Evaluation of Educational Achievement.

Fisher, C., & Hiebert, E. (1990). Characteristics of tasks in two approaches to literacy instruction. *Elementary School Journal, 91,* 3-18.

Fry, E. (1996). California students do poorly on reading tests. *California Reader, 29* (2), 9-11.

Gibson, L. (1993). *Status of California public libraries: Final report, abbreviated version.* Sacramento, CA: California State Library.

Glass, G. (1978). Standards and criteria. *Journal of Educational Measurement, 15,* 237-261.

Guthrie, J., Kirst, M., Hayward, G., Odden, A., Adams, J., Cagampang, H., Emmett, T., Evans, J., Geranios, J., Koppich, J., & Merchant, B. (1988). *Conditions of education in California, 1987-88.* Berkeley, CA: Policy Analysis for California Education.

Guthrie, J., Kirst, M., Koppich, J., Hayward, G., Odden, A., Rahn, M., & Wiley, L. (1993). *Conditions of education in California, 1992-93.* Berkeley, CA: Policy Analysis for California Education.

Krashen, S. (1993). *The power of reading.* Englewood, CO: Libraries Unlimited.

Krashen, S. (1995). School libraries, public libraries, and NAEP reading scores. *School Library Media Quarterly, 23,* 235-237.

Krashen, S. (1996). *Every person a reader: An alternative to the California's Reading Task Force Report.* Culver City, CA: Language Education Associates.

Lance, K., Wellborn, L., & Hamilton-Pennell, C. (1993). *The impact of school library media centers on academic achievement.* Castle Rock, CO: Hi Willow Publishing.

Levine, A. (1996, October). America's reading crisis: Why the whole language approach to teaching has failed millions of children. *Parents, 16,* 63-65, 68.

McQuillan, J. (1996a). SAT verbal scores and the library: Predicting high school reading achievement in the United States. *Indiana Media Journal, 18* (3), 65-70.

McQuillan, J. (1996b, August). *The effects of print access on reading acquisition.* Poster session presented at the 1996 Whole Language Umbrella, St. Paul, Minnesota.

National Center for Education Statistics (NCES). (1994). *Data compendium for the NAEP 1992 Reading Assessment of the nation and the states.* Washington, D.C.: U.S. Department of Education.

Schmittroth, L. (1994). *Statistical record of children.* Detroit: Gale Research, Inc.

Snyder, T., & Hoffman, C. (1996). *Digest of education statistics, 1995.* Washington, D.C.: U.S. Department of Education.

Stanovich, K., & Cunningham, A. (1992). Studying the consequences of literacy within a literate society: The cognitive correlates of print exposure. *Memory and Cognition, 20,* 51-68.

Stewart, J. (1996). The blackboard bungle: California's failed reading experiment. *LA Weekly, 18* (14), 22-29.

White, H. (1990). School library collections and services: Ranking the states. *School Library Media Quarterly, 19,* 13-26.

17 California, Whole Language, and the National Assessment of Educational Progress (NAEP)

Kenneth S. Goodman
University of Arizona

In the opening section, Goodman notes problems with the 1994 analysis of reading that have been acknowledged by the Educational Testing Service itself, which conducts the NAEP assessments. Further, he points out that comparing the 1992 scores with the 1994 scores is problematic, since there were significant differences in the two tests. In addition, he quotes two NAEP documents cautioning that "differences in reading performance among states most likely reflect an interaction between the effectiveness of the educational programs within the state and the challenges posed by economic constraints and student demographic demands." Nevertheless, the media and politicians have boldly declared that instructional methodology itself has been the problem: that, in fact, the alleged decline in test scores is the fault of whole language teaching. Goodman continues by focusing on NAEP data that have been ignored by the media and the politicians—data which show children in phonics-intensive classrooms to have earned lower proficiency scores than children receiving less instructional emphasis in phonics (an object of inquiry in only the 1992 NAEP), and data indicating that the students of teachers who used predominantly trade books scored higher than students receiving only basal reading instruction. In concluding this section, Goodman summarizes: "Nothing in the two NAEP tests suggests that moving from basal toward trade books has been anything but beneficial."

Further drawing on the NAEP data, Goodman discusses reading for fun at home and reading silently in school, both of which correlate with higher test scores. For example, opportunities to choose what they read in school correlates strongly with higher NAEP scores; nationally, there was a 20 point mean difference in 1992 and a 16 point difference in 1994 between those who chose their own reading daily and those who rarely got to choose. Goodman notes that nothing he could find in the NEAP data justifies the claims that whole language is responsible for low test scores. Unfortunately, Goodman says, there is no evidence in the 1994 assessment "that phonics is either beneficial or not" in reading development.

The next major section focuses on factors contributing to California's low mean scores on the NAEP. These include problems relating to the NAEP test itself and how it is reported; school conditions (class size, spending per pupil, absenteeism); and teacher characteristics, such as temporary certification and teacher experience. Goodman begins his final section by summarizing: "This critical analysis . . . shows a very different pattern of trends and important findings from those widely claimed by the test makers, public officials, and the media. It shows remarkable evidence for the beneficial effects of many key aspects of whole language, and it provides no support for the assumed cause-effect relationship between low test scores and whole language." In conclusion, he explains why and how "the irresponsibility associated with misstating and overreacting to misunderstandings of the 1992 and 1994 NAEP assessments has been widespread with plenty of blame to go around."

In April 1995, amidst a national press conference, the Department of Education issued *NAEP 1994 Reading: A First Look* and promised a complete report by September 1995. A revised *First Look*, dated October 1995, was not issued until well into 1996. In it the writers acknowledged "two technical problems" in the procedures used to develop the reading scale and achievement levels in both the 1992 and 1994 tests and the "Trial State Assessments." The more complete reports—the *Cross-State Data Compendium*, dated December 1995, and the *NAEP 1994 Reading Report Card*, dated January 1996—were available only in late spring and early summer of 1996. What effect the "technical problems" had on the results announced in April 1995 is not possible to determine from the reports released. I am beginning with this history to make clear why this critical analysis of the 1994 NAEP reports is possible only fifteen months after the flawed *First Look* was released.[1]

The National Assessment of Educational Progress has been conducted every two years in several school aspects, including reading, by Educational Testing Service (ETS), a private corporation under contract from the U.S. Department of Education. In 1992, NAEP changed considerably, establishing three arbitrary achievement levels and a mix of

---

[1] In the interest of reading ease, I refer to these three NAEP reports throughout the essay by the following shortened titles: *First Look, Compendium,* and *Report Card.* These reports can be found in the References list under their full individual titles: *NAEP 1994 Reading: A First Look* (Revised Edition); *Cross-State Data Compendium for the NAEP 1994 Grade 4 Reading Assessment;* and *NAEP 1994 Reading Report Card for the Nation and States.*

types of test items. As a result, this should have been considered an experimental test, and in fact changes were made between the 1992 and 1994 tests. How extensive these changes were, and what procedures were followed in assuring that the tests are equivalent, is not clear from the reports. In 1992, NAEP began the Trial State Assessment in grade 4 reading, and this assessment was repeated in 1994. In addition, a sampling of administrators, teachers, and pupils were asked to respond to a questionnaire to provide background information. The questions on the 1992 and 1994 interviews were not identical, with some dropped, some added, and some changed. No information is provided as to why the changes were made in the reports.

The national scores reported in the *First Look* for fourth and eighth grades were not significantly different, statistically, from 1992 to 1994. Twelfth-grade means were significantly lower in 1994 than in 1992. However, the main focus in the April press conference and the subsequent press reporting was on fourth graders from a group of eight states which had significantly lower scores on the reading test in 1994 compared with 1992—and the focus was particularly on California. The press and political leaders saw California's drop as the result of a shift in education toward whole language over the previous decade.

Both the *First Look* and the more complete *Compendium* contain the following caveat: "The reader is cautioned against making simple or causal inferences related to subgroup membership, effectiveness of public and nonpublic schools, and state educational systems. . . . [D]ifferences in reading performance among states most likely reflect an interaction between the effectiveness of the educational programs within the state and the challenges posed by economic constraints and student demographic demands" (*Compendium*, p. 3). Here is an example of reporting from *LA Weekly* (March 7, 1996), reprinted in *The Sacramento Bee*, *The San Jose Mercury News*, and other papers: "But whole language, which sounds so promising when described by its proponents, has proved to be a near disaster when applied to—and by—real people. In the eight years since whole language first appeared in the state's grade schools, California fourth-grade reading scores have plummeted to near the bottom nationally according to the National Assessment of Educational Progress (NAEP). Indeed, California's fourth graders are now such poor readers that only the children of Louisiana and Guam—both hampered by pitifully backward education systems—get worse reading scores." Similarly, the California legislature was so convinced of a relationship between whole language and NAEP test scores that it gave immediate effect to two "ABC" bills which "require, in part, 'systematic, explicit phonics, spelling and basic computational skills'" (Eastin, 1996, p. 1).

Clearly these journalistic and political responses not only ignore the caution that NAEP advises in interpreting its data; they also go far beyond what the NAEP studies have shown. There are only two state studies over a two-year period, so there is no NAEP data about California scores "plummeting" over an eight-year period. Furthermore data from the 1992 NAEP study showed that literature-based, integrated, and whole language emphases had beneficial effects on scores while heavy phonics emphasis produced lower scores than did the absence of phonics emphasis.

The fact that 98 percent of students in the 1992 assessment had teachers giving at least moderate emphasis to the integration of reading and writing suggests an overwhelming consensus among teachers on the usefulness and appropriateness of this approach for fourth-grade students. It would also appear that a majority of students are being taught by teachers who have embraced aspects of whole language and literature-based reading as a part of their reading instruction. Teachers reported that these methods were being given at least moderate emphasis, with the approaches reaching 82 percent and 88 percent of the fourth graders, respectively (1992 NAEP Executive Summary pp. 33–34).

Phonics continued to be an element of reading instruction for fourth graders (in 1992), but for more than one-third (39 percent) of them phonics played either a very small part or no part in their instruction. Teachers reported that only 11 percent of the students were receiving heavy instructional emphasis in phonics and they had lower proficiency than students receiving less instructional emphasis in this approach. The heaviest use of phonics in 1992 was in Mississippi, Louisiana, Guam, and particularly the District of Columbia—all of which had low mean scores on NAEP.

No data in the NAEP reports for 1994 relates explicitly to phonics. The District of Columbia withdrew from the comparison in 1994. Guam, which was also relatively high in use of phonics in 1992, had the lowest scores of any jurisdiction reporting in 1994. However, it is unclear whether the Guam data includes schools attended by military dependents (or whether these schools are treated as overseas defense department schools). If they are not included in Guam, then the Guam data refers largely to a Micronesian population for whom English is a second language. Due to this uncertainty, I have not included Guam in any of the comparisons which follow.

In this critical analysis the focus will be on data reported by the 1992 and 1994 NAEP reports.

Whole Language Evidence in the 1994 NAEP Data

The 1994 NAEP questionnaire asked teachers about topics they had "training in." Three topics seem to relate to whole language: Teaching Critical Thinking, Combining Reading and Writing, and The Whole Language Approach to Reading. Nationally, on training in critical thinking, 83 percent of responding teachers said yes in 1992 and 79 percent in 1994. On combining reading and writing, 89 percent said yes in both years. On whole language, 80 percent said yes in 1992 and 85 percent in 1994 (*Compendium*, pp. 126–28). There seemed to be no advantage for scores earned by students whose teachers did or did not report such training in any of the three areas, a fact which may simply reflect the low percentage of teachers reporting no training in these three areas. There is no information on teachers reporting *use* of whole language in the 1994 data.

In all three areas, for both years, California teachers reported training above the national mean. For critical thinking, those saying yes constituted 89 percent and 85 percent in the two assessments; for combining reading and writing, 97 percent in both years; and for whole language, 93 percent and 94 percent (*Compendium*, pp. 126–28).

It is not clear why NAEP chose to ask teachers about these areas and why they did not ask about phonics and other topics. It is also unclear why they asked teachers what they were taught but not what they *used* in 1994. Since NAEP did not ask teachers about their use of whole language and phonics in 1994, there is no way to see directly whether the trend teachers reported toward less use of phonics in 1992 continued in the 1994 data.

Movement away from basal readers

What should have been reported as the biggest story of the 1994 NAEP reports is the remarkable shift away from basal readers to the use of real literature (trade books) and the superior performance of pupils using trade books over those using basals. The policy shift initiated in California in the last decade was not so much to whole language as to use of real literature in the place of basals. The California Department of Education told publishers they would consider for adoption only programs that provided real literature for young readers, including trade books.

The NAEP data shows that the trend away from primary reliance on basals, begun by California, was continued and related to higher scores on NAEP. Table 1 shows the national data for 1992 and 1994 that documents the shift away from basals indicated in 1992 and continued in 1994. Estimates before 1992 indicated that 95 percent of classrooms used basal readers either exclusively or as the major material in reading instruction. The 1992 data showed 12 percent of teachers nationally saying they used primarily trade books and 49 percent reporting they used both trade books and basals. For 1994 these figures moved to 19 percent and 57 percent. Only one out of five teachers said they used only basals. Furthermore, students using primarily trade books showed higher mean scores than those using primarily basals. Notice that with the sharp shift away from basals, the advantage of using trade books remains appreciable in 1994, with those in trade-book-dominant classes showing a mean score of 219 versus 212 in basal-dominated classes.

This instructional material shift also shows in the California data and some comparison states. (In reporting California figures, I have included two other states [Louisiana and Hawaii] with similar low mean NAEP scores, as well as the top three NAEP 1994 states [Maine, North Dakota, and Wisconsin]. I hope thus to show similarities and contrasts.) For Louisiana (low) and North Dakota (high) the shift is from basals to mixed use of trade books and basals. Neither state reports much primary use of trade books, an absence which probably reflects state policies. It is probable that those reporting mixed use of basals and trade books are using the so-called literature-based basals which

Table 1

Materials for Instruction: Basals and Trade Books

		Basal		Trade		Both		Other	
		1992	1994	1992	1994	1992	1994	1992	1994
National	%	36	21	12	19	49	57	3	3
	Mean	216	212	223	219	218	215	208	202
California	%	11	3	15	37	66	52	7	8
	Mean	196	—	208	200	202	199	203	180
Hawaii	%	38	18	11	21	45	52	7	9
	Mean	203	198	192	197	204	205	211	190
Louisiana	%	67	52	2	3	31	44	1	0
	Mean	203	199	—	—	205	195	—	—
Maine	%	11	7	34	54	54	38	1	1
	Mean	224	224	231	232	226	225	—	—
North Dakota	%	62	35	1	4	36	59	1	2
	Mean	224	226	—	223	228	225	—	—
Wisconsin	%	25	17	13	25	61	56	1	1
	Mean	224	217	227	226	223	226	—	—

Sources: Report Card, p. 68; Compendium, pp. 65–66.

include sets of trade books in their packages. In virtually every state, over half of all teachers reported using a mix of basals and trade books in 1994. Maine, which topped all states on the NAEP scores, also shows the highest percentage of primary use of trade books (54 percent), quite a bit higher than California's 37 percent. Primary use of basals in California is down to 3 percent, too small to generate a mean score. Those who have blamed California's low scores on a shift to whole language must be ready to credit Maine's high scores to the same shift. Nothing in the two NAEP tests suggests that moving from basal toward trade books has been anything but beneficial. It should be noted that while use of trade books is a strong feature of whole language classrooms, they may also be used in non-whole language classrooms, and, in fact, recent calls for "balanced" programs call for use of trade books with direct instruction in phonics. NAEP provides no data directly related to such "balanced" programs.

NAEP also provides no information on what is included under "other." That would be the logical place to find skill and phonics packages, but it could include other instructional materials. In the 1994 NAEP report, Hawaii and California show 9 percent and 8 percent "other," figures that are near the 7 percent in each state reporting daily use of reading kits in teaching reading, but it is not clear how these figures might fit together (*Compendium*, p. 110).

Reading for fun at home

Of all the NAEP data, the part that is most encouraging to whole language teachers is the number of pupils who read at home for fun almost daily. In both 1992 and 1994 almost half of fourth graders nationally (44 percent and 45 percent) said they read almost every day for fun. Another 32 percent in both years said they read for fun once or twice a week. Only one out of eight said they almost never read at home for fun in fourth grade. Sadly, the figures for eighth and twelfth grade, also stable in both years, show less than one-fourth of pupils reading at home for fun almost every day, and just as many said they never or hardly ever read at home for fun (*Report Card*, p. 74). This drop-off may reflect the heavy homework and social agendas of adolescents. But perhaps a trend will carry over as 1992 and 1994 fourth graders reach eighth grade.

Remarkably, fourth graders in every state reported very similar patterns to the national pattern. In California, in both years, 45 percent reported reading at home almost every day. Louisiana and most Southeastern states show around 40 percent in 1994. In Iowa and Wyoming the figures get up to 50 percent. Louisiana and Mississippi with 16 percent have the highest percentage of kids saying they hardly ever read for fun at home. In four Northeastern states that figure drops to 8 percent. Though California and Louisiana were close in mean fourth-grade scores, they look very different in this aspect of home reading for fun and many other aspects (*Compendium*, pp. 132–33).

Not surprisingly the more kids read at home, the higher the mean scores on the two NAEP tests (see Figure 1). Nationally, in both 1992 and 1994, those reading almost every day averaged about twenty-five points higher than those never or hardly ever reading for fun at home. Even greater differences show in eighth and twelfth grades (*Report Card*, p. 74). All states also show similar differences, except Louisiana, Mississippi, and Alabama, which show more even scores regardless of home reading patterns. There is, of course, a circularity here. Kids who read better have more fun reading, so they read more and that helps them read better. But there is also a connection to the quality of what they are reading which the NAEP data does not examine. In whole language classrooms, young readers are introduced to a wide

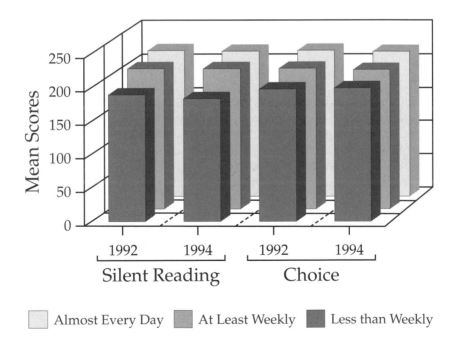

Figure 1. Silent Choice and Reading: Means.

range of literature through literature circles and author studies. There are classroom libraries which make books easily available. Paperback book clubs are also utilized. So it is not surprising that children are spending time reading at home for their own pleasure.

Holistic experiences in school

Responses by students to some other questions indicate that having holistic experiences in school relates to higher scores. One such beneficial experience is having frequent opportunities to read silently. Nationally, and in every state including those shown in Table 2, roughly two-thirds of pupils in both years reported that they were asked to read silently almost every day. In most cases, kids who read silently almost every day score better than those who read silently at least weekly. But the sharp disadvantage is for kids who rarely read silently in school. They scored about thirty points lower on average in both years than daily silent readers. In California, the difference is also about thirty points.

While silent reading is a characteristic of whole language programs, it is found in other programs as well. But silent reading appears to sharply divide more and less effective instructional programs. It would help to know how time available in some classrooms for silent reading is being used in other classrooms. There may be a double effect with silent reading aiding reading development and alternative activities hindering it. The NAEP data does not help with this question. An amusing anomaly in the NAEP data arises in the contrast between how teachers and pupils reported opportunities for silent reading. The table below is based on student responses. Among teachers, 75 percent said they have almost daily silent reading and hardly any said that they assign it less than weekly (2–3 percent). It can only be that some of the teachers are reporting not what the pupils are experiencing but what teachers believe they should be experiencing (*Compendium*, pp. 91–92).

Whole language teachers place a strong value on pupils having choice in what they read. As shown in Table 3, both NAEP assessments indicate that more than half of all pupils nationally report having time to read books of their own choosing almost every day in school. And as with silent reading, there is strong evidence in the relative mean scores that choice is beneficial. Nationally in 1992 there was a twenty-point mean difference between those who chose their own reading daily and those who rarely did so, and in 1994 the difference was sixteen points. In California the contrast is particularly sharp in both years, with a difference of twenty-seven points in 1992 and nineteen points in 1994. Every state showed similar patterns, although in Louisiana only 42 percent and 40 percent of pupils reported daily choice in the two assessments. All of the

Table 2

Silent Reading Reported by Pupils

Silent Reading		1992			1994		
		Almost Daily	At Least Weekly	Less than That	Almost Daily	At Least Weekly	Less than That
National	%	67	22	11	64	23	13
	Mean	221	213	193	220	213	188
California	%	68	20	12	69	20	11
	Mean	210	201	180	208	192	177
Louisiana	%	60	27	13	57	29	15
	Mean	208	206	188	202	198	184
Hawaii	%	66	21	14	65	20	15
	Mean	210	201	188	209	196	185
Maine	%	75	18	7	76	16	8
	Mean	229	229	210	232	224	211
North Dakota	%	65	24	11	67	25	8
	Mean	229	228	211	228	227	203
Wisconsin	%	70	22	8	73	18	8
	Mean	228	221	205	228	224	209

Source: Compendium, pp. 93–94.

Table 3

Pupil Reports of Time in School to Read Books They Choose

Choosing Own Books	1992			1994		
	Almost Daily	At Least Weekly	Less than That	Almost Daily	At Least Weekly	Less than That
National %	55	27	18	53	29	18
Mean	222	214	202	220	212	204
California %	57	25	18	56	27	16
Mean	213	200	186	208	194	189
Louisiana %	42	33	25	40	35	25
Mean	206	205	201	202	199	193
Hawaii %	53	28	19	54	28	18
Mean	210	202	203	210	200	189
Maine %	59	24	17	60	26	14
Mean	230	226	220	233	227	218
North Dakota %	57	27	16	55	20	15
Mean	229	226	216	230	222	219
Wisconsin %	58	28	14	63	25	12
Mean	229	221	221	230	220	214

Source: Compendium, pp. 96, 97.

states with less than 50 percent reporting daily choice in 1994 were Southeastern states: Alabama (47 percent), Mississippi (44 percent), Tennessee (43 percent), and West Virginia (46 percent).

Reading books at home

NAEP asked pupils in both years how many books they had read in the previous month. Clearly those who read none had the lowest mean scores nationally and in all the states. In addition, there is a wide difference in scores between those who read no books and those who read five or more books per month, though only 7 percent of pupils in 1992 reported no books read, and 9 percent in 1994. In California only 5 percent and 6 percent reported reading no books at home. Nationally the mean scores were about the same for those reading three to four books and those reading five or more. Even those who read one or two books a month were sharply better in both assessments than those who read none, with the margins at sixteen and eighteen points (*Compendium*, pp. 134–35).

There is again a circularity here. One who reads well reads more, and one who reads more reads better. But there has been a boom in the sales of children's books and in circulation in the children's rooms of public libraries over the last ten years. In the first six months of 1995, sales of children's paperback books rose 39.2 percent nationally over the previous year, which was 17 percent over the year before. Many publishers and children's authors credit whole language with the increased interest in children's books. Warwick Elley reports that a reading program he calls "book flood" was highly successful in developing island nations in the South Pacific which made a large number of trade books available to pupils (Smith & Elley, 1996).

California is surely part of the trend toward greatly increased popularity of children's books. Over sixty bookstores in California either are dedicated exclusively to books for children and young people or have major children's departments. In fact, according to the NAEP figures, 94 percent of California's pupils read one or more books a month, 66 percent read more than three, and 42 percent read five or more. In 1992 the figures were even higher with 70 percent reading three or more and 48 percent reading five or more. Yet in the 1994 study, the mean score for these prolific readers of five or more books in California was only 201 (as compared with the national mean of 215). And it is hard to reconcile the home reading habits of California pupils with the NAEP report for 1994. If 56 percent of California's fourth graders were reading below the "basic" level, how could 66 percent read more than three books a month? If only 18 percent are at the proficient level, why are 42 percent reading five or more books a month?

Whole language in the NAEP data: a summary

In the three NAEP reports that I examined for the 1994 NAEP, I found nothing that provides any support for the claims in the press and by politicians that whole language is to blame for low test scores. Nothing in the reports shows whole language as anything but beneficial. Use of trade books, children reading silently in books of their own choosing in school, and reading a number of books a month for fun at home all point to positive contributions of whole language to reading development. Nor could I find any evidence in the 1994 reports that phonics is either beneficial or not beneficial in reading development. Phonics simply is not examined in the 1994 NAEP reports. There is evidence that relying primarily on basal readers in reading instruction is not as effective as using trade books. Fortunately the major trend the NAEP data shows is a strong shift away from relying primarily on basals to mixed use of basals and trade books and beyond that to primary use of trade books.

Factors Contributing to California's Low Mean Scores

There is no evidence in the NAEP data that whole language is the cause of any decline in reading in California or anywhere else. Yet there is no doubt that California—as a whole—scored relatively low on the NAEP test in 1992 and even lower in 1994. Though the press has made much of California's next-to-last showing in the fourth-grade comparison, statistically California was one of nine states with no significant difference in mean scores. The others are Delaware, Arizona, Florida, New Mexico, South Carolina, Mississippi, Hawaii, and Louisiana (*First Look*, p. 34). In the following section, I will examine other evidence in the NAEP data that suggests some factors which might help to explain the overall poor showing. Some of these factors relate to the "economic constraints and student demographic demands" that NAEP refers to in its cautionary note quoted above. But there are some other factors worth further investigation as well.

Problems relating to the NAEP test and how it is reported

This is not a critique of the National Assessment of Educational Progress; in fact I have taken the reported NAEP data at face value. However, several issues involving the test itself need to be mentioned since they are potentially involved in the results of the test and how they are interpreted.

1. The test is based on an evolving view of what literacy is and how it can be measured.

The performance of the national sample and of the state samples are as much a measure of the test as of the students who took it. It is up to the test makers to continually examine the results to provide evidence that it indeed measures reading proficiency and that it does so fairly to all groups who took the test. Nothing in the reports (except the confession of data analysis errors) addresses this issue.

2. The three levels—"basic," "proficient," and "advanced"—were established in consultation with professionals who estimated how well test takers should do.

The results of the tests need to be used to reexamine how much those levels can be justified. The distributions on both the 1992 and 1994 tests appear to be at odds with other evidence. Some of this evidence is reported above, such as the amount of reading fourth graders are doing at home. Fewer pupils achieved each of the three NAEP levels than should have on the basis of other evidence such as scores on achievement tests, SAT's, and College Boards, as well as general success in school.

It is not clear in any of the NAEP documents what the test makers predicted in terms of percentages of students reaching each level. If, for example they expected 40 percent of the fourth graders would score below the "basic" level, then that was why they set the level where they did, and it should not be surprising that 40 percent nationally did so.

Educational Testing Service and the federal agencies that contracted with it have an obligation to examine their own arbitrary cutoff scores on the basis of 1992 and 1994 pupil performance. There has in fact been much criticism of the NAEP 1992 and 1994 tests in the testing community. Lissitz and Bourque, themselves involved in the setting of the NAEP standards, sum up the situation: "Despite the fact that progress has been made since the sixties, much of it does not appear likely to culminate in anything resembling finality or success. . . . For example, a great deal of subjectivity appears inevitable in the setting of standards no matter what approach is taken . . . and there are a number of unanswered questions which still need further research" (Lissitz & Bourque, 1995).

The National Center for Education Statistics seems to have taken a first step in considering how NAEP cutoff scores may have been misinterpreted. The Associated Press, on June 17, 1996, reported that NCES issued a document, *Reading Literacy in the United States*, authored by Marilyn Binkley, addressing data from the 1992 IEA study in which American fourth graders' mean score was second only to Finland

(Binkley, 1996). The scores for fourth graders on NAEP were low, whereas the scores for American nine-year-olds in the thirty-two-nation IEA study were high (Elley, 1992). AP quotes Binkley as indicating that the NAEP test measures U.S. students against government goals whereas the international study compares students of different countries. The IEA report explains the apparent difference in the two studies of American children's reading:

> In the case of the IEA . . . [s]tudent performance in one country is compared to student performance in the other participating countries. . . . As such the point of comparison is a relative rather than an absolute comparison. . . .
> Alternatively, much of the NAEP reporting is based on comparisons between actual student performance and desired performance. . . . As such, the reporting is referenced to a description of the tasks that students are expected to be able to do, or that someone thinks they should be able to do. (Binkley, 1996, pp. 13–14)

The score treated by NAEP as basic is in fact a government goal, what "someone thinks" constitutes basic literacy. American kids compare very well with those in other countries in reading, but they did not meet the arbitrary goals set in the NAEP assessments. Scores on tests are a function of the tests as well as the test takers. It is up to the NAEP test makers now to look carefully at the disparity between what they expected from American pupils and what the pupils actually did on the tests.

3. Changes in the test from 1992 to 1994 introduce the possibility that differences in performance are the result of the test changes and not of changes in reading proficiency.

Perhaps the lower twelfth-grade scores occurred because the test got harder. Perhaps biases were introduced which adversely affected some populations. We must consider these possibilities unless NAEP can provide information that would eliminate them.

4. Two major issues involve how the results are reported.

These issues can lead to misunderstandings by the public, the press, and the politicians.

A. Any comparison between performances on a test administered at intervals to each of three grade levels, as the NAEP is, can give the impression of providing longitudinal data. But we must remember, and the reports should remind us, that the 1994 fourth graders are a different group of pupils than the 1992 fourth graders. When the 1992 fourth graders are in the eighth grade in 1996, we might be able to see trends in their development—but only if the same sample is used. One reasonable conclusion of the significant difference in scores of California fourth graders in 1992 and 1994 (assuming the test is comparable) is that the two populations differ in significant ways. Such differences *could* include differences in their instructional experiences. But they also could include differences in the populations, the schools they go to, and the teachers they have.

B. *A common error in reporting test performance is to confuse the test scores with what they purport to test.* Over and over, in the NAEP reports, and in the press reporting of the results, test scores are simply referred to as "reading proficiency," as in this quote: "This chapter presents the overall average reading proficiency of students in grades 4, 8, and 12" (*First Look*, p. 7). In philosophy such a maneuver is called *reification*—treating a measure or symbol for something as if it were the reality it represents. This is no small distinction. No test, however cleverly it is constructed, can ever do more than sample what it seeks to examine. The scores are test scores—not reading proficiency. This is a particularly important issue when it is related to the arbitrary level-cutoff scores. The press is reporting almost 60 percent of California fourth graders cannot read at a basic level. What the data shows is that 56 percent of the California sample scored below the cutoff score labeled "Basic" on the 1994 test.

5. In a country as large, as populous, and as diverse as the United States, what do mean scores on any measure tell us?

Even if we divide the sample into subgroups, how does an average score relate to the complex realities which affect the performance of those in the group? So too, what is the importance of a mean score in California, which educates one-sixth of the nation's pupils and has almost as much diversity? What can it mean when states as different as California, Louisiana, and Hawaii have statistically equivalent low means, and Maine, North Dakota, and Wisconsin have statistically equivalent high means? The data I reported above shows how much difference can be covered by statistically equivalent scores.

But now let us consider the ethnic breakdown of three top-scoring states and three low-scoring states (see Table 4). I have added Arizona to include a substantial American Indian population. In 1992, NAEP used a single category that grouped together people who in 1994 would be categorized separately as either Asian or Pacific Islander. When the category was divided in 1994, a sharp contrast showed up

Table 4

Racial Composition of Different States and Mean Scores for 1992 and 1994

	White		Black		Hispanic		Asian/Pac.* Islander	Asian	P.I.	American Indian	
	92	94	92	94	92	94	92	94	94	92	94
National %	69	69	17	16	10	12	2	2	1	2	2
Mean	223	223	192	186	199	186	215	231	216	206	200
California %	46	44	7	7	35	33	11	8	5	2	2
Mean	219	211	185	182	183	174	213	211	213	—	—
Louisiana %	51	51	41	36	5	8	1	1	0	1	2
Mean	217	213	191	180	188	175	—	—	—	—	—
Hawaii %	20	17	5	3	11	11	61	19	46	2	1
Mean	218	219	192	189	194	185	204	219	191	—	—
Arizona %	56	58	4	4	29	29	1	1	1	10	8
Mean	222	220	201	183	198	188	—	—	—	185	181
Maine %	92	92	0	1	4	5	1	1	0	2	2
Mean	229	229	—	—	210	218	—	—	—	—	—
North Dakota %	93	88	0	1	3	6	0	1	0	3	4
Mean	228	228	—	—	222	212	—	—	—	212	197
Wisconsin %	83	84	6	5	8	7	1	2	0	2	2
Mean	229	228	201	197	211	211	—	—	—	207	—

Source: Compendium, pp. 14–16.

* Figures for Asian/Pacific Islander treated as a single group in 1992.

nationally between the two groups; in fact those classified as Asian had the highest mean score, 231, nationally. Use of the term Pacific Islander is not adequately explained in the NAEP reports. In Hawaii the term seems to have served as a residue for all those not classified as White, Black, Hispanic, or Native American, thus constituting almost half the population (46 percent), with a low mean score of 191. But whether Hawaii's substantial Filipino population is counted as Asian, Pacific Islander, or Hispanic is not clear. The figure of 11 percent Hispanic seems high unless it includes Filipinos. This question indicates a general problem regarding who is included in each category within each state. In California, those categorized as Asian score about the same as those categorized as Pacific Islander, thus suggesting that California includes different subgroups than Hawaii does. California has a substantial population of refugees from the region known as Indochina as well as recent poor Chinese immigrants who are probably included in the Asian group.

The three top-scoring states have small populations categorized as Hispanic who seem to score considerably better than the national Hispanic mean and better than the large Hispanic groups in California and Arizona with quite low means. This difference suggests that the populations are quite different in their composition. Similarly the small groups of American Indians in some of the states reporting here look very different in mean scores than the more substantial Arizona group. New Mexico shows 10 percent American Indians in 1994, with a mean of 185. Montana's 9 percent has a mean of 203. American Indians attend a variety of public, contract, and Bureau of Indian Affairs schools, and it is not clear which are included in the public school data here.

Even with these problems regarding who is included and excluded from each group in different states and regions, the clear pattern here is that those who are not classified as White, with the exception of some categorized as Asian, are not doing as well on NAEP as those categorized as White. In fact, for the categories White, Black, and Hispanic, scores are more similar within each group across different states than they are across different groups within the same state. I would guess that few of the differences between states in each ethnic group would be statistically significant, though I do not have the means to test that (NAEP could). Nationally, the mean scores for those categorized as Black and for those categorized as Hispanic were significantly lower in 1994 than in 1992, and that was also true for both categories in some states. Only in Delaware was there a significant drop in the mean for those categorized as White. What we can conclude from these figures is that a large part of the difference between mean scores of states is accounted for by the proportion of people not categorized as White (excluding some categorized as Asian) in the states. The effect could be even more dramatic than it initially appears: some students classified as Limited English Proficient (LEP) or special education (IEP) were excluded from the test sample if they were deemed unlikely to be able to finish the test. Those categories are much more likely to include to include people of color, so the actual percentage of people of color in the schools may be higher than shown in this data, which may exclude the lowest-achieving members of such groups.

Another issue is whether the relatively low scores of students not categorized as White reflect biases in the test items. I have no way of judging that, but it is a well-recognized problem in all testing.

School conditions

Several factors that would influence learning and teaching are reported by NAEP. The most striking are these:

Class size: Only 14 percent of California teachers reported having fewer than twenty-five pupils in their classes, in contrast with a national figure of 59 percent. No state matches California in large classes, and only two states—Utah and Florida, with 24 and 38 percent of teachers respectively reporting classes with fewer than twenty-five pupils—even come close. Class size is a measure of financial support as well as state policy. All of the Texas teachers (100 percent) and 95 percent of Maine teachers reported classes under twenty-five pupils (First Look, p. 55). Currently, California's governor has earmarked a tax surplus, legally mandated to be spent on schools, to be used to reduce class size to twenty in primary grades. While this reduction is much needed in the short term, it appears to be triggering a shift of qualified teachers from the less affluent to the more affluent schools, leaving a vacuum which can only be filled by recruitment outside the state or by unqualified non-professionals. No relief of the shortage of qualified teachers is possible in the long term with the decreasing support for teacher education in the state.

Spending per pupil: NAEP provides a summary of 1991–92 per-pupil expenditures. Nationally, the average was $5,421. California spent $4,746; Louisiana spent $4,354; and Hawaii's per-pupil expenditure was $5,420. Among the three top-scoring states, Maine spent $5,652; North Dakota $4,441; and Wisconsin $6,139. These figures, of course, need to be considered in terms of the relative costs in each state. Connecticut, New York, and New Jersey all spent over $8,000 per pupil. California's spending is comparable to much poorer states. Ironically, California teachers are relatively well paid, about $5,000 a year above the national average in 1992–93, the year NAEP reports. But these salaries are achieved at the price of very large classes (First Look, p. 58).

Absenteeism: In California 29 percent of pupils go to schools with high rates of absenteeism (see Table 5). Not counting Guam, only Arizona shows a higher rate (34 percent). Interestingly, the other border states, Texas and New Mexico, both have 25 percent rates. Border states are particularly affected by continuous recent arrivals from Latin America. Southeastern states also exceed 20 percent absenteeism. In contrast the top-ranking states—Maine, North Dakota, and Wisconsin—each have rates of 5 percent or less. The next three states by rank—New Hampshire, Massachusetts, and Iowa—had less than 7 percent or less (First Look, p. 55).

   In California's case, these figures about class size and per-pupil spending reflect the long-term effects of Proposition 13 and other restrictions on support for schools. All three factors—class size, per-pupil spending, and absenteeism—reflect possible changes in the school population which are not reported in the NAEP data but which may contribute to test performance.

Teacher characteristics

NAEP 1994 provides some data on the background of teachers which could affect pupil performance. Over a long period, California has had a somewhat different history of certification than other states, de-emphasizing professional education with more focus on non-education majors, and this difference is reflected in the NAEP data.

Table 5

Percentage of Schools Reporting at Least Moderate Absenteeism

States with High Rates	Percent	Rank	States with Low Rates	Percent	Rank
Guam	34	41	Dept. of Defense Schools	0	15
Arizona	34	33	North Dakota	3	2
California	29	39	Wisconsin	4	3
Arkansas	26	29	Maine	5	1
Texas	25	25	Massachusetts	5	5
Tennessee	25	24	New Hampshire	6	4
New Mexico	100	35	Iowa	7	6

Source: First Look, p.55.
Note: National mean was 16 percent.

Undergraduate majors reported for teachers reflect the state certification policies. Nationally, 69 percent of teachers major in education, 12 percent in non-education majors, and 20 percent in English, reading, or language arts. These figures reflect a tendency for elementary teachers to have an education degree and secondary teachers to have a specialized subject degree. But in California, only 39 percent of teachers have education majors (lowest of all states), 39 percent have non-education degrees (highest of all), and the rest (22 percent) have specialized degrees in reading, English, or language arts. Only 29 percent of California teachers have degrees above the bachelor's, whereas the national figure is 41 percent and some states are markedly higher. Kentucky, for example, has 82 percent, and Indiana has 84 percent. Of teachers with master's degrees in California, 65 percent are in education, meaning that one in five California teachers has an education master's degree. This markedly different pattern of educational background of teachers must be considered in looking at the California NAEP scores (*Compendium*, pp. 120, 121).

Temporary Certification

NAEP reports whether certification is general or specialized in reading or English/language arts, and these figures reflect state certification laws. Curiously, there is no figure reported for teachers with temporary or emergency certification, yet all states do issue temporary certificates to unqualified applicants when a sufficient supply of certified teachers is not available. Los Angeles has consistently employed 2,500 or more unqualified teachers with temporary certification each year. It is unclear whether these teachers were excluded from the sample or their temporary certification is lumped with regular certification. It would surely be important to know how pupils fared who were being taught by unprepared teachers. Consider that many school beginners may be trying to learn to read with a succession of temporary unqualified teachers and that it is entirely possible for a child to reach fourth grade without ever having had a professional teacher.

Experience

California shows a deviant pattern in the NAEP teacher data that reports years of experience. Table 6 shows figures for 1992 and 1994. In 1992, 41 percent of California teachers had ten years or less of experience, compared with 31 percent nationally. By 1994, over half of all California teachers had ten years or less of experience, but the national figure was only 33 percent. Thus, California already had a larger proportion of less experienced teachers than the national pattern in 1992, and the differences became sharper in 1994. This is a notable change over a mere two-year period in the relative experience of the teachers that California pupils had. The data does not suggest whether these less-experienced teachers include substantial numbers of unqualified teachers, though this would be a logical assumption since most teachers with more experience would be tenured, which requires regular certification.

Summary: Possible Causes of California's Poor Showing on the NAEP Tests

Analysis of data provided in the NAEP reports suggests several factors which very probably contributed to California's poor showing on the NAEP tests. There is a substantial difference in mean scores among those counted as White, those counted as Asian, and those counted in other categories used for people of color. California also suffers from the legacy of Proposition 13 and de-emphasis on professional education of teachers. These factors are reflected in meager financial support and large class size. California stands alone on class size, with no state even coming close to its very large classes. Changes in the school population are reflected in high rates of absenteeism, a problem shared with other states that border Mexico. The patterns of teacher education and certification in California differ markedly from those in most other states and appear to have resulted in notable differences in the educational background of California teachers, as a whole, compared with those elsewhere. Furthermore a sharp trend toward the loss of teachers with over ten years of experience occurred between 1992 and 1994 in California.

Table 6

Years of Teaching Experience

	1992			1994		
	0–10 yrs.	**11–24**	**25+**	**0–10 yrs.**	**11–24**	**25+**
National %	31	51	18	33	48	19
Mean Scores	212	219	216	210	214	216
California %	41	40	19	51	31	18
Mean Scores	197	205	205	197	198	201

Source: Compendium, pp. 122, 123.

The Need for Further Analysis and Critical Study

This critical analysis, which I was able to do easily once the much-delayed reports of the 1994 NAEP were available, shows a very different pattern of trends and important findings from those widely claimed by the test makers, public officials, and the media. It shows remarkable evidence for the beneficial effects of many key aspects of whole language, and it provides no support for the assumed cause-effect relationship between low test scores and whole language. There will be some who will say that the results of my analysis reflect my professional and personal commitment to whole language. Let them do, then, what they should have done before they drew their own conclusions—critically analyze the actual NAEP data.

The irresponsibility associated with misstating and overreacting to misunderstandings of the 1992 and 1994 NAEP assessments has been widespread with plenty of blame to go around. ETS, The National Center for Education Statistics, the Office of Educational Research and Improvement, and the U.S. Department of Education should have been much more complete and careful in their *First Look* and subsequent reports. Despite their brief cautionary note about overinterpretation of the results, ETS and the federal agencies involved in NAEP should have publicly corrected the widespread misrepresentation of the NAEP results. They should have been much more careful in focusing attention on state scores and much more cautious in reminding people that the mean state scores cannot be easily related to single factors such as curricular policies. They should also have taken much more responsibility for examining the possible flaws and inadequacies of the test itself. They owe it to the public and the profession to publicly consider how the test itself may have contributed to the patterns of performance and how they were interpreted. Particularly, they need to be honest about arbitrary cutoff levels and test designs.

In turn, the California school authorities and legislature should have demanded from the federal agencies a much fuller accounting of the evidence from the NAEP data about which teachers, which pupils, and which schools did better or worse and what factors contributed to better performance. And instead of quickly proclaiming a crisis and leaping to unwarranted conclusions about the relationship of whole language curricula and policies to low test means, California politicians and school agencies should have considered the full range of conditions, realities, and policies which could be contributing to the performance of California pupils on the NAEP tests. Particularly they need to consider the long-term effects of Proposition 13, low per-pupil expenditures, and large class sizes. They also need to examine the possible effects of California's teacher education and teacher certification policies. And they need to look carefully at changes in the school population and how schools are supported— or not—in coping with these changes.

The press has its own share of responsibility for failing in its job of investigating and exposing to scrutiny the NAEP data and the realities which should be examined to understand this information. Instead they have reported speculation unrelated to the NAEP results—most particularly on the importance of phonics in reading instruction, a topic singularly unsupported by the NAEP data. In fact the word phonics never occurs in any of the NAEP reports. The lack of any serious responsible journalism is evident in article after article following the same pattern beginning with the "abysmal" scores on NAEP and attributing them to whole language. Instead of going to the data, these writers quote each other, creating the news rather than reporting it.

The research community also has neglected its responsibility. Instead of careful analysis of the NAEP reports and the databases they produced, many researchers have responded to reports by the press and politicians by offering pet theories on why the scores were low and how high scores can be achieved. If they want to use the NAEP reports to support their positions, they need to go far beyond speculating on low mean scores. They need to look at the data.

I raised some of these issues in an open letter to President Clinton and U.S. Secretary of Education Richard W. Riley. In response, Anne Sweet, Senior Research Associate in the National Institute on Student Achievement, Curriculum, and Assessment, at the U.S. Department of Education, said:

> The fact that an increasing number of children have begun to read books of their own choosing for pleasure at home on a daily basis is highly significant. When this pattern translates into NAEP test score gains, you can be sure that the Department will make the connection more explicitly.

The evidence, as I reported above, is in the NAEP data. The Department of Education owes it to American teachers and students to make that public.

References

Binkley, M. and Williams, T. (1996). *Reading literacy in the United States.* Washington, DC: National Center for Education Statistics, U.S. Department of Education.

Cross-state data compendium for the NAEP 1994 grade 4 reading assessment. (1995, December). Washington, DC: Report prepared by Educational Testing Service for the National Center for Education Statistics, Office of Educational Research and Improvement, U.S. Department of Education.

Eastin, D. (1996, May). *A balanced comprehensive approach to teaching reading in grades pre-kindergarten–3.* Sacramento, CA: California Department of Education.

Elley, W. (1992, July). *How in the world do students read?* The Hague: International Association for the Evaluation of Educational Achievement.

Lissitz, R. and Bourque, M. (1995, Summer). Reporting NAEP result using standards. *Educational Measurements: Issues and Practice*, 14–31.

NAEP 1994 reading: A first look (revised edition). (1995, October). Williams, P. Washington, DC: Report prepared by Educational Testing Service for the National Center for Education Statistics, Office of Educational Research and Improvement, U.S. Department of Education.

NAEP 1994 reading report card for the nation and states. (1996, January). Washington, DC: Report prepared by Educational Testing Service for the National Center for Education Statistics, Office of Educational Research and Improvement, U.S. Department of Education.

Smith, J. and Elley, W. (1996). *Learning to read in New Zealand.* Katonah, NY: Richard C. Owen.

VI From Instructional Myths to Meaningful Instruction

18 The Schools We Have.
The Schools We Need.

Richard L. Allington
University at Albany

In the introduction to this chapter, Allington discusses his concern that, historically, American education has had different standards and goals for different children, and thereby promoted success for some and failure for others. He refers to evidence from a variety of sources indicating that "the differential curricula used in different tracks and reading groups [has] limited the opportunities of some children to achieve anything but the most basic levels of educational proficiencies." Allington argues that we should operate from the assumption that virtually all students can achieve the kinds of literacy that perhaps only a quarter of our students have historically attained. One important starting point is to recognize factors that we as educators and the public have historically confused, and then to reject our false assumptions. Allington explains in detail how we have confused experience and ability; the kind of curriculum we've provided for labeled learners (a slowed-down curriculum) with what they need (an accelerated curriculum); the difference between merely sorting students and providing them with the extra assistance they need to succeed; the distinction between curriculum and instruction; the importance of books, as opposed to filling in blanks; the concept of teaching as different from assigning, and of understanding as different from remembering. The last two sections of the chapter focus on ways of beginning to create the schools we need.

If we were to believe the reports about American education that dominate the media we would have to conclude that the quality of U.S. schools has diminished significantly over the past several decades and that radical reforms are immediately necessary. But, one should never believe everything one reads. A more accurate summary of the current state of affairs is that American schools are doing quite well at what society once wanted them to do, but today society wants schools to accomplish more than in the past. This seems especially true in the area of literacy development.

My professional career spans roughly a quarter century. Across this period I have been primarily concerned with the school experiences of children who find learning to read and write difficult. The work I have done, both alone and with my colleagues, has almost invariably addressed the rather straightforward premise that children are more likely to learn what they are taught than what they are not. This simple premise, when applied to the educational experiences of children who find learning to read and write difficult, raises some interesting and disturbing issues (Allington, 1977, 1983; McGill-Franzen & Allington, 1991) and suggests that achieving the new goals set for our schools will necessitate some substantial shifts in what is commonly taught.

I was asked to write in this article about the "instructional/practical implications" of my work. As I pondered the invitation and grappled with composing an article, I returned to the same ideas again and again. Much of what I have written about for nearly 2 decades has been drawn from what I learned while observing in schools and puzzling through (usually with assistance from teachers and colleagues) how to best explain what I had seen. For me, observing usually was more confusing than enlightening—at least initially.

In this article I explore some of the confusions that upset my educational equilibrium and seemed then (and often still) to limit our view of both the problems we face as teachers and teachers of teachers and the potential solutions we might pursue. These confusions, or competing explanations of educational phenomena, foster and sustain much of the uncertainty that marks our profession today. Uncertainty always accompanies change, and there is no doubt that American education is involved in substantial change. Our schools now educate larger numbers of children to higher levels of proficiency than ever before. Still, there exists a general impression that schools no longer work very well. Our schools meet or exceed the goals that have been held historically but fail to meet the more recent expectations set by society. After nearly a century of expecting schools to develop the basic literacy abilities of most students, but expecting advanced literacy to be learned by only some, today schools have been challenged, or expected to develop, advanced literacy in virtually all students. In other words, society now expects schools to educate all students to levels of proficiency expected historically of but a few (Marshall & Tucker, 1992).

We can debate whether such a shift in goals is necessary to sustain the changing economy (Shannon, 1993) and debate how such a shift might be best accomplished, but schools, especially publicly funded schools, are expected to adapt to shifts in public expectations. How might schools begin to adapt to the expectation that virtually all children achieve the sorts of literacy proficiencies that, perhaps, one quarter of students historically attained? We can see adaptations that are already underway in the elimination of tracking in many high schools and the move away from reading groups in elementary schools. Because evidence from a variety of sources indicated that the differential curricula used in different tracks and reading groups limited the opportunities of some children to achieve anything but the most basic levels of educational proficiencies, elimination of differential goals and differential curricula has been set as an immediately needed adaptation (Wheelock, 1992).

But the notion of differential standards for different children has a long history in American education. Differential goals are anchored in understandings about human intelligence and human learning that have come under increasing attack as human learning is better understood (Tharp & Gallimore, 1988). It simply is not necessary that some children fail to learn to read well. Unfortunately, that is how society has historically understood the bell-shaped curve that was created at the turn of the century to represent the normal distribution of a wide range of supposedly innate human abilities. It is time to reject the notion that only a few children can learn to read and write well. For too long we have set arbitrary but limited literacy learning goals for some children, usually those children whose scores fell at the wrong end of the normal curve distribution. This design virtually ensured some children would not receive instruction sufficient to develop their potential as literacy learners.

With the accumulation of overwhelming evidence that schools have better served advantaged children than disadvantaged children (Cooley, 1993), the notion of differential goals has come under attack as violating basic tenets of education in a democratic society. After nearly a century of attempting to identify what is wrong with poor children or their families, many are instead suggesting that schools need to be dramatically restructured in order to better serve disadvantaged children. Because my work has focused on children whose educational needs were often not well met in schools, issues of differential goals and expectations, accompanied by differential curriculum and instruction, have literally permeated my writing and my confusions and uncertainties.

But such confusion and uncertainty has not undermined my belief that schools can meet the more recent and more substantial expectations that challenge the profession today. Nor have the confusions and uncertainties undermined my belief that our schools must adapt in order to educate historically underachieving children to the levels of proficiency achieved by their advantaged peers. No, my confusions and uncertainties lie more in precisely how to change the schools we have in order to achieve the higher levels of proficiency we expect. I would like all children to achieve the sorts of proficiencies that my own children have attained. I am quite certain that we must work to create schools where all children achieve, not just children with the "right" parents.

But for schools to accomplish such adaptations, several current confusions about literacy teaching and learning must be resolved. These confusions that limit our ability to adapt our schools stem from a turn-of-the-century behaviorist psychology and what I have dubbed "the cult of the normal curve." The first confusion, mistaking limited experience with limited ability, occurs often even before the child actually arrives at the classroom door.

Experience vs. Ability

When children begin school with few experiences with books, stories, or print, we generally confuse their lack of experience with a lack of ability. Children who lack experiences with text before school usually perform poorly on any of the kindergarten screening procedures now common in schools, regardless of whether the assessment emphasizes isolated skills acquisition or holistic understandings. The poorer performance, compared to that of their classmates with more experience with books, stories, and print, is too often understood in school as evidence that the children's capacity for learning may be somehow limited. Children with few experiences with books, stories, and print are described with phrases such as *at risk, unready, limited ability, developmentally delayed, immature, slow* and other terms that confuse limited literacy experience with intellectual limitations (McGill-Franzen, 1992).

In a similar manner, once in school, children who read little are the children least likely to read well and most likely to be described in terms that suggest a limited capacity for literacy learning. The phrases used to describe children who find learning to read difficult often contain the words *low* or *slow* (e.g., low group, low readiness, low ability, slow learner). Such children typically experience lessons designed in ways that restrict how much reading they do in school. These children read little in school compared to classmates whose reading development is more advanced (Allington, 1983; Hiebert, 1983).

The premise of one of my earliest articles was that we so emphasized skills activities with children who found learning to read difficult that these children did not have the opportunity to read much in school (Allington, 1977). A number of more recent and larger studies have continually reaffirmed the original premise that children who become good readers routinely read a fair amount both in and out of school. In other words, sheer quantity of reading experience is an important factor in children's literacy development. Still, when we hear talk of children who find learning to read difficult it remains unlikely that we will hear much discussion of the lack of reading experiences as the source of the difficulties. Professional discussions about a 12-year-old child who is still experiencing substantial difficulty reading independently will commonly involve talk of potential neurologically based learning disabilities and only rarely talk of the evident lack of experience with reading.

The design of instructional interventions for limited-experience children has similarly failed to emphasize expanding substantially their opportunities to read, write, and listen to stories. Rather than creating interventions that immerse low-experience children in print and texts, remedial, compensatory, and special education interventions focus more often on providing participating children with more skills lessons.

Children with few preschool experiences with books, stories, and print have not often attended classrooms or experienced literacy curricula that immersed them in a rich array of literacy activities. Even our preschool programs for disadvantaged children have rarely created settings where limited-experience children are immersed in a rich print and story environment (McGill-Franzen & Lanford, 1994). Here, again, we confuse the lack of experience with limited capacity. Because of this, we design preschool curricula that effectively limit the opportunities that disadvantaged children have to experience the sorts of literacy events that more advantaged children routinely experience in their preschools and in their homes. Far too often limited-experience children are viewed as having limited potential and the pace of introduction of the book, story, and print curriculum is slowed for them, while social skills, self-esteem, and rote learning are emphasized.

Acceleration vs. Slowing It Down

Because we confuse experience with ability, we tragically lower our expectations for literacy learning in children lacking experiences with books, stories, and print. We just do not expect kids who started out behind to ever catch up. Once we had developed the assessment tools that ostensibly allowed us to measure reading achievement and intellectual capacity, we began to use these tools to limit the opportunities that some children would have to become literate. The reading tests indicate some children are behind others in their literacy development.

Many children with limited experience with books, stories, and print also perform poorly on the tests of intelligence. This has been interpreted to mean that children who begin school behind or fall behind once in school have some impaired capacity for learning. It has been generally assumed that this presumed impairment was hereditary—intellectually impaired parents, the poor, unemployed, and not well-educated ones, pass this intellectual impairment on to their children. Our most enduring label for these children—slow learners—makes the assumed link between delayed literacy development and intellectual capacity quite clear. The label also clearly suggests that this supposed limitation in intellectual capacity makes it unlikely that these children will ever learn to read with or as well as their peers.

Of course, children who read well score better on the tests than students who do not read so well. We now know that one reason for the correlation is that intelligence tests usually measure things that are likely learned in school, from books, and in middle-class homes (Gould, 1981; Stanovich, 1993). However, when we take a broader view of the human intellect (Gardner & Hatch, 1989), it becomes painfully clear just how tenuous any relationship between literacy development and intellect must remain. But even if the old view of intelligence as narrow, verbal, and largely unmalleable were true, there need not be any strong correlation between literacy achievement and intellectual capacity. Rather, even the old view could easily be seen as providing an estimate of how much instructional effort might likely be required to develop literacy in individuals of differing intellectual capacities (Allington, 1991). We might use the tests to estimate who will need more and better teaching rather than predicting who will learn to read well and who will not. In fact, part of the argument for compensatory education programs in the 1960s was that providing supplemental instruction to some students would overcome the disadvantage of living in poverty or having parents who were not well educated.

Unfortunately, few designed remediation in ways likely to foster substantially accelerated literacy development in children (Johnston & Allington, 1990). Often the designs reflected deeply held beliefs about the assumed limited capacity of some children as literacy learners. Even those who have led the way in the development of early, intensive intervention (e.g., Clay, 1991) admit that the powerful demonstrated potential of such remediation was surprising. The "recovery" of so many young readers experiencing difficulty in such short periods of time (12-15 weeks) violated widely held professional beliefs and called traditional remedial and special education practices into question. Since the turn of the century, experts had advocated slowing down curriculum introduction for children who experienced difficulty learning to read. But as instruction was slowed and made *more concrete,* readers in trouble became less and less likely to ever catch up. Many still believe that literacy learning will necessarily be delayed for such children and that most will never catch up. When such beliefs drive the design of intervention programs we cannot be surprised that remedial instruction is usually insufficiently intensive to accelerate literacy development and allow children to catch up to their peers.

Sorting vs. Supporting

Much of the institutional energy that is expended on children who find learning to read difficult is focused on sorting children into categorical groups rather than on creating enhanced instructional support for learning to read. We have confused sorting and labeling children with supporting their learning. Across the past 25 years we have expanded the array of labels we use and the number of special programs and special teachers available in schools. In fact, today about half of all adults employed in elementary schools work in some role other than that of a classroom teacher (Allington, 1994).

Our schools have become places where readers in trouble are assessed, sorted, labeled, and then segregated from their peers for all or part of the day. The tests we administer usually tell us more about the instruction the child has received at home and school than about the children themselves, but assessment results are rarely translated in this way. Instead, assessments are used to assign children to one or more of the special categorical programs.

Concern about the increasing use of labels and the increasing segregation of ever-larger numbers of children has resulted in a series of federal initiatives to return harder-to-teach or inexperienced-with-print children to the regular classroom for increasing amounts of time and instruction. There is a good reason for these initiatives. The evidence has accumulated that special programs, special teachers, and segregated instructional programs simply cannot match the effects of high-quality classroom instruction (Cunningham & Allington, 1994).

We spend enormous amounts of money trying to sort kids into different special programs. These costs accumulate before a child receives any instructional services. We spend large sums each year to identify which low-achieving children will be placed in which categorical programs. Testing children to identify who will be labeled as handicapped now occupies the time of large numbers of school psychologists, speech teachers, and special education teachers, many employed in professional support positions that were nonexistent just a few years back. Testing to identify which children will be eligible for federally funded Chapter 1 compensatory services has been an annual ritual in most schools. But the tests only help sort and label children. Tests do not tell us what providing sufficient instruction might entail.

Labeling is not instruction. Labeling was originally intended as a sort of shorthand for describing the needed instruction, but it just never panned out. Tests just do not provide the sorts of information needed to design supportive instruction. In fact, tests provide little reliable information even for sorting children. Today, the labels we give children communicate virtually no useful information beyond which agency funds the intervention to be provided. Children identified as learning disabled, for instance, cannot be readily differentiated from those served in remedial programs or those identified as dyslexics (Algozzine & Ysseldyke, 1983). In addition, no one has been able to demonstrate that any particular curriculum or teaching style works better with some groups of children than others.

Curriculum vs. Instruction

Our professional history is replete with debates about teaching methods and curriculum focus. Following a pendulumlike persistence we swing from more child-selected, holistic, literature-based curriculum to more adult-selected, atomistic, empirically derived curriculum (Larger & Allington, 1992). But curriculum would seem an unlikely source for debate given the evidence on how little curriculum focus really seems to matter. In study after study, curriculum materials and teaching methods have not proved as critical to literacy development as how well and how intensively children were taught. These many studies always found larger differences between the more-effective and less-effective teachers using any given curriculum than differences in the effectiveness between curriculums being compared. In other words, some teachers achieve better results regardless of the curriculum in place. Children's access to high-quality instruction is what seems to matter and high-quality instruction can be achieved within a variety of curriculum frameworks. We have known for at least 25 years that access to high quality classroom literacy instruction with substantial opportunities to read and write is more important than curriculum focus— but we continue to debate curriculum and method. However, across this long history of curriculum debates one pattern stands out: Some children, usually poor children, are not nearly as successful in developing literacy as other, more advantaged, children. It was this hard fact that led——to the passage of the U.S. Elementary and Secondary Education Act of 1965 and provided schools with additional reading teachers through the federal Title 1 program (now Chapter 1).

Chapter 1 compensatory education programs were founded with enormous expectations. It was expected that supplemental Chapter 1 instruction would be the solution to the difficulties so many economically disadvantaged children experienced in schools. But by the time the program celebrated its 25th year, substantial evidence had accumulated that the program had failed to live up to these high expectations (LeTendre, 1991). It was not that Chapter 1 had failed, exactly. Participating children typically made small gains, but the literacy development of few children was accelerated sufficiently or rapidly. Most children had continued eligibility for program participation. Others tested out, only to return a year or two later to the program rosters. Chapter 1 programs improved the futures of participating children only modestly while failing to foster advanced literacy proficiencies in most children served by the program (Allington & Johnston, 1989).

But the most common design of Chapter 1 interventions was an unlikely candidate to achieve such goals. Historically, Chapter 1 programs were designed as pull-out instruction operating during the regular school day. Thus, no additional instructional time was actually made available. In addition, most participating children were pulled out of the regular classroom during some part of classroom reading and language arts instruction, ensuring that no added literacy instructional time was available. Usually Chapter 1 programs involved small group instruction for 5-7 children for 30 minutes several times a week. These instructional groups were similar in size to the classroom reading groups, and so intensity of instruction was rarely increased. Because Chapter 1 teachers often worked with larger numbers of children each day than did the average classroom teacher and worked with these children for rather brief periods of time, instruction was rarely personalized. Instead, the most common Chapter 1 program designs literally precluded instruction of the sort that might be expected to accelerate achievement (Allington, 1987; Allington & McGill- Franzen, 1989a; McGill-Franzen & Allington, 1990). Unfortunately, the same has been true of the most common program designs implemented for the instruction of children with learning disabilities (Allington & McGill-Franzen, 1989b).

However, the debates that have dominated the professional literature of remedial reading and learning disabilities have typically argued curriculum matters. These debates largely ignored the critical features of the instructional interventions and environments provided participating children. In focusing on which curriculum to use, the inadequacies of the intervention designs were ignored. As the limited effects of these programs became clearer, design issues have finally been addressed. Thus, today we can find substantial experimentation in the design of remedial and special education programs. Generally, the redesign discussions focus on how to actually expand instructional time, how instruction might be better personalized for students, and how intensity of the intervention can be increased (Allington, 1993).

As the reauthorization of various federal educational programs proceeds, issues of instructional program design, not curriculum, seem to dominate (Commission of Chapter 1, 1993; Rotberg, Harvey, & Warner, 1993; U.S. Department of Education, 1993). But while curriculum debates are largely and fortunately absent, a focus on the types of literacy activities that children accomplish across the school day is needed. It is important that all children have substantial opportunities to engage in reading and writing activity. It is especially important that instructional interventions intended to accelerate literacy development ensure that participating children read more and write more than other children. But reading and writing are still not popular activities in American schools.

Books vs. Blanks

It is true that American elementary school students today read and write more during the school day than they did just 10 years ago (Langer, Applebee, Mullis, & Foertsch, 1990). Still, reading and writing activity occupy less than 10% of the school day! While we have increased the time children spend actively engaged in reading and writing and decreased the time they spend in seatwork activity, children still read and write little in school (Allington, Guice, & Li, 1993). Much of the traditional fill-in-the-blank seatwork has been removed from the school day, and there is no reason to mourn the loss (Jachym, Allington, & Broiku, 1989). However, replacing traditional seatwork are maps, webs, journals, and question-generating and question-answering activities that still occupy much time that might be spent reading and writing. New to the school day routine are the presentations of books, in which the whole class sits and listens as each reader describes his or her current reading. These instructional activities can offer powerful support for children's developing understandings of how to read skillfully and thoughtfully. But such activities still prevent children from actually reading and writing. We need to ask ourselves as we plan, "Is this activity a better way for children to spend their time than engaging in reading or writing?" Children need time to read in school.

We continue to organize the school day such that most children have little opportunity to actually read or write.

Another reason that children read so little in school seems to be the lack of anything much to read. No basal has enough reading material for anyone to become a good reader and yet in too many classrooms basal anthologies are just about the only reading material available. In our recent work we have found that some schools have books and magazines available for children to read, but very few schools could be described as having a wealth of books available (Guice & Allington, 1992). In the schools we studied, children's access to books and magazines was directly related to the number of children from low-income families that attended the schools. In other words, schools with few poor children had about 50 percent more books and magazines than schools that enrolled many poor children. This may account for the limited use of literature in schools that enroll large numbers of poor children (Puma, Jones, Rock, & Fernandez, 1993).

However, even in schools with the largest school and classroom libraries there was often still little variety in the reading material available. Library collections were often dated and classroom collections offered multiple copies of a few titles rather than single copies of many titles. The short supply of easy, interesting material was especially troublesome for children who were finding learning to read difficult. If we carefully examine the materials available in classrooms, the lack of a ready supply of diverse, interesting, and manageable material becomes readily apparent. Most classrooms still have a larger supply and variety of skills materials available than good books and magazines. Without easy access to comfortable, interesting materials, many children go about their daily work but never actually experience real reading.

I suggest that the essence of reading is getting lost in a story—literally entering the text world—but we organize the elementary school day in ways that more often prevent such reading behavior. It is difficult to "step into" (Langer, 1990) a good book in the short periods of time that dominate literacy lessons in most classrooms. Imagine, for instance, attempting to read a wonderful novel in a series of separate 8–10-minute encounters. Children too rarely spend any sustained school time just reading (by sustained I mean 30–60 minutes or more). Teachers seem to feel uncomfortable when children just read. Sustained reading seems more like a leisure activity than educational work to adults. But actual involvement in reading remains the most potent factor in development of reading processes. Truth be told, the current organization of the school day leaves teachers with little opportunity to schedule longer blocks of uninterrupted time for sustained reading. For a number of reasons, including a dogged adherence to another remnant of turn-of-the-century psychology, distributed learning, the current school day seems organized around 10-20 blocks of time. In other words, there are multiple, separate activities that fill up the school day and multiple interruptions of potential learning time across the day. Children need fewer brief, shallow literacy activities and many more extended opportunities to read and write.

The situation for children who find learning to read difficult is especially fragmented, since they are most likely to be scheduled for special program participation during the school day. Such participation usually interrupts some part of the classroom reading and language arts lessons (U.S. Department of Education, 1993). Thus, children who are most in need of substantially greater opportunities to actually read are often, by design, the children who receive the shortest and least well-linked opportunities to read and write. Over the past 25 years schools have added a number of special programs to address the difficulties that some children experience in acquiring literacy. Today, these various well-intended efforts seem as likely to impede the design of an effective educational intervention as to foster it. In too many schools classroom teachers have no single hour-long block during the school day when all children are present in the classroom! Special program participation and special content class schedules (e.g., art, music, physical education, library) all interfere with efforts to create coherent blocks of time when students might engage in sustained reading and writing. This interference with the regular education program has influenced the call to dramatically restrict the segregation of some children that has been created by special programs and special classes. Instead, there is a renewed effort to focus attention on enhancing the quality of classroom literacy lessons for all students. Thus, we see calls for more inclusionary education for children with handicaps and more in-class support instruction or after-school and summer school programs for children needing remedial or compensatory educational services.

Schools are experimenting with schedules for special classes and special programs in an attempt to counter the current enormous fragmentation of the daily classroom schedule. Some schools are incorporating "block schedules" that provide all classroom teachers with daily protected time periods of several hours in length. During these periods no special classes are scheduled and no children participate in special programs. In other schools, special instructional programs operate outside the regular school day or school year—before or after school, on Saturdays, or during the summer months. Some schools are trying team-teaching models, pairing classroom and specialist teachers together in the regular classroom for extended time blocks. The impetus for such changes lies in the recognition that children need time to read and write and that our current programs are often designed in ways that literally reduce such opportunities.

But providing children with access to a rich array of reading materials and sustained blocks of time to read them is not enough. All children need some instruction in order to acquire the complex cognitive process we call reading. But many children require more and better instruction as well as expanded opportunities to read.

Teaching vs. Assigning

Unfortunately, we assign children work to complete and confuse that with teaching. What all children need, and some need more of, is models, explanations, and demonstrations of how reading is accomplished. What most do not need are more assignments without strategy instruction, yet much of the work children do in school is not accompanied by any sort of instructional interaction. Rather, work is assigned and checked. Teachers talk to students when assigning, but the talk usually involves presentations of procedures, not instructional explanations of the thinking processes needed to complete the activity. Children are told to "Read pages 12 to 15 and answer the questions at the end (or on the Ditto, in the workbook, or in a journal)." They are assigned story maps to complete with no modeling or demonstrations of how one might discover the structure of a story. Children are assigned to write persuasive essays with no models or demonstrations of how to develop an argument or support it. Some children get vowel Dittos to fill in with no instruction in word structure patterns. Most children are interrogated after reading but have limited opportunity to receive instruction in the comprehension strategies needed to answer the questions posed. In short, we too often confuse assigning and asking with teaching. Omitting the instructional component enormously reduces the potential of many activities (e.g., maps, webs, summary writing, response journals) for supporting the acquisition of complex literacy strategies and understandings. Without a strong instructional component children are left to their own devices to discover the strategies and processes that skillful readers and writers use. Many children attempt to puzzle through the activities but never discover the thinking patterns that skillful readers employ (Delpit, 1986; Johnston, 1985). We now label these children and schedule them for special instructional programs. It is time, instead, to teach them what they need to know.

The teaching activities, modeling, explaining, and demonstrating, have much in common. Teachers model the reading and writing processes by engaging in them at times when children can observe. Simply reading aloud to children, for instance, provides a model of how reading sounds and how stories go. Writing a list of things to do on the board provides a model of one function of writing. Sharing a newspaper story or a poem provides models as does presenting a reaction or response to a story or book. But models do not provide the child with much information about how one actually accomplishes such feats.

Explanations are one way, and probably the most common method used in schools, to help children understand how one goes about reading and writing. But explanations get bulky and often require a specialized language. For instance, traditionally when we attempted to help children understand the alphabetic principle that underlies English orthography we talked about vowels and consonants and long and short sounds. Such specialized and abstract vocabulary often served to confuse some children. In actuality, children do not need such specialized vocabulary to acquire the understandings needed to become effective in the use of decoding strategies. But whenever we attempt to explain the process, we have invariably become tangled up with a focus on the specialized vocabulary of the abstract explanation. Thus, some children labored at learning the specialized vocabulary but never did learn to effectively employ knowledge of the alphabetic principle when reading. These children could mark long and short vowels, but they could not read well. At other times we used explanations like "the main idea is the most important idea" in our attempts to foster children's comprehension. Unfortunately, explanation by definition is often unhelpful—children now can define main idea, for instance, but they still cannot construct an adequate summary reflecting the important information in a text. Explaining a process is an improvement over simply assigning students work, but many children do not benefit from explanations alone.

Demonstrations include teacher talk about the mental activities that occur during the reading and writing processes. Demonstrations usually involve modeling and explanation along with the teacher's description of what sorts of thinking occur during the process. For instance, when a teacher composes a story summary on an overhead projector in front of the class (Cunningham & Allington, 1994), he or she provides a model of the writing process and a model of a summary. If the teacher works from a story map that has been constructed following an explanation of the essential story elements, then explanation has been available. But demonstration occurs when the teacher thinks aloud during the composing, making visible the thinking that assembles the information from the story map, puts it into words, and finally creates a readable story summary. Likewise, when a teacher talks children through a strategy for puzzling out an unknown word while reading a story (here are things I can try: read to the end of the sentence; ask myself what makes sense here; cross-check what makes sense against word structure; reread the sentence using the word that makes sense and has the right letters), the teacher demonstrates the complex mental processes that readers engage in while reading. When the teacher demonstrates such thinking and demonstrates how thinking shifts from incident to incident (here I can look at the picture to get a clue; I think the word will rhyme with *name* because it is spelled the same way, etc.), the child has the opportunity to understand that skillful strategy use is flexible and always requires thinking, not simply rote applications of rules or knowledge.

Many children only infrequently encounter demonstrations of this sort. Instead their days are filled with memorizing rules and completing isolated tasks with no accompanying demonstrations. These children see the teacher and other children engaging in reading and writing activities or serving as models, but they are left with the puzzle "How do they do it?" All children need instruction, but some children need incredible amounts of close, personal instruction, usually clear and repeated demonstrations of how readers and writers go about reading and writing (Duffy, Roehler, & Rackliffe, 1986). Without adequate demonstrations these children continue through school always struggling to make sense out of lessons and rarely accomplishing this feat. These children never really learn to read and write, they just learn to score better on tests.

Models, explanations, and demonstrations of how we go about reading and writing are essential elements of an effective literacy instructional program. However, as we plan literacy instruction we must focus our lessons on the processes real readers and writers engage in as they read and write.

Understanding vs. Remembering

In our classes and on our tests we have focused children's attention primarily on remembering what they have read and routinely underemphasized facilitating or evaluating their understanding. American children are, for instance, more likely to be asked a simple recall question about material they have read than they are to be asked to summarize that same material. They are more likely to be assigned work that requires that they copy out information from a text than they are to be assigned an activity that asks them to synthesize information from two or more texts. They are more likely to be interrogated about the facts of a story than involved in a discussion of the author's craft in producing the story. Our lessons do not often involve much thoughtful reflection on what has been read or written, as several recent analyses of American elementary and secondary schools have demonstrated (e.g., Brown, 1991; Goodlad, 1983). Often our lessons have little relationship to reading and writing outside of school.

Somewhere along the way we confused comprehension with question-answering (Allington & Weber, 1993). School questions are different from the questions we pose outside of school. In school we ask known-answer questions—we interrogate. Outside of school we ask authentic questions—questions we do not know the answer to but are interested in having answered. When we talk with friends about things they have read, we do not engage in the sort of interrogation that follows the completion of a reading assignment in elementary or secondary school. (To see just how odd such behavior would be, readers might interrogate colleagues or family members about materials they are currently reading using questions at each of three comprehension levels.)

To foster understanding, children will need substantially less interrogation and substantially more opportunities to observe and engage in conversations about books, stories, and other texts they have read. Children from homes where parents provide few models of such literate talk about texts will learn how to enter and participate in such conversations only when we provide them with the models and opportunities in school. For these children the demonstrations provided at school offer the only opportunities to acquire literate understanding.

The popularity of the known-answer question in schools and the tendency for such questions to focus on literal detail found in texts may, in fact, work to impede children's understandings of how literate people actually read and discuss the materials they read. The focus on detail may work to create readers who never actually enter the text world, concentrating instead on remembering the sorts of detail that most literate readers omit when summarizing or discussing texts. For instance, I have long believed that the primary reason that answers to textbook questions were placed in parentheses in teachers' guides is that normal people do not typically remember the sorts of story details these questions asked for! Those children most likely to be asked the largest number of such questions— the children having difficulty learning to read—would then have their attention turned from more authentic and holistic engagement and toward a careful attention to details. These children would improve their question-answering achievement but never learn to enter a story or to summarize or discuss material read. Recent reports from the National Assessment of Educational Progress seem to indicate just this result—more evidence that children learn what they are taught.

For most children to acquire the advanced literacy proficiencies that allow one to summarize, synthesize, analyze, and actually discuss the ideas found in texts of various sorts, the nature of classroom conversations will necessarily have to change. Applebee (1993) has suggested that we might consider the nature of the conversations we want children to be able to enter and complete as a primary basis for thinking about the sorts of curriculum we create. Literate talk, usually conversational, is not often heard in classrooms of the schools we have. Instead, interrogation is the most common form of discourse between teachers and students. Until we realize that question asking does little to foster thinking and that question answering provides little good evidence of understanding, we should not be surprised that only few students ever develop advanced literacy proficiency.

Creating the Schools We Need

American schools have long been better organized to sort children than to support them in their quest to develop literacy. Sorting children, as Bloom (1976) pointed out, always takes less effort than supporting children. But this sorting, based upon turn-of-the-century hereditarianism and supported by behaviorist psychology and psychometry, has always benefited children of the advantaged classes more than it benefited less advantaged children. I am certain that we can create schools that lessen the current inequities in literacy learning opportunities (Allington, 1994). There is little reason to doubt that we can have schools where children develop advanced literacy proficiencies regardless of the parents they have. But designing such schools requires that we discard many of the long traditions of American schooling and replace many widely held historical beliefs about human learning.

As long as we continue to believe that some children, usually children with the wrong parents, cannot learn to read alongside their more advantaged peers, there will be little reason to attempt to design instructional programs that ensure all children succeed. If we remain ensnared by hereditarian beliefs concerning the limited potential of some children, there will be little reason to work intensively to accelerate their literacy development. We must not continue to confuse lack of experience and opportunity with lack of ability. Some children will always require closer, more personalized instruction in larger quantities than other children if we are to help them achieve their full potential. Some children will need more and better models, explanations, and demonstrations than other children if they are to learn together with their peers. These are the children that need greater access to interesting books that they can comfortably read as well as expanded opportunities to read those books in and out of school.

Creating schools that better support children who find learning to read difficult will require more and closer collaborative educational efforts on the part of both the classroom teacher and the special teachers we employ to help support readers in trouble. Schools will undoubtedly have to expand the school day and school year for some children in order to expand their instructional opportunities. We can create schools where virtually all children achieve the sorts of literacy proficiencies that in the past have been attained by only a few children. But there will necessarily be much changed in the design and delivery of our literacy lessons before this will occur. I am quite certain that children are more likely to learn what they are taught than what they are not. I am also quite certain that our schools, our classrooms, and our lessons are organized in ways that often impede our progress toward change and that impede the progress of the children we teach toward advanced literacy. I am less certain about how to accomplish the changes that are needed, but I think the changes are unlikely if we continue to adhere to the turn-of-the-century psychology and turn-of-the-century school organizational structures that dominate our practice today.

How We Might Begin

As a first step we will have to reemphasize the importance of the classroom teacher and classroom lessons in developing literacy in all children. Even though we have doubled the number of adults working in elementary schools since 1960, virtually all of those new personnel are specialists and support staff. Little of the real increase in educational spending has gone to support enhanced classroom environments. Instead, we have invested enormously in people and programs that often seem to be more likely to inhibit high-quality classroom instruction than to enhance it. We must create schools where classroom literacy instruction is continuously adapted and improved. In these schools the primary role of special program funds and personnel would be to enhance the quality of classroom literacy instruction available to children finding learning to read and write difficult and to expand their opportunities to engage in literacy learning activity.

Many schools have already undertaken initial reorganization of instruction for readers in trouble by reemphasizing the importance of classroom instruction that serves all children well. We can see this in schools where children who find learning to read difficult are no longer segregated for all or part of the school day but, instead, receive additional supportive instruction in their classrooms. Collaborative teaching models, where classroom and special program teachers work together—side by side—to effectively support literacy learning, take time to learn, but it is time well spent (e.g., Standerford, 1993). It is children who find learning to read difficult who can least tolerate fragmented instruction. Rather than continuing the fragmentation of the curriculum and the school day, collaborative teaching models foster coherent and consistent instructional efforts.

A second step is reorganizing the school day and week. Teachers need long, uninterrupted blocks of time to teach, and children need such time to learn. Instead of planning for a daily series of separate short lessons for a variety of subjects, the day and the week need to be substantially reconfigured. Perhaps it is time to schedule literacy lessons on only Monday and Tuesday—but all day Monday and Tuesday! Just think how planning changes if two whole, uninterrupted days of literacy lessons become available. Activities that now "take too much time"—like reading a whole book, producing a dramatization of a story or even a scene, researching a topic rather thoroughly for an oral presentation, composing a truly well-formed story, report, or poem, from drafting to illustrating to publishing, and so on—could actually become part of the regular planning. Imagine the new roles that specialist teachers might play if they worked a half day once or twice weekly in such classrooms. But until we imagine such reorganization we will remain trapped in the schools we have.

Similarly, these schools would not operate on the 8:30–2:30 schedule that seems so common in the U.S. today. Rather, schools would change to meet the needs of children in a society that has changed much since we designed the schools we have. Schools would open earlier and close later. In some cases, schools might remain open well into the evening to provide parent education and homework support. But schools would routinely extend the instructional day for some children—those who need increased instructional opportunities to accelerate their learning. The schools we need would not operate as though most parents are home at 3:00 to help with homework—since most are not (Martin, 1992). They would be redesigned in recognition that in most families with children both parents work, and more parents work longer hours today than they did when the schools we have were designed. Such shifts have already taken place in some communities. Some schools open at 7:00 in the morning and close at 9:00 in the evening. In these schools a variety of learning activities are scheduled after the formal school day. Children can learn to dance, sew, cook, act, play the piano, juggle a soccer ball, or deliver a karate kick. In these schools children have a quiet place to do homework, with library resources at hand, and, often, an adult to provide assistance. Some of those adults who work into the evening might be drawn from that half of the professional staff currently in schools who are not classroom teachers.

Linked to reorganizing the daily and weekly schedule is reworking our approach to curriculum design. A third step will be to throw out the old notion of distributed learning that fostered the current approaches to instructional planning. In its place we put the notions of engagement, involvement, and *flow* (Csikszentmihalyi, 1990). We replace the broad curriculum of today with a deep curriculum—a *post-hole* approach (Dow, 1991)—one that develops deeper levels of integrated understanding of far fewer topics. It is difficult for anyone to be thoughtful about topics that are understood only shallowly. In fact, lots of brief lessons on multiple unrelated topics literally force shallow thinking. If we are to create schools where understanding replaces simple remembering until the test has been taken, our curriculum will necessarily change. Again, some schools have already begun to move in this direction. Integrated language arts curriculum, thematic lessons, monthlong expertise units, whole day project periods, and the like are all examples of preliminary movement in this direction (Walmsley, 1994).

A fourth step is replenishing the classroom and the classroom teacher. Few of the classrooms we have studied are well equipped for the schools we need, and few classroom teachers are well supported with ongoing professional development activities. For instance, even though schools are moving to literature-based curriculum in an attempt to create more thoughtful instruction, few teachers are very expert in the area of children's literature, and few classrooms have sufficient collections of books and magazines (Allington, Guice, & Li, 1993). It seems a rare school where developing such expertise is part of the ongoing professional development plan. Few of the schools implementing literature-based instruction seem to have in place any sort of structure for fostering teacher familiarity with the new children's books that are published each year. Few have a long-term plan for building school library and classroom collections of books. If children are ever to become readers, many more will need the sorts of access to books that only a few have today (Allington & McGill-Franzen, 1993). Schools that serve large numbers of poor children, especially, will need a tenfold increase in the numbers of books, magazines, and reference materials that children might use.

Such changes could be funded, in large part, from the funds that currently support the schools we have. For instance, in an elementary school with 300 students and 13 classroom teachers we might forego hiring one specialist staff member and use the costs recovered to fund the replenishing. If we use a US$37,000 base salary and a 21 percent fringe benefit cost we have about $45,000 available annually—or about $3,500 per classroom. We might spend $1,000 of this amount each year to purchase books for the classroom and $1,000 for the school collection (or an additional $13,000 per year). The remaining funds might be used to fund professional development opportunities for each teacher. These might include conference attendance, summer curriculum development workshops, videos, professional library collections, college courses, and so on. Over a 10-year period we would invest $35,000 in replenishing each classroom and each classroom teacher. Would such an investment accrue benefits to the children who find learning to read difficult that were at least comparable to the benefit accumulated through the employment of that one special teacher? Without a far broader view of how schools might invest special program funds to better meet the needs of children who find learning to read difficult, it is likely the question will never be raised, much less answered.

Finally, the schools we need will reformulate the processes of evaluating student learning. Evaluating programs will become a different sort of enterprise than it is today. While standardized achievement tests will probably remain as one indicator, these tests would play a substantially smaller role than they do today. Students taking standardized tests and high-stakes assessments associated with program evaluation would complete the tests anonymously. No student identification would be attached to those test results. School personnel, legislators, and policy makers would still have the achievement test information for program evaluation purposes, but these narrow and very fallible instruments would not be used to sort students or to plan instruction. The evaluation of student learning, or exploration of their learning difficulties, would become a personalized process with a heavy reliance on close, careful examination of a student's work (Johnston, 1992). Again, we can see movement in these directions as schools work to develop portfolios, performance, and student self-evaluation processes. We can see it in the debate over report cards (Afflerbach, 1993) and the current experimentation in how best to convey student progress to parents, employers, and to the students themselves (Pearson, 1993; Purves, 1993). The testing and reporting procedures so common today were better suited for the low-level curriculum goals of the schools we had, but those procedures simply do not work for the schools we need.

In the end it will all come down to putting children together with expert teachers who have the time and resources necessary to support the diverse groups of children assigned to their classrooms. We can and should rethink many of the features of the schools we have, but it ultimately comes down to schools staffed with high-quality classroom teachers, especially for the futures of children who find learning to read and write difficult.

References

Afflerbach, P. (1993). Report cards and reading. *The Reading Teacher, 46*, 458–65.

Algozzine, B., & Ysseldyke, J.E. (1983). Learning disabilities as a subset of school failure: The oversophistication of a concept. *Exceptional Children, 50*, 242–46.

Allington, R.L. (1977). If they don't read much, how they ever gonna get good? *Journal of Reading, 21*, 57–61.

Allington, R.L. (1983). The reading instruction provided readers of differing abilities. *Elementary School Journal, 83*, 548–59.

Allington, R.L. (1987). Shattered hopes: Why two federal programs have failed to correct reading failure. *Learning, 13*, 60–64.

Allington, R.L. (1991). The legacy of 'slow it down and make it more concrete.' In J. Zutell & S. McCormick (Eds.), *Learner factors/teacher factors: Issues in literacy research and instruction* (pp. 19–30). Chicago National Reading Conference.

Allington, R.L. (1993). Michael doesn't go down the hall anymore. *The Reading Teacher, 46*, 602–5.

Allington, R.L. (1994). What's special about special programs for children who find learning to read difficult? *Journal of Reading Behavior, 26*, 1–21.

Allington, R.L., Guice, S., & Li, S. (1993). *Implementing literature-based literacy instruction in schools serving many at-risk children*. Manuscript submitted for publication.

Allington, R.L., & Johnston, P.A. (1989). Coordination, collaboration, and consistency: The redesign of compensatory and special education interventions. In R. Slavin, N. Karweit, & N. Madden (Eds.), *Effective programs for students at risk* (pp. 320–54). Boston: Allyn & Bacon.

Allington, R.L., & McGill-Franzen, A. (1993, October 13). What are they to read? Not all children, Mr. Riley, have easy access to books. *Education Week*, p. 26.

Allington, R.L., & McGill-Franzen, A. (1989a). Different programs, indifferent instruction. In D. Lipsky & A. Gartner (Eds.), *Beyond separate education: Quality education for all* (pp. 75–98). Baltimore: Brookes.

Allington, R., & McGill-Franzen, A. (1989b). School response to reading failure: Chapter 1 and special education students in grades 2, 4, and 8. *Elementary School Journal, 89*, 529–42.

Allington, R.L., & Weber, R.M. (1993). Questioning questions in teaching and learning from texts. In A. Woodward, M. Binkley, & B. Britton (Eds.), *Learning from textbooks: Theory and practice* (pp. 47–68). Hillsdale, NJ: Erlbaum.

Applebee, A.N. (1993). *Beyond the lesson: Reconstruing curriculum as a domain for culturally significant conversations* (Report No. 17). Albany, NY: University at Albany, SUNY, National Research Center on Literature Teaching and Learning.

Bloom, B.S. (1976). *Human characteristics and school learning.* New York: McGraw-Hill.

Brown, R.G. (1991). *Schools of thought: How the politics of literacy shape thinking in the classroom.* San Francisco: Jossey-Bass.

Clay, M.M. (1991). Reading Recovery surprises. In D. DeFord, C. Lyons, & G.S. Pinnell (Eds.), *Bridges to literacy: Learning from reading recovery* (pp. 55–75). Portsmouth, NH: Heinemann.

Commission on Chapter 1. (1993). *Making schools work for children of poverty: A new framework.* Washington, DC: Author.

Cooley, W.W. (1993). The difficulty of the educational task: Implications for comparing student achievement in states, school districts, and schools. *ERS Spectrum, 11,* 27–31.

Cunningham, P.M., & Allington, R.L. (1994). *Classrooms that work: They can all read and write.* New York: HarperCollins.

Csikszentmihalyi, M. (1990). *Flow.* New York: HarperCollins.

Delpit, L.D. (1986). Skills and other dilemmas of a progressive Black educator. *Harvard Educational Review, 56,* 379–85.

Dow, P.B. (1991). *Schoolhouse politics: Lessons from the Sputnik era.* Cambridge, MA: Harvard University Press.

Duffy, G.G., Roehler, L.R., & Rackliffe, G. (1986). How teachers' instructional talk influences students' understanding of lesson content. *Elementary School Journal, 87,* 4–16.

Gardner, H., & Hatch, T. (1989). Multiple intelligences go to school: Educational implications of the Theory of Multiple Intelligences. *Educational Researcher, 18*(8), 4–10.

Goodlad, J.I. (1983). *A place called school: Prospects for the future.* New York: McGraw-Hill.

Gould, S.J. (1981). *The mismeasure of man.* New York: Norton.

Guice, S., & Allington, R.L. (1992, December). *Access to literacy: Variations in schools serving low-income children.* Paper presented at the meeting of the National Reading Conference, San Antonio, TX.

Hiebert, E.H. (1983). An examination of ability grouping for reading instruction. *Reading Research Quarterly, 18,* 231–55.

Jachym, N., Allington, R.L., & Broikou, K.A. (1989). Estimating the cost of seatwork. *The Reading Teacher, 43,* 30–37.

Johnston, P.H. (1985). Understanding reading failure: A case study approach. *Harvard Educational Review, 55,* 153–77.

Johnston, P.H. (1992). *Constructive evaluation of literate activity.* New York: Longman.

Johnston, P.H., & Allington, R.L. (1990). Remediation. In R. Barr, M. Kamil, P. Mosenthal, & P.D. Pearson (Eds.), *Handbook of reading research, Vol. II* (pp. 984–1012). New York: Longman.

Langer, J.A. (1990). Understanding literature. *Language Arts, 67,* 812–23.

Langer, J.A., & Allington, R.L. (1992). Curriculum research in writing and reading. In P.W. Jackson (Ed.), *Handbook of research on curriculum* (pp. 687–725). New York: Macmillan.

Langer, J.A., Applebee, A.N., Mullis, I., & Foertsch, M. (1990). *Learning to read in American schools: Instruction and achievement in 1988 at grades 4, 8, 12.* Princeton, NJ: National Association for Educational Progress.

LeTendre, M.J. (1991). Improving Chapter 1 programs: We can do better. *Phi Delta Kappan, 72,* 577–80.

Marshall, R., & Tucker, M. (1992). *Thinking for a living: Education and the wealth of nations.* New York: Basic Books.

Martin, J.R. (1992). *The schoolhome: Rethinking schools for changing families.* Cambridge, MA: Harvard University Press.

McGill-Franzen, A. (1992). Early literacy: What does "developmentally appropriate" mean? *The Reading Teacher, 46,* 56–58.

McGill-Franzen, A., & Allington, R.L. (1990). Comprehension and coherence: Neglected elements of literacy instruction in remedial and resource room services. *Journal of Reading, Writing, and Learning Disabilities, 6,* 149–82.

McGill-Franzen, A., & Allington, R.L. (1991). The gridlock of low-achievement: Perspectives on policy and practice. *Remedial and Special Education, 12,* 20–30.

McGill-Franzen, A., & Lanford, C. (1994). Exposing the edge of the preschool curriculum: Teachers' talk about text and children's literary understanding. *Language Arts, 71,* 22–31.

Pearson, P.D. (1993). Standards for the English language arts: A policy perspective. *Journal of Reading Behavior, 25,* 457–75.

Puma, M.J., Jones, C.C., Rock, D., & Fernandez, R. (1993). *Prospects: The Congressionally mandated study of educational growth and opportunity.* Bethesda, MD: Abt Associates.

Purves, A.C. (1993). Setting standards in the language arts and literature classroom and the implications for portfolio assessment. *Educational Assessment, 1,* 174–99.

Rotberg, I.C., Harvey, J.J., & Warner, K. (1993). *Federal policy options for improving the education of low-income students, Volume 1: Findings and recommendations.* Santa Monica, CA: Rand Institute on Education and Training.

Shannon, P. (1993). Developing democratic voices. *The Reading Teacher, 47,* 86–95.

Standerford, N.S. (1993). Where have all the sparrows gone? Rethinking Chapter 1 services. *Reading Research and Instruction, 33,* 38–57.

Stanovich, K.E. (1993). Does reading make you smarter? Literacy and the development of verbal intelligence. In H. Reese (Ed.), *Advances in child development, Vol. 24* (pp. 141–62). Orlando, FL: Academic Press.

Tharp, R.G., & Gallimore, R. (1988). *Rousing minds to life: Teaching, learning, and schooling in social context.* New York: Cambridge University Press.

U.S. Department of Education. (1993). *Reinventing Chapter 1: The current Chapter 1 program and new directions.* Washington, DC: Office of Policy and Planning.

Walmsley, S.A. (1994). *Children exploring their world: Theme teaching in the elementary school.* Portsmouth, NH: Heinemann.

Wheelock, A. (1992). *Crossing the tracks: How untracking can save America's schools.* New York: The New Press.

Index

Editor

Constance (Connie) Weaver is professor of English at Western Michigan University, where she specializes in the teaching of language arts (reading, writing, and grammar). She is author and editor of numerous publications, including *Creating Support for Effective Literacy Education* (1996), *Teaching Grammar in Context* (1996), *Reading Process and Practice* (2nd ed., 1994), *Success at Last! Helping Students with Attention Deficit (Hyperactivity) Disorders Understand Their Potential* (1994), *Theme Exploration* (1993), *Understanding Whole Language* (1990), and *Grammar for Teachers* (1979). In addition to the NCTE companion volume, *Practicing What We Know: Informed Reading Instruction*, another edited volume, *Lessons to Share: On Teaching Grammar in Context*, is forthcoming. Dr. Weaver has also authored a videotape, *A Balanced Approach to Reading and Literacy*, and has co-authored another, *Reading Strategies and Skills: Research into Practice*. From 1987 to 1990, she served as director of the Commission on Reading of the National Council of Teachers of English. In 1996 she received the Charles C. Fries award for distinguished leadership in the profession from the Michigan Council of Teachers of English. Weaver is also co-founder of Michigan for Public Education, a nonprofit grassroots organization advocating equality and excellence in education.

Standards in Practice, Grades K–2

Linda K. Crafton

Viewing the English language arts standards developed by NCTE and the International Reading Association as a point of departure rather than a final destination, this book presents a number of ways to increase student ownership of learning. Crafton details a pedagogy that recognizes, respects, and builds from individual language strengths and experiences, and in each chapter presents a rich classroom portrait of the standards at work in student-centered, real-world experiences and activities. Standards in Practice Series. *121 pp. 1996. Grades K–2. ISBN 0-8141-4691-0.*

No. 46910-4041 .... $15.95 ($11.95 for NCTE members)

"You Gotta BE the Book"

Teaching Engaged and Reflective Reading with Adolescents
Jeffrey D. Wilhelm

Jeffrey Wilhelm's vital book looks at what "reading really is": a social practice and a search for meaning. The author presents a thorough overview of theory and research in reading, and develops a powerful alternative to traditional models of close reading and bottom-up reading instruction. *You Gotta BE the Book* then moves theory into the classroom again, where teacher research becomes a window into students' evolving reading practices. *Winner of the NCTE Promising Researcher Award. 191 pp. 1997. NCTE and Teachers College Press. Grades 6–12. ISBN 0-8077-3566-3.*

No. 10924-4041 .... $21.95 ($15.95 for NCTE members)

The Culture of Reading and the Teaching of English

Kathleen McCormick
1994 Shaughnessy Prize Winner

This award-winning book aims to help create a more active dialogue among reading teachers and researchers, and to encourage those in literary and cultural studies to enter the conversation about reading. Wide-ranging, ambitious, and accessible, McCormick offers perhaps the most fully developed articulation of literacy studies and cultural studies yet proposed. *227 pp. 1994. Manchester University Press. Coll. ISBN 0-7190-3245-8.*

No. 09985-4041 .... $25.95 ($18.95 for NCTE members)

NCTE National Council of Teachers of English
1111 W. Kenyon Road, Urbana, Illinois 61801-1096
Telephone: 1-800-369-6283 or 217-328-3870   Web site: http//www.ncte.org